NEW YORK OBSERVER

PRESENTS

THE KINGDOM OF NEW YORK

Knights, Knaves, Billionaires, and Beauties
in the City of Big Shots
As Seen by *The New York Observer*

INTRODUCTION BY PETER W. KAPLAN

◇◇◇◇◇◇

HARPER

An Imprint of HarperCollins*Publishers*
www.harpercollins.com

ACKNOWLEDGEMENTS

Thanks to: Amanda Urban and Jennifer Joel at ICM.
Tim Duggan and Allison Lorentzen at HarperCollins. John D. Sicher,
Joe Conason, Eric Etheridge, Mark Lasswell, Craig Unger, Aimee Bell,
Tom McGeveran, Mary Ann Giordano, Elise O'Shaughnessy,
Lauren Ramsby, Jesse Wegman, Shazia Ahmad, I-Huei Go,
Jake Brooks, Beth Broome, Josh Benson, Marcus Baram, Lisa Chase,
Bettina Edelstein, Renee Kaplan, Nick Paumgarten, Jay Stowe,
Christine Muhlke, Maria Russo, Jason Gay, Tom Acitelli, Hillary Frey,
Tom Scocca, Zachary Roth, Suzy Hansen, Choire Sicha, Matt Haber,
Barry Lewis, Brian Kroski, John Vorwald, Joe Pompeo, Mary Dixie Carter
and the entire staff, past and present of The New York Observer.

THE KINGDOM OF NEW YORK

Editors: Alexandra Jacobs, Peter W. Kaplan, Peter M. Stevenson

Art director: Nancy Butkus

Managing editor: Oliver Haydock

Historian: George Gurley

Associate editor: Will Heinrich

Designers: Alisha Neumaier, Barbara Sullivan

Production manager: Tyler Rush

Photo editor: Alana Kaloshi

Copy editor: Chris Cronis

Assistant editor: Karla Alindahao

Production assistant: Peter Lettre

Editorial assistants: Stephanie Lee, Morgan Pile, Reid Pillifant

OUR ILLUSTRATORS

Blitt

Barry Blitt has been contributing weekly caricatures to *The Observer* since 1991, when then-editor Graydon Carter called and asked for a portrait "the size of a softball." Mr. Blitt's work also appears regularly in *The New Yorker*, *The New York Times*, *Vanity Fair* and many other publications. *Pages: 3, 22, 27, 30, 31, 46, 53, 61, 64, 65, 69, 78, 79, 82, 93, 96, 98, 99, 140, 141, 166, 178, 179, 185, 187, 189, 196, 197, 203, 205, 210, 216, 225, 230, 231, 232, 233, 237, 250, 252, 253, 270, 276, 287, 288, 292, 293, 298, 299, 338, 339, 342, 343, 344, 354, 356*

Burke

Former "angry young man" **Philip Burke** first met Peter Kaplan at *New Times*, to which, along with *The Village Voice*, he was contributing mostly political caricatures. Among copious other magazine and newspaper work, he had long-running stints at *Vanity Fair* and *Rolling Stone* before joining *The Observer's* rotation in 1994. *Pages: 80, 111, 112, 125, 131, 139, 147, 148, 171, 184, 188, 192, 201, 210, 223, 230, 248, 258, 259, 287, 301, 303, 312, 316, 323, 326, 332, 346, 360*

Friedman

Aside from illustrating a monthly cover for *The New York Observer* since 1993, **Drew Friedman**'s work also appears in *Time*, *Newsweek*, *The New Republic*, *The New Yorker*, *Mad* and many others. *Pages: Cover, 32, 94, 100, 109, 112, 113, 116, 123, 128, 129, 132, 133, 137, 138, 153, 156, 159, 160, 161, 165, 171, 172, 174, 182, 186, 191, 195, 200, 202, 205, 206, 207, 214, 218, 224, 225, 234, 244, 251, 254, 257, 261, 276, 278, 280, 296, 302, 308, 315, 319, 320, 322, 325, 340, 348, 355, 362, 367*

Grossman

Robert Grossman has done cover illustrations for more than 500 issues of national magazines such as *Time*, *Newsweek*, *Sports Illustrated*, *Rolling Stone* and *The New Republic*. Today his work can be seen regularly in *The Nation*, *The New York Times* and *The Observer*. His 1977 animated film, *Jimmy the C.*, earned an Academy Award nomination. *Pages: 104, 122, 124, 130, 136, 144, 153, 154, 162, 170, 190, 222, 241, 243, 246, 266, 271, 272, 279, 314, 321, 328, 334, 342, 345, 349, 354, 364*

Juhasz

Victor Juhasz has drawn for *Time*, *Newsweek* and *The New York Times* as well as (since 2005) *The Observer*. He is a frequent contributor to the National Affairs section of *Rolling Stone* and serves on the board of directors of the Society of Illustrators. *Pages: 18, 48, 119, 120, 124, 146, 176, 185, 219, 225, 256, 264, 265, 267, 274, 281, 286, 298, 300, 302, 307, 310, 313, 321, 324, 325, 329, 333, 343, 345, 346, 347, 353*

Cover Illustration by Drew Friedman

FIRST EDITION
Library of Congress Cataloging-in-Publication Data is available upon request.
ISBN: 978-0-06-169540-7
09 10 11 12 13 ID/QWT 10 9 8 7 6 5 4 3 2 1

CONTENTS

THE KINGDOM OF NEW YORK

BY PETER W. KAPLAN

CAMELOT IT WASN'T.

But the Kingdom of New York that *The New York Observer* was founded to cover was an island paradise with fiefdoms, rulers, turf battles, borders and a brutal hierarchy that seemed impossible to describe to Boston or San Bernardino. Its voracious royals thought a great deal of themselves, bought a lot for themselves, dressed accordingly, traded in secret insults, spent fortunes on town cars, lounged at ritzy restaurants, brought their battles into private schools and charity balls with the idea that it was a game worth winning.

They were our beat. They picked up their own phones! And they were endlessly available: socialites who climbed mountains, debutantes who joined the Colony Club, authors at each other's throats, bistros clawing for clienteles, TV executives struggling for prime time, senators sucking around presidents, first ladies trying to become senators. And physical torment: classy ladies pioneering nether grooming, botulism in the forehead, high colonics, special formula enemas, face-lifts, private-school kids snorting Ritalin. Sex, and plenty of it, in the City.

The Kingdom was a topography of power, with its Manhattan moats and turrets, its courts in media, politics, society, its residues of Edith Wharton, Walter Winchell and Weegee. It may have been a generated nether haze, but it was all ours.

There were other papers, but they didn't seem to be having much fun. The city was going through a revolution, up from the muck of the 1970s when it was razzed by TV comedians, and Central Park West apartments were being given away for cigar money. New Yorkers gave the keys to the Kingdom to the hard-nosed mayor in exchange for security, cleanliness, order. Money seemed to self-propagate. The city hummed with a focused purpose. Now and then in its history, New York makes sense, has a middle class, takes care of its kids and its streets, its businesses.

Into this territory waded *The New York Observer* in 1987. Arthur L. Carter, who owned *The Nation* magazine, and *The Litchfield County Times* in Connecticut, had the idea of publishing a power elite weekly. At first, *The Observer* mystified the town of killers with what seemed to be a quiet little invention, embroidered with pen-and-ink drawings and a photograph of Central Park on Page 1. The paper began somewhat gently and innocuously, stacked up in the lacquered lobbies of Upper East Side apartment buildings. But it changed quickly. *The Observer* couldn't have been spawned a minute earlier than it was. The rise of the money culture created a lovely narcissism, which made the 1990s the screwball decade it became. Its driven, self-fascinated cast of well-dressed characters—gorgeous and grotesque, cruel and generous, utterly without a concept of where they would live if there were no New York—generally got pleasure from being onstage.

Most of them had to be personally experienced to be believed. There was Alfonse D'Amato, the junior senator who proposed to the glamorous gossip columnist Claudia Cohen and called himself "The Frog Who Got Kissed by a Princess" before the relationship ended; Fred and Mary, the celebrity newsstand owners on Hudson Street in Tribeca who served as the downtown media gossip filling station; Julian Niccolini, the smooth Vittorio De Sica–like co-owner of the Four Seasons; Robert De Niro, the world's greatest screen actor, who was determined to turn Tribeca into the movie capital of the East; John F. Kennedy Jr., the rollerblading Superman of North Moore Street; Harvey Weinstein, who looked like he didn't have taste, did, pummeling Hollywood into a supplicant's kneel; Puff Daddy; P. Diddy; Sean Combs; Mary Boone; Huntington Hartford; Shoshanna Lonstein; Al Sharpton; Cindy Adams; Christian Curry; Mark Penn, the pollster who failed; Lucianne Goldberg; Col Allan; Liz Smith; Ethan Hawke; Donna Hanover; Judith Regan; the Friars Club ... They were each gifts that kept on giving.

Of course, they had wonderful story lines. The ideal, which hardly ever happened, was that you could follow them week-by-week like characters in a 19th-century novel published in weekly installments, showing up, disappearing for a few weeks, returning much changed with a new wife or a business triumph or a nice embezzlement. Manhattan in the 1990s was a giddy, baroque city where the stock market rose and crime numbers went down while the unflinching mayor became a national celebrity by ruling his city like an ambiguous hero-villain right out of *Batman*. Some found life impenetrable. Some took it seriously.

More and more, *The Observer* reported on mad meritocrats, billionaires and socialites, on the mayor and on which kids got thrown into jail after the prom. We told our writers and editors to speak to its readers just as reporters speak to other reporters—directly.

The paper was born into a Georgian red-brick townhouse on East 64th Street that Arthur Carter had once planned to live in himself. There were four-legged bathtubs on two of the floors, which were quickly packed with newspapers, and the bedroom that Arthur had promised to one of his former partners at Carter, Berlind, Potoma and Weill became the office of the gossip columnist. There was a tiny cage-door elevator that groaned endlessly up and down between the newsroom on the fourth floor and the production offices on the first floor.

One floor down was the publisher's office, where Arthur sat at a green-leather-topped partner's desk among a lot of good 19th-century furniture, black-and-white photographs of Albert Einstein and Thomas Mann, a giant red-paisley wingback armchair and a long formal dining table that a series of secretaries kept in high-polish. Up from the center hallway ran a rather grand curved staircase on which trod some of the most enterprising call girls in New York, who showed up to buy personal ads in the classified section. And blurred visitors: Bill Murray, Mike Wallace, Norman Mailer gallantly struggling to the elevator on a pair of canes with a suitcase of cartoons he was determined to put in the paper weekly.

NEW YORK WAS STILL A BIG NEWSPAPER TOWN, WHICH most people never thought would be an antique term—except for anyone who was watching closely. *The Observer* was a newspaper reaction to *The New York Times*, the greatest newspaper in America, which continued to dominate the psyche of the literate New Yorker as nothing else ever has or ever will. *The Times* was magnificent, but its infallibility demanded a retrofit stand-in for all the beaten broadsheets of New York: the *Herald Tribune*, the *World*, the *Telegram*. In the absence of anything else, the Off the Record column acted partly as an ad-hoc ombudsman for a city that otherwise had to take the reporting in *The Times* as received truth.

When Jayson Blair was caught fabricating stories in *The New York Times*, we were well prepared. Our Off the Record reporter, Sridhar Pappu, staked out Blair's house in Brooklyn until he was invited in and got the following quote of his dreams: "So Jayson Blair the human being could live, Jayson Blair the journalist had to die." *The New York Times* is the most important newspaper in the world and *Observer* reporters have always been told to cover it the way *The Times* covers the State Department.

The Observer is often mistaken for a comedy newspaper. Irritated subjects called it "snarky." It's not—it just refuses to be guileless, a pathetic accomplice to big shots. We're yappers and nippers, but we report by the Marquis of Queensbury rules—on the record and with fact-checkers. *The Observer* reports on everything that is being written and talked about and thought in a city that can't bear to have thoughts that don't show up in print. It's not parody, or postmodern; it's just a little newspaper with its own persona. My old boss Clay Felker used to call it a "newspaper of interpretation." As a matter of fact, it battled what was being called the Age of Irony—we didn't believe in irony.

We reported on the distillation of a certain Manhattan sensibility, the New York that the rest of America thinks of as New York. We also gorged on the media. Hollywood has movie studios—Warner Bros., Fox, Paramount. But New York has its own big studio system: Condé Nast, *The New York Times*, Rupert Murdoch's *New York Post* and *Wall Street Journal*, Hearst, Time Warner, the *Daily News*, plus NBC, ABC, CBS, CNN and Fox. There was an argument by the right-wing nuts that this crowd controls American perception and information. That's attributing an inconceivable cohesion among them.

Even within *The Observer* there has never been any particular cohesion. The paper's bunch of loud, brilliant critics occasionally jumped across the columns at each other's throats until it was dictated they were off-bounds to each other, and even that didn't quite do the trick: Hilton Kramer, who had been the super-erudite, emphatic, regal art critic of *The Times*, took whacks from Michael M. Thomas, the idea-spouting financial-social critic who wrote the Midas Watch column; Andrew Sarris, the dean of American film critics, jousted with Rex Reed, the nightlife-loving astringent culture gadfly who had become a kind of latter-day Waldo Lydecker—who later took on John Heilpern, the raffish, literate drama critic. They were none of them cubs; they wrote directly, without condescension; they were contentious grown-ups who had no use for the dead weight of phony manners and objectivity that had mucked up the polite media.

The first editor of the paper, John Sicher, made a few crucial choices. What Hilton Kramer or Michael Thomas thought was meant to be Page 1 news. Power in New York would be stated in buildings bought and sold, or brokered in a small room. To that end, both Charles V. Bagli, who saw real estate as a brutal battle for square feet, and Terry Golway, a lyrical political expert from Staten Island well versed in the lives of Al Smith and the Molinaris, occupied the top of the big broadsheet front page, week after week.

The paper trundled along a little sleepily until Arthur Carter had the inspiration to hire the hugely talented co-founder of *Spy*, Graydon Carter, as editor in 1991. Graydon Carter ran *The Observer* for only 12 months, but he remade it with ambition and panache, brought in antique furniture, super-smart acolytes, community journalism, society reporting, British newspaper excerpts and a hopped-up work ethic. The paper immediately bloomed; it hit a note that New Yorkers, particularly Upper East Siders, picked up on. It suddenly stated the case that needed to be made: New York was combat turf but actually fun!

The Observer became visible. Then, the near-inevitable: Graydon Carter eloped, swept away by S. I. Newhouse to run *Vanity Fair*. Next came the advent of Susan Morrison, No. 2 at *Spy*. Beautiful, quirky, a demanding editor of tremendous intelligence who understood the subversive fusion of humor and fact, Susan Morrison went to the *New York Post*'s Page Six and raided Frank DiGiacomo, a tough gumshoe reporter with a literary ear and an armadillo-size, key-locked Rolodex. DiGiacomo treated gossip as reporting, not the other way around.

Susan Morrison also promoted a couple of deadly choirboys with the cold glint of reporters: Peter Stevenson, a 33-year old writer with hyper-developed literary instincts, wrote features, and Jim Windolf, a cultural omnivore who could absorb almost anything, took on the press column. Stevenson and Windolf hunted phonies by day, read novels at night. So it was all set: real estate, politics, society, gossip, attitude.

ONE AFTERNOON IN 1994, ARTHUR CARTER SUMMONED me to his apartment on East 67th Street. His living room was lined with Picassos and Kandinskys and Legers, with a grand piano the length of a Duesenberg. He was wearing a cashmere sweater and sneakers. He was focused and rather serious. We somehow established that his mother had given my grandmother French lessons in Long Island in the 1940s.

By June 1, I was at the paper. I had three main goals:

    1. To state New York as the center of the universe.
    2. To assign subjective narrative reporting.
    3. To hire great cartoonists.

By 1994, New York was creating its own new comic story line, a resurrection of the narrative started by Woody Allen and Sidney Lumet in the 1970s that New York was the only place that mattered. The New York romance had gone cold when the economy did. By 1994, however, it picked back up: NBC's Thursday-night urban comedies *Seinfeld* and *Friends* romanticized the city reminiscent of how Hollywood studio screwball comedies and gangster pictures had in the 1930s. David Letterman's *The Late Show* was a powerful statement of the city's sudden ability to embrace regular, touristy Americans and endow them with a postmodern ironic sensibility, as they tromped into the Ed Sullivan Theater to see the Indiana boy who suddenly, triumphantly owned New York. New York seemed to be a city of wise guys, long-legged working girls, cute college graduates in giant exposed-brick apartments with mysterious means of financial support and funny neighbors. Who wouldn't want to live there?

Half the parents who bought their kids one-bedrooms as family "investments"—little did they know they were securing the city from urban flight when things would get tough later—believed the adorable *Friends* fantasy. And it became true! Their sons and daughters graduated from Wharton and N.Y.U. Law, dropped into ludicrously high-paying gigs, found their corner deli owners adorable, their gay neighbors accessible, their bittersweet Saturday nights erased by Sunday brunches in Soho. Manhattan became a haute-bourgeois theme park.

For them, *The New York Observer* became a kind of pet Pekinese, a hometown paper that was naughty, cheeky, yappy, occasionally thoughtful, reporting on a population that exulted in its own parties, manners and marital breakups. We became the joyful, exuberant reporters of their image-madness. Sometimes we thought of ourselves as enablers. But what reporters could resist these people? It would

> *A topography of power, with its Manhattan moats and turrets, its courts in media, politics and society, its residues of Wharton, Winchell and Weegee.*

have been malpractice to turn away. No matter how mad they were, they generally called to buy their own front-page caricatures.

We culled from the great *New York World* of the 1920s, the newspaper of newspapers—stylish, fun, writerly, liberal, legendary—the monumentally designed broadsheet that towered above the city, covering politics, culture and society while below, other papers chased ambulances and closed nightclubs. "This is New York," Ben Hecht had written in his newspaper comedy, *Nothing Sacred*, "skyscraper champion of the world ... where Truth, crushed to earth, rises again more phony than a glass eye." A few of us sat on the floor with crumbling copies of the *World* from 1924 and lifted the headline voice.

At *The Observer*, Jim Windolf became a particular master of the Homeric headline; epigrams abounded: Alfonse D'Amato became "our beloved Alfonse." Tina Brown became the "Intellectual Property Mogul." Meanwhile, Peter Stevenson brought back in a writer who was a close friend of his, a skinny, glint-eyed blonde with perfect teeth, Candace Bushnell. Stevenson and I felt pretty strongly that the paper was a little arid and detached from life as we understood it in the city. And Candace was a writer who understood the price—and the value—of everything. We asked her if she would write a column about sex for the paper. If there was one thing about Candace, it was that she was game.

"Sex?" she said. "In New York?" Her eyes were mysteriously azure. "Sure."

I often can see the keys of *The Observer's* last typewriter as we banged out the words: S-E-X-A-N-D-T-H-E-C-I-T-Y. We knew right away it was good. It was so good that we immediately tried to change it to something cleverer. Candace's first column was a pretty standard report on a downtown sex club. But after a few weeks, Carrie Bradshaw showed up and that was that.

We knew it was a hit when angry readers, particularly single women scraping the walls and floor of the dating market, began calling to cancel their subscriptions.

The paper began picking up. It got press and developed a national reputation. It was the 1990s, and I have to tell you, we thought we were a little bit in heaven. We had four amazing front-page illustrators, each with a different style—Robert Grossman, Victor Juhasz, Philip Burke and Drew Friedman—who were like a great four-man starting rotation of pitchers, with the astonishing caricaturist Barry Blitt as the closer. We knew we were getting somewhere when it was reported to us, apocryphally or not, that Michael Eisner, the CEO of Disney, had slammed down a Drew Friedman front-page illustration of his No. 2, Michael Ovitz—as Mickey Mouse's beleaguered Sorcerer's Apprentice—in front of Ovitz on the Disney board table.

The Observer believed that there was some importance in letting the reporters go for it, even if it occasionally meant losing the owner acquaintances who had portrayed themselves as his friends. Arthur Carter didn't mind turning the whole town—billionaires, restaurateurs, gallery owners—into Margaret Dumont to the paper's Groucho. I sat with him a couple of times where social acquaintances literally turned their backs on him. Arthur generally preferred the paper to cronies. At lunch one day, I asked him if he liked making his friends angry. He looked at me seriously, as though I were not only insane but deeply insensitive. "I don't like it," he said. "Not one bit."

But occasionally maybe he did like it one little bit. He told me he had gotten a wake-up call in bed one Wednesday morning from an angry mayor who didn't like the fact that *The Observer* had run a feature on one of his country homes. "But Mayor," Arthur said, "why didn't you call me yesterday, before the paper came out? I could have done something about it then!"

For a few minutes, we at *The Observer* were what Hildy Johnson called "the white-haired boys." We went to Elaine Kaufman's bar, and Elaine bought us drinks. Frank DiGiacomo's Transom was making running characters of Pat Buckley, Pat Cooper, Triumph the Insult Dog, Anna Wintour and Harvey Weinstein. New York was a movable feast, a banquet table where the dessert talked back.

Why? Maybe it was that we were new and honest, and the old guys were getting older. We were, and they were. Across the room from me right now is a big bound edition of *The Observer* from 1995, with a story that could only be loved by an archivist of exquisite trivialities: "THE OBSERVER 500: Power! Measured N.Y. style — In Gossip Inches." In agonizing, pre-digital hours, we compiled a list of who had been mentioned most in the New York news columns, by number of mentions. Here's how it went:

1. O.J. Simpson
2. Madonna
3. Mayor Rudolph Giuliani
4. President Bill Clinton
5. Barbra Streisand
6. Michael Jackson
7. Donald Trump
8. Diana, Princess of Wales
9. John F. Kennedy Jr.
10. Elizabeth Taylor

That was another world. New York was suddenly perceived as a new kind of power capital. The stock market kept rising. People began chortling about the "World Wide Web." It was going to be our great new communications industry! You could dial it up. Mobs of jolly suburbanites roamed the streets at night. Sushi joints and gourmet pizza places began opening on every street corner and people had the money to buy art. When middle-class people start buying art, you can tell your grandchildren, something is seriously out of whack. The Yankees won four World Series in five years and even the Mets won a pennant. Skinny ladies mobbed Cipriani and La Goulue, and Julian Niccolini seated the Four Seasons like it was the U.S. Senate.

Harvey Weinstein, the co-owner of Miramax, devoured the moment. He did what New York movie producers had been trying but failing to do for decades—he hijacked Hollywood. He beat Steven Spielberg for Best Picture in Spielberg's own hometown. Meanwhile Graydon Carter's *Vanity Fair* party replaced Swifty Lazar's—it was a New York conquest. Rap stars consorted with CEOs, and bought tables at the Metropolitan Museum's Costume Institute Ball and became real es-

tate moguls, and Robert De Niro's crew established Tribeca as the nether glamour sector of the city, confirmed by the residence of the star of stars, chiseled, gleaming, unmatchable John F. Kennedy Jr., so transparently heroic that women dropped in his path and *Seinfeld* devoted an episode to Elaine's aerobics-class lust for him.

The entire thing astonished us. When at last there was a national crisis, it turned out there were endless wirings between the chubby, mirthful intern who managed to deliver a pizza to Bill Clinton and New York: Monica fled here; her family was here; so was Linda Tripp's tireless right-wing literary agent, Lucianne Goldberg, who manned the phones day and night, guiding reporters. Was there no sitcom plot to be left unexplored? And when the president decided to recompense his wife with a power base of her own, he called Congressman Rangel and installed her—where else? She became our senator.

> What were those papers about? A civilization that loved itself a little too much and created its own inky portrait. Now the world has changed.

NEW YORK WAS SEIZED BY A SEINFEL-dian bantering amorality. It was a sushi and ice cream town. Money voyeurism prevailed, coddled by Clinton Years prosperity. By 1998, Carrie Bradshaw and her HBO buddies were trawling the city for practical love. New York was the world's richest, coolest burg, a never-never land on a perpetual Thursday night. Everybody worked, few bled. It was implausible that anything could go wrong. But by the time it did, we could console ourselves with one thing: We knew it wouldn't last.

Needless to say, it didn't. I won't weigh you down with our particular version except this: A newsroom that had rarely wept found itself that Tuesday, a day that we were planning on the usual weary coverage of the mayoral primaries, charged with making a screaming shift from a Drew Friedman cover illustration of Michael Jackson's birthday party to printing up a headline that said only: September 11, 2001. I had been tromping all the way down Second Avenue as the firetrucks went roaring by, heading south from the Bronx and Westchester.

I remember coming into the office and finding our toughest editor slumped on his desk, his head covered with his hands. We were not, as Ma Joad told Tom, kissing people, but there was a great deal of hugging that day. I called Drew Friedman and he faxed in a black-and-white drawing of the Statue of Liberty besieged in black billows; we hand-tinted it in the production department. By evening, we could smell the first wisps of that particular acrid, chemical smoke blowing up to East 64th Street from downtown.

The giddy days were done. New York was no longer a comedy.

But in many ways, *The Observer* became a better newspaper. It wasn't that it sobered up and stared deeper into its beats. It's that the generation of reporters who showed up became more committed to reporting the city. It was after 2001 that we got some of our best reporters and editors, resolute young hard-nosed journalists who loved print but began taking charge of the Internet. They just seemed to keep landing at the doorstep of East 64th Street, then when we moved, to lower Broadway. More and more, they knew journalism and politics and carried their own little digital cameras and wanted to write not once a week, but as often as they could file. Less and less did they buy a copy of any newspaper. When I first started at *The Observer* my standard question to applicants was: How many days a week do you buy a daily newspaper? The age kept going up and up, until relatively few bought anything beyond the massive Sunday *Times: Sic transit gloria* Monday.

A great deal has changed in New York City for newspapers since 2001. One thing, of course, is the World Wide Web. *The New York Observer* was made to be, designed to be, a newspaper paradigm. But it is no longer a newspaper.

IN LATE 2006, JARED KUSHNER, A SMART, HANDSOME REAL estate scion who saw the future of newspapers, bought *The Observer*. Jared brought new swagger to the paper: He liked it, bulked up the newsroom, but wanted to publish it as a paper for the new digital present, not the remote fading past. We made two huge, significant changes. The first was that we remade ourselves as a tabloid, a kind of *New York Post* goes to college. It was like buying a miniskirt. David Carr, the press columnist for *The New York Times*, wrote that *The Observer* had used "stacked headlines and narrow columns, to play against type: it unleashed a waterfall of improbable display language splattered with exclamation points, ellipses and question marks that created a libretto before the reader even started the article." The big front page was a beautiful cacophony. But the world is moving quickly, and the broadsheet paradigm doesn't have the same intrinsic satiric bite it once did: The gold standard has changed.

The other change was that we leaped into the Internet revolution. It was bracing and it was good. More than that, it was imperative. And it worked. *The Observer's* Web site was not only beautiful and stylish, it made sense for the paper. By the homestretch of the 2008 presidential election, our political and media reporters—in Iowa and New Hampshire, through the primaries and the Hillary saga, then into the conventions and the election—had put the paper at the front of the pack. We broke big stories in the campaign. On the very day Joe Biden announced his candidacy for president, a story by political reporter Jason Horowitz quoted him describing Barack Obama as "the first mainstream African-American who is articulate and bright and clean and a nice-looking guy." Bingo! By the last month of the election, the *Observer* Web site was being visited by two million readers a month. It was a game-changing concept.

But what about the newspaper itself? The ink-smeared salmon-tinted newsprint? Would it become another smoking hulk on the media battlefield? Print has its own metaphysical power to bite back. A tactile, physical page has a relationship with a reader that nothing else does. It's meant to be engaged and absorbed. An electronic culture is stripped of nuance. Clifford Odets wrote that life shouldn't be printed on dollar bills—it also can't be counted in Web page views. The Internet may be the most democratizing event in media history. It has already affected American society and global politics in a way that nothing ever has. And it's still only primitive. All the wonderful news Web sites we've become addicted to—Drudge and Gawker and the Huffington Post—are untethered churners.

Lately, there are Web Geniuses who tell you that editors are a superfluous prophylactic between the information and the reader. I don't know. One of the few good things I've ever heard said about editing was Harold Ross' comment that "All an editor can do is have a net handy to grab any talent that comes along, and maybe cast a little bread on the waters." Our own critic Andrew Sarris stated the Auteur Theory of movie directors. Surely, for anyone who cares deeply about the media, it makes sense that Clay Felker and Milton Glaser of *New York* magazine, Harold Ross of the *New Yorker*, Jim Bellows at the *Herald Tribune* and Arthur Gelb of *The New York Times* were auteurs like John Ford and Howard Hawks. It doesn't matter if it was in print or it's on little screens—it's the catalytic combination of sensibility, aesthetic, storytelling, reporting and morality that matters. The new media is waiting for its Orson Welles—someone who can electrify the literature.

THE NEW YORK OBSERVER HAS ADAPTED TO THE NEW World. Our Web site reports—we're not really bloggers. We were given the chance to do this through enlightened publishing. The Web Geniuses are nice people, but page views, traffic and emphasis are their business. Aggregation isn't journalism. It isn't sensibility or chemistry, and it isn't comedy or tragedy, either. It's collecting with a bias. You can't report by aggregation, or deepen the culture. The aggregators are as essential to the current media crisis as home lenders were to the financial collapse of 2008. They pull up chairs at the table with empty mugs and say, "Fill 'er up—and you're buying!" These seers will be replaced in the long run; they are the powerful primitives in the media evolution. If journalism is the first draft of history, Web sites are the first draft of journalism.

If newspapers and magazines fold up and go away, it will be a disaster for democracy. Bob Hope had a great joke in the 1950s: "When vaudeville died, television was the box they put it in." There is a box being built for newspapers as well: an iPhone that your kid will stuff into his back pocket and sit on and smash the screen, which is about right—newspapers carry the protection of the First Amendment but they are not meant to be treated well. Recently, one of *The Observer's* reporters wrote: "Readers want to get their news fix and they can't wait for newspapers to come once a day on their doorstep, or even once an hour, like on blogs. It's going to start getting streamed right to their fingertips, on mobile devices." Not shocking to you as a concept, and not so different from newsboys screaming "Extra!" Newspapers are living things that bite and yap, they are essentially beautiful, but they are meant to get streamed right to you, and then mostly disappear. A few of the ideas stay.

Was it really a kingdom? We thought so. Nobody cares about the rococo tales of newspapers but reporters, any more than anyone can make sense of the majesty of the dragon of the printing press itself, with its roar and black ink issue. Now that those dragons are fading, the tales are heading into mythology. What were those papers about? They were about a civilization that loved itself a little too much and created its own inky portrait. Now the world has changed. Will the papers persevere? They will, if they can buy safe passage into the new era. Great cultures are always being declared washed up. The Kingdom isn't dead. It will exist as long as there's a reporter and an editor to conjure it. Long live the Kingdom of New York!

THE NEW YORK OBSERVE

© 1987 The New York Observer Company, Inc.

VOL. 1 NO. 0   AUGUST 31, 1987

Tuberculosis Cases Increased by 46% In City Since '80

Disease Hits Hardest at the Homeless Who Exist in Cramped Conditions

By SHERYL FRAGIN

After decades of progress toward its eradication, tuberculosis is quietly spreading in New York City once again. The infection rate in impoverished pockets of the city is equal to that of many third world countries and is "epidemic" among the city's growing homeless population, according to many medical authorities.

By the City Health Department's count, there were 2,223 new, reported cases of tuberculosis in New York last year, up 46 percent from 1980, while cases in the rest of the country were generally declining. "New York City has by far and away the largest number of cases," said Dr. Dixie Snider, director of the division of tuberculosis control at the Centers for Disease Control in Atlanta. "The thing that's most disturbing is the trend in New York. We've never had an increase of 46 percent before in history."

Infected Droplets

TB is spread by infected droplets carried through the air by coughing. Health authorities say that the risk to the general public in casual contact with an infected person is minimal, but that the risk increases exponentially in crowded conditions. "People on subways and buses are in a risky situation, no question about it," said Dr. Snider. "But ... the magnitude of risk is not very great. It's not as risky as being closed up with a co-worker who has a chronic cough."

The real risk, many experts say, is to the homeless in shelters. "If you or I were to sleep in a shelter one night," said Peggy Rafferty, a board member of the Coalition for the Homeless, "we'd inhale some particles, but we'd get rid of them. But if you're malnourished and maybe beaten up, you're a lot more susceptible to disease." According to a recent report issued by the Centers for Disease Control, the incidence of latent TB among the homeless may be as high as 22 percent to 50 percent.

Equally Vulnerable

Equally vulnerable are residents of the city's poorest neighborhoods, where drugs, alcohol, AIDS and malnutrition have ravaged many people's immune systems. Last year, central Harlem had 130 tuberculosis cases per 100,000, up from 110 in 1985. Among black men ages 35–44, the rate was 263 per 100,000. These figures contrast sharply with affluent areas such as Manhattan's East Side, where the rate was 9.1, or Maspeth-Forest Hills, Queens, where it was 7.1.

"Central Harlem has the highest incidence both of disease in general and

Neal McGraw at work in Central Park's Sheep Meadow.

Philip Greenberg

Well-Dressed Men Plunder Posh Pads

Break in to Upper East Side Co-ops; Rob Valuables

By DAVID FRANCE

Two stately gentlemen have strolled into a dozen or more posh uptown apartments in recent weeks and, with a nod and friendly assistance from the doormen, have skipped away with a fortune in jewels, silver and other treasures. Their pretexts are varying, but their success in thwarting detectives at the 19th Precinct, perhaps since early June, is unwavering.

The two—both white men in their forties, around 5'10", "middle-class and good dressers," according to police—have posed as architects, engineers, designers or general contractors to talk their way past tight security in buildings from Fifth Avenue to Park, from 76th Street to 96th Street.

Murdoch Seems Bent on Keeping The Post; Sale Deadline Looms

By PETER GRANT

As Rupert Murdoch's deadline for selling The New York Post approaches, newspaper-industry analysts and observers are becoming increasingly convinced that he is determined to hold on to the brash tabloid that is one of his prized possessions.

Mr. Murdoch has to sell The Post according to the Federal Communications Commission's 1985 ruling, which allowed him to purchase six television stations, including WNEW-TV in New York, from Metromedia, Inc. The FCC gave him two years from the closing of the deal to comply with its rule that prohibits the same company from owning both a broadcasting station and a newspaper in the same market. That deadline expires in March 1988, but Wall Street analysts expect Mr. Murdoch to find a way around it. They say they see no evidence that he has begun looking for a possible buyer, which he would be doing by now if he intended to meet the deadline.

and prestige of owning the paper is worth a great deal to him.

"Owning a paper in New York gives you clout in the world of finance and the world of Madison Avenue," noted J. Kendrick Noble Jr., a media analyst for PaineWebber. "It gives you political clout with the Mayor, the Governor and even the President. New York also is where Murdoch lives."

The Post's losses, meanwhile, are minuscule when put into the context of Mr. Murdoch's media empire. His News Corporation Ltd.—which owns newspapers, magazines, television stations, publishing houses and movie production and distribution firms in 31 cities across four continents—is worth an estimated $9 billion. The corporation earned $119.8 million in 1986 compared to $58.4 million in 1985.

Mr. Murdoch could not be reached for comment. A spokesman for News America, the U.S. holding company that owns The Post, would only say that

Dinkins Join Koch and St And Draws

Shelter Vote Ril Golden, Shulm

By TOM ROBBINS

Even before the Board of E had cast its final vote last week the way for construction of 11 for the homeless, Mayor Ko downstairs in the City Hall trumpeting his coup.

"What we saw upstairs," s Mayor, "was a grand slam. A man who hit the home run wa Council President] Andy Stein. under enormous pressure, a weak would have buc

News Analysis Almost as an aftert the Mayor credited hattan Borough Pr David Dinkins as well. But it w a decidedly secondary role, li of a utility player who had co the bench in the late innings ar the infield's defense tight.

Actually, the Mayor hadn' anything at all. He had spent t hours of the unprecedentedly Board of Estimate meeting liste the proceedings through a spe his office. Mr. Stein also sat i tempest upstairs in his own of City Hall's east wing. This le Dinkins sitting stony-faced at the shoe table, casting the assentin to put each of the shelters top, and listening in silence to i ingly rancorous denunciations other board members. When the dar clerk slipped and called Brooklyn and Manhattan to Brooklyn Borough President Golden interrupted: "Please, w nothing to do with Manhattan

Ire Aimed at Dinkins

When the borough presidents Bronx, Queens and Brooklyn emerged from the chambers, w drawn and angry faces, none c darts were aimed at Mr. Stein, t the Mayor cited for the starrin in carving the narrow 6–5 majo favor of the administration's shelte

Instead, their ire was aimed ex ly at their counterpart from M tan. And a fierce ire it was. To Borough President Claire Shulm Dinkins was a "backstabber;" nando Ferrer of the Bronx, "clubhouse politics." And Mr. of Brooklyn asked how Mr. could "face the mirror in the mc

There were a number of reaso borough leaders may have been resentful of Mr. Dinkins than of M or Staten Island Borough Pre Ralph Lamberti, who also cast he with the Mayor. For one thin Dinkins had publicly embraced a report issued last spring by hi task force on homeless familie report was called "A Shelter a Home," and it forcefully rebut Mayor's plan, arguing instead fc manent homes carved out of abar

1987-1990

Salmon-colored weekly newspaper joins New York City's media mob

Tom Wolfe roasts yuppie tycoons in *The Bonfire of the Vanities*

Yow! The Dow Jones Industrial Average plunges 800 points

Buyout king Henry Kravis, designer Carolyn Roehm storm high society

The Whitney bulges with Robert Mapplethorpe's naughty male nudes

New Yorkers fear nighttime walks in their nabes more than AIDS

Dazzling Diane Sawyer shuns CBS for ABC, marries Mike Nichols

The Ayatollah proves big publicity boost for Salman Rushdie's *Satanic Verses*

 Tina Brown's *Vanity Fair* is essential reading for the nouveau riche

Takeover titan Saul Steinberg spends $1 million on his 50th birthday party

Manhattan Borough President David N. Dinkins elected city's first black mayor

---

C Will Announce
adquarters Plan
ithin Two Weeks

LEASE IS UP IN '97

ork Eyes Trump's TV
ty and New Jersey
As Alternatives

By GINGER DANTO

National Broadcasting Company
announce by Labor Day whether
s to remain at its present Manhat-
adquarters, relocate to one of four
n New Jersey or set its sights
nald Trump's proposed "Televi-
City" on the Upper West Side,
vork official said this week.

are still evaluating all of the
ilities, including Trump's Televi-
ity," said Dom Giofre, manager
rmation at NBC, which has been
ng for more than a year where
ve once its current lease at
feller Center expires in 1997.
e looking for the best offer," said
iofre, adding that rent, taxes and
in its future location are among
ctors NBC is weighing in its

At Site Since 1933

C has occupied the RCA building
1933, renovating for television the
s originally built for radio. While
ompany still has ample time to
a new home for its 4,000
yees before its lease expires, Mr.
said, "We want to make a deal
o if anything has to be built we
time to do it."

e want to keep NBC in New
" said Alair Townsend, Deputy
r for finance and economic
opment. "Being in New York is
tant to NBC, and NBC is impor-
o New York."

Townsend said that while negotia-
between NBC and Mr. Trump
ed to be moving along," the city
rking to make it attractive for the
rk to remain. Dollar for dollar,
aid, it may cost NBC more to
in Manhattan, but there are
le advantages, such as proximity
er aspects of the industry. "We
we can put together a package
oes a great distance to keep NBC
w York," she said, adding that
the city considers Television Ci-
iable site for the network, it "will
ive Donald Trump carte blanche
everything he wants to do."

Trump, Mayor Feud

Trump, meanwhile, is doing his
o keep NBC from leaving New
While such efforts were initially
tent with Mayor Koch's agenda,
eveloper and the Mayor began
g over the best way to negotiate
the network.
Koch has not taken a formal
on on Television City, but at a

1987-1990

AUGUST 31, 1987

THE NEW YORK OBSERVER EDITORIAL

54 East 64th Street, New York, New York 10021

A Note of Explanation The copy of *The New York Observer* that you have in your hand is a prototype of a new newspaper devoted to covering Manhattan. The editorial content is real and is an indication of what's to come. The advertising is simulated copy to help convey what our paper will look like this fall, when we go into regular publication.

Manhattan is, above all else, unique. From Harlem and Inwood in the north, through the commercial and residential areas of midtown, and south through TriBeCa to Wall Street and Battery Park City, Manhattan constitutes a huge city complex of 1.6 million people. It contains one of the greatest concentrations of wealth in the world and some of the worst poverty. The rich and powerful in politics, business, media and entertainment make their homes here, and it is the culture capital of the world. But the city is also a place where countless people live in despair and desolation, many without homes. These extremes are only part if what makes Manhattan a complicated, fascinating and somewhat awesome place.

Covering the city is a tremendous challenge and a huge job. Our goal in launching *The Observer* is to publish a paper that is lively, penetrating and honest. This is the only way we can expect to attract readers and advertisers. We plan to work hard to create the best newspaper we can each week.

The Bartered Result The political art of the smoke-filled room prevailed last week as the Board of Estimate settled on a compromise that will result in the construction of 11 of the 15 homeless shelters proposed under the original plan offered by Mayor Koch. In exchange for the vote of Manhattan Borough President David Dinkins, a vote Mr. Koch needed desperately for the plan to go through, the mayor promised only one shelter in Manhattan, rather than the proposed three, and agreed to renovate 1,000 city-owned apartments for homeless families.

The construction of 11 new shelters seems on its face a victory for the homeless, and to a degree it is: Any positive step to ameliorate this tragedy is welcome. Yet several aspects of the vote require closer scrutiny.

Shelters are temporary. Many who opposed the plan from the beginning urged the mayor instead to rehabilitate city-owned housing as standardized permanent units. Mayor Koch said this is too time-consuming and expensive. But he was finally forced, under the deal with Mr. Dinkins, to agree to renovate the 1,000 units. Will the city ever get the permanent housing it needs?

What happened in Clinton? Community Board 4, which contains Clinton, was the only board of 15 to agree to accept a shelter, though it suggested moving the location by 50 feet. But no shelter is going up in Clinton. Why?

What happened in Far Rockaway and Co-op City? Shelters were proposed in two largely white neighborhoods with political clout, neighborhoods where many residents did not want shelters. City Council President Andrew Stein, who voted with the mayor, opposed both these sites. Now, a shelter is being constructed in neither location. They ended up in Harlem; in Bushwick; in East New York; in the South Bronx—in other words, largely in minority neighborhoods with very little political clout. A coincidence?

Some action is being taken for the homeless—11 shelters will be built. And Mayor Koch may have won his political victory. But temporary shelters provide only a temporary solution. A real solution requires compassion and commitment and cannot be hurriedly bartered by Board of Estimate members the day before the vote.

Intent of the Framers? Broadcasting's "fairness doctrine"—the federal regulation that required radio and television stations to offer airtime to groups or persons with dissenting views—has worked as its name implies. It has helped those with a different viewpoint gain access to the airwaves. It has helped promote public debate and the exchange of views vital to democracy. The Federal Communications Commission's decision to abolish this protection is a mistake.

Some have praised the F.C.C. decision as, among other things, a victory for free speech. Government should not, they argue, dictate to broadcasters what views they must put on air. In so dictating, the government, they say, violates the constitutional guarantee of freedom of the press.

Writers of the Constitution were familiar with the printing press and with newspapers. They did not, however, foresee radio and television, each of which is strictly licensed by government. They did not foresee the creations of huge broadcasting empires controlled by such companies as General Electric and Westinghouse. The framers of the Constitution envisioned a living document. As such, it must be continually construed to guarantee the right to dissent and freedom of speech in today's high-tech, electronic age.

Access to the major networks and stations only for those who can afford to buy airtime is a distorted kind of freedom. The freedom represented by the fairness doctrine is, by contrast, something that the framers of the Constitution would have understood very well indeed. It helps ensure that others will have the power to make their voices heard. It is a freedom consistent with the spirit and intent of 1787.

OCTOBER 12, 1987 BY JEAN NATHAN

HEALTH WORRIES LEAD TO REMOVAL OF SAND FROM PUBLIC PLAYGROUNDS

OF THE 143 PLAYGROUNDS IN MANHATTAN, 101 HAVE SANDBOXES. OF these, only 52 have sand in them. They are used as shooting galleries, outdoor ashtrays, garbage pits and toilets for people and animals. Razorblades, glass fragments and fleas also defile them. The days of an occasional sand-encrusted popsicle stick being the only debris there are long gone.

The Parks Department, overwhelmed by such problems, has reacted by quietly phasing out the sandbox. Of the 20 projects now on the boards to design new and renovate existing playgrounds, only one includes a sandbox. Parks Commissioner Henry J. Stern acknowledges the problem, saying "It crept up like tooth decay."

The question of what to be done with Manhattan's remaining public sandboxes is very much on the minds of Parks Department officials, parents and doctors, many of whom have affectionate memories of times they and their children have spent there.

The Parks Department policy for the future of the city's sandboxes is not a blanket one. "Our sandbox policy is empirical," said Mr. Stern. "We judge by experience. If in any community it works, and the people and animals keep it clean, then fine, we like the sandbox. There is a different chemistry in each area." "The sandbox requires a higher level of social responsibility than some of our citizens possess at this time," said Mr. Stern. "We don't want to expose children to disease and injury."

◇◇◇◇◇◇◇

OCTOBER 12, 1987 BY BELLA ABZUG

Why Must Women be Perfect?

A MALE DEMOCRATIC CONSULTANT WAS QUOTED LAST week on the occasion of Congresswoman Pat Schroeder's withdrawal from the presidential race, "Women in politics have to be perfect—that's just a nasty fact of life."

He was, of course, referring to the fact that Ms. Schroeder cried when she made her statement, and his observation was echoed by more than one commentator.

Who says that women politicians have to be perfect? Moreover, who says that crying makes you imperfect?

What human is perfect?

It's to cry, all right baby, as well as a nasty fact of life that politics has slipped more and more away from reality and humanity. Every day we are robbed of the opportunity to expect real and honest emotions which, after all, we all initially possess whether we are politicians or not.

It's to cry, baby, and a nasty fact of life that Pat Schroeder, a Class A act as qualified or more so than most of the men running, decided not to run. She served 15 years in Congress trying to reverse the arms race. She spent 15 years moving to preserve the environment, 15 years embracing the concerns of family and the nurturing of children, and as co-chair of Congress' caucus on issues promoting human rights.

It's to cry, baby, and a nasty fact of life that she started to test the

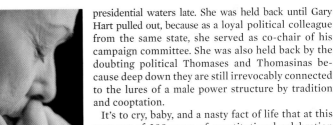

presidential waters late. She was held back until Gary Hart pulled out, because as a loyal political colleague from the same state, she served as co-chair of his campaign committee. She was also held back by the doubting political Thomases and Thomasinas because deep down they are still irrevocably connected to the lures of a male power structure by tradition and cooptation.

It's to cry, baby, and a nasty fact of life that at this moment of 200 years of constitutional celebration we continue a government supplied by man alone. In the words of Frederick Douglass, a government supplied by man alone is a government only half supplied and like a bird with one wing unable to soar to the highest and the best.

You're a proud woman, serious member of Congress, terrific wife and mother and a person of deep feelings. Suddenly your dream is shattered. The frustration is overwhelming. You know you are needed but are forced to withdraw. You let it honestly happen. You let it all hang out. You share your feelings with your family, your friends, your supporters—and the people.

No—it's not to grin and bear it or to smile—it's a nasty fact of life and—IT'S to cry.

OCTOBER 19, 1987
BY MOIRA HODGSON

A CRITIC'S VIEW: DINING AT WINDOWS ON THE WORLD: TOO BAD YOU CAN'T EAT THE VIEW

A RESTAURANT THAT OFFERS both good food and a view is as rare as a clean subway. But when Windows on the World opened on the 107th floor of the World Trade Center in 1976, it seemed that such a restaurant might finally have arrived in Manhattan. At the time, it received favorable—even ecstatic—reviews. But restaurants change. Visitors from all over are still pouring into Windows on the World, which seats 350 and has the best view in New York City. But recent experiences here have been more reminiscent of eating on an airplane than in a good restaurant.

Nothing beats the experience at dinner of looking out over inky rivers and twinkling lights, to the Empire State and Chrysler Buildings, all the way up the George Washington Bridge, with the Brooklyn Bridge on your right. But if you have dinner at Windows on the World, make sure it's on a clear night.

NOVEMBER 23, 1987   BY FRANCINE DU PLESSIX GRAY

A CRITIC'S VIEW: WOLFE'S NEW NOVEL: RICH PROSE, THIN CHARACTERS

AT THE AGE OF 38, HE LIVES IN A 14-room, $2.5 million Park Avenue apartment purchased with a $1.8 million bank loan; his mortgage alone costs him 21,000 a month. This patrician graduate of Buckley, St. Paul's and Yale wears $650 British shoes and $2,000 custom-made suits from Savile Row.

Sherman McCoy is the hero of Tom Wolfe's first novel, *The Bonfire of the Vanities*, and he may become our decade's most memorable emblem for a generation of yuppie tycoons who were flaunting their wealth with an exhibitionism unprecedented in the history of New York City ... until a few weeks ago. Few contemporary novels have been so uncannily recursive. The blow dealt by Wall Street's Black Monday collapse to the fortunes of McCoy's real life counterparts might well parallel McCoy's landslide into penury.

Tom Wolfe's satiric, pitiless black comedy is a classical fable of high hubris. Beyond crass insensitivity and an astounding lack of self-knowledge, his hero's fatal character flaw is his belief that he is a "Master of the Universe," entitled to "the simple pleasures due all mighty warriors."

Yet there is a curiously disturbing aspect to this gifted book: It is populated by sumptuously described material possessions rather than by fully fleshed people. Apart from McCoy's love for his little daughter (expressed by cloying bathos), no emotion inhabits these individuals beyond occasional lust, ethnic paranoia, and greed for still more status-laden objects. A neat summing up of the ethos of the late 1980's: tone deafness to the reality of pain, passive resignation to inequities.

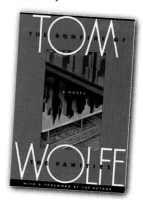

FEBRUARY 1, 1988   BY MARK J. PENN AND DOUGLAS E. SCHOEN

Observer Poll: In New York, Marriage Satisfies, Beckons

A KEY TO HAPPINESS FOR NEW Yorkers appears to be having A successful marriage, according to *The New York Observer* Poll.

The poll showed that marital bliss is somewhat related to frequency of sexual intercourse. People who reported having sex at least once every two weeks reported the same levels of happiness as those who said they have sex several times a week. But once sex dropped to once a month or less, marital satisfaction declined precipitously.

Surprisingly, frequency of sexual intercourse in a marriage did not appear to rule out affairs. On the contrary, 21 percent of married men who said they were having intercourse with their wives more than once a week said they also had an affair.

Indeed, the poll found that the happiest people were those who are married, followed by those who are close to it—living with someone. And people who date just one person are happier than those dating a range of people.

Among the tenth of the sample who said they are divorced, 92 percent said they had made the right decision while only 8 percent regretted it. But not nearly as many of those going through separations and divorces said they were "very happy" with their lives as married New Yorkers.

APRIL 30, 1990   BY MICHAEL M. THOMAS

MILKEN'S GREEDY GAME IS FINISHED, THE BIG BEETLE GOT STOMPED FLAT

"I'VE HAD THIS TERRIBLE dream that Diane Sawyer was interviewing Marla Maples."

"That was no dream, you jackass! Why ..."

Delicacy forbids me to transcribe the further deliriums of a woman whose perceptions are obviously still clouded by Morpheus.

As I skulk downstairs to deal with my chores, it all comes back. Aye, so t'was: I wasn't dreaming. Indeed, indeed there on my set, before my very eyes, the blond goddess of ABC had in

fact "interviewed" the Prince of Swine's alleged squeeze.

Now what, I wondered, could have made her do that? Not Ms. Maples, that plays itself. Too much hair, major gazongas and strong into the leg division. I'm too much a gentleman to draw I.Q. conclusions from what I heard on the tube.

My lament is: "Say it ain't so, Diane." I can understand she had good reasons for chucking CBS and *60 Minutes* for ABC, like three big ones a year and never having to airkiss Larry

Tisch again, but somewhere must have lurked the notion that real journalistic options were hers for the seizing, and now this! Simper City! Give me a break! Maybe it would have been better if *Primetime Live* had brought in a ringer for this one-shot special, someone like Alec Baldwin, say, or Kevin Costner, and no holds barred. Then we might have been given a true zinger, none of this "I have to get on with my life" bullbleep, but Miss M. strutting her best stuff.

MAY 21, 1990
BY HELEN THORPE

Observer Poll: Most Fear Streets At Night; Mixed Grades for Police

MOST NEW YORKERS FEEL EIther uncomfortable or afraid walking alone in their own neighborhoods at night and almost one-fifth feel uncomfortable or afraid doing so in daytime, according to *The New York Observer* Poll. At the same time, many members of the public seem dissatisfied with the NYPD.

A clear majority of New Yorkers say the police force acts in a biased manner, according to *The Observer* Poll. Only 17 percent of respondents said the police treat all groups of people the same, while 68 percent thought the police treat some better or worse. And while most city residents consider the police to be both friendly and helpful, one-fourth consider New York City police in general to be corrupt.

FEBRUARY 8, 1988   BY JEFF SHEAR

Felker Still Pursues Publishing Power After 20 Years and 7 Publications

THE WRITER GAY TALESE TELLS a story about magazine editor Clay Felker.

"We were arriving home in a taxi in the East 50's one evening," he says. "It was sometime during the mid-60's. It was winter. We had been drinking at some forgotten restaurant downtown, Clay still had an empty glass in his hand.

"It was the only time I ever saw him do something dramatic," he said. "Usually you would see him loping through the Four Seasons, not taking anything around him very seriously or paying much attention. Of course, he was, he never missed anything.

"But now, unexpectedly, he took a hook shot with the glass, a skyhook in the pre-Abdul Jabbar style, casually, slowly, looping the glass over the avenue."

Before it crashed against the curb, the two men had walked on, without so much as a word about the toss. "He gave no impression of his feelings," Mr. Talese said, although he was left with the sense that there was something to be understood in Mr. Felker's gesture, an odd aplomb, a signature perhaps, or an augury.

This April, as *New York* magazine celebrates its 20th anniversary, Clay Felker will mark his eighth month as editor of *Manhattan, inc.*, a magazine that had begun four years ago as the hot new magazine in town but has grown, as it says in its latest direct-mail subscription campaign, into "a relatively new magazine."

It is also a publication that has been reeling from a dispute that left it without an editor for a month last June and prompted a raft of departures from its masthead.

The crippling dispute occurred when the magazine's founding editor, Jane Amsterdam, quit after a power struggle with publisher D. Herbert Lipson. The issue was reportedly the degree of influence that advertising interests could exert on the editorial staff. Ironically, it is the sort of power struggle that has dogged Mr. Felker's career.

Mr. Lipson was vacationing in Caneel Bay, St. John, and could not be reached for comment. He has said in the past that he has complete confidence in Mr. Felker's judgment.

Still, the seeds of contention are there, and wherever Mr. Felker goes, drama follows. Power may drive him, but conflict stalks him and ultimately undoes him. The shattering of the glass against the curbs of publisher Herbert Lipson's power seems only to be a matter of time.

MARCH 14, 1988
BY MARILYN HARDING AND MARJORIE S. DEANE

FOR NEW FASHION ROEHM, IT'S A LONG WAY FROM ST. LOUIS

CAN CAROLYNE ROEHM, THE DAUGHTER OF A SCHOOL PRINCIPAL, have it all? Can a little girl from the Midwest grow up to be a slick Seventh Avenue designer? Can a cheerleader from St. Louis wed one of New York's wealthiest businessmen?

Nan Kempner, a matron of New York society by virtue of her marriage to broker and financier Thomas Kempner, an international representative for Christie's auction house, said: "Have you ever seen anyone as handsome as Henry Kravis? I would kill to sit next to him at a dinner party." But however Mrs. Kempner may position herself at a charity banquet, Carolyne Roehm is the one Mr. Kravis takes home.

Married for some five years, after both had divorced previous spouses, the Kravises have taken New York by storm. He, as the noted founder and partner of the firm Kohlberg, Kravis and Roberts, specializing in leveraged buy-outs. These are the guys who pulled off the big acquisition of Beatrice Foods and are now buying Stop and Shop. And she, launching her own designer label in 1985, one of the first to offer European tailoring and attitude geared to the moneyed American women. This is the very same couple who, within the past six months, have found their lavish lifestyle—a 17-room apartment on Park Avenue, a house in Connecticut and a gateway ski retreat in Vail; a major art collection; private Lear jet travel, and an assortment of the richest, most attractive friends—swept up by an avalanche of media hype that follows them.

It's high-profile country when *Women's Wear Daily* coins the very frivolous phrase "Nouvelle Society" and tacks it to your persona.

MARCH 14, 1988   BY NANCY JONES

TRANSFORMING AEROBICS INTO A FITNESS EMPIRE

CALIFORNIA'S PRINCESS OF FITNESS, GILDA MARX, BREEZED INTO town in September 1980 with a new program of aerobic exercise, and very nearly blew the competition away. Exercising in those days meant calisthenics at Lotte Berk, killer runs around the reservoir at 7 A.M., swinging from a trapeze at Alex and Wlater's or, at the very least, staring into a full-length mirror for a 15-minute work-out with two Campbell soup cans.

Today Gilda Marx owns three studios in Manhattan, with others in Washington, D.C., and Stamford, Conn., and every six weeks she jets back and forth from the West Coast to oversee details of what has become a multimillion dollar operation. Privately held Gilda Marx Industries projects revenues of $40 million for 1988, up from half a million in 1976.

Ms. Marx, who said she was born in Pittsburgh some 50-odd years ago, started exercising back in the 60's, moving around to music with her friends in her California living room. By 1975 she had opened her first Body Design by Gilda studio in Century City, and movie stars started to drop by. In the 70's, Ms. Marx and her husband, Robert, son of the least known Marx Brother, Gummo, created Flexatard Bodywear, a line of exercise clothing that they say is currently the country's best-selling exercise line.

◇◇◇◇◇◇◇◇

MAY 9, 1988   BY VALERIE BLOCK

Books & Co.: A Browser's Idea of Heaven

FOR A SPECIAL BOOKS & CO. COMMEMORATIVE BOOKLET SHE plans to publish in September, Jeannette Watson has been ask-ing friends and patrons to write down their experiences in the store, which she opened 10 years ago on Madison Avenue at 74th Street.

Writer Harold Brodkey characterized his experience in the store as "symphonically important to me." Writer Hortense Cal-isher called Books & Co. "wild and pleasant and comfy." Publisher Roger Straus of Farrar, Straus, Giroux, wrote of his delight upon finding his favorite out-of-print authors arranged alphabetically.

The 10th anniversary is a milestone for the store, according to Ms. Watson, because in their first year of business, she and her then-partner, Burt Britton, previously of the Strand Bookstore on Broadway, nearly went bankrupt as a result of an emphasis on book buying over bookkeeping. "There were times when publish-ers would call and ask for me and I would say, 'I'm sorry, she's not in right now, can I take a message?' and they would say, 'Yes, tell her we're suing her for nonpayment.' I went home every night and cried."

"Eventually, I just started calling up publishers and saying, 'I know I owe you a lot of money. I want to pay you this money, but I'm going to have to do it monthly.' The publishing companies were support-ive, she said, and eventually the store was in the black.

JUNE 20, 1988 BY GINGER DANTO

From Couples in 'Holy Deadlock,' Lawyers Earning Mega-Buck Fees

AFTER THE OPULENT WEDDING, the Champagne receptions, the lavish honeymoon, the Concorde trips, the expensive interior redecoration ... and then the love lost, comes the million-dollar divorce. That's how New York divorce attorney Raoul Felder sees it, every time he scans the wedding announcements to see where divorce lurks. "Marriage is the first step towards divorce," Mr. Felder said matter-of-factly, citing statistics that show one in every three marriages ends in divorce, and divorce now accounts for more than 50 percent of all court proceedings. But even such numbers are misleading "because there are so many people in the throes of divorce and no way of counting [others] getting out-of-country divorces," claims Mr. Felder. "The vast number of people are unhappily married, living together in holy deadlock."

Through the late 1970's, divorce settlement involved a simpler, if inequitable, arrangement. As New York was a "title state," each spouse in a New York divorce theoretically had the right to keep whatever belonged to him or her. With men generally earning and purchasing more than women, however, divorce often left the wife with far less materially than she had enjoyed during the marriage. Time spent raising a family while the husband worked, for instance, did not translate into a packet of assets in the event of divorce.

The equitable law distribution of 1980 created "marital property" so that assets acquired during a marriage by either spouse became common property divisible at divorce time. If loud arguments were part of divorces prior to 1980, they would now rise to crescendo in the disagreements over who should walk away with what.

JULY 25, 1988 BY MICHAEL M. THOMAS

THE MIDAS WATCH: THE PUNISHING HAMPTONS SOCIAL SCENE OF '88

IT'S EARLY IN THE SEASON YET, but already the pace and intensity of the Hamptons social punishment are the most daunting in memory. For the last few years, the July Fourth holiday has marked the entrance of a tunnel of time from which, some 60 days later, the survivors will emerge in a condition that makes survivors of the siege of Stalingrad look like recent graduates of the Golden Door. Over the holiday weekend, for example, the powers that be up the road in Smarthampton had the novel idea of staging what by the accounts of those who participated was nothing short of a social triathlon.

Indeed, one of the things that most interests me about the current season is what a hard time guests are giving their erstwhile hosts: always behind the back, of course, in the best high-society tradition. Ask someone if they had a good time the night before, and what you get is, well, about what you'd expect if you consulted Mario Buatta on the professional merits of, oh ... let's say Richard Feigen. It may be objective, intended as a commendable earnest of intellectual honesty, but as a post-mortem summary of a major nosh of prime Beluga and '47 Haut Brion it can have a chilling effect. Stirred into this long-fermenting human cocktail, this mélange of muslin and dimity old-timeliness, were some of the glorious butterflies, dressed to the nines, off to celebrate the 20th anniversary of a marriage that few of them had attended and most of the rest of us had. For us plain-spoken folks, it afforded a welcome chance to see the New Society on parade. Such spangles, sequins, bustles and well, I never ...!

Suddenly, there was a buzz, a stir, and the spectacle was enlivened by the arrival of the cadet branch of the Swine family. I naturally pressed close, as I do whenever major hogs are rumored in the vicinity. Kindness precedes me from saying more except that I now understand what the estimable John Fairchild's coinage of "Fashion Victim" can mean at its zenith. If victimization's the name of the game, this poor child was put together by the fashion equivalent of Jack the Ripper, from the lace-over-something jacket that looked capable of stopping a dum-dum bullet, down to the six-inch stiletto pumps. Now travel down the highway a piece and look at the ladies of art, themselves women of a certain age, or a few years to either side. An age where the black bird's footprints can be found. Still, look at these relaxed faces: Gloria Jones, Elaine Benson, Nora Ephron, Jessie Wood, Carol Ryan, Penny McCall, the lady who puts up with me—a whole glorious caboodle of them, and yet not a tough line in the lot.

That's what art does for one, you see. It doesn't just yield beauty and truth, it's good for the complexion.

JULY 25, 1988   BY LOU CHAPMAN

EXPERTS WARN OF IMPACT OF GREENHOUSE EFFECT ON CITY

THE SAME ENVIRONMENTAL forces that many scientists believe are raising the temperature of the earth's atmosphere will cause an increasing amount of salt water to flow up the Hudson River, worsen the effects of major, unpredictable ocean storms and contaminate the underground aquifers of fresh water beneath Long Island—that area's critical source of drinking water. All of that, government officials and environmental experts warn, could have severe consequences for New York City's drinking-water supplies, tunnels, storm sewers, sanitary sewers, and coastal development, and could hamper the complex workings of John F. Kennedy and LaGuardia airports. Many researchers say higher ocean levels and the incursion of salt water into freshwater estuaries will be two results of the "greenhouse effect," a man-made phenomenon that most atmospheric and weather scientists now agree is gradually warming the earth's climate. The greenhouse effect gets its name because it is doing to the surface of the earth exactly what a man-made greenhouse does for plants: It lets heat from the sun in but not out.

The U.S. Geological Survey had proposed a study that would cost more than $1 million and take more than three years, to allow planners to predict the impacts of a variety of changes to the Hudson River, including increased salinity and higher sea level. The city is counting on that study on a major state-orchestrated review of water management throughout New York to help decide how to prepare for the future, Mr. Englehardt said.

◇◇◇◇◇◇◇

AUGUST 22, 1988   BY HILTON KRAMER

A CRITIC'S VIEW: Mapplethorpe Show at the Whitney: A Big, Glossy, Offensive Exhibit

IN THE ROBERT MAPPLETHORPE retrospective that is currently installed at the Whitney Museum of American Art, there is so much that is highly problematical and so much that is simply offensive—so much indeed that many people will still want to consider it pornographic—that we have no choice but to conclude that it was precisely its air of scandal and provocation that commended the work to the museum's staff and made it seem not only a suitable but an irresistible subject for a large, glossy, sensational exhibition. The impression—that it is Mr. Mapplethorpe's subject matter that is primarily, though not solely, responsible for this large-scale show—is reinforced, moreover, by the fact that he is in many other respects a photographer who contributes little that is new to the language of photography. The formal conventions within which he works clearly owe much to the style that Edward Weston and his many followers perfected years before Mr. Mapplethorpe was born, and this is not a style that in its original form could be expected to elicit much interest nowadays at the Whitney. The best of Mr. Mapplethorpe's pictures are those that are concentrated on the bodies of nude figures—mostly male figures. Some of these bear a remarkable resemblance to certain sculptures of Gaston Lachaise. By and large, however, these photographic celebrations of exemplary physiques, with their theatrical lighting and arty poses, combine the familiar conventions of fashion photography—especially that of Irving Penn and Richard Avedon—with the formalist conventions of the Weston style.

As for Mr. Mapplethorpe's famous framing devices—the use he makes of fabric, mirrors, etc., in order to turn his pictures into one-of-a-kind art objects—all one can say is that they represent a tacit recognition that the photographic images are often not in themselves of sufficient power or interest to stand on their own. If you have a taste for campy minimalism, you will probably love these devices. I find them pretty trashy.

The truth is, there are about a dozen pictures in this show that have some real artistic quality—but you couldn't mount a major retrospective on an accomplishment of that size. And so it has been left to the "forbidden" subject matter to carry the burden of the show. There is no denying that the result is a sensational exhibition—but the sensation in question doesn't add much to the experience of art.

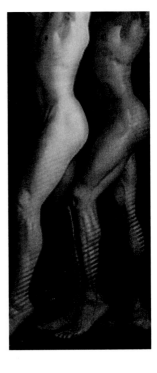

MAY 7, 1990 BY DANIEL LAZARE

Evans-Brown Team—or Is It Brown-Evans?

HARRY HADN'T NOTICED IT, BUT TINA WAS INCENSED. "Yuppies," she snorted. "That's what they are, complete yuppies. What's yuppie about it is the perception that you have to keep doing one thing all your life, and if you don't you're a failure.

"Harry," she went on, "who was the triumph of English journalism, who edited the best paper in the world, what [newspaper] would he want to edit here? There's nothing to edit, absolutely nothing."

Tina is Tina Brown, editor of *Vanity Fair*, favorite magazine of the nouveau riche. Harry is Harold Evans, former editor of the *Sunday Times* and *Times* of London, now in charge of *Condé Nast Traveler*. The alleged yuppies are the editors and writers of *Spy* magazine, who did a nasty little number in a recent issue on Si Newhouse's leading husband-and-wife team.

The *Spy* feature opens comic-strip-style in the 1970's with Tina, 22 and fresh out of Oxford, refusing to budge from Mr. Evans' doorstep until the great man of English journalism consents to see her. Then it flashes forward to 1981 when Rupert Murdoch, having just purchased the London *Times*, is unceremoniously giving Harry the boot while Tina (by then his wife) is piling accolade upon accolade as the swinging editor of *Tatler*, a society monthly. It winds up in contemporary Manhattan where Tina edits *Vanity Fair* while poor Harry, as *Spy* sees it, oversees articles on iguana stew and sunblock SPF's. "Harry's on the phone," an assistant calls out. Replies Tina, in the midst of some glamorous fashion shoot: "Take a message."

Moral: how the mighty have fallen, how the worm has turned, etc. All of which is rather carry on *Spy*'s part, but not entirely inaccurate. True, he's bounced around a bit since being canned by Mr. Murdoch in March 1982 (not 1981, as *Spy* reports) for showing insufficient loyalty, in the Australian's view, to Britain's monarch, Margaret Thatcher. He served as a director of Gold Crest Films & Television in London. He wrote a book, *Good Times, Bad Times*, about his experience working at, and being fired from, *The Times*. He taught journalism at Duke University. He served as editor of Atlantic Monthly Press. He participated in a short-lived but unsuccessful attempt to start up a competitor to the *Hartford Courant* in Connecticut. He spent two years at *U.S. News & World Report*. Now he edits stories about budget hotels in Manhattan and travel bargains in Budapest.

Though at age 60 Harry Evans is no longer rocking the foundations of British government, as he seemed to do every couple of years in 1970's, he says he's satisfied.

"My fortunes haven't fallen," said Mr. Evans, a short, somewhat rumpled figure. He sits in a corner office decorated with front pages from the *Sunday Times* in the 70's, a huge map of the world and a Helmut Newton photo of a woman standing naked in the middle of Prague.

"I actually am as happy as I've ever been and as fulfilled as I've ever been," he said in a recent interview. "Clearly, I did not like losing the editorship of *The Times*, but I don't read what I've done since as down. I'm a bit defensive about that. I've been asked to edit three papers in England since leaving *The Times*, but I didn't want to do it. That part of my life was over. I wanted to do something fresh and different."

"Doing a magazine is harder," he added in a follow-up conversation. "It's invented anew every month, whereas at a newspaper any old fool can follow the flow of events. When I was at *The Times*, I would start a flow of reports coming in and then would tell the staff, 'Do this,' or 'Do that.' On a magazine, you don't have that sort of conveyer belt.

"In England, the feeling is that Harry Evans is coasting," said a reporter for *The Economist*.

The Village Voice's editor-in-chief, Jonathon Z. Larsen, said: "People who don't know Harry tend to view him as the fifth wheel to Tina, but in fact the guy is incredibly good. I remember I went out to lunch with him when he was just starting *Condé Nast Traveler*, and I told him it wouldn't work, that no one reads travel magazines and I thought, my God, this guy has really pulled it off. ... While all the other start-up magazines are going down the tubes, here's one that really works."

If *Condé Nast Traveler* is a step down, the lower perch has been doing pretty well. Last year, ad pages rose 53 percent over the year before. In the first four months of 1990, they rose 17 percent over the same period in 1989—a mite slower but still a decent gain considering that the average monthly lost about 3 percent over the same period, according to the *Media Industry Newsletter*. Circulation has climbed to about 750,000, according to executive editor Thomas J. Wallace.

Unlike most travel journalism, which is a variant of brochure-writing devoted to describing the best three-star restaurants and the most elegant hotels, *Condé Nast Traveler* takes pains to describe the downside as well. In addition to giving the lowdown on 60 picturesque Mediterranean islands, a recent issue had playwright David Mamet grousing about the quality of English food ("I don't think most Londoners can identify a vegetable with a gun to their heads"), plus a rather acerbic comparison of the merits of New York and Los Angeles.

Of course, editing a new travel magazine is one thing; being the Queen of Glitz is quite another. That's Ms. Brown's department. She doesn't so much edit a magazine as sit astride an arc stretching from New York's junk-bond-borne Nouvelle Society to the purveyors of mass entertainment in Hollywood. The result, depending on whom you ask, is either a magazine that is the embodiment of this fast-moving set or simply a glossy tip sheet on who in this milieu is at the moment and who is not.

Fumed a well-known New York journalist of Ms. Brown's magazine: "It's the embodiment of everything obscene about the Reagan 80's."

"It's brilliant," acknowledged another, "no question about it, but it fills me with disgust."

One former *Vanity Fair* writer, recalling the time he proposed a story about a certain bright-burning celebrity, said: "My editor, in anticipation of what Tina would say, asked, 'Do you know these people well?' I said, 'No, I don't know them at all.' And he said, 'Well, you know, we want it to look like you belong in this world.' The standard viewpoint that the journalist should be objective, they're not interested in that."

Ms. Brown, not surprisingly, adheres to the view that *Vanity Fair* "works" because it's like a three-course meal mixing trifles with more substantial fare.

Of course, editing a new travel magazine is one thing, being the Queen of Glitz is quite another. That's Ms. Brown's department.

SEPTEMBER 19, 1988   BY JOSEPH C. GOULDEN

'FIT TO PRINT: A.M ROSENTHAL AND HIS TIMES'

FOR ALMOST A YEAR, I HAD BEEN INTERVIEWING PEOPLE IN New York who either worked for or otherwise knew A.M. Rosenthal, then executive editor of *The New York Times*. Oddly, in all those months I caught only a fleeting glimpse of my subject across a crowded luncheon room at an East Side café. When commencing my research, I wrote Rosenthal, told him what I was doing, and expressed the hope we could talk eventually. Rosenthal's reply, in effect, told me not to expect any of his time; that he was a busy man and had more important things to do.

Fit to Print: A. M. Rosenthal and His Times is about the power and insecurity of Abe Rosenthal, and how his talent and persona combined to make him one of the more successful newspaper editors in America—and also one of the more detested. Professionally, Rosenthal was *sui generis*, a newsman who excelled at every job he undertook, from copy boy to foreign correspondent to editor. "The smartest son of a bitch who ever walked into a newsroom," his old friend Theodore H. White, the political writer, said of Rosenthal a few months before his 1986 death.

Rosenthal is not a very likable human being. He is a man of strong emotions, both negative and positive. He sends flowers to friends in the hospital, and he expects cards on his birthday and other occasions. But friends also know he is hypersensitive to any criticism, however mild, either of himself or to *The Times*. A person who often offends Rosenthal can find himself suddenly, brutally and permanently cut out of his circle. He also likes to pass along personally the good news of a promotion or a raise. Friends see in his behavior a desire to be loved; a hope that people would look beyond what he calls "my dark side" and find someone who truly cares about humans.

Rosenthal can only hope, for about the nicest adjective I heard about his conduct over two years was "abrasive," with "unfortunate" a close second. Rosenthal is a shouter, a curser, a whiner ... and he can hold grudges for years. He is a small man physically but his rages are so violent that he intimidates persons twice his size. "Much of Abe's supposed bravery in shouting at other men lies in the fact that he can say those two little words, 'You're fired,'" one of his deputies said. "Otherwise, they'd have carried him out on a stretcher with a busted jaw back in the 1960's."

FEBRUARY 20, 1989   BY LOU CHAPMAN

IS SAWYER'S FUTURE A STELLAR PROSPECT?

Sawyer

WHEN DIANE SAWYER REcently confirmed she was jumping ship at CBS News to join rival ABC, the story made the front pages of newspapers across the country.

After all, Ms. Sawyer had been the first and so far only female correspondent on *60 Minutes*, America's most watched news program and, week after week, among the 10 top-rated television shows of any genre. She was making an estimated $1.2 million as a *60 Minutes* correspondent and is rumored to have clinched a deal worth $1.5 million a year at ABC, even though her previous assignment, co-anchoring *CBS Morning News* with Bill Kurtis, was a flop.

Besides, Ms. Sawyer was in the news last year when she was married to Mike Nichols, the movie director and producer, after having dated or had continuing relationships with men about town including Henry Kissinger, the developer Mortimer Zuckerman and the Carter Administration official Richard Holbrooke. And the former all-America Junior Miss (in 1963, when she was 17) was 42 when she married, making her a magnet for industry mavens and reporters searching out the perfect woman with whom to discuss the biological clock syndrome.

Not to mention that Ms. Sawyer was a press aide to former President Richard Nixon and spent almost four years after his resignation working for him in California, researching his memoirs.

It all looks stellar. But is it? And what does it mean? Maybe it means simply that Diane Sawyer, generally considered to be dazzling, intelligent, hard-working, competent and

ambitious—and someone who, if she never really added a unique dimension to *60 Minutes*, is a fine journalist nonetheless—is getting something she wants at ABC that she doesn't see in the tea leaves at CBS.

Insiders and experts seem to think that regardless of what happens at ABC, Ms. Sawyer can't lose. So far, things seem to have gone that way for her.

"She's not likely to be blamed if the new show fails," Tom Shales, who won a Pulitzer Prize last year for his television criticism in *The Washington Post*, said in an interview. "Theoretically, she could fail. She could perform very poorly on camera. But given her experience and track record that is highly unlikely. I mean, she came back from *Morning News*, the debacle of debacles, to do *60 Minutes*. Basically, if it fails, it's just one more prime-time magazine that fails ... one in a line of many."

MARCH 6, 1989 BY MICHAEL M. THOMAS

THE MIDAS WATCH:
RUSHDIE AFFAIR: IRAN KICKS SAND IN AMERICA'S FACE

ONE CANNOT BLAME HARRY Hoffman or any other bookseller who took *Satanic Verses* off the shelves. One bookseller of my acquaintance was visited by a couple of hulks, whose acquaintanceship with the tenets of Islam was obviously faint but who were just looking for any excuse to make trouble. Let me say this, however: If we grant the right of the chains and others to suppress Mr. Rushdie's book in the face of threats, is it right that their pusillanimity, no matter how justified, should be rewarded with extra profits? Without the Ayatollah, who for all I know may be an ad hoc as-

signment to Viking's publicity staff, *Satanic* might have done 50,000 copies. Instead, it'll probably do four times that, even more if Viking can find a way to efficiently suppress word-of-mouth on the book once it begins to be read.

The chains and others are therefore getting a windfall from a book they ran from, which is money they don't deserve. Let me therefore propose that Walden and the rest set aside a substantial percentage of these excess unwarranted profits and contribute them to my pal Mary Elizabeth Smith's Volunteers for Literacy.

◇◇◇◇◇◇

MARCH 13, 1989 BY SHERE HITE

THE *OBSERVER* POLL:
Does Getting AIDS Virus Worry Most New Yorkers?

BY NOW WE HAVE ALL HEARD OF AIDS, THE GREAT MENACE "OUT there" somewhere, ever present. But when faced with a rubber condom and the Actual Situation, many New Yorkers, it turns out, sheepishly turn away and hope that "just this time" they won't get it.

The *New York Observer* Poll asked a random sample of adults in New York City how concerned they are that they could eventually get AIDS and what measures they are or are not taking to prevent that from happening. Only 28 percent said they are "at all worried" that they someday might contract AIDS.

As one young woman in the poll explained in a follow-up interview: "When I first met him, I was head over heels in love, just crazy about him. I was dying to go to bed with him. But in the back of my mind, there was always this looming question I knew I would have to face at some point: Was he going to offer to use a condom? Would he turn off if I said something? Would I ruin the moment? Definitely! ... So I admit it, I didn't stop him. I didn't say, How can we be sure? Where's your condom? And neither did he. ..."

APRIL 24, 1989   BY LOU CHAPMAN

AT *THE NEW YORKER,* THE NEWHOUSE ERA BRINGS A NEW LOOK

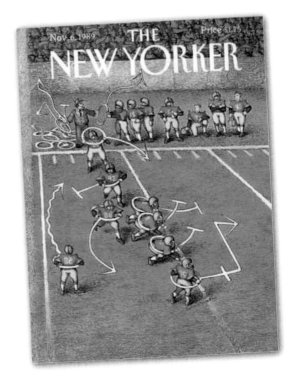

DANIEL MENAKER, AN EDITOR AND WRITER FOR *The New Yorker*, tells a story from 1970, when he was working as a freshman fact-checker for the venerable magazine that has been fertile soil for writers ranging from Lillian Ross to James Thurber to Jay McInerney.

A decision had been made, Mr. Menaker recalled in a recent interview, to create a larger, more complete table of contents to appear on the same page, in the same format, each week. At the time, the table of contents appeared wherever it fit within a section called Goings on About Town, in minuscule type and sketchy detail.

None of the Reader's Business

Mr. Menaker remembers turning to an associate who had worked at the magazine much longer than he and mentioning that a more complete and readable table of contents was a good idea, that it would help the reader know what was in each issue. "She said to me, 'It's none of the reader's business what's in the magazine,'" Mr. Menaker said.

The anecdote typifies how, for many years, there existed among many at *The New Yorker* an aloof attitude toward the magazine's audience. This accompanied an inviolate wall between the magazine's editorial and business sides.

Today, after almost four years under the ownership of S.I. Newhouse and his family-controlled company, Advanced Publications Inc., and after 26 months under the editorship of Robert Gottlieb, former editor in chief and, later, president of Alfred A. Knopf Books (also owned by Advance Publications), the walls at *The New Yorker* seem at least to be shrinking a bit.

From Research to President

"There is still a separation of Church and State," said Steven T. Florio, president and chief executive of The New Yorker Magazine Inc, brought in to run the publication when it was bought by Advance Publications for about $170 million in May 1985. "But I think the Church is rooting for the State, and the State is rooting for the Church."

Mr. Florio is proud that the average age of *The New Yorker* reader under his leadership has fallen from 43 to 40—a trend that may result partly from tightly targeted, direct-mail marketing campaigns—and that readers' average income has risen, from a reported $38,000 to $40,000.

He is pleased that Mr. Gottlieb, the magazine's third editor in its 64-year history, is known for his fondness of kitsch; for his interest in modern culture as well as in the classical arts; for his desire to draw in young writers on popular culture while at the same time carrying a sensibility for the unique styles of respected *New Yorker* writers such as Brendan Gill, E.J. Kahn Jr., Andy Logan and Lawrence Weschler. Mr. Gottlieb in fact edited books by several *New Yorker* writers while he was editor in chief at Knopf.

Since Advance bought *The New Yorker*, and since March 1987 when Mr. Gottlieb abruptly replaced 79-year old editor William Shawn in what was regarded by many staff members as a personal affront by Mr. Newhouse and Mr. Florio, things have indeed changed, particularly on the business side.

The Goings on About Town section has itself been revised to provide new batches of distinctly separated listings. The section has been spiffed up with caricatures and other artwork, reminiscent of the section in the 1930's and 40's.

Of more concern to some staff members and readers has been the addition to Goings on About Town of brief reports and recommendations. "It's about choices now and opinions, not just listings," Mr. Florio explained. "It's saying, hey, we realize you people reading this may never have heard of Rosemary Clooney, but you really ought to go hear her."

In those ways and others, *The New Yorker* has begun to adapt to the style and offbeat interests of its new editor. One recent profile, for example, was of Paul Shaffer, bandleader of the David Letterman talk show. A recent article in Talk of the Town was about a collector of plastic guitar picks. Still, there's no confusing *The New Yorker* with *Rolling Stone*. Mr. Gottlieb's *New Yorker* still publishes long pieces on such challenging subjects as Uruguayan politics and the Oxford University Press.

"It is eminently logical that Bob Gottlieb is going to bring in new writers, writers of his own standards and style," said Mr. Kahn, a staff writer at *The New Yorker* since 1937 and author of the book *About the New Yorker and Me*. "But a piece on a collection of plastic guitar picks? I don't know. Then you read it, and you find out that it wasn't even the world's best collection of plastic guitar picks. It was the second best collection. Mr. Shawn would never have approved of that."

AUGUST 21, 1989 BY MICHAEL M. THOMAS

THE MIDAS WATCH:
Steinberg Party: Start of Decline and Fall

THE PHONES STARTED RINGING FIRST THING MONDAY morning. Had I seen it? Well, of course I had. I'm up with the dawn, and by the time the first call came in, I'd not only read the *Daily News*'s Aug. 7 story of Saul Steinberg's 50th birthday celebration, I'd had time to ponder what, if anything, it meant.

Not much is my guess. The reason's simple: Out here on the East End of Long Island, nothing competes with real estate. Your typical black-tie dinner party conversation will go like this:

Man: "Six million two."

Woman to his right: "I heard seven."

Woman to his left, eavesdropping: "Absolutely not! My masseur says five million eight and not a penny more!"

Man across the table, shrugging: "More like, six four, six five, if you ask me."

Anyway, we're stuck with the Steinberg party as a Current Hot Topic. I have a feeling a lot of ink will be spilled on the "Late Roman-ness" of the shindig, and I must confess that I got down Juvenal and Petronius, figuring the latter, at least, might provide a fruitful comparison between Trimalchio and the pudgy green-mailer of 740 Park Avenue, but no soap. I'm therefore going to leave Gibbonian dialectic to others.

Facts Let's start with facts. The party is supposed to have cost $1 million. (The guy on the adjacent stool here at the Candy Kitchen just looked at what I've written, put down his paper, gave me an all-time "you schmuck" look and muttered: "Eight hundred grand, meathead!") There were 250 guests, all the usual suspects.

There were a couple of omissions. The Swine family appears to have been presented only by the cadet branch, the Prince himself being otherwise engaged. Where can that fellow have been? What is he up to these days? One hears all kinds of neat stories.

The big news was the "living art" that carried out the theme of the evening: "An Evening of 17th Century Old Masters in Celebration of Saul's 50th Year." Models were posed in simulation of great paintings, none of which the chubby Maecenas owns, beginning with (I understand) "the Arnolfini Wedding" by Jan Van Eyck, a painter active around 1430, but what's a cen-

tury or two among friends. Vermeer and Rubens were also among the emulees, but the lion's share of post-party attention has gone to the nekkid girl who disposed herself after the fashion of Rembrandt's *Danae*.

This picture, painted in 1636, was an interesting choice. For one thing, it hangs in the Hermitage in Leningrad, so I suppose it could be construed as a gesture toward Glasnost. Then, of course, the Danae myth teaches that the way to get the girl is to come on to her in a shower of gold coins, and I really don't think I need say any more than that in this context.

Now, according to which society scribe you read, the Danae vitrine was at various points in the evening subject to attempted encroachment, at some point, by Time Warner supremo Steve Ross and later by Jim Wolfensohn. Press accounts are silent as to whether either of these gentlemen was thereafter taken by the ear by his lady wife and made to go home, after the fashion of a "Maggie and Jiggs" cartoon. I think we should be told.

Obviously, it was a spectacle. The people I've talked to invariably dwell on how it was done, and of course we're living in a world where if something is well done, it doesn't seem to matter what it is. Comparisons are advanced with the Besteigui party in Venice in the 50's (although nothing can come up to the photos of gondolas full of catamites disembarking at the Palazzo Whateveritwas at that affair) and Truman Capote's "Black and White Ball" 20 years ago.

Anyway, does it matter? Suppose a tidal wave had swept in and carried off the lot, would American capitalism be better off? Probably—but who'll ever know?

What do I keep coming back to are a few lines from one of this century's great masters of revels (I'm doing this from memory, so there may be a slip or two).

"I went to a mah-velous party with Noonoo and Nana and Nell; it was in the fresh air, and we came as we were, and stayed as we were —which was hell!"

If we deconstruct those last two lines of Noël Coward's to read in terms of a stretch of time longer than the several hours of mere party duration, to encompass, say, a lifetime ... oh, hell, let me put it this way, by rephrasing Winston Churchill's famous riposte to the homely woman who accused him of being a drunk: "Indeed I am, but tomorrow I will be sober, and you will still be Saul Steinberg."

NOVEMBER 13, 1989
BY CHARLES V. BAGLI AND MICHAEL TOMASKY

Dinkins Wins, Will Govern a City Beset by Problems

NEW YORKERS HAVE BEEN ELEC-ting mayors since 1665, but not until Nov. 7, 1989, did they elect a black mayor.

Manhattan Borough President David N. Dinkins, an ex-Marine who came up through Harlem politics, emerged from a bitter fall campaign to defeat Rudolph Giu-liani and win election as the city's 106th mayor.

Shortly after the polls closed, Mr. Dinkins was declared the winner, based on exit polls, by all three major television net-work's local stations.

Jubilant Atmosphere

Mr. Dinkins, who is 62, will take over on Jan. 1 from Ed-ward I. Koch, the three-term incumbent who lost in the Democratic primary.

The atmosphere at the Dinkins campaign headquarters for the evening, the Sheraton Centre Hotel, was jubilant. In the Grand Ballroom, where large video screens where set up to bring the news to the 1,000-strong crowd, at 8:40 the band struck up "Take the A Train," the Billy Strayhorn song that helped give identity to the mayor-elect's home neigh-borhood. At Suite 2150, where Mr. Dinkins, his wife, Joyce, and close friends and supporters gathered, security was so tight that several elected officials were turned away.

Throughout the fall, experts almost unanimously predicted a Dinkins victory, which would make New York one of the last big cities in the country to elect an African-American as mayor. In a process that began in 1967 with the election of Carl B. Stokes in Cleveland and Rich-ard G. Hatcher in Gary, Ind., African-American mayors now hold office in a host of large cit-ies: Atlanta, Baltimore, Birming-ham, Ala., Detroit, Hartford, Los Angeles, Newark, New Orleans, Philadelphia, Washington.

Mayor-elect Dinkins's elation at his historic victory was sure to be tempered by the daunting economic and budget problems he will face upon taking office in January. The job growth the city enjoyed for much of the 1980's has come to a halt and the boom in development has slowed sub-stantially. Mr. Koch recently was forced to submit a revised spending plan designed to close a budget shortfall estimated at $550 million. Next year, the gap is expected to widen. Little help can be expected from the Cuomo administration, which faces its own budget problems and last month instituted a 2 percent cut in spending by all state agencies to offset a projected $277 million shortfall in revenues.

"Six months from now, every-one will forget we elected the first African-American mayor," said a prominent union leader who backed Mr. Dinkins. "The rocks will start flying. It will be arithmetically impossible to meet the expectations of the coalition that elected him. I think the best thing we can expect is a change in problem solving: trying to bring people together and work out a compromise. I'm just pointing out the problems. I think it will be great for the city."

JANUARY 1, 1990 BY HILTON KRAMER

New Round of Controversy Hits the Whitney Museum

NOW THAT THE POWER STRUG-gle raging at the Whitney Musuem of American Art has become a public scandal and prospect is bright—brighter, any-way, than it has been in years—that Thomas Armstrong, the museum's director, will at long last be sent packing, perhaps we can all begin to think seriously again about what the mission of this institution, the only one in New York specifically devoted to American art, ought to be and what it'll take to set the museum on a proper course.

At this writing there is no guar-antee, of course, that Mr. Arm-strong's directorship—which has been such an unmitigated disaster for the life of art in New York—will actually be terminat-ed. But the signs are promising. Some of the less docile members of the museum's board seem fi-nally to have awakened to the true dimensions of the debacle over which Mr. Armstrong has so long presided.

It's too soon for euphoria, to be sure, but even the possibil-ity of a change at the top of the Whitney is the best news the New York art scene has had all season. Clearly the museum is at a crossroads. It can ei-ther continue to be what Tom Armstrong has made it into—a bazaar specializing in fads, fashions, and art-market pro-motions, an institution devoid of serious standards—or it can be turned into a museum that commands respect because of the stringent aesthetic values it espouses and the distance it enjoys from the commercial hurly-burly that now disfigures so much of the New York art scene. Which is to say, it can ei-ther remain part of the problem that we face or become a leader in finding the solution that we so desperately need.

JANUARY 15, 1990   BY ALFRED KAZIN

UNDRESSED COCKTAIL PARTY: WHEN VIDAL AND MAILER COME FOR DRINKS

I HAVE BEEN WRAPPED UP FOR days in *The Writer's Chapbook*, a delicious book put together by George Plimpton from the long-standing *Paris Review* interviews with leading American, British and European writers of the century rapidly coming to a close. The book puts them all in New York, babbling away at George Plimpton's house at the end of East 72nd Street.

Tennessee Williams, poor guy, is explaining, "I try to work every day because you have no refuge but writing." Adds that he has to drink wine in the morning in order to get going. This annoys the French novelist and poet Blaise Cendrars, who in a *Paris Review* interview not sufficiently used in this selection, says writers exaggerate the difficulties of writing in order "to make themselves sound interesting." Writing is a privilege, Cendrars thunders, "compared with the lot of most people, who live like parts of a machine, who live only to keep the gears of society pointlessly turning." With a curl of the lip he tells Norman Mailer (who is too busy talking to Virginia Woolf to hear anyone else) that the greatest danger for a writer is to fall victim to his own legend.

JANUARY 29, 1990   BY CHARLES V. BAGLI

The Night Wall St.'s Kings Romp with Princes in Drag

THE TUMULT BEHIND THE doors of a room on the first floor of the Plaza Hotel threatened to rock the glass chandeliers in the plush hallway.

Suddenly, silence. Then a door was flung open, emitting a procession of husky men, dressed in skirts, dresses and pumps. The hair from a long-haired wig hung between the massive artificial breasts of one man. Glamorous "hostesses" directed the group toward the Baroque Room, where scores of men dressed in tuxedos. A convention of transvestites?

A bachelorette party? The filming of *Animal House II*?

'A Good Time'

None of the above. The gaggle of bewigged and bedressed men were "neophytes" being initiated into Kappa Beta Phi, a secret fraternity comprised of some of the most powerful and celebrated figures in the world of business, finance and law: Felix Rohatyn, Lazard Freres & Co.; William R.. Saloman, Salomon Brothers Inc.; Arthur Levitt Jr., former president of the American Stock Exchange; George L. Ball, Prudential-Bache Securities; Peter A. Cohen, Shear-

son Lehman Brothers Inc.; John F. McGillicuddy, Manufacturers Hanover; Stanford I. Weill, Primerica Corporation; James D. Wolfensohn, chairman of the board of Carnegie Hall; Joseph H. Flom, Skadden, Arps, Slate, Meagher & Flom; Martin Lipton, Wachtell, Lipton, Rosen & Katz; Robert E. Rubin, Goldman, Sachs & Company; E. Gerald Corrigan, of the Federal Reserve Bank of New York; John S. Chalsty, Donaldson Lufkin & Jenrette Inc.

Grand Swipe & Grand Smudge

To some, fraternity is simply "a good time," an opportunity to let your gray hair down among your bothers. Others say Kappa, like Bohemian Grove in California and similar men's clubs, aids and abets social cohesion among the elite, to the exclusion of women, African-Americans, Latinos, Asian- Americans. Indeed, among Kappa's 226

frat brothers there are no women, no African-Americans, no Latinos, and no Asians.

Founded during the Depression, when some "brothers" were tossing themselves out office windows, Kappa Beta Phi has a simple Latin motto: Cantamus et Biberamus, We Sing and We Drink. So what do they do? A reporter was barred from further investigation at Kappa's 58th annual dinner Jan. 18 by a frat brother from Chicago who stood at the entrance. Over the next several days, two dozen Kappa members contacted by *The Observer* were no more forthcoming. "You have to talk to the Grand Swipe," said Frederick A. Kingenstein of Klingenstein, Fields & Company, who is a member of the frat's Grand Council. "I don't talk to the press. It's against my religion."

"I don't know how you found out about it," said 1989 Grand Swipe E. John Rosenwald Jr., 59, vice chairman of Bear Stearns & Co.. "We really don't like publicity. It's a secret organization, and we like to keep it that way."

One Kappa Beta Phi member did agree to talk about the frat at some length but requested ano-

nymity. In preparation for the annual dinner, the neophytes, or pledges, compose skits, songs or poems that are both ribald and barbed paeans to their firm, chairman or colleague. Dressed in tutus, dresses or even as cops and robbers, the men are paraded into the annual meeting during the cocktail hour. Hostesses, who are hired for the occasion and in some years are "scantily clad," the source said, mingle with the brothers, who are dressed in black tie.

When the performances begin, all hell breaks loose, with the audience pelting the performers with food. The source said: "I think the story is just the fact that the elite of the business community in New York carries on like a bunch of fraternity members, throwing food, hooting and howling, jeering, while their colleagues put on a performance that's outrageous."

"The men proceed to make fools of themselves," explained Pat Hill, who was hired through Charles V. Ryan modeling agency and has served as hostess at a number of Kappa dinners, including this year's. "Let's just say some men never grow up."

OCTOBER 26, 1987 BY MICHAEL M. THOMAS

THE MIDAS WATCH: Drop of the Dow:
Bulls Spooked, Herd Stampeded Out of Control

HOW DEADLY IS THE CANKER IN THE ROSE? IS THIS the beginning of the end or merely the end of the beginning? As this is written, the Dow has plunged over 800 points in four sessions. Is the greatest financial party in history over—or about to be?

My own guess is that we're getting there. I can't say I base my conclusion on experience: I wasn't born in 1929, had other things on my mind in 1958, was marginally involved in Wall Street in 1974. I claim no acute knowledge of Prechterian fiscal thermody-namics, nor of the relationships between bond and stock prices so artfully and convincingly elaborated by my learned friend Alfred Malabre in *The Wall Street Journal*. Indeed, if pushed to the wall, I must need confess that my conclusions on the matter are compounded as much from schadenfreude as from ratiocination, as much from a visceral wish that the ungodly get theirs (always less than one would like) than from sweet reason.

Still, I've read a little history and the portents seem to be there. It's all rather like *Macbeth*: Someone casually mentions that the brindled cat hath mewed thrice, and before you know it, the whole damn castle's fallen down. The thing is not to look primar-ily for specific cyclical or typological parallels to earlier crashes. Some of these are certainly on hand. The gratifying news that the collective wealth of the Forbes 400 advanced 41 percent last year must certainly comfort those who see "1929" writ in the tea leaves of wealth concentration. That's just one example. For my own part, I've been wondering for some time just how long we could leave a trillion dollars of pension fund wealth outside the tax orbit and viably finance the economy.

Every man's entitled to choose his own portents. The markets like things simple—no surprise that, given the intellectual equipment of those who man them—so right now they're zeroed in on the trade figures. Big deal: Two years ago, interday trading swung on interest rates; before that, it was M-1. Markets don't cause crashes, markets crash. Leading indicators do little more than lead.

For Small Minds

Excessive reliance on specifics, factual parallels, is a foxhole for small minds. What counts in the meaningful examination of his-tory are structure and the zeitgeist, something we were taught at Yale, before that institution dedicated itself simply to providing vocational training for future options brokers.

Here things start to get interesting. I've been researching a Wall Street novel that will run from 1924 to 1990, which has taken me into unfamiliar territory as regards to 1929, and jiggled my memory with respect to 1974. I'm not going to go into a catalogue of structural equivalencies, but here's what I think happens in a crash. You can decide for yourself whether it applies to the present.

Markets exist to line the pockets of those who purvey them, so inevitably they evolve in the direction of excess, in the pen-ultimate stages of which "catchpenny schemes," as the great economist Charles Kindelberger has called them, flourish with a vengeance. If fueled by vast quantities of essentially purposeless,

indeed almost disembodied, liquidity and credit, this evolution can be nothing short of spectacular. Witness the fact that Avis seems to change hands every week at exponentially higher prices.

Now the fun begins. As the price of pieces of paper rockets ever higher, increasingly detached from economic and political reality—and a sine qua non of every collapse is that things in the real world ain't as good as the securities markets make them seem—an unspoken disquiet creeps forth on the face of the land. Can something indeed be rotten in the state of Denmark? No one says anything, but respectable men are seen to edge closer to the door. Disquiet becomes unease; that rankness once so faint in the nostrils now stinks outright, is given sporadic confirmation by events verging on the grotesque, such as "Makeover-of-the-Century," Asher Edelman's attempt to convert his Columbia Business School stu-dents into finders (and to chisel them, at that). Piece by piece, prop by prop, the psychological stage is set. Without being quite sure how it got there, the market finds itself all on edge; not the slightest prod—in 1929, a speech by Roger Babson; in 1987, the trade numbers—causes it to jump like Don Knotts, a reaction which worries it further.

What happens at the next prod, or the one after that, all depends. It may be that structures have grown in place that guarantee a retreat becomes a rout, in which case you get a 1929, instead of the slow bleeding of 1974. Do you prefer cancer or a heart attack? Most of us have seen or read enough Westerns to know that there's something in the souls of cattle that makes them spookable, sets them stampeding out of control for no apparent reason. It seems to be the same with markets; each bull market evolves its own particular susceptibility to stampedes. In 1929, margin loans and calls set the snowball rolling out of control. Are there 1987 equivalents? Well, program trading and electronic fund redemptions come to mind. What about Japan? To every man his own demon.

If I was tending the herd, I'd be right restless. Not least because Wall Street seems to be pulling in its horns, in the manner of a host packing up the crystal and the china and the good Scotch, leaving his own party, happy to let the drunken fools trash whatever's left, because after all, the place was only rented, and with their own money.

> *Most of us have seen or read enough Westerns to know that there's something in the souls of cattle that makes them spookable, sets them stampeding out of control for no apparent reason. It seems to be the same with markets; each bull market evolves its own particular susceptibility to stampedes.*

GEORGE GURLEY INTERVIEWS ARTHUR CARTER

What made you decide to start *The New York Observer* in 1987?

I had *The Litchfield County Times* and I also had *The Nation* magazine. I'd given some thought to starting a paper in a city. I considered Boston, because it would be less competitive. But New York was my hometown, so I decided to do it here. Newspapers had interested me for some time, and the one I started in Connecticut turned out to be a very well-thought-of newspaper. And the world of journalism, the world of what I call opinion journalism—there weren't many things around. I became interested in the world of newspapers. I had to study a lot of them, such as *The Emporia Gazette*—William Allen White bought it when it was an unknown paper, and it became a prominent national publication, a small-town paper that reached a kind of notoriety in the national scene. The other one was *Le Canard Enchaîné*, a French publication started around 1915. When de Gaulle became president of France, it became a very strong voice attacking the establishment. It became a terrific publication with a significant circulation, not only in Paris but throughout the provinces. I'd thought about being a publisher since the early 1970s, even before I ventured into finance and Wall Street. So I'd given it some thought, but it never really crystallized until I bought a farm up in Connecticut and started *The Litchfield County Times*. I had been asked to consider something in the political arena and I decided against that. I didn't think I was the right person or had the right attitude to run for office.

Can you tell me about the first *Observer* writers?

I hired that whole group—Hilton Kramer, John Heilpern, Rex Reed, Andrew Sarris and Michael Thomas. Hilton was on television. I was watching him give an interview, and I always knew about Hilton, so I called him up and said, "Let me come down and see you." I asked him, "Would you like to write for us? Cover the art scene?" He had left *The Times*. He thought that I'd last for about two weeks.

Michael Thomas?

I knew his father quite well, because of my first job at Lehman Brothers—his father was a partner there. And I thought Michael would be a terrific writer; he's a very amusing, talented guy. And he started at Lehman Brothers himself, so he knew Wall Street. So his column the Midas Watch became a perfect vehicle for Michael.

Rex Reed?

I knew Rex a little bit. Very talented man. Then Richard Brookhiser: I had a very good relationship with Bill Buckley, and one day I said, "Listen, you wouldn't mind if I called Brookhiser?" I ran this by Bill Buckley, he'd invite me over to his house and have these little dinners from time to time. And I wanted a very strong con-

servative voice in the paper. I didn't want us to be considered a left-wing paper or a right-wing paper. So Brookhiser wrote for us on the conservative side and Joe Conason was sort of the other side.

Two months after you started *The Observer*, the stock market crashed, in October 1987. What made you keep the paper going?

I thought we would go into some kind of downturn and I thought that we could be in trouble, but I decided to stay with it.

What purpose do you think *The Observer* has served in New York media?

I think that people got a lot more tough-minded in other publications because they saw what we were doing. So we raised the bar higher in terms of critique.

When you started it, did you have a plan, a manifesto?

No. Trial and error. Now the peach paper, of course, it gave a message. You have the three or four peach papers in the world, and they are all very sophisticated publications. Broadsheet peach. The *Financial Times*, of course.

Why did you locate *The Observer* in the 64th Street townhouse?

You ask why did I put them in the townhouse? Because I owned the townhouse.

Over the years, several of your friends in high places were enraged at articles *The Observer* published about them.

You can't run a newspaper and be worried about that, you can't go picking and choosing who you're writing about. We have no sacred cows, which I thought was the only way to make the paper a serious paper. I didn't want us to pull any punches. We were not going to make a real dent in our world unless we did it that way. If we wanted to be a real factor in the industry and the community, we had to do that. If we were doing the best we could to say what we really believed, and did the homework behind it, I thought that we were in the right place. We're one of the few New York publications willing to say it like it is.

Can you think of any specific occasion when you were at a party and someone you knew yelled at you?

All the time. My standard reply was, I don't write the pieces, I don't assign the pieces, I only see them after the whole thing comes out.

How did you feel when people like the mayor or governor called you up and screamed?

Well, if it was about an editorial, for many years I did assign the editorials. So on the editorial page, clearly, I could take responsibility. I tell you, if we said something on the editorial page and I had assigned it—which in most cases, I had for quite a few years—I thought we were on solid ground. I wasn't going to apologize for something I said, that the newspaper said, that I thought was solid. And so many times, all it became was, "This is my opinion and that is your opinion." I wasn't going to apologize for what the paper said.

*Arthur Carter is the founder of The New York Observer.
Arthur Carter: Sculptures, Paintings, Drawings is published by Harry N. Abrams.*

Like the editorial that said "If Hillary Clinton had any shame, she would resign"?
That was a tough editorial. She had done some marginal stuff that could be attacked, comfortably attacked. A few things that were very, very dicey.

Let's talk about your editors.
Graydon Carter?
Terrific talent. One of the best. I was disappointed when he left after a year. I'd read *Spy* and then I met him up in Connecticut. He had a house up there and we hit it off. And I'm sorry that he had that [*Vanity Fair*] offer from [Si] Newhouse and he took it. But I didn't blame him. But I think he made a powerful difference in the paper. And then, I knew Susan Morrison was his number two at *Spy*, and after Graydon left, I hired her. Susan was terrific, very talented and exceptional; I liked her a lot. After a few years, she told me she was thinking of alternatives—she ended up at *The New Yorker*—and I thought, well, I'm going to have to come up with some other possibility. I had seen Peter Kaplan was at *Manhattan, inc.* magazine in the 1980s, and at this time he was Charlie Rose's producer. So I called him up out of the blue. He came up to the apartment, and within five minutes we realized his grandmother took French lessons from my mother—*and* his grandfather was best friends with my uncle. And I remember his grandmother and grandfather very well. It was amazing. So we chatted, and this was what he wanted to do, and I knew Susan wanted to go, so he came aboard. Graydon and Susan took the paper to a range of levels that it wasn't at before. They were both extraordinarily talented and I was lucky to have the both of them.

So Peter takes over in 1994 ...
I knew very early on that he was the right guy.

You're still involved with the paper but no longer the majority owner; you own 20 percent.
I was losing millions and after 20 years, it can be difficult. Personally. Economically, certainly, but even beyond that. It was something I decided I wasn't willing to do anymore. So I had three or four candidates who were interested in buying the paper, and I thought Jared Kushner was a perfectly decent guy to do it. He had the resources.

You've established yourself as a sculptor and have a book coming out this year published by Abrams. How is your art related to *The Observer*?
When I started *The Litchfield County Times*, I became its graphic designer. We had a very wonderful guy who did all that, his name was Gary Gunderson, and at the beginning—don't forget, he was a very experienced guy—he and I'd get into a lot of arguments, but you know, I owned the paper. It was the same at *The New York Observer*. I designed *The Observer*, every detail. I had a few people who came with me, who were working there, they executed my design. I had no background. I was a serious classical pianist, yes. But that's not graphic design. So not

many people knew that. Even the people at *The Observer*. Like what type do we use, every aspect of it. I became very interested in that, never knowing that this is what I liked to do. And then I started to sketch a little bit, because of the graphic design. And I had hired two brothers who were carpenters and contractors up in Connecticut to work on the farm there. We have a lot of houses, facilities. So I'd done three or four sketches and I said to these guys, "Let's build something," first out of wood. And then we built it out of steel. And then I took pictures of these up and down Madison Avenue, talked to a few of the galleries and sure enough, one of them said, "We'd like to have a show." I had a show and everything sold. So I built a workshop for myself, a design studio up in Connecticut, and I've been doing it ever since.

When you walk by a newsstand and see *The Observer* do you think, "That's my creation, I did that"?
Well, I *know* I did. I don't *think* I did.

Is it true that when you would interview people to work at *The Observer*, you would ask about their SAT score?
I think it's true.

And this would be for editors?
Anything. The colleges use it, so why shouldn't I? You don't get into Harvard or Princeton or these other places—they make you take that test. So why shouldn't I have a little guideline: This is a smart guy, this is a dumb guy.

And did you always get an answer?
People would always be a little shocked, like, "What?" If they went to Harvard, you don't have to ask them what their SAT scores were.

Whom did you have a good working relationship with?
I liked Terry Golway, I liked Peter Stevenson, Frank DiGiacomo—the three of them were wonderful to work with. Jim Windolf. Terrific. Super-talented guy. Very sad to see him go.

You and Peter Kaplan would have a weekly lunch.
Once a week. Gino's, a few other places. Half the time we would talk about everything else, like what you're doing in your life. Just a fun lunch. I did it with Susan, with Graydon. A fun lunch and often it was some issue we wanted to resolve: In other words, are we hiring somebody or are we firing somebody?

Did you do most of the talking?
Are you kidding? With those three?

What do you miss?
The day-to-day relationships I had with a lot of people who were there.

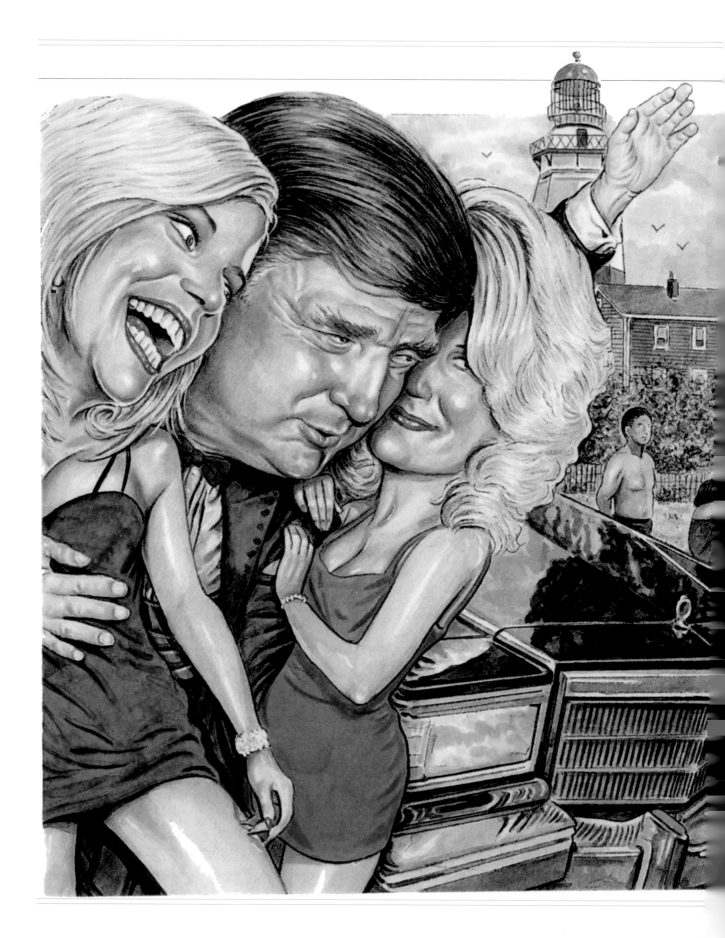

1991-1992

▶ Donald Trump plots riverside towers as courts parse his post-nup

 Mario Cuomo totes up 10 years as governor of New York

▶ Literary Brat Packers Jay McInerney and Bret Easton Ellis face sophomore slump

▶ The new *New Yorker*: Staffers hold noses as  Tina Brown brings *Vanity* flair

▶ Grown-up guys form Iron John drumming circles, then glue selves to Game Boys

▶ "Too-tall" building on Upper East Side lops off a dozen stories

 Madonna generates flashbulb frenzy with rockumentary *Truth or Dare*

▶ *Vox* in socks: bearded, beaming Nicholson Baker writes best-selling phone-sex novel

▶ Charlie Rose's talk show is the way to spend the hour between 11 p.m. and midnight

▶ Miramax movie moguls  Harvey and Bob Weinstein court controversy, critics

▶ George Herbert Walker Bush prepares to yield his WASP-y White House to Bubba

1991-1992

MARCH 18, 1991 BY ROBIN POGREBIN

THE *OBSERVER* POLL:
Lawyers Overpaid,
Not So Honest

O.K., SO MAYBE STEVEN BRILL IS incapable of mellowing. Maybe he will always retain the mercurial, blustery streak that is by now the stuff of legend. But let a reporter from another publication into the lion's den at *The American Lawyer* and the reputedly pugilistic Mr. Brill practically purrs.

That could well be because the president and editor in chief of the magazine is a savvy journalist who knows when to turn on the charm. But there is also the possibility that working with established media experts on his new, 24-hour cable Courtroom Television Network has taught the consummate boss that Steve Brill

doesn't always know best.

The cable network, otherwise known as COURT TV, is due to start broadcasting in July. According to its planners, it will offer gavel-to-gavel coverage of trials all over the country, and reporting from legal journalists in the field will be supplemented by occasional commentary from prominent trial lawyers such as Arthur Liman, Floyd Abrams, David Boies, Robert Bork and Barry Slotnick. On weekends, COURT TV will offer continuing legal education programming provided by bar associations and other legal groups nationwide that is directed at the legal profession as well as the general public.

MARCH 18, 1991 BY ADAM BEGLEY

POET BECOMES A GURU
OF THE MEN'S MOVEMENT

ROBERT BLY'S *IRON JOHN: A Book About Men,* published in November by Addison-Wesley, has been on the nonfiction best-seller list for 17 weeks, and in the number one spot for six weeks, including a four-week stretch during which the ground war in the Gulf erupted; even *The Prize,* Daniel Yergin's timely history of the geopolitics of oil, could not match its rate of sale.

The success of Mr. Bly's book has taken the publishing industry by surprise. Save for a small number of editors and publishers aware of an ill-defined but rapidly growing men's movement, nobody thought that a complex, poetic meditation on "male initiation and the role of a mentor" (to quote the flap copy) could attract such a wide audience.

Iron John contains Mr. Bly's prescription for how to rehabilitate the wounded male psyche. He argues that many of the "soft males" of the 60's and 70's, the kind of man who grew up with feminism, "are not happy," and he urges the development of the "inner warrior." He is careful to distinguish the kind of masculinity he favors from crude "macho" insensitivity. Mr. Bly

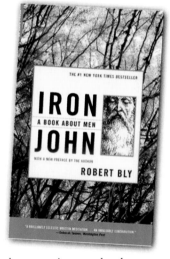

has not written a vulgar how-to book but *Iron John* does offer a battery of suggestions for self-improvement.

In years to come, the publication of *Iron John* may be seen as a watershed event, the first of a major trend. Enthusiasts argue that the men's movement is as yet in an embryonic state; they make extravagant claims for its future potential. But even if the trend proves to be a passing fad, the current success of *Iron John* is certainly sufficient to prod a me-too publisher.

APRIL 1, 1991 BY ALFRED KAZIN

AMERICAN PSYCHO: HORROR SHOW OF MONOTONY, HEAVY-HANDEDNESS

THAT NOW-CELEBRATED ITEM known as *American Psycho* (Vintage Books, $11), by a 27-year-old from Los Angeles named Bret Easton Ellis, confirms something I have long been afraid to disclose. It is perfectly possible to have a certain amount of literary talent yet to be as dumb as hell.

Nothing I had heard or read about this book—outside the routine mutilations, disembowelings, stabbings, shootings, eye gougings, ridiculously acrobatic sex trios and utterly passionless rapes with assorted mechanical devices (at one point, as more than mere voyeur, a large, starving rat)—had prepared me for the terrible earnestness of this author. This is a relentlessly moral tract, a cautionary tale by an almost

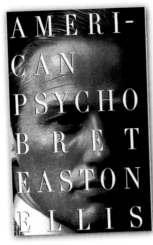

entirely humorless writer. He is attempting a satire on the super-yuppiedom of various horribly spoiled young gentlemen on Wall Street during

the now-universally execrated 80's Reagan boom. Abandon all hope, ye who still dream of entering upon a life of hideous extravagance and pleasure!

What we have here—in intention—is not exactly pornography. No one decently interested in sex is likely to get a jump out of this horror show. The book is really a heavy-handed attack on a madly trendy New York subculture during the 80's that was self-indulgent to the point of hysteria—wasteful, cruel mindless, ignorant. Yet above all it was fashionable, having more to do with designer labels than (at least in this book) with the acquisition of money.

Early in the book, virtually a whole chapter is given over to Patrick's state-of-the-art living room. White marble and gran-

ite gas-log fireplace. An original David Onica. A 30-inch digital TV set from Toshiba.

Of course Tom Wolfe too had to research a lot for *Bonfire of the Vanities*; he even had to locate something called the Bronx. But Bret Easton Ellis doesn't know the difference between a novel and the Hammacher Schlemmer catalogue. He thinks that if you hammer the reader page after page with designer names—ARMANI, ELLIS, BLASS, GIO PONTI, SANUI, ETTORE SOTTSASS—you have shown up such people for the trash they are.

Our author is a jerk. His book is a satire of itself. *American Psycho* is at the very heart and center of the New York it wants to denounce.

◇◇◇◇◇◇

JULY 1, 1991 BY ANDREW SARRIS

THE ACCIDENTAL AUTEURIST: Madonna's *Truth or Dare* Offers Witch's Brew; Lee, Too, Lacks Art

MADONNA AND SPIKE LEE TURNED OUT TO BE THE MOST PUBlicized personages at this year's Cannes Film Festival, although neither has come close to being universally admired and probably neither ever will be. Indeed, Madonna is not even a real movie star, and Mr. Lee has yet to win personal recognition from a Cannes jury after two hyped-up tries. Still, Madonna generated more flashbulb frenzy for disrobing to her metallic-sheen underwear than more voluptuous women have traditionally done posing au naturel.

For his part, Mr. Lee received more press coverage for losing the Golden Palm than the less charismatic Coen brothers did winning it. But once we stipulate that Madonna and Spike Lee are prodigiously shrewd self-promoters, is there all that much more to say about them? My own feeling is that there is both less and more than meets the eye in the careers of these two cutting-edge phenomena. I have grave reservations about their "art," but they remain indisputably "there" whether I like it or not, and I must come to terms with the challenges they have posed.

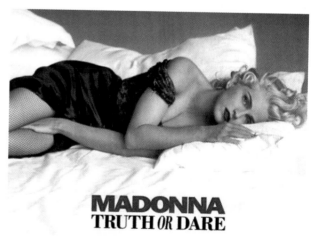

SEPTEMBER 16, 1991   BY HELEN THORPE

Miramax Brothers Court Headlines Like This One; Business Booms

NOW SHOWING IN THEATERS near you are *Paris Is Burning* and *The Pope Must Die,* two films distributed by Miramax Films Corporation. Now featured in newspaper headlines are the same two movies, both embroiled in controversies over their content. Which is just how Miramax likes it.

When *Paris Is Burning,* an acclaimed documentary about drag queens in Harlem, was released nationally in August, it was met by protests from fundamentalist Christian groups. Press coverage followed. Meanwhile, advertisements for *The Pope Must Die,* a British comedy about a fictitious pope who advocates safe sex and birth control, were refused by ABC, NBC and CBS and amended by some newspapers, including *The Boston Globe,* to read *The Pope Must ... .* Miramax responded by retaining celebrity lawyer Alan Dershowitz to "monitor the networks." What Mr. Dershowitz also did was hold a news conference, generating additional stories about his involvement in the spat.

Two Brothers From Queens

Most companies avoid controversies at all costs. Miramax feeds on them: Since advertising budgets for its films are miniscule in comparison to widely released studio pictures, controversy is a bless-

ing. And the Manhattan-based distributor has an uncanny gift for generating free publicity from disputes involving issues of censorship and freedom of expression—subjects dear to the press. In addition, many Miramax films have received considerable critical acclaim.

Among the films Miramax has distributed are *Scandal,* about the Profumo affair that rocked the British government; *The Cook, The Thief, His Wife and Her Lover,* the violently scatological drama of manners by British director Peter Greenaway; *Truth or Dare,* Madonna's tell-all documentary; and the film that gave hope to models aspiring to be actresses, *Sex, Lies and Videotape.*

Harvey and Bob Weinstein, the brothers from Queens who founded Miramax and are still its co-chairmen, are an incongruous pair to sit atop a small empire that has made its name distributing art films: They resemble car salesmen in both appearance and manner, have a management style that supporters call "energetic" and detractors call "brash," and have earned a reputation for playing hardball—in an industry not known for playing any version of softball. At least one producer of an award-winning film told *The Observer* that he is battling the Weinsteins for money he claims they owe him, and it is rumored that other producers also have complaints with their business style. The Weinsteins dispute such assertions. Boosters and critics agree that as the field of independent distributors has thinned and Miramax has grown, the Weinsteins have come to wield considerable muscle.

SEPTEMBER 30, 1991   BY CLARE MCHUGH

ENTREKIN MAKES ATLANTIC PRESS A HOUSE OF MORGAN

BECAUSE MORGAN ENTREKIN IS the person he is—a highly social, supremely self-confident, youngish man in a traditionally stodgy field—finding telling anecdotes about him isn't difficult. And most are anecdotes he'll repeat himself, happily.

The one about the start in publishing involves Kurt Vonnegut Jr. Mr. Entrekin, then 23, had come to work for Seymour Lawrence at Delacorte Press as an assistant. Mr. Vonnegut was turning in his 11th novel at the time, and Mr. Lawrence let Mr. Entrekin take a look at the manuscript. Mr. Entrekin, who comes from Nashville and had been to Stanford, where he'd studied modern fiction and even written some himself before realizing he neither had the patience nor the stamina for that kind of work, dissected the novel in a lengthy memo and provided suggestions for its improvement. His boss was very impressed—so much so that the publisher forwarded the memo to Mr. Vonnegut, who was similarly impressed. Mr. Vonnegut made all the changes the young

assistant suggested, or so Mr. Entrekin remembers. The novel duly appeared, titled *Jailbird.*

Mr. Entrekin was not long for assistantdom. He stayed only a couple of years at Delacorte before moving on to Simon & Schuster, where he rose to the rank of senior editor, acquiring nonfiction and fiction. It was to Mr. Entrekin that *Fatal Vision* author Joe McGinniss sent a first novel written by one of his students, Bret Easton Ellis. Mr. Entrekin bought the book, which became the successful *Less Than Zero,* but he left the company before it was edited, turning the task over to Bob Asahina, who also edited Mr. Ellis' third novel, *American Psycho.*

Meanwhile, Mr. Entrekin was getting cash together to emulate his mentor, Mr. Lawrence, by founding his own imprint. He joined Atlantic Monthly Press as an independent publisher in 1986, soon after a fellow Tennessean, Carl Navarre, bought the small, Boston-based firm from Mortimer Zuckerman and moved it to New York.

MAY 4, 1992   BY DEBORAH MITCHELL

TALK OF *THE NEW YORKER*

READERS WHO WERE SHOCKED AT THE FIRST "Notes and Comments" in *The New Yorker*'s "Talk of the Town" of April 27 can only imagine what the piece was like before it went through the magazine's exhaustive editing process. The story, about four young women who drove from New York to Washington, D.C., for the pro-choice march on April 5, was written by 24-year-old Elizabeth Wurtzel. "Whatever else feminism may have accomplished," her essay begins, "it hasn't got rid of the automotive double standard." First the women have to find a car, then they have to find a woman who can drive it. That takes a column and a half. Then "the car ride turned into a Homeric catalogue of gynecological ills," before they discovered, around about Maryland, that they were driving in a convoy of women going to the march. "Which was fortunate," the hapless writer continues, "since we'd forgotten to take a map." Ms. Wurtzel then allows that she "felt a little funny" chanting and carrying a placard at the march. Ready to call it a day at 4 P.M., she and her friends were flummoxed when their car wouldn't start. Fortunately, a man driving a taxi came by, looked under the hood and fixed the carburetor.

"'I guess we didn't manage to make this trip without help from any men,'" one of the author's friends observes. "This seemed a sorry note to end on, but, of course, women can't get pregnant without any men, either," Ms. Wurtzel continues.

Several *New Yorker* staff members were not impressed with the original piece and shared their opinions with the magazine's deputy editor, Chip McGrath, who edits "Talk." Mr. McGrath says the article was sent in on Tuesday and was revised on Wednesday, Thursday and twice on Friday—which he calls "par for the course." Several insiders took great pains to explain that dissenting views are common at *The New Yorker* and Mr. McGrath says he took some of his colleagues' objections into account while editing. The editor of *The New Yorker*, Bob Gottlieb, says he didn't hear any complaints. "I thought it was rather funny that, to the extent that there was guff, it was Chip who had to deal with it, while I stood around being Olympian," says Mr. Gottlieb.

◇◇◇◇◇◇◇

SEPTEMBER 14, 1992   BY JIM WINDOLF

Tina Brown's Debut: Oct. 5 *New Yorker* has Vanity Flair

"I'M THE HAPPIEST GIRL IN THE WHOLE U.S.A.," ROBERT GOTTLIEB declared the other day, describing his state of mind upon leaving his job as editor of *The New Yorker*. The remark, a reference to a 1972 country and western hit by Donna Fargo, was typical of the man known for his fascination with popular culture and kitsch.

Although some of his staff portrayed him as "zombie-like" and depressed since publisher S. I. Newhouse announced in July that he would be replaced by *Vanity Fair* editor Tina Brown, Mr. Gottlieb insisted that he couldn't be more content. "I am feeling absolutely fine, like a helium balloon that's waiting to be untethered," he said. "Of course I'll miss it, but I am also looking forward tremendously to being free of it." When asked what he might do next, Mr. Gottlieb became reflective. "The older I get, the less need I seem to feel to be a player," he said. "But if interesting work comes along—not in publishing!—I suppose I'll give it a try."

Ms. Brown moved into *The New Yorker*'s offices at 20 West 43rd Street on Sept. 8, a week after returning from a vacation on a dude ranch in Wyoming.

NOVEMBER 25, 1991   BY JOSEPH OLSHAN

MANHATTAN LIFE: INTERVIEW: HAROLD BRODKEY: PROUST OR JUST POUTY

With Mr. Brodkey's **The Runaway Soul** *no longer long overdue, but actually out, Joseph Olshan discovers that sitting down with the author to talk about the novel is to invite the scrutiny of a world-class scrutinizer.*

Few novels have been so anxiously awaited as *The Runaway Soul*. The 835-page book tracks every psychological nuance in the life of its narrator-hero, and has been nearly 30 years in the writing. The author has been teasing the public with rumors of its completion for nearly half that time. In 1977, the anticipation of an imminent publication of the novel, then called *Party of Animals*, reached such a pitch that the normally unflappable *New York Times* reported on the front page, "Brodkey Delivers." Never before has there been an unpublished novel so discussed, or second-guessed. Thus far the author of only two books of short stories published with a gap of many years between, Mr. Brodkey has been compared, by the major players of the New York literary-industrial complex, to Proust, Wordsworth, Milton, even Shakespeare.

I met Mr. Brodkey under the awning of his apartment building on West 88th Street. Although the evening was mild, the imposing 6-foot 2-inch author was dressed in a raincoat and a foul-weather hat with a crenulated brim. Out of sync with the weather, he peered down at me, his ink-colored eyes at once fiercely calculating and soft, his beard fashionably trimmed.

Now, in a small Japanese restaurant on the Upper West Side, Mr. Brodkey sits glaring at me. Our conversation is barely 10 minutes old, the food is not yet ordered, and we are being harangued by a woman dining next to us, who keeps making suggestions about the menu.

She only further irritates Mr. Brodkey, who has just been asked what he considers an audacious question: whether, according to an interview published in *The Washington Post* in 1986, he appropriated some of the aforementioned critical comparisons and wondered publicly if his own writing might be "the rough equivalent of a Milton or Wordsworth." Or even Shakespeare?

Mr. Brodkey is constantly misunderstood and misinterpreted, which is hardly surprising in someone who is both a genius—as he unquestionably is—and an egomaniac. The problem is only exacerbated by the fact that he speaks in long sentences, freighted with insights, which invariably plunge into unintelligible mumbling.

"Not only did I make these comparisons, I don't understand them," Mr. Brodkey now continues. "If the person making a remark is a critic [like Harold Bloom or Denis Donaghue], someone you respect highly, do you say, 'What's the joke?' Or do you smile and blink? It may be the only praise you'll ever get. You obviously can't accept that remark. You translate it to be 'That must mean I'm really good.' The quickest way to push somebody out of society is to call them a genius."

The next moment he is reaching next to him into the puddle of cloth that is his raincoat. Is he leaving? Is he going to shoot me? "You don't mind if I tape this, do you?" he says coolly, presumably to protect himself from being misquoted. Naïve on one hand, fervently ambitious on the other, he nevertheless comes across as a bit paranoid. At this moment, the animosity between us is palpable. Mr. Brodkey now admits that he's frightened of how *The Runaway Soul* will be received. "Although I, like anyone else, may have my own private dreams of how good I am, I'd rather be mediocre," he claims. "That I could live with more easily, because at least I would understand what the critics were saying. What's happened in the past is that people have cited greatness and then gone on to undermine their praise with condemnation. All I really want is to be accepted."

If the critics Harold Bloom and Denis Donaghue did compare Mr. Brodkey to Milton, Wordsworth and Proust, each seems to have remodeled his compliment. In a 1985 article for *Vanity Fair*, Donaghue wrote, "As good as Proust? Why not? Proust, too, was a not-so-young man who couldn't make up his mind where the next bit should go."

"I did not mean to compare him to Proust," Mr. Donaghue says. "Rather, what I meant is that the mode in which Mr. Brodkey's writing operates is Proustian. There is the same elaborate working-over of memory. The same autobiographical impulse."

"To compare Mr. Brodkey to Wordsworth and Milton is to doom him," Mr. Bloom says. "There is no point. He is ruminative, given to reveries and many nostalgias, which is Whitmanesque." He maintains, however, that Mr. Brodkey is a great and powerful writer, whose prose, at its best, is more powerful than any other American writer except perhaps Philip Roth. "But the writing is almost without humor and without much narrative continuity. You have to be part of an elite, with the patience and application to read someone thoroughly who is minutely concerned with the problem of self. He is a difficult writer who has become more difficult."

The Runaway Soul may be difficult, it may be long to excess, it may dare to spend a score of pages on a single fit of masturbation, and even longer on a sexual act. But it is a painstaking work of great emotional candor and audacity. Mr. Brodkey has strived to illuminate the tics of personality, the lilt of speech, the idiosyncratic language of the decades succeeding the 1930's. He has also worked out an elaborate philosophy, which, though difficult for even the most assiduous reader to fathom, is offset by many incandescent passages and one-liners that speak volumes. One is compelled to forgive the novel's faults for its sheer lyrical brilliance, its intricate psychological depth. And Mr. Brodkey may well earn the distinction of being able to characterize the ethos of New York City in a single phrase, as "raw envy acting as if it were intelligence."

In an effort to veer away from literary comparisons, Mr. Brodkey steers the conversation into gossip about the recent publishing party for Norman Mailer's *Harlot's Ghost.* "If you'd gone, you wouldn't have seen Norman and me standing together. I get very claustrophobic. And the party got so crowded that I was forced to spend time out on the balcony talking to Fran Lebowitz. And then I ended up going downstairs in the lobby where I met other guests who were claustrophobic."

Such fear finds an antecedent in Mr. Brodkey's very unusual childhood. He was born Aaron Roy Weintraub in Illinois in 1930. When Mr. Brodkey was 17 months old, his mother fell ill and died from an infection six months later. Upon her death he passed into a self-inflicted catatonia, as though courting death himself. Mr. Brodkey was subsequently adopted by his father's second cousin, but in his early adolescence his adoptive parents died within a few years of each other. It's no wonder that his early life was punctuated with a series of breakdowns, that it is hashed and re-hashed in his second collection of fiction, *Stories in an Almost Classical Mode,* as well as in *The Runaway Soul.*

If, for the last 25 or 30 years, Mr. Brodkey has been intensely preoccupied with bringing into focus the prisming light of early life, this may explain why he has done a lousy job protecting his public persona. According to a 1988 interview in *New York* magazine, for example, Mr. Brodkey claimed that John Updike had him in mind when creating the character of the Devil in *The Witches of Eastwick.* "Some of the things the Devil said, I have said," Mr. Brodkey told his interviewer. "I tend to be in a number of Updike books, either offstage or in lesser roles onstage."

When queried about this, Mr. Brodkey winces. "Why bring this up? Why don't you let it die? The Devil began as a composite of

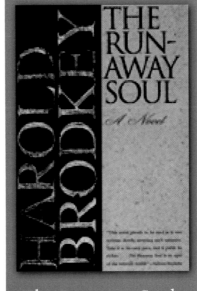

The Runaway Soul *may be difficult, it may be long to excess, it may dare to spend a score of pages on a single fit of masturbation, and even longer on a sexual act.But it is a painstaking work of great emotional candor and audacity.*

other writers, of Ozick, of Roth. When the film came out, I kept getting phone calls from people who recognized things. It was all very upsetting at the time it happened. And it's not important now. I've lived in New York for 30 years and lots has happened, lots have been said." (An intriguing coincidence is that his second and present wife, writer Ellen Schwamm, published a novel in 1983, *How He Saved Her,* about a woman who leaves her husband and children for the Devil.)

One wonders if such gifted man is a literary lemming. In 1988, Mr. Bloom was quoted as having said: "There is in Brodkey what Freud characterizes as 'the need to fail.' There is an intense psychic suicide going on. The question is whether the creative and personal psychology will sabotage him or will allow him to properly organize and bring forth his work."

We finally leave the restaurant and, at Mr. Brodkey's suggestion, take a stroll through Riverside Park, along a pathway that glints beneath lamplights with a powder of crushed glass, and descends toward the bank of the Hudson. I ask him why the novel has bounced between publishers since it was signed up in 1964. "These situations are two-sided. In one case, the publisher died, in another case it was somebody I liked a lot but I was out of sympathy with. In another case, it was a matter of money. Neurosis went into it. The problem is the way I write. The book at first reading is not completely acceptable."

Now ambling through a more forsaken area of the park, we pass an assembly of sinister men, who size us up with feral-looking eyes. Hearing rapid footfalls behind us, I turn to Mr. Brodkey. "This is your neighborhood. Is it safe to be walking here?"

"No."

"So why did you bring me?"

"A while back you said you liked to take risks."

"Not this kind. Let's get out of here," I say.

Picking up the pace, we soon find a set of stone steps that lead back up to Riverside Drive and manage to climb away from the late-night menace. As Mr. Brodkey stands before me catching his breath, I reflect that he has taken a far greater risk in waiting so long, perhaps too long, to publish.

DECEMBER 9, 1991 BY MICHAEL M. THOMAS

THE MIDAS WATCH: YO, WASP, PULL UP THOSE TUBE SOCKS

LAST WEEK WE DISCUSSED THE INTERESTING WAY HERBERT Hoover Poppy is CEO-ing the country, which he seems to view as some kind of gigantic corporation and therefore susceptible to the same management techniques that have, over the last 25 years, made American industry the glory of the developed world.

He is evidently trying to accomplish in the public sector what he never could in the private: to prove himself a glinty-eyed effective manager. Given the utter lack of ability and character which he brings to the task, I suppose you could say H.H.P. is making heroic strides. Nevertheless, as a WASP, I feel about the president the way my Jewish friends feel about the Dersh: God help us, every one.

He certainly doesn't have much feeling for the symbolic gesture. Twenty-eight bucks' worth of tube socks and whatever at the local Penney's isn't going to turn the nation's economic morale around. And frankly, I'm not too impressed with the net net net, cash-to-cash aspect, either: not when I factor in the cost to the taxpayer of the limousines, security people, press hounds, et cetera, needed to get the great man to the mall. I'll bet we're talking $10,000 for a bottom line of minus $9,972, although you can bet that we, the taxpayers, got stiffed for the $28, which will find its way into "miscellaneous" on the White House P.R. budget. So it's $10,000 out of (our) pocket any way you look at it.

'Too Tall' Apartment on Upper East Side to Lose Top Floors

THE BEHEADING OF THE "TOO Tall Building" on the Upper East Side, whose travails have attracted international attention, is set to begin within six weeks.

In an unusual challenge for demolition experts, contractors are planning to lop off the top 12 floors of a 31-story tower at 108 East 96th Street, just east of Park Avenue, which has remained empty since it was built 53 months ago. The job is expected to take about 37 weeks, costs $1 million and require some 500 dump trucks to cart away 3,000 tons of concrete rubble.

The task, which requires the use of hob-knockers, ho-rams, loader dozers, acetylene torches, jackhammers and chain-falls, is not impossible, but it will be extremely tricky. "It's a dangerous project, not because you can't take down 12 stories, but because you have to preserve the integrity of the floors below," said Richie Baris, president of Avalanche Wrecking, a demolition contractor based in Carlstadt, N.J. "The pneumatic equipment could shake the floors below and possibly loosen the facebrick. There's also a question as to how much heavy equipment you can use in demolishing the structure."

The beheading is the result of an accord reached last April among city officials, the neighborhood planning group Civitas and Queens developer Laurence Ginsberg, whose building is 12 stories taller than allowed by local zoning regulations.

The 12-story error was the most egregious in the memory of city officials, and the severity of the punishment also appears to have set a record.

FEBRUARY 24, 1992   BY CHARLES BAGLI

THE UN-ZABAR WANTS OUT OF STORE; FOOD FIGHT ON THE UPPER WEST

THOSE FELLOWS AT ZABAR'S ARE at it again.

Murray Klein, not a Zabar, but certainly a driving force behind the success of the Upper West Side food emporium, claims his partners, Saul and Stanley Zabar, are working him to death.

In court papers seeking to dissolve the partnership, the 68-year-old Mr. Klein said the Zabars have repeatedly refused to sell him the business, or buy his one-third share for $6 million. Behind this tactic,

Mr. Klein claims, it an attempt to prevent him from retiring, so the Zabars can buy him out when he dies for half of what he says is the true value of the business.

The Zabars, in turn, dispute Mr. Klein's claim, saying their white-haired partner is simply attempting to subvert the partnership agreement and force a sale. A hearing in State Supreme Court is scheduled for later this month.

New Yorkers, meanwhile,

continue to jam the aisles of what has become a two-story institution that stretches for most of the West Side block of Broadway between 80th and 81st streets, generating sales of $39 million and making Zabar's the most profitable specialty food store in the country.

"This is the longest-runnning horrendous partnership in the history of the world, except that it works," said David Liederman, the cookie king who tried to buy Zabar's in 1985.

◇◇◇◇◇◇◇

MARCH 9, 1992   BY CHRISTOPHER HITCHENS

CURTAIN UP ON MCINERNEY NOVEL

HITCHENS HADN'T EVEN FINISHED READING *Brightness Falls*—it was late afternoon and he was de-icing the silver cocktail shaker preparatory to some old-fashioned, feet-up literary immersion—when his telephone trilled its urgent summons. A brisk voice inquired in a friendly but more than just inquisitive tone what precisely he meant by "profiling" Jay McInerney and what, in any case, he meant by reviewing a novel before its official publication date. This was Hitchens' first ever call from Gary Fisketjon—he knew of people who had waited in vain for such a call from such a one—and the emotions of flattery and curiosity contended for mastery in his finely but oddly chiseled features.

Hitchens dialed Julian Barnes in his London snooker speakeasy.

"Call me collect one more time, Hitch," he quipped, "and I'll break your arm."

"Listen, Jules, I need a soundbite. Your mate McInerney seems to have a lot of protection. His roman is very good, but it's not as much á clef as I'd been told. Please advise."

"The thing to notice," said Barnes, "is that Jay's literary development is completely disconnected from his social curve. I think the real curve—the writing curve—goes steadily upward. Whereas in terms of the literary-social melodrama, he's seen as someone with a terrific early success who then wrote two dogs."

Julian Barnes may be right in decoupling McInerney's fiction from his life, but anyone who knows the publishing racket is still going to be spotting the members of the real-world literary bestiary. There is what could be a misprint in my copy, where a reference is made to the industry of "Proesy and pose." Mistake or not, it ought to stay in. Here we meet cynical ex-radicals on the make, Jewish paranoid belletrists who spend a Borgesian lifetime constructing unreadable fictional labyrinths and cool black dudes who lend cred, absorb the diss and split the diff. Also, since this is set in the age of the arbitrage casino and the reign of funny money, there are some lycanthropic *Bonfire* ingredients lying combustibly about the place.

Ignoring, or perhaps better say reisisting, a heavy-lidded glance from Carol Azul, Hitchens gave the silver shaker a gelid twirl. "Look here," he said grandly to Fisketjon, "I can't believe you're holding this book until June. I bet it's in the stores before then. But if you do have time, let me save you from a blunder. Victor Propp the fraud is described as being in his 60's and also as having a father who claimed descent from Isaac Babel. Now if Babel had lived he could still be technically alive, so if you're going to make not one but two learned references to Russian Jewish letters, you had better ... Hullo? Hullo? Hullo ... operator?"

MARCH 16, 1992 BY MARTIN AMIS

MASTER OF THE TELEPHONE EXCHANGE

WRITERS' LIVES ARE ALL ANXIETY AND AMBITION. No one begrudges them the anxiety, but the ambition is something they are supposed to shut up about. The two strains are, of course, inseparable and symbiotic. Early on in his autobiographical meditation on John Updike, *U and I*, Nicholson Baker considers some likely responses from the great man:

"Updike could react, feel affronted, demolish me, ignore me, litigate. A flashy literary trial had some fantasy appeal, except that I knew that I would burst into tears if cross-examined by any moderately skillful attorney. But it probably wouldn't come to that."

No, it probably wouldn't come to that. A few pages later, Mr. Baker attends a literary party in Boston, hoping Mr. Updike will be there. His "foolish beaming pleading" gaze eventually seizes on an acquaintance, the novelist Tim O'Brien, who quickly reveals that he "goes golfing" with Mr. Updike. "I was of course very hurt that ... Updike had chosen Tim O'Brien as his golfing partner," writes Mr. Baker, although he doesn't know Mr. Updike and can't play golf. Perhaps the golfing friendship will solidify at some later date? (Out on the fairway, as he masters the game, Mr. Baker's book chat will soon have Mr. Updike thinking, "Hm, I guess that Nick Baker is not to be underestimated.") But that's not good enough: "I want to be Updike's friend now!" All writers will recognize the truth of these childish desires. It took Nicholson Baker to own up to them, and to realize their comedy. Writers want to disdain everything yet they also want to have everything; and they want to have it now.

Well, everything—in the form of a capitalized success—is on offer. I arrived in New York for our meeting, and there it all was: the Hiltonic hotel room, the appalling schedule, the tuxed waiter bearing the club sandwich on his burnished tray, the soothing prospect of a public reading (that night) and a transcontinental plane ride (the next morning), and finally, another interviewer coming through the door with all his dreams and dreads and character flaws. ... The cult author of *The Mezzanine* and *Room Temperature* has now come cruising into the commercial mainstream.

Stark Naked

Mr. Baker's third novel, *Vox*, is the season's hot book, sexually explicit, much promoted, ambivalently received; for the moment it seems to stand there, stark naked, in the primitive fever of scrutiny and demand.

Although I was of course very hurt that *Vox* was doing quite so well, it should be said—to get the B-and-Me stuff at least partly out of the way—that I entered Mr. Baker's domain with an air of some knowingness. I myself had granted many an interview, if not

in this very hotel room (it was a nonsmoking room on a nonsmoking floor; Mr. Baker doesn't drink, either), then in this very hotel, and I was a stupefied veteran of the writer's tour that Mr. Baker now contemplated with such disquiet. He was, on the other hand, inadmissibly young (36), and never before had I interviewed a literary junior. This imagined hurdle turned out to be a liberation and a pleasure, but I somehow found it necessary to pre-devastate Mr. Baker with the news that one of *Vox*'s supposed coinages (a synonym for masturbation) had been casually tossed out by me two novels ago. Mr. Baker was duly devastated and the interview began.

Pointlessly Tall

Those who know and therefore love his books might expect Mr. Baker to prove barely capable of sequential thought, let alone rational speech. The novels suggest a helpless egghead and meandering pedant whose mind is all tangents and parentheses. His radical concentration on the mechanics of everyday life—the escalator, the shoelace—prepares one for a crazy professor, even an idiot savant. One is also steeled, by his own self-mockery, for Mr. Baker's physical appearance; a balding, four-eyed, pinheaded drink of water.

He is, to be sure, fabulously and pointlessly tall, tall beyond utility, and waveringly plinthed on his size 14 shoes. But these impressions soon fall away, just as the cold surface of his prose is warmed by the movement of his inner ironies, as they ceaselessly search for intricate delight. Mr. Baker, it turned out, was both droll and personable. I might even have glimpsed a quiet charisma behind his barbered beard, his messianic spectacles. Or was that just Manhattan and the dawn glow of celebrity?

"There are a lot of numbers now," said Mr. Baker when I asked him about his current ascendancy. "The fact that success is quantified is very exciting." After just three weeks on the *New York Times* best-seller list, *Vox* has already moved to number three. "But that's not good enough. Only number one will do." But then how long will it be number one? There is, after all, the very worrisome example of Stephen Hawking. Perhaps two years. But why not three? Why not forever? "Actually, I thought *The Mezzanine* was going to be a best seller," said Mr. Baker. "The writer's mind is always leaping forward." So in that sense he is fully prepared, as all writers are—even the most obscure, even the unpublishable. In their minds, they have all been best sellers, and golfed with John Updike, and lost sleep (as Mr. Baker has) over acceptance speeches for prizes they haven't even been entered for, let alone won.

"I felt as famous as I ever wanted to be with

The writer may scheme and dream, but the words on the page are always free of calcula-tion. He lingered to chat, and to defend his book ("I meant it to be human and touching"; "I like it more than any of the oth-ers—I ... love it").

U and I. And I thought when you wrote a best seller you were ... rich. It isn't the case. But there are prices for ideas, for certain bits of information. Like a piece of software. You can design a good Argyle sock or a bad Argyle sock." So perhaps *Vox* can be seen as a "needed" or gap-filling product. *The Mezzanine*, in particular, reveals a sober respect for market forces as one commercial process succeeds another, and Mr. Baker admits to being less interested in fashion and accident than in the firmness of the merit-value equation. "You can get very fired up about these things. It's what drew me to the stock market."

Ordeal Readiness

"Don't let Nick fool you," Mr. Baker's editor had said. "He wants to be rich and famous." Perhaps Mr. Baker should be grateful that this remark came from his editor rather than someone really central, like his publicist. In any event, I sat in the audience at the Manhattan Theater Club where Mr. Baker was to read that night, trying not to let Nick fool me. As he loped up on to the stage, his neck and knees were bent in what might have been ordeal readiness, or simple height effacement. And of course, he didn't read aloud from *Vox* (which would have tested anybody); he read aloud a piece about reading aloud.

After handing *Vox* in, Mr. Baker explained, he told his publishers he would not do "any public performances of any kind." There was evidently some discussion at Random House, though, because when the proofs arrived, Mr. Baker saw on the back the following italicized promise: National Author Reading Tour. His stance at the lectern was impressively rigid and spavined, but the performance felt assured and effective. In conclusion Mr. Baker offered to field comments on *Vox*, and a tentative Q-and-A session began.

Performing writers can usually count on at least one strong-minded holdout in any silent audience, and finally an elderly lady (a stranger to this author's habitual indirection) came up with: "How can you ask for questions when you haven't read from it? What are we supposed to do? Guess?" Mr. Baker hesitated. "This book is in its fifth printing," he said. "Someone is reading it."

When I breakfasted with him the next morning, before he flew out to Los Angeles, Mr. Baker confessed that this unguarded remark had supplied the grist for the previous night's insomnia. He suffers from insomnia, also arthritis, also psoriasis (a link with Mr. Updike, who "had one unfortunate fictional representative vacuuming out the bed every morning"). Mr. Baker was, in addition, percolating anxiety about a trip to England. "They're going to be disappointed by *Vox*. Why should I be there while they're being disappointed? Why should I fly into disappointment?"

This is from *U and I*: "When excessively the shy force themselves to be forward, they are frequently surprisingly unsubtle and over-direct and even rude; they have entered an extreme region beyond their normal personality, an area of social crime where gradation don't count. ... The same goes for constitutionally ungross people who push themselves to chime in with something off-color—in choosing to go along they step into a world so saturated with revulsions that its esthetic structure is impossible for them to discern. ..."

One would like to apply the above, not so much to *Vox* (where a sortie of this kind is attempted, and nothing much actually happens), but to the standard Baker prose paragraph, where scarily delicate senses are exposed to the Brobdingnag of workaday life. So placed, Mr. Baker stares with the clean eyes of a child, and speak with a child's undesigning but often terrible honesty.

In Albany 10 Years, Cuomo Has Failed to Leave His Mark

WHEN THE CITIZEN'S BUDGET COMMISSION PROPOSED SEVERAL months ago the New York's ailing state government adopt a series of budget reforms, including such fiscal mom-and-apple-pie stuff as elimination of risky short-term borrowing and adoption of a truly balanced budget, the reaction in Mario Cuomo's Executive Chamber was telling.

"Impossible!" the State Budget Office replied in not so many words. "Can't be done! Nobody else does it!"

An almost reflexive reaction against change, for better or for worse, has been a hallmark of the Cuomo administration, which will celebrate its 10th anniversary next January. Ten years is hardly an insignificant amount of time for a political chief executive, yet New York political insiders (except for those employed by the Cuomo administration) often remark that so little has changed in Albany since that January day in 1983 when Hugh Carey retired from office, his interest in his job having lapsed some time short of its official termination. Making note of the gap between the governor's words and their implementation has become journalistic boilerplate—two years ago, *New York Newsday*'s endorsement of Mr. Cuomo contained the following subtitle: "Gov. Cuomo talks like a man with a vision. Now he must turn it into a reality." This after the Governor had been in office for eight years.

Johnny? Jay? Heeere's ... Charlie!

RIGHT NOW, CHARLIE ROSE IS LIKE KIPLING'S OLD MAN KANGAROO: "Very truly sought after." His eponymous public television talk show is being hailed as *the* way to spend the hour between 11 P.M. and midnight; Mrs. Astor has asked him to dine with the Reagans; the glossy magazines have called about profiling him. Mr. Rose says he doesn't quite understand what all the fuss is about. He makes lots of references to himself as a country boy—a sort of "Charlie in Wonderland," Wonderland being the wonderful world of New York's glitterati—and claims that "I'm sort of bewildered by New York."

Despite the hoots of laughter that should, and do, greet that last statement, there is indeed a country boy named Charlie Rose, albeit one on fast forward. The man *TV Guide* has dubbed "the stealth bumpkin" is tall, a bit disheveled and rather charmingly manic as he dashes about from the library (where he's boning up on his prospective guests), to "this thing for Mike Nichols," to the Channel 13 studios on West 58th Street. He grew up in Henderson, N.C., retains a Southern accent, and owns quite a bit of land in the next county over, including a farm of which he is clearly very fond of and to which he repairs on the weekend whenever possible. "I have my purest thoughts there," he says at one point during an interview, picking up the theme later with a hymn to the sounds of a birdsong. And yet, when he's taken to lunch at Arcadia, one of the Upper East Side's more exquisite restaurants, he has been there before—and knows the chef, Anne Rosenzweig, who appears at the end of the meal to chat. She's been on his show.

OCTOBER 5, 1992   BY JIM WINDOLF

Off the Record

AS PREDICTED, THE CHANGING OF THE GUARD HASN'T BEEN entirely smooth at *The New Yorker*. Someone at the magazine, clearly a loyalist to long-deposed editor William Shawn, pinned two notes to the bulletin board just outside the temporary office of the new editor Tina Brown during her first week. One was the February 1987 farewell to the staff written by Mr. Shawn: "We have done our work with honesty and love," Mr. Shawn wrote. "*The New Yorker*, as a reader once said,

has been the gentlest of magazines." The second message pinned to the board was a 1985 Notes and Comment written by Mr. Shawn after the magazine had been acquired by S.I. Newhouse for Advance Publications. In the note, Mr. Shawn affirmed his vision of the magazine, emphasizing the independence of the editorial side from the business side: "The idea of *The New Yorker* ... cannot be bought or sold." The two notes were removed soon after Ms. Brown and her crew showed up for work.

Ms. Brown has caused murmurs among staff members with her habit of wearing sunglasses in the West 43rd building, especially when she keeps them on during art meetings. And an anecdote making the rounds of *New Yorker* writers has not helped the new editor's cause any: Ms. Brown, it seems, asked George W.S. Trow to write a profile of the diminutive Hollywood agent Irving (Swifty) Lazar. Mr. Trow said he wasn't interested. Ms. Brown next asked fashion writer Kennedy Fraser to write it, making the special request that she write the profile "in the George Trow style." Ms. Fraser politely declined.

Bootlegged galleys of parts of Ms. Brown's first issue were circulating in the publishing world several days before the official publication date. The galleys contained editors' comments set off in brackets. At the end of a particularly roiling sentence in James Wolcott's piece about the marketing of the novel *Suicide Blonde* was the following: "[QA: Huh?]". The last chunk of sentence, which included the phrase "wicky-wacky ball of wax," did not make it into the debut issue.

Finally, some staff members felt insulted the morning of Sept. 29 upon finding that *The New York Times'* review of Ms. Brown's first issue appeared under the byline of Walter Goodman, the television critic.

◇◇◇◇◇◇◇

AUGUST 17, 1992   BY CHARLES BAGLI

NEW YORKER, NATION EDITORS BATTLE FOR A DREAM (RENT: $375) APARTMENT

IN THE MEATPACKING DIStrict, where lifeblood flows each day into the gutter, two members of the literati are battling over Manhattan's seemingly most precious commodity: real estate. Rick Hertzberg, the incoming executive editor of *The New Yorker*, is wrestling with Andrew Kopkind, an associate editor of *The Nation* magazine, over a rent-controlled apartment at 67 Gansevoort Street, in the drab West Side neighborhood below 14th Street.

There is already some literary history behind Gansevoort Street, where workmen still trundle sides of beef, corned briskets and bologna across the cobblestones at the edge of the Hudson River. In the late 1800's, Herman Melville labored as an outdoor customs officer on the once-bustling dock, inspecting incoming goods to be hauled away to the area's meat markets and warehouses. At night, he trudged home to work on his last novel, *Billy Budd*.

Both Mr. Hertzberg and his wife, Michelle Slung, from whom he

is separated, are planning to move back to New York from Washington, D.C., where Mr. Hertzberg was editor of *The New Republic*. And they want the apartment they sublet to Mr. Kopkind in 1979, which still contains the couple's 4,000 books, Mr. Hertzberg's collection of *Mad* magazines and Ms. Slung's 1970's wardrobe.

In what is perhaps a variation on the anarchist slogan, Property is Theft, Mr. Kopkind and his roommate, John Scagliotti, refuse to budge. Mr. Kopkind accuses Mr. Hertzberg of profiting from his tenancy by over-charging for a rent-controlled apartment. He has not paid any rent since sometime in 1988, but he believes he has some unassailable right to what has been his home for the past 13 years. Mr. Hertzberg, who continues to pay rent on the apartment, said he feels betrayed by a journalist he once admired. "I think it was an outrageous abuse of trust," Mr. Hertzberg said of Mr. Kopkind. "They've deluded themselves into thinking this is a fight for truth and justice against mammon and evil."

SEPTEMBER 28, 1992 BY CLARE MCHUGH

Let's Go to the Video Journalist!
Stellar Month for New York 1 Debut!

IF THERE'S A GOD WHO RULES THE FATE OF TV NEWS EXECUTIVES, he, or she, chose to smile upon Paul Sagan for two weeks during the middle of September. Mr. Sagan, 33, is the vice president for news and programming at New York 1, the 24-hour, all-news, local cable television station that made its debut Sept. 8 on Channel 1. During the station's first fortnight, Mr. Sagan was blessed with several meaty stories to cover, stories well-suited to the continuous news format and sexy enough to attract the attention of a wide spectrum of New Yorkers.

Just as covering Operation Desert Storm played to CNN's strengths, the continuing tension between police and residents of Washington Heights, a suspenseful election night, the nasty police demonstration on City Hall's steps and the subsequent daylong City Council hearings on the all-civilian review board provided rich fodder for New York 1 and its team of 20 "video journalists" who are deployed across the city, carrying their own cameras on their backs.

"When I first saw how easy it was to go live for a decision on the Washington Heights case, I was blown away," said Mr. Sagan. "Even though we'd been practicing for months, I didn't realize how it would feel—what ability we'd have to respond to the big stories immediately."

◇◇◇◇◇◇

OCTOBER 19, 1992 BY PETER KAPLAN

TV DIARY: BUSH'S VALEDICTORY, CLINTON'S SELF-HELP

I. PREGAME WARM-UP

What a morning! On *Meet the Press*, the mad caricaturist's match-up between the strangely feline James Carville, an R. Crumb creation out of *Fritz the Cat*, and, from the Bush camp, a gum-drop-eyed man named Charles Black who evoked Dondi as a 45-year-old. Between them was beaming Tim Russert, watching as Mr. Carville pistol-whipped Mr. Black, who just kept blinking. Next door on *Face the Nation*, we had a made-for-TV movie in which Bush spokeswoman and Carville girlfriend Mary Matalin mud-wrestled Clinton spin-mistress Mandy Grunwald, who kept smiling and calling the Bush campaign "sad."

II. WHAT WE DIDN'T SEE

Howard Stringer, the president of CBS Broadcast Group and former president of CBS news, decided to broadcast the American League baseball playoffs in Oakland, which was strolling toward extra innings. Mr. Stringer called it a "Faustian bargain of epic proportions" and watched the debate himself. Somewhere, Dan Rather was chewing and spitting out wallpaper.

III. WHAT WE SAW

Uh-oh! Bill Clinton's really John Bradshaw! This is pretty interesting since we support him, and even though we've had boring presidents before, we've never had self-help presidents. So this is what he does on the air. He is, among other things, purposefully calming—a soporific. He conveys self-taught inner worth. His attacks are gentle, never personal, and his self-defense is that of the universally aggrieved: "You were wrong to attack my patriotism. I was opposed to the war but I love my country and we need a president who will bring it together." That's political context but it's family talk. He has a calming effect, Bill Clinton, like a counselor in some kind of program, and he uses Alcoholics Anonymous and psycho-language.

The president conceded. Mr. Bush had a choice to make, and he knew what it was. He could make a big noise or he could pretend he was finishing up his second term and deliver a valedictory, which is what he did. He's been through these things before.

A Booth of Their Own: Tammy Faye Bakker, Imelda Marcos, Zsa Zsa Gabor and Leona Helmsley were sisters in scandal

1993

Media mega-magnate Rupert Murdoch buys the *New York Post*—again

Truckload of explosives is detonated at World Trade Center, killing six

Former Le Cirque star chef Daniel Boulud opens his own restaurant

 Details editor James Truman is crown prince of Condé Nast

Beauty Myth's Naomi Wolf convenes salon of "culture babes"

Broadway is uplifted by Tony Kushner's  *Angels in America*

The aroma of Seattle espresso bars wafts over the East Coast

Updike up in arms at American Academy of Arts and Letters

 NBC late-night goes Gen X with lanky Harvardian Conan O'Brien

1993

◇◇◇◇◇◇

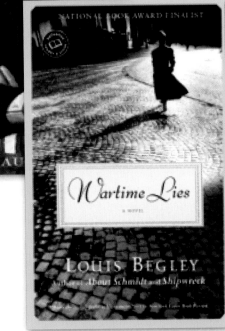

JANUARY 25, 1993 BY JAMES COLLINS

THE OBSERVATORY:
LOUIS, LOUIS

UNTIL THEY ATE HAMBURGERS TOGETHER ON JAN. 14 AT THE Mark Hotel on 77th Street and Madison Avenue, Louis Auchincloss and Louis Begley had only had one encounter, an indirect one, of any significance. Mr. Auchincloss, of course, is the prolific, 75-year-old romancer of an all-but-vanished, brownstone-mansion New York and a former partner in the law firm of Hawkins, Delafield & Wood; his new book *Three Lives* has just been published. Mr. Begley, 59, is the masterly chief of the international department at Debevoise & Plimpton who two years ago wrote the most celebrated first novel in memory, *Wartime Lies*, which concerns a young Polish Jew's experience of the Holocaust; his second book, *The Man Who Was Late* (Knopf), has also just been published.

"Your *Great World of Timothy Colt*," Mr. Begley told Mr. Auchincloss, "almost stopped me from becoming a lawyer. It was the first book I read about the place I was headed, which was Wall Street. I had almost no idea what went on in those precincts and I said, 'Holy mackerel, this is what it's going to be like.'"

The Great World of Louis Auchincloss and The Great World of Louis Begley would be perfectly apt titles for novels in which each was the hero; for a couple of hours recently, bracketed by Mr. Auchincloss' vodka martini and Mr. Begley's second double espresso, these worlds orbited each other, as the two men discussed New York law firms, anti-Semitism, writing, writers, steak tartare and the perils of being named "Louis."

"Oh please call me Louis," said Mr. Auchincloss. "We have the same first name—you're Louis not Lewis, aren't you?"

"I'm Louis—"

"Yes, Louis, like me. I detest being called Lewis. Lewis is L-E-W-I-S!"

"It's an enormous problem. Either that or people call me Lou." This prompted a knowing rueful laugh from Mr. Auchincloss.

"They say Lou right off!" Mr. Auchincloss broke in. "'What's your name?' 'Louis Auchincloss.' 'Oh, hi, Lou.'"

FEBRUARY 8, 1993   BY PETER STEVENSON

WNBC NEWS STAFF CHAFES AS BOLSTER DRAGS STATION INTO BUTTAFUOCO ERA

ON MONDAY, JAN. 25, THE LEAD story on WNBC's 5 P.M. newscast was the murder outside C.I.A. headquarters in McClean, Va. But when the tape rolled, viewers instead saw 45 seconds of footage, of New York City police closing in on a hostage-taker in the Bronx.

It was only the latest of a series of on-air meltdowns for WNBC News. Last Sept. 18, anchorman Chuck Scarborough was left hanging for 30 seconds while producers scrambled to find the video for a Woody Allen story. And in November, during the crucial ratings sweeps, viewers who tuned in to the newscast one night found themselves staring at a blank screen for a full two and a half minutes—a television eternity.

Taken alone, these gaffes would be a large blotch on the record of a news operation that had until recently been considered the best in the city. But the on-air gaps are minor compared to the abyss that has opened up inside 30 Rockefeller Plaza between WNBC management—specifically, the new WNBC president and general manager, Bill Bolster, and the new news director, Bruno Cohen—and the correspondents, anchors, writers and producers who work for them.

Channel 4 has always prided itself on having reporters who not only won Emmy Awards, but were also local superstars—most notably Gabe Pressman and John Miller. This combination of grit and glamour brought the newscast five Emmies in a row in the late 1980's. But since Mr. Bolster arrived in the fall of 1991, the station's reputation has changed with remarkable speed.

◇◇◇◇◇◇◇

FEBRUARY 15, 1993   BY WARREN ST. JOHN

Rrring! Rrring! Hello, Jerky Boys? Time Warner Courts Prank Callers

SOMETIMES, FAME IS THE RESULT OF YEARS OF DILIGENT WORK. Sometimes it arrives unbidden, a bolt from the blue. Take the case of Dr. Steven Rosenberg of Manhattan. For the past several years, Dr. Rosenberg's name and the Upper East Side business address have circulated around the country on an underground tape recording of a prank telephone call to his office. In the call to Dr. Rosenberg, we hear the doctor trying to placate a dissatisfied customer who keeps claiming, in an annoyingly, high-pitched voice reminiscent of Bugs Bunny, "I bought some glasses there the other day and now my eyes is goin' cra-a-a-zy."

The principal architect of Dr. Rosenberg's involuntary fame is Johnny Brennan, 31, of Flushing, Queens. He passed the tapes around to his friends, who copied them and passed them around to their friends. As the circle of listeners widened, so did the fame of Dr. Rosenberg and numerous other victims of the Jerky Boys, as Mr. Brennan and his cohort, Kamal (Kamal has "just one name, like Sting," said an associate), call themselves.

MARCH 8, 1993   BY ROBIN POGREBIN

Former Le Cirque Star Returns

THE SPACE IS A SKELETAL SHAMBLES OF DUST AND debris. With power tools scattered among ladders and poles, and hulking workmen traipsing over temporary floors, it is difficult to envision a refined restaurant emerging out of so much rubble.

But Daniel Boulud doesn't even have to use his imagination. The 5,200-square-foot restaurant that will open late next month on the street level of the Surrey Hotel on East 76th Street is his baby. Daniel, the restaurant, is the realization of what Daniel, the famed former Le Cirque chef, has been dreaming of for years.

Where there is now exposed insulation and chunks of cinder block, he sees a Maplewood bar with banquettes upholstered in red-checked burlap where customers can converge even at non-meal hours for afternoon tea or an after-work cocktail. Where there are metal pipes sticking up out of gauged concrete, he sees gleaming stoves, walk-in refrigerators and ice cream machines. In the dark, dim basement, he sees a florist, a prep station, a wine cellar.

"It's getting more exciting," said the French-born Mr. Boulud (pronounced BOO-loo), a diminutive man who looks much younger than his 37 years. "The fun part is starting."

Opening a restaurant at a time when others are still reeling from a recession that has withered expense accounts and discouraged New Yorkers from eating out, Mr. Boulud exudes a daredevil's confidence. He signed a 20-year lease on the restaurant that was formerly Les Pleiades and insists his optimism is justified.

"I really feel it's going to be a beautiful, charming restaurant," he said in an interview at his temporary office in a second-floor suite at the Surrey. "I have a good feeling people will feel very receptive to what I will try to do." Nevertheless, Mr. Boulud shares the concern of New York's restaurateurs that President Clinton's proposal to cut the percentage of deductible expense account spending to 50 percent from 80 percent will hurt their lunch business period. "Let's hope it never happens," Mr. Boulud said. "But I'm not trying to be on the upper, upper scale, so I'm not too worried about it."

◇◇◇◇◇◇◇

MARCH 15, 1993   BY IAN WILLIAMS

SHEIK PROBED IN TRADE CENTER BLAST GIVES INTERVIEW TO REBUT SUSPICIONS

SHEIK OMAR ABDUL RAMAN'S demeanor can only be described as jolly, although his smile is somewhat disconcerting. The milky white irises of his eyes show the blindness that has afflicted him since infancy. The shiek's disfiguring disability notwithstanding, he and his followers have been accused of involvement in the assassinations of, among others, the late Egyptian President Anwar el-Sadat and Rabbi Meir Kahane, and now in the bombing of the World Trade Center. In Egypt, Sheih Abdul Rahman is held responsible for murderous attacks on tourists and assaults by Muslims on the nation's Coptic Christian minority.

When I spoke to him on Feb. 20, the Saturday before a truckload of explosives went off under the Trade Center, he denied all knowledge of such crimes. Besides, Sheik Abdul Rahman has an obvious defense to all the charges involving his followers: Was the pope guilty because Al Capone went to mass? In turn, the Immigration and Naturalization Service has ventured its own exotic variation on the Federal Government's Capone gambit. Unable to prove substantive criminal charges, they eventually got the mobster for tax evasion; more recently they have been trying to deport the sheik for, of all things, polygamy.

APRIL 5, 1993 BY JOHN DIZARD

WALL ST. DIARY: Clues Behind Murdoch's *Post* Gamble Point to Foxy Media Plans in Boston

WHY WOULD ANY SANE PERSON want to buy the *New York Post*?

Let's rephrase that question: Why would Rupert Murdoch want to buy the *New York Post*? We already know the answer his friends are giving—that he loves the *Post*, that he hated the idea of being run out of New York in 1988 by the likes of Teddy Kennedy, and that there's nothing he enjoys more than ripping up a front page at the eleventh hour and dictating a new story and a new headline.

His triumphant return to South Street certainly emphasized the emotional benefits mentioned by those close to the Australian media baron. "He's full of beans," said a friend, one of several associates who asked that their names not be used. "Never been happier—he loves the idea of Mario Cuomo and Teddy Kennedy and Ernest Hollings calling him and begging him to do this. At the time he was forced to sell it, the *Post* was nothing better than a $50 million executive toi-

let. But if it makes him happy, then the whole organization will work better."

"None of us thought he should buy it," added a business adviser. "[His wife] Anna was arguing against doing the *Post* right up to the last minute. The only way we were finally persuaded that it was all right for him to go ahead with it was by being convinced he could limit the time he'll spend on it—Fox [the TV network and the movie studio] has to be the priority."

◇◇◇◇◇◇◇

NOVEMBER 15, 1993 BY PETER STEVENSON

'CULTURE BABES' FILL GODDESS ROLODEX; SALON OF WOMEN WHO RUN WITH THE WOLF

LAST WINTER, SEVERAL DOZEN women working in media in Manhattan received a two-page invitation printed on hot pink paper. The letter opened with "Dear Babes," and contained phrases such as "Babes! We love you for your minds," and was signed "Yours in babehood." The letter was co-written by Naomi Wolf, 31-year-old best-selling feminist author (*The Beauty Myth* and a new book due out this month) and scourge of Camille Paglia. It was an invitation to an upcoming meeting of "Culture Babes," the name of Ms. Wolf's feminist networking salon that convenes at various apartments and bars in Manhattan once a month.

According to the pink invitation, a typical Culture Babes gathering

would be "a good place to eat excellent food, drink good wine, smoke by the window and play in the Zeitgeist toybox." The target of Culture Babes, according to the letter, was "the white boys' Rolo-

Naomi Wolf

dex." Ms. Wolf proposed instead "the Goddess Rolodex."

The first gathering of Culture Babes was held at Ms. Wolf's apartment on a snowy afternoon in February. Ms. Wolf's plans for Culture Babes called for a projected $20 million escrow account to back women's projects, sponsorship of debates on gender issues and a "women and politics" talk show (she called it "an anti-*McLaughlin Group*"). While those projects are still being discussed, the gatherings have evolved into essentially an all-woman cocktail party, with Ms. Wolf as Hostess, and networking and mentoring the main thrusts. Most Culture Babes seem to prefer it that way and are pleased to have a venue in which to meet other women in positions of power.

APRIL 12, 1993
BY RICH COHEN

CURTAINS OPEN FOR WINDOWS ON THE WORLD, OR OPEN IN TIME FOR MOTHER'S DAY?

FOR A RESTAURANT, THE ONLY thing worse than rats in the kitchen is bombs in the basement. "It may be even more damaging than food poisoning," said Michael Bartlett, the editor of *Restaurants and Institutions* magazine. "Being blown up, that's a serious setback." Mr. Bartlett was referring to Windows on the World, the landmark restaurant that has topped One World Trade Center since the tower opened in 1976. Unlike other tenants forced to cease operations in the wake of the recent terrorist attack, some in the restaurant business say Windows on the World, in its current configuration, may never reopen. "In the end, it might prove the tragedy's biggest loser," said an industry insider. "The Port Authority, who owns the space and has long been unhappy with its management, may use the bomb as an excuse to remake the restaurant." Windows on the World management insists the restaurant will reopen next month—a claim the Port Authority disputes.

APRIL 19, 1993 BY CANDACE BUSHNELL

THE OBSERVATORY: MANHATTAN TRANSFERS

O N ANY GIVEN DAY, IT IS POSSIBLE TO WALK INTO A coffee shop in Minneapolis and find the sort of trend-setting Armani-draped New Yorkers you'd expect to see hanging out in Miami's South Beach. You might even see, for instance, Nick Beavers, the youngest of the Manhattan Beaver brothers (famous for operating the Surf Club in the 80's), who, along with his sidekick, Terry Prem, a former model and fashion stylist, is opening a nightclub called the Rogue Bar in Minneapolis' landmark warehouse district—and has hired Dante, the former doorman at Tatou, to be his head bouncer. Then there's Andrew Zimmern, who used to manage Elio's and Petaluma, and is now the chef at Minneapolis' own Un Deux Trois (a satellite of Un Deux Trois on West 44th Street), and a regular on the local TV show, *Great Chefs of Minneapolis*. Other displaced Park Avenue offspring include Taylor Burr and Josh Holland, of the Burr/Holland recording studio (their motto: "We're Burr/Holland. We're from New York"), photographer Adam Gaynor, securities broker Billy Grace and lawyer Josh Levy.

They are not here for the scenery, although some grow to appreciate and even like the long straight roads that stretch right to the horizon, and Minnesota's many lakes have a certain austere beauty. Nor are they here for the weather. On a recent morning in late March, for instance, it was 83 degrees in Miami versus a whopping 1 degree in the Twin Cities.

Rather, this gang of the formerly glamorous have come to Minneapolis as night-life refugees, lured by the area's famous drying-out facilities such as Hazelden Foundation and the Fairview Riverside Medical Center. And once on their feet, they are kept here by the abundant halfway houses and coffee shops, and by the continued presence of rehabbed sophisticates like themselves. Here New York sends its partied-out, its drug-addled, its rich kids yearning to be addiction-free. New Yorkers go to Miami because they want to. They come to Minneapolis because they have to.

"They don't call this state Minnesober for nothing," said Michael Morse, a craggy-faced bearded man in his early 40s who peers sharply over the top of his reading glasses. Mr. Morse used to manage Un Deux Trois in Manhattan. He came to Hazelden to kick heroin in 1989 and now owns the Minneapolis version of the restaurant, which is a second home to the city's displaced East Coast natives. There are dozens of treatment centers and halfway houses in Minneapolis. The New Yorkers who have settled here have been through "the program" at Hazelden or Fairview Riverside (some, several times), and they've been advised that it would be a good idea if they remain in Minneapolis (overcutely referred to by many as the "Mini-apple"), if not for the rest of their lives, then at least for a year or two. "When they tell you this, you just get really angry, especially if, like me, you just came here to look reasonably healthy again," said Billy Grace.

"Right now, most of us don't have a choice. We have to stay here," said Mr. Zimmern, 31. He lives in a Victorian house in St. Paul near Summit Avenue, where F. Scott Fitzgerald used to wander drunkenly from house to house, crashing dinner parties. "Back then you could get in anywhere if you had the right accent," Mr. Zimmern noted wistfully.

Mr. Zimmern declares his stylistic kinship with Soho (and makes a point of standing out from his distinctly Midwestern neighbors) by alternating between pairs of blue, pink and yellow Cole Haan sneakers. In a yellow pair and over his third cup of coffee, he explained: "New York is the place where we did our using. There are too many temptations. If we go back to New York and use, two things happen: We either end up in jail or we die."

"You can have a lot more real friends here than you can in New York," said Mr. Prem, the former stylist, who hastened to add that he grew up in an apartment sandwiched between Peter Duchin upstairs and Roy Lichtenstein below. "In New York, you have a thousand acquaintances and two friends. Here, it's easier to differentiate between people who really like you for you, and people who only want to know you because they want something from you, mostly because people here are so bad at that kind of manipulation."

Some of Minneapolis' ex-New Yorkers haven't been back to the mother city for years; when they do return, it is usually for short, clandestine visits. ("I get pavement paranoia immediately," said Mr. Gaynor.)

When Hazelden's new recruits arrive at Minneapolis International Airport ("This place is not as backwards as people think—they have an international airport," Mr. Morse said), they're told to go to carousel 14, where they will be picked up by the Hazelden staff. Like Mr. Zimmern, who had 15 stiff drinks on the plane, most arrive at this quiet, clean and spacious airport drunk, high and clinging to their portable phones. "I kept thinking, 'How will they know me?'" Mr. Zimmern remembered. It wasn't a problem.

The main Hazelden treatment center, founded in 1949, is a series of low, modern buildings on 488 wooded lakefront acres about 45 minutes out of the Twin Cities. In-patient treatment here lasts for about 28 days. New arrivals tend to feel that "a terrible mistake has been made; there's someone sleeping in your room, and more important, you have to make some phone calls," in the words of Mr. Grace. After the 28-day treatment, many patients are free to return to their former lives. But some are not. The most difficult cases are assigned to the Jellinek Center, an extended treatment house for those who still have a hard time admitting they're addicts. Patients there spend the next four to six months writing 5,000-word essays (called "sections") on all aspects of their lives, from family relationships to business, among other therapies.

Other graduates go directly into a Hazelden-run halfway house in St. Paul, which, said Mr. Zimmern, is like taking a course in Daily Life 101: "You learn how to do the little things: Get up in the

> *New Yorkers go to Miami because they want to. They come to Minneapolis because they have to.*

morning, make your bed, return phone calls." Part of the program's prescription for rehabilitation is taking a menial job. Mr. Beavers scooped frozen yogurt in a mall; Mr. Zimmern cleaned toilets; everyone knows former bankers who washed dishes and lawyers who sold shoes.

When they talk about their new home, Minneapolis' New York transplants sound an awful lot like suburban apologists earnestly justifying their moves from Manhattan to Westchester or New Jersey: "You can go to the movies and not have to stand in line, or pull your car right up to the bank," said Mr. Morse. But Minneapolis, unlike Scarsdale, perhaps, is also the sort of place where the locals "have trouble pronouncing lasagna. They call it 'lagonia,'" said Adam Gaynor, who works nights in an Italian restaurant and delivers potato chips two days a week.

In Minneapolis, almost everyone lives with a roommate—sometimes up to four at a time. ("Here, you're like a raw, exposed nerve, pulsing and vulnerable. You don't want to be alone," Adam Gaynor said.) In the evening, people travel in packs of up to 10. ("I still go out every night, but I never stay anyplace long," Mr. Prem said. "In New York, you leave a party because you don't want to miss the next big thing. Here, you leave because it's boring.") Although some rehab graduates, like Mr. Prem, go to nightclubs and can handle hanging out with "normies"—annoying recovery speak for people who can drink and take drugs and still get to bed by 1 A.M.—the preferred venues for socializing are coffee shops like the aforementioned Day-By-Day Café or Muddy Waters.

At Muddy Waters, Mr. Gaynor's black-and-white photographs of fellow Hazelden graduates hang on the walls—sharp in the middle and blurry around the outside—in serene contrast to the atmosphere:

blaring new rock 'n' roll and leather-jacketed punks, some with nose rings as thick as worms. "Strange things can happen to people in recovery," Mr. Gaynor said.

"Everything's easier in Minneapolis, but you've got to do something, you can't just hang out or you'll go crazy," said Taylor Burr, sitting in the office of the Burr/Holland recording studio in the Uptown section of Minneapolis, an area that is "sort of what I imagine Greenwich Village must have been like in the 60's." (Transplanted New Yorkers never tire of analyzing their adopted city in terms of Manhattan equivalencies.)

Two things happen to the New Yorkers who remain here, he said: "They either lose all their ambition and drop out, going to meetings and working their menial job and paying $300-a-month rent." Or, like Messrs. Beavers, Morse, Burr and Holland, they embrace the big-fish-in-a-small-pond theory of life, in which being a New Yorker is a distinct advantage. "Coming from the streets of New York has given me a savvy I can take anywhere," Mr. Morse said.

Mr. Burr puts it this way: "When I was in New York, I felt lost. There you are, this young man who wants to do all this cool stuff, and no one cares. Here, we're one of the three cool recording studios. We couldn't do this in New York."

"In New York," said Mr. Beavers, "you start off trying to get what the other guy's got. There's always that pressure to be the amazing one-shot deal. I wanted to produce movies, but I didn't want to work at it. I'd get fucked up and call Jack Nicholson's office, and then three days later it was like, whoa, the guy's not calling back.

"Minneapolis is about reality," continued the man who, during one of his last nights in New York, used an umbrella to destroy a plant at the Mark Hotel because he saw snakes in it. "If you want to do something here, you can do it. And for about one-fifth of the cost."

"It's really about economics," said Jon Levy, 30, a partner in a local law firm who's lived in Minneapolis for six years. "I want my kids to have the kind of [Park Avenue] upbringing I had, but I don't think it's possible in New York anymore. It's not safe.

"On the other hand, what's kind of cool is that it's real white bread here. No one has any idea what we as New Yorkers have been through and seen. No one really knows how bad it gets. Sometimes I feel like I'm living in a movie directed by David Lynch."

Others feel the same, though for different reasons. "I believe that Minnesota is a spiritual vortex," said Jim Lynden, a Californian who has been in Minneapolis for 20 years and is an uber-sponsor for recent New York recruits like Mr. Zimmern and Billy Grace. Gray-haired and dressed in jeans and a flannel shirt, Mr. Lynden has the sort of serene, unwrinkled face that is due either to a careful avoidance of the sun or an untroubled soul. "When the glaciers receded, they left a lot of ferrous iron in the ground, and this iron is acting as a magnet, drawing people here. They're coming in on a spiritual quest, and they're learning humility. I don't think all of them will stay here, but I imagine these creative, intelligent people learning to be humble, and then going out all over the world to create and spread the message."

"If that's true," said Chuck, a local hardware store owner, "then it's time to move out of Minneapolis."

MAY 17, 1993 BY ROBIN POGREBIN

A STAR RISES AT THE MESA GRILL

HE CALLED HIMSELF THE SUSAN LUCCI OF THE JAMES BEARD Awards. But this year, unlike the soap opera star who has been nominated 14 times for the Daytime Emmy Awards without winning, Bobby Flay broke his losing streak. On May 3, after being nominated in 1991 and 1992, Mr. Flay, the chef and part-owner of New York's Mesa Grill, was finally named Perrier-Jouet Rising Star Chef of the Year at the Beard Awards.

His victory brought to a close two long years of pretending not to care, yet kind of caring, two years of watching other chefs go up onstage to accept the award.

It wasn't as if Mr. Flay desperately needed the award for his ego, which seems healthy, or for his business, which is booming. The 28-year-old chef has already been widely hailed as a kitchen Wunderkind, earning two stars from *The New York Times* in 1991 and accolades nationwide. And although the James Beard Awards have been called the Academy Awards of cooking, they are only three years old and have yet to translate into significant publicity or profit for its winners.

Nevertheless, the awards, established by the James Beard Foundation in Manhattan and given to cookbook writers as well as chefs, are one of the few tributes of their kind in the restaurant world. And since candidates are selected from all over the country, the possibility of being honored before a black-tie audience of distinguished peers, decorated with a gold-plated medallion engraved with the late Beard's bald image and sent off with an oversize bottle of Perrier-Jouet Champagne on a pedestal, has become downright appealing to chefs like Mr. Flay.

Mr. Flay, whose closely cropped red hair and freckles give him a boyish look, breezed in wearing an Armani checked jacket and khaki pants. "This year, I'm very relaxed," he said. "I haven't thought about what I'm going to say if I win. I'll just get up there and wing it."

◇◇◇◇◇◇◇

JUNE 21, 1993 BY PETER STEVENSON

That's Mrs. Parker to You, Broderick!
The Brat Pack in Round Table's Clothing

DURING THE LAST WEEK OF APRIL, A SMALL, FINE-BONED WOMAN with straight auburn hair checked into the Algonquin Hotel under an assumed name. She requested a suite on an upper floor and a refrigerator stocked with Evian water and fruit juice. She spent a good part of each day at a secluded table in the hotel's Rose Room, chain-smoking and chatting with guests who had come at her request. The mystery woman was actress Jennifer Jason Leigh, gathering nuance and information for her role as Dorothy Parker in the Fine Line Features film *Mrs. Parker & the Round Table*, which is being produced by Robert Altman and directed by Alan Rudolph.

The film, which started shooting June 14, is the most expensive and ambitious project in what seems to be a new Dorothy Parker-and-the-Round-Table feeding frenzy. In early June, guests at the Algonquin could pay $50 to eat "Lunch at the Algonquin" alongside such postmodern Round Tablers as Jules Feiffer, Roy Blount Jr. and Phyllis Newman—sponsored by Toyota. And on Aug. 20, the hotel is offering a "Dorothy Parker Weekend Package," part of the month-long Dorothy Parker Centenary in honor of what would have been the cranky writer's 100th birthday.

JUNE 28, 1993
BY MIMI SHERATON

MEMO TO SEATTLE: HOLD THE COFFEE!

"I love coffee, I love tea ... I love the java jive and it loves me ..."

LOVE IT OR NOT, JAVA JIVE IS hitting the charts again, but not as the coolly hot jazz classic of the early 1940's. Today's ubiquitous jive hypes the new-wave espresso bars that are sprouting up all across the country and, most recently, in Manhattan. With a breathless, messianic zeal probably induced by caffeine high, food writers everywhere are heralding the coming of coffee paradise.

Converts to this new religion turn northwest when worshipping, facing the mecca that is Seattle, and Starbucks is their prophet. A coffee importer, roaster and wholesaler since 1971 and, in 1987, the creator of the Seattle-style espresso bar, Starbucks is represented along the West Coast and in Chicago, Washington, D.C., and Boston, among other cities.

In truth, Americans nationwide imbibe oceans of miserable, overheated, weak, acrid coffee, a combined result of penny-pinching by restaurateurs and the customer's lack of discernment.

Yet, as a frequent visitor to Seattle, I have never really grasped the appeal of Starbucks' espresso. I have also been disappointed with beans from the similarly celebrated Peet's of San Francisco and by cupfuls at the Coffee Connection in Boston's Quincy Market.

Better than New York coffee shop coffee they are, but is better than terrible necessarily good?

MAY 17, 1993   BY WARREN ST. JOHN

SCHLESINGER, UPDIKE UNITE IN REVOLT AT AMERICAN ACADEMY OF ARTS AND LETTERS

ARE CERTAIN OF AMERICA'S most illustrious artists and literati more illustrious than others? That question has tormented the 250-member American Institute of Arts and Letters for 89 years, and the dispute has recently come to a head. At issue is an elite, 50-member inner chamber known as the American Academy of Arts and Letters. From time to time, egalitarians in the institute have tried to break down the walls of the inner sanctum, only to be defeated by elitist factions. But late last year, a group led by historian Arthur Schlesinger Jr., economist John Kenneth Galbraith, painter Jack Levine, composer Lukas Foss and author Elizabeth Hardwick succeeded

in persuading academy and institute members to unite.

Of course, many in the academy think unification is an extremely bad idea. The opposition was led by Henry James biographer Leon Edel and counted among its ranks eminences like novelists Louis Auchincloss and Ralph Ellison and painter Andrew Wyeth. When members gather on May 19 at the McKim, Mead & White–designed West 155th Street headquarters for the annual awards ceremony, they will go as equals, for the first time since 1904. Now everyone will be a member of the academy; the less distinguished institute has been abolished.

The issue flared again in the late 1980's, when some academy members approached Mr. Updike, then the academy's chancellor, and suggested that the matter be reconsidered. Mr. Updike, cautious to a fault, declined. "When I was chancellor, I didn't want to be the one who presided over the dissolution of the academy," Mr. Updike told *The Observer*.

◇◇◇◇◇◇

SEPTEMBER 6, 1993   BY ROBIN POGREBIN

Scenes From the Stein Marriage

THEY BREEZE INTO THE CARlyle Hotel like movie stars, flashing white smiles and looking summery chic: former mayoral candidate Andrew Stein in a beige suit and blue shirt, attorney Lynn Forester in a cream-colored pants ensemble that highlights her loose yellow hair.

She sends the lemon wedge back in favor of milk for her cup of tea and says airily that their breakup, which they announced in early August, is all for the best. There will be no alimony or fight over belongings; it couldn't be more amicable. He adds earnestly that seven of their 10 years married were one long honeymoon until a few years ago, when they just stopped communicating.

Yet there is something contra-

dictory in the otherwise smooth demise of the Stein's union. Why, after the Council president announced his decision to leave the public sector for the comforts of private life on June 29, did he and Ms. Forester choose to surface only five weeks later on the front page of the *New York Post* with an "exclusive" hand-delivered to gossip columnist Cindy Adams about their pending divorce?

Perhaps the former couple's Aug. 3 publicity blitz was necessary because, despite their studied, rather self-contained effort to portray their parting as healthy and friendly, the picture

wasn't quite so perfect.

Ms. Forester—formerly known as Lynn Forester Stein—was more forthcoming on the subject. "It's true that two or three years ago we knew we didn't have a fabulous marriage," she said. "But at the same time, he was embarking on the most important moment in his career."

MAY 3, 1993 BY PETER STEVENSON

Heeere's Conan! NBC Goes Generation X: is 6'4" Harvardite the Next Letterman?

WHEN JAY LENO INTRODUCED CONAN O'BRIEN TO a surprised nine million people on *The Tonight Show* on April 26, it seemed that no one was more surprised than Mr. O'Brien himself. Repeating the phrase "I'm just thrilled," and looking demurely at the floor, the redheaded, 6-foot 4-inch, 185-pound successor to David Letterman as host of NBC's 12:30 a.m. *Late Night* show exuded a little of the shocked disbelief of a beauty pageant winner.

It was Mr. O'Brien's second appearance on *The Tonight Show* stage. On the afternoon of April 13, he had rummaged through the closet in his apartment on the edge of Beverly Hills, pulling out all his sport jackets and ties. He had just been summoned to the Burbank set of *The Tonight Show*, and he didn't know what to wear.

A few weeks earlier, *Saturday Night Live* executive producer Lorne Michaels had called Mr. O'Brien and asked if he was interested in producing the as-yet-uncast *Late Night* replacement that NBC had charged him with developing. Mr. O'Brien, a supervising producer (that means writer) for *The Simpsons*, had answered swiftly that what he really wanted to do was work in front of the camera.

Amazingly, NBC took him up on it. Mr. Michaels, who had hired O'Brien as a writer at *Saturday Night Live* in 1987, arranged for him to audition to be the host of the show. He would be on the stage where Johnny Cason and Mr. Leno had come to rule after many years of struggling, five days before his 30th birthday.

Mr. O'Brien arrived at *The Tonight Show* set for his audition around 7 P.M. The audience, which he had helped select, was packed with comedy writers, many of them fellow alumni of the *Harvard Lampoon*—ordinarily a very tough crowd. A live feed had been set up to Mr. Michaels' offices in New York, where the producer and NBC executives would watch the audition. Communicating over the monitor from New York, Mr. Michaels watched as Mr. O'Brien tried on his pile of assorted jackets and ties, and finally told him which ones to wear.

At 9 P.M., Mr. O'Brien walked onstage to

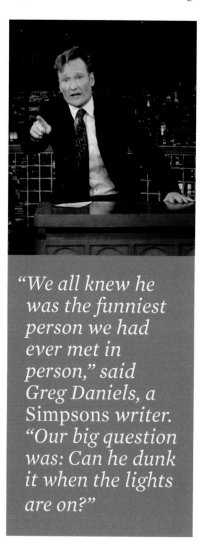

"We all knew he was the funniest person we had ever met in person," said Greg Daniels, a Simpsons *writer.* "Our big question was: Can he dunk it when the lights are on?"

taped *Tonight Show* theme music, wearing a beige jacket and jeans. The *Lampoon* alumni in the audience held their breath. "We all knew he was the funniest person we had ever met in person," said Greg Daniels, a *Simpsons* writer. "Our big question was: Can he dunk it when the lights are on?"

Apparently, he could. During the monologue, which he performed without cue cards, Mr. O'Brien told NBC executives why they should hire him. "You've got a very narrow window of opportunity," he said, pointing to his large, square head. "I've seen my uncles, and in three years, I'm going to have a big, fat, meaty Irish head."

He then sat in Mr. Leno's chair and interviewed *Seinfeld*'s Jason Alexander and actress Mimi Rogers. He had been giving prep cards for the two actors. Ms. Rogers started to tell Mr. O'Brien how hard it was to be a model. He listened politely for a few seconds, then said, "Hey, wait a minute. Being a model is not a hard job. Turning a crank in a factory, now that's a hard job!"

Mr. O'Brien's contract with *The Simpsons* runs through November, but Gracie Films, the company that produces the show, has been very supportive of his career move, according to a source at the show. During the weeks between the audition and the announcement, observers were amazed to see Mr. O'Brien's Ford Taurus still parked each day in the Fox lot. "The people he was negotiating with were shocked to find out he's still at work, writing *Simpsons* episodes," Mr. Daniels said. "They expected him to be in his apartment, chewing his nails."

On April 18, Mr. O'Brien celebrated his 30th birthday with a few friends. They ate chicken wings in his sparsely furnished apartment, near the old ICM building in Beverly Hills. Mr. O'Brien said he worried that Mr. Shandling might drag out negotiations. Then he amused his friends with stories about the model who lives downstairs from him, who thinks he is a nerd. Someone remembered a cartoon Mr. O'Brien had drawn 10 years ago for the *Lampoon*. In the cartoon, a pharaoh is looking out over the pyramids that have just been built in his honor. "I like it," the pharaoh is saying, "I really like it."

SEPTEMBER 20, 1993 BY A.D COLEMAN

PHOTOGRAPHY: A Kiss is Just a Kiss? Doisneau le Poseur

A CURIOUS AND (FOR ME) REGRETTABLE CHANGE HAS OVERTAKEN my relationship to Robert Doisneau's often marvelous photographs of Parisian life: I've stopped believing them.

Recent events surrounding Mr. Doisneau's images, "Le Baiser de l'Hôtelde Ville" ("Kiss by the Hotel de Ville"), made in Paris 1950, suggests that it is necessary to discard one analytical strategy and adopt another in regard to this photograph—and by implication, to large chunks of the œuvre of Mr. Doisneau, who is now 81.

After seeing a magazine reproduction of the famous photograph in 1988, Denise and Jean-Louis Lavergne—now in their 60's—maintained that they were the young lovers immortalized in this now internationally iconic image, and insisted that they were entitled to share in the profits.

The reason they lost the case was not just that they'd failed to meet the burden of proof. The photographer's representatives produced irrefutable evidence—in the form of contact sheets showing the couple in the photograph at different locations around the city, and contracts—proving that this photograph was part of a series commissioned by *Life* magazine, and that Mr. Doisneau had hired his subjects (who were definitely not the Lavergnes) to play roles in this staged tableau.

A statement issued on Mr. Doisneau's behalf makes the point that while the photographer is known for his candid photographic style, he has "never claimed that he does not use models." This is, to say the least, disingenuous; the 1950 issue of *Life* in which the image first appeared—as part of a spread of Doisneau pictures of kissing couples—included text that described them all as "unposed pictures," an assertion the photographer never repudiated.

SEPTEMBER 20, 1993 BY CANDACE BUSHNELL

WALLFLOWERISH PRINCE OF CONDÉ NAST IS BEAVIS AND BUTT-HEAD'S OWN MENCKEN

JAMES TRUMAN WAS HOLDING a gift-wrapped sexual device in his hand.

Seconds earlier, on the rooftop party deck at the downtown offices of *Details*, Mr. Truman, the magazine's editor in chief, had been asked to present the device to the managing editor. She was getting married in three days. Mr. Truman, who has the wiry haunted looks of a 60's rock star, approached the device with a gangly sort of trepidation, then picked it up gingerly between thumb and forefinger. An expression of horror, amusement and confusion crossed his face. Without missing a beat, he turned the device on through the wrapping. "One should never give gifts without the batteries," he said.

When the bride-to-be gushed her appreciation for the presents—which in addition to the sexual device included antique mother-of-pearl-handled fish forks—Mr. Truman gave his

trademark Oriental bow. It is a gesture that seems designed to smooth over those awkward moments when a kiss on the cheek would be too familiar and a handshake too cold. Mr. Truman has his explanation for the bow: "I get very embarrassed when people are nice to me," he said.

These days a lot of people are being very nice to James Tru-

man. This was not the case three years ago when the mop-topped Englishman presided over the complete deconstruction and reconstitution of *Details*. Founded in 1982 as a hiply deadpan black-and-white guide to downtown club life, the magazine was purchased by S.I. Newhouse's Condé Nast Publications in 1988 with the aim of polishing it into a national twenty-something men's fashion glossy, with politics and culture subsumed under style. Suddenly, there were articles on basketball sneakers and rave parties, feature stories on River Phoenix and Vanessa Williams; teen sex surveys! It was MTV on paper. Wayne-and-Garth's and Beavis-and-Butthead's favorite magazine. Readers of the old *Details* hated it.

But with its 268-page September issue, *Details* is one of the hot magazines of the year, with circulation up from 355,000 to 455,000 this year and ad pages climbing steadily. Not yet 40, Mr. Truman is the

young prince—complete with modified pageboy—in the decidedly hierarchical court of Condé Nast. "James invented the magazine from inside his head," said Mr. Newhouse, who is said to dote on *Details*.

Mr. Truman's editing style is easygoing. "I learned at *The Face* that the editor is not an all-powerful figure. I've always found that people's own standards are higher than any standards you can impose on them. If they're not, you don't want them around you anyway," Mr. Truman said.

For all his boyish elusiveness, Mr. Truman and *Details* now share a history. He's even starting to reminisce. "In the third issue, we ran an article on penises," said Mr. Truman with a fond grin. "It seemed like a unifying characteristic of our readers. Advertisers thought it was disgusting that we even acknowledged the existence of penises."

Heh heh heh heh. Cool.

◇◇◇◇◇◇◇

OCTOBER 18, 1993 BY TERRY GOLWAY

Biker, Screenwriter, Club Crawler ... Add Top Finance Aide to O' Donnell's C.V.

LAWRENCE O'DONNELL JR. SHOWED UP ON TIME FOR HIS 8:15 P.M. appointment in a fashionable Capitol Hill restaurant, an extraordinary achievement in a city of very important people who always seem to have one more call to make and one more fax to receive before leaving their offices. Right away, Mr. O'Donnell, who is the staff director of the Senate Finance Committee, made clear that in Washington, he is a little different.

But then there are other ways to reach that conclusion. After all, he did roar up to the restaurant aboard a huge Harley-Davidson.

"Yes, I'm part of the cult," he said, stripping off his black leatherbiker's jacket, his helmet gripped in his left hand. "I go to Harley-Davidson dealers the way other people go to museums." His face, unlined, with a prominent chin, sports a 5 o'clock (in the morning) shadow. Just then, a limousine-load of important people in the uniform of

imperial Washington went by, sizing up Mr. O'Donnell with puzzled looks.

"This is behaviorally the most conservative city in America," explained Mr. O'Donnell, switching effortlessly from biker mode to sociologist mode. "There is a uniform code of dress and a uniform code of behavior and a uniform code of ambition. And it is the uniform code of ambition that enforces the other two."

Mr. O'Donnell, however, seems to revel in breaking the code. As staff director, under its chairman, Senator Daniel Patrick Moynihan, of the Finance Committee—the institutional gatekeeper on matters relating to funding and taxation, which is to say, all matters—Mr. O'Donnell ordinarily would be among the keepers of the code. Instead, he is that most uncommon of species, a free spirit adept in the ways of power.

MAY 10, 1993 BY JOHN HEILPERN

CRITIC AT LARGE: *ANGELS IN AMERICA*: INDEED, THE MILLENNIUM APPROACHES

THERE CAN BE NO DOUBT THAT TONY KUSHNER'S *Angel's in America* is as great a play as you have heard. Part one, titled *Millennium Approaches*, which has just opened at the Walter Kerr, is triumphant—the finest drama of our time, speaking to us of a murderous era as no other play within memory.

Its scope and daring, fully realized in George C. Wolfe's superb production, sends us reeling from the theater, convinced we must have witnessed some kind of miracle. As with all great stories, it evokes these three compelling words: What happens next? At the end of three and a half hours—and 30 mesmerizing scenes—I'm certain I was far from alone in thinking, "Tell us what happens next! Bring on part two!" The angel-messenger has arrived, crashing through space and closing part one. That's some end, some fantastic beginning.

Heralding what? Perhaps hope, or salvation, in this contemporary epic cradled in sorrow. Yet the story within Mr. Kushner's vast apocalyptic canvas is intimate (and often wildly funny). It is ultimately mind-bending. There is one gay couple: a young Jewish self-loathing liberal and courthouse word processor who deserts his AIDS-stricken WASP lover. There is a married Mormon couple: A Republican lawyer and closet homosexual, working in the same courthouse, who deserts his unloved, hallucinating wife. And there's Roy Cohn, Saint of the Right or Antichrist. From that small, unexpected base, Mr. Kushner weaves his glorious tapestry of an entire 1980's era and the collapse of a moral universe.

His specific message is a call to arms to the homosexual community in the AIDS era to march out of the ghettoized closet, as the rabbi in the opening scene reminds us of the heroic journey of the persecuted 19th-century Jews from the ghettos and shetls of Europe to the Promised Land of America. The spectral embodiment of Roy Cohn, mythical witch-hunter and closet homosexual dying of AIDS, offers pragmatic guidance to his Prodigal Son, the repressed Mormon lawyer. "Was it legal?" he says of fixing "that timid Yid nebbish on the bench" during the Rosenberg trial. "Fuck legal. Am I a nice man? Fuck nice. You want to be nice or you want to be *effective*?"

Angels in America is subtitled *A Gay Fantasia on National Themes*, though I didn't quite see it that way. It is memorably about heartlessness and responsibility during the Reagan years and beyond. Its supreme achievement is its portrait of America Lost, perhaps to be regained. In its richness and pain—"Children of the new morning, criminal minds. Selfish and greedy and loveless and blind. Reagan's children"—I saw *Millennium Approaches* more as a modern morality play, with a debt to the guilt, justice and iconography of the Old Testament rather than the New. It is, among other things, about Good and Evil, the disintegration of tolerance and cities and dreams. It asks: Where is God? And yearns for an answer, a prophet, a messiah or salvation. It is, in its searing essentials, about love.

Mr. Kushner is too witty to be preachy. To the contrary, this near-feverish outpouring of visions and ideals is rooted in an episodic economy of means and a wonderful theatricality. For some time, possibly a lifetime, I have been searching in vain for the new American drama of imaginative ideas, a form of magic realism transcending the bourgeois or the naturalism of movies. *Angels in America* is that landmark drama.

It is, on the one hand, painfully concrete; on the other hand, it delights in the theater of magical images. The playwright is good-humored; "*Very* Steven Spielberg," says the dying Prior Walter, an esthete, as the world splits open before his eyes (and ours.)

This writer of plays is therefore justifiably playful. The ambitious narrative sweep takes us seamlessly from Manhattan to Antarctica. You cannot second-guess it for a moment. At the same time, the sheer pleasure Mr. Kushner takes in theater itself empowers him to establish his own conventions and take us anywhere he wishes. It seems reasonable, and irresistible, when, for example, the 13th- and 17th-century British relatives of Prior Walter visit his deathbed for a chat. Those two cheerful angel's heralds, ghostly survivors of historic plagues, are a theatrical riot. So the ghost of Ethel Rosenberg appears to the dying Roy Cohn to say, "The shit's really hit the fan, huh, Roy?" Actors double in virtuoso walk-on parts; actresses play male roles, not always, let it be said, with equal success. But the delight of a true ensemble is created and with it, another dimension, a timeless troupe of Traveling Players.

I could have sworn that there were 15 or so actors in the cast. In fact, there are eight. At least four of the performances scale the heights. The reptilian bravura of Ron Liebman as Roy Cohn gets as near to going over the top as all the great bravura performances must. Is this the role of his career?It would seem brilliantly so (though watch for his brief reincarnation during the action as a campy Tartuffe). Stephen Spinella's Prior is so transcendentally moving that it is impossible to imagine anyone else playing the role or equaling his mysterious saintly aura. Joe Mantello as Louis, lover of Prior and self-loathing posturing intellectual in search of easy absolution, is exactly right. Marcia Gay Harden as Harper, unloved Mormon in search of escape and a fantasy New World, was first cautious, I felt, in capturing the lyrical (her comic flair is beyond question), but she is a wonderful actress. David Marshall Grant, as her Mormon husband in torture rectitude—again, terrific. So, too, the immensely gifted Jeffrey Wright as Belize, nurse, ex-drag queen and conscience, a role that could easily spill over into high camp, but doesn't.

That we have an ensemble as fine as this, and a production as great as this, is due to the genius of director George Wolfe and the spare, emblematic poetry of his design team (Robin Wagner, Jules Fisher and Toni-Leslie James). In one astonishing scene, Mr. Wolfe frees the stage for a quartet of characters, the gay couple and the Mormon couple. They are separate, emotionally explosive scenes happening simultaneously, like a split-movie screen. They are about the pain and death of love; both scenes, both worlds, become spellbindingly one. At times, it is just incredible what we see at work and at play here.

I have run out of space and superlatives. Part one of Tony Kushner's *Angel's in America* has arrived! Bring on part two! *Save us!* Though in *Millennium Approaches*, I have already seen the miraculous.

DECEMBER 6, 1993 BY JOHN HEILPERN

THE ANGEL HAS LANDED: *PERESTROIKA* HITS MARK

IN THE HISTORY OF BLIND DATES, WE haven't looked forward to anything with quite so much nervous anticipation as part two of Tony Kushner's *Angel's in America*.

But the angel that crashed through the ceiling at the close of part one turns out not to be the fantasy redeemer of our dreams. Mr. Kushner's fabulous three-and-a-half-hour *Perestroika* is no sweet fable. It is more uncompromisingly realistic than that, more ambitious than part one, denser, furious (and therefore funnier), sprawling, flawed, more challenging, a feverishly imaginative achievement. In theater terms, George C. Wolfe's production exists almost literally on another planet. In its thrilling sweep and ambition and chaos, *Angels in America* remains the landmark drama of our time.

"Change! Change!" cries the old Bolshevik, blind prophet of the prologue at the dawn of the new age of perestroika, of the exploding of history and the death of all old orders, Reaganism included. Give the old Bolshevik warrior a new theory and system, and he'll be there at the barricades! Apocalypse or paradise? Doom or change in the AIDS era? Mr. Kushner's answer is that there is no perfect answer—no system, no book of divine revelation, no God, no savior-angels. In the turmoil, there is Truth, if you will, and the hope that humanity can change, confronting the wreckage and lies of our American lives. "Stop!" the angel seems to be saying on orders from above. "Stop, and look around you."

Yet the more painful the message, the funnier Mr. Kushner becomes. Has there ever been a more mesmerizing comic and ultimately pathetic figure than Ron Leibman's prince of darkness, Roy Cohn? Now dying of AIDS in a Manhattan hospital, cared for by the ex-drag queen Belize (Jeffrey Wright, terrific again), dosed with AZT, symbol of illicit power and money, Mr. Liebman's monumental monster creation can even touch our sympathy. "Hold!" he screams to approaching death, as if pushing the button on his third arm, which is his phone—his wire to the outside world, as his deathbed tangle of tubes is his lifeline. Cohn and that leftish intellectual weasel, Louis (Joe Mantello), are the only characters in part two who do not grow and change. We cannot say, then, that Mr. Kushner is "unfair" to both the left and the right. But for me, the whining, overtalking wimp Louis is a case of a dramatic character who has outstayed his welcome. Only once does he speak with blazing conviction. Breaking with his new lover, the Republican Mormon lawyer Joe (David Marshall Grant), he pleads to passionate effect that gays are not a legal technicality, but equal citizens. (And for God's sake, think and do the right thing.)

How glad we are when Joe's wife and Valium fantasist, Harper, finally leaves him in the dust, hopefully to get her ill-fated life in shape. Marcia Gay Harden has grown wonderfully as Harper and gives another superb performance—as does Kathleen Chalfant playing, among other roles, the Mormon Hannah Pitt, a sensible, generous mother, it turns out, and grace note of the play. The extraordinary Stephen Spinella could not be finer as the dying Prior. He's wickedly comic. "The stiffening of your penis is of no consequence," the angel tells Prior, who's at the point of orgasmic ecstasy. "Well, maybe not to you," he replies. At the same time, Mr. Spinella brings to his character a heroic dimension, taking the ravaged Prior from terrible fear, and even cowardice, to graceful understanding and courage, in the time he has left on earth.

That's a kind of miracle! And, let it be shouted from the rooftops, this is a miraculous production. In its spare, fluent magic-realism, George Wolfe and his team have created visions for us. Set designer Robin Wagner and lighting designer Jules Fisher have achieved their very finest work. The vast, dizzying canvas moves effortlessly from epic fantasy to reality—from mad dioramas at the Mormon's Visitor Center, to Roy Cohn ripping his IV from his body in a shattering nightmare image of blood and plague, to the ultimate vision of heaven in chaos as a celestial San Francisco at the barricades.

Yet I feel in my gut that all concerned would have still killed for three or four weeks more work on part two. In the heat of Broadway deadlines and Mr. Kushner's urgent last-minute rewrites, there is looseness to some of the writing within the colliding scenes. The muscularity of the drama dips, for example, in the reunion of Harper and her gay husband; the moving and forgiving kaddish for Roy Cohn, spoken with the help of the ghost of Ethel Rosenberg, is undercut by a graceless "Sonofabitch!"; and Louis' amazement at being in bed with a gay Republican would be an easy laugh in an underground theater. There can be too many jokes, though not necessarily in the sense of the Emperor's advice to Mozart, "Too many notes."

I mean the missing note of the genuinely spiritual. The angel, jokey, novice, speaking in tongues, is as much an angel of death offering the potential prophet Prior death. (Die to be reborn as prophet or savior.) In the most moving speech of the play, the dying Prior rejects prophetdom and chooses life: "I want more life." And the heaven he witnesses shows the gods in disarray, and God heartlessly absent. I wish only that Mr. Kushner had brought the leading player on stage. Bring God on! For had there been a genuine debate between them, Prior's choice of life on earth would have been more astonishing, the dice would not have been loaded, and this fantastic drama would have looked into the vision of light.

It is, if you will, the legitimacy of the spiritual that I feel is missing. And God knows how Mr. Kushner might have achieved *that*. But when in the quiet, peaceful, almost wistful end, we are left with the near-blind Prior and his friends by the stone angel of Bethesda Fountain in Central Park, it is his courageous spirit that speaks of longed-for change. In this messy, scintillating, turbulent drama of loss and betrayal, of an entire era of American life and death, his spirit asks for change in all of us, for understanding, commitment and love. In its entirety, *Angels in America* has been an unforgettable journey.

GEORGE GURLEY INTERVIEWS MICHAEL M. THOMAS

Arthur Carter came to see me in the fall of 1987. I'd been writing a column for *Manhattan, inc.*, but I had quit because Herbert Lipson, the publisher, wouldn't run a humorous column of mine about Ralph Lauren, because he was trying to get advertising. And so I started up at *The Observer*. My column, the Midas Watch, generated attention, I think, because, well, I'm a great believer that the bad guys have names and that if you don't *name* the names, the whole point of the exercise is lost, you just keep saying, "*unnamed sources*." Also, I grew up in this world of Wall Street, and I knew a lot of the people and I wasn't very impressed. The one thing that most of them lack is a sense of humor about themselves, so you could tweak in pretty short order. I used to be a sort of mainstream person in New York society, and I soon found myself on the outside. I had to resign from certain boards I was on, because I was going to write about the people who were on them. And the reason I called the column the Midas Watch is because of the transmutational power of gold. Everything Midas touched turned into gold, and my take on it was, we were living in a society in which, increasingly, everything that gold touched turned into some kind of *virtue*.

I always thought that the worst thing that ever happened to journalism in New York was when [*New York Times* publisher] Punch Sulzberger accepted the presidency of the Metropolitan Museum, because that meant he would be soliciting money from people his newspaper might want to write about. I used to say that the problem today is most journalists want to dine *with* people they ought to want to dine *on*. And to me, *gossip*, properly defined, is what people really *don't* want said about them. In one of my first columns, I wrote, "This is not a bulletin board for PR people the way Liz Smith's column is." Liz Smith stopped speaking to me. A friend of mine!

Do you think that if more people on Wall Street had been reading your column, it might have made a difference in the current crisis?

The people who were trying to spray water on this Wall Street thing over the last few years, like Jim Grant and myself, see it was a young man's game, we don't have an *effect*. We're living in a world in which young people haven't paid much attention to their elders. I told *60 Minutes'* Steve Kroft two years ago that all hell is going to break loose in the subprime mortgages and he ought to go talk to Jim Grant; this is going to be a huge deal. But they don't want to do it before the fact, they'd rather do it after the fact, when they can go around pointing fingers.

So one of the reasons I decided to give up writing the column is that at the end of all that time, it had made no difference. If you think that going into the Century Club and have three septuagenarians come up and say "Well, I love reading you in *The Observer*" is the be-all and end-all of life, well, that's something else.

I will say, blame for the mess on Wall Street lies with guys my age, people in

their 70s. You'd bump into them and it's always the same; they'd look at you and say, "I don't know what these young guys are doing, but they're making me a lot of money." Whereas when I was starting out, and dealing with 70-year-olds at Lehman Brothers, they were all scared shitless—they'd *been there* in '29. They'd been through it, and they were watchful. That's the one thing that you can indict my generation for, completely, is allowing this to happen on Wall Street, for not warning the new guys by pointing to the lessons of our parents' generation. The new guys had seen nothing but *up*. We should have known better. The 50-year-olds couldn't have known better, they were in thrall to their computers, they believed what their computers would tell them.

What's your take on Bernie Madoff?

Well, first, the last thing any of these people involved with the Madoff thing were was greedy. They were conservative! When you have capital, you wish to increase it. That's not greed; that's just common sense. Greed is an overused word. Where Madoff was so smart was that he delivered conservative returns but he appeared to be doing so consistently. I mean, a *greedy* person goes for the gold ring every time! But look, his clients were experienced businessmen. You can't feel sorry for people who have no excuse for being that stupid. This isn't some window cleaner who's being offered a $600,000 mortgage. These are people with hundreds of millions of dollars, with broad experience of finance. These are people who could have picked up the telephone, but it just worked all so nicely. They were making a lot of money, it was consistent, it was safe.

What do you think needs to happen?

We have to somehow de-velocitize trading. It doesn't make any sense if Citicorp stock goes up 7 percent one day, down 7 percent the next. The other thing this does is that it's almost eliminated Buffet-type investing, because you can't feel safe. It doesn't matter if you own a good stock. You own Apple, Apple's got 10 billion in cash, its earnings go up 20 percent a year. But if these guys at the hedge funds want to beat up on it in the short term, they can ruin the stock! It becomes what they call a broken stock. Great company, broken stock. So how do you invest?

Is it similar to what happened in 1987?

Eighty-seven was nothing, '87 was over in a couple weeks. This is systemic, with all this liquidity worldwide, where suddenly we're discovering that U.K. police departments in places like *Nottingham* can't pay their officers because they've lost all their fucking money in an *Icelandic* bank. Now I ask you, what business does a Nottingham police department have in putting its operating funds there just because some smartass in Nottingham said, "This Icelandic bank will give you 12 percent."

You've written a lot about the Hamptons.

When I started going there—I have a picture of me sitting on my mother's lap in 1938; it says "Mrs. Joseph A. Thomas and her son Michael, prominent members of Southampton Summer Colony." There was nothing out there.

Michael Thomas, a former partner at Lehman Brothers, has written the Midas Watch column, on and off, since 1987. His eighth novel, *Love or Money*, will be published this year.

Now, everything is denser. This money seeped in everywhere.

What New York characters did you like writing about the most?
Well, the people I picked on! The premise of the column was that if you call attention to your advantages and to your wealth often enough and loudly enough, it's going to occur to someone else to come and take them away from you. And it was fun to tweak these guys. To me, the all-time bad guy during this period was Greenspan. Alan Greenspan was full of shit the first day I met him, which was 20 years ago. Basically what I was looking for was to pop the personal balloons. I mean, I like Henry Kravis, he's a nice guy, but when Henry was being the little king, he needed to be tweaked! And he'd get pissed off at me! Mort Zuckerman's the same way. Poor Mort's been publishing the same fucking newspaper for years. Nobody's ever said to him at a dinner party, "Gee, Mort, that was interesting what I read in the *Daily News* today." So he's kind of fun to tweak. The key to the column was, I really had no ambitions, George, that would be compromised by speaking my mind in the column in any way that I thought would get the job done effectively. Whether it was tweaking or hammering or piercing or whatever. I didn't care about being invited places.

What about [Sotheby's former chairman] Alfred Taubman?
Ah, Lord Tubman! Now he *certainly* did *not* like me, poor Lord Tubman. But I called Alfred that because he'd show up at these parties in Southampton dressed as if he was going shooting for a weekend at Blenheim. It used to just kill me.

You were destroying these people.
No, I was not destroying them. Because if I *had* destroyed them, or if *anyone* could have destroyed them, they would have been destroyed. They weren't! They went on, they got richer, the invitations continued to pile up. I'll give you a good example. I had written a column, must have been '91, which asked how high did the bodies have to be piled at American Express before we could figure out who's at fault. So I'm sitting at home in Bridgehampton and I get a call from Jimmy Robinson, who was the CEO of American Express. And he said, "You wrote this about me in the paper and blah, blah, blah." And I said, "Jimmy, for Christ's sake, this is a newspaper read by about 18 people." And he said, "Yeah, and I've heard from all 18 of 'em."

But you know, if you're getting rich with the taxpayers' money and you're worth millions of dollars and you have this massive publicity machine, all I'm doing is, I'm the pea in the princess-and-the-pea act. You've got 99 mattresses and if you can feel *me* down there, you must be pretty sensitive. But they *are* sensitive, because they have very little sense of humor about themselves. I grew up among rich people, and I came from a privileged family myself; I kind of know where the Achilles' heel is. The important thing is to figure out what people like least about themselves, or are most insecure

about, and emphasize those qualities. Or where just something is in such horrible taste. I used to have fun with Ralph Lauren; I used to say, "You've got to admire somebody who can turn a pad of tracing paper and the 1947 L.L. Bean catalog into a billion dollars." I like nicknames, so he became the Wee Haberdasher. And Jerry Della Femina hated me. I called his daughter out on that stupid Hamptons guidebook. I didn't understand why, if you go to a place for haven, you try to make a buck out of it by selling the best routes and the back roads and everything else.

Tell me a little bit about your relationship with Peter Kaplan
My relationship with Peter is complicated only by the difference in our schedules, I guess is the best way to put it. I'm sitting over here with nothing to do, George, so I can answer any email within five seconds. Peter has answered two emails in 20 years. I love Peter. I am completely devoted to him; I know how hard he works. You know, he's a kind of hero. I mean, without him, there's no paper.

Did you ever regret writing a particular column?
No, I have no regrets about the column. Well, I mean, yes, I once wrote a column about the Fanjuls, after which Poppy—my late stepmother—called me up and said, "Darling, I have to live in this town."

You wrote about your father a number of times, described him as "a man who minced precious few words and the scene will not see his like again." You wrote that he "once entered a lavish resort drawing room—"
Oh, yes, Palm Beach. He looked around and asked the hostess, "Did you invite these people or advertise for them?"

How has New York changed in the past 20 years?
George, I think everything is pretty much the way it used to be, only with more zeros. A couple years ago, when I had my 70th birthday, we went to Wolfgang's down on Park Avenue, and you know, I'd almost forgotten that the *vilest* place on earth is a Manhattan steakhouse at the height of a trading bull market. Because you've got all this testosterone in there and all these *animals* with the cigars, eating steaks practically with their bare hands, but it's all such *bullshit*. Because if you've worked on Wall Street, you know what it is that they *do*, and if you know what it is that they do, it just becomes almost inconceivable that they get paid the money they do. For doing *that*. What Jefferson called "legerdemain tricks on paper." In my time, I'd get corporations to float bond issues in Europe because I wanted to go to Europe. So I would suggest, "I think we ought to do a $20 million euro dollar, blah, blah, blah." Next thing you know, off we go to sell the deal in the capitals of Europe. And all the expenses—the hookers at Madame Claude and the meals at Maxim's and all that shit—that got charged right to the deals. It's just bullshit! It's just bullshit.

1994

Candace Bushnell's *Sex and the City* column debuts with tales of swinging

First Lady of Fifth Avenue Jacqueline Kennedy Onassis dies

Zuckerman on the rebound? Writer Philip Roth calls it quits with actress Claire Bloom

Upper East Side parents grovel to get tots admitted to elite preschools

Voters pick George Pataki, the pride of Peekskill, as new governor

Cocaine returns to New York nostrils, sometimes cut with heroin

 City Harvest salvages 500 pounds of food from Trump-Maples wedding for homeless

Tale of hard Knopf: Prestigious publishing house fires editor Gordon Lish

Ed Kosner leaves *New York* magazine to become the 10th editor of *Esquire*

1994

◇◇◇◇◇◇◇◇

JANUARY 17, 1994 BY PHOEBE HOBAN

Coming Soon to a Bookstore Near You

PHILIP ROTH'S ART AS A WRITER often imitates his life as a man, but there's a sad new fact in his life that has not yet made it into his fiction: the celebrated author and his companion of nearly 20 years, the British actress Claire Bloom, have separated. She's moved out of their country house in Cornwall Bridge, Conn., and their Upper West Side apartment. Mr. Roth, who was recently spotted without her at a party in Manhattan (Zuckerman on the rebound?), is deep into work on his latest book. (This year marks the 25th anniversary of perhaps his most famous novel, *Portnoy's Complaint*.) And Ms. Bloom is in Cambridge, Mass., rehearsing for the American Repertory Theater's production of Chekhov's *Cherry Orchard*, which opens Jan 21.

"Philip and Claire were perfect," said a friend who knows them both. "I think the fact that she could tolerate him was kind of amazing, and the fact that he gave in to her was kind of amazing. Claire is patient and Philip is manic."

"They are two extraordinary people that we love and admire. Our hearts are broken," said Francine du Plessix Gray, a close friend and a Connecticut neighbor.

MARCH 12, 1994   BY CANDACE BUSHNELL

COCAINE RETURNS TO PARK AVENUE NOSTRILS; NEW 'SHNOOF-SHNOOF' OFTEN CUT WITH HEROIN

ON A RECENT THURSDAY NIGHT, A TALL, HANDSOME MAN—we'll call him "Giuseppe Crostini"—parked his late-model Ford in front of a small prewar doorman building in the East 70's in Manhattan.

Upstairs in 3c, Mr. Crostini was greeted eagerly by a tall, preppie blond woman.

A quick and nearly undetectable exchange of an aluminum foil packet for cash took place, and Mr. Crostini left. On his way out, he thanked the doorman for watching his car.

Despite all that we keep reading about the so-called new sobriety, "Mr. Crostini" and his blond customer are part of a recent trend: the comeback of cocaine. While the perception persists that most (read: fashionable) people gave the drug up in the late 1980's as hopelessly passé, an informal investigation conducted by *The Observer* would lead one to believe that plenty of people are still secretly snorting away their paychecks and inheritances. There are even new pet names: the "Bolivian marching powder" popularized by Jay McInerney's *Bright Lights, Big City* is out; it has been replaced by equally cutesy terms: "schnitzie," "shnoof-shnoof," "naza" and "You-Know-What."

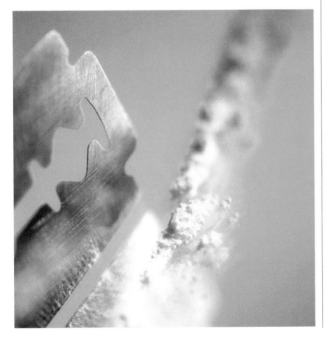

MARCH 28, 1994   BY FRANK DIGIACOMO

Dueling Swiftys? Tina and Graydon Vie for Attention of Oscar's A-List

THE MARCH 14 PARTY CELEBRATING *THE NEW YORKER*'S OSCAR-pegged movie issue wasn't scheduled to start for 30 minutes, but already the first celebrity had emerged from the corridors of the lilac-perfumed Hotel Bel Air: Lassie. Following close behind was *New Yorker* writer Lillian Ross. Interestingly enough, in a 1948 article about the Hollywood blacklist, Ms. Ross had written, "Almost the only motion-picture star who is taking conditions in his stride is Lassie."

The piece had been rerun in the magazine's "The New Yorker Goes to the Movies" issue, which was being celebrated on that night. The magazine's Los Angeles bureau editor, Caroline Graham, suddenly appeared with a video camera and captured the reunion of writer and subject. Standing just out of the frame, Lassie's trainer commanded the dog to sit, raise a paw and speak.

Would that all celebrities were so easily persuaded! (Or were, at least, so mindful of their handlers' instructions!) Such were the feelings of editors and publicists at *The New Yorker*—and also at *Vanity Fair*, which sponsored an Oscar-night party at Morton's in West Hollywood—as both of the Condé Nast publications competed to assemble the ultimate Hollywood party of this year's Academy Award season. For weeks, *The New Yorker*'s Tina Brown, *Vanity Fair*'s Graydon Carter, and their staffs had been working the phones with publicists and agents, trying to pull together party lists glittering enough to fill the gap left by the death of the high priest of Oscar pomp, Irving Paul (Swifty) Lazar. For some three decades, until he died late last year, Lazar had hosted Hollywood's indisputably A-list Oscar-night bash, in recent years at Wolfgang Puck's Spago restaurant.

The hierarchy needed Swifty on Oscar night to concentrate on Hollywood's power crowd and play bad cop when, for example, the governor wanted to bring bodyguards. (He wasn't permitted to, but Madonna was.) Lazar's passing had left a void, and the hierarchy-happy top editors in S. I. Newhouse Jr.'s magazine empire, among others, seem to be raring to fill it.

APRIL 24, 1994
BY LISA GUBERNICK

DE KOONING'S UPTOWN UPSTART ART DEALER SLOUCHES TOWARD SUCCESS DESPITE SLUMP

IT WAS 30 MINUTES INTO HIS gallery's second exhibition of the year and already he wanted out. "I feel like a sitting duck," he said, hands clasped together at his waist, head tilted to one side.

These are times that call for a certain anxiety. In the three years since Mr. Marks opened his Madison Avenue art gallery, the market for contemporary art has been nothing short of disastrous. Prices at auction are a fraction of what they once were, prices at private sales often worse. Scores of galleries have shut their doors. Where the 80's called for a certain flash and sinew, the 90's are soft-spoken, restrained. Matthew Marks, retiring, his carriage the fleshy stoop of someone used to weighing considerably more than he currently does, is a man of the 90's.

APRIL 24, 1994
BY PETER STEVENSON

A MOODY 70'S SCION GOES HOME

RICK MOODY SAT UP IN THE PAS-senger seat of a rented Dodge sedan, in nervous anticipation of his first trip in years to the monied ur-WASP town that lies at the core of his new novel and of his own half-conquered anxieties.

Besides rereading Mr. Up-dike, the other thing Rick Moody did before writing *The Ice Storm* was take a long drive with his father. "I figured the drive would be a way to have a heart-to-heart about what I was planning to write," he said.

The elder Mr. Moody, now an investment consultant in Manhattan, was reticent about the idea of his son writing a novel about New Canaan in the early 1970's.

"Why do you want to write about all of that?" he asked.

"It's my life," said Rick.

"No, it's not," said his father. "It's my life."

"And that," said Mr. Moody, "was the end of the conversa-tion."

MAY 30, 1994 BY D. T. MAX

Gourmet Garage, Eli Zabar's Food Fight Proves Cherimoyas, Ciabatta Don't Mix

THE UNEASY RETAILING EMBRACE BETWEEN ELI ZABAR, THE two-fisted proprietor of the pricey 20-year-old Madison Avenue restaurant E.A.T., and the three partners of the 1 1/2-year-old discount Soho vegetable emporium Gourmet Garage is officially over, bringing to an end what one customer characterized as "a six-month war of attrition between chicken pot pies and mesclun salad." The two organizations will disentangle their merchan-dise and fixtures by June 1, when the cavernous warehouse store they shared near York Avenue on East 91st Street, whose exact name has always remained something of a mystery, will officially become Mr. Zabar's to stock as he pleases under the name Eli's Vinegar Factory.

It will cost Mr. Zabar, who bought the building from a condi-ment maker late last year with an eye to collaborating with Gour-met Garage, roughly $600,000 to get out of his relationship with the produce company, most of whose profits come from filling the greenery needs of fine restaurants. He characterized the payment as a voluntary gesture on a handshake deal in the hopes everyone would walk away happy.

Now that the marriage is over, both sides are emphasizing their warm feelings: Mr. Zabar now promises to continue to stock most-ly Gourmet Garage produce at East 91st Street, where he will soon open a restaurant on the second story. He has already installed a new varnished floor. Mr. Arons and his partners are scouting for large spaces in the Sutton Place area and the Upper West Side, and have big plans to move their crowded wholesale and retail opera-tions from Wooster Street to a 10,000-square-foot space nearby, which will include a two-level café and perhaps even prepared foods, and pots and pans, in direct competition with nearby Dean & DeLuca. "The great thing about restaurants," said Mr. Arons, sounding a lot like Mr. Zabar, whose bread he said he will stock exclusively, "is they're c.o.d."

JULY 11, 1994   BY RALPH GARDNER JR

THE OBSERVATORY: THE PRESCHOOL GROVEL

ON A RAINY MORNing in May, almost 200 smartly dressed mothers and four or five dads filled the Marymount School's auditorium on the Upper East Side for a symposium on how to get their toddlers into preschool. Once called nursery schools and considered optional, preschools, as they are known, are now obligatory steps in the cutthroat competition to get into the right kindergarten, and from there, the best elementary schools, prep schools and colleges. These parents were hoping their children might win places in the city's premier preschools a year and a half later, in the fall of 1995. Some of the children were not yet 2 years old. Nevertheless, the parents sat in respectful silence, jotting down notes in their Filofaxes, as the heads of four preschools talked about application deadlines, age requirements, and tried to quash the park bench rumors about how arbitrary and elitist the admissions process is. "There's this huge Upper East Side mentality that you've got to get into the right private school, and the right private college," explained one mom. "Most of us think it's bullshit, but you get caught up in it. You just know everyone is making the phone calls, so you say, 'Oh my God, I better do this, too.'"

Getting into elite preschools such as the All Souls School, the Episcopal School and the 92nd Street Y Nursery School, on the East Side, and at the Montessori School, on the West Side, is tougher than getting into Harvard, Princeton or Cal Tech—much tougher. Even the cream of the Ivy League schools has admission-rejection ratios of 1 to 5, or 1 to 6, but the odds at these preschools can be three or four times as bad. At All Souls, for example, 550 hopeful families telephoned for applications in the first four days after Labor Day last year. The school conducted a lottery where 130 lucky names were plucked out of a hat and sent applications. Of those, only 30 were accepted.

Often, more than half the available spots are claimed by younger siblings of children who already attend, by kids whose families belong to the churches and synagogues many preschools are affiliated with, and by legacies, children whose parents attended the preschool themselves. "People are really thinking of themselves as graduates of preschools," observed Robert Friedman, the president of New Line Television and an Episcopal School father.

There are many criteria to consider when deciding where to apply, including the preschool's educational philosophy. One mom said the staff at her son's pre-preschool (infant academies that teach everything from tumbling to French) persuaded her to send her child to the Temple Emanu-El Nursery School and Kindergarten instead of All Souls because it was "more academic." "They have all these specialty teachers," she explained. "There's a cooking teacher, a gym teacher, a nature teacher. You kind of got the feeling that it was enough that [All Souls] was a nice place."

Location is also key for anyone who had to shlep a howling 3-year-old to school at the crack of dawn with the wind chill at 40 below. But because you live around the corner from your favorite preschool is no guarantee your child will get in. One Park Avenue mother phoned the 92nd Street Y the day after Labor Day—and got a recorded message asking her to call back the day after Labor Day. When she finally got through, all the applications had been taken. "I've lived in this neighborhood for 20 years," she said. "Who are these applications going to?"

"There's nothing more difficult for powerful, achieving parents than to be in a situation they feel they have no control over," Jean Mandelbaum, the director of All Souls School, explained.

"I heard somebody describe it as the death of the perfect child," Nancy Shulman said.

JANUARY 10, 1994   BY PHILIP WEISS

THE OBSERVATORY: LET THEM EAT CAKE

THE FOOD STARTED COMING BACK DOWN TO THE Plaza kitchen from Donald Trump's wedding at 11:30 p.m., and it kept coming for the next hour and a half. The guests had gotten to their dinner late, and all in all had not eaten too much of it.

First to arrive were the racks of lamb. Scores and scores of them rested daintily on metal trays, and the trays were set into tall file-cabinet-like warmers with Sterno going in the bottom. Robert Crawford lifted the trays out and put them on a steel table. The rib tips of the racks poked up waxily and he used them as handles to drop them into the crimped-aluminum food trays he pulled from a cardboard box.

A big, soft-spoken man of 46, Mr. Crawford had been making pickups all night for City Harvest, a nonprofit organization that takes leftover food from restaurants and parties and brings it to the poor. December is a big month for City Harvest's two constituencies. The Plaza had called City Harvest the afternoon of the Trump wedding. Even hours before Donald Trump and Marla Maples exchanged vows, it was a certainty that there would be too much food.

Mr. Crawford had come into the Plaza at 11 p.m., but it had taken him 30 minutes to walk to the gymnasium-size kitchens, past the elaborate security, the guards wearing earpieces, the early leavers in furs and tuxedos, the press with their cameras. Mr. Crawford shouldered two cardboard boxes and wore a dark green coverall reading City Harvest. He's created a minor incident by walk-

ing through the Plaza's Edwardian Room. Guests had looked up from candlelit tables. The maitre d'hotel made no effort to disguise his horror.

"Excuse me, sir, but if you would kindly not walk through the public areas," he said.

Mr. Crawford had arrived at the great back stage of the wedding as the fete was winding down. Waiters in tails sank wearily against food trucks. Bottles of half-finished Cristal Champagne sat in a big bucket of melting ice. An armful of long-stemmed white roses lay crushed on the streaked tile floor.

Now it was midnight and food cascaded back to the kitchen. The roasted baby winter vegetables were arranged artistically, the carrots in a spray at the center bedded on baby squashes, translucent onions and eggplants the size of a thumb. The salmon had begun retruning, tray after tray of it. Heart-shaped steaks, grilled perfectly, covered with a beurre blanc morel mushroom sauce that was no longer fresh. Shrimp in a green curry sauce. Sliced duck breast, a cou-

ple of silver trays of that, too. Several whole-roasted turkey breasts speckled with coriander and rosemary. Fluffy beds of white rice.

And still there was more. Rolled pieces of lox on a silver fish-headed tray. Ziti in marinara with zucchini. Vegetable pate in pretty layers of green, beige and brown. Lobster tail cut into one-inch rounds, a whole silver platter of it barely disturbed by Mr. Trump's friends. Into the aluminum vat it tumbled, over curried shrimp.

At 1 a.m. the presentation dishes, the ones no one was meant to eat, made their appearance. A giant whole red snapper standing up on its belly and encased in shiny gelatin, ringed by shiny crawfish. A 10-pound lobster, also varnished in gelatin. Baskets of asparagus tips with the same treatment. White wax figures of dolphins, horse's heads and owls.

There was so much food, and so little of it apparently eaten, that the feeling of waste was almost nauseating. Hours before the Plaza chefs had labored over the food, they had created trompe l'oeil checkerboards of black-and-white colored gelatin on the bottoms of the players. Now they tilted those same players in the air over garbage bags with deadened contempt.

"You don't want any of this, it's sat out too long," a large chef told Mr. Crawford, dumping out several pounds of pate de foie gras.

Another chef, also in the Plaza uniform of white double-breasted tunic and black-and-white checkered pants, lifted a three-foot circular form of braided bread like a giant fish. He turned it upside down to shake out a mass of smoked sturgeon pieces, as though he were dumping an ashtray. "See this, $20 a pound," he said.

Mr. Crawford calmly arranged his haul on a food truck for the long trip out. Sealed aluminum trays towered and teetered up toward the ceiling. Nearly 500 pounds of food.

There were a couple more stops that night for Mr. Crawford and Brian Jones, the driver, down the dark, empty streets of Manhattan, and it wasn't until 2:45 that they pulled into the McAuley Water Street Mission on Lafayette and White streets in Tribeca. The mission is a three-story brick building with a religious bareness about it. There is cheap wooden paneling on the walls and fluorescent lighting. A toothless man named Bob Wasman who writes religious poetry was manning the desk. He wore a wool knit hat and a silver fringe beard and a raised sole on one shoe. When City Harvest arrived, Mr. Wasman called Eric Richards from a cinder block room where he was sitting up studying the Bible. Mr. Richards is the mission's director of security, a good-looking black man of 37 with a confident manner. He opened the back doors.

The men from City Harvest brought the food inside. Streaks of leaking green curry sauce formed on the cardboard boxes they used as pallets. They stacked food by the elevator, near a pile of six-pound peanut butter tins donated by the U.S. Government. Mr. Richards woke the resident cook and the two of them stayed up the rest of the morning sorting and storing, and gorging themselves on lobster. How long would it be before he saw lobster again, Mr. Richards asked himself.

Upstairs, a hundred men lay asleep in steel bunk beds, barely a foot apart. Most of them had been given beds in a lottery 12 hours earlier. Large wooden cutouts on the walls were painted with Bible verses. Other signs laid out the mission's many rules. A hang-lettered sheet by the bathroom door said to ask the man at the desk for soap. "We Also Provide ... Baking Soda for Shoes," it said.

The next day at lunch, some reporters came to the Water Street Mission to see what had become of the Trump food. James VarnHagen, the mission's director, passed around a history of the place. The mission was started a century ago by an Irish-born thief named Jerry McAuley after he found God in Sing Sing. The history had illustrations of Sing Sing. Some of the prisoners wore iron cages over their heads, bolted at the neck, a special form of humiliation for petty offenders. The men at the Water Street Mission are not all that different from the ones who came a century before. It is a place marked by suffering. "You don't have to tell them they're sinners, they know they're sinners," Mr. VarnHagen said. "They've had failures, they're looking for hope. We encourage them to trust God."

There is no pride at the Water Street Mission; there is the opposite of Trumplike vanity. Eric Richards said plainly that he had had a drug habit since he was 12 years old. He was a telemarketer before he lost his job a year ago and went onto the streets. In the mission, he has found his way: He has been rescued the way that McAuley set out to rescue people. "If you don't have a broken and contrite heart, you're not going to be able to give up the hold the Devil has on you," Mr. Richards said.

At lunchtime, the food was set out in the basement dining room on a wooden table with a plaid cloth. Mr. VarnHagen said a prayer to thank God, working through Mr. Trump. Some men called the bounty a blessing. One man wondered if Mr. Trump was just getting a big tax deduction. Then the men pulled back the plastic wrap. The cooks had cut up the filet into neat pieces and arranged it simply on a clear plastic platter. They surrounded it with pieces of duck breast. Next to that was an aluminum tray with turkey breasts and smoked sturgeon and lettuce. Ringing that tray were disks of lobster tail.

Only a dozen or so men came to lunch, but that night 200 homeless people came for the 5, 6 and 8 o'clock dinners. At 5, the cooks served

All food inhabits its particular social conditions, no matter where it comes from. A soup line must move fast, several hundred pounds in an hour, and the soup must stick to a hungry man's rib.

rack of lamb. Then at 6, they served soup made from Trump filet and Trump turkey and mission beef stock, with Trump winter vegetables and Trump rice. Soup is typical fare at a soup kitchen. It stretches was meat the cooks have, and it addresses the primary concern of the providers—fairness, that no one should get what another cannot have. There may not have been enough beef filet for 100 people.

The homeless filed in wearing their coats. They ate quickly, bent over their soup bowls. They complained about the food. They joked that they had found a human finger in it or they said it lacked flavor, or they said that the mission reused plastic spoons and so the spoons were greasy. And if the spirit of the Trump wedding was boundless self-exaltation, the spirit of the Water Street Mission was something else, ashen humiliation that many in the place struggled against. A young woman, one of the few women served, put on lipstick after dinner, and a man named Robert, who said he would be riding the subways that night, pocketed the salt and pepper shakers he had brought with him to make the food more palatable.

A man could get seconds and thirds later. But first he had to go upstairs to the chapel for service. There were metal chairs there, and a chaplain. The message was generally a traditional one, one of man's personal responsibility to free himself from Satan's curse of darkness. No talk of dysfunctional families or society's unfairness. On the chapel wall a Bible verse spoke to the social conditions the food had traversed.

"For There Is No Difference: For All have Sinned and Come Short of the Glory of God. —Romans."

After chapel service, there was more soup in hard rubber bowls. Mr. Gilliard's small kitchen was far cleaner than the Plaza kitchen. Every surface was wiped and gleaming. There was no waste. Ladles were carefully replaced on the stove hood. The menu was simple, and somehow much more thoughtful than the Roman-style menu of the wedding night.

But what the men said about the food was true: It wasn't tasty anymore. It was a bit of a mishmash, with its clashing ingredients, bland and gluey. All food inhabits its particular social conditions, no matter where it comes from. A soup line must move fast, several hundred pounds in an hour, and the soup must stick to a hungry man's ribs. The chef has no time to plan; he discovers the identity of his diverse perishable ingredients that morning. His meal cannot be salty because some of the men have hypertension. And so forth.

Donald Trump's splendid food had become a sort of fodder. Now and then, the tongue hit a bit of gristle.

Many men did not wait for more. They said goodnight and went out the front door. As they did so, they passed an old doorstop set out on the counter. A page thumbtacked to the bit of wood had vital information.

"WEATHER," was the heading. "Low 40's. Rain. TOMORROW. Low 40's. Wind."

MAY 30, 1994 BY MICHAEL M. THOMAS

THE MIDAS WATCH: Jackie's Quiet Elegance Ennobled the Nation

I WONDER WHAT MRS. ONASSIS WOULD THINK OF what's been written about her in recent days. For example, the notion that she was an "embryonic feminist." I expect, were she in a position to comment, that she would have some pithy response.

I only met her once, about a dozen years ago. A mutual friend brought her to a small cocktail party I was giving for an English friend. She asked me why I wrote such awful things about people. She had a fine, wry way about her and a twinkle. I replied, as I recall, that awful is as awful does.

Mrs. O. was quality, folks. That is, she ended her days as such, which was no small feat considering she came from an East Hampton social scene that, intellectually, made Newport look like the Macdowell Colony. How hard it is to remember that she was only 31, younger than most of my children, when she precipitated into the White House. She was a kid, and thank God for that, because she brought a kid's enthusiasm, liveliness and joy in things to her official role.

In the last decades, Mrs. O. withdrew from a world she had been so instrumental in creating. Having preached the Crusade, as it were, she took a hard, frank look at the way her parfit Christian knights were behaving, and betook herself to a nunnery. She was by all accounts a damn good editor, and in that respect alone will be sorely missed, for such are few. I remember some years ago encountering my beloved mentor John Pope-Hennessy, the greatest expert of painting and sculpture of the Italian Renaissance. Aware that his memoirs were being prepared for publication, I mildly asked who was editing them.

The "Pope" looked down his nose at me, like a sharpshooter squaring up in cross hairs, and in a voice dripping with the natural scorn of the cosmopolite for the rube, said: "Why, Jackie O., of course!"

In that offhand "of course" was articulated a world of respect.

◇◇◇◇◇◇◇

JUNE 20, 1994 BY ERIK HEDEGAARD

'PLEASURE PLUS IN THE 12-PACK, PLEASE!' A BOUTIQUE FOR 'NO GLOVE, NO LOVE' ERA

IT WAS A WARM FRIDAY NIGHT in Manhattan, on the cusp of summer, birds flickering, and it was extra crowded inside the Greenwich Village specialty shop known as Condomania. There were college students there, Kenneth Cole preppies, hipsters, double-daters, blacks, whites, Asians, weary, grinning Hoosier tourists.

A female customer entered wearing a jumpsuit, a backpack, and her hair in a twist. Seeing what she wanted, she snapped it up and presented it to Arli Silver, the long-haired fellow at the cash register.

"Pleasure Plus in the 12-pack!" Mr. Silver said. "That'll be $11.75."

The woman paid and took her condoms in a white plastic bag decorated with the Condomania logo, which is a squiggly silver-edged condom enclosing the word "Condomania."

What Condomania sells—

condoms and condom-related merchandise—it sells more of than any other store on the face of the planet, and it hopes to be selling a lot more of it beginning June 18. That's when the Gay Games start here. Condomania, which grosses over $200,000 a year in condom sales, has more than doubled its inventory of condoms to try to cover any surge in demand.

Actually, Condomania, which is located at 351 Bleecker Street, is both store and chain, with two outlets in Florida and another in Los Angeles. Though pharmacies and supermarkets continue to dominate the $400 million condom industry, Condomania Inc. more than holds its own on a per-store basis. The average U.S. drugstore sells $12,000 of condoms a year. The average Condomania sells 10 times that amount.

Condomania owner Adam

Glickman has plans, too. Industrywide sales have been relatively flat since the go-go years of the late 80's, which followed former

Surgeon General C. Everett Koop's announcement that only condoms can protect against H.I.V. But that doesn't deter Mr. Glickman.

JANUARY 31, 1994   BY MARION HUME

THE OBSERVATORY: The Best Customer in the West

NAN KEMPNER IS THE COUture customer. She has earned her prized ringside seat in the gilded salon of the Hotel Intercontinental in Paris not by being a movie star, like Catherine Deneuve; nor by being a doyenne of the press, like Suzy Menkes; but by spending. And spend she does.

Nan has known Yves Saint Laurent since he was young and skinny. They met when her mother, Irma Schlesinger, took her daughter to Paris and to Dior in 1958. There, Nan, who claims she had only been slightly embarrassed to turn up at school wearing white gloves and carrying a hand-painted lunchbox each day, fell in love—with a white, sleeveless sheath dress and matching white overcoat with ermine cuffs, which costs far more than her clothes allowance.

So she cried. And she cried and she cried, until a gawky boy in glasses, the assistant to Mr. Dior, emerged to see what the fuss was about. Nan kept on wailing until the vendeuse reduced the price to within her not inconsiderable means. The pattern of a lifetime was set.

Saint Laurent is stocky now, but Nan is still slim, "the same size as I was when I married," she said—to Thomas Lenox Kempner, a banker, and now chairman of Loeb Partners in New York. Nan's exaggerated slimness has benefits. "Yes, it is useful," she explained, "because I get to buy the mannequin's dresses at discount."

It is also useful because Yves has always designed best for a skinny tall body, the female body shape that most resembles his own as it was once, in a prime that had him posing gaunt, lanky and naked for his own perfume advertisements.

This mother of three and grandmother of six has said, memorably, that she wants to be buried naked, "because there are bound to be stores where I'm going." What she leaves behind will join the clothes she has already given to the Metropolitan Museum of Art, "or be sold at Christie's, wouldn't that be marvelous?" she mused.

◇◇◇◇◇◇◇

AUGUST 22, 1994   BY FRANK DIGIACOMO

SOCIETY DAME OR HOLLYWOOD POLITICO? THE TRIALS OF MS. DUFF, PERELMAN'S FIANCÉE

PATRICIA DUFF SPOKE QUIETLY and hesitantly, as if her words were meant more for someone at her end of the telephone call. "I don't want to talk on the record. Ronald would prefer that I don't," she said. "I don't think I should, either."

Ms. Duff was referring to Ron Perelman, the billionaire cosmetics and media mogul whose child she is expecting in January and who, judging from the number of times she excused herself from the conversation, was hovering while she tried to explain why she did not want to be profiled.

"People in Los Angeles weren't that interested in my life," said Ms. Duff. "It's strange to me that there seems to be all of this interest now. I don't get it."

Quite frankly, Ms. Duff's life has become much more interesting since last August, when rumors that she had been seen at Mr. Perelman's sprawling East Hampton estate, the Creeks, preceded the public announcement in September that she and her husband, former TriStar Pictures chairman Mike Medavoy, had separated.

OCTOBER 3, 1994   BY JIM WINDOLF

BROWN'S TWO YEARS AT *THE NEW YORKER*: 'I FINALLY THINK WE'VE GOT IT RIGHT'

FOR HER FIRST COVER OF *THE NEW YORKER*, DATED Oct. 5, 1992, Tina Brown, the fourth editor in the magazine's 69-year history, held an informal contest among the magazine's artists to see who could come up with a scene commenting on the state of the magazine in general and the editor's tenure in particular. Edward Sorel was the winner, and he has drawn covers commemorating Ms. Brown's anniversaries ever since.

The 1992 cover showed a wizened punk with a Mohawk haircut (no doubt Ms. Brown) lounging in a horse-drawn carriage. The top-hatted driver (in the role of the magazine's unsettled staff) looks uneasy as he clutches the reins. A year later, for the issue dated Oct. 4, 1993, Mr. Sorel drew a voluptuous scene wherein a middle-aged Pan-like creature, his head horned, his feet cloven, holds a crisply folded *Wall Street Journal* in one hand and a stogie in the other; beside him is a plump woman, fully naked, her eyelids large and lazy, her head resting on his shoulder. The cover coincided with what many staff members said was a brief Pax Romana in Ms. Brown's reign: She had enlivened the magazine, raising its circulation and its profile in the media, but she had yet to unmake the delicate property that had been passed down to her from editors Harold Ross, William Shawn and Robert Gottlieb.

This year's Sorel cover, commemorating Ms. Brown's second anniversary, is different. Like the other two, the illustration has an autumnal backdrop. But this year, it's an Upper East Side Adam and Eve being banished from Central Park. The cover is melancholy, a modern take on the gloomiest scene in human lore, and it comes after a summer that saw *The New Yorker* undergo a number of staff changes as it was seduced by the triple temptations of access, heat and sensation.

Adam and Even have been exiled from paradise; with them, *The New Yorker*. What does it mean? In her two years as editor, the magazine has traveled from its sacrosanct position in the garden of print—unassailed and mysterious—to a new position in the larger media world. More accessible and less mysterious, *The New Yorker* has been driven into the outside world. You can even find it online, in something called the Electronic Bookstore. Her magazine is part of the noise, part of the belching All-American hype-entertainment news machine.

Two years ago, the magazine's political coverage consisted of dispatches from one detached and almost unreadable Washington correspondent; its show business or media reporting was a rare and exotic event; its crime reporting was an occasional literary exercise. Now that the magazine has quit Eden, it is burgeoning but still losing money as it draws new readers. It is more fun to read, better-looking, less distinguished, preppier, accessible, often anti-literate and generally rolling in the barnyard of American journalism. Once *The New Yorker*—yes, *The New Yorker*!—it is now ... a magazine.

"When some of the detractors of the new *New Yorker* say there was another way the magazine could have been changed, I would say, yes,

there was indeed another way," she wrote. "It would have been to curtail the very long, arcane pieces and simply bet on hot journalism. Much that I loved editing it, I did not want to do a weekly *Vanity Fair*. To me, the challenge was always to find a way to make quality and intellectually challenging articles reach a much wider audience, to turn on the generation drifting towards television by making use of our weekly frequency with a two-strand mix of more immediate material and the slower, more thoughtful material. Visually, that has meant more contemporary presentation and marketing ideas.

"Of course, some of the older *New Yorker* writers resent the implications of this. They prefer to think there is a choice and that the choice is simply to go on publishing the slower, exceedingly long kind of piece of the past. It is unpalatable, I guess, for them to admit to themselves that the audience for this has depressingly shrunk, just as in book publishing."

Ms. Brown's push to make *The New Yorker* more topical and her knack for orchestrating mini-sensations in the media have led to a great increase in the number of magazines sold. At the end of 1992, three months after her tenure began, circulation stood at 628,014; as of June 30 of this year, the number had climbed to 816,615. A two-million-piece direct mail drive, sent by first-class mail at great expense, kicked off the circulation surge early in her tenure; but since that time, the magazine has won subscribers out of readers who buy copies off the newsstand, the number of which has doubled on average since she got started. *The New Yorker* has also made it easier for people to subscribe than it was in the pre-Brown era by offering subscriptions at a base rate of $32 a year, with occasional special offers at $16. The sale days will come to an end in Januarry 1995, when the subscription price will rise to $36.

It remains an immense question whether or not she can make the magazine profitable. Thomas A. Florio, who became president of *The New Yorker* in January, said that 60 percent of his subscribers are new to the magazine and 40 percent are longtime readers.

And while the number of advertising pages has been down roughly 10 percent over the number of ad pages that ran last year, the magazine sees the drop as a result of a "get tough" policy instituted by Mr. Florio soon after he took over.

The more important gauge of advertising revenue shows the magazine up 2.4 percent over this time last year, according to Publishers Information Bureau. And the magazine will help itself with advertisers with its planned all-fashion issue—a Tina Brown extravaganza set for November that will venture into the territory staked out by her "*The New Yorker* Goes to the Movies" and "Broadway Jubilee" special issues.

Magazines, magazines; *The New Yorker* is still an important magazine. But, as E.B. White once wrote in a caption, I say it's spinach, and I say the hell with it.

> *Magazines, magazines;* The New Yorker *is still an important magazine. But, as E.B. White once wrote in a caption, I say it's spinach, and I say the hell with it.*

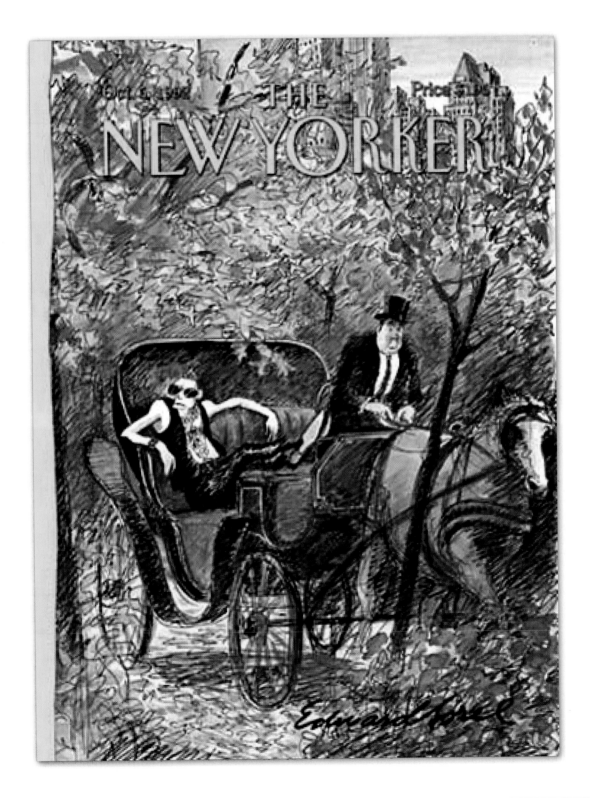

OCTOBER 31, 1994
EDITORIAL

ECCE CUOMO: A Flawed Giant Over a Passionless Opportunist

FOR THE FIRST TIME SINCE 1982, New York voters will be choosing a governor without considering that they may be voting for or against a future president of the United States.

Time and circumstances have dimmed Mario Cuomo's once-brilliant star, with reason. Mr. Cuomo's act seems tired after 12 years. His rhetoric has lost its edge. His defense counsel posture is exasperating.

But Mr. Cuomo has brought it on himself, simply by being Mario Cuomo, stubborn and contrarian to the end. He could have retired as Joe DiMaggio did, with the memory of his grace and understated elegance fresh and unsullied. But now, a potentially involuntary and embarrassing departure risks comparisons with Willie Mays' final year, which ended ignominiously in the 1973 World Series, with the once-nimble center-fielder flat on his back, his legs and agility having betrayed him. He had stayed a season too long.

NOVEMBER 14, 1994   BY TERRY GOLWAY

GOVERNOR PATAKI! PRIDE OF PEEKSKILL DROPS CUOMO; JUMPY VOTERS DECIDE 12 YEARS OF MARIO IS ENOUGH

GEORGE PATAKI, WHO ONLY A matter of months ago was a political unknown with an odd name and a bland demeanor, has put an end to Mario Cuomo's long reign as the Democratic Party's best-known voice of hard-knuckled liberalism.

According to network projections, the state senator from upstate Garrison won in surprisingly handy fashion. Exit polls showed him with about 49 percent of the vote, compared with the Governor's 45 percent. Third-party candidate Thomas Golisano, whose free-spending intrusion into the race was thought to be Mr. Cuomo's salvation, took only 5 percent.

"The Pataki victory is not based so much on his strength, but on voter exhaustion with the Family of New York," said Mitchell Moss, director of New York University's Urban Research Center.

The Cuomo campaign may have seen this coming. As he cast his vote early on Election Day, a grave-sounding Mr. Cuomo said that his prayer would be not "Lord, help me to win," but "Lord, help me to understand the results and deal with it." And one of the governor's operatives told *The Observer* just before the polls closed that he was advising his colleagues to ask for divine intercession.

◇◇◇◇◇◇◇◇

NOVEMBER 28, 1994   BY CANDACE BUSHNELL

SEX AND THE CITY: Swingin' Sex? I Don't Think So ...

IT ALL STARTED THE WAY IT ALways does: innocently enough. I was sitting in my apartment, having a sensible lunch of crackers and sardines, when I got a call from an acquaintance. A friend of his had just gone to Le Trapeze, a couples-only sex club, and was amazed. Blown away. There were people naked—having sex—right in front of him. Unlike S&M, where no actual sex occurs, this was the real, juicy tomato. The guy's girlfriend was kind of freaked out—although, when another naked woman brushed against her, she "sort of liked it." According to him.

I started imagining all sorts of things. Beautiful young hardbody couples. Girls with long, wavy blond hair wearing wreaths made of grape leaves. Boys with perfect white teeth wearing loincloths made of grape leaves. Me, wearing a super-short over-one-shoulder, grape-leaf dress ...

What did we see? Well, there was a big room with a huge air mattress, upon which a few blobby couples gamely went at it; there was a "sex chair" (unoccupied) that looked like a spider; there was a chubby woman in a robe sitting next to a Jacuzzi, smoking; there were couples with glazed eyes; and there were many men who appeared to be having trouble keeping up their end of the bargain. But mostly, there were those damn steaming buffet tables, and, unfortunately, that's pretty much all you need to know.

Le Trapeze was, as the French say, Le Rip-Off.

DECEMBER 19, 1994   BY JIM WINDOLF

OFF THE RECORD: Granta Claus Coming to New Yorker Town

THE NEW YORKER NAMED BILL BUFORD, THE EXPATRIATE EDITOR of *Granta* since 1979, as its new fiction and literary editor on Dec. 13. Mr. Buford will replace Charles (Chip) McGrath, who will leave the magazine in February to edit *The New York Times Book Review*.

Mr. Buford's new job—which begins April 1, 1995—will give him first crack at manuscripts by famous writers who habitually send their work straight to *The New Yorker*. "In a lot of ways, *The New Yorker* was a kind of irritating model for everything I was doing at *Granta*," he said. "People were always sending their stories to *The New Yorker* first. If we ever got a story from a well-known author, we could usually dust it and detect *The New Yorker*'s fingerprints."

Mr. Buford, 40, was born in Baton Rouge, La., and is the author of *Among the Thugs*, an account of hooliganism among British soccer fans. Under his direction, *Granta* went from a Cambridge University student magazine with a few hundred readers to one of the most acclaimed and widely read journals of fiction and reportage, with a circulation of 100,000. Mr. Buford, who is also the publisher of Granta Books, said his successor will be selected by Rea Hederman, the publisher of *The New York Review of Books* who is also *Granta*'s principal shareholder.

Granta was the first magazine in Britain to publish such writers as Raymond Carver, Richard Ford, Tobias Wolff and Jayne Anne Phillips—a school the magazine dubbed "Dirty Realism" in a 1983 issue.

Mr. Buford said he might remain in Cambridge even after he begins working for *The New Yorker*. "I'm going to hold on to the house in Cambridge," he said. "Europe is a very dynamic place right now. The collapse of the Soviet Union has opened up Europe in a way that is fascinating to witness."

DECEMBER 19, 1994   BY PETER STEVENSON

EDITOR OVERBOARD! KNOPF JETTISONS LISH, JUMPSUITED SUPERGURU OF NEW FICTION

A FEW DAYS AFTER HE HAD been fired from the Alfred A. Knopf publishing house, Gordon Lish sat in a bar where he has gone for a number of years because "no one in the building comes here"—the building, of course, being 201 Alfred A. Knopf and its parent company, Random House.

Still strikingly handsome at 60, though smaller than one expects given his outsized reputation as a combative, charming, blue-eyed Svengali to an entire school of fiction—not to mention to scores of writing students—Mr. Lish was oddly costumed for midtown Manhattan: He wore a beige jumpsuit with a zipper from neck to crotch, unzipped enough to show a white long-john shirt. He also wore a wide brown leather belt with its end dangling, and brown leather ankle boots. A lifelong sufferer of psoriasis, his hands looked painfully raw, and he twisted them together as he spoke.

Mr. Lish's voice was hoarse—from the six-hour classes he teaches and from grief: In early fall, his wife, Barbara, died of Lou Gehrig's disease ("At the end we were up to nine nurses"), a loss that, when it came to his own fictional inspirations, left him feeling, he said, "emptied out. ... The desire has gone out of it, and fear doesn't take its place so much as a sense of absence."

"It's best to understand that the meeting at which this was presented consisted of myself and Sonny Mehta," he said. "It's fair to observe that the matter between us was self-evident. This might seem a wonderfully ironic thing to say: a minimalist approach to spoken language was altogether effective."

1995

"Oprah ... Uma ... Oh no" ... David Letterman flops as host of the Oscars

Models Naomi Campbell, Elle McPherson and Claudia Schiffer front Fashion Café

Magician David Blaine casts kooky spell on downtown celebrities

Boy toy at the Bowery: Jann Wenner steps out with clothing designer Matt Nye

Nix on Triple-X! Mayor Rudy Giuliani scrubs sex shows from city

Entertainment reporter Claudia Cohen and Senator Alfonse D'Amato are an item

Literati chew up author Martin Amis for visiting high-priced New York dentist

Pollsters Mark Penn and Douglas Schoen plug away for Bill Clinton

Gossip columnists Rush and Molloy are *Daily News*' Nick and Nora

1995

FEBRUARY 6, 1995
BY ANDREW COHEN AND ALEX KUCZYNSKI

THE OBSERVATORY: NOT-SO-VICIOUS CIRCLES

EVERY FRIDAY NIGHT AT 8 o'clock, in a worn brownstone across the street from the Nuyorican Poets Café, 10 or 15 writers crowd into Steve Cannon's living room and convene another session of the Stoop on East Third Street. Stoop members read each other's work, ridicule one another's literary tastes ("Is this an aesthetic or a mental condition?") and drink Ballantine Ale 40-ouncers, while Mr. Cannon, former City University professor and fixture of the Nuyorican, shouts abuse and encouragement. At first glance, the assembled M.F.A. candidates, Puerto Rican hip-

hop poets and single mothers from Brooklyn don't much resemble the *toujours gai,* poker-playing Round Table, or the front room at Gertrude Stein's Paris flat. But trade the beer can for a martini glass and the plaid shirts for pearls, and the idea is generally the same: Steve Cannon and cohort Bob Holman, director of the poetry program at the Nuyorican, have given birth to a salon.

Mr. Cannon's Alphabet City apartment—which, in true Stein fashion, includes a small gallery ("I'm the only blind man I know who has an art gallery in his apartment," said Mr. Cannon, who lost his eyesight to glaucoma two years ago)—is also a stopping place for painters, performers and photographers. It's one of many multicultural salon scenes that have recently sprung up around the city, accommodating the growing numbers of freelance writers, independent artists and filmmakers and other seekers of community in the naked city. Along with Dorothy Parker's poetry, salons are coming back.

FEBRUARY 13, 1995   BY FRANK DIGIACOMO

THE TRANSOM: Why, Claudia? $80 Million Gossipeuse One-Ups Ron Perelman With ... D'Amato

REGIS PHILBIN STARED AT THE sheet of paper he had just lifted from the fax machine. It was the first fax on the Feb. 3 *Live With Regis & Kathie Lee,* a new interactive segment on the show. "We should have a conference about this," said Mr. Philbin as he handed it to co-host Kathie Lee Gifford. "Easy," he warned her. "Don't read out loud."

Ms. Gifford deliberated silently, then delivered her opinion. "I think we can answer that now," she said. "It's been out." Mr. Philbin then confirmed what the viewer had asked. Claudia Cohen, *Live*'s entertainment and gossip reporter, was indeed "dating" the junior senator from New York, Alfonse Marcello D'Amato.

The studio audience broke into healthy applause. A few even cheered. "They're very comfortable together. It's a lot of fun. It really is," said Mr. Philbin. "It's nice to see Claudia happy," added Ms. Gifford, who told the audience about a dinner party at her home the new couple had attended, along with Mr. Philbin and his wife, Joy. Before an audience of eight million viewers, Mr. Philbin and Ms. Gifford had advanced New York's heterosexual-romance-of-the-moment beyond the gossip stage and into legitimacy.

Their duty done, Mr. Philbin and Ms. Gifford promptly dropped the topic, thus ignoring the obvious follow-up: Why, Claudia?

MARCH 6, 1995   BY CANDACE BUSHNELL

A BABY HOUDINI OF THE BOWERY BAR

"I'VE HEARD SO MUCH ABOUT YOU," MOLLY RINGWALD SAID TO David Blaine,the 21-year-old society happening and illusionist, as he slipped in gracefully next to her at a booth in the Bowery Bar.

Ms. Ringwald, her hair in a smooth flip, was sitting with her publicist Jason Weinberg, who also represents Mr. Blaine. "I just ran into all these people who know David but all from different places," said Mr. Weinberg. "It's amazing. Have some champagne." He motioned for more glasses.

Mr. Blaine smiled and lit a cigarette. He was wearing his signature tiny blue sunglasses and a Dolce & Gabbana jacket. He leaned towards Ms. Ringwald and began talking to her quietly. Ms. Ringwald asked someone for a quarter. A few seconds passed and then Ms. Ringwald exclaimed, "Omigod!" Mr. Blaine was pushing a cigarette through the center of the quarter.

"Usually when people build someone up, you're disappointed when you actually meet them," said Ms. Ringwald. "But he's truly incredible!"

David Blaine has become a white-hot player on the downtown social circuit. A combination of card wizard Ricky Jay and one of those handsome, downtown-actor types, he entertains—but only on his own terms. People think that Mr. Blaine is going to be big, big, big, and he thinks it himself.

◇◇◇◇◇◇◇

MARCH 11, 1995   BY FRANK DIGIACOMO

THE TRANSOM: Wenner, Nye Step Out in the Age of Outing

"YOU HEARD WHAT FRAN SAID ABOUT THEM THEM, DIDN'T YOU?" The stage-whispered call and response began to make the rounds of the Bowery Bar just moments after Jann Wenner and Matt Nye walked into Mary Boone's party for Ross Bleckner.

When scandal punctuates the world where the Velvet Mafia merges with the media elite, it is Fran Lebowitz who usually validates the moment with the first punch line.

The line? Informed that Mr. Wenner had left his wife for Mr. Nye, Ms. Lebowitz is said to have replied, "I wouldn't leave a chair for Matt Nye."

Of course the largely gay crowd at the Bleckner party loved the remark because it was so bitchy. But humor was also a means of grasping a relationship that for two months had been frustratingly slippery.

But Mr. Wenner has not yet learned to wear his sexuality with the self-confidence that is second nature in Mr. Bleckner's crowd. Mr. Wenner's notorious need for control has long been at war with his equally legendary impulsive and compulsive personality, and here was a prime example: At the same time that Mr. Wenner had been privately acknowledging that he was happily involved in a serious gay relationship, he had been actively thwarting the press' attempts to update his public persona.

JUNE 5, 1995

SEX AND THE CITY: WHAT HAS TWO WHEELS, WEARS SEERSUCKER AND MAKES

A FEW WEEKS BACK, I HAD AN ENCOUNTER WITH A Bicycle Boy.

It happened at a book party that was held in a great marble hall on a tree-lined street. While I was surreptitiously stuffing my face with smoked salmon, a writer friend, a guy, rushed up and said, "I've just been talking to the most interesting man."

"Oh yeah? Who?" I asked, glancing around the room with suspicion.

"He used to be an archeologist and now he writes science books ... fascinating."

"Say no more," I said.

I had already spotted the man in question—he was dressed in what I imagined was the city version of a safari suit—khaki trousers, a cream checked shirt, slightly shabby tweed jacket. His gray-blond hair was raked back from his forehead, exposing a handsome chipped profile. So I was motoring, as much as you can motor in strappy high-heeled sandals, across the room. He was in deep conversation with a middle-aged man, but I quickly took care of the situation. "You," I said. "Someone just told me you were fascinating. I hope you won't disappoint me." I bore him off to an open window where I plied him with cigarettes and cheap red wine. After 20 minutes, I left him to go meet some friends for dinner.

The next morning, he called me while I was still in bed with a hangover. Let's call him "Horace Eccles." He talked about romance. It was nice to lie in bed with my head throbbing and a handsome man cooing into my ear. We arranged to meet for dinner.

The trouble began almost immediately. First he called to say he was going to be an hour early. Then he called back to say he wasn't. Then he called to say he was going to be half an hour late. Then he called and said he was just around the corner. Then he really was 45 minutes late.

And then he turned up on his bicycle.

I didn't realize this at first. All I noticed was a more than normal dishevelment (for a writer), and a slight breathiness, which I attributed to the fact that he was in my presence. "Where do you want to have dinner?" he asked.

"I've already arranged it," I said. "Elaine's"

His face twisted. "But I thought we'd just have dinner at some neighborhood place around the corner."

I gave him one of my looks and said, "I don't have dinner at neighborhood places around the corner." For a moment it looked like it was going to be a standoff. Finally, he blurted out, "But I came on my bicycle, you see."

I turned around and stared at the offending piece of machinery, which was tethered to a lamppost.

"I don't think so," I said.

Mr. New Yorker and His Three-Speed

This was not my first encounter with a Manhattan literary-romantic subspecies I've come to call the Bicycle Boys. A while back, I was at a dinner with one of the most famous Bicycle Boys, whom we'll just call Mr. New Yorker. Mr. New Yorker looks like he's 35 (even though he's quite a bit older), with floppy brown hair and a devastating smile. When he goes out, he usually has his pick of single women, and not just because the women want to get something published in *The New Yorker*. He's smooth and a little sloppy. He sits down next to you and talks to you about politics and asks your opinion. He makes you feel smart. And then, before you know it, he's gone.

"Hey, where's Mr. New Yorker?" everyone was asking at 11 o'clock. "He made a phone call," one woman said, "and then he took off on his bike. He was going to meet someone."

The image of Mr. New Yorker, stealing through the night in his tweedy jacket, pumping like mad on his three-speed bike (with fenders to keep his pants from getting dirty), haunted me. I pictured him pulling up to an Upper East Side walk-up—or maybe a loft building in Soho—leaning against the buzzer, and then, pant-

A SUCKER OUT OF ME? A BICYCLE BOY BY CANDACE BUSHNELL

ing slightly, wheeling his bike up the stairs. A door would open, and he and his inamorata would be giggling as they tried to figure out where to put the bike. Then they'd fall into a sweaty embrace, no doubt ending up on some futon on the floor.

The Bicycle Boy actually has a long literary tradition in New York. The patron saints of Bicycle Boys are white-haired writer George Plimpton, whose bike used to hang upside down above his employees' heads at the *Paris Review* offices, and white-haired *Newsday* columnist Murray Kempton. They've been riding for years, and are the inspiration for the next generation of Bicycle Boys, like the aforementioned Mr. New Yorker, the writers Chip Brown and Tom Beller, literary agent Kip Kotzen and scores of young book, magazine and newspaper editors and writers who insist upon traversing Manhattan's physical and romantic landscape as solitary pedalers.

Bicycle Boys are a particular breed of New York bachelor: Smart, funny, romantic, lean, quite attractive, they are the stuff that grown-up coed dreams are made of. There's something incredibly, er, charming about a tweedy guy on a bike—especially if he's wearing goofy glasses. Women tend to feel a mixture of passion and motherly affection. But there's also a dark side: Most Bicycle Boys are not married and probably never will be, at least not until they give up their bikes.

Why John F. Kennedy Jr. Is Not a Bicycle Boy

"Riding a bike is not necessarily a power move," said Mr. Eccles. "It's best done by power people like George Plimpton. Otherwise, you have to hide your bike around the corner and surreptitiously take your trousers out of your socks."

Bicycle Boys don't ride their bikes for sport, like those silly guys you see riding around and around the park. They ride partly for transportation and, more importantly, to preserve an eternal literary boyhood. Think of twilight at Oxford, riding over the cobblestones, while a woman waits down by the Cherwell River, wearing a flowing dress, clasping a volume of Yeats. That's how Bicycle Boys think of themselves as they pedal Manhattan, dodging cabbies and potholes.

While John F. Kennedy Jr. is certainly New York's most famous and sought-after bike-riding bachelor, his rippled athleticism disqualifies him for Bicycle Boydom. Because a Bicycle Boy would rather bike through midtown in a seersucker suit than in shorts and a chest-hugging tee. And Bicycle Boys spurn those skin-tight bike pants that have cushy foam padding sewn into the butt. Bicycle Boys are not averse to the chastising pain of a hard bike seat—it helps the literature.

Which may be one reason Bicycle Boys, more than their athletic cousins, tend to get physically attacked. The other reason is they ride at any hour, in any physical condition, anywhere.

"Drunks roar out of their windows at night to send you into a tailspin," said Mr. Eccles.

One Halloween, Mr. New Yorker was wearing a British bobby's cape when he rode into a group of 12-year-olds who yanked him off his bike. "I said, 'I can't fight all of you at once. I'll fight one of you.' They all stepped back, except for the biggest one. I suddenly realized I didn't want to fight him either." The whole gang jumped on Mr. New Yorker and began pounding him, until some innocent bystander started screaming and the gang ran away. "I was lucky," said Mr. New Yorker. "They didn't take my bike, but they did take some records I had in my basket." (Note that Mr. New Yorker was carrying "records," as in vinyl albums—not CD's—another sign of a true Bicycle Boy.)

Mr. Eccles recalled a similar story. "Two days ago, I was riding through Central Park at 10 at night, when I was surrounded by a 'wilding' gang on rollerblades," he said. "They were almost children. They tried to capture me in a flank maneuver, but I was able to bicycle away even faster."

But an even bigger danger is sex, as a *New York Times* reporter we'll call Chester found out. Chester doesn't ride his bike as much as he used to because, about a year ago, he had a bad cycling accident after a romantic interlude. He was writing a story on topless dancers when he struck up a friendship with Lola. Maybe Lola fancied herself as Marilyn Monroe to his Arthur Miller. Who knows. All Chester knew was that one evening she called him up and said she was lying around in her bed at Trump Palace, and could he come over. He hopped on his bike and was there in 15 minutes. They went at it for three hours. Then she said he had to leave because she lives with someone and the guy was coming home. Any minute.

Chester ran out of the building and jumped on his bike, but there was a problem. His legs were so shaky from having sex they started cramping up just as he was going down Murray Hill and he crashed over the curb and slid across the pavement. "It really hurt," he said. "When your skin is scraped off like that, it's like a first-degree burn." Luckily, his nipple did eventually grow back.

> *The image of Mr. New Yorker, stealing through the night in his tweedy jacket, pumping like mad on his three-speed bike (with fenders to keep his pants from getting dirty), haunted me. I pictured him pulling up to an Upper East Side walk-up—or maybe a loft building in Soho—leaning against the buzzer, and then, panting slightly, wheeling his bike up the stairs.*

MARCH 11, 1995
BY CANDACE BUSHNELL

SEX AND THE CITY: A Portrait of a Bulgy Calvin Klein Hunk: Bergin Pops Out of His Giant Billboard

THE FIRST TIME YOU MEET MICHAEL, AT BOWERY BAR WITH CLIFford at his side, you want to hate him. He's 25. A model. Et cetera. You pretty much sense that he wants to hate you, too. Is he going to be really stupid? Besides, you don't think sex symbols are ever really sexy in person. The last one you met reminded you of a worm. Literally.

But not this one. He's not exactly what he appears to be.

"I have different personalities with different people," he says.

Then you lose him in the crowd.

About two months later, you're at that model Amber Valletta's birthday party at Barocco and you run into Michael. He's standing across the room, leaning against the bar, and he's smiling at you. He waves. You go over. He keeps hugging you, and photographers keep taking your picture. Then, you somehow end up sitting across the table from him. You and your friend are having this huge, never-ending, heated argument.

Michael keeps leaning over and asking you if you're O.K. And you say yes, thinking he doesn't understand that you and your friend always talk to each other that way.

Michael lives in a tiny studio that has white everything: white curtains, white sheets, white comforter, white chaise. He has 31 pairs of Calvin Klein underwear. He says he's given away hundreds. When you're in the bathroom, you look to see if he uses special cosmetics. He doesn't.

Michael grew up in Naugatuck, Conn. His father was a homicide and narcotics detective with the Connecticut State Police. His father let him do whatever he wanted—except drugs. "Are you kidding?" Michael says. So, when Michael was in high school, he couldn't hang out with the cool kids. He hung out with the benchwarmers on the football team. They looked up to Michael.

Every morning, Michael goes to the Bagel Buffet in the West Village for breakfast. You and Michael are hungry, so you go there at 6 in the evening on a Sunday. Two female cops sit in the corner smoking. People are wearing dirty sweat clothes. Michael eats half of your ham and cheese sandwich. "I could eat four of these sandwiches," he says, "but I won't. If I eat a hamburger, I feel so guilty afterwards."

Michael cares about the way he looks. "I change my clothes about five times a day," he says. "Who doesn't look in the mirror about a hundred times before they go out? I go back and forth between the two mirrors in my apartment like I'm going to look different in each one. It's like, yeah, I look good in the mirror, let me see if I look as good in the other. Doesn't everyone do that?"

MARCH 20, 1995   BY PETER STEVENSON

PLAYING RUDY'S STONEWALLING GIRL FRIDAY, LATEGANO DRIVES ROOM 9 REPORTERS NUTS

WHILE A STUDENT AT RUTGERS University in the mid-1980's, Cristyne Lategano, who is now Mayor Giuliani's press secretary, was a coxswain on the male crew team. That meant she sat in the bow of the boat and told the men how to row. Now, as Mayor Rudolph Giuliani's press secretary, she is sitting in the bow of the City Hall pressroom. But she's stopped calling strokes, and the press corps is certainly not rowing in her direction.

"Cristyne," said WNBC's Gabe Pressman, "is a distillation of the mayor's emotions—both his benign moments and his angry, hostile moments."

◇◇◇◇◇◇◇

APRIL 3, 1995   BY JIM WINDOLF

TV DIARY: TV BOY AT THE OSCARS: DAVE GETS THE SWEATS

"UMA … OPRAH." YEAH, WELL, screw it. I'm out there every single night. And one tiny night out of the 3,000 nights a year I'm on the air, one night I'm not at the top of my game for the first 10 minutes of the show. And I have to be exiled because of it. Well, screw it. Yeah, buddy, that's right, you try entertaining night in and night out, you try it and then you can get back to me and then we can talk. Because I'm telling you, I'm serious now, I'm going to floor those people next year. I'm point-ing the car at the Grand Canyon and we're going all the way until the wheels fall off and the chassis burns and all those big-time movie-star jewelry-rattlers run screaming to the hills.

Crystal loves those people. He can pretend he's Catskill Boy all he wants, but he's Hollywood to the bone. Like I'm going to go out there and sing a little song. Like I'm Mike Douglas opening the show with a number. Like I'm Merv.

Steve Martin made the joke you should have made. 'I think Dave's monologue was really funny. But then again, anything would have been funny after Arthur Hiller.' Beautiful. Well, that's why Steve has eight months off every year and you're TV Boy.

Eighteen writers, and not one of them can give you an Arthur Hiller joke? Come on. Johnny made that joke on Jack Valenti for years.

Isn't Ovitz supposed to prevent just this kind of disaster?

APRIL 10, 1995   BY PETER STEVENSON AND JIM WINDOLF

THE OBSERVATORY: MAG MAX

On April 12, magazine editors from all over town will gather in the Waldorf-Astoria Ballroom for the handing out of this year's National Magazine Awards. The winners will take home Ellies, the Oscars of the magazine industry. PETER STEVENSON and JIM WINDOLF dope out the judging process, handicap the chances of the 75 nominees and reveal this year's likely winners.

THEY WILL TELL YOU OTHERWISE, THEY WILL TRY to play it cool, they will claim it means nothing. They will say "It's a thrill just to be nominated" so often you'll think you're in Hollywood.

But don't listen to them. Because, oh, how they want it.

It, of course, is the Ellie, the prize given at the National Magazine Awards, the Alexander Calder-designed sculpture thing that's supposed to represent a modernist pachyderm but looks more like a sculpture of a Rorschach inkblot. The American Society of Magazine Editors has bestowed it upon grateful editors for the last 28 springs, and this year will present it to lucky winners in 14 categories over lunch at the Waldorf-Astoria on April 12.

Editors of nominated magazines aren't supposed to know if they've won until the lunch. This year, for the first time ever, an accounting firm, Price Waterhouse, was brought in to handle the ballots. "We're trying to preserve an Oscar-like secrecy," said Richard Stolley, founding editor of *People* and an ASME judge.

Here's how the judging process works: By Jan. 10, more than 300 magazines had submitted more than 1,300 entries. In February, a panel of 156 top and executive-level magazine editors holed up in the Hotel Macklowe in Manhattan to screen those entries. They broke up into groups of 10 to 20 to focus on a particular category, like General Excellence or Photography. Their job was to take, say, 115 entries and pare the list down to five or six finalists. It wasn't pretty. "Every year, there is very spirited debate," said Ms. Levine.

When the screeners finished, the 1,300 entries had been pared down to 75 finalists. Then, on March 15 and 16, the judges—54 current and former magazine editors, art directors and journalism professors—gathered in the World Room at Columbia University's Journalism Building to choose the 14 winners.

For the most part, this year's judges are the same ones who've judged the past few years, although, two years ago, according to Ms. Levine, "we cut out the judges we felt had lost touch."

Still, there are consistent complaints that the panel is weighted toward graying eminences. "The judges are all elderly," said an anonymous screener. "There may have been someone around 40, but no one younger. I'm not sure that's a good thing."

"They've turned it into the Grammys," said a 29-year-old editor who did not wish to be identified. "Safe choices are rewarded, alternative choices go home empty."

Up at Columbia, the judges broke up into groups of three to five, each taking a category. When they had made their choices, a member of each group rose and announced it; the selections then had to be ratified by secret ballot by a majority of the 54 judges. "This year we had a secret written ballot for the first time," said ASME's Ellen Levine. "Fewer people know who's going to win than ever before."

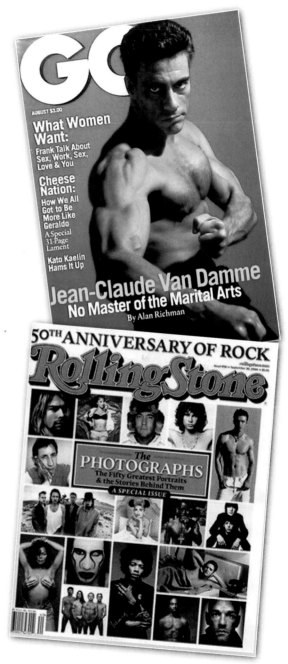

APRIL 24, 1995   BY JIM WINDOLF

NOW PLAYING NICK AND NORA AT THE NEWS, RUSH AND MOLLOY FEED THE GOSSIP BEAST

WITH THEIR COLUMN SAFELY filed away for the next day's editions of the *Daily News*, George Rush and Joanna Molloy tried to unwind one recent evening in their adjacent cubicles, seven floors above the grid of 42nd Street. The couple—who share not only a bed, but 25 inches of column space five days a week— were trying to impress a visitor by listing the high points in their careers as gossip writers for the *News* and, before that, the *New York Post*. Was it the item about Don Johnson's love child, the bit concerning Harvey Keitel's pet chicken, or the revelation that Scientologists witnessed the wedding of Michael Jackson and Lisa Marie Presley?

"Who cares about any of this crap," said Ms. Molloy as she fussed her way through years of clips. "This is so goddamn depressing."

Mr. Rush, as usual, sounded a little more relaxed than his wife.

"Darling," he said in his best William Powell drawl, "we're just feeding the beast."

The *News* tag-team Tattlers joined forces professionally on Feb. 20, when the column once known simply as George Rush became Rush and Molloy. Even their competitors had nothing but kind words for New York's self-styled First Couple of Gossip. *Post* columnist Neal Travis said, "The *News* is a mess, but George and Joanna seem to know what they're doing." The usually acerbic Khoi Nguyen of the *Post*'s Page Six agreed: "After my own page, it's the next thing I read every morning." Liz Smith, who gushes about something or other each day in her *New York Newsday* column, couldn't help but gush over Rush and Molloy. "It's nifty, lively and on the ball," she said.

APRIL 24, 1995   BY FRANK DIGIACOMO

THE TRANSOM: IS FASHION CAFÉ TROIKA A FRONT?

THE SKEPTICISM REMAINED EVEN AFTER THE THICK FUMES OF hype had dissipated from the newly opened Fashion Café at 51 Rockefeller Plaza. Supermodels Naomi Campbell, Elle Macpherson and Claudia Schiffer have been touted as partners in Manhattan's newest theme-park restaurant ever since the first press release on Fashion Café was issued back in October.

But even though Naomi, Elle and Claudia did their best to sound resolute about their involvement in the Rockefeller Center eatery ("It's our baby. We make all the decisions," Ms. Schiffer told *Time*), they didn't quite seem to sell the notion of themselves as restaurateurs. And this was a trio whose repertoire of bedroom looks and runway prowling has moved millions of dollars of designer merchandise.

Perhaps, in the end, the multinational mannequin troika didn't believe their own hype. A check of New York State Liquor Authority records indicates that the Fashion Café is owned by an alliance consisting of general partners and brothers Tommaso and Francesco Buti, who own 28 percent of the business, and limited partner Dr. Guido Bracchetti, a Los Angeles oral surgeon who has the remaining 72 percent.

"None of those gorgeous models are owners," State Liquor Authority spokesman Richard Chernela told *The Observer*'s Daniel Green. "It's a promotional gimmick. I'm sure those women got a few bucks, more than a few bucks, to help market Fashion Café. According to our records, the models have no interest, either direct or indirect, in the restaurant. If they did, it would indicate fraud."

APRIL 24, 1995 BY CANDACE BUSHNELL

SEX AND THE CITY: NEW YORK'S LAST SEDUCTION: LOVING MR. BIG

A 40-ISH MOVIE PRODUCER I'LL CALL "SAMANTHA JONES" walked into Bowery Bar and, as usual, we all looked up to see whom she was with. Samantha was always with at least four men, and the game was to pick out which one was her lover. Of course, it wasn't really much of a game, because the boyfriend was too easy to spot. Invariably, he was the youngest, and good-looking in the B-Hollywood-actor kind of way—and he would sit there with a joyously stupid expression on his face (if he had just met Sam) or a bored stupid look on his face (if he had been out with her a few times). Because at that point it would be beginning to dawn on him that no one at the table was going to talk to him. Why should they, when he was going to be history in two weeks?

We all admired Sam. First of all, it's not that easy to get 25-year-old guys when you're in your early 40's. Second, Sam is a New York inspiration. Because if you're a successful single woman in this city, you have two choices: You can beat your head against the wall trying to find a relationship, or you can say "screw it" and just go out and have sex like a man. Thus: Sam.

This is a real question for women in New York these days. For the first time in Manhattan history, many women in their 30's to early 40's have as much money and power as men—or at least enough to feel like they don't need a man, except for sex. While this paradox is the topic of many an analytic hour, recently my friend Carrie, a journalist in her mid-30's, decided, as a group of us were having tea at the Mayfair hotel, to try it out in the real world. To give up on love, as it were, and throttle up on power, in order to find contentment. And, as we'll see, it worked. Sort of.

Meeting Mr. Big

As part of her research, Carrie went to see *The Last Seduction* at 3 in the afternoon. She had heard that the movie portrayed a woman who, in pursuit of money and hot sex and absolute control, uses and abuses every man she meets—and never has a regret or one of those expected "Oh my God, what have I done?" epiphanies.

When she came out, she kept thinking about the scene where Linda Fiorentino picks up the man in the bar and has sex with him in the parking lot, gripping a chain-link fence.

Carrie bought two pairs of strappy sandals (there is sexual power in women's shoes) and got her hair cut off.

On a Sunday evening, Carrie went to a cocktail party thrown by the designer Joop. A man walked by with a cigar in his mouth, and one of the men Carrie was talking to said, "Oooooh. Who is that? He looks like a younger, better-looking Ron Perelman."

"I know who it is," Carrie said.

"Who?"

"Mr. Big."

"I knew that. I always get Mr. Big and Perelman mixed up."

Carrie had seen Mr. Big once before, but she didn't think he'd remember her. She was in this office where she works sometimes and *Inside Edition* was interviewing her about something she wrote about Chihuahuas. Mr. Big came in and started talking to the cameraman about how all Chihuahuas were in Paris.

At the party, Mr. Big was sitting on the radiator in the living room. "Hi," Carrie said. "Remember me?" She could tell by his eyes that he had no idea who she was, and she wondered if he was going to panic.

He twirled the cigar around the inside of his lips and took it out of his mouth. A high-testosterone male. He looked away to flick his ash, then looked back and said, "Abso-fucking-lutely."

Another Mr. Big (at Elaine's)

Carrie didn't run into Mr. Big again for several days. In the meantime, something was definitely happening. She bumped into a writer friend she hadn't seen for two months and he said, "You look like Heather Locklear."

"Yeah? Is that a problem?"

Then she went to a party after one of those Peggy Siegal movie openings and met a big movie producer who impulsively gave her a ride in his car to Bowery Bar. Mr. Big was there.

Mr. Big slid into the banquette next her. Their sides were touching.

Mr. Big said, "So. What have you been doing lately? What do you do for work?"

"This is my work," Carrie said. "I'm researching a story for a friend of mine about women who have sex like men. You know, that they have sex and afterwards they feel nothing."

Mr. Big eyed her. "But you're not like that," he said.

"Aren't you?" she asked.

"Not a drop. Not even half a drop," he said.

Carrie looked at Mr. Big. "What's wrong with you?"

"Oh, I get it," said Mr. Big. "You've never been in love."

"Oh yeah?"

"Yeah."

"And you have?"

"Abso-fucking-lutely."

MAY 8, 1995 BY ALEX KUCZYNSKI

Incidental Information on Martin Amis: Don't Look a Gifted Author in the Mouth

HALF AN HOUR AFTER MARTIN AMIS' BOOK PARTY WAS supposed to be over on May 1, he was standing in the small back room at Match on East 60th Street. Usually at a book party, the author is an afterthought, as the literati spread out and talk shop among themselves, deigning perhaps to stop by and shake the humble author's hand; at his party Martin Amis was its collective thought.

Mr. Amis, in a lavender shirt and subdued chalk-stripe suit, was accompanied by his American girlfriend Isabel Fonseca, also wearing lavender. There was a bottleneck at the door. The sushi bar was four deep. And when Mr. Amis' agent Andrew Wylie arrived to chat with Mr. Amis for a few minutes, it was like watching welding sparks; the most unfazable New Yorkers stared even though they knew it was bad for their corneas. Mr. Amis, verifiably, incontestably, irritatingly, had become a celebrity. Not just a book-world celebrity. A mondo-celebrity celebrity.

So: Why wasn't Mr. Amis smiling?

Three days earlier, Mr. Amis was preoccupied.

"If I had known that my teeth would become a theme of public debate and make headlines in the tabloids and *Time* magazine," said Mr. Amis, "I would have committed suicide without hesitation a year ago."

Mr. Amis was about to fly to New York, to kick off the three-week American book tour for his new, celebrated, vilified novel, *The Information*. This novel about literary envy has aroused wrath in England for the size of its advance ($750,000), and sparked public fascination about Mr. Amis' teeth, which are now surely literature's most famous diseased body part since John Updike's psoriasis. Mr. Amis, who is being fitted with new teeth by a high-priced New York dentist, has been attacked in England as a sort of corrupted, treasonous Brit, for his decision to replace his suitably ghastly English chompers with an American Colgate smile. It was as if, by fixing his teeth, he was embracing the smug, rich, sexually prolific, best-selling Gwyn Barry character in the new novel, and abandoning the rotting, impotent, unpublished, powerless-but-lovable (and very British) Richard Tull.

"The work wasn't really a cosmetic job," explained Mr. Amis, "it's profound reconstruction."

He went on. "Our teeth are the way by which we actually live, and I had become very neurotic about mine. They are your naked bones. They are the sensory focus of your life."

◇◇◇◇◇◇

MAY 15, 1995 BY FRANK DIGIACOMO

THE OBSERVATORY: IT'S 1 A.M. AS SIX GREAT CHEFS FEAST ON THE CITY THAT HAS MADE THEM STARS

IT WAS WELL AFTER MIDNIGHT at the Blue Ribbon restaurant on Sullivan Street in Soho, but Laurence Kretchmer, the 29-year-old co-owner of Mesa Grill and Bolo restaurants, hadn't yet ordered the first bottle of wine. Most of the boys hadn't shown up yet.

The boys happened to be a regular gathering of six of New York's hottest young chefs who meet after work most Saturday nights at the Blue Ribbon to gossip and trade secrets.

Most Saturday nights at the Blue Ribbon, the table closest to the entrance is occupied by this den of chefs. And just as the Algonquin Round Table of the 1920's and 30's gathered to commiserate about their literary careers and their love lives, and to zing wisecracks at each other, the Blue Ribbon round table gathers to share horror stories about customers from hell, culinary techniques, business gossip and, of course, the trials of making a romantic relationship work on a chef's insane work schedule.

The crew includes Bobby Flay, the celebrated red-haired 30-year-old chef of Flatiron District restaurants Mesa Grill and Bolo; his business partner, Mr. Kretchmer; Tom Valenti, 36-year-old chef of Cascabel; Alan Harding, chef at Tribeca's farmer-friendly Nosmo King; Matthew Kenney, the darkly

handsome, quiet, 30-year-old chef-owner of Matthew's on the Upper East Side; and Mario Batali, the 34-year-old bearded, ponytailed chef-owner of bustling Pó in the West Village.

Mr. Kenney sat down. He was swaddled in a bulky sweater topped by a heavy coat. "I'm freezing," he said quietly. "Whenever I leave the kitchen, I'm ice cold." Then Mr. Harding

sat down. Mr. Batali peered at the wine bottle. He did not appear cheered by the label.

"What was that face for?" Mr. Flay said.

"It's a little early for pinot noir for me, Mac," said Mr. Batali.

"We should order some oysters," someone said.

"Where's Valenti?" Mr. Flay wanted to know.

"I think Valenti went home," said Mr. Batali.

"He's a punk," said Mr. Flay. But five minutes later, as if summoned, Tom Valenti arrived.

And the Blue Ribbon round table was complete. Mr. Flay sat back into the plush red-orange fabric of the banquette that his crew occupied and smiled.

JUNE 5, 1995   BY TISH DURKIN

ANOTHER FINE MESS: PENN AND SCHOEN, LEAKPROOF POLLSTERS, RUSH IN FOR CLINTON

O N THE WALL BEHIND THE RE-ceptionist hangs a picture of Ed Koch, circa 1977, and behind him stand two young lords of the realm: one rotund, rumpled and bookworm-like; one thin, taut, bookworm-like.

Ah, but that's not why we're here, on East 92nd Street. Why we are here has rather to do with the piece of paper on the front desk. It is a questionnaire that starts off, "If the election were held today, would you vote for ... ?" The men over Mr. Koch's shoulder are the pollsters Mark Penn and Douglas Schoen, and, in December, the Democratic National Committee put Penn & Schoen Associates on retainer. Now they are the men behind the president of the United States.

How two low-profile workhorses came to acquire a role in the fortunes of a politically embattled chief executive is, according to some, a great New York story of how two fast kids from Horace Mann hooked up at *The Harvard Crimson*, stuck together through the thick and thin of political warfare from Manhattan to Mobile to Manila, and landed at the front door of the White House. Or, say others, it is a rather tidier tale of how two guys got a deal that's better than they are.

In 1994, Mr. Penn and Mr. Schoen were working for a Mississippi Democrat named Ken Harper. Mr. Harper lost the Senate race to incumbent Republican Trent Lott, who was getting advice from Dick Morris, an old acquaintance of Mr. Penn and Mr. Schoen. Mr. Morris had in recent years become a Republican consultant, but not before forging an unbreakable bond with Bill Clinton. Friends say Dick Morris brought Mr. Penn and Mr. Schoen to the attention of the D.N.C. because Mr. Clinton needs first-class polling. Period.

But Washington whispers that Mr. Clinton really wants to hire Mr. Morris, but that he cannot afford to be seen getting advice from a Republican. Not to put it too bluntly, but some are saying that Penn & Schoen are, in effect, beards for Mr. Morris.

"My understanding is that Dick Morris will be paid through Penn & Schoen," said the head of a major Republican polling firm in Washington, D.C. "You have to be honorable to one side or another in this business. ... Dick Morris has decided he can have it both ways."

"It would be unseemly for the D.N.C. to write checks to the same guy Trent Lott is writing checks to," echoed an equally prominent Democratic pollster, who expressed doubt that Mr. Penn and Mr. Schoen have ever spoken with the president. (They say they have.)

But perhaps Washington's most stunning comment on the subject

of Penn & Schoen, received from all the Clinton colleagues contacted by *The Observer*: silence.

Polling Horace Mann.

Both Mr. Penn and Mr. Schoen came to their passion for electoral politics—statistical division of—alarmingly early. Above one of Mr. Penn's couches hangs the first poll he ever took, circa 1968. Eighth-grader Mark Penn found the faculty of the Horace Mann School to be more liberal than the average American.

Mr. Schoen had graduated from Horace Mann two years earlier. At 16, convinced that his would never be the athletic glory of which he had dreamed, Mr. Schoen found an outlet for his competitive juices in the City Council race of his mother's friend from temple, Robert Low. Soon young Mr. Schoen was ringing doorbells; one of his first campaigns was that of Assembly candidate Dick Gottfried, whose campaign manager happened to be Dick Morris.

By the time the two arrived at Harvard and hit *The Crimson*—day editor Mr. Schoen sent cub reporter Mr. Penn to cover a women's softball game—they were already consultants, masquerading as undergraduates.

As an Oxford Ph.D. candidate, Mr. Schoen wrote a book about the Tory populist Enoch Powell. Meanwhile, Mr. Penn, the computer scientist, having graduated from Harvard in 1976 and gone on to Columbia University's law school, so engrossed himself in the campaigns of Brendan Byrne, Ella Grasso and others that he stopped "maybe a course" short of getting his law degree.

By 1976, the combination was going full-throttle out of Mr. Penn's apartment. Political consultant David Garth, once a summer boss of Mr. Schoen's, brought them on board Ed Koch's 1977 mayoral race, where, said Mr. Schoen, "we developed constant daily tracking, but saw how Garth used it to develop a winning strategy."

They seem to have no New York Democratic connection left unmade—including that with Clinton confidant Harold Ickes, who hired them to poll for David Dinkins in 1989. "Harold is a very shrewd political actor," said Mr. Schoen. "He's always been very kind about our work."

But Washington is determined to keep them under a hot lamp. "Penn & Schoen's numbers are fine, but their analysis is mediocre at best," said one prominent pollster. "If you had to come up with the top 10 list of pollsters, they would not be on it."

"The Beltway rap," Mr. Penn said, "is, 'They're accurate, but can they tell you what it means?' No—we just throw darts at it."

JULY 17, 1995
BY JIM WINDOLF

THE NEW YORK WORLD: THE N.Y. LUNCH RITUAL

SET A LUNCH DATE TWO TO three weeks from the date of your call—but be vague about the place and time. Then, on the morning of the lunch date, fail to call your partner. If he or she also fails to call you, you've both got it made—lunch is off!

If your lunch partner remembers to call you, mention how "crazy it's been around here lately," and then say, off handedly, "You know what? Tomorrow would be a lot better for me." If tomorrow's no good for the other person, lunch is postponed indefinitely!

If the other person is free for lunch tomorrow, promise to call the following morning to set the time and place. Next morning, conveniently forget to make the call. Most likely, your lunch partner will be too proud to call you—and lunch is off forever!

JUNE 12, 1995 BY ANDREW JACOBS

Chastity Zones to Scrub Up Sex City: Talese, Sailors Weep for Dirty Old N.Y.C.

EXCEPT FOR THE GREASY SCUFF mark that sullied one leg of his bell-bottom sailor's pants, a man who gave his name as Keith Lancaster was blindingly white, a vision of purity in a sinful city. That is, if one could ignore the nearly naked blonde wriggling on his lap.

"This is what makes New York so great," the 21-year-old midshipman said with a sigh, just moments after "Cleopatra" had finished performing atop his military whites at Church Street's All-Star Harmony Theater in Tribeca.

He isn't the first stranger in town to enjoy the snares of New York's prolific sex industry and he surely won't be the last. But if the Giuliani administration has

its way, future visitors to this city will be hard pressed to find the licentious charms that led one mid-19th-century traveler, Ole Raeder of Norway, to call New York "the Gomorrah of the New World."

All this month, community boards throughout the city are debating the merits of a dramatic zoning change that would force up to 90 percent of the city's peep shows, topless bars and triple-X video outlets to relocate or close altogether. Of the 177 sex establishments counted in 1993 by the Department of City Planning, all but 25 would have to unplug their flashing lights within a year of the new zoning rule's passage, which lawmakers hope to have in place by Thanks-

giving. A few might manage to survive by moving to unfriendly industrial strips on the fringes of all five boroughs, but then only with a 500-foot buffer zone between each business and with an equal gap between a given sex establishment and a school, church or residence.

Combined with the invasion of superstores and Disney's planned foray into Times Square, the new plan could help to zone unwholesome fun right out of the heart of the city. Critics of the proposed zoning restrictions maintain that such changes would not only turn New York into a bland, sexless metropolis, but threaten the city's tradition of unfettered artistic expression.

SEPTEMBER 11, 1995 BY JAY STOWE

OFF THE RECORD: *New Yorker* Staff Heckles Tina's Roseanne Folly

THE LATEST ATTEMPT BY *NEW Yorker* editor Tina Brown to fold some Hollywood glitz into her venerable magazine started, naturally, in Brentwood, Calif. That's where Ms. Brown met with feminist sitcom mama Roseanne in the dining room of her manse on July 25. Roseanne's latest husband and former bodyguard, Ben Thomas, "left us alone to let our hair down," Ms. Brown said.

As a result of the meeting, Roseanne will serve as a consulting editor for an upcoming double issue of *The New Yorker* focusing on women.

Another result: A number of *New Yorker* writers are grumbling again about Ms. Brown's judgment. Most notable among them is veteran *New Yorker* staff writer Ian Frazier, who quit soon after he learned of the latest departure from the magazine's traditions.

New Yorker editors David Kuhn, Deborah Garrison and Ms. Brown herself will go west on Sept. 25 to meet with Roseanne for a three-day brainstorming session at the home of the crass comedienne. Ms. Brown said she will use Roseanne as an "interesting sounding board."

AUGUST 21, 1995
BY CANDACE BUSHNELL

SEX AND THE CITY: CITY IN HEAT! SEXUAL PANIC SEIZED RUDY AND MR. BIG

THE CITY'S IN HEAT. DAYS OF 90-plus-degree weather strung together one after the other. Everyone is cranky. No one can work. Women wear almost nothing. August is the month New Yorkers think about sex more than all the other 11 months combined. Everyone is amorous—even the mayor and his lovely wife, Donna, who embraced on WNBC on Aug. 10 at 6:45 A.M., while most of New York was still sleeping. The papers duly reported that the Mayor's wife was "beaming."

New York—meaning Manhattan, not the Hamptons, which, thanks to the ocean breezes and chilly social caste system, cannot be said to ever truly be in heat—is a completely different city in August. Like living in some South American country with a corrupt and drunk dictator, skyrocketing inflation, drug cartels, dust-covered roads, clogged plumbing—where nothing will ever get better, the rains will never come, so might as well turn off the air-conditioner and have some fun.

AUGUST 7, 1995 BY JEFFREY HOGREFE

LEROY'S FINAL INSULT TO 57TH STREET: RUSSIAN TEA ROOM GOES THEME PARK

IN THE ONE MONTH SINCE Faith Stewart-Gordon agreed to sell the Russian Tea Room to Warner LeRoy, the celebrity restaurateur has been besieged by phone calls from many of her regular customers, whose ranks have included Lauren Bacall, Raquel Welch, Woody Allen, Candice Bergen, Roy Scheider and powerhouse agent Sam Cohn, who eats lunch in a front booth every day. Said Ms. Stewart-Gordon, a soft-spoken native of South Carolina who has owned the West 57th Street landmark since 1967, "they have complained that they'll be left homeless" once she turns over what she refers to as "the tearoom" to Mr. LeRoy on Jan. 1. "Nonsense," she said she has told the regulars. "Warner will take

good care of you."

That, it seems, is exactly what they are afraid of. A flamboyant child of Hollywood whose grandfather founded Warner Brothers,

Mr. LeRoy, 60, is the proprietor of Tavern on the Green in Central Park and the creator of Great Adventure, the amusement park in Jackson, N.J.

DECEMBER 25, 1995   BY FRANK DIGIACOMO

POWER! MEASURED N.Y. STYLE – IN GOSSIP INCHES

WALTER WINCHELL MAY HAVE REVOLU-tionized the culture of gossip, but some-where between the birth of Page Six and coming of age of the cyber generation, this black-sheep offspring of traditional journalism emerged as a legitimate media commodity. Because those being gossiped about are increasingly defined, not by what they were born to, or where they dine out, or even whom they marry, but whether they can shell out $5.7 billion to buy MCA, or turn the Gulf Western building into "The Most Important New Address in the World."

For some time now, *The Observer* has been saying that a rar-efied version of the meritocracy—that over-stimulated group of elite professionals who dominate the corporate, entertain-ment, media and design worlds—has overtaken the aristoc-racy, the moneyed socialites who do not work for a living, in the city's social hierarchy. New York's original social elite was, of course, defined literally as the 400 couples who fit into Caroline Astor's Fifth Avenue ballroom, and their inclusion conferred upon them a certain amount of power. But the fin de siècle advent of the camcorder, America Online and Bill Gates has opened up the ballroom considerably. Coincidentally, the Microsoft Era has made more accessible a national obsession that has existed since Winchell's day. "The thrust of almost ev-erything in American life is toward celebrity," said Neal Gabler, the author of *Winchell; Gossip, Power and the Culture of Celeb-rity.* "That's the currency of American life."

If celebrity is the currency, then gossip is the coin of the realm, an alloy of information and fame that can create oppor-tunities, careers, even people. But gossip also has the power to destroy what it creates. And there is really only one forum where the unique New York confluence of power, money, ce-lebrity and controversy is dissected on a daily basis: the city's gossip columns. That is where the agenda is set. "The columns don't report on celebrity," said Mr. Gabler. "They make celebrity."

By conducting a census of nine New York-based columns in newspa-pers and magazines over a period of 12 months and determining quan-titatively who appears in boldface most often, *The Observer* staff has assembled a ranking of New York's gossip star-system: *The New York Observer* 500. Those who made the cut also enjoy a certain power, the power that celebrity brings in a society that, as Mr. Gabler noted, is ob-sessed with it.

Gossip has evolved into what Mr. Gabler called a "common database for all Americans," but much of that data is generated here. Celeb-rity has many facets—social, corporate, artistic, international—and no other city can offer as many of them in one concentrated location as Manhattan, an island that also happens to be the media capital of the world. The density and complexity of life here are ideal condi-tions for the art of gossip. "One of the fascinating things about living in New York is that you know that you are close to power and mon-ey and influence and prestige. But a lot of it is hidden behind doors and buildings," said Jay Rosen, professor of journalism at New York

University and director of the Project on Public Life and the Press. "The combination of proximity to and distance from" these hidden worlds of power and influence "creates a natural demand for a form of news that can't emerge from official channels and conventional journalism and approved newsgathering."

Then there's the other reason: "New York is the No. 1 hometown of the professional yenta," said public relations executive Dan Klores.

Professional yentas, pay attention: The *New York Observer* 500 was culled from the *New York Post*'s Page Six, Neal Travis and Cindy Adams; *Newsday*'s Liz Smith (who ended the year at the post); the *Daily News'* Rush and Molloy and Hot Copy; *Women's Wear Daily*'s Suzy column; *New York* magazine's Intelligencer page; and *The New Yorker*'s Talk of the Town section. A small army of staff members and freelancers logged all of the names that ap-peared in these columns between Dec. 1, 1994, and Nov. 30, 1995. Approximately 40,100 entries were fed into a computer program that tabulated and cross-indexed the entries. From that database, the 500 names with the most mentions were chosen, the first annual 500.

In addition to demonstrating who is foremost in the minds of the city's gossips, the 500 names on this census, and order in which they appear, form a sort of pointillist portrait of New York culture over the last year. At the top, no surprise, is O.J. Simpson. The 359 mentions that Mr. Simpson received—177 more than the No. 2 finisher, Madonna—demonstrates just how much Mr. Simpson's story dominated the media last year, especially since the lion's share of the "trial of the century" was found in the news pages and not in the gossip columns.

Between his Bronco ride and the verdict, Mr. Simpson and his case often became the New York media equivalent of white noise: distracting, yet devoid of any real value for the city. Underneath, real issues percolated, but no one seemed able to focus on them.

Rudolph Giuliani's third-place finish indicates that the state of the city is an issue we could focus on. The mayor has promoted himself as a much-needed architect of change for the city. And anyone who promises change in a city of seven million opinionated cynics—especially when it comes to government—immediately becomes a conflict magnet. Conflict, of course, is the infrastructure of any great gossip item. Mr. Giuliani's *Observer* 500 ranking also suggests that he may have been overly concerned that his police commissioner, William Bratton, was stealing too much of his public relations thunder. Although Mr. Bratton (87) ranked within the top 100, his 38 column mentions paled in comparison to Mr. Giuliani's 174.

Among the rumors contributing to the mayor's big finish were those linking him to his press secretary, Cristyne Lategano (460). Regardless of their veracity, the gossip suggested that Mr. Giuliani was spending a lot of time at the office.

Glancing through the top 20, there is only one person who stands out as not being an active member of the meritocracy: Elizabeth Taylor (10), who is essentially a lapsed member. Save for her cameo in *The Flintstones*, Ms. Taylor has not acted in a film for years. As work-related matters go, 1995 was another big year for media moguls. Deals were made and broken; executives were hired and fired. Many of these deals can be found in the top 100: Steven Spielberg (21), David Geffen (35) and Jeffrey Katzenberg (83) of Dreamworks SKG; Edgar Bronfman Jr. (34), the new chief of MCA; Michael Ovitz (28), whom Mr. Bronfman almost hired, but who ultimately landed at Disney, nearly wrecking his old place of business, Creative Artists Agency. (Memo to Michael Eisner: Compare your ranking to Mr. Ovitz, but not before taking your heart medication.)

In fact, much of the 500 is revealed to be a hardworking albeit glamorous crowd. There aren't too many Brenda Fraziers on the list. Socialites and the international aristocracy comprise only 10 percent (see chart). The rest of the finishers, with the exception of certain players in the O.J. Simpson opera—see Kato Kaelin (29)—are careerists of some sort.

What's interesting is that the nouveaux riche, whose conspicuous consumption and decadent entertaining were the sources of many items (and much derision) in the 1980's, were dropped or were pushed from sight. Henry Kravis (192) and Susan and John Gutfreund (371 and 410) placed, but hardly in the high style to which they are accustomed.

And Saul and Gayfryd Steinberg, who once hired models to pose nude as statues at one of their soirees, did not even make the list. This only exception to the rule seems to be Ron Perelman, who ranked 31st. Last year was a big one for Mr. Perelman. He got married to Patricia Duff (213) and added another child to his brood. And his liaisons with Rupert Murdoch (213) and Brandon Tartikoff seemed to have bolstered his media and mogul image. Nevertheless, his high ranking suggests that the press might want to stop referring to Mr. Perelman as publicity-shy.

Hitching one's star to the Hollywood power clique greatly increases the chances of anointment in the columns. Left Coast commodities both behind and in front of the camera racked up 167 spots, accounting for a full third of the list. Movie stars and moguls have long been staples of the New York columns. Some of it has to do with the fact that Los Angeles is a company town where the *Los Angeles Times* edits the city's only newspaper gossip column, Liz Smith's, with a mighty heavy hand. That makes the New York columns the primary outlet for film industry scuttlebutt. And Hollywood coverage by the New York columns has only increased since New York society ran for cover and left a big void.

But this year, Hollywood's showing may have been aided by another phenomenon. Some of Hollywood's leading lights, tired of earthquakes and mudslides and riots, began spending more time in Manhattan. In some cases, those who didn't already have places in the city bought them. And New York columnists seemed to respond to those stars who visited home turf. With the exception of Sylvester Stallone (16), who left Los Angeles for Miami, the highest-placing film celebrities were those who either kept a home in New York or spent a lot of time here. In the top 50, there's Mr. Spielberg, who recently traded in his apartment in Trump Tower for the San Remo and who spends a lot of time at his East Hampton estate; Julia Roberts (35), who recently moved to Greenwich Village; Tom Hanks (36); who bought on Fifth Avenue; Woody Allen (38) and Robert DeNiro (39), who have long made New York their home; Long Island boy Alec Baldwin (43) and even Brad Pitt (44), who always seemed to be in town.

There is one practice in public relations to which few self-respecting flacks want to be linked. It's a practice that has existed since the days of Winchell and is perhaps the most concrete example of a celebrity's currency. In that process, a publicist will feed a columnist a number of juicy items that have no fingerprints and no strings attached to any of the publicist's clients. To reciprocate, the columnist will then place a "contract" item—an item that lacks the usual gossip edge and promotes the publicist's client. Thus the celebrity of one person is traded to gain celebrity for another.

Sometimes, the result is that one publicist steps on another's toes, such as when Nick & Toni's regular Peggy Siegal plants items about the East Hampton restaurant's star-studded patrons before the restaurant's own publicists has a chance. Often the trade-off is conducted for personal gains—Hillary Rodham Clinton, under fire from the press, went to America's database and brokered an exchange with a number of female journalists, including Cindy Adams and Liz Smith. More than once, Mrs. Clinton allowed access to both herself and the White House, and in return, she was humanized by the columnists.

> *If celebrity is the currency, then gossip is the coin of the realm, an alloy of information and fame that can create opportunities, careers, even people.*

OCTOBER 16, 1995   BY CHARLES V. BAGLI

GIULIANI TOPS WHITMAN WITH SICKLY SWEET BID TO KEEP COMMODITIES

THE GIULIANI ADMINISTRATION HAS PUT TOGETHER THE LARGest corporate subsidy package in New York history to keep the city's commodity exchanges from moving to New Jersey.

With the governing boards of the Coffee, Sugar & Cocoa Exchange scheduled to vote Oct. 11 on an offer from Gov. Christine Todd Whitman of New Jersey, city and state officials in New York suddenly countered on Oct. 3 with a package of cash and tax breaks worth up to $80.5 million if the exchanges remain in New York. Taken together with the $183.9 million in subsidies granted to the Mercantile Exchange last year, New York has offered more than $264 million to the commodity industry, at a time when city and state governments are slashing budgets for transit, job training, education and welfare.

But it's unclear whether the Giuliani administration can derail the deal in New Jersey. On Oct. 10, the directors of the Cotton Exchange voted unanimously to accept the Jersey offer.

New York's strenuous effort to keep the exchanges has raised eyebrows even in the financial community. "There's something screwy here," said Michael Keenan, deputy chairman of the finance department at New York University's Stern School of Business. "It sounds like a lot of money for the benefit. There are questions about the long-term viability of the exchanges and their actual contribution to the economy."

◇◇◇◇◇◇◇

OCTOBER 16, 1995   BY ERIK HEDEGAARD

Meet Ms. New York—Penny Crone! A Spiky, Fiery, Lusty, Fox 5 Gal

AS FAR AS FOX NEWS IS CONcerned, Penny Crone is a lot more than Penny Crone. At a minimum, of course, Penny Crone is the 48-year-old, Emmywinning, *10 O'Clock News* Fox reporter with the spiky, nativehut hairdo; ever-flapping mouth; short skirts ("They can't hurt"); ankle bracelet ("Is that stupid? Is that out of style?"); nails-inher-windpipe laugh; and deep, barfly-type voice that once spent some time calling Yogi Berra Yogi Bear. About her and her work in the city, everybody has an opinion. Jerry Nachman, vice president of news at WCBS-TV, said, "I find her fascinating. I can't not watch her; it's sort of

like a train wreck: horrific and compelling. Sometimes I'll tell my reporters, 'Watch Penny Crone.' She's got contempt for the camera, which is a great fucking trick; if there was a giant anchovy hanging out of her nose, she'd keep on talking." A veteran newsman who likes to speak anonymously said, "I admire her doggedness and her tenacity but, Jesus Christ, I find her sort of a pain in the ass."

Penny herself takes this view of the situation: "I'm just Penny." You have to agree that's saying a lot; Fox, however, knows it is still far from the truth. Over at Fox, they like to say, "Penny is

New York!"

On a day in early October, at 2 P.M., shortly before her workday began, Penny dropped into an outside seat at Soleil, a Third Avenue restaurant.

"Right now, I'm in contract discussions with Fox," she went on. "So I'm sitting with my agent outside somewhere talking about salaries, with these two old ladies eating their lunch and listening to us talk. Something came up about another reporter making some huge kind of money and I went ballistic. My agent said, 'This person has lots of contacts with cops.' I said, 'Contacts? I've fucked 6,000 cops!'"

Penny roared.

NOVEMBER 6, 1995
BY THOMAS HUDSON

MAD MARIO CANTONE ON BROADWAY: 'LOVE ME, LOVE MY HAIRY ASS!'

IN A RARE FEW HOURS OFF from his burgeoning career in the legitimate theat-ah, Mario Cantone arrived 15 minutes late at Carolines comedy club in Times Square. A gaggle of photographers shot his picture by the bar. The club was sold out, and Mr. Cantone surveyed the crowd. He has alarmingly white teeth, a slightly hooked nose, big sunken eyes, thick eyebrows, a shock of bushy black hair.

"Yeah, I'm a Broadway actor now, but I used to have a kids show," he said into the microphone, referring to his days as host of *Steampipe Alley*, a low-budget program of pure kiddie mayhem. "It was five years of booze and dope." Mr. Cantone was in good voice and so he unleashed a Jerry Lewis-like howl: "Five years of pills and drugs!"

A rush of laughter from the cocktail tables. There was Mortimer Zuckerman busting a gut. Yes, the people there were with Mario Cantone, feeling they'd stumbled upon what all New Yorkers crave. That is, Someone New.

NOVEMBER 27, 1995   BY CANDACE BUSHNELL

SEX AND THE CITY: He Loves His Little Meeskeit, But He Won't Take Her Home to Mom

WALDEN'S FIANCÉE WAS OUT of town at a collagen convention. On his own, Walden always got lonely. It reminded him of a time when he had really been lonely, for months on end that seemed to drag into years. And it always brought him around to the same memory, of the woman who had made him feel better, and of what he'd done to her.

Walden met her at a party filled with very pretty people. This being Manhattan, she was nicely dressed in a short black dress that showed off breasts that were on the large side. But she had a modest face. Beautiful long black hair, though. Ringlets. "They always have one great feature," Walden said, and took a sip of his martini.

Libby had gone to Columbia undergrad, Harvard grad school. She talked to him about law. She told him about her childhood, growing up with four sisters in North Carolina. She was 27 and had a grant to make a documentary. She leaned forward and removed a hair from his sweater. "Mine," she said, and laughed. They talked for a long time. He finished a second beer.

"Do you want to come over to my place?" she asked.

Libby was definitely a one-night stand. She wasn't pretty enough to date, to be seen with in public.

"But what does that mean, really?" Stephen interrupted.

"I just thought she was uglier than me," Walden said.

When they got to Libby's apartment—a basic two-bedroom in a high-rise on Third Avenue that she shared with her cousin—she opened the refrigerator and took out a beer. When she bent over in the refrigerator light, he saw that she was a little on the heavy side. She turned around and unscrewed the cap and handed the bottle to him. "I just want you to know," she said. "I really want to have sex with you."

"I found myself very uninhibited," Walden said. "Because she wasn't pretty. The stakes were lower; the emotion higher. There wasn't any pressure because I knew I couldn't date her." He fell asleep with his arms around her.

"The next morning," Walden said, "I woke up and felt at ease. Very relaxed. I'd been feeling tormented for some time and, with Libby, I suddenly felt peaceful. It was the first honest emotional connection I'd had in a while. So I immediately panicked and had to leave."

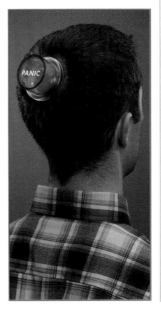

DECEMBER 11, 1995
BY JIM WINDOLF

HE DID HER, SO MERRILL DOES DAVE: CONFESSIONS OF EX-MS. LATE NIGHT

SHE CAME UP WITH A SOLUtion for the introduction problem. David Letterman could come out and say: "And now, the only guest this evening with whom I've had oral sex, Merrill Markoe!"

Instead, Dave introduced her in his polite and sincere mode: "Our next guest had a long relationship with this show and, uh, yours truly."

It would look funny if the host of *Late Show With David Letterman* didn't refer to their past. On the other hand, she's got a book out in paperback now, and people should know she's a writer and she's doing all right and she certainly doesn't think of herself as Dave's ex, so why introduce her that way?

"She has since been lucky enough to move on to greener pastures and this is a copy, now in paperback, of her very, very funny book, *How to Be Hap-Hap-Happy Like Me*. Ladies and gentlemen, please welcome back Merrill Markoe. Merrill!"

GEORGE GURLEY INTERVIEWS GRAYDON CARTER

Well, I really had a wonderful time at *The Observer*. At one point after we sold *Spy*, I wanted to start up a newspaper that would cover the city socio-professionally, rather than geographically. I was sort of off-handedly raising money for it, when I bumped into Arthur Carter at a dinner party in Connecticut, and asked him if he'd be interested. He said, "Listen, why don't you come and do it at *The Observer*?" I don't know if you've looked at those early *Observer*s, but they were pretty sleepy. But I thought I might as well learn the newspaper game on somebody else's dime, so I accepted Arthur's offer.

I took two weeks off after leaving *Spy*, and worked on a 9-month, 12-month, 18-month plan, so that the day I walked in there, I would have a rough idea of what I was going to do. The first two days were just spent cleaning house. I don't mean firing people and such. I mean, physically cleaning the offices, which were a mess.

Aimee Bell, who I brought over from *Spy*, and I then went to work on the actual newspaper. Have I mentioned how sleepy it was? It was like the most dreary Metro section you've ever read in your life. Acres of stories about community board meetings and photographs of park benches. A number of the columnists were seriously dusty. But for the first three or four months, I just let them be and the dustiest of them just gradually faded away. I thought I shouldn't knock what was there when I arrived, and that it was best not to alienate the old readers before I got some new ones.

Also, we had no money. One thing I used to do was to take all the British newspapers home on the weekend, and tear out all these great profiles of literary and theater figures, stories on books that were about to come out, and wonderful features about New York. Aimee and I would get on the phone Monday morning and scoop up the syndication rights, often for as little as a pound. I'd then get Barry Blitt to do an illustration, and that was the way a lot of our features found their way into the paper.

I had a small, narrow office in the *Observer* townhouse and had a long desk built in. I bought a refractory table and this beautiful green leather barrel chair for guests. I assume it's still in Peter Kaplan's office. I loved coming over to the

> *It was sort of the mop-up period from the '80s. There were still these bloated human floats from the '80s parade, and the '90s hadn't established themselves.*

East Side; I would arrive most mornings at 6:30 and be the only person there for two or three hours. There was a casement window at the end of my office that had a lovely view of the garden below. I was really very happy there.

Did you have fun with Arthur at lunch?
Lunch was just O.K. I do remember once at Lutece, Richard Nixon came over to say hello, and it sticks in my mind that he gave us a business card, which I thought was very funny. Anyway, after about the first six months, people started actually reading the paper. But I wanted my friends outside New York to read it as well, so I came up with a hundred-person comp list and I would mail the paper to them every week. Now unbeknownst to me at the time, Si Newhouse makes a twice-yearly world tour of his properties, and he's in Europe, this is like the spring of 1992, and everywhere he goes, in Paris and London, his editors have a copy of this pink newspaper on their desk. I think he came back with the thought that "everybody's reading this thing!" and that the editor must be onto something. A couple of months later, he called me up for a chat.

Small circulation doesn't matter if you find the right 10,000 readers?
Back in the day, before blockbusters like *Jaws* and *Star Wars*, movies were platformed—they'd open in a couple of theaters in New York and L.A., lock in their reviews and some good word of mouth, and then roll out to other cities. At *Spy* we knew we didn't have much money and we aimed for an initial circulation of 25,000—a small number, but if we got the right 25,000, we figured we could build it out from there. And *The Observer*'s circulation was similarly small—and still is, relatively, but it hits the audience that it is going for.

There were like 13 of you in that one-half of the fourth floor? And the bathroom situation—not so good?
I brought a brakeman's cup to the office.

And the staff that was there?
I didn't go crazy. I've never been one to immediately come in and toss a lot of people out. One of the people who I found instantly difficult to deal with was Charles Bagli, who covered real estate. I got into lots of fights with him. But about six months in, we got to know each other, and I grew to appreciate that he was the most valuable reporter on the staff. He now works for *The Times*.

What about the transition from the *Spy* sensibility to *The Observer*?

Graydon Carter is editor of *Vanity Fair.*

George Gurley Interviews Graydon Carter

Well, if it's a newspaper that's coming into your house every week, it's got to be a lot cheerier and kinder than a satirical monthly. Also, I wanted to avoid using all the same tricks we had used so effectively at *Spy*. So I went out of my way not to make it mean. I meant it as sort of a cozy publication for the Upper East Side. I was very influenced by P. G. Wodehouse's *Psmith, Journalist*, which is set in the teens in New York City. Psmith, who is one hell of a character, steps in and takes over a small, sleepy paper and endeavors to bring it to light. I was very inspired by that book.

I'm told that every Wednesday you would put Post-It notes on each reporter's desk with their assignments for the next week. How did you know what you wanted from each?
I would go out at night and come back with tons of little scraps of paper with ideas on them and sort of empty them out on my desk and divvy them up among the reporters.

What were you paying people?
A hundred dollars a week or something. Not a lot.

Do you remember a moment that you thought this was really working, clicking?
Well, you'd go to a dinner, and all of a sudden, for the first time, someone would say, "I read that article about such and such in the paper." I also started getting calls—this was before email and just after faxes. You can tell in an instant when what you're putting out there is beginning to be read. About six months in, I knew that the paper was hitting that certain segment of New York I was looking for.

What about that time in N.Y.C., 1991, was that a good time to be doing this?
It actually was. It was sort of the mop-up period from the '80s. There were still these bloated human floats from the '80s parade, and the '90s hadn't yet established themselves.

What about what the other publications were doing at the time?
Other publications—like *The New York Times* and *The Wall Street Journal*—told you about the world. But my goal for our readers was to tell them about their world. If you lived between 53rd Street and 96th Street, and Fifth Avenue and the East River—that's who we were going for in that first year. And my plan was that once we knocked out the East Side, we'd go down to the Village and come up the West Side.

So you needed another four years or something?
Three years, for quote-unquote total New York domination.

Were there certain people you couldn't write about?
No, in fact, it was the opposite. One time when I was having lunch with Arthur, I said, "Listen, I just wanted to give you a heads up, we're going to do a story on Sandy Weill." And he said, "Oh no, fine, do it, do it, it's fine." And I thought, "My God, what a great person to work for," because Sandy Weill and Arthur had been partners in their brokerage firm in the '50s and '60s, and I thought, editorial-independence-wise, "That's encouraging." A little later, I told him we were going to do a story on Arthur Leavitt Jr. (another of his former partners) and that the piece might be a little tough in places. And Arthur said, "Absolutely fine!" And then I thought, "Wait, is he playing a game of chess I don't know about?"

So you got a call from S. I. Newhouse in June of '92?
Yes. As I said, he kept seeing *The New York Observer* on his rounds. And we knew each other socially. He asked if I was interested in either *The New Yorker* or *Vanity Fair*.

Which were you thinking?
The New Yorker—we had spent five years ridiculing *Vanity Fair*. And so for two weeks, I worked on a plan for what I would do at *The New Yorker*, and then one day it changed to *Vanity Fair*. I have no idea what happened, but I assume it had something to do with Tina Brown. Years later, I told him about the comp list and that that was why he kept seeing it during his travels back in 1991. He just laughed.

What do you think of *The Observer*'s future?
I can't figure out why it doesn't make money. I think it's a seriously great paper. It's a top-notch paper, it matters and it's read by a certain number of the right people.

We have the same shirt on, don't we?
How very good of you—the hallmark of a great reporter.

1996

▶ **Bill Clinton celebrates his 50th birthday at Radio City Music Hall**

 Gallerist Mary Boone ditches "homogenous" Soho for uptown digs

▶ **Mike Ovitz, over? CAA power agent now: Walt Disney's No. 2**

Does my butt look big in this bankruptcy? Barneys files for Chapter 11

▶ **David Foster Wallace's 1,079-page novel *Infinite Jest* gives readers hernias**

 Private-school kids snort Ritalin for that extra oomph

▶ **Journalist Michael Kinsley quits print for clean Slate on the World Wide Web**

Rich New Yorkers stream into clinics for high colonic irrigation

▶ **Madcap Manhattanite Sandy Pittman** social-climbs Mount Everest

1996

◇◇◇◇◇◇◇◇

JANUARY 8, 1996   BY ROB SPEYER

N.Y.C. Sperm Count Tops That of L.A. in 20-Year Sample

UNBEKNOWN TO THEM, NEW Yorkers may possess the ultimate weapon in their struggle against Los Angelenos for bicoastal bragging rights. Dr. Harry Fisch, a Park Avenue urologist and fertility specialist, has discovered that New York City men have more potent sperm than their Los Angeles rivals. Dr. Fisch is expected to present his finding at a conference of the American Urological Society in May in Orlando, Fla. Until then, the good doctor, who conducted his research at Columbia-Presbyterian Hospital, is offering few specifics about his report: "I'm very concerned that it will come out in *The National Enquirer,*" he said from his car phone. "I want to be

famous in an academic sense, not as a joke."

Dr. Fisch studied sperm samples donated over the last 20 years by men to sperm banks in New York and Los Angeles. He found that New Yorkers consistently have both higher sperm counts and better semen quality, according to several medical sources familiar with the report. Appropriately, the New York semen was collected at a depository in the Empire State Building, that phallic monument to the city's virility.

Medical experts contacted by *The Observer* believe that Los Angelenos can blame the inferior state of their semen—which can have a major impact on one's ability to conceive children—on several factors: warm weather, pollution and drugs. Not to mention that carefree L.A. lifestyle. Dr. Joseph Feldschuh, director of Idant, the Manhattan sperm bank that Dr. Fisch used, suggested that L.A. men may simply be having too much sex. "Sexual frequency makes a difference," said Dr. Feldschuh. "If you have an ejaculation every day, your sperm count drops." The doctor paused thoughtfully. "It's a real possibility."

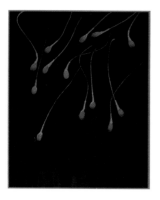

JANUARY 15, 1996   BY PHOEBE HOBAN

MARY BOONE DITCHES SOHO FOR THE UPTOWN BOONIES

DOWNTOWN IS DEAD. AGAIN.

At least according to Mary Boone, who ought to be in a position to know. After nearly 20 years on SoHo's main street, the Boonette, as Robert Hughes once dubbed her, will this spring vacate her thrice renovated premises at 417 West Broadway and move uptown—to 745 Fifth Avenue, just across from Bergdorf Goodman and cater-corner from the Warner Brothers Studio Store, with her own Eloise-style view of the Plaza. After years of looking for a suitable space, Ms. Boone is finally bidding the downtown art world goodbye. And, as far as she's concerned, not a minute too soon.

Dressed in an emerald-green Hermés jacket over a lapis-blue catsuit, Ms. Boone dug the spike of one high-heeled boot into the limestone floor in her office. "I think the energy and focus of art has shifted uptown," she announced. "I feel there's a lack of specificity downtown right now. It's just about a kind of homogenous tourism. What was once an asset—being accessible on the ground floor on West Broadway—is now a liability. There are people who come down here and go in every door."

JANUARY 15, 1996 BY PETER STEVENSON

'Buffalo' Buford, Literary Gambler, Tries His Luck at Tina's *New Yorker*

ONE AFTERNOON BEFORE Christmas, Bill Buford slid his barrel-chested frame into a U-shaped banquette at "44," the restaurant in the Royalton Hotel. As *The New Yorker*'s literary and fiction editor, Mr. Buford was awarded one of the restaurant's best booths, a luxury he seemed neither to mind nor indulge.

When Mr. Buford came to *The New Yorker* last April, there was talk—slivers of it reportedly coming from him—that he was editor Tina Brown's heir apparent. After all, as an expatriate American in London he had made *Granta* the most talked about literary quarterly in the world. He was intimate friends with writers like Martin Amis, Julian Barnes and Salman Rushdie. He himself had written a well-respected book. He was ferociously social, a big personality. His leaving *Granta* for *The New Yorker* made front-page headlines in England.

But just before the New Year broke over Manhattan, Ms. Brown announced the elevation of two other editors—David Kuhn, to features director, and Dorothy Wickenden, to executive editor. The power seemed to lie with the nonfiction editors, who could bring in the more "glamorous" pieces about, say, Michael Ovitz or CBS. Mr. Buford's corner of the magazine—fiction and gritty literary reportage—was secure—but still just a corner.

At lunch, Mr. Buford said he wasn't giving much thought to being editor of *The New Yorker*. "It hasn't been discussed," he said, then continued: "One of the reasons I left *Granta* was because I had become 'Mr. *Granta*'. ... I had derived enormous pleasure from writing a book, and wanted to write more books, and I could see I was never going to be able to as long as I was this 'Mr. *Granta*'." He paused, then laughed. "*The New Yorker* would be so much worse—it's a fucking weekly." He flashed a smile. When Mr. Buford smiles, his eyes are full of dark, manic glee.

His own turf, rest assured, will be fiercely guarded. "The intermittent interest in things nonliterary, that now appears in *The New Yorker*, shouldn't obscure the fact that it is the only publication that is overwhelmingly committed to text," said Mr. Buford. "It's a text magazine, and it's trying to stimulate the kind of writing nearly a million people will buy."

Among the writers he has brought into—or back to—the fold are Paul Theroux, Leonard Michaels, V.S. Naipaul, Tobias Wolff, Amos Oz and Peter Carey.

"What I want to do is get writers to start using the magazine, exploiting the magazine, as a valid and important place to play," he said. "Writers have become alienated by magazines. ... It's going to take a while,

persuading the Peter Careys and Paul Austers not to be so jumpy, not to mention the Don DeLillos and Thomas Pynchons."

Mr. Buford took a swallow of his red wine. "The business doesn't have a sense of play about it. Everything's become business. It's become the book that has to sell this many titles, earn out the advance, meet this sales rep's target, then publicity: 14 cities, 17 cities, 42-city tour—that's not fun. I want to get some fun in the magazines again."

'BILL BUFFALO'

In the early 1980's, the British poet James Fenton threw a party at his home in Oxford. The cusp of British literary bad-boyhood was there: writers Martin Amis, Ian McEwan, Redmond O'Hanlon. There was also a relative newcomer, an American named Bill Buford. He was in his late 20s, and editor of *Granta*, a Cambridge undergraduate literary magazine that had collapsed in the early 1970's when the treasurer took all the money and ran off with a girl to Paris. The American was on a mission to revive it.

"We weren't used to someone packed with so much testosterone," said Mr. O'Hanlon.

"He looked like some sort of exotic creature from the plains," said novelist Julian Barnes, who met Mr. Buford around that time. "He quickly acquired the nickname 'Bill Buffalo.'"

Bill Buffalo was there to drink and do some business. "By the end of the night," said Mr. O'Hanlon, "he'd signed us all up."

A dozen years later, Mr. Buford would come home to his Cambridge house to find Tina Brown had called four times. Why he agreed to come back to America is a matter of some speculation among his friends.

"He felt he'd done 50 issues of *Granta*, and *The New Yorker* was offering such a lot of money he couldn't refuse," said Mr. O'Hanlon, "and a lot of debts may have been building up, we don't know."

"He had made a decision to be in exile and remake his life here," said Mr. Barnes by phone from London. "There must be some emotional and atavistic need to remake your life in your own country."

"Men in their 40s either have a difficult time, or they don't," said Mr. Amis. "Life either goes in a straight line, or it takes a curve or two. I think Bill falls into the latter, as do I. He's going through a bit of that right now."

THE LAW IS A JEALOUS MISTRESS

JANUARY 22, 1996   BY ERICA JONG

Spare the Rodham?
Hillary Storms New York

WHEN HILLARY RODHAM CLINTON FIRST APPEARED ON THE NA-
tional scene a few years ago, she was a blast—not a breath—of fresh
air. Here was a woman like most American women: a breadwinner,
a working mother, outspoken in her opinions and visibly strong.
Unlike Nancy Reagan, who secretly manipulated the White House
schedules with the aid of her astrologer, or Jacqueline Kennedy, who
always cooed softly that husband and children came first, or Barbara Bush, who never tried to influence George with her sensible
views of abortion, H.R.C. was a woman of the next century—unafraid
of seeming as powerful as she was. Her very demeanor said: Times
have changed; now even women have to watch their backs. The protection racket is over, and it's every Amazon for herself.

Hillary Clinton makes a lot if people nervous because she *is* the
new American woman. She knows nobody is going to protect her—
quite the opposite, they're going to try to *kill* her. She knows she has
to be twice as tough to get half as far. She is the woman created by
the decline of the American economy. She can no longer afford conspicuous consumption. Even if she *wanted* to stay at home with the
kid, she couldn't *afford* to. She can hardly remember the last time she
got laid and she ain't mellow. The Republicans created her but they
don't seem to like her very much. As for the rest of us—we'd better
get used to her: She's the New Woman of the Next Century and she's
here to stay.

JANUARY 29, 1996   BY FRANK DECARO

BETTER BANKRUPTCY THAN TACKY:
BARNEYS IS MANHATTAN STYLE

THE YOUNG CLERK, IN A TOO-
short skirt and too-high heels,
stood just beyond the handbags
that look like *peau de soie* origa-
mi. She was squared off against
a 50-ish blond customer in
stretch jeans and Etonic sneakers who clearly was not having
a good hair day one recent Saturday morning at Barneys New
York. "We're not going out of
business," the clerk assured the
frowzy woman. "We have no
cash flow problems!"

That likely is true. But the
owners of Barneys New York—
the Pressman family, led by the
Levi-wearing,   cigar-smoking
son named Gene—have fallen
on hard times. A few weeks ago,
the Pressmans filed Chapter 11
proceedings in U.S. Bankruptcy
Court and sued their Japanese
partner, Isetan Company. The
Japanese retail monolith, as we
all know by now, had funded
Barneys' expansion from its
original Chelsea location, at
Seventh Avenue and 17th Street,
to its more swank, $270 million
uptown digs and beyond.

Barneys New York—once a
purveyor of off-price suits whose
slogan was "No bunk, no junk, no
imitations"—now has stores in
Beverly Hills, Chicago and other
cities in America and Japan.

These days, though, the Pressmans are on the receiving end of
that attitude. The Barneys bankruptcy has touched a nerve with
New Yorkers and, at least among
journalists, set off a kick-'em-
while-they're-down   backlash.
Maureen Dowd ripped the store
in her Jan. 18 column in *The New
York Times*, describing it as "an
NOCD (Not Our Class, Darling)
joint" that "features designers
so avant that no one has heard
of them." A *Newsweek* column by
senior writer Johnnie L. Roberts
ran in that magazine's Jan. 22 issue with the overline "Revenge"
and the headline "It Couldn't
Happen to a Nicer Store." Mr.
Roberts, who contends he was
a victim of racism when he was
accused of shoplifting six years
ago at Barneys in Chelsea, wrote,
"See you at the Going Out of
Business sale."

FEBRUARY 5, 1996:
BY ADAM BEGLEY

BOOK REVIEW: Three Pounds of Literary Literature for Gen X: Go Ahead, Read Yourself to Death

Infinite Jest
by David Foster Wallace.
Little, Brown & Company,
1,079 pages, $29.95

INFINITE JEST IS A THREE-BRICK novel, a hernia risk, a forest slayer. The 1,079-page tome is brilliant, funny and dauntingly difficult, the magnum opus of a hitherto underknown 33-year-old wunderkind. But come February, when it lands with a thud in bookstores, what people will twig to is that it's big, "the biggest novel of the year," Little Brown confidently boasts. A teasing series of six postcards, sent out over the last eight months to reviewers, editors and booksellers, announced "Infinite Style. Infinite Substance. Infinite Writer." A reader's edition signed by the author; a nine-city reading tour; three more postcards, blurb-adorned; an advertising campaign—the hype is a kind of sign language meant to impress both booksellers and the media with the publisher's unwavering commitment to the product.

FEBRUARY 26, 1996   BY SARAH FRIEDMAN

TALES OUT OF SCHOOL: NEW PRIVATE SCHOOL CRAZE: KIDS SNORT THEIR RITALIN

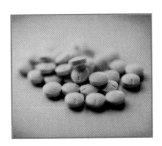

ON A DECEMBER MORNING DURing finals week, an upperclassman at the private Dwight School and her friends were sitting at the back of an Upper West Side coffee shop. The table in the popular Dwight hangout was hidden from the street. The girl opened her bag and removed a vanity mirror, the barrel of a clear Bic pen and a tiny black and yellow tub of Carmex lip gloss, from which she extracted a small white pill. She placed the pill on the mirror and mashed it up with her driver's license. The she leaned forward and, using the pen barrel, snorted the pulverized pill up through her nostril, Later that day, she had a history exam.

The white tablet was not something she bought from a stranger on the street, nor anything smuggled across a border or manufactured in an illicit lab; it was Ritalin, the drug prescribed to sufferers, mostly preteenagers and teenagers, of Attention Deficit Disorder. Kids who have A.D.D. and swallow the prescribed dosage of Ritalin (usually from 10 to 60 milligrams) find it quells hyperactivity, helping them to focus, concentrate and calm down. But you're not supposed to snort it. More importantly, the Dwight student didn't have A.D.D., and neither do many of the New York private school kids who, mirroring a nationwide trend, have made Ritalin something of a trendy drug, used for its reputed ability to boost a grade and boost a party. In those who do not have A.D.D. and tend to double the dosage and snort it, Ritalin produces a burst of energy and euphoria, which can last for a few hours.

On the Upper East Side on a recent Saturday night, several Riverdale Country School students were getting ready to go out to a club. Preparations included hair combing, collar adjusting and Ritalin snorting. The boys weren't concerned with increasing their powers of concentration. "It juices you, it makes you really excited and happy," said one. "It makes for a fun night and you can drink a lot." None of the kids present had been diagnosed with A.D.D. Conveniently, however, many of their friends had, and had plenty of Food and Drug Administration-approved, physician-prescribed Ritalin to give away or sell.

But it isn't just kids who are abusing Ritalin; parents, too, have been accused of hauling uncooperative, misbehaving offspring off to the doctor and basically demanding Ritalin. "I cannot tell you how many times a child has been brought in diagnosed with A.D.D. and it turns out the mother's just run away to Arizona and the father's married someone a couple of years older than the kid," said Dr. Miller. "There's a kind of hysteria in which people want to explain away all sorts of other causes for what looks like rising A.D.D." According to one teacher at Dwight, Ritalin at the school is "widely overprescribed."

Several Dwight students interviewed by *The Observer* estimated that, between licit and illicit use, about half the high school is using Ritalin. Whether or not they are exaggerating, their comments point to how deeply Ritalin

has penetrated into the New York private school subculture. Dr. George Kamen, the school psychologist, said he knows of only five students with Ritalin prescriptions, but pointed out that students often have outside therapists who may issue prescriptions without notifying the school. "I'm not aware of that," he said when asked about recreational Ritalin use. "I'm surprised."

Nationally, Ritalin prescriptions have increased more than 600 percent over the last five years, according to the Drug Enforcement Agency. More than 2 million children have been prescribed Ritalin. "Over the last 20 years, the diagnosis of A.D.D., with or without learning disability, has been widely recognized," said Dr. Miller. Previously, he explained, "if a child was behaving badly or doing poorly in school, we looked at him as bad and stupid. It's possible, if it's gone too far, to claim all badness is madness, and everyone is mad. You'll end up with every adult on Prozac and every child on Ritalin."

There is no definitive test for A.D.D.; a doctor bases his or her diagnosis on an evaluation of the patient, and on the subjective evaluations from parents and teachers. A.D.D. often coexists with other problems, such as learning disabilities and conduct disorders. Children suffering from other problems may end up with a Ritalin prescription at the behest of ambitious, worried parents. "It's a quick fix for parents who want their children to get an extra edge academically," said a Manhattan doctor who specializes in adolescent medicine. "If parents hear of something that's going to help kids' grades, they'll want it. They press doctors to prescribe it."

JANUARY 8, 1996   BY WM FERGUSON

THE OBSERVATORY: IN CYBERIA, NO ONE CAN HEAR YOU SCREAM

IF THE WORLD WIDE WEB DOESN'T GO THE WAY OF THE CB radio—and it might yet—the autumn of 1995 will be remembered as the birth of a medium. It was certainly the first time that anybody was making any real money on the Internet—namely, a 24-year-old software Wunderkind. The day in September that Marc Andreessen's Netscape Communications went public, Mr. Andreessen, who had developed the much-touted Netscape Web browser, made $58.3 million. And if you needed proof of a willing audience, *The New York Times*—on the front page, no less—elevated the World Wide Web to mass medium status. (*The Times* tempered its blow to its luddite readers, identifying the Web as "a newer-fangled medium.")

Those luddite readers received another jolt: Michael Kinsley, one of journalism's glamour boys, was going to Cyberia! He was moving to Seattle! He was off to edit a Webzine.

"Someone is going to produce good stuff on the Web," Mr. Kinsley said, repeating his new-media mantra. "I'm absolutely, totally convinced of that. Whether it's me ..."

However self-deprecating Mr. Kinsley's remarks may be, they have a caustic edge: the assumption that there's nothing of value on the Web. That would likely be contested by the hundreds of journalists who already publish in the datasphere. Some are from television; some from magazines and newspapers; more than a few come from absolutely nowhere. But because of his reputation, and the fact that he has chosen his digital exile, Michael Kinsley has been elevated to spiritual leader of the content providers (1).

If a generalization must be made, it's this: In Cyberia, it's hard to tell who's waving and who's drowning.

Before Mr. Kinsley, the perception was that online journalism was a graveyard. Much like the striking writers of the *Detroit Free Press*, whose final option was to put up a Web site, journalists in the datasphere were viewed as lost souls. If you were a cyberjournalist, there were two reasons: Either you couldn't get work anywhere else, or you were in exile, like some deposed media shah (2) waiting for an opposing faction to be ousted so that you could go back to Quark Copy Desk and an office (with a door) at 350 Madison.

Susan Mulcahy, who was Page Six editor at the *New York Post* and editor in chief of *Avenue*, was already in a sort of exile when Tom Phillips, previously publisher at *Spy*, called her in early 1994. He was interested in starting an online gossip service. Living in a small town in Oregon and not expecially enjoying the freelance life, Ms. Mulcahy accepted his offer. After expanding the gossip mill to be a general entertainment service, she became editor and chief publisher—job descriptions are up for grabs in cyberspace—of Mr. Showbiz. Her colleagues in New York reacted two ways:

"Some people recoiled: 'Computers? That's so sad.' The other half of my friends were like, 'That's where things are going, that's so smart, you're in on the ground floor,' But in New York," Ms. Mulcahy said, "most people were in the Oh My God That's So Sad camp."

The perception of digital exile may be dependent on geography. "There's a complete East Coast-West Coast split on that," said Dave Talbot, editor of Salon, a literary Webzine. "In some ways, it was despera-tion that got us here. But San Francisco, for the first time since *Rolling Stone* and *Mother Jones* [started], is feeling like a publishing center." So when Mr. Kinsley announced that he would be vacating the East Coast power corridor for Seattle, where his Microsoft magazine will originate, his news was greeted by his colleagues as visionary—or the equivalent of going over to the dark side of the Force.

Ms. Mulcahy, like most of the content providers who have been laboring in obscurity, views his intentions with genteel skepticism. "I think some of the people in the industry were sort of stunned by the statements that Kinsley made," Ms. Mulcahy said.

Suck, a Webzine, was a bit more explicit: "[Mr. Kinsley's] recent public musings that 'Someone is going to create the first great magazine on the Web—maybe it could be me' tends to reinforce our initial impression that we've got another vainglorious newbie (3) on our hands."

NEW(BIE) JOURNALISM?

Even alongside that most Dylan Thomas of adjectives, the word newbie is a tip-off to the digital myopia of Web writing at the moment. To anyone who isn't an aspiring computer geek, the term—derogatory Webspeak for neophyte—has about as much pejorative power as sillyhead. No matter. The lexicon is about to be rewritten. The content providers have arrived.

Whether any of them know what they're doing is another question entirely.

Maybe Mr. Kinsley is vainglorious, but he'll also admit to not having a clue. He has expressed a disdain for hypertext (4)—only the raison 'd être of the WWW—and all the bells and whistles of multimedia. In fact, he tends to play up his lack of technical savvy. When asked if he's seen anything on the Web worthy of cribbing from, Mr. Kinsley replied: "My computer's all packed up," this being the month of his cross-country move. "What I've been doing is writing down on little scraps of paper the names of Web sites that people recommended," he said. "I've got a lot more browsing to do." It's a charming image—little scraps of paper!—and it clearly positions Mr. Kinsley as a writer among the technophiles.

"I think he's gonna have his head handed to him," said Joshua Quittner. Mr. Quittner is the editor of The Netly News, a site on Time Warner's pathfinder service. Pathfinder (http://pathfinder.com) is not so much a Webzine as a sprawling database comprising selections from virtually all of Time Warner's media holdings. While most of the sites listed in Pathfinder are simply archives of repurposed text—*Sports Illustrated*, *People*—The Netly News has no print counterpart. Mr. Quittner wrote about the digital world for *Newsday*, *Wired* and then *Time*, where his proposal for a Webzine was approved. If he comes across as a bit of a digital zealot, it is because he's found his niche. And he digs the technology. "There are all these new devices that will fit into the journalist's bag of tricks. And Kinsley best learn how to use them. It makes no sense to come online and try and reproduce a magazine. They do not survive the transition to a computer monitor."

"If The Netly News has a strength, it would be that Quittner has a history of doing pretty decent pieces," said Joey Anuff, the editor of Suck. "But his strength is not in operating a Web site. He doesn't

If a generalization must be made, it's this: In Cyberia, it's hard to tell who's waving and who's drowning.

know shit about operating a Web site."

Technological mastery is a sore sport for the content provider. Reasonably, many Web-tempted print journalists argue that they aren't expected to know the ins and outs of printing presses or the distribution networks of their publications, so why should cyberjournalists have to be familiar with every facet of their medium?

"Kinsley has said that what he's going to do is not a technical but journalistic thing. So what's the point?" asked Jon Katz. "It doesn't play to the strength of the Web." Mr. Katz, who writes for *Wired* and whose book about the war between the literary and computer cultures, *Virtuous Reality*, is due from Random House in October, predicts a mass migration back to print in a couple years.

"The journalists who have gone online don't have a clue," he said. "I do some work for the Web. I have no desire to do it full-time. As a writer, I would be very anxious about not being in print."

But even for those who do know how to operate a Web site, the hype of the new technology is well beyond its availability. As yet, multimedia is a solution in search of a problem.

For example, ex-*Rolling Stone* editor and writer Michael Goldberg's Addicted to Noise sports some of the most vivid graphics of any Webzine; consider that both a draw and a warning. Addicted to Noise literally vibrates on your screen. In fact, as with any site so loaded with visuals and hyperlinks, partaking in ATN requires a remarkable commitment. Never mind the 2 minutes, 18 seconds it can take to download the eye-numbing contents page even with a fast modem. As for content, Mr. Goldberg has corralled some big rock writers—Dave Marsh, Ira

Robbins, Greil Marcus. But considering the pace at which information travels through telephone wires, Mr. Goldberg's boast that Addicted to Noise is "90,000 words of rock-and-roll a month" sounds like a veiled threat. So the technology is not there—yet. Yet is important. It is the hope of all content providers.

1 **Content provider is the new media term for ... those who provide content!** It describes both a Webzine and its writers. Its current vogue reflects the shift away from repurposing text—taking a *Time* article and dumping the words online, for example—to providing original material.

2 After less than two years as Time Inc.'s editor of new media, Walter Isaacson abandoned the brave new world of online journalism for a more conventional role, managing editor of *Time* magazine.

3 Despite the Webzine's adolescent moniker, the Suck newbie critique is not to be taken lightly. In interviews for this story, virtually every person held up two Web sites as examples of "doing it right": their own venture and Suck.

4 Hypertext is the language of the World Wide Web. Short for Hypertext Markup Language, or HTML, it works by linking documents on the WWW. For example, certain words in a Web document will be underscored, signifying them as links. By clicking on a link, you are sent to information germane to the highlighted word—usually.

MARCH 18, 1996
BY MICHAEL M. THOMAS

THE OBSERVATORY: SOCIETY SAFARI

AS WITH SO MANY CONSEQUEN-tial events in my life, the tale begins with a phone call from My Beloved Stepmother, or M.B.S.

"Darling," she said, "I want you to join me on a safari." "Gee," I responded, "I didn't know they had safaris to Taillevent."

Well, it turned out Paris wasn't what she had in mind. Africa was. It seemed like the Wildlife Conservation Society, on whose board M.B.S. sits, was sponsoring a bunch of trips to East Africa in celebration of its 100th anniversary. She felt that a fortnight out under the wide equatorial sky looking at nature pure in instinct and deed might do wonders in relieving me of an entirely unhealthy preoccupation with the socioeconomic or cultural parasites responsible for the way we live now.

How could I but agree? Not only had I never been to Africa, I had never traveled as part of an organized or affinity group. The late Robert Benchley had observed that there were two classes of travel: first, and with children. I had long suspected, and was curious to see for myself, that even lower than the latter in the descending circles of Travel Hell must be "Group"—when 10 or more adults are brought together more or less randomly into the metaphorical equivalent of the sealed railway car in which—in 1917—Lenin was transported across Germany to the Finland station.

I am someone, mind you, who bears the scars of family ski vacations, where many are always at the mercy of the one who forgets mittens, or ski pass, but such slips are, if irritating, inadvertent.

MARCH 25, 1996   BY ALEX KUCZYNSKI

THE NEW YORK WORLD: OVERLOADED NEW YORKERS HOOKED ON HIGH COLONICS

IN THE REPORTS FROM DI-ana's impending divorce from Charles, the list of her annual expenditures includes: $153,000 for clothes, $6,400 for hair treatments and $15,3000 for psychotherapy, aromatherapy and ... *colonic irrigation.*

"They take all the aggro [aggravation] out of me," the Princess of Wales has reportedly said about the process. Now, an increasing number of New Yorkers, who certainly have their own share of "aggro," are turning themselves over to practitioners who shoot between 15 and 20 gallons of distilled water through their bodies in 45-minutes sessions.

It should come as no surprise that these high-powered enemas are catching on here. For this is the city that pours too much *into* people, a city that overloads the senses, a city of food and smoke and booze and taxi exhaust. A good colonic is meant to give residents of this thankless town a chance to *let it all out.*

Acolytes claim colonic irrigations rid their bodies of that ill-defined, New Age bugaboo—*toxins*—and help prevent colon cancer; some people do it to kick-start a diet, although it's clear that you don't lose fat from a colonic.

How does it work? Rudy M.

Cooper, who has practiced colon therapy on New Yorkers for the past 12 years, explained every last detail: "A speculum, or scope, is inserted in the rectum. The scope, or speculum, has two tubes attached, one for water to enter and one for waste to exit. The therapist has control over the water entering the person, er, client. And after the speculum or scope is lubricated and inserted in the rectum, the water is brought into the system, slowly, until the colon itself is filled to the extent that it is able to be filled.

"And the colon therapist—I guess people have different styles—but then they start massaging the abdomen and bringing in the water as needed for the procedure of breaking down the old waste and helping the system to evacuate organically."

At Ismail Kibirige's office at the SoHo Professional Health Center, one wall is plastered with head shots of the models and actresses who are his regular clients. Mr. Kibirige said he sees about 250 regular clients.

A reporter who wanted to have a little something in common with the princess decided to pay a visit to Mr. Kibirige's immaculate office. Mr. Kibirige played an inspirational tape about colonic irrigation and got started.

As the tube was inserted, the reporter remembered Grandma's thermometer; as the water flowed in, she felt a little seasick; as the stuff traveled out through tube No. 2, she got that woozy-in-the-intestines feeling typical of a terrible hangover. The session lasted nearly an hour. The bill came to $65.

"I'd say in the last two years membership has nearly doubled," said Bill Tiller, president of the International Association for Colon Hydrotherapy. "We now have about 1,000 members who are practitioners. It's a very large movement."

APRIL 1, 1996 BY JIM WINDOLF

THE NEW YORK WORLD

IN THE NEW ISSUE of *Harper's*, novelist Jonathan Franzen almost knocks himself out trying to explain why serious fiction is still relevant in a culture dominated by TV. He makes his argument in a fake

prose that makes you want to reach for the nearest remote.

Some lines from Mr. Franzen's essay are quoted below, followed by appropriate remarks:

"I, too, was dreaming of escape ..."

I, too, *am an ass.*

"A quarter century ..."

Wouldn't that be the same as *25 years*?

"When I got out of college in 1981 ..."

Ah, the heady days of '81!

"I found a weekend job that enabled both of us to write full time ..."

One of those $50,000-a-year weekend jobs that you hear so much about.

"Broadcast TV breaks pleasure into comforting little units ... the way my father, when I was very young, would cut my French toast into tiny bites."

Oh, the pathos!

"When the Ayatollah Khomeini placed a bounty on Salman Rushdie's head, what seemed archaic to Americans was not his Muslim fanaticism, but the simple fact that he'd become so exercised about a *book*."

I knew *something* seemed archaic to me about that.

"My Hollywood agent, whom I'll call Dicky ..."

Dicky? Naughty, naughty, Mr. Franzen!

"... television has killed the novel of social reportage."

No, you did.

"... elitism doesn't sit well with my American nature ..."

But it sure sits well with Edith Sitwell.

"My belief in manners would make it difficult for me to explain to my brother, who is a fan of Michael Crichton, that the work I'm doing is simply better than Crichton's."

Give me your brother's number. I'll tell him how you feel.

"I took a job teaching undergraduate fiction-writing at a small liberal arts college."

Just tell us the *name* of the college, you big wimp.

"I happen to enjoy living within subway distance of Wall Street and keeping close tabs on the country's shadow government."

I'm sure you do, junior. I bet you ride the rails every couple days to give those guys a good going over.

"I'm still waiting for the non-German-speaking world to get the news that Kafka, for example, is a comic writer."

Extra! Extra! Kafka Comic Writer, Sez Dopey Young Novelist!

"... ours is a country to which hardly anything really terrible has ever happened. The only genuine tragedies to befall us were slavery and the Civil War."

There *was* that little slavery problem but otherwise ...

"I spent the early 90's trapped in a double singularity."

That's funny. I spent the early 90's trapped in an elevator.

"I got a letter from Don DeLillo."

Me, too. That Don. Nice enough guy, but his letters really get on your nerves.

MAY 6, 1996 BY ALEX KUCZYNSKI

Sandy Pittman Social-Climbs Mt. Everest

BASE CAMP, MOUNT EVEREST, APRIL 22: "THIS IS SANDY HILL PITTMAN ... And I'm calling from base camp, at 17,500 feet ..." Sandy Pittman's voice broke and she bent forward, collapsing into the rasping hack known to Tibetan mountaineers as Khumbu cough. She brought the phone back to her mouth to finish the sentence: "... at Mount Everest."

She paused, then went on in a whisper, gripping the phone in hands bigger than many men's. "It's bitterly cold tonight. The temperatures are subzero"—she coughed the wheezing, hard cough—"and it's pitch black." The wind, which can reach 100 miles per hours at base camp, was whipping the camp tents in the background. "It's so dry up here. We're doing extremely strenuous activity and it's extremely cold and dry. It burns"—she coughed—"*burns* the insides of your lungs."

New York, April 26: 41-year-old Sandy Hill Pittman, madcap Manhattan socialite, former fashion editor and avid outdoorswoman, is attempting for the third time to conquer the summit of Everest, first reached by Sir Edmund Hillary and his Sherpa companion Tenzing Norgay in 1953.

The base of the Lhotse face, April 19: "We spotted the bottom half of a human body," said Ms. Pittman. "It was dressed in a climbing suit, leather boots and crampons. There was no head or arms. The discovery was a macabre ending to an otherwise successful climb."

Sharon Hoge's Park Avenue apartment, April 25: "Would you ask her whether I should bring a long-sleeve or sleeveless dress for Katmandu?" said Ms. Hoge.

Base Camp, Mount Everest, April 25: "I'm standing on Mount Everest," said Ms. Pittman. "And I'm not wearing a dress. So I really don't know what to say."

JUNE 24, 1996 BY CANDACE BUSHNELL

SEX AND THE CITY: SEX LIVES OF SERIOUS JOURNALISTS: HE'S A FEMINIST, SHE'S A REAL MAN

MEET JAMES AND WINNIE DIEKE. THE PERFECT COUple. They live in a five-room apartment on the Upper West Side. They graduated from Ivy League colleges (he, Harvard; she, Smith). Winnie is 37, and James is 42—the perfect age difference, they like to say. They've been married nearly 10 years. Their lives revolve around their work and their child. They love to work. Their work keeps them busy. Their work separates them from other people. Their work, in their minds, makes them superior to other people.

They are journalists. Serious journalists.

Winnie writes a politics-and-style column for a major newsmagazine. James is a well-known and highly respected journalist—he writes worthy 5,000- to 10,000-word pieces for publications like *The New York Times Magazine* and *The New Yorker*.

Here are a few of the things Winnie and James agree on: They hate anyone who isn't like them. They hate anyone who is wealthy and gets press. They hate people who do drugs. They hate people who drink too much (unless it's one of their friends, and even then, they complain about the person often). They hate the Hamptons (but take a house—there, anyway, in Sag Harbor). They believe in the poor. They believe in black writers. (They know two, and Winnie is working on becoming friends with a third.)

Winnie believes (no, knows) that she is smarter than James, and as good a journalist as he is, and as good a writer. She often thinks that she is actually better than he (in every way, not just journalism), but he (being a man) has gotten more breaks. James' style of writing and her style of writing (which she picked up from James, who picked it up from other writers of his tall, gaunt, khakis-and-button-down ilk) was not hard to figure out how to do, once she understood the motivation.

Winnie is deeply bitter and James is deeply bitter, but they never talk about it. James is scared of his wife. She doesn't seem to be scared of anything—and that scares him. When Winnie should be scared—when she has an impossible deadline, or can't get people to cooperate on interviews, or doesn't think she's getting the assignments she wants, she gets angry instead of scared. She calls people and screams. She faxes, she e-mails. She marches into her editors' offices and has "hissy fits."

Everyone is just a tiny bit scared of Winnie, and James is scared that one of these days, she won't get the assignment, or she'll get fired.

But she always does get the assignment. At the potluck suppers ("our salon," they call it) they host every other Tuesday night (they invite other serious journalists like themselves, and discuss the political implications of everything from the V-chips to rent hikes, to what's happened to the journalists who were fired from *New York Newsday*, to the scandal of *60 Minutes* pulling its planned segment on the Clinton Whitewater book), Winnie will discuss whatever story she is working on. Everyone will be sitting with Limoges plates on their laps, and they will be eating iceberg lettuce with fat-free salad dressing and skinless chicken breasts, and maybe some rice, and then there's fat-free frozen yogurt for dessert, and Winnie will say, "I want to know what everyone thinks about the new NBC 24-hour news channel. I'm doing my column on it this week." When she started doing this, a few years ago, James thought it was cute. But now he gets annoyed. (He never shows it.) Why is she always asking everyone else what they think? Doesn't she have her own thoughts? And he looks around the room to see if any of the other men (husbands) are sharing the same sentiment.

He can't tell. He can never tell. Maybe if people got drunk—but they only drink little, wee glasses of wine. No one they know drinks hard alcohol anymore. James often wants to ask these other husbands what they think of their wives. Are they scared of them, too? Do they ever have fantasies of pushing their wives down on the bed and ripping off their underpants and ... (James sort of tried something like that with Winnie, but she slapped him and wouldn't talk to him for three days afterward.) Mostly he wants to know: Are other men scared of Winnie?

There are times when James doesn't feel like the man in the relationship. But then he asks himself what Winnie would say if he told her that. She'd say, "What does it mean to 'feel like a man', anyway? What does 'a man' feel like?" And since he never can answer those questions, he has to agree with Winnie.

Fed Chair Alan Greenspan as the Grinch

◇◇◇◇◇◇◇

JULY 15, 1996 BY TODD LAPPIN

THE OBSERVATORY: Lord Kinsley Is Here to Tame the Web

MICHAEL KINSLEY HAD HIS ONLINE DEBUT ON JUNE 24, AND EVER since, the Internet has been coughing him up like a hairball.

Accepting the noble cause, Mr. Kinsley, Harvard graduate, Rhodes Scholar Anglophile, former editor of *The New Republic*, former co-host of CNN's *Crossfire* and prodigy of the cultural elite, set out to create an outpost of civilization in the heart of digital darkness.

The World Wide Web is an anarchic wild of untamed energy and uncertain geography, populated by hordes of information hunter-gatherers and uppity villagers who add their voices to an unrehearsed chorus of commentary, critique and opinion.

They see Mr. Kinsley as the embodiment of a smug East Coast media establishment that for decades doled out information to them, like so many beneficent aristocrats handing out pennies to the huddled masses. The Web is nothing if not a forum for class anger against the cultural elite, and it bestows a curious mixture of personal power and humbling populism upon its users. For $10 a month, the cost of an America Online account, anyone can become her own broadcast network. Yet she does so knowing that she's only one of thousands upon thousands of people spouting off, maybe into the void at that.

That's the paradox of the Web, and its beauty, and it is what Mr. Kinsley doesn't seem to get. As he told Ken Auletta in *The New Yorker*, "I don't want to seem like an Internet fascist, but there is a reason why some people get paid as writers and some don't."

THE OBSERVATORY: WHY AREN'T YOU AT WORK?

AS YOU SLIP OUT OF THE OFFICE to a doctor's appointment, you can't help but notice them. You see them through the windows of Starbucks, lounging with their tall frappuccinos, laptops on their laps.

I accosted 100 of these lay-abouts over two recent work-days and asked them: *Why the hell aren't you at work?*

Their answers suggested they don't believe that the purpose of living in Manhattan is to fulfill grand ambitions. All the city's bustle and noise serve them as a mere backdrop for their own private musings.

Unlike the slackers who were the subjects of books, movies and countless articles in the late 80's and early 90's, this Manhattan breed doesn't stew in its own misery. Their constant presence in Barnes & Noble and Starbucks shows they have no hard feelings toward corporate America, and their inactivity shouldn't be construed as a form of silent protest. These people are quite content, thank you. If they have a goal, it's to lead lives of relative ease in a harsh city.

Oh, they may seem harmless enough—but if these happy loafers are not stopped, they will turn Manhattan into an Eastern Seaboard version of San Francisco, where nothing much happens, except that it gets a little chilly at night.

Here we've got all this brain-power and it's all going to waste in the clean comfort of the Barnes & Noble Starbucks. It's the middle of the morning, after all, prime working time. The Amish have been out in the fields for hours. The traders on Wall Street are crazed and hoarse. But here ...

people are watching one another drink coffee. And it's like this all over Manhattan, in the borough's 22 Starbucks locations.

But must we blame the loafers themselves for drifting through the part of the day prized by the hard worker? Shouldn't Starbucks itself bear some of the blame for bringing Manhattan to the level of some West Coast burg?

In a telephone interview, Starbucks spokeswoman Jeanne McKay says, "It's a casual setting, a meeting place to make connections."

Yes, yes, Ms. McKay, but *isn't it true* that Starbucks provides people with even more opportunity to fuck off?

Ms. McKay maintains her caffeinated cool. "That's an individual's choice and it's not my place to judge," she says. "We're just a business serving coffee. We can't take responsibility."

Can't take responsibility, Ms. McKay? Very nice. Very nice, indeed.

AUGUST 19, 1996: BY ALEX KUCZYNSKI

THE OBSERVATORY: NEW YORK IS GERM CITY! AN INVASION OF E. COLI, OTHER NASTY MICROBES

YOU MIGHT WANT TO THINK TWICE BEFORE USING THE NYNEX pay phone on the northwest corner of Madison Avenue and East 71st Street. You may want to avoid taxis—at least for the month of August. And that idea you had of taking the kids to see *Across the Sea of Time* at the high-tech Sony Imax Theater on Broadway and West 68th Street? Skip it.

According to an *Observer* investigation, that pay phone harbors flesh-eating bacteria; taxicabs are depositories for infectious respiratory microbes; and one pair of 3-D glasses at the Sony Imax Theater carries Escherichia coli, or E-coli bacteria, one strain of which, not *necessarily* the one found in our sample, was responsible for the food-poisoning illnesses of hundreds of people who ate contaminated hamburgers in the Northwest in 1992 and 1993.

A team of reporters, armed with Starplex microbiology transport swabs, collected viable cultures from the surfaces New Yorkers touch, sit on, lean against and drink from every day. Such as the engagement ring counter at Tiffany, the cafeteria in the Time & Life building, Harry Cipriani restaurant, the front door at Condé Nast headquarters, a suit hanger at Barney's New York, the Plaza Hotel, a Citibank automatic teller machine, Zabar's celebrated cheese counter, and *60 Minutes* executive producer Don Hewitt's favorite perch at the Candy Kitchen Diner in Bridgehampton, L.I.—to name just a few. The swabs were placed in sterile plastic tubes and brought to Dr. Philip Tierno, director of microbiology and diagnostic immunology at New York University Medical Center-Tisch Hospital.

The preliminary conclusions? You'll never go out into the city without wearing long pants again.

SEPTEMBER 2, 1996
BY FRANK DIGIACOMO

THE TRANSOM: A Hillary-Whipped President Parties

HARVEY KEITEL WELCOMED President William Jefferson Clinton into his sixth decade with a line originally uttered by William Powell in the 1948 movie *Mr. Peabody and the Mermaid*. Standing on the stage of Radio City Music Hall, Mr. Keitel looked down into the audience at the sleekly turned out Mr. Clinton and told him that 50 was "the youth of old age" or "the old age of youth." And then the star of *Mean Streets* added, "Choose your delusion."

President Clinton's birthday celebration was just beginning, but already it was clear that there would be many delusions from which to choose on this 18th day of August, 1996. The Clintons and their support team had landed in New York all right, but it might as well have been a sound-stage replica of the Big Apple. This was high Hamptons season, and save for a handful of loyal Democratic V.I.P.'s and wannabes, the city's overclass had abandoned its muggy concrete canyons to the tourists. Hillary Clinton and the Democratic National Committee had chosen to celebrate the president's birthday in a city devoid of its soul.

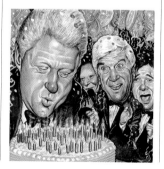

SEPTEMBER 16, 1996:
BY JIM WINDOLF

To Neurotic New York, Seinfeld Is News at 11

EACH WEEKNIGHT AT 11, BEFORE a shrunken audience, Chuck and Sue are still doing their old routine on Channel 4. But in the last year, these anchors have lost a good number of viewers, and even some of their authority, to a mere rerun.

That is because the rerun in question is *Seinfeld*, and *Seinfeld* delivers the real news for a city marked by cutthroat ambition and the accompanying fear of success.

In the gamey warmth of good old brown-hued Channel 11, WPIX-TV, *Seinfeld* gives the city the same nightly dose of clarity and community that an ideal newscast would provide. Since *Seinfeld* debuted as a rerun last September in the old *Cheers* slot, it has made local television history as the station's first 11 p.m. show to beat all three newscasts in the ratings, pulling off this feat more than once.

SEPTEMBER 23, 1996 BY NIKKI FINKE

Poof! From Sorcerer to Shmo

Now he's Eisner's No.2, a mere employee who can't hold media in his spell; His old power base—that mini galaxy of C.A.A. stars—can't help him now

*T*HE WALL STREET JOURNAL USUALLY GETS IT RIGHT. Nevertheless, there was a glaring error in a Sept. 12 story about the turmoil at Sony Pictures, in which the newspaper noted how Michael Ovitz, the "powerful president" of Walt Disney Company, has had the ear of Sony Corporation president Nobuyuki Idei. For weeks, rumors have been circulating that Ovitz, who could conceivably escape his contract at Disney, might be the next chief executive of Sony Corporation of America.

At issue wasn't the accuracy of the reporting. Instead, Hollywood executives were baffled by the business journal's continued use of the word "powerful" to describe the No. 2 Disney executive. "Seeing that in print brought home, as nothing else could, what everybody knew," said a former Sony executive, "that calling him 'powerful' could only be attributed to sentimentalism."

Mr. Ovitz still intimidates enough people—except for maybe David Geffen—that almost no one will speak on the record about him. But in the last few weeks, there's been a fundamental sea change in Ovitzology, and it is this: People are beginning to trash him and the press is beginning to write about it.

Suddenly, Mr. Ovitz has become Merlin without his spells, the Wizard of Oz without his curtain. Worse yet, he's no longer the sorcerer; just the sorcerer's apprentice. It's been almost a year since Mr. Ovitz gave up the chairmanship of Creative Artists Agency to become, literally, Michael No. 2 (his nickname around the Disney lot) to Walt Disney Company chairman Michael Eisner's Michael No. 1. Mr. Ovitz, the most powerful man in Hollywood, has become just another executive (albeit a well-placed, well-paid one) with less clearly defined areas of responsibility than even Al Gore.

Call it hubris, but Mike Ovitz made the same mistake many former agents make in assuming that his power would follow him out the door of Creative Artists Agency. Stripped of his superstar client roster—Tom Cruise, Brad Pitt, Demi Moore, Tom Hanks, etc.—his "good cop" partner Ron Meyer; his "Young Turk" foot soldiers; his I.M. Pei office replete with mood lighting; even his affectation for Asian mysticism, Mr. Ovitz is standing naked and vulnerable for everyone to see. "He doesn't have a buffer zone around him anymore," explained one close colleague. "So every day he takes a walk, he bumps into a door."

He can no longer control the media, much less Hollywood moguls. Which is why the Disney president, beleaguered by bad press and bracing for still more, spent 20 minutes haranguing the company's elite at an Aspen retreat in early September about the dangers of leaking to the media.

Mr. Ovitz's concern is justified; the sharks know blood when they smell it. For instance, the recent resignation of the senior vice president at ABC Entertainment, Mike Rosenfeld Jr., would hardly rate a second glance. But Mr. Rosenfeld, a former C.A.A. TV agent and son of one of the agency's five founding partners, was no ordinary executive. He'd been brought to the network personally by Mr. Ovitz, who had promised him privately that he was heir apparent to ABC Entertainment president Ted Harbert whenever Mr. Harbert moved up or out. But then, much to Mr. Rosenfeld's dismay, Disney, after sending out a feeler to television producers Marcy Carsey and Tom Werner, hired NBC prime-time wunderkind Jamie Tarses as Mr. Harbert's second in command. Adding insult to injury, Mr. Rosenfeld was inexplicably left off the invitation list for the Aspen retreat.

On Sept. 9, Mr. Rosenfeld walked into Mr. Ovitz's office and announced that he was quitting. The Disney president erupted: "You can't quit, because it would be personally embarrassing to me," according to a source familiar with the conversation.

There are as many anecdotes about the two Mikes bickering as there are of Michael No. 2 claiming credit for things he had little to do with. For instance, earlier this month at an animation meeting involving a sequel to *The Lion King*, Mr. Eisner and Mr. Ovitz disagreed in front of the participants over how a plot problem should be solved. When Mr. Ovitz wouldn't let it go, Mr. Eisner growled, "Don't even try to win a creative battle against me."

It's little wonder that speculation now centers on Mr. Ovitz possibly looking to Sony Corporation as a life preserver to escape the sinking situation he finds himself in at Disney. However, questions remain about whether he can extract himself from his contract there. On the other hand, the betting on the Disney lot is that Mr. Eisner might be more than happy to help him abandon ship.

After a recent sleepover with a group of grade-school boys from the John Thomas Dye School, which Eric Ovitz attends, a playmate of Eric surprised even his business-savvy parents with his up-to-date knowledge of Mr. Ovitz's situation. "Yeah, Eric's father used to be powerful," the boy told his parents. "But now he's the No. 2 guy over half of Disney."

OCTOBER 7, 1996: EDITORIAL

BOB DOLE, THE RIGHT CHOICE FOR '96! A VOTE FOR CHARACTER OVER SLEAZE

Y ES, BOB DOLE IS A TERRIBLE CAMPAIGNER. Yes, the Republican Party is filled with neo-Puritans who would like nothing better than to codify their notions of morality into civil law. Yes, the religious right and the right-to-lifers are wild-eyed fanatics who threaten our hard-won liberties.

None of these concerns, however, argues against a Dole presidency. Bill Clinton's party, after all, is not without its radicals and crackpots, and Mr. Clinton's skill on the campaign trail points to everything that is wrong about his performance as president.

In this election year, character is not merely one of several issues demanding our attention. It is the only issue. That makes our decision easier. Bob Dole has character, and Bill Clinton has none. So Bob Dole is our choice.

The president has spent much of the last year or so cultivating the image of First Father, the man to whom we would gladly entrust our children. The notion, of course, is ridiculous.

If the president wishes us to think of him as a member of the family, two comparisons come to mind. There's Mr. Clinton as the scarred and terribly insecure child who will do or say anything to get in good with the cool kids in the schoolyard. Then there's Mr. Clinton as a salacious, middle-aged uncle who disrupts the holidays by passing lewd remarks in front of his teenage nieces and talking smugly about his days in Canada during the Vietnam War. While both spectacles are embarrassing for different reasons, Mr. Clinton's presidency has been embarrassing for many reasons.

There have been administrations worse than Mr. Clinton's, but rarely, if ever, has there been one that so often inspires shame. We have been embarrassed for nearly four years. We have suffered too long the sins of those yahoos Mr. Clinton transported from Arkansas, so many of whom seem to have spent the entire term answering prosecutors' questions. There was a time when the nation looked at the White House as a symbol of leadership, of resolve and of character. The president served not only as an elected leader, but as a bastion of the qualities we liked best in ourselves, qualities that we liked best about America.

In turning the White House into a better-dressed version of *Animal House*, Mr. Clinton has managed to squander the respect that the American people always have had for the office of the presidency, even when they disagreed with the person who held the title. Instead of a role model, we have a floozy who will consort with anyone if it means a bump in the popularity polls. Instead of a man of character, we have a bunch of characters, most of them acting with all the discretion and sophistication of the denizens of Dogpatch, U.S.A.

Mr. Clinton has damaged the office to which he was entrusted and the nation over which he presides. There actually once was a time when the president of the United States was thought to be the leader of the free world. After four years of Mr. Clinton, the president is now just another figure on tabloid television. We used to ask our presidents about the great issues of war and

peace. We ask Mr. Clinton about his underwear. Worse, he gives us an answer. In the end, he is nothing more than a *flâneur* and a poseur, "at best mistaking the shadow of courage for the substance of wisdom," as F. Scott Fitzgerald wrote.

Mr. Clinton's wife, Hillary, has been a full partner in this sickening spectacle. Her self-righteousness and transparent piety have not averted our eyes to her slimy dealmaking and fanciful fiction-telling. She once thought of herself as the scourge of Richard Nixon. Nowadays, as a practitioner of the politics of paranoia and self-pity, all she lacks are hunched shoulders and a five o'clock shadow. She virtually ran as Mr. Clinton's running mate in 1992. Now we have a chance to rid ourselves of both. A perfect twofer.

The Republican Party has provided a flawed but highly acceptable antidote to the dumbing-down of the White House and the trivialization of the nation's highest office. Bob Dole is everything Bill Clinton isn't. (The same could be said of Elizabeth Dole and Hillary Clinton.) After more than 40 years of service to his country, Mr. Dole has shown himself to be a man of character, a man who has put the nation ahead of self. So, too, is he a man who has no need to consult pollsters and swamis to figure out what he thinks. He is a decent man, and decency is what he will bring to the White House.

We believe Bob Dole can return the Presidency to its now-shattered sense of majesty and importance. His sacrifice in honorable pursuit of a better world represents the best of America.

Our history is filled, unfortunately, with contests in which ill-fated candidates fell to victors who had neither their character nor their abilities. Several spring to mind: Adlai Stevenson, Barry Goldwater, Walter Mondale, Wendell Willkie and Al Smith.

On Election Day, Bob Dole may well join this list of honorable losers, for the American public has long been a sucker for the "Slick Willies" of the world. It's a cliché, but it's true: Sometimes lost causes are the only ones worth fighting for. Given a choice between a man who has displayed nothing but contempt for the traditions of his office and a man who so clearly reveres his country's institutions and is humbled by his service to them, we will choose honor over expediency.

> *After more than 40 years of service to his country, Mr. Dole has shown himself to be a man of character, a man who has put the nation ahead of self. ... He is a decent man, and decency is what he will bring to the White House.*

It is hard not to remark upon the paths these two men have taken and the choices they have made. Both Mr. Dole and Mr. Clinton hail from small-town America, that mystical place whose natives are blessed with common sense, decency, patriotism and, yes, character. Mr. Dole's life, service and sacrifice sum up all that the American imagination associates with places like Russell, Kansas. Mr. Dole understands that freedom is dearly won and forcefully defended, that the life of a nation matters more than the life of an individual, and that hard work and sacrifice (and not indulgence and quick-buck scamming) are the nation's bricks and mortar.

He is a small-town man New Yorkers can embrace because he also happens to be blunt, sardonic and utterly immune to the hooey that is second nature to Mr. Clinton.

Mr. Clinton, coming from a similarly underprivileged background and rooted, you would think, in traditional values, is but a caricature of a generation that decided it was bigger than the nation, the system and the dreaded Establishment. His governing style is a product of his generation's self-indulgence and Little Rock's loose political morals. He knows nothing of sacrifice and little of the real world, for he has been talking, and talking, and talking, for the last quarter-century. Historians will one day note that in 1996, the oldest presidential nominee in U.S. history was a man of action, while one of the youngest incumbents was a sedentary yapper.

Mr. Dole entered politics to *do* something. Mr. Clinton did so to *be* something.

The president's supporters haul out the threadbare argument that a Dole presidency would be a disaster for the Supreme Court. What makes them so sure Mr. Clinton, the hypocrite who signed a welfare reform bill so fundamentally abhorrent to his alleged values, would appoint liberal justices? Besides, the track record of Republican Supreme Court appointees isn't so bad: Sandra Day O'Connor, Anthony Kennedy and David Souter are fine thinkers and political moderates.

Mr. Clinton and his surrogates have expended much energy snickering at Mr. Dole's proposal to cut income taxes by 15 percent. They, of course, are much more comfortable with soaking the rich to pay for their constituency's favorite social programs. Mr. Dole's proposal could be fundamentally sound, provided he cuts the fat out of the bureaucracy's bloated payroll. We think he will do just that.

Ultimately, though, all these issues are so much background noise. Character is all that matters. If granted another four years, Mr. Clinton will continue to embarrass himself, the presidency and the country.

The American Century's signature generation has been Bob Dole's—born in an age of muscle and sweat, tested by unknowable sacrifice and, in its maturity, providing an example of lives well lived, of causes well fought and of victories well earned.

Not for himself but for America and for the presidency, Bob Dole deserves one more victory.

You say D'Amato: Senator Al, solo again

OCTOBER 14, 1996 BY CANDACE BUSHNELL

SEX AND THE CITY: GOODBYE, MR. BIG! THE END OF THE AFFAIR JUST ONE OF THOSE THINGS— THAT TOAST AT '21' COULDN'T SAVE A LOVE GONE SOUR; ENTER THE FEMALE GOLF PRO; WELCOME BACK, DISGUST, MISERY AND SELF-LOATHING

MR. BIG CAME INTO THE villa. "Get off the phone," he said. "I want to go into town." She hadn't particularly wanted to go into town, but she didn't particularly want to stay at the villa. She didn't particularly want to be there at all; or, she wanted to be there, but not with him.

It was coming home from the St. Barts week that Carrie allowed herself to acknowledge the fact that the relationship with Mr. Big would probably not last the summer.

What happened between April and the middle of July was nothing. A few incidents stand out: the explosion of TWA Flight 800. The hurricane. The fights.

The fights were: She wanted to talk, he didn't. She wanted more attention; he

CARRIE THOUGHT THIS WOULD BE HER LAST NIGHT IN MR. BIG'S HOUSE.

YOU CAN'T ACT LIKE YOU'RE TWELVE... YOU CAN'T COME HOME AT FOUR IN THE MORNING.

MOST TWELVE YEAR OLDS DON'T COME HOME AT FOUR IN THE MORNING.

didn't want to make the effort. "Now you sound like all of my ex-wives," he'd say. "Always demanding something. Don't ask for anything and maybe you'll get it. Don't tell me what to do."

One day at the beginning of July, on another lousy gray day in the house in East Hampton where Carrie had stayed out for the week, some friends dropped by.

"I'd break up with him tomorrow if I could. I'm dying to get out of here," she said, slamming cupboard doors. She'd just hung up from yet another remote conversation on the phone, all about logistics.

Why not end it then?

That would be inconvenient.

Instead, she was doing laundry (why? They had a maid), she was making sure the kitchen was stocked with food (with things they would never eat, like packages of yellow rice), and she was watering the vegetable garden. The relationship was over before they had any vegetables, but the garden was useful because it gave her something to talk about with him and his friends. Everything was growing but nothing was ripening. No sun.

In the evenings on the weekends in the Hamptons, they'd have dinners, or go to dinners. Everyone got drunk, very fast and very early, and went to bed by 11.

Carrie found herself complaining about how the guy at the Red Horse Market never sliced the smoked salmon thin enough. Then Mr. Big would tell a story about how he'd refused to buy a six-dollar pound of butter at Thieves and Bitches.

Occasionally, she stopped herself from calling him "dad." As in, "Yes, Dad, I will take out the garbage. Yes, Dad, I will drive carefully."

On Fourth of July weekend, Mr. Big kept disappearing in Mr. Marvelous' Hummer. They claimed they were going to the store. They claimed they were going to the store six times in two days. They came back with pickles. Then they claimed they were going rollerblading. Carrie wasn't

paying attention.

As soon as Mr. Big left, she'd turn the stereo all the way up and dance around the house. K.C. and the Sunshine Band. "You're Out of Control."

"What are you going to do with your life?" he'd ask.

"I'm going to become famous."

"That is so sad. You won't like it when you get there."

"Get off our planet."

Then he'd go and smoke a cigar and sulk, or go to the store again with Mr. Marvelous.

In the middle of July: "Is there somebody else?"

"This is not about anyone else. This is about us."

"That's not answering the question."

"This is about us."

"It's a yes or no question. Is there somebody else?"

"No."

"Liar. You've been coached, haven't you?"

"What are you talking about?"

"Someone's been coaching you on what to say."

"This is about us. Not about anyone else."

"See? There you go again."

"Why do you have to make this harder?"

"I'm not making it harder. I have to get a cigarette."

"I have to go to sleep. Why won't you let me sleep?"

"You don't deserve to sleep."

"I haven't done anything wrong."

"You haven't done anything right, either. I want to get to the bottom of this coaching business."

"What are you talking about?"

"Someone's been telling you what to say. It's an old shrink trick. When you're in a difficult situation, you keep repeating the same phrase over and over again. That way, you can't have a conversation."

One hour later:

"What are you doing? Who are you seeing? What time are you getting home?"

"Early. I'm getting home early."

"You're out of control."

"I am not. I'm home at 11."

"Don't lie to me."

"Don't lie to me."

"I could have you followed. How do you know that I'm not already having you followed? I'm rich enough to have you followed."

This was several weeks after Carrie had begged to be taken to a mental institution.

(To be continued ...)

OCTOBER 21, 1996 BY BEN PROFUME

THE NEW YORK WORLD: OFF THE MENU

THERE'S A DEEPLY SICK TREND overtaking Manhattan's restaurants.

It used to be that only the very rich had the narcissistic arrogance to order "off the menu" at their favorite lunch spots. Remember the vile Roy Cohn, biting into an off-the-menu tuna sandwich at "21"?

Well, like many bad habits, ordering "off the menu," or O.T.M., has dribbled down to the common folk. Go into any diner and you'll see some fellow sticking his nose into the kitchen, asking something like, "What meat do you have fresh today?" Said fellow doesn't bother to consult the menu—that's for the little folk, not Diner Man.

We're not talking about the well-known "high-maintenance eater"—you know, the person who asks to switch sauces, or get dressing on the side, etc. O.T.M.'ers are much more hard-core: They're into power, not taste. Only an idiot, they think, would order from the actual menu.

If you, too, would like to feel that little throb of power, there are distinct rules:

Consult the menu, find the most complex item, which the chef has clearly spent days or weeks creating—but ask for it done plain, no sauces, no spices, etc., thereby insulting the chef's intelligence. For example: "I'll have the red snapper with mango chutney in whole wheat phyllo pastry—but can I just get the snapper, broiled plain, and a lemon slice? *Thanks.*"

Set the menu aside, look sincerely into the waiter's eyes and say, "You know something? I'd just like a peanut butter and jelly sandwich today. *Thanks.*" By ordering something so ridiculously, anachronistically plain (a favorite O.T.M. ploy), you'll seem *haimish*, etc.

Ask for Diet Coke "but with ice on the side." This lets your fellow diners know that you're hip to the New York custom of overloading a glass with ice to displace the costly soda.

Call the beleaguered manager by his first name—clasp his hand, smack him on the back—even better, speak to him in his native Greek, Italian or Spanish. This shows your pals what a man of the people you are. Never mind that the manager has dreams of shoving a metal spike through your throat.

A noteworthy O.T.M. subspecies is the Gourmet Coffee Shop O.T.M.'er. It takes lots of training to join this group, since many of the wait staff at gourmet coffee shops are recovering O.T.M.'ers and can easily out-attitude the neophyte O.T.M.'er. But an expert practitioner was seen recently at Commodities Coffee Shop in TriBeCa. He clearly had years of experience, so don't try this at your local joint:

He approached the woman behind the counter, leaned his face over the stack of bran muffins, and said in a faux-intimate voice, "I'd like a coffee with a little skim milk—but not as much as yesterday. *Thanks.*"

With this one simple request, the customer's arrogance and narcissism dovetailed beautifully. Notice how he simply *assumed* that the woman behind the counter would remember *exactly how many millimeters of milk* she had poured into his cup the day before, that she has had nothing better to do with the last *24 hours of her life* than remember how much skim milk this guy likes in his coffee.

We'd say more, but our waiter is here.

NOVEMBER 18, 1996   BY LORNE MANLY

MEDIA UPSTART FELIX DENNIS SERVES MANY MISTRESSES, MANY MAGAZINES

FELIX DENNIS, BRITISH MULTI-millionaire, international playboy and self-described "mad fucker," whirled back into the living room of his East 49th Street apartment and thrust a sheet of paper into a reporter's hand.

"I'm going to let you read it for three seconds. Read fast!"

The words "Bank of Bermuda" and "account balance" flashed by, followed by a number—a big one, higher than $13 million. Just then, the swingin' Londoner turned publishing mogul snatched the document and danced back to his place on the couch.

Mr. Dennis, 48, was in Manhattan on an autumn afternoon

last month to check up on the preparations for bringing his London-based men's magazine, *Maxim*, to the United States.

Maxim is a kind of *Cosmpolitan* for men, with cleavage on every cover and sex and money advice on the pages inside. With this rag for the regular guy, Mr. Dennis hopes to shatter the "cozy cartel" of men's magazines turned out by Condé Nast Publications and Hearst Corporation—such stalwarts as *GQ*, *Details* and *Esquire*.

"I've got 10 or 15 million to burn, and I don't care if I lose it," Mr. Dennis said.

But for now, despite his fortune of roughly $250 million, Mr. Dennis cannot rightly count himself in the company of S.I. Newhouse Jr. and Jann Wenner and other New York media *machers*. Until he ac-

tually cracks the American market with a general-interest publication—he's just a crazy Englishman with a big idea and money to burn.

If *Maxim*'s lowbrow formula doesn't work in the United States, Mr. Dennis said, he won't try again to break into the market. "If *Maxim* flops, I'm out," he said.

Whatever happens, his regrets will be few. "If most men knew how I live and have lived my life for the last 25 years," he said, "they would happily take out a shotgun ... and they would shoot me without a second thought. And I wouldn't blame them. Because if I was them, I'd shoot me."

NOVEMBER 25, 1996   BY FRANK DIGIACOMO

Four-Star Feud:
Aprés Bouley, le Déluge

THE REMNANTS OF THE SATURDAY LUNCH CROWD LINGERED over their coffee and petit fours as Daniel Boulud described what it has been like, lately, to feed them. "You know when you try to put a 100-pound pressure into a 10-pound pipe?" said Mr. Boulud, as he shifted in his chef's whites. "I mean, *Pchgh!*"

Mr. Boulud unclenched his valuable fingers, pantomiming the explosion.

The chef affected a harried look. He was not convincing.

Mr. Boulud has to know that, in this winter of culinary discontent, he may not be the last chef standing, but he is the best. That is why a lot of powerful people are kissing the former Lyons farm boy's derriere.

Mr. Boulud seems determined to capitalize on his heightened power and popularity. In April, he and his pastry chef, François Payard, will open Payard, a bistro and patisserie on Lexington Avenue at East 74th Street. But what really has the culinary world talking is the chef and restaurateur's interest in taking over a familiar and hallowed piece of turf that once belonged to Sirio Maccioni, Mr. Boulud's boss from 1986 to 1992: the space in the Mayfair Hotel that housed Le Cirque.

"I did not ask them to do this," Mr. Boulud said of Mr. Bouley's and Mr. Maccioni's decisions to close, then relocate, their establishments. He laughed a dry laugh that turned into a wheeze.

1997

- Twilight of the literary beasts: Roth, Mailer, Bellow, Updike roar in their senescence

- Bill Clinton rings in second term with Washington power orgy

- Good golly! Molly Shannon is *Saturday Night Live*'s star klutz

- Pucker up, Park Slope: Author Kathryn Harrison tells of incest in *The Kiss*

- Sex or sanity? Prozac, Paxil and Zoloft dull depressives' libidos

- Woody Allen lobbies in vain to save beloved Books and Company

- The age of expressionless-ism: New Yorkers inject botulism toxin to fight wrinkles

- *Zut alors*, the bistro is back: Keith McNally opens Balthazar

- Al Sharpton, Ruth Messinger battle for Democratic mayoral nomination

1997

JANUARY 6, 1997 BY ALEX KUCZYNSKI

Minimalist Chic Shrinks the Big City

IT WAS A WINDY MIDWINTER night in Manhattan, and two women in their 20's stood outside an apartment in a postwar building. One of them pressed the buzzer.

"Welcome," said the young man, a lawyer, who opened the door wearing a mandarin collar jacket and black pants. "Oh, and before you come in, could you remove your shoes?"

The two women exchanged glances—what kind of party did you say this was?—but politely discarded their shoes and entered the four-room apartment, furnished in little more than an expanse of off-white carpet. In the kitchen, an expensive-looking stainless steel pod served as a garbage receptacle. In the bedroom, a mattress covered with a rough cotton duvet rested on a wooden square. There were no doorknobs anywhere in Apartment 4F. No piles of mail, no loose sweaters, no stray gym socks, no television remote controls. There was Nothing, and there was a whole lot of it.

"Don't you love it?" said the lawyer, surveying his blank kingdom and sipping a glass of club soda (no red wine allowed in the apartment). "Isn't it so"—his voice dropped a tone—"so min-im-al-ist?"

Minimalism is the latest social-aesthetic disease to sweep Manhattan. After the opulent 80's and the lackluster early 90's, minimalism, fueled by the recovering economy, is devouring our retail spaces, our bookstores, our literature, our public figures.

"There has been a definite return to an appreciation of what most people call a minimalist aesthetic," said Manhattan architect John Fifield. "It's accessible, for one. You don't have to know the history of architecture to appreciate the beauty of a simple concrete floor."

Also, unlike doing your place up in Sister Parish splendor, it doesn't really take taste to create a convincing minimalist space.

FEBRUARY 3, 1997
BY FRANK DIGIACOMO

OH, DONNA! DON'T CALL HER MRS. GIULIANI

SINCE SHORTLY BEFORE CHRISTMAS, THE GOSSIP MILL, TABLOIDS and even *The New York Times* have carried curious stories about the separate public lives that Donna Hanover and her husband, Mayor Rudolph Giuliani, seem to be leading. The last time the couple appeared together in public was New Year's Eve.

There is also Ms. Hanover's renewed career focus, which an invitation to a Dec. 12 reception at Gracie Mansion put succinctly: "Broadcast journalist and the First Lady of the City of New York Donna Hanover requests the pleasure of your company." Note that the career comes first, the city second.

And of course there was the name change. Donna Hanover had appended "Giuliani" during her husband's second mayoralty campaign. "The mortgage is Donna Hanover Giuliani; the taxes, Donna Hanover Giuliani. In the campaign, and if Rudy is elected, I would prefer Donna Hanover Giuliani, although in a professional capacity, I would continue to use Donna Hanover," the first lady told a *Newsday* reporter in July 1993, adding: "I'm comfortable with any combination." (In the same interview, she also said, "My husband is the most virile man.")

JANUARY 27, 1997
BY NICK PAUMGARTEN WITH
GEORGE GURLEY

BILL CLINTON'S PRESIDENTIAL POWER ORGY

IT HAD THE MAKINGS OF A BAD Beltway joke: Alan Greenspan, Bob Woodward and Andrea Mitchell were strolling arm-in-arm down the ground-floor corridor of the Willard Hotel on the eve of the 53rd Presidential Inaugural. And no one even lost their lunch.

When folks talk about the corridors of power, they don't usually mean carpeted hotel lobbies or the vast public tundra of the Mall. But in Washington, D.C., during inaugural weekend, the entire city became a thoroughfare for people more often confined to tighter hallways, boardrooms, mastheads and TV screens. It was a vast farmers market of power. And the Willard, on several occasions, teemed with strange and unnerving alliances, byproducts of an incestuous life in the nation's second-largest one-industry town. The story of Inauguration Day, as delivered on the evening news, was of the temporary truce between the two political parties and of the relative non-pomp of a second inaugural. But what made the day such a sight to behold was the constant flaunting of the cozy relationship between the press and the politicians, between those who deliver information and those who guard it, and those who describe power and those who wield it. And New Yorkers—from Mark Green to Graydon Carter to Tabitha Soren to Bobby Zarem—came to slip under the covers and get a piece of whatever it is people come to Washington to get.

FEBRUARY 3, 1997:   BY JIM WINDOLF

Klutzy, Desperate Molly Shannon: Superstar in White Cotton Undies

MOLLY SHANNON IS 32 AND LIVES ALONE in Greenwich Village. She usually walks to work, more than 40 blocks up to NBC, sometimes in a lavender thrift shop coat with a fake fur collar. People are beginning to go up to her, even if they don't know her name, and she's already had a stalker.

Sometimes on days off, she'll walk all the way up into the 100's. Or she'll walk downtown, along the Hudson, listening lately to the Smashing Pumpkin's *Mellon Collie and the Infinite Sadness* on a Walkman. In the evenings, she'll get a magazine and have what she calls "a lady's dinner alone." Late at night, when she can't sleep, she might smoke seven Marlboro Lights in a row, reading self-help books like *Codependent No More* or watching her video of George Cukor's *The Women*. The *Saturday Night Live* schedule can screw you up, and sometimes she's in a diner at 4:30 in the morning.

In the coffee shop by Studio 8H, a beautiful guy gave her an I'm-hitting-on-you look, and she held his stare.

"Do you like that?" I said.

"No!" she said. "God, no."

Days of Fiennes and Roses: Miramax's Bob and Harvey Weinstein flank The English Patient's *Ralph Fiennes*

FEBRUARY 10, 1997 BY WARREN ST. JOHN

THE SAUCY, LITERARY HARRISONS PUCKER UP

THE NOVELIST KATHRYN HAR-rison was sitting erect in the cafe of the Regency Hotel in Manhattan, her blond hair pulled back and strikingly set off by a black velvet scarf and beaded black lamb's-wool sweater. It was an afternoon in late January, and she reluctantly agreed to talk about her decision to write *The Kiss,* a memoir to be published in April by Random House, in which she admits a consensual four-year love affair, from age 20 to 24, with her father, a preacher. The galleys of *The Kiss,* had been circulating among Manhattan's literary set for weeks, where it has achieved a kind of haute seamy status.

"For me, writing is a transaction by which I try to come to terms with myself, and in this case, my past," said Ms. Harrison. "We'll see if I'm laying the tinder at my own stake."

The tinder is already smoldering. A recent *Vanity Fair* article by Michael Shnayerson, who did not interview Ms. Harrison, accused her of shameless opportunism. "The article portrayed me as

calculating and mercenary," said Ms. Harrison. "It stung." More articles are on the way from *Vogue, Mirabella,* and *Harper's Bazaar*; *The New Yorker* is preparing an excerpt.

But by deciding to merchandise her pain, Ms. Harrison surely knew what she was getting into. She is, after all, one-half of an ambitious literary couple: She is married to novelist and *Harper's* magazine deputy editor Colin Harrison, who has just signed a $1 million, two-book deal with Farrar, Straus & Giroux. Some of the sniping over *The Kiss* may be a case of envy. The Harrisons have the kind of life not a few New York media types aspire to: two writers chipping away at their respective novels in their Park Slope brownstone, sharing child-care duties and talking about books and ideas late into the evening. The fact that Ms. Harrison has written a book that may pass muster with both *The New York Review of Books* and Oprah Winfrey is also not insignificant.

But certain facts—that it was Ms. Harrison's agent, Amanda (Binky) Urban, who suggested she write *The Kiss*; that Mr. Harrison is writing an article for *Vogue,* about being married to the author of *The Kiss*—have led some people in the publishing business to agree with one editor who knows the couple, who calls their prepublication behavior "The Colin and Kathryn Harrison show."

Time Inc.'s Norm Pearlstine scales the Henry Luce heights

◇◇◇◇◇◇◇

FEBRUARY 17, 1997 BY KATHERINE EBAN FINKELSTEIN

Abortion-Inducing Drug to Make Manhattan Debut, Beating RU-486 to City

A DOCTOR AT COLUMBIA-PRESBYTERIAN MEDICAL CENTER IS ABOUT to make available to New York City women, for the first time, a generic version of RU-486, the compound that chemically induces abortion.

Before March 10, the controversial drug, mifepristone, will be provided at one of Columbia-Presbyterian's downtown clinics, *The Observer* has learned. Carolyn Westhoff, an associate professor of clinical obstetrics and gynecology at the Columbia School of Public Health, has been given the go-ahead by the Food and Drug Administration to administer the drug to women on a first-come, first-served basis. She joins only five other doctors in the country who have been given permission to do so.

As ibuprofen is to Advil, mifepristone is to RU-486. Two years ago, the F.D.A. approved its use in the United States following almost a decade of lobbying by abortion-rights activists. Yet RU-486 is still not available in America. Its distribution has been held up pending the result of a nasty Federal court battle between the Population Council, a nonprofit organization, and Joseph Pike, a lawyer and businessman who invests in health care products.

Lawrence Lader, a Manhattan-based abortion rights activist, was so frustrated that he got the generic form of RU-486 approved by the F.D.A. as a stopgap until the problems with RU-486 could be resolved. He found a Columbia University scientist to replicate RU-486, goosed the F.D.A. into signing off on the use of mifepristrone for abortions in less than two years, found a manufacturer to make it and enlisted Dr. Westhoff and Columbia-Presbyterian.

MARCH 3, 1997   BY WARREN ST. JOHN

Mike Nichols' All-Star Clinton Gamble

IS IT POSSIBLE TO MAKE A FILM version of Joe Klein's satirical novel *Primary Colors* without pissing off President Clinton and the first lady?

That's a question director Mike Nichols has been grappling with in recent weeks, as he gets ready to start shooting *Primary Colors*, the movie. Mr. Nichols has the makings of a hit: John Travolta has been cast as the pudgy, randy Southern governor based on Mr. Clinton, Emma Thompson as the candidate's bulldog wife, Oscar nominee Billy Bob Thornton as the quasi-Tourettic redneck campaign staff member based on James Carville, and British actor Adrian Lester as the African-American translation of George Stephanopoulos.

Mr. Nichols, who paid $1.5 million of his own money for the property, has a $65 million budget. Sources at Universal said he has been given total control of the film's content. And his former comedy partner, the writer and director Elaine May, has created a compressed, astringent screenplay that asks some complicated, nasty questions about politics in our times.

So what's to worry?

Already, Mr. Nichols is feeling the pressure of earning back $65 million from a political satire. And there is a social cost to *Primary Colors* as well. An associate close to the project said Mr. Nichols "wants to move the movie away from the book's specific identification with the Clintons." But: "Without the candidate fucking people or being a lecherous guy, you don't have a movie," said one Universal higher-up. "That's what you're selling."

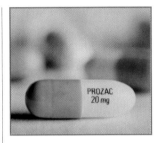

MARCH 10, 1997
BY JENNIFER KORNREICH

THE OBSERVATORY: SEX OR SANITY?

WITH THE HELP OF OUR LITTLE friends Prozac, Zoloft, Paxil, et al., anyone can be happy nowadays. But something has gone terribly awry in the brave new world of medicated Manhattan: Everybody functions smoothly now, at work or at social functions, but in those private moments, in the quiet of the bedroom ... nothing.

More and more frequently, psychiatrists in New York have been bumping into monsters of their own creation: patients who, having cured their depression with those wildly popular anti-depressants, are experiencing a new kind of misery now that the drugs' most outrageous side effect has left them with practically no libido.

So here it is, a depressing Catch-22 for the not-so-gay 90's. The urbanite must choose between the agony of depression and the fleeting moments of ecstasy inherent in a robust sex life. It's all in there, in a recent issue of *Primary Psychiatry*: The journal estimates that between 40 and 50 percent of people taking the S.S.R.I. (selective serotonin reuptake inhibitor) class of anti-depressants—which includes Zoloft, Paxil, Luvox and Prozac—suffer from sexual dysfunction.

And in the New York City of 1997, most fashionably medicated, formerly depressed people are choosing Prozac over sex.

MARCH 24, 1997   BY JIM WINDOLF

THE OBSERVATORY From Best Years to Our Years

Fifty years ago, a top-of-the-line Hollywood studio product, *The Best Years of Our Lives*, stole the Oscars away from Frank Capra's *It's a Wonderful Life*. Jim Windolf explores William Wyler's unsentimental tear-jerker with some help from one of the movie's surviving stars, Teresa Wright.

O N MARCH 13, 1947, the president of the Screen Actors Guild, Ronald Reagan, opened the Oscar ceremony at the Shrine Auditorium in Los Angeles with a few words before a movie montage. Then Jack Benny took over as the emcee in the first nationally broadcast Academy Awards show. In the Audience sat producers and directors from the five nominated films for best picture: Clarence Brown's *The Yearling*, Laurence Olivier's *Henry V*, Edmund Goulding's *The Razor's Edge*, Frank Capra's *It's a Wonderful Life* and William Wyler's *The Best Years of Our Lives*.

The Best Years of Our Lives nearly swept: Wyler won an Academy Award as best director; Robert Sherwood won one for his screenplay; Frederic March won as best actor; Harold Russel (who lost his hands while handling dynamite during the war) won as best supporting actor, and after the ceremony, with the press taking pictures, Cary Grant leaned over to Russel and whispered, "Where can I get a stick of dynamite?"

Sam Goldwyn, who produced the movie, went home, sat down alone in his darkened living room with his Oscar for best picture and his Irving R. Thalberg award, and wept.

Fifty years later, as *The English Patient*'s producer Saul Zaentz prepares to do some Goldwyn-style weeping with his prospective Oscar, and the Academy Awards also-ran *It's a Wonderful*

Life has entered the cultural vocabulary of every other schoolchild in America, *The Best Years of Our Lives*—which went on, in 1947, to become the second biggest grossing movie of all time, after *Gone With the Wind*—is a nearly forgotten artifact, without cult or fan club, network showing, remakes, miniseries versions or digitally enhanced reissues. And yet, it is as good a movie as it ever was—not antiqued or made laughable by time; in fact, quite

the opposite. Its integrity has aged it into a kind of permanent American artifact, with values that are so rock-bound and understated that they put this society, in 1997, into stunning relief.

Of the three veterans returning home in the film, one was a bank executive on the verge of middle age, one was a handsome former soda jerk, untrained to enter the postwar employment market, one was an amputee who had to face his family and who was deter-

mined to convince his fiancée to dump him because of his infirmity. For these three, Wyler cast the now pouch-eyed former matinee idol Frederic March as the bank executive, Dana Andrews as the soda jerk, and—after searching through disabled hospitals—was watching a documentary when he spotted an amputee named Harold Russel, whose sincerity struck him. He cast Myrna Loy as March's wife, Teresa Wright as his daughter (who falls in love with

the soda jerk), Virginia Mayo as Dana Andrews' bombshell cheating wife, and Cathy O'Donnell as Harold Russell's fiancée.

The best-known scene in the film—and there are a number of greatest hits—is a long, undialogued sequence of the desperate Dana Andrews, about to leave town, sitting in the nose of a junked B-17 recalling his battle experiences. He is interrupted by a man who gives him a job as a laborer. It is a victory.

When Bob Dole accused the Clinton generation of never having suffered, never having done anything real, it sounded like the voice of a stern former warmonger chiding the children of postwar prosperity.

But those semifamous ("I'm just a man") lines were written by a child of the baby boom, Mark Helprin, and perhaps they more accurately reflected the baby boomers' fear and awe of the men and women who fought a successful war on two fronts than the feelings of the victors themselves. For *The Best Years of Our Lives*, made when the memory of war was so fresh that it was still unexamined, shows the weakness and

> *The movie is certainly a product of the Hollywood factory, but it manages to do something that has always been rare in the movies: It shows life as it is lived.*

unconscious remorse of the men coming home, and women flexing the new muscles they gained while the soldiers were fighting.

With the help of cinematographer Gregg Toland, who added to the stylish bombast of *Citizen Kane* with his pioneering use of deep focus but brought a kind of centered clarity to this movie, Wyler told the story of three veterans with an unmannered sincerity and directness. He told his cast to buy their costumes off the rack at department stores and to use as little makeup as possible. It is a long way from the perfume-commercial-slick tragedy of that new supposed classic of the war's aftermath, *The English Patient*.

Dana Andrews, an actor with matinee idol looks and a drinking problem, played the damaged bombardier who can't adjust to his sudden loss of status now that he's a civilian. With his teeth clenched, he delivers the final stinging lines of the movie—a bitter marriage proposal offered to Peggy Stephenson, played by Teresa Wright. It's a pretty tough ending for a movie that won seven Academy Awards. Fred's proposal goes like this:

"You know what it'll be, don't you, Peggy? It may take us years to get anywhere. We'll have no money, no decent place to live. We'll have to work. Get kicked around." When Andrews reached the end of the phrase, "get kicked around," he lands on an off note. It's like he's on the verge of uttering some final sweet nothing that will smooth down the sharp edge of his proposal and make for a more harmonious ending.

Instead, the phrase just hangs there—get kicked around.

And so it goes with Dana Andrews' crumpled marriage. He comes home one afternoon to find a guy named Cliff in his

apartment with his wife, Virginia Mayo. "Did you know him while I was away?" he asks.

"I knew a lot of people," answers his bombshell bride. "What do you think I was doing all those years?"

"I don't know, babe, but I can guess."

"Go ahead, guess your head off! I could do some guessing myself. What were you doing in Paris and London and all those places?"

And then the unhappy little marriage breaks up: "I've given you every chance to make something of yourself," Virginia Mayo says. "I gave up my own job when you asked me. I gave up the best years of my life, and what have you done? You flopped. Couldn't even hold that job at the drugstore. So I'm going to work for myself, and that means I'm gonna work for myself and in case you don't understand English, I'm going to get a divorce. What have you got to say to that?"

It's a great touch, that Virginia Mayo's shallow, fed-up character, who wants to get on with it and stop obsessing and remembering, is the one to speak the words "the best years of my life." It undercuts the title's seeming tinge of wallowing self-indulgence; it also plays off the indescribably compressed war experience. The phrase refers, ironically, to the war years, when the movie's characters were apart and scraping to survive. So it's tacitly understood that the protagonists' best years are gone, invested in their country's future, and they've spent their youth and now they must try to find a way to negotiate the aftermath. And the aftermath is even more daunting than the war itself—just life—now that the characters are no longer part of a grand cause and must figure out for themselves what

to do with the endless years that lie ahead. They have to make their own lives, a condition that has been a given in this country for at least a generation. This purposeless peacetime, in other words, has been hell, with the result that people have distanced themselves as much as possible from what they had during the war: a community at large.

Teresa Wright says the movie shows her character, Peggy Stephenson, waking up. "She probably would not be as advanced in her thinking without the war," Ms. Wright said. "As she was, the war made her grow up a lot, as it made a lot of people grow up. Even grown-ups grew up a lot. But there came a time after the war when there was a new kind of prosperity—people needing new cars and new homes and things they couldn't get during the war. And so a softness set in, even a softness in thinking. I don't think the people we saw in the film—I don't think Fred's (Dana Andrews') family would go backwards at all, but the average family probably regressed a bit."

It has become a cultural maxim that the baby boom generation behaved as it did in rebellion against the war generation. But the war veterans in the film who questioned their former place—the unsatisfied drugstore cowboy, the unhappy bank bureaucrat—seem like precursors to the wild characters of the 60's. It's not really such a long way from *The Best Years of Our Lives* to another seminal three-hour movie, *Woodstock*. But it's a very long way from *The Best Years of Our Lives* to its supposedly contemporaneous putative best picture, *The English Patient*, the entire purpose of which is to show the best year in the life of Count Laszlo de Almasy, who, in real life, was a spy for the Nazis.

J.F.K. Jr. (#8) and Rudy Giuliani (#4) were among those on '97's Power 100

◇◇◇◇◇◇◇

MARCH 31, 1997 BY RON ROSENBAUM

THE EDGY ENTHUSIAST, WOODY ALLEN SERENADES BOOKS & CO.; WILL THE WHITNEY LET IT SURVIVE?

"WHAT ARE THEY GONNA RE-place it with," Woody Allen asks glumly, "another expensive foreign clothing store?"

"Maybe a nail salon," I suggest bitterly.

We'd been speculating about the Whitney Museum of America Art's plans for the Books & Company space if the museum succeeds—as it now seems intent on doing—in killing the beloved bookstore a second time.

The Woodman had called to express his support for the campaign to save the bookstore. He'd already put in a call to Leonard Lauder, chairman of the Whitney board, who now seems to be the last slim hope for saving the store, as Mr. Lauder's underlings at the museum seem to be engineering a quiet suffocation of this vital New York City institution through bureaucratic sleight of hand. The Woodman

is both impassioned and persistent: He's enlisting friends in the campaign, and when Mr. Lauder, who has been traveling, did not immediately return his call, Mr. Allen faxed him requesting a talk as soon as he returned. It is to be hoped that all book-loving *Observer* readers who did not respond to my plea in a previous column to write or fax Mr. Lauder drop everything and do so now, because the situation has become even more dire. The way the Whitney is going about disposing of the bookstore is turning into a classic case study of how power operates in New York, the way a powerful institution deals with potentially embarrassing public relations challenges: by putting on a public face of sweet reason while quietly using bureaucratic maneuvers and delays to strangle the inconvenience it wishes to dispose of.

TV DIARY: Happy Midlife, Dave! What, You Worry?

THIS ISN'T EXACTLY DREW BARRYMORE TURNING HER BACK ON the audience and getting up on the desk in the old Ed Sullivan Theatre and giving you a flash of her breasts (*Late Show With David Letterman*, April 12, 1995), but: Happy birthday, Dave, happy birthday to you.

This is what it has come down to, after all the hard work on those Indianapolis radio and TV stations (1969-1975) and the slugging it out alongside Jay Leno and Jeff Altman at the Comedy Store in Los Angeles (1975-1978) until the long hard years at *Late Night With David Letterman* (1982-1992) which led not to your rightful place in Burbank, Calif., but to a retrofitted stage in a monstrous, dark, rat-exterminated Ed Sullivan Theater for a maddening network, CBS, which looked so promising when you signed on for $14 million a year, but has since lost the Olympics, National Football League games and truckloads of viewers, but went on to sign ... Bryant Gumbel.

Dave, you're first and foremost a broadcaster, unlike Jay Leno, who is just a comic, and to some extent like Ted Koppel and certainly unlike Bill Maher, who is stealing viewers from you between midnight and 12:30 a.m. but who is truly a scavenger, relying on such grisly grist as the death-cult suicides to provide his show with its only reason for being.

But as Nick Carraway said to Jay Gatsby, you're better than the whole lot of them put together. (That's not completely true, but it's your birthday.) And it's time for you to grow up!

Pataki Pack: Governor George Pataki yuks it up with pals Senator Alfonse D'Amato and Charles Gargano

APRIL 21, 1997 BY WARREN ST. JOHN

KATHRYN HARRISON'S DAD RESPONDS TO HER MEMOIR

AUTHOR KATHRYN HARRI-son's father is a retired Protes-tant minister, living in a small Southern city, who claims he knew nothing of his 36-year-old daughter's best-selling memoir *The Kiss*, with its ac-count of their four-year con-sensual incestuous relation-ship, until contacted on April 11 by *The Observer*.

Allowing that he was "pretty shaken" to learn of his daugh-ter's book, he said, "You say that Kathryn has said that she had an affair with me? I guess if people want to believe that, golly."

Asked if he had a sexual rela-tionship with his daughter, he first replied, "The girl writes fic-tion." Pressed, he said, "I don't want to do anything to bring Kathryn into a bad light. My im-mediate reaction is that you've got me with something that I don't even know a thing about. You've asked me about a book that I didn't know was published. I guess I'm going to have to find out real quick.

"I don't want to call my daugh-ter a liar," he said, "I don't want to bring her into question about her standing—but obviously I've been brought into question about mine."

Reached overseas, where she was promoting *The Kiss*, Ms. Harrison gave a statement through Random House spokes-person Carol Schneider: "In writing this book, I exposed my-self and not my father, and every-thing I have to say is in the book. I have no further comment."

MAY 5, 1997
BY LORNE MANLY

OFF THE RECORD: AFTER DECLARING DEATH OF DOWNTOWN, JAMES TRUMAN OUSTS DETAILS EDITOR

◇◇◇◇◇◇◇

MAY 5, 1997 BY DEVIN LEONARD AND GREG SARGENT

Brave New Rents Would Make Manhattan a Cold Place

THERE WAS A TIME WHEN PEO-ple might have been forgiven for believing there was at least some paltry reward for sticking it out in Manhattan. Sure, they

had to brave the cursing cab-bies, the hostile bus drivers, the in-your-face panhandlers, the junkies shooting up in door-ways, the muggings, the Third World infrastructure. But there were people so enthralled with Manhattan and all of its grit and glittery promise that they couldn't imagine living any-where else, including the outer boroughs.

"This sounds a bit elitist," said Andy Humm, editor of *Social Pol-icy* magazine. "But in some ways, living in the boroughs doesn't fit with what attracted me to Man-hattan in the first place."

So they hacked out an exis-tence, rehabbed a tenement apartment in Chelsea, fought for a local park, did battle with the landlord and agitated for better schools for their children. To those hardy souls willing to go to such ends to live here, Man-hattan offered something in return: shelter from the whims of its notoriously profit-hungry real-estate speculators. Now, it seems, the deal is off.

DETAILS EDITOR JOE DOLCE kept hearing rumors that a head-hunter was offering his job to a number of magazine editors in town. So on the afternoon of April 28, the editor put in a phone call to his boss, Condé Nast Publications editorial director James Truman.

By the end of the phone call, Mr. Dolce was out of a job.

"I just hear the rumors one too many times, so I called James on his vacation in Brazil—and I re-signed," Mr. Dolce said. "I guess I ruined his vacation. Or maybe not. Maybe I made it good."

Back in February, Mr. Truman said he wanted to remake *De-tails*, changing it from a magazine aimed at ultra-hip young men into a more mainstream publi-cation catering to would-be ex-ecutives. "I have an intuition that downtown is dead as a subject," Mr. Truman said at the time. He added that Mr. Dolce would be keeping his job.

MAY 12, 1997 BY GEORGE GURLEY

BLUEBLOOD BELLES, LOST IN NEW YORK

A GROUP OF YOUNG WOMEN with one foot in *Vogue* and one foot in the Social Register is now coming of age. These modern-day belles of the Manhattan blueblood set still shell out big money to attend black-tie fund raisers for diseases and museums, and they still hang out at such exclusive enclaves as the Colony Club and the River Club, but they're also trying to make names for themselves outside of their own sphere.

Some of the blueblood belles recently found themselves in a rented space in the garment district. The occasion was a press fashion show held for one of their own, Alexandra Lind, and her line of clothing.

At a Madison Avenue bistro one night soon after her small triumph, Alexandra Lind spoke for her clan: "We all share a common interest in making our own statement about who we are instead of who our family is," she said. "I don't think any of us would use our last names."

What if the family name opened a door that might otherwise be shut?

"I think it can help," Ms. Lind said. "If my father is a good friend of an editor in chief of some magazine, my God! All the more power to me. Or if I found other private investors through friends of my parents, that's a great advantage. Or your parents supporting you financially to start up a company, that's something that's really valuable."

But you and your friends don't fall back on that?

"Exactly."

Senator Moynihan enters Penn Station

◇◇◇◇◇◇◇

MAY 12, 1997 BY ALEX KUCZYNSKI

NEW YORK WORLD: Botulism Becomes You, My Dear—But Get Ready to Lose That Scowl

HERE'S AN IDEA. GET YOURSELF INJECTED WITH BOTULINUM TOX-in A, the neurotoxin that causes botulism, to smooth out those wrinkles in your face.

It may sound gruesome, but dermatologists and plastic surgeons across the city have lately been luring hundred of patients into their chairs with this novel use of the deadly toxin. A shot of Botox, as it's known commercially, paralyzes the muscles that cause wrinkles, leaving those who receive the treatment with faces as smooth as carved soap.

New Yorkers endure a lot to earn those scowl lines and laugh lines—but in their panicky battle against the all-too-visible effects of aging, men and women as young as 30 have gone to the extreme of having themselves injected with the botulism toxin. One bizarre side effect of the treatment leaves patients unable to make certain expressions, lending the Botoxified face a "Stepford wife" quality. Strangely, the typical patient who goes in for the botulism treatment comes to like having a face with a permanently blasé appearance.

"A scowl is a totally unnecessary expression," said Dr. Pat Wexler, a dermatologist with an office on East 32nd Street who says she injects two dozen people a week with the toxin. "Scowls are negative. And who needs a squint? It's not the most positive thing in the world."

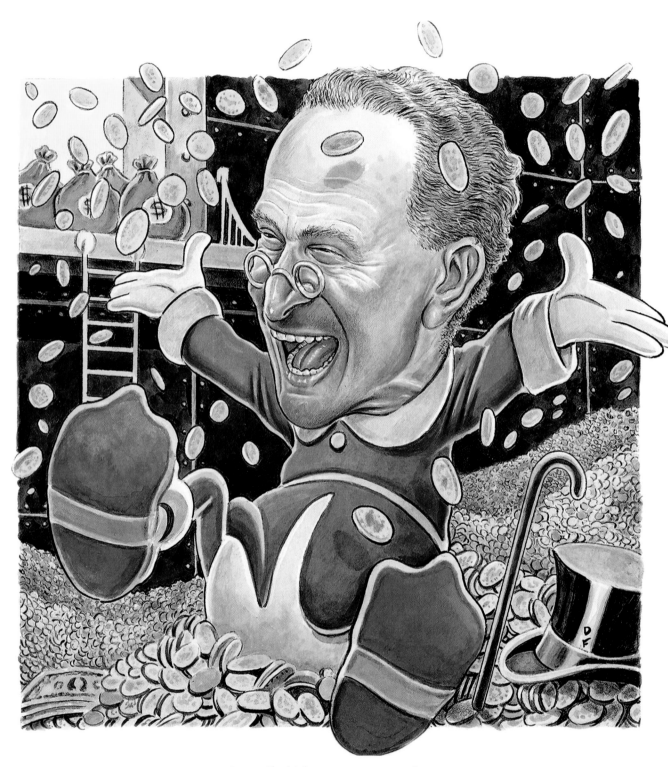

Senator Chuck Schumer as Scrooge McDuck

MAY 19, 1997 BY FRANK DIGIACOMO

THE OBSERVATORY: BISTRO OF BURDEN

KEITH MCNALLY HUNCHED over Table No. 70 at Balthazar and methodically began to shred the paper placemat. "I'm not wishing for this to be over," he said, "but I can't appreciate something until it's finished." The dark pouches under his eyes complemented the skinny black tie that hung loosely beneath his open shirt collar. "I can really enjoy things afterwards, but right now, I'm too wrapped up in the *things* that aren't quite right."

At 4 p.m. on May 9, a Friday, Balthazar, the brasserie that Mr. McNally opened on April 21, looked well under control. A number of people dallied over their lunches; an expensively dressed elderly woman sat alone savoring a cup of coffee. But Mr. McNally was nursing a look that suggested disaster would be arriving with the dinner crowd.

"I'm really anxious about tonight. There are too many reservations," Mr. McNally said. As a result, he had had to deny the art dealer Mary Boone a table, and she had been a regular customer at his other ventures. There was more. "I'm anxious now because the music's not on at all. It should be on a little bit in the afternoon. The lighting's a little bit too bright now." Mr. McNally stopped and coughed a nervous cough. "I'm worried about a lot of things right now," he said.

Keith McNally has walked this tightrope of neuroses before, but never at this height and never alone. Yes, there is Pravda, the Russian-themed vodka bar and cafe that Mr. McNally opened last year, but as the financier and Balthazar regular Steven Greenberg said, "Pravda was a paragraph in the book of Keith's life. Balthazar is an entire chapter."

In the three weeks since it had opened, Balthazar had generated instant heat. With no advance publicity, the brasserie's red awnings and interior sienna glow seemed to materialize overnight on a piece of Spring Street that had never before merited a second glance. The socialite Brooke Hayward remembered walking by the restaurant at noon on the first day that Balthazar served lunch and seeing a largely empty restaurant. "I thought, 'This looks interesting,'" she said, "But when I came back at 1, I couldn't get a table. I've never seen anything like it."

The buzz right now is that Balthazar is a downtown institution-in-the-making, one that could eventually eclipse the Odeon, the seminal TriBeCa hangout that Mr. McNally, his wife, Lyn Wagenknecht, and his older brother, Brian McNally, opened in 1980. But Keith McNally knows all too well that the frenzy and the media coverage that has greeted the opening of Balthazar will not mean a whole lot a year from now if he doesn't worry about the details. The danger of instant heat is that is can dissipate just as instantly.

"I don't want to roll the dice again or whatever they say. This is it for me," Mr. McNally said as he took the shredded strips of paper he had torn from the tablemat and began to crumple them into little balls.

MAY 26, 1997
BY JIM WINDOLF

AGENTS! BABES! SUITS! NEW YORK IS TV TOWN

ABC INC. PRESIDENT ROBERT Iger assumed his position behind the podium on the Radio City Music Hall stage and started flagellating himself and his network for the benefit of the advertising executives in the audience.

"It's nice to be here in Radio City Music Hall," he said in a staccato delivery. "I think it's the closest I've been to NBC all season. A few years ago, A European politician said, 'Today we stand on the brink of a great precipice, tomorrow we will take one step forward.' I decided not to use a speechwriter for my remarks today."

Toward the end of his quick statement, he offered a tepid endorsement of the head of ABC Entertainment, 33-year-old Jamie Tarses. "We realize we can't solve all of our problems at once, but the ABC television network and the company stand behind Jamie Tarses and the people responsible for our prime-time programming," he said, still reading his lines off the teleprompter in a rapid-fire monotone.

Mr. Iger's straightforward words were in violent contrast to the mad spectacle to come.

OCTOBER 13, 1997 BY SVEN BIRKERTS

TWILIGHT OF THE GREAT LITERARY BEASTS ROTH, MAILER, BELLOW RUNNING OUT OF GAS

HOW TO SAY THIS? HOW TO BE TACTFUL AND PROPERLY grateful for everything they have given us—we have scarcely had time to reckon the gift yet—but also how to say what needs saying and preserve one's sense of honor as a reader and critic. I mean—*out with it!*—that our giants, our art-bemedaled senior male novelists (and this will only deal with males) are not connecting. Not the way they did. Once they seemed to shape the very cultural ectoplasm with the force and daring of their presentations. Their books had, in any publishing season, the status of *events*. Now they don't. They have been writing manifestly second-rate novels in recent years and they are not—much—getting called onto the carpet for it.

I'm talking now about Philip Roth, John Updike, Norman Mailer and, to a degree, Saul Bellow, though one wouldn't need a shoehorn to get a few others on the list. There have been other changes, granted. The publishing world has been ravaged by corporate greed and has, in recent years, suffered a deep crisis of confidence. But that can't account for the books. The latest novels are weak, makeshift and gravely disappointing to all who believed that these novelists had a special line on the truth(s) of late modernity. Not one of the books can stand in the vicinity of their author's finest work.

Oddly (or not, depending on how jaundiced is your view of the backstage machinations of the literary world), with the exception of Mr. Updike's newest, which has been K.O.'d right at the starting bell, the critical community has been kind to the grandees.

But when this body of recent work is viewed alongside the writing of the younger brothers—Thomas Pynchon, Don DeLillo, Robert Stone and John Edgar Wideman, to name several—the contrast is striking. These authors seem to be looking at the larger world, assessing the twin claims of politics and spirit. We feel in their books, certainly in *Mason & Dixon* and *Underworld*, some of the pressure of seriousness that we were once so sparked by in their elders. But these elders are no longer spinning the stuff of our times into lasting art. The once-thrilling researches into the self have proved exhaustible. No less important, they are not holding themselves to the literary standards they did so much to establish.

I'm talking about narcissism now, the male variety, with its attendant exalted belief that one is in some way co-terminous with the world, steering it with will and desire. The pathology that in one version at least, needs over and over to gain the admiring (as in *ad mirare:* "to reflect back") love of women, that struts pridefully forth holding sexuality—the penis—aloft as its talisman.

But the story doesn't end here with the male eternally rampant. Youth declines into maturity, maturity sinks toward dreaded old age. The lion paces a weary circle and lies down. No one would reasonably expect the artist to carry on in his former style. Opportu-nities for quiet recusal, for edging from the race, abound. But—Mr. Bellow excepted—these writers have kept on drilling out roughly a book a year—each, for as long as anyone can remember, holding the spotlight on himself by main force. Surely they are no longer striving to keep the wolf from the door. What gives?

The narcissist is no more immune to time than anyone else. As my wife, my therapist, formulates for me: "Aging is a narcissistic injury." When the narcissist faces the loss of the self and its reflected glory, he reacts with rage. And indeed, checking in on some of the works of later years by our masters, we are overwhelmed by dissonant music from the downside of the artists: Mr. Bellow's Dean Corde in *The Dean's December* snarling at the underclass; the cataracting vituperations of Mickey Sabbath in *Sabbath's Theater* ... We see anger at promises not kept, at prerogatives usurped, and deep bitterness about an America that has betrayed its youthful innocent promise. But also, with scorching vindictiveness at times—especially in Messrs. Updike and Roth—comes the lashing out at women. Women, the supposed adoring ones, whose job it was to keep the illusion of perpetual youth and power intact. Dare we tie this, as Mr. Updike seems to in his new book, to the failure in age of the sexual fix? Could the whole business really have been driven by the say-so of an upstanding phallus? A frightening thought.

OCTOBER 13, 1997 BY DAVID FOSTER WALLACE

BOOK REVIEW: TWILIGHT OF THE GREAT LITERARY BEASTS: JOHN UPDIKE, CHAMPION LITERARY PHALLOCRAT, DROPS ONE; IS THIS FINALLY THE END FOR THE MAGNIFICENT NARCISSIST?

"Of nothing but me ... I sing, lacking another song."
—John Updike, *Midpoint*, 1969

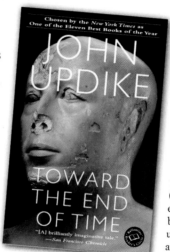

TOWARD THE END OF TIME CONCERNS an incredibly erudite, articulate, successful, narcissistic and sex-obsessed retired guy who's keeping a one-year journal in which he explores the apocalyptic prospect of his own death. It is, of the total 25 Updike books I've read, far and away the worst, a novel so mind-bendingly clunky and self-indulgent that it's hard to believe the author let it be published in this kind of shape.

Mr. Updike has for years been constructing protagonists who are basically all the same guy and who are all clearly stand-ins for the author himself. They always live in either Pennsylvania or New England, are unhappily married/divorced, are roughly Mr. Updike's age.

Always either the narrator or the point-of-view character, they all have the author's astounding perceptual gifts; they all think and speak in the same effortlessly lush, synesthetic way Mr. Updike does. They are also always incorrigibly narcissistic, philandering, self-contemptuous, self-pitying ... and deeply alone, alone the way only a solipsist can be alone. Though usually family men, they never really love anybody—and, though always heterosexual to the point of satyriasis, they especially don't love women. The very world around them, as beautiful as they see and describe it, seems to exist for them only insofar as it evokes impressions and associations and emotions inside the self.

The clunky bathos of this novel seems to have infected even the prose, John Updike's great strength for almost 40 years. *Toward the End of Time* has occasional flashes of beautiful writing—deer described as "tender-faced ruminants," leaves as "chewed to lace by Japanese beetles," a car's tight turn as a "slur." But a horrific percentage of the book consists of stuff like "Why indeed do women weep? They weep, it seemed to my wandering mind, for the world itself, in its beauty and waste, its mingled cruelty and tenderness" and "How much of summer is over before it begins! Its beginning marks its end, as our birth entails our death" and "This development seems remote, however, among the many more urgent issues of survival on our blasted, depopulated planet." Not to mention whole reams of sentences with so many modifiers—"The insouciance and innocence of our independence twinkled like a kind of sweat from their bare and freckled or honey-colored or mahogany limbs"—or so much subordination—"As our species, having given itself a hard hit, staggers, the others, all but counted out, moved in"—and such heavy alliteration—"The broad sea blares a blue I would not have believed obtainable without a tinted filter"—that they seem less like John Updike than like somebody doing a mean parody of John Updike.

Besides distracting us with worries about whether Mr. Updike might be injured or ill, the turgidity of the prose also increases our dislike of the novel's narrator (it's hard to like a guy whose way of saying his wife doesn't like going to bed before him is "She hated it when I crept into bed and disturbed in her the fragile succession of steps whereby consciousness dissolves"). This dislike absolutely torpedoes *Toward the End of Time*, a novel whose tragic climax (in a late chapter called "The Deaths") is a prostate operation that leaves Turnbull impotent and extremely bummed. It is made very clear that the author expects us to sympathize with and even share Turnbull's grief at "the pathetic shrunken wreck the procedures [have] made of my beloved genitals." These demands on our compassion echo the major crisis of the book's first half, described in a flashback, where we are supposed to empathize not only with the textbookish existential dread that hits Turnbull at 30 as he's in his basement building a dollhouse for his daughter—"I would die, but also the little girl I was making this for would die. There was no God, each detail of the rusting, moldering cellar made clear, just Nature, which would consume my life as carelessly and relentlessly as it would a dung-beetle corpse in a compost pile"—but also with Turnbull's relief at discovering a remedy for this dread—"an affair, my first. Its colorful weave of carnal revelation and intoxicating risk and craven guilt eclipsed the devouring gray sensation of time."

Maybe the only thing the reader ends up appreciating about Ben Turnbull is that he's such a broad caricature of an Updike protagonist that he helps us figure out what's been so unpleasant and frustrating about this gifted author's recent characters. It's not that Turnbull is stupid—he can quote Kierkegaard and Pascal on angst and allude to the deaths of Schubert and Mozart and distinguish between a sinistrorse and a dextrorse Polygonum vine, etc. It's that he persists in the bizarre adolescent idea that getting to have sex with whomever one wants whenever one wants is a cure for ontological despair. And so, it appears, does Mr. Updike—he makes it plain that he views the narrator's impotence as catastrophic, as the ultimate symbol of death itself, and he clearly wants us to mourn it as much as Turnbull does. I'm not especially offended by this attitude; I mostly just don't get it. Erect or flaccid, Ben Turnbull's unhappiness is obvious right from the book's first page. But it never once occurs to him that the reason he's so unhappy is that he's an asshole.

JUNE 2, 1997 BY WARREN ST. JOHN

The Secret Selling of Thomas Pynchon

IT WAS AN ODD PLACE FOR A THOMAS PYNCHON SIGHTING: ALONG-side John Grisham, Mary Higgins Clark, Danielle Steele and Dr. Seuss in the upper reaches of the *New York Times* best-seller list for June 1. Every Pynchon novel, of course, is an event: They arrive like comets, once every decade or so, carrying not just fine writing but faint radio signals transmitting clues about Pynchon himself. *Mason & Dixon*, however, answers more questions about the book-buying public than it does about its famously reclusive author. For the book's audi-ence has expanded hugely beyond Mr. Pynchon's loyal, inbred literary groupies; the 773-page, $27.50 novel with the gorgeous peach-toned cover is this summer's book to be seen with. The fact that it is a very difficult book to read has only increased its cachet as an intellectual fashion accessory. But that's just fine with Mr. Pynchon's publishers, Henry Holt and Company, who are success-fully pulling off a cheekily misleading marketing campaign for the invisible author's challenging novel.

Mason & Dixon is actually being called the "easy" Pynchon novel. Echoing a number of critics, Yale University professor Harold Bloom said, "It's remarkably relaxed and, for Pynchon, a happy book. ..."

Cathy Melnicki, the book's publicist at Holt, said *Mason & Dixon* is "a really accessible, kind of familiar, two-guys-go-into-the-woods story ... the ultimate Odd Couple, a 'friend' book." Then she men-tioned the bonus: "Reading Pynchon makes people feel smart," she said, "and people like to feel smart."

JUNE 9, 1997 BY PHILIP WEISS

LAY OFF THE SOCIALITE! JON KRAKAUER LEADS VILIFICATION OF EX-MRS. PITTMAN

I'M AN ASTERISK TO THE GREAT Everest disaster of 1996. A couple of months before she left for base camp, I went shopping for gear with Sandy Hill (then Sandy Hill Pittman). We dipped into a little hardware store on 17th Street, and in a minute she had the yar-mulked owner and everyone else swarming at her elbows trying to find stuff for her. She was wearing Prada boots and a $500 crocodile belt and lectured me briskly about the best duct tape and how to pee out the leg of your shorts. "I'm not doing anything like hiking." I felt put down.

My schadenfreude toward Sandy is today a popular feeling.

Among the tents of Manhattan base camp, there's an almost universal feeling that Ms. Hill is evil. As Peter Wilkinson said in *Men's Journal*, she's the "chief villain, the Susan Lucci" of the Everest trip.

The destruction of a bold, single woman, once the toast of the town on her MTV husband's arm, has been a ghastly thing to watch. It's happened because of a lot of sniggering articles reporting the climb, because of gossip and because of Jon Krakauer's best seller, *Into Thin Air* (Villard).

Mr. Krakauer isn't the first person not to like Sandy Hill.

Countless magazine profiles and whispered comments por-tray an insensitive and material-istic woman who knows how to use people. Those faults might be excused in a greater talent, but her failure to display ap-propriate humility post-Everest angered others, causing them to overlook the truly impres-sive aspects of her character. And the belief that she killed anybody on Everest is absurd and cruel. Yes, she was gross, but a close study of the facts in Mr. Krakauer's splendid ac-count shows that if fault for the deaths is to be found, it must be found elsewhere.

Senator Bill Bradley plays keep-away from Al Gore

AUGUST 4, 1997 BY GEORGE GURLEY

HAMPTONS '97: THE NEW-MONEY DUDES ARE HERE

EAST HAMPTON, JULY 29—THE Vipers were out on Route 27, big throbbing Dodge Vipers. In the driver's seats of these $60,000 sports cars were guys who looked like that newest breed of weekend Hamptonite, the bonus babies of the rising Dow. They were ready to spend whatever it took to get in on the glamorous scene they had heard so much about, but guess what. There they were, stuck in traffic, all revved up with no place to go.

This season, many of the long-time summer residents and the A-list party creatures have made a decided effort to go into a kind of social hibernation. For this is the summer the Hamptons rebelled against being the East Coast Hollywood.

Steven Spielberg's house, a little mansion in East Hampton called Quelle Barn, has been quiet lately. And among other movie people and celebrity moguls—with notable exception of Long Island natives Billy and Alec Baldwin—the notion of putting oneself on display at a party heavy with publi-

cists and paparazzi is no longer considered good form.

Robert De Niro, for one, has been spending time in Montauk this summer—but by staying away from the usual hot spots, he has managed to avoid serving as the subject of gossip items and paparazzi shots. Michael Douglas also managed to get in some golf at the National Golf Links without drawing any attention. Steve Martin, too, has been coming out this summer—but only to see his actual friends, rather than enduring the scrum of parties. Billy Joel is also in hiding. The only one out of synch with the times, it seems, is Donald Trump, who got photographed the other weekend bashing a piñata with a stick at a child's birthday party; unfortunately, Mr. Trump was not wearing a blindfold.

Meanwhile, standing behind counters of gift shops and taking the orders in the restaurants and country clubs, are the townspeople—some of whom are growing more and more restless with the beautiful invaders.

SEPTEMBER 22, 1997 BY TISH DURKIN

Al Sharpton Wins in Never-Never Land

THE REV. AL SHARPTON WAS ABOUT TWO HOURS LATE FOR HIS Sunday-night stop at the Mount Calavary Fire Baptized Holiness Church in Bushwick, Brooklyn, but with someone else at the wheel in his purple campaign van, he could sit back and make big plans. "You've got to get Don King to get the Garden," he said to a reporter along for the ride. "James Brown to open it up, and Rudy and I to debate. A great New York night!"

It was a great New York thought, and at that moment, before talk of uncounted absentee ballots started to smudge the sureness of the fact that Mr. Sharpton had forced Manhattan Borough President Ruth Messinger into a runoff for the Democratic mayoral nomination to face Mayor Rudolph Giuliani, it sounded almost sane. Only the other night, Mr. King had addressed a rally of star-reaching Sharptonites at the National Action Network in Harlem. And just an hour or two before, Mr. Brown, a longtime father figure to Mr. Sharpton, had introduced him onstage at a twilight concert in Central Park. Mr. Giuliani might not be up for Madison Square Garden with all the trimmings, but then, if he were obliged to debate Mr. Sharpton under any circumstances, the spectacle would take care of itself.

Not a few reporters were secretly cherishing the prospect, however remote, that a general campaign otherwise crumb-dry of charisma might be overtaken by a figure positively pouring with it, and vaguely, warily wondering what such a campaign might drag to the surface of the city.

NOVEMBER 17, 1997 BY FRANK DIGIACOMO

JUDITH REGAN DRIVES TWO AUTHORS BONKERS

WHEN THE MORNING DELIVERY OF *THE NEW YORK TIMES* BROUGHT news on June 27 that Harper Collins had canceled more than 100 titles from its publishing list to cut costs, Ellen Hawkes turned to her longtime companion, Peter Manso, and said: "We should be so lucky."

At the time they read the article in their Berkeley, Calif., home, Ms. Hawkes and Mr. Manso, accomplished book authors both, had been collaborating for almost a year on a biography of the deceased model and actress Margaux Hemingway for Regan Books, the Harper Collins-owned imprint run by publishing's brash wonderwoman, Judith Regan.

But all was not well between the authors and their editor. They claimed they had not been in contact with Ms. Regan since September 1996. She had, however, made her presence felt in a phone call on June 6 to Ms. Hawkes' agent, Marion Rosenberg. "They are assholes, unprofessional beasts, reprehensible, unprofessional motherfuckers," she told Ms. Rosenberg (who took notes).

The authors themselves were no shrinking violets when it came to memos. "Judith (and we) have all along thought of this as a 'woman's' book," they wrote to Mr. Manso's agent, Elaine Markson, when they learned that Ms. Regan wanted a shot of Hemingway "with breasts visible under [a] sheer wet dress" on the book's cover. Ms. Markson at one point wrote Harper Collins' general counsel, James Fox: "Please inform Regan Books that, like E.E. Cummings, there is some shit I will not eat."

◇◇◇◇◇◇◇

DECEMBER 15, 1997 BY PHILIP WEISS

The Dark Bourgeois Heart of Woody Allen

WOODY ALLEN OFTEN LIKens his work to magic, and his haunts in the Manhattan Film Center inside the Beekman apartments feel a little like the magician's back rooms. On Dec. 2, the day after Mr. Allen's 62nd birthday, I was shown into a screening room that was also doing double duty, with record albums on one wall and canisters of film along the other.

I sat in a brown armchair and then abruptly, like a trick, Mr. Allen appeared on the muskrat-colored couch, wearing a tasteful muted palette of gray and olive and black scuffed shoes and gathering a dark pillow defensively to his stomach, said, "I'm at your disposal," in a gentle voice.

"Do you have a name for your penis?"

Woody Allen looked aghast.

"What?"

Maybe it was the wrong question to start with. I guess I'd felt justified because it's a bit from Mr. Allen's new movie *Deconstructing Harry*.

But seated across from me now, he seemed white-faced, sincere.

"You know, it's in the movie. 'Do you have a name for your penis?'"

He shook his head. "No. But that is the strangest question I've ever gotten from a journalist."

GEORGE GURLEY INTERVIEWS JIM WINDOLF

You started the New York World column ...
We looked at old newspapers like *The New York World* in the '20s, and they had a column in there called the Conning Tower, and it was kind of modeled on that. The Conning Tower was by Franklin Adams; he was on the outskirts of the Algonquin Round Table.

In the Transom you had the news about things that happened that week, and New York World was more of the feeling of the city or things that may not have been news, but described the mood of the city. And funny things. I wrote a short one: "Lunch Excuses." Nice little hundred words. There were a lot of hundred- or two-hundred-word things and Talk of the Town didn't have that. So that was one of the things we could do differently. Sparrow I liked because when I was covering the media, I covered his protest of *The New Yorker*. Sparrow was in this group of poets called The Unbearables who protested *The New Yorker*, and Sparrow had this great quote: "Our poetry is as bad as anything published in *The New Yorker* so we deserve to be in there as much as anybody else." And when I actually read the stuff I really liked it—it was so beautifully readable and funny, as opposed to the crap in *The New Yorker*.

What was it like when Graydon was the editor?
I'd been a teacher—taught English at Friends Seminary, and I decided I didn't want to be a teacher anymore, so I applied to 20 newspapers and the only place I got a response was *The New York Observer*. Luckily, I really knew *Spy* well: At the interview I was able to know what I was talking about because I'd read *Spy*. I started on November 11th, 1991. Helen Thorpe was writing Off the Record, Charlie Bagli doing real estate, Terry Golway doing politics, Claire McHugh doing the Transom and Robin Pogrebin doing a mix of Broadway, feature stories, news stories—for some reason she had the Andrew Stein beat. I think she was the one who reported he had 30 wigs for the month, so that it looked like natural hair coming in—he'd start each month with his shortest wig and then work his way through as the month went on. I thought that was a great detail and that made me realize that there was something different in *The Observer*. It wasn't the same as reading *The Times*.

Before Graydon took over, this guy John Sicher was the editor. He wasn't really a journalist. I think in the first issue of *The Observer* the cover was a picture of a duck pond in Central Park. Kind of this pastoral view of New York: Let's treat New York like it's a quaint small town. When Graydon came

Jim Windolf is a contributing editor at *Vanity Fair*.

in, he brought in the satire, the insider's look at different industries, especially media and gossip. He did it with the writers who were there. *Spy* was a magazine made up of writers who were witty; *The Observer* was different because you had someone like Charlie Bagli, who was just a straight-ahead reporter who got news. And Terry Golway was serious about city politics. He came from the *Staten Island Advance* and it was not a joke to him. And Graydon took people like that, with their heart and seriousness, and brought in the hard edge and satire. Graydon had yellow Post-It notes and before the reporters got there, he would put a Post-It note on each desk; he would have their assignment on that Post-It. I was amazed. How does he know what's going to look good in the paper a week from now? The other thing was, Graydon at that time had a side deal to write for *Vogue*. One of my jobs was to fax his article to Anna Wintour and it really was a shock to me—like, "So he's working with them?" Like somebody *Spy* had mocked.

And I was an old intern. I was 28, and I was an intern. I'd go to the library for the reporters: three hours of working microfilm and Xeroxing stuff and bringing it back. And we had a van and Graydon wanted to put wood in his office, so we picked up the wood that was going to be the built-in shelves. We picked up the wood and then [Graydon's assistant] Kirk hit the brakes too hard and the wood cracked the windshield on our way back. Another time I was bringing Graydon coffee and I completely spilled—like lunged forward—he had a beautiful white shirt and I doused him. And he was nice about it and he told me some story where he had done the same thing to Si Newhouse. The first articles I did were covering community board meetings. Graydon said, "You go to these meetings and there's always a story, because some people want something and they're either going to get it or they're not. And that's a story." I got $50 a week for each one. The first real feature story that I did was when adults were starting to play Gameboy. This was 1991; that primitive version of Gameboy. And it was so cool because I never had a Gameboy and I had to get one and figure out how it works. This was the time when adults would play Tetris on their computers. Graydon said he couldn't understand why adults would do that when they should, at the end of the workday, be getting home for dinner or their kids. When I wrote the article, I wanted to write the most fantastic article of all time, so I wrote this ridiculous 300-word introduction that was complete crazy bullshit, really bad beatnik prose, and the editor said, "If I show this to Graydon, you'll no longer be working here." Then I understood: You're not writing for yourself, you're writing an article for other people to read. One thing I remember is we were going to have this special daily election issue come out for the 1992 convention. And then Graydon announced he was leaving. And during the meeting where he announced it, Robin [Pogrebin] said, "Well, are you going stick around for the convention?"

> *There were a lot of things flying out of Kaplan's window. We'd be like, "Did you see this article in New York magazine?" and he'd throw it out the window.*

And he said, "No, I'm going fishing." He was going to take two weeks off before his next job [as editor of *Vanity Fair*] started.

I was made the media columnist, writing Off the Record. The first week I wrote the column, Tina Brown took over *The New Yorker*. Luckily, I knew the history of *The New Yorker* really well from reading all the *New Yorker* books as a hobby. It wasn't like I was preparing to be a media journalist. I just knew that stuff. I enjoyed reading it. And right before I took over Off the Record, one day on the car radio, I heard—just flipping around on AM stations—this song, "I'm the Happiest Girl in the Whole USA." It was the No. 5 hit of 1971—really bad country pop song by Donna Fargo. So when Tina got the *New Yorker* job, I called Robert Gottlieb, who was the outgoing editor. And he didn't give many interviews. He answered his phone and I said, "How do you feel leaving *The New Yorker*?" and the first thing he said was, "I'm the happiest girl in the whole USA." So I said, "Donna Fargo, right?" and just because I could say Donna Fargo, he stayed on the phone.

And then through a friend of a friend, I knew one person who happened to have a job at *The New Yorker*. So when Susan Morrison, who came in after Graydon, said, "I need to know what's happening inside," I had a mole. I called him at night: "Now what's happening? Where's Tina's office going? Who's been fired?" For two months: the source that was complete luck. So when something like that appeared in *The Observer*, the people at *The New Yorker* would be, "How are they getting this?" And they couldn't connect me to this person who was working there. I met him once in person but I freaked him out. I felt, "Now I have to act like a real journalist," so I took him to the Oyster Bar and dinner was 88 bucks. And since he was telling me stuff in secret, when we met in public, suddenly it was like if you're doing something naughty and you're doing it in public. Sometimes it's better to keep your sources very quiet. You don't want to bring him out in the open and have a good party about it. If I hadn't had my little mole and my Donna Fargo, I would have failed doing Off the Record and been out of the business in a couple of months.

I had some things that were funny. *GQ* wanted to see what their readers were thinking, so they put readers in this room and had them look at their magazine. They had a one-way mirror, and Art Cooper, the editor of *GQ*, was sitting on the other side. The focus group leader said, "Would you read this article?" And the people in the focus group were like, "This sucks, I like *Esquire* better than this piece-of-crap magazine." And they kept on going, and Art Cooper got so pissed that he opened the door and went into the focus group. They didn't even know there was a one-way mirror, so they're

thinking, "Who the hell is this?!" And he told them all off: "You idiots!"

Tina Brown was really my main subject, the person I really had the strongest feeling about, and the most mixed emotions. I did a big story on her. By that time [Peter] Kaplan was there. That was a great story for me to learn how to write. I learned how Kaplan edited something, which was different from how Susan Morrison edited. Whenever I turned in a column, she would always appear slightly unsatisfied, except she would laugh at something and then she would send it back to me for certain details like, "What color was the truck?"—that kind of stuff, which was good because you learn how to do it. And when you're starting out, you forget that those details are important. I remember it was often, "What color ..." Kaplan asked me the same thing another time—"What color was Wes Andersen's SUV?" With Kaplan, he didn't line-edit the way Susan did. Kaplan was more like before you wrote it, he really wanted to sit down and talk.

And the pranks?

When [Peter] Stevenson arrived, it became mayhem. That's when we started calling George Stephanopoulos and stuff. That was in 1994, Clinton's midterm. And I used to do Maya Angelou's voice to prank-call people. The best one was George Stephanopoulos. I would get such a laugh at the fact that once you started calling people, you realize that everybody's reachable and there is no line between you and other people. That's one thing you learn from journalism. Everybody is findable. When I was a kid I thought that there was a wall between you and the people who were on the other side of the TV screen and other people who were doing stuff—but there isn't any. To call George Stephanopoulos, all I had to do was call the White House switchboard—the number that's in the phone book! So I called using the Maya Angelou voice and said: "Yeees, may I speak with Geooorge Stephanopoulos, puhleeeeeaase?" And his assistant bought it. Clinton had had Maya Angelou read at his inaugural. And this was when Whitewater was starting, right before Monica. I was calling to offer to read a poem at his midterm. And Stevenson and I had written a fake Maya Angelou poem that had a Whitewater rafting conceit: "I riise on my whitewater raft ..." And Stephanapolous was listening. I had him. And he's just silent, listening. Finally he goes, "Who is this?!" Then he starts cracking up. He bought it for long enough so that it was really funny. I also used to pose as a Singaporean political donor—we called Hillary Clinton's senatorial campaign and said we wanted her to pose with an exotic mountain cat. And if she would, I would consider giving a large sum to the campaign. And we had these Clinton people for weeks, negotiating finer points! I ▶

would hint that the amount I wanted to donate was in the millions—cash—just to see what would happen. We didn't tape it. Just me and Stevenson. What happened was the rhythm of the *Observer* week: You kill yourself Friday, Monday and Tuesday. Then Wednesday you're still dead. Then we'd do these crank calls Wednesday afternoon, then it's back to work.

What about the transition from Susan to Peter?
I feel like Peter [Kaplan] opened it up. Graydon made it relevant to New York City. The first thing he did was make sure that people from other publications read it—so you get a magnified sense of how important it is, because *The New York Times* is going to mention you. You can have a small circulation but if you reach people in the media, suddenly, it has a bigger impact. Look at where almost all the *Observer* reporters went from there: They went almost immediately to *The New York Times*—like 15 people.

Graydon gets a ton of credit. He did that first transformation and Susan Morrison continued that. Then she did a great thing—she brought in Peter Stevenson and Rich Cohen. Then I also wrote feature stories as well as the column. And so I just remember, in a given week, we had a really strong lineup where Peter, Rich—and after a while Warren St. John—we had a lot of people writing feature stories. You had the top of the fold of the front page, which gave the paper gravity, and then you can do all this bullshit on the bottom half of the page, which was usually what I was involved in. So it was a good mix. The paper didn't look like a flyaway thing. It had some news in it.

So Kaplan takes over in 1994 and there was a redesign in 1996?
Kaplan was very big in this thing: One thing I got involved in with him was writing the headlines every Tuesday. I'd sit in there every morning and that would be a two-hour thing—writing the front-page headlines. And it was a lot of fun. He would say this thing over and over again: "You've gotta talk directly to the reader."

Kaplan had a different mentality from *Spy* because he had a warmer voice, because he comes out of a slightly different tradition, which is Clay Felker's *New York* magazine. Kaplan's style is, you're looking at a moment in time that's happening right now as if you're looking at it five years from now. There were also a couple of different voices. There was this old guard thing that [*Observer* owner] Arthur [Carter] would call "an underground paper for the Upper East Side"—for the elite, which it was. The underground paper for billionaires. It got more and more open with Kaplan—less clubby. The '90s were a happy little time. It was a time that was like the '20s—when comedy comes to the fore because they were easy times. When the Trade Tower was bombed in 1993, it was taken so unseriously that I did a story on it and it's on page 18. I went down to the Manhattan Correctional Center and I visited the guys in jail. That's all the story was, the conditions they were being held in, under 23-hour lockdown, they got to go to the roof one hour a day. That was it. And they prayed. I looked at their cells, they looked

at me—it was kind of cool. Like, "Who are the crazy goofballs who attempted to do that? Of course you can't bring down the World Trade Center!" When the Clinton sex scandal is in the newspaper every day, you're reading in a time of farce, not tragedy. "The Monica Diaries" that Stevenson wrote were hilarious. And Kaplan was the type who was interested in what the president meant for the country, how it affected the times. He loves to see things like that. There's Rudy, the mean-ass mayor, and you have a really intelligent president who's involved in a sex farce. Sex and the City was perfect. That was a great post-Reagan view of New York City, because instead of *The Village Voice* in the '60s, which was "Come to New York City and be an artist, live in the rubble!", the message of Sex and the City was "Come to New York City and be FAAAAABULOUS!" But the weird thing about Sex and the City is that it's the most depressing column in the world if you actually read it in *The Observer*. Every one of those columns basically ended with, "I've come here to New York City in pursuit of love and I've failed again, reader." Candace didn't get married at the end of that. There was no happy ending. The column had a measure of contempt for the same things it was showing people were cool.

And the attitude the paper had?
It's capturing that time. Everyday life and how it felt at the time. The atmosphere Kaplan created, it wasn't like I'd go to him and say, "Heya boss! I got this idea!", where I had to write a proposal and then he has to say yes or no. Instead I'd interview a hundred people, cut it down and we had an article! To me that sums up the mood. There were things happening and you just looked at everything like it was a story. There was one where I'd heard people complaining, saying they couldn't wait to leave the city because it's so annoying. So you do a story where you report on people who keep saying they want to leave the city, but never do. Articles like that aren't stuffy things you expect to see in a newspaper, they're things you expect to see on page 210 of a novel.

Can you talk about the 64th Street office?
The townhouse was cute because it was crowded, but I despised that neighborhood. You walk outside and you would see boutiques and expensive stores. La Perla one day showed up and Kaplan looked and went "WWWOOOOOOW!" Then there was Books & Company, which went out of business. It was very quiet and felt like a library and Stevenson and I would go in there on our gigantic Wednesday lunches. Sometimes we'd eat by Central Park Zoo and watch how the German tourists always wanted to take pictures of this fierce, muscular-looking goat statue.

You went after Michael Pollan in a book review, right?
My Michael Pollan review was one of the meanest. He'd built a hut in the woods, and then he wrote a book about building a hut in the woods! And he wrote the book in the hut! It drove me absolutely crazy. In the last paragraph, I challenged him to a fight.

> My Michael Pollan review was one of the meanest. He'd built a hut in the woods, and then he wrote a book about building a hut in the woods! And he wrote the book in the hut! It drove me absolutely crazy. In the last paragraph, I challenged him to a fight.

What about the National Magazine Award winners you predicted?

Somebody who knew who the winners were going to be leaked it to me and Stevenson. Kaplan assigned us to write a forecast of the event, to choose which articles and magazines we thought would win. We read every article that was nominated and said we're going to pick our own winners. And the source gave us 13 out of 14 actual winners. I guess they gave us one wrong on purpose to hide their asses. We wrote "Here's Who Should Win / Here's Who Will Win" and then at the event, we went and everybody had seen our predictions. And one by one, our predictions were coming true as each editor or publisher went up onstage to get their award, and then they realized we had a source. Which showed how connected the paper was. And after that, they really shut down their process so that there aren't any leaks. Now they make sure no one person knows all the winners.

Was it a normal, healthy work environment?

One time I was on deadline—Tuesdays would be crazy. I'd be editing and people would be calling constantly, and something pissed me off and I smashed my keyboard and the letters jumped off the keyboard and I went down to [office manager] Barry [Lewis] and said, "I need a new keyboard." They gave me one and I went back upstairs and plugged it in and just went back to work. Kaplan kept coming in, so I closed that door and I barred it with a filing cabinet.

When did Kaplan start throwing stuff out the window?

Once he tried to throw my computer out the window. There were a lot of things flying out of Kaplan's window. We'd be like, "Here, did you see this article in *New York* magazine?" and he'd be, "Fuck that article!" then he'd throw it out the window.

And it wasn't like after work we'd head to the Waverly Inn the rest of the night. It was kind of gross: We were there late and we were exhausted; we didn't go out after work. We joked around at lunch and at the office but I was always married and had kids so I was always running home.

What about some of your profiles?

Well, I did Jon Stewart in 1995. That was after he left MTV. I interviewed him at this bar down by N.Y.U. and after the interview I realized that he had lied to me about his age, which pissed me off. He's since corrected it. He used to shave four years off.

David Letterman?

He wouldn't cooperate so I had to write an essay. That was a desperate cover story where Kaplan was like, "Letterman's turning 50, we need something!" And I had to pull something out of my ass in two days. I learned to think for the publication as a whole—that was what's fun about being an editor. You weren't just one writer; you were trying to look at the paper as a whole—what makes a good cover illustration and a good front page headline, and can you make a piece that at least is decent enough to hold?

Larry David. You wrote the first profile?

Kaplan and I were *Seinfeld* fans and watching the show and really getting into it and realizing that Larry David was the head writer and nobody knew who he was. Those were great scripts. So I saw his name in the credits and I'm like, "Who's that?" And I started calling people about him; then I tracked down Kenny Kramer, the real Kramer, who gave me his home number, and I called Larry David at home and I thought he wouldn't give the interview and he said, "O.K., go ahead!" And it was one of those nights—Monday, late and I'm talking for two hours with Larry David and I knew the show so well that I could say this episode this, this episode that. ... And when somebody in his position gets a phone call like that, he's glad that it's somebody who really knows his work.

What about Elvis Costello?

That was another thing where I called him—somehow I got his home phone and it was gonna be like 20 minutes, but I knew his stuff so well that we stayed on the phone for two hours. I couldn't believe it.

> It was one of those nights—Monday, late and I'm talking for two hours with Larry David, and I knew the show so well that I could say this episode this, this episode that.

You did a piece on Hemingway.

That was a good one. I wanted that to be a cover because it was Hemingway's centennial celebration all over the country and I thought New York should step in and say, "Here's the New York take on Hemingway." I interviewed Lillian Ross for that. She gave me pictures of him and I still have to give them back to her. I did a piece on the movie *The Best Years of Our Lives*, for it's 50th anniversary. I got obsessed with that movie. That was the kind of thing where I, on my own, got obsessed with that movie and then I told Kaplan and he of course knows everything about it, and he gets me deeper into it and then maybe I can do a piece. I saw it on TV one night and was like, "Holy fuck, what's this?"

I couldn't believe it because it had a reputation for being a soap opera tearjerker and it was not like that at all and then I rented it. Got into it. I thought it was one of those bad movies that wins a lot of Academy Awards, but it turns out that it was one of those good movies that wins a lot of Academy Awards.

Any other secrets from back then?

You learn that any place is accessible. I was watching *Saturday Night Live*, I wanted to go to the party they have after the show. So I took a name off the credits, and I went to Rockefeller Center, and I said this name of a random cameraman and they said go right in.

But you know, I was really reading from Kaplan's training—really going back into the New Journalism pieces from the late '60s and '70s and trying to do a version of it in a shorter space in *The Observer*.

I found a good item, about guys off the menu—guys who would go into the kitchen.

Guys who would not order things on the menu! Those guys were too cool to order things on the menu—even in a diner. What dopes. See, a little thing like that with nice little details. You're just noticing little things about the city, getting them in print before they fade away.

1998

▶ **Much ado about nothing? Seinfeld's eponymous sitcom ends a nine-season NBC run**

▶ James Cameron's *Titanic* has jaded New York teenagers drowning in tears

▶ **Super-Pfizer me: Men pop Viagra as women try Brazilian bikini waxes**

▶ From here to eternity: consummate crooner Frank Sinatra dies at age 83

▶ **Government goes gossip-crazy and White House rocked by Lewinsky scandal**

▶ The mother of all chick lit: *Bridget Jones's Diary* arrives stateside

▶ **Sean "Puffy" Combs throws Black and White Ball at Cipriani**

▶ Partnership of restaurateurs Warner LeRoy and David Bouley in crumbs

▶ **David Granger, former protégé of *GQ*'s Art Cooper, starts men's-mag war at *Esquire***

1998

◇◇◇◇◇◇◇◇

JANUARY 26, 1998   BY LORNE MANLY

The New *Esquire* Man Pops His *GQ* Mentor

*Who's the Alpha-Male Editor?
The Youngish 90's Guy or His Bearded 70's-Style
Mentor? David Granger Wanted His Own Shop,
So He Broke Up Pappy Cooper's Happy Crew*

EVERY SUMMER, THE EDITORS and writers who work at *GQ* magazine go on a retreat at the Connecticut country home of the magazine's editor in chief, Art Cooper. At night, in the dining room of the Hopkins Inn, they go through cocktails and dinner and bottles and bottles of wine. The mood is pleasant and raucous. But then *GQ*'s food writer and resident gourmand, Alan Richman, unveils the many cheeses he has brought up from Zabar's or Fairway, and those present are expected to say whatever is on their minds, no matter how nasty. Someone will suggest an idea for a story or a cover, and someone else

will stomp all over it with glee.

It was a little different cheese time in the summer of '96. *GQ*'s editor in chief, the bearded and patriarchal Mr. Cooper, had a question for his crew: "What is the good life to you?" he said. "Define it in two words or less."

David Granger was among the 20 or so people at the long table. He was Mr. Cooper's protégé, the editor who developed most of *GQ*'s best writers. Colleagues said he was like the son Mr. Cooper never had.

"I need three," Mr. Granger said as he prepared his answer. Then he gave his three-word definition of the good life: "editor in chief."

About 10 months later, the ambitious Mr. Granger was gone. He took the editor in chief job at *Esquire* and then he convinced a number of *GQ* writers and editors to come with him. In the testosterone-laden environment of men's magazines, this meant war. "It's not enough for Art to stay on top," said someone who has worked with both men. "I think he needs David to fail."

FEBRUARY 23, 1998   BY DEIRDRE DOLAN

NEW YORK'S STREETWISE ADOLESCENTS DROWNING IN THEIR *TITANIC* TEARS

**'I couldn't stop crying and my parents came home and they were like, "What's wrong? This isn't right—you've seen lots of movies."'
—Jamie Beilin, student at the Spence School**

NOT SINCE FRANK SINATRA OR THE BEATLES HAVE NEW YORK CITY teenagers found themselves so willing to surrender themselves en masse to a pop cultural sensation. But this time, the subject of hot adolescent devotion is not a sexually liberating singer, but a decorous movie—*Titanic*, that gaudy romantic blockbuster—and the boys are expected to shed tears right along with the girls.

The movie has captured teenagers, but it wasn't really intended for them. Ancient virtues and vices—love, honor, pride, courage, cowardice, greed—are all up there on the screen, writ large with the help of the record-setting $235 million budget. For kids who have grown up in a broken-down, whacked-out metropolis and who have been educated in a climate where parents and teachers and therapists tell them there are no real answers, this is something incredibly new.

So in *Titanic*, supposedly jaded city kids have found something they can really throw themselves into, body and soul. They enter the theater knowing they're going to witness a doomed love story and the horrible deaths of 1,550 passengers, and that's why they go see *Titanic* again and again—so that they can feel something, so that they can weep.

But the act of seeing the picture over and over, and sobbing along with it each time, is something that might not sit well with parents. Jamie Beilin, a 17-year-old junior at the Spence School who said she's only applying to colleges with film schools, is a seven-timer. "The first time I went and saw it was on a Monday and I came home and my parents weren't home and I was just crying so much and I couldn't stop crying and my parents came home and they were like, 'What's wrong? This isn't right—you've seen lots of movies,'" she said, all in one breath.

APRIL 27, 1998
BY GEORGE GURLEY

RECLUSIVE HEIR HUNTINGTON HARTFORD EMERGES FROM HIS BROOKLYN LAIR

GEORGE HUNTINGTON HART-ford II, the 87-year-old heir to the A.&P. grocery fortune, was worth $100 million about 50 years ago. Now he lives in a four-room apartment on Ocean Avenue in Flatbush, Brooklyn. From his bedroom window on the eighth floor, he can see graffiti on walls and subway trains running above ground. He said he hasn't set foot outside in a year.

Things started off all right for Mr. Hartford. He was a rich boy in the roaring 20's, graduated from Harvard in 1934 and served in the Coast Guard during World War II. Then he came into all that money.

Now he was facing the TV, lying in bed. Bill Cosby was on, but the sound was off. Mr. Hartford's white hair reached almost to his shoulders. On the bedside table were five coffee cups, a *TV Guide*, a tube of Ben-Gay, cashews, a squeeze bottle of chocolate syrup, and a photo of his daughter Juliet.

"Here I have all the money and everything—I probably have more trouble than a guy who didn't have any money," he said.

APRIL 27, 1998 BY WARREN ST. JOHN

Tom Wolfe's Magnum Opus Is Ready!

FOR A LITTLE OVER A WEEK NOW, the most coveted invitation in the Manhattan magazine world has been for a seat at a wooden table in a conference room at Farrar, Straus & Giroux's Union Square West offices. There, Tom Wolfe's new novel, *Red Dogs,* exists as a foot-high stack of paper, typed in his usual triple-spaced lineation. Mr. Wolfe and his publisher have been keeping the novel under wraps, inviting fiction editors from the few magazines Mr. Wolfe considers worthy of excerpting his work to peruse the manuscript in Farrar's offices. Bids for first serial rights were due in the fax machine of Mr. Wolfe's agent, Lynn Nesbit, by 11 A.M. on April 21.

The catch here is that Farrar, Straus & Giroux, Ms. Nesbit and Mr. Wolfe are hoping to reap close to $1 million for first serial rights to the novel, an unheard-of sum for any magazine to pay for a novel excerpt. Bidders say a figure approaching $100,000 is much more likely.

For days now, those lucky few fiction editors have scurried to the publisher's office to have a look at one of the most anticipated novels in the last few years. *Vanity Fair's* Doug Stumpf has come by for a peek, as has *The New Yorker's* Bill Buford and *Esquire's* Adrienne Miller. Jann Wenner, editor and publisher of *Rolling Stone*, is the only other potential bidder for the serial rights.

A longtime friend and patron of the author, Mr. Wenner would seem to be a natural partner for Mr. Wolfe's next big book. He got Mr. Wolfe started on *The Right Stuff* in 1973 when he hired him to write four articles on astronauts for *Rolling Stone*, and shelled out big bucks to serialize an early version of *Bonfire of the Vanities* before its publication in 1987, as well as *Ambush at Fort Bragg*, a novella outtake from *Red Dogs*, in December 1996. He has his own copy of the book, provided by Mr. Wolfe.

Adopting typically Wolfian hyperbole, some who have seen the manuscript describe it as "a huge world-creating social satire." That has not, however, kept the magazine bidders from losing their heads. As *The Observer* was going to press, at least one magazine had balked entirely at Farrar's implied starting price of $500,000 for the book.

Farrar publicist Jeff Seroy would say only: "Negotiations are in progress, and it would be foolish to talk about them at this time."

Mr. Wolfe had a hard time settling on a title for his latest work. The novel has gone from being called *The Mayflies* in summer 1995 to *The Stoics* and *Chocolate City* before becoming *Red Dogs*. (Sources at Farrar said that Mr. Wolfe is considering *Cracker Heaven* as a backup title.) In late August 1995, Mr. Wolfe told guests at East Hampton's Guild Hall, who had gathered to hear him read from his work in progress, that his novel was about real estate development, banking and working-class life—in New York City, of course. At the time, the hero of the book was a 60-year-old tycoon from Georgia living in New York City. Supporting a 29-year-old bride with expensive tastes, he suddenly finds himself $200 million in the hole, not long after *Forbes* has calculated his net worth at $900 million. Rather than sell off his beloved quail plantation or Gulfstream IV jet, he decides to deal with his coming bankruptcy by laying off some of his workers.

MARCH 11, 1998 BY PETER KAPLAN

Warren Beatty Shampoos the Sleazy 90's

While the country gets ready to line up for Godzilla and killer comets, 61-year-old Warren Beatty thinks he can go out and make a brave political comedy with (shhh) ideals. Is he crazy? PETER W. KAPLAN shares nuts with him

IN THE PAST 30 YEARS, SINCE HE has taken control of his own career, Warren Beatty has made at least one big, significant movie in each decade. Now he has directed and co-written a movie for 20th Century Fox called *Bulworth*. It is the best political comedy of its generation, and one of the best ever made by a Hollywood studio. It's as good-willed, brave, idealistic, funny, as complicated as the best movies of the 70's. Most of all, it has a startling optimism about race and America, positing as no studio product has in years that Americans descended from Africans and Americans descended from other places still have a chance to be merged into one country.

Bulworth is direct about race in a way that movies have not been for some time. When Eldridge Cleaver died recently, the papers were filled with the sadness of his gnarled life, with his wild return to America and his crazy crawling to the Republican Party. But *Bulworth* has a memory about black America, that the 60's were not a wasted time. When the 26-year-old woman whom Bulworth falls for, played by Halle Berry, begins spouting her own doctrine in the movie, she explains that her mother knew Huey Newton, who was socially active in the hood.

"Huey was tightly wound," said Warren Beatty. "If you said 'Hi, Huey!' it would be like that table." He knocked on the table. "He was like that all the time. He had a good sense of humor. I remember being at a party with him one night, and he says, 'Nixon's going to be gone.' And I said, 'I don't think so, Huey.'

And he said, 'Nixon's going to be gone.'" Mr. Beatty laughed. "And I said—oh, I tell this story in the movie—oh, no, I cut it out of the movie. I told this story, and I cut it out of the movie. 'So you want to make a bet?' And I said, 'Yeah.' He says, 'How much?' And I said, 'I'll bet you ...' I think we bet $100. And we put it in a lamp that was hanging from the ceiling, and finally Nixon was gone. I went back there five years later, and I got a stepladder and I went up to the lamp. It was still there." He laughed, then stopped. "Huey was dead," he said.

But he blames the decline of quality in American politics on "money" and on the 30-second ad.

"It's money. Money and technology. It should increase democ-

ratization. But the technology is not controlled democratically. Technology's owned by wealthy interests, and so advertising serves the advertiser. And this goes across the board in all areas, in fast food, or politics, or movies, or newspapers." The last part of which brought up the following question: Would Rupert Murdoch support his movie, the most directly liberal movie in years, a movie that curries applause from an audience when some baby street-gang members packing heat get to tell the L.A.P.D. to go fuck themselves? "Well, I think there's really only one question," Mr. Beatty said. "Will they spend the money you have to spend on movies? And the answer to that is ... I don't know. I hope so."

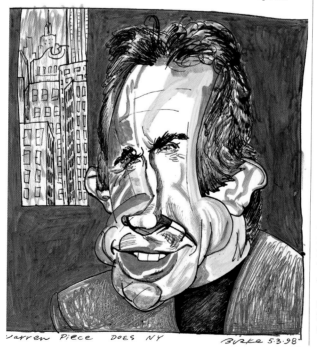

/arren Piece DOES NY   Burke 5·3·98

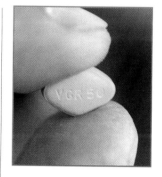

MAY 4, 1998
BY WILLIAM NORWICH

FEAR OF PFIZER? THE NEW VIAGRA

WEDNESDAY, APRIL 22, V-DAY, THE day of my Viagra trial.

"Are you really going to write about this?" my friend asked. "It's like a bad scene from *Heartburn.* The film."

Fifteen minutes later, still awkward silences. Then my friend observed that my face and scalp had gone beet red.

"Maybe I'm having a stroke. Do you have the phone number for an ambulance, in case?" I asked.

Then we noticed something else. How to say this in a family newspaper? Well, one found at one's middle in the middle of one's life something that hadn't been quite so quite in a spell. Perky. Very perky. Really rock hard. That was a little bit of all right. Dr. Lamm had mentioned a handy test. Give a few taps to oneself and see if it remained erect. It did. This pertness remained the case throughout the entire, lovely experience that followed, except for the odd minute of deflation when (1) I pictured my friend's people in Philadelphia reading this and (2) I found myself thinking about how much *Vanity Fair* writers are paid.

"So what did you do with the rest of the pills?" a friend asked the morning after. "Throw them away?"

No comment.

MAY 25, 1998 BY GAY TALESE

THE OBSERVATORY: THE MAN WHO KNEW HOW TO SAY GOODBYE

WHEN I WAS GROWING UP IN THE 1940'S, DURING World War II, an impressionable acne-speckled youth in parochial school being insulted daily by the Irish, I also knew I was on the wrong side of the war because most of my uncles and older cousins were in Mussolini's army, fighting against the Allied invasion of my immigrant father's hometown in the Southern Italian hills. While this hardly made me feel secure as an American, the reason I was not emotionally driven underground during this time was the music on the radio being sung by a skinny crooner who was the star of the Lucky Strike Hit Parade. To me in those days the only thing that did not seem so terrible about being Italian was Frank Sinatra.

What other Italian-Americans were there in the American mainstream? There was, to be sure, the ever-silent and self-centered Joe DiMaggio, who, while he also served in the American Army, never spoke out in defense of anyone, including himself. He was and remained an interior man, ever distant, cautious, never in the forefront with a social conscience. At best, a male Garbo.

In the political arena there was, of course, the famous Little Flower, Fiorello La Guardia. But he was born in a manner that was less typically Italian, less insular, more savory; he had a Jewish mother, and he was a Protestant. And the other ethnic Italian headliners in those days were the wiseguys—Lucky Luciano, Frank Costello and their confederates in the Mafia.

What I am perhaps overemphasizing here is that the Italian-American experience during the World War II years was marked by a good deal of shame and self-loathing; and for most of the next 50 years, from the 1940's to the end of the century, the only national figure of Italian origin who spoke out against prejudice and injustice, and who managed to find broad acceptance within the vast American landscape, was Francis Albert Sinatra. To those of us among the 14 million Americans of Italian origin, Sinatra more than anyone else embodied egalitarian opportunism, and was a one-man force for affirmative action, defending not only his own kind but all other minorities.

He was also the one Italian-American movie actor who in his films played romantic roles in ways not done today even by such active Italian-American actors as De Niro and Pacino, to say nothing of all those antisocial Italo types who are habitually cast as overheated heavies—except for this year's newcomer aboard the *Titanic*, young Leonardo. Before Sinatra, to find an Italian-American matinee idol who dressed with any stylish elegance on the screen and got the girl, one had to extend back to the silent era of Rudolph Valentino.

Sinatra also had the capacity to change his life, to take risks, to say goodbye and move out, which is inherent in the nature of every true immigrant, to uproot one's self from all that is familiar and predictable.

This is a nation navigated by boat people, but the Italian immigrants' offspring in America tended to be conservative, politically and socially, marrying within, identifying with a group, searching for security and a guaranteed existence. Sinatra was about stepping out and many goodbyes—leaving the plumber's daughter in Hoboken, for instance, to remarry with Ava Gardner, which in my view is not necessarily a social step up. Still, it was Frank breaking the patterns and breaking hearts, a quintessential American's quest for the kind of fantasy fulfillment that he also sang about.

America made love to his music, necked and lied to one another in parked cars in unacknowledged gratitude to his singing. But I remember talking once to Sinatra's valet in Los Angeles, back in the 1960's when I was doing a magazine article, and hearing the valet concede that he sometimes overheard Sinatra dialing one telephone number after the other, trying without luck to get a Saturday night date.

I do think that Sinatra was often very lonely, although he dwelled luxuriously within loneliness. In this loneliness, in this solitude, there was a kind of narcissism where his art dwelled in a most selfish and singular way. He could not appease his creative craving and his romantic relationships simultaneously for very long, for I think he was possessed by an overriding need to experience affection on a massive scale, to have one-night stands with the world.

MARCH 23, 1998

THE NEW YORK WORLD: **The Monica Diaries**

Continued excerpts from several hundred loose pages, wrapped in brown paper and tied with string, which were dumped on The Observer's front stoop and labeled, "The atached (sic) is my story, the story of a white house intirn (sic), in my own words, not that bitch Linda. ML."

dear diary,

so I go to WH and betty's like He's in there and i give her the look that says AS IF I DID NOT KNOW THIS?? And he's in there standing by the window and he's like Hi Mon how are you? and i'm like fine Sir which always makes him crack up a little and he's like I have a meeting in 10 minutes but they can wait with you looking so good and he sits back in his chair and starts unbuckling and so I sort of sit on the desk and say We need to TALK ... and he's like well is something wrong in your job?? and i'm like NOOOOO, silly--about US ... and he's like Well, what aBOUT us? and i'm like, Well, we need to TALK ... and he's like, YESSSS? and so i say, You know--REALLY TALK? and he's like, Mon, we ARE talking ... and i say Yes, that's true, but we're not really TALK-ING, you know? and so he's like What do you want to talk about? and I'm like, US ... and so he says, Go ahead, but i have this meeting ... so i say we need to talk now about how he never shares his feelings?? and I have feelings too?? and we must grow or die which is what that book that L. gave me said, but now i'm feeling like a dope cause i'm starting to cry which is not in the plans and he stands up and looks in my face and says Mon I care very deeply about your feelings and he's got his hand on my shoulder and I think he's going to hug me and give me the comfort but I feel his hand pushing me down and I say Wait I need more talking and he's like Well talk is what I do all day I love the way you and I have the DEEPER connexion and I hear the L-word in there but I realize he did not actually say it as meaning he loves MOI and then he says Mon we know each other SOOOOO well we don't need to talk and then he says something about sounds of silence which I guess is from that poetry book and I see he does have a point but then I think about what L. said about why don't I get the pleasure and the stuff she said about the two kinds of female orgasms and so I say why don't you ever at least take me out to DINNER?? we could say its just business, and he's like Mon i'll try to work that out one day soon i promise and i'm like well good cause I still get hungry ya know? and he's like well want me to have betty order you something? and I can tell he's getting pissed cause his face is all red and his jaw has that twitch so i'm like no i'm not hungry never mind and he sits back down sorta pulling me down with him so my face is in his lap his belt buckle is like ice on my cheek so I give the BJ and after he's like Mon you made my day with all these meetings you are the fresh air and i'm like What-ever, so he'll know its MY turn to be pissed ... but he gets no hints just buckles up and takes me to the door his hand on my elbow and I say Next time can't we just sit and TALK? And he's like yes, let's do that, and I say promise? And he's like sure and then I drop the bombs and say oh by the way, I TOLD MY DAD ABOUT YOU!!! ... and Creep looks like he's about to wig out so i say JUST KIDDING!

Oct. 12, 1996, 11:15 P.M.
dear diary,

Nancy wants me to come over monday and watch MP [presumably, the TV drama, Melrose Place--ed.] and I feel all conflicted cause Tracey told me how Nancy told her she thinks I'm a total bitch and that I'm conceeded about my looks and great job and my feelings are, like, why doesn't Tracey just like look in the mirror--hel-lo!--and maybe she'll see who's the b-i-t-c-h!!! Also I lent nancy my black pumps last year and she's never given them back!!! so now do i ask her for the pumps back and maybe cause a situation, or do i go out and buy new pumps?? ....saw ellen at the mall after that and she goes on and on about her bitch of a sister and i wish i was strong enough to tell ellen to tell her sister to bug off! after the mall i stopped by the white house and gave the President a BJ (no swallowing) ...

Nov. 3, 1996, 11:45 P.M.
dear diary,

God i want to like die!!! so yesterday was Janet's party? the one i've been so totally looking forward to? Because i am just slightly very much in total lust with janet's brother Tom? so i got my short black dress the one with the fur cuffs back from the cleaners and it's 5 PM and i'm drying my hair and the phone rings and wouldn't you know it's the Big He and he's like Come over I need you, so i say Ok i'll come over after the party and he's like No, no, no, no that will be too late, i need you now, and for some dumb reason i'm like, Ok, and i go to WH and he's there in his office and sudenly he's like kissing me and telling me how much he cares about me and he's pushing meanwhile me down and he's got his thingy out so i go down and say better make it quick i have this party and he's like i know i know i'll have a car get you to the party and wouldn't you know he like pulls his thingy out and he spooges all over the collar of my dress and i'm like holy shit and i say why why why did you do that, you ruined my dress and i have the party and i'm crying a little and he seems to sincerely feel bad and he's zipping up then he says dont move i'll be right back so i like wipe off the spooge with a napkin that says president on it and then he bursts back in and he's holding this, like, thoroughly heinus dress all flowery and dopey laura ashley and i'm like hel-lo, what is that? and he's like it's one of chelsea's dresses it will fit you quick put it on and i'm like are you friggin nuts i am not putting that crap on my body and he's like well suit yourself and i realize that it's either me at the party in that ugly dress or no party so i say Ok, and next thing i'm standing on P ave and there's no cabs and i'm in this loser dress and of course when i get to the party tom is nowhere in sight which might be good cause if he saw me in that dress he'd be like see ya ...

Oct. 12, 1996, 11:15 P.M.
dear diary,

saw ellen at the mall and she goes on and on about her bitch of a sister and i wish i was strong enough to tell ellen to tell her sister to bug off! after the mall i stopped by the white house and gave the President a BJ (no swallowing) ...

March 3, 1997, 11:58 P.M.
dear diary,

well Creepo BLEW UP at me tonite over NOTHING and i am listening to the radio for love songs that will make me cry and i decide to reminiss about our first kiss back when they called the intirns to say the govurnment was shut down so all intirns had to keep the country moving and i was like YES! and i put on a shortish skirt with opake tights and the gray Banana Republic sweater set that makes my boobs look good and my chunky heel loafers...and i get to the WH and some cute guy gives me envelopes to stuff and im like I DON'T THINK SO so i hand them to this dweeb intirn charles that we call charles in charge like a joke and i sort of wander around the WH and these intirns have this pizza for the President and i say better let me take it to him and they are SUCH Losers they say Ok, and this one extra cute secret service guy says Ok too so i carry the pizza to the O.O. and the secretary is like go on in he's hungry so i go in ... and he's on the phone and he's wearing this dark blue suit that is SOOO HANDSOME but a HEINUS tie and i'm like PIZZA PARTY! but he just points to a table so i put the pizza down but first i put napkins under the box and he says thank you without words just moving his mouth but if he's expecting me to leave he is way mistaken so i take out a slice and he hangs up and says well HELLO THERE its good to see you again and i'm like its an honor mr. president and he gets diet cokes from this little fridge and gives me one and says he's so greatful the intirns are running the country because of the republicans and i feel him staring at the pizza so i say DIG IN and he does and i pick the pepperonis off my slice and he asks me about my duties but i'm looking at his blue eyes which are so pretty and then he looks at me and says With intirns this gorgeous, hell, i wish we had a govurnment shut down EVERY DAY! and inside i'm like OH MY GOD so i say maybe the shut down will last forever and we laugh and he says he's seen me around the WH a lot and has always thought I was a very beautiful woman and then we are kissing and i put my hand on the back of his head and his hair feels NICE and i'm thinking GOD is he romantic and i think i almost had a swoon and then he is sort of pushing me down and his thing is out so i give him the bj and then he zips up and i'm feeling like dizzy so i sit down and he says We both better get back to the countries business and i'm like i hope i see you again soon and he says sure and sort of holds my arm and leads me to the door and says let's keep this just between us Ok and i'm like OF COURSE and I try to give him a kiss but he turns away and says pizza breath ...

September 2, 1997, 11:15 P.M.
dear diary,

at lunch i left pentogon to drive to see this new shrink and the waiting room smells like cigars and the door opens and i go Whoa because that Carvel guy that hangs with Big Creep walks out quick like he doesnt see me and i figure this must be a fancy shrink if the Carvel guy is seeing him and the shrink comes out and he's like Hello, Monica and its this chubby guy who looks real familiar wearing a dark blazer and way tacky black turtleneck and hes like Wont you come in? and its dark with big leather chairs and a couch and he says Would you like some tea and he brings me some tea that tastes gross and he's like Your mother is worried about you, and Im like, What else is new? and he laughs and says mothers tend to worry too much and Im like Oooh, big newsflash, and he says, But nevertheless a persons young 20's are a hard time because the pressures of life make their imaginations run wild, and Im like Uh-huh, and im feeling weird from the tea and hes like Why dont you tell me about you, are you dating anyone special? and Im like Well I assume Mom told you I am the Presidents girlfriend? and he's like Ah yes, she did mention you were under that impression, and Im like, Well its no impression bucko its the real love, and hes like Monica its a known fact that children of divorce are suskeptical to fantasies about father figures that their minds can create a whole relashunship that is not real and Im like Well my boyfriends not the figure of my imagination hes the President and the shrink just sits there and everything feels dizzy and the shrink says Ok Monica, lets start again, Why dont you tell me about you, are you dating anyone special? and Im like Hello? Earth to doc? I am dating ... the ... President? and he sighs and Im feeling way sleepy and then the shrink says, Ok, lets start again, Why dont you tell me about you, are you dating anyone special? and then i cant remember what he said next because the next thing i know its after dark and im at home in my bed

September 5, 1997, 11:09 P.M.
dear diary,

i get home from pentogon today in a bitch of a mood cause Big Creep has still not returned a single call and at home i see this dweeby guy sitting on our couch hes got a short haircut and a shiny face and this blue blazer with tacky gold buttons and kåki pants and little brown shoes and so im like um, Mom, who is this? and she says dont be silly monica you know as well as i do hes your boyfriend Ted and this guy stands up all fake polite and he comes to kiss me and im like Back off, loser, and he says My my, someone had a bad day today, and im like Excuse me i have never set the eyes on you in my life and he puts his arm around my showlder and hes like Thats my monica always the jokester! and he smells like soap and i want to puke so i push him off and Im like Touch me again and youll be sorry, and moms like, Monica whatever has gotten into you in the three years you and Ted have been dating youve never acted this way to him and Im like, Hello? Ive never seen him before, and hes like standing there all smiling and i cannot deal so i turn around and walk to my room and theres the second freakout cause there's a picture of me and this dweeb Ted in a silver frame on my nitestand and hes dressed in the same weenie outfit

MAY 25, 1998 BY PETER BOGDANOVICH

THE OBSERVATORY: I'll Be Around

THE FIRST THING I REMEMBERED WHEN I HEARD THAT FRANK Sinatra had died was his parting wish to a concert audience at the Royal Albert Hall in London one of the times I saw him perform there: "May you live to be 100," he had said, "and may the last voice you hear ... be mine!" And something like 10,000 British people had cheered wildly, as though death would surely lose its sting were it to be accompanied by the sounds of Sinatra. Certainly his voice had been present at so many of what the French call *les petits morts* the world over: How many kisses, how many climaxes had been reached with Sinatra singing in the background?

The first actual contact I ever had with Sinatra was a nasty telegram he sent me. Cybill Shepherd and I were living together then, and I had just produced a Cole Porter album for her and sent copies to several performers we both admired, hoping for some endorsements we could use as liner notes. We got two or three, and then came Frank's wire: "Heard the record. It's marvelous what some guys will do for a dame. Better luck next time. Sinatra." Well, Cybill and I tried to pretend to each other that there was a missing period after "marvelous," and let it go. I finally met him not too long afterward, when he hosted the American Film Institute's Life Achievement tribute to Orson Welles. I actually thanked him for his telegram, and he looked slightly bewildered; but when I added that we thought it was funny, he smiled a bit uncomfortably and said, "Yeah, I thought you'd get a kick out of it." The subject never came up again.

One of the things that most moved me during the world's first reaction to his death on May 14 was when the Empire State Building, an unofficial symbol of New York, New York, turned its lights blue the night of his passing: a poignant tribute from a city to a 70's invention of Sinatra's, only the last in a career that began as the voice of the 40's. It reminded me of my reaction to hearing that all the lights of Las Vegas had been turned off for a minute the night they heard Frank's pal, Dean Martin, had died. Both were gestures more potent that lowering a flag to half-mast, from both the private sector and the public, a bow of respect to say in silence that someone very special had gone from our midst.

BOOK REVIEW: Will Sex and the Single Girl Sell Again in America?

Bridget soldiers on despite the notorious perfidy of almost every unattached male.

Bridget Jones's Diary,
by Helen Fielding. Viking, 271 pages, $22.95.

IT'S VERY POSSIBLE THAT WITHin a month every American book buyer will know the name of Bridget Jones, a 30-something Londoner whose diary records in hilarious detail a ceaseless search for thinner thighs, inner poise and a nice boyfriend. Bridget is the creation of Helen Fielding and a monster hit in England: More than 900,000 copies of *Bridget Jones's Diary* have sold in the last six months. Salman Rushdie bestowed a magnificently blunt blurb on the book: "Even men will laugh."

It could have been otherwise: Bridget mocked, dismissed as childish, vapid and whiny or cute and cloying. She is obsessed with her weight and fixated on gooey romance. A chronic slob, her attention span is not just short but perpetually misplaced. She has never sustained a serious thought—at least not if there's a phone within arm's reach. As one not-very-nice boyfriend remarks, "If Bridget had a child she'd lose it."

All the same, she's hugely likable. Part of it is the dirty-dishes honesty of her diary. Each entry begins with the day's vital statistics, hard facts accompanied by commentary. Here, for example, is the tally for a Sunday spent waiting for a phone call from that same not-very-nice boyfriend: "126 lbs., alcohol units 5 (drowning sorrows), cigarettes 23 (fumigating sorrows), calories 3,856 (smothering sorrows in fat-duvet)."

In *Middlemarch*, George Eliot rolled out this sonorous pronouncement: "That element of tragedy which lies in the very fact of frequency, has not yet wrought itself into the coarse emotion of mankind; and perhaps our frames could hardly bear much of it." Ms. Fielding is mining the element of comedy from the very fact of frequency—and it turns out that we can bear quite a lot of it. But Bridget's creator would surely agree with Eliot's conclusion: "As it is, the quickest of us walk about well wadded with stupidity."

Bridget's signature stupidity, her foolish faith in a brighter future, is also her most lovable trait. Ms. Fielding wisely refrains from showing us the spectacle of our heroine satisfied, content, at last possessed of inner poise—that is, smug. Like most of us, Bridget is at her best with something to look forward to. Did I mention that there's a sequel in the works?

JULY 6, 1998 BY FRANK DIGIACOMO

Four-Star Food Fight: LeRoy vs. Bouley

THE WELL-KNOWN RESTAU-rateur on the other end of the phone line was searching for the proper word to characterize the deteriorated state of relations between Russian Tea Room owner Warner LeRoy and his former partner, four-star chef David Bouley.

"There's, like, hate," said the restaurateur. "Warner's like India. He's going to test the hydrogen bomb."

On June 11, Mr. LeRoy filed suit against Mr. Bouley in State Supreme Court in Manhattan. The gist of the suit is that Mr. Bouley violated the terms of his contract with Mr. LeRoy over Bouley Bakery, the first venture in what was to have been an ambitious partnership between the two strong-willed food moguls.

Eleven days later, on June 22, Mr. Bouley's attorney, Andrew Rahl, told The Transom that his client and Mr. LeRoy had a "handshake" agreement to settle the lawsuit out of court. Still, Mr. Rahl called Mr. LeRoy's lawsuit "nonsense" and said it was a "given" that Mr. Bouley and Mr. LeRoy were going their separate ways.

New York's culinary establishment was hardly surprised by the news. An inevitable and ugly falling-out between the two men has been predicted ever since they announced their intentions to join forces in late 1995. Mr. Bouley represents the culinary pinnacle in Manhattan; Mr. LeRoy, with restaurants like the Russian Tea Room and Tavern on the Green, is the expert showman. In the last three years, he has had to deflect a lot of derision as his friends and colleagues told him, and anyone else who would listen, that he would not be able to rein in the clearly talented and charming but incredibly independent-minded Mr. Bouley.

JULY 20, 1998 BY WARREN ST. JOHN

OFF THE RECORD: TINA GOES CHEEK TO CHEEK WITH MIRAMAX

ON JULY 13, TINA BROWN TOOK time from taking meetings to take a call on her cell phone. She was downtown, in Miramax country, and her mood was something approaching delirium. "I'm in the TriBeCa Grill having a meeting with the acquisitions staff," she chirped. "I'm exhilarated by my change—exhilarated. I'm having a fantastic time. I've never had such dynamic meetings in my entire 19 years of being an editor in chief. The meetings are so exciting right now.

"I'm learning a lot, I'm learning a lot," Ms. Brown continued. "I guess when you're learning you're excited and refreshed. It's a very exciting thing. I could always be excited by the journalistic exchange, but now I'm getting exchanges on every kind of level—I move from the journalistic to the business back to the logistical. I'm involved in so many talks at the moment." Ms. Brown sounded as if she was about to lose it.

What about the rumor that you'll never start a magazine and the new venture will be pared down into a run-of-the-mill development office? "That is total nonsense," Ms. Brown said. "The magazine is the core excitement here. ... It certainly will not get in the way. It's the cultural search engine which is going to drive the company!"

Is Ms. Brown prepared to part with the Condé Nast editor's sense of entitlement and run a tight ship? "It's a very terrific financial box in which to complete a structure," she said, sounding a bit more serious. "That's fine; I completely understand that. Ron [Galotti] and I are going to work with the Miramax financial people to create a business plan that will be ready by the fall, and in that business plan will be the budget, and in that budget we will live inside."

Even outsize Rudy Giuliani could feel dwarfed by the mayoral office

THE BALLAD OF BURT AND ELVIS

ELVIS COSTELLO AND BURT Bacharach climbed aboard the stage in the basement of the Virgin Megastore on Union Square. It was not the hippest room in town.

The Virgin Megastore is a monstrosity. A disk jockey sits in a booth, overlooking the floor like a cheap god. There are tables where you can have coffee and croissants. There's an escalator. It's part state-of-the-art record store, part hell.

"This is the first time I've played in a concert hall with an escalator in the middle," Mr. Costello said into the microphone.

Mr. Bacharach, 70, tinkled the first few notes of "Toledo," a bouncy ballad from the just-released album *Painted From Memory*. The new duo seemed tentative, not quite acquainted with each other or the song. Mr. Bacharach played in an easy, decorative style that might have sounded mushy to fans of venomous Costello songs like "Pump It Up" or "I Want You." And Mr. Costello was singing in a voice that could easily put off fans of Mr. Bacharach's work with pop divas and "divos" like Dionne Warwick, Dusty Springfield, Tom Jones and Luther Vandross. But then he sloughed off his jitters

for the third song, "Painted From Memory." It's a ballad about an artist who paints a portrait of his ex-lover, only to imagine, jealously, that "those eyes, they smile for someone else." Mr. Costello brought the song to life. It was raw. It was great. So this record store basement might not have been the hippest room in town, but that didn't matter anymore.

After writing one song with Mr. Bacharach for the 1995 movie *Grace of My Heart*, the monumental ballad "God Give Me Strength," Mr. Costello had asked Mr. Bacharach if they might continue the collaboration for his first Polygram album. Soon he was meeting his hero for songwriting trysts in New York hotel rooms.

Some reviews for *Painted From Memory* have called it a masterpiece, some have called it crap. "It's very hard to avoid them completely," he said.

Wasn't he curious to see what they were saying about Mr. Bacharach? "I'm more than familiar with the casual rudeness of modern writing and the overfamiliarity of people who imagine that through the price of admission that they get a license to insult you personally. And I would be very unhappy, and I can be extremely vindictive, about people who do those things needlessly, particularly when it's visited on somebody who's perhaps not expecting it, whereas I'm kind of expecting it all the time. I would be sad to see that done needlessly and mindlessly to Burt, somebody I really admire and who I've invited into a world that is slightly different in the way things are appraised. I don't think it's healthy for people to be completely critically inoculated, but it's about time that people started to recognize the real substance of his music."

SEPTEMBER 7, 1998 BY GEORGE GURLEY

A Sexual Standoff in the Naked City

She's so lovely. He's so frustrated. GEORGE GURLEY gets himself mixed up with women, men and the whole sex problem on the streets of Manhattan

IF ANYTHING CHARACTERIZES THE STREET SCENES LATELY, IT HAS to be the huge number of lovely women who just walk on by, one after the other. Following the successful reintroduction of the miniskirt and minidress, and with the advent of the belly shirt, the see-through blouse and extra-tight spandex tops, not to mention those fetching open-toed shoes, oh, what a paradise it seems! But with every pleasure afforded by the sight of each passing beauty comes a little pain.

While the happy gains of post-feminism may have given women permission to wear skimpy garments in the city heat, the earlier and more sober gains of feminism have made it very uncouth indeed for any civilized man to acknowledge the delights that meet his eye. And so there has been something of a standoff between men and women in the public spaces of Manhattan. The women are gorgeous, in their spaghetti strap shirts and sandals, and the men, in their sensible khaki slacks and Oxford shirts, are blithering dopes who find themselves in constant hummana-hummana mode all summer long. The women claim they're dressing for comfort and they seem perfectly oblivious to the intense effect they produce in the men, who fall instantly and hopelessly in love with every woman who approaches, only to pass out of their lives forever.

MAY 25, 1998 BY WOODY ALLEN

THOUGHTS OF A KNOW-NOTHING FAN

I AM ALWAYS ASKED TO WRITE ABOUT BASKETBALL. PEOPLE labor under the mistaken impression that, since I attend the Knicks games and have done so regularly for over 25 years, I've learned something or that I have insights and observations that are worth listening to, but they are wrong. I have only opinions and feelings based on nothing much but emotions, and I have gripes and theories, often crackpot. Mostly, I sit quietly at the Garden hoping for a close game, hating the blowouts, even if it's the Knicks on top, enjoying the fans, marveling at the dancers and barely tolerating the endless insipid promotional stunts during timeouts.

When asked why it is so important that the Knicks win, since at the end of the game or even the season, nothing in life is affected one way or the other, I can only answer that basketball or baseball or any sport is as dearly important as life itself. After all, why is it such a big deal to work and love and strive and have children and then die and decompose into eternal nothingness?

To me, it's clear that the playoffs or 61 home runs, a no-hitter, the Preakness, the Jets, or human existence can all be much ado about nothing, or they can all have a totally satisfying, thrilling-to-the-marrow quality. In short, putting the ball into the hoop is of immense significance to me by personal choice and my life is more fun because of it. Not that I ever thought of becoming a basketball player. My height was insufficient for a serious career, although to this day, if I play in a game with kids 8 years and under, I am a tremendously effective shot blocker.

Now, a favorite crackpot notion of mine is the following: I think the Knicks never regained their past championship form because they sinned by trading Walt Frazier to Cleveland. I can't prove this, but those who have read "The Rime of the Ancient Mariner" know what the shooting of that bird did. Not that Frazier was an Albatross. Quite the contrary. He was, in my opinion, the greatest of all Knickerbocker players, and he was for a time not only the soul of the team but one of the spirits of this city.

I recall him after a routine night of superb basketball, tooling around in his chauffeured Rolls, dressed, to put it mildly, like an extrovert and lighting up the various night spots of Manhattan like he had just lit up the Garden. Clyde came up with the Knicks and was a major cog in the peerless machine that took two championships. It should have entitled him to tenure in New York forever. Dealing him to the Cavaliers upset some balance in the cosmic order, and the fruit of this curse could be felt from the days of Spencer Haywood, through Bob McAdoo, Michael Ray Richardson, Lonnie Shelton, the Bulls, the Rockets, Rick Pitino, Hubie Brown, Mike Fratello, last year's brawl in Miami, many heartbreaking late baskets by Reggie, by Michael, even by Sam Cassell.

Incidentally, I should mention here that I'm totally prejudiced toward a guard-oriented or small forward-oriented game. I've never enjoyed center-focused basketball, and watching Wilt Chamberlain, great as he was, or David Robinson or Shaquille O'Neal get the ball down low and put it in is not my idea of a thrill. That's why, when Pat-

rick Ewing got hurt, the Knicks became a much weaker but much more exciting team. There's no question Ewing is the franchise player and one of the greats in all the years of this sport. Can you imagine if he had been properly staffed over the past decade? Picture the Knicks without him. They would have languished near the bottom.

Now conjure up an image of Patrick over the past decade on the Bulls. With a center like Ewing, given their team, Chicago would have gone undefeated. Ewing would be my all-time Knick center on a team comprised of himself, Walt Frazier, Earl Monroe, Dave DeBusschere and Bernard King. Some might lobby for Willis Reed and while I'd want him on my team, I wouldn't start him. Yet as soon as Ewing was lost to injury the games became thrilling, often being decided by a point or two in the final seconds. The guards ran the club, the guards and Larry Johnson, a forward of incredible agility (and fragility) with super moves that make him, like Hakeem Olajuwon, an unusually exciting low post player. (Olajuwon is the one center who has been some fun for me to watch perform over the years.)

As far as the other Knicks guards go, I think both Charlie Ward and Chris Childs have certain fine individual skills and could learn from one another. If a science-fiction machine were available to combine both these guards into a single player, New York would have its great point guard.

And finally, what can one say about Charles Oakley? Or can one say enough? Oakley has been a consistently tremendous ballplayer for New York who contributes mightily night after night, season after season, and actually gets better with age. Of course I'd hate to wake up in the middle of the night and find him hovering over my bed with that look on his face, but on the court he's worth every cent they pay him.

I also admire the Knicks' coach, although I, like Larry Bird (one of the many ways we're similar), am a firm believer in the limits of coaching. It has been said that a good coach is someone who, if you give him a good team, will not screw up with it. I've always felt, if Jeff Van Gundy had coached the Bulls over the past decade and Phil Jackson guided the Knicks, that for the most part the record books would stand pretty much the way they are written today. The truth is, I always believed that I could have coached the Lakers in the years of Magic Johnson, Kareem Abdul-Jabbar and James Worthy and if not me then certainly my mother.

Having given you a number of my emotional feelings about the Knicks, a team I love, let me give you a few of my less socially acceptable notions.

First—I happen to like Reggie Miller. I liked it when he hit the three-pointer that tied the game with the Knicks. It set the stage with a drama that Reggie, who deserves to be a Knick and play in New York, seems to possess. The only thing that went wrong in my fantasy scenario was that the Knicks did not utilize the five-plus seconds they had left to win the game and make the afternoon a thrilling one for New York. If, as Reggie claims, he saw in the eyes of the home team that the heart went out of New York in the overtime, then that is unforgivable. The Knicks had the Pacers in a tie at the end of regulation at friendly Madison Square Garden. It's a situation wherein they should dismantle their opponents.

Another unpopular archvillain I always liked to watch, and wished in years past was on the Knicks, was Bill Laimbeer. Constantly accused of being a dirty player, he would have been a huge plus for New York despite all the derision he got when he competed against us. I feel that way about Dennis Rodman, too. The fans in Chicago love him and we would, too, if he paraded his psychotic vaudeville here.

And what about Marv Albert? I'd like to see him back doing the New York broadcast. I miss that voice, full of city street urgency. He made the games exciting to listen to, and to deny him his place as the voice of the Knicks is unworthy of those who are empowered to hire. (Not to get off the subject of basketball, but I'm a firm believer that a Baseball Hall of Fame that excludes Pete Rose embarrasses itself.)

And what is all this postgame praying? Those new fashionable prayer huddles—what goes on? They can't be thanking God for winning, because how do the teams with the losing records explain things? ("The Lord loves our team—He sabotages us so we can get a high draft pick.") The players also cannot be thanking God for keeping them from injury, because they're injured all the time. My theory is they're thanking God for the huge increases in salaries over the past few years. Only a very benevolent Supernatural Being could be responsible for some of those numbers certain players earn.

My favorite player in the league is Charles Barkley. Not only has he been thrilling over the years, but his performances have been original and funny. I find his attitude of wanting a championship ring, but not letting it be a life-threatening event should he fail to obtain one, quite refreshing. He, like Dennis Rodman (although he brings it off with much more flair and aplomb), does not give an inch to the sanctimony that permeates professional sports.

Incidentally, lest the reader not think I'm totally blasphemous in my tastes and feeling, I should point out that I experienced a true religious epiphany watching the All-Star Game this year when the "torch" was passed from Michael to Kobe Bryant. For a minute, I thought I saw angels at Madison Square Garden. My feeling about Kobe is that he is a knockout talent and they should encourage him to play a complete game with assists, rebounds and defense and not use him to come in and make circus shots. But the concept of passing a torch I did find a hoot, no matter how many times the television announcers used the phrase; it's a concept alien to basketball, which is a team sport, and Michael Jordan has not created a holy order like the papacy, where there is a line of accession. (If the smoke is light gray, the new Pope is Kobe; if it's dark gray, Grant Hill's been chosen.)

Finally, I would not like to end this little rumination without an interview that I dedicate to an old favorite writer of mine, Frank Sullivan, whose appreciation of clichés would have hit a new high had he lived long enough to hear one of today's basketball players.

INTERVIEW BETWEEN FRANK SULLIVAN'S CLICHÉ EXPERT AND AN N.B.A. STAR:

Int: In the upcoming playoff game, where will your team be staying?

Star: We're going to try and stay within ourselves.

Int: But you'll be trying to take your game where?

Star: To another level.

Int: By having your point guard do what?

Star: By raising his game a notch.

Int: And where do you plan on finding the game?

Star: I'm going to just let the game come to me.

Int: By hitting who?

Star: The open man.

Int: And staying--

Star: Focused.

Int: And what kind of minutes will your bench give you?

Star: Quality minutes.

Int: And how would you characterize your aging superstar?

Star: Oh, he's a warrior.

Int: So why didn't you win yesterday?

Star: We didn't take care of business.

Int: What didn't you get done?

Star: We didn't get the job done.

Int: Rather than being voted M.V.P., what would you rather have?

Star: A ring.

(With this, the referee, who has been listening to this drivel, awards a double technical and the show is over.)

OCTOBER 19, 1998   BY KATE KELLY

Ex-Hotshot Banker at Morgan Stanley Faces Fraud Charge

CHRISTIAN CURRY HAD EVERY-thing going for him. Fresh out of Columbia College, he was working as an investment banker at Morgan Stanley Dean Witter & Company during the greatest stock-market surge of the century. He was dining at Le Cirque 2000 and checking out strip clubs like Flashdancers and Ten's with clients. But in April of this year, everything fell apart.

First, nude photos taken of a visibly aroused Mr. Curry appeared across eight pages of *Playguy*, a gay pornographic magazine. Soon after the pictures began circulating at Morgan Stanley, Mr. Curry was bounced from his job. And

then things got worse. On Aug. 20, in a small park on East 43rd Street, Mr. Curry was arrested on five felony counts, including computer trespass, tampering with physical evidence and fifth-degree conspiracy.

The police say Mr. Curry, who is black, tried to hire someone to hack into the Morgan Stanley computer system as part of an attempt to paint himself as the victim of racial discrimination. He was, according to police, trying to plant racist interoffice e-mails that could serve as evidence in a potential lawsuit against the company. But there was a big problem: The hacker Mr. Curry allegedly

asked to help him with this job was actually an undercover New York City police officer.

"He was surprised," said New York Police Department deputy inspector Robert Martin. "He thought he was dealing with some rogue hacker, and we moved in."

Mr. Curry declined to comment either on his arrest or on the criminal charges. But his girlfriend, Marisa Wheeler, said he disputes the police claims.

Morgan Stanley has repeatedly said that Mr. Curry was fired for abusing his corporate expense account. The company would not comment on Mr. Curry's claims of discrimination.

◇◇◇◇◇◇

NOVEMBER 16, 1998   BY PHILIP WEISS

Wife Buys $800 Sweater, Drives Husband Crazy!

I WAS TALKING TO MY FRIEND JIM ON THE PHONE when he said that his office mate, who is a friend of my wife, and my wife had gone shopping and encouraged one another to buy $800 sweaters. I don't think that happened, I said. Maybe my wife's friend bought an $800 sweater, not my wife. Jim said, Gosh, I hope I haven't created any problem. I said No, because that had to be wrong.

I only asked my wife about it that weekend. We were driving to Home Depot.

"But I showed it to you," she said. "That black one."

I vaguely remembered her coming down the stairs several weeks before. Not that she'd said a word about the price.

Then she said, "Look, this is none of your business, Jim never should have told you that."

I was stunned and didn't know what to say (she was driving, she has a learner's permit). I wasn't sure whether to fold on it not being my business and burn inside, put it down to my wife's superior wisdom, or make something of it. But the more I tried to be quiet, the more something rose in me, my values. "But we don't do that, that's beyond extravagance," I said.

She started to quarrel then; I could sense her quailing just in her

cheeks and, seeing the advantage, I poured it on. When someone we know spends money like that, you say it's gross, I said. That what you could get for $800 was a ticket to India. I don't know if I could be married to someone who spends that much money on a sweater.

My wife said she'd been planning to return it. Amazingly, she still had the receipt.

Then the next day when I brought it up, she said, "If you say another word about that sweater, I'm going to paint the bathroom in it."

I went to lunch with Jim near the Flatiron Building.

"It's not that we can't afford it," I said. "But those values are appalling."

He held up his hand. "I'm sorry. It was naïve of me, but I didn't know that there existed this sphere in your wife's life to which you have no entree."

"But of course there's that sphere."

"And you accept that?"

"I don't have any choice."

"But what is in the sphere?"

"If I knew what was in it, it wouldn't be the sphere, would it?"

I liked his word. "I have no idea what's in there."

NOVEMBER 16, 1998 BY FRANK DIGIACOMO

THE TRANSOM: Puff Daddy's Black and White Ball

SEAN (PUFFY) COMBS WAS ON the phone from a yacht in the Bahamas, and he was laughing.

"When Penny Marshall comes to my joints, she gets buck wild!" Mr. Combs said with admiration in his polite voice. "Every time she comes to one of my parties, she gets ..." he paused, then continued excitedly, "Penny Marshall stopped the music and sang 'Happy Birthday.' I love her, man. I love her energy. You know, when I'm old, when I'm 60, I'm gonna remember that."

Lord knows if, three decades from now, anyone else will remember Ms. Marshall's nasal serenade of Mr. Combs, but for the next few months, they will be talking about the party where it happened.

Get past the confusion at the door and the white noise thrown up by the publicists of the celebrities who didn't get inside. Instead, talk to the people who attended the 29th-birthday party of Mr.

Combs at Cipriani Wall Street on Nov. 4, and many of them will agree that it marked a moment in New York's social history.

While Truman Capote's "Black and White Ball" at the Plaza Hotel in 1966 honored the crème de la crème of society, Mr. Combs was celebrating the kind of high-profile commercial success and notoriety that knows no racial or class bounds. On the night of his party, Mr. Combs attracted and presided over a group of local, national and international celebrities such as Donald Trump, Martha Stewart, Ronald Perelman, Sarah Ferguson, Kevin Costner and Ms. Marshall, who either have that kind of success, are trying to regain it, or are yearning for their first taste of it. And for at least this evening, as the television cameras caught them partying with Puffy, they caught a bit of the buzz that Mr. Combs has worked so hard to generate.

NOVEMBER 23, 1998 BY GEORGE GURLEY

What's New, Pussycat? 90's Women Adopt Sleek New Look Down Below

IT'S NOT YOUR MOTHER'S VULVA ANYMORE.

In a town house on West 57th Street, six Brazilian sisters are helping to bring about a private fashion revolution among stylish Manhattan women. Where once there was hair, now there is none, except for perhaps a tiny decorative strip on the *mons pubis*. The women at the J. Sisters International salon call it the "Brazilian bikini wax," but it's also known as the "thong wax" or "*Playboy* wax." It has long been the norm for strippers and porn actresses. Now this painful process is increasingly part of the regular beauty regimen for the Prada set.

The J. sisters, whose first names all begin with the letter J, perform the service for roughly 100 women a day. They do haircuts, manicures and pedicures, and they've been offering the special wax for the last five years. Brazilian bikini wax appointments for the week before Valentine's Day are already booked solid at J. Sisters.

"It makes you sexy," said Jonice Padilha, the youngest J. sister. She was wearing oval glasses and a black Donna Karan suit as she talked about it in the town house the other day. "Makes you fashion. When I don't have my bikini wax, I don't feel like to have sex with my husband. I feel dirty. And even himself say, 'Try a bikini wax!' I feel free. I feel clean. I feel sensuous even when I take a shower. I feel like I've been taken care of."

As Gold as It Gets! Jack Nicholson and Oscar

"Oh, Monica ...": Bill Clinton, bodice-ripper?

DECEMBER 21, 1998 BY GEORGE GURLEY

New Yorkers, Meet Your Media Elite

IT WAS BIG. AND, THE *POST*'S *Richard Johnson, Liz Smith* and *Cindy Adams* told GEORGE GURLEY, it was a year in which the dogs wagged and so did their tongues.

NYO: Why write so much about only a few people?

Ms. Smith: I can't go back over a year's worth of columns to tell you exactly why we wrote about such and such. For one reason or another, these people were on our minds or in the news. I mean, can you even question Bill, Hillary and Monica? Madonna is a perennial—the most famous woman in the world—and not just for us, we just don't trash her. Sinatra died, Elizabeth Taylor endures, no matter what, Leo and Brad and Matt are hot young stars, Cher is having a comeback, Rosie's still very big, and she's done so much for Broadway, Sharon has incredible glamour and attitude, Anne Heche is hot and gay! Barbra got married. Come on, why do I have to explain this?

NYO: Which boldfaced names are you most sick of?

Mr. Johnson: Puff Daddy.

NYO: But you've written about him more than anyone did!

Mr. Johnson: Right.

NYO: Brad Pitt told Oprah Winfrey that he didn't know how gossip columnists could look their kids in the eye and tell them what they do for a living.

Ms. Adams: Well, I don't have a kid. And that's one of the reasons. But what I would say is … I write short stories. As short as possible. I write about what everybody wants to read. It's not Shakespeare, but then Shakespeare couldn't do what I do. Possibly Brad Pitt has had too many mentions. But with more pictures like *Meet Joe Black*, he won't have to worry about that anymore.

Mr. Johnson: I think my kid already has a fine appreciation for what I do since I've been able to take him to, like, Broadway openings and took him on a junket to the Bahamas. And he likes stretch limos already.

NYO: So, what would you tell your kid that you are?

Mr. Drudge: A reporter who toils away on these wonder wires and who is not afraid to take on authority.

◇◇◇◇◇◇◇

DECEMBER 21, 1998 BY FRANK DIGIACOMO

THE GOVERNMENT GOES GOSSIP-CRAZY

How would you like to be Bill Clinton, closed in on by the fervent gossipocracy? Well, writes FRANK DiGIACOMO, here they are, the 500 most noted people in New York, as calculated by appearances in the very media that make them what they are today: trapped

YOU THINK YOU KNOW WHAT happened in 1998: You remember January and the explosion, the wagging finger, the near immolation of a president, the long siege that followed; you think you're tired of this terrible series of unanticipated events; you just want them to end.

But it was done for you. It was custom-made for you, voracious American consumer. The Starr Report was a government document tailored to this cybertabloid age. It was a referral with a sexy nar-

rative that had been co-written by Stephen Bates, a lawyer who had studied fiction at Harvard and had written nonfiction features for *The Nation* and *Playboy*.

Just as in the 1930's, when the argument was made that the federal government shouldn't be building dams and providing electrical power because that was something best done by private industry, this year the federal government usurped the celebrity culture and the press.

This was the year the Government became the Gossips.

1999

Book business hops into bed with "that woman," Ms. Lewinsky

 Talk editor Tina Brown, latest Miramax starlet, throws party on Liberty Island

The billionaire and the sex bomb: Ron Perelman courts Ellen Barkin

Swipe again, suckers: Straphangers toss tokens for Metrocards

Internet stock trades are new sanctioned narcotic of upper middle class

 John F. Kennedy Jr. dies in self-piloted plane at age 39

Women warriors Williams, Kournikova, Hingis invade U.S. Open

Hello, possums! Dame Edna Everage spreads gladness

 Hej-Hej, Gap: Swedes invade with cheap-chic H&M

1999

◇◇◇◇◇◇◇

MARCH 1, 1999
BY ALEXANDRA JACOBS

THE NEW YORK WORLD: THE METROCARD BLESSING

JANUARY 18, 1999 BY DINI VON MUEFFLING

Bloomingdale's or Bust! The Rise of Shoshanna Lonstein (Jerry's Ex)

JERRY SEINFELD'S EX-GIRL-friend, Shoshanna Lonstein, now 23, who became a household name as the teenage girlfriend of America's most famous TV funnyman, is about to get the last laugh.

While many New Yorkers have some inkling that Ms. Lonstein has branched into the fashion business, few are aware that her clothes—which are smart and cute, like cotton dresses in gingham and Liberty prints with matching bags (matching thong tucked inside)—are *moving*. The clothes—which Stefani Greenfeld, owner of the hot East Side boutique Scoop, calls "lingerie-inspired sportswear"–are extremely well priced (the dresses go for about $130) and geared toward large-breasted young women. Women who, like Ms. Lonstein, have a hard time finding flattering clothes to fit their physiques. After Ms. Lonstein's initial splash at Bloomingdale's, Kal Ruttenstein, the sneaker-clad fashion director, has reordered her resort line, placed a large order for spring, and asked Ms. Lonstein to design a line exclusively for the store.

But will Ms. Lonstein ever be able to avoid having her name in the same sentence as Jerry Sein-feld? If there's one place she might be able to do it, it's back home in her city, not the one Mr. Seinfeld created on a stage set in Hollywood. It is here that Ms. Lonstein has won the respect of Mr. Ruttenstein and other high-end fashion buyers, evolving from the gossip columns' "bosomy Shoshanna" to president of a company with three full-time employees and which she predicts will have sales of $1 million in 1999. And who strikes those who meet her as much more beautiful than her grainy tabloid pictures and who is, by all accounts, disarmingly ... nice.

And while her ex seems caught in terminal romantic adolescence—witness his brazen, tabloid-ready swiping of newlywed Jessica Sklar from her husband of three months—Ms. Lonstein waves away her Seinfeld past with, "That's a part of my life that's so over. I really don't think about it. It was a relationship, that's all."

Ms. Lonstein said she didn't exactly miss all the attention. "I couldn't imagine some of the past criticism of my life. I never felt like I did anything wrong, so it never bothered me." Still, she admitted, she found relentless hounding, and the media obsession with her chest, trying. "Rather than 'Shoshanna,'" she said, "It's always 'shapely Shoshanna.' To have it be a sexual part of your body is very difficult. It's different if it's long legs."

YOU HAVE YOUR LUDDITES, WHO still refuse to buy it because they like the "tactility," or whatever, of tokens. You have your paranoids, who think Big Brother is using its magnetic strip to monitor their every move. And then ... and then you have your addicts, whose lives will never be the same because of those little gold passes to freedom.

"I am obsessed with my unlimited Metrocard," said Jake Kreilkamp, 25, who lives in Washington Heights and works for PEN American Center. He happily fronts $63 for his monthly card. "It makes you feel like the train is working with you to lower your transportation costs. Which is so not New York, you know? New York is all about, you know, 'Yer gonna pay.'"

James Tupper has a recurring role on *As the World Turns*—and lots of auditions. "I used to walk everywhere, it's true," he said. "Now I just jump on the subway."

The swipe, the dip, the beep-acceptance.

"Oh, my God. There's a moment there, definitely," said Mr. Tupper. "I feel accepted. I do. It's like a green light. Like, I feel that all is well. No, really, I do. For a tiny moment there, all is well."

MARCH 29, 1999   BY FRANK DIGIACOMO

HARVEY WINS IN HOSTILE HOLLYWOOD

HARVEY WEINSTEIN, THE CO-CHAIRMAN OF MIRAMAX FILMS, rested his pale, meaty hand at the base of the burnished gold statuette on the table before him. It was 1:30 a.m., and Miramax's Oscar party at the Beverly Hills Hotel was standing-room-only, save for the small strip of guarded V.I.P. territory where Mr. Weinstein, his wife, Eve, and a small group of well-wishers sat. It was time for the annual post-mortem. The moment when, after a neck roll or two, Mr. Weinstein defined Hollywood's high holy night in New York terms and Queens English. But in the early hours of March 22, he smiled at this *Observer* reporter and said simply, "It's good to be alive."

Maybe it was. But Mr. Weinstein had the look more of one of Steven Spielberg's soldiers in the picture he had defeated, *Saving Private Ryan*. Yes, he had made a successful landing on a foreign shore. But, oh, those mortars!

Harvey Weinstein, the New Yorker, they said, had broken the rules; he had spent tens of millions; he had thrown the wrong kind of party, mixing movie people, press and civilians. But mostly, they were mad because, like Yankee soldiers in Atlanta, like Bill Clinton in the Congress, Miramax had come and beaten them on their home field.

◇◇◇◇◇◇◇

APRIL 5, 1999   BY ALEXANDRA ZISSU

THE OBSERVATORY: Hey, Barneys ... Remember Me? Jeffrey Kalinsky Sets Up Shop on 14th

PETITE RETAILER JEFFREY Kalinsky stuck an Hermès dingo boot out of his lady-chauffeured Lincoln Town Car onto far West 14th Street on a recent sunny Saturday afternoon. A few men in white, blood-stained aprons and a couple in errand wear were the only other living be-

ings on the carcass-filled street in the meatpacking district. The air smelled of dried blood and guts. Mr. Kalinsky emerged, dressed in head-to-toe Madison Avenue: cream-colored Helmut Lang jeans, a white Yves Saint Laurent belt (with a mother-of-pearl buckle), a fitted, black Gucci T-shirt, a sky blue Yves Saint Laurent cashmere cardigan and a navy leather Hermès jacket. He stared out from behind Katharine Hamnett sunglasses.

On Aug. 2 (his 37th birthday), Mr. Kalinsky, a former shoe buyer for Barneys, will open Jeffrey New York, a 12,000-square-foot former warehouse on the corner of 10th Avenue packed with expensive garments, reminiscent—in inventory, at least—of his former employer.

What Jeffrey lacks in name recognition and square-footage compared to Barneys (and everyone is comparing his store to Barneys), Mr. Kalinsky intends to make up for in pampering and Southern charm. The son and grandson of retailers and owner of three successful Atlanta stores—Bob Ellis, Jeffrey and Jil Sander (he owns her franchise)—will offer up his Manolo Blahniks with a healthy dose of hospitality, which may prove to be a welcome antidote to Madison Avenue, where the salespeople are almost always too hip to help. If you have ever been to one of Jeffrey Kalinsky's stores, you have probably met him, and chances are he remembers your shoe size.

Bag designer Judith Leiber calls Mr. Kalinsky her "terrific shoe man." And when wedding-cake designer Sylvia Weinstock, who has been shopping with Mr. Kalinsky for 10 years, heard he was coming to New York, she called him to say, "I can't wait! I have my charge card ready!"

Retailers are less giddy. In fact, Barneys is said to be ticked off. Jason Weisenfeld, vice president of public relations, tried to take the high road. "We are thrilled for Jeffrey as we are for all Barneys alumni that go on and excel in the world of retail," he said. "In Jeffrey's case, we are particularly flattered because he has always been very vocal about the enormous amount he learned during his tenure at Barneys."

MAY 3, 1999
BY FRANK DIGIACOMO

HOTHEAD COMEDY GENIUS PAT COOPER OUTLASTS ALL THOSE SHOWBIZ PHONIES

IN THE LULL BETWEEN LUNCH and dinner, Pat Cooper sat in the second-floor bar room of the Friars Club. He wore an under-stated gray turtleneck, a black baseball cap with an embroi-dered Fox Movietone News logo, and gold-rimmed aviator-style glasses that evoked an earlier era of Bryl-Creem and Harvey Wallbangers. On the back of his chair hung a lush, black motor-cycle-style leather jacket that Mr. Cooper had removed about 20 minutes earlier. As a waiter delivered the glass of red wine the comedian had ordered, the interviewer asked Mr. Cooper how long he had belonged to the Friars Club. "I am an honorary member. I don't pay dues," he replied. "I pay back with my tal-ent." Mr. Cooper closed his mouth around the word talent like he was sealing it in a vault. "If they need me for a roast, if they've got special shows, I'm here. They're nice people. They've always been nice to me."

JULY 12, 1999
BY FRANK DIGIACOMO

THE TRANSOM: A Word to Ellen: Watch It, Girl! Life With Perelman Is Film Noir

IF THERE WAS ANY QUESTION that things had gotten serious between billionaire Ronald Perelman and the actress Ellen Barkin, the answer lies in the hairstyle that Mr. Perelman has been showing off, along with his date, at a series of public events in the city, including the 40th anniversary of the Four Seasons restaurant.

Mr. Perelman, who has always kept his male-pattern bald head remarkably well-coifed, has got-ten the billionaire's equivalent of a buzz cut. While certainly not in the stubbled league of, say, the lead singer of Rage Against the Machine, it is safe to say that Mr. Perelman has done the one thing (short of growing a goatee) that a 56-year-old bald man can do to make himself look hipper to a 45-year-old Hollywood sex bomb such as Ms. Barkin. And that says one thing: That Mr. Perelman—a man known to be a relentless seducer both in his professional and personal life—has begun his full court press for the exclusive enjoy-ment of Ms. Barkin's irresist-ible crooked smile.

JANUARY 11, 1999 EDITORIAL

EDITORIAL: ZUCKERMAN, KOSNER AND BRILL

ALL OF THE MEDIA'S NARCISSISM CAN BE SUMMED UP IN A PHRASE: Zuckerman, Kosner and Brill. Mortimer Zuckerman, publisher of the once-great *Daily News*; Edward Kosner, late of *Esquire*, now the *News*' Sunday editor; and Steven Brill, proprietor of the much-hyped *Brill's Content*: These three men truly believe they are the publish-ing *machers* of the city. But with nary a drop of wit, mirth or humor among them, these three fatuous wannabes are determined to drive away all would-be readers and bore us all to tears.

Hats off to Mr. Zuckerman, who has managed the seemingly im-possible: He has made a tabloid unreadable. With even politics now part of the tabloid news cycle, the *Daily News*, which exemplified American tabloid journalism for decades, *should be* in its glory. In-stead, it induces in readers a permanent state of narcolepsy. Why? It certainly doesn't help that Mr. Zuckerman has never met a tabloid reader, wouldn't know where to find one and wouldn't understand his or her concerns. Imagine Mr. Zuckerman stumbling across a *Daily News* subscriber: What would he say?

No doubt he would find reason to boast of his latest impersonation of a senior statesman while a guest on *The Charlie Rose Show*. Mr. Zuckerman's pretensions, his utter cluelessness, became evident when he announced that Mr. Kosner was being hired to revamp the tabloid's Sunday edition. It was inevitable that these two smug, back-scratching mediocrities would find each other. Mr. Kosner is fresh from running *Esquire*, turning an eminent literary showcase into a men's consumer pamphlet about the six best mustards in town and premature baldness. No doubt Mr. Kosner is going to bring that same sensibility to the *Daily News*, which will further dilute the newspa-per of the New York worker into a dispensable curiosity, a pale simu-lacrum of its former self.

The Sunday *Daily News* has been hemorrhaging readers for the last sev-eral years. And Mr. Zuckerman's solution is to hire Mr. Kosner—the only editor around who would work for him. Their task is made considerably more difficult by the likely fact that neither man reads the *News*, anyway.

Now, if the puffed-up Mr. Brill reads his own publication, we feel sorry for him. Only someone as profoundly solipsistic as Mr. Brill could have invented *Brill's Content*, which sounds like hair cream ("A Little Dab'll Do Ya!") and should be. In fact, if you happen to use hair cream, then you must like this dull, humorless, self-important maga-zine. Still, it must have taken real brainstorming to create a magazine about journalists that even journalists don't read. Mr. Brill, whose screaming tirades have scared away anyone who worked for him who had a modicum of talent and self-respect, thought he could sell a mass-market magazine on the premise that America just couldn't wait to read about conflicts of interest in book review sections. Amazing! And this man presumes to judge the news judgment of the nation's editors. The very premise of this magazine is a stunning dis-play of arrogance and pomposity, and its conceit offers a revealing glimpse of Mr. Brill's absurd pretensions. Steven Brill, the arbiter of American media?

Please. Willian Allen White, maybe. But not Steven Brill.

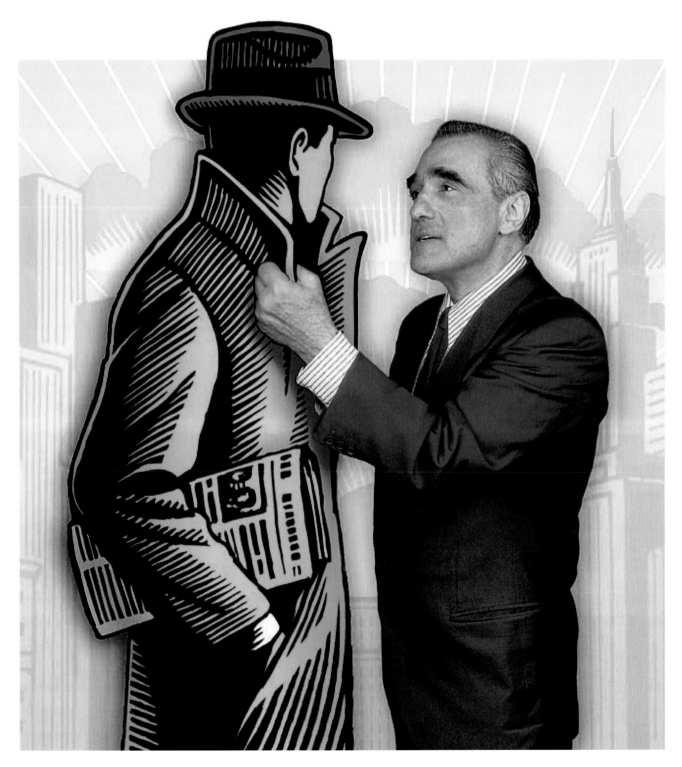

Director Martin Scorsese confronts The Observer's *avatar*

JUNE 28, 1999 BY GEORGE GURLEY

HEY! YEAH, YOU ! WHAT'S YOUR GAY QUOTIENT?

In New Ambiguous Age (Hello, Brad Pitt!), It's No Longer Easy as 'Gay' or 'Straight'; Liv Tyler, Pete Hamill, Bob Grant, Kurt Andersen Take Part in our Casual Survey

IT USED TO BE EASY. YOU WERE EITHER GAY OR YOU WERE straight. Maybe certain oddballs belonged to that category known as "bi," especially in the 70's. But for the most part, you got to identify yourself as one thing (heterosexual) or the other (homosexual), and that was that. That was O.K. But how about this: Just how gay are you? What percentage? Editor-turned-novelist Kurt Andersen described his own gay quotient. "I often talk to certain friends of mine, certain heterosexual friends, I might add, I often say, 'Well, that's be-

cause I'm gay,' as a jocular explanation of, for instance, the fact that I don't like sports, to take the coarsest example of my gayness," he said.

So what's the percentage? Mr. Andersen asked if he could assign himself two separate percentages: "If I could give myself two scores, one on the sexual, one on the cultural, I would put myself much higher on the cultural," he said. "I'd say 0 to 1 on the sexual and, like, 20 on the cultural, or maybe more." As evidence of his cultural gayness, Mr. Andersen offered: "I do all the cooking in my household. I dress up in women's clothing most nights. That's a joke. I read *Rules of Interiors* with an unseemly degree of interest." Architecture? "Yeah, architecture, there you go, that's a gay interest. What else? I actually like gay people. I would say if you gave me 10 random heterosexuals and 10 random homosexuals, I would like more of the homosexuals than the heterosexuals."

Later in the interview, Mr. Andersen revised his level of sexual gayness: "I have never had, faintly, a sexual feeling about a man, I don't think," he said. "So '1' if you want to be p.c., but '0' if I were going to be honest." All this artful hemming and hawing brings to mind the great Henry James, God rest his probably gay soul. If he gazed upon his own era and saw in it *The Awkward Age*, let us look at our own and declare it the Ambiguous Age. Even the greatest, most solid American historical personage of all, Abraham Lincoln, the rail-splitter himself, is entering the terrain of sexual uncertainty. Two upcoming biographies—one by sex researcher C.A. Tripp and one by gay firebrand Larry Kramer—will argue that Lincoln had a ho-

mosexual bond with his dear Illinois friend, Joshua Speed. The two men shared a bed, upstairs of Speed's general store, when they were struggling bachelors. There have already been some homoerotic hints in the beautifully made 1998 biography *Honor's Voice: The Transformation of Abraham Lincoln*, by Douglas L. Wilson. Mr. Wilson reported that Lincoln and Speed "regarded themselves not only as close friends but as something like soul mates" and that both were miserable upon getting married. "When this shall reach you," Lincoln wrote in a letter to Speed in 1841, "you will have been Fanny's husband several days. You know my desire to befriend you is everlasting—that I will never cease, while I know how to do anything."

This touchy area is the kind of thing that interests scholars now. In the Bill Clinton era, during which one cultural hero after another has been revealed to be frail and human, people can accept shades of gray. There was a lot of hooting, but Mr. Clinton managed to stay in office—and with an approval rating higher than Jimmy Carter's. In the Ambiguous Age, the pinup boys come complete with ... interesting questions. The latest heartthrob, the Latin singer Ricky Martin, has told members of the press: "What I say about sexuality is, I leave it for my room and lock the door." That didn't stop *The Advocate*, a gay magazine, from trying to break that door down, with a cover story titled "Ricky Martin: The Gay Connection." And yet the girls are still screaming; they're comfortable in that sexual gray area. Another case: Movie star Brad Pitt is exposed in a 30-page photo spread in *W*. The pictures show him with his mouth wide open; lying on a cement floor, face down, with his naked buttocks visible; standing near a grizzly bear in a holding cell; with his hands in his pants; and making various ecstatic facial expressions.

"They had a photo of Brad Pitt the other day," said Bob Grant, the very conservative talk-show host on WOR-AM. "I said, 'Gee, I wish I had that waistline, I wish I had that chest.' But that doesn't mean I want to go up to Brad Pitt and give him a big *hug*." He was asked if he might be 2 percent gay. "I couldn't even quantify it," he said. "It's nonexistent. I'll tell you one thing: I can admire a good-looking guy, I can see somebody like Tom Cruise, somebody like that, and say, 'Gee, I wish I looked like him.' That doesn't mean I want to take him to bed."

Sexual theorist Edward Stein is working on a book called *The Mismeasure of Desire: The Science, Theory, and Ethics of Sexual Orientation* for the Oxford University Press. Mr. Stein, who earned his Ph.D. in philosophy at M.I.T. and is now working toward a law degree at Yale Law School, believes those mid-1990's notions of sexual identity will soon seem stale. That elaborate University of Chicago survey from 1994 that found less than 10 percent of the adult male population to be gay? "Take it with a grain of salt," he said. And he will seek to cast doubt on the ideas that sexuality is genetically or neurologically based.

"Most of that research of which I am critical assumes that sexual orientation is like a light switch—either you're gay or you're straight," said Mr. Stein. "Or it assumes that it's more like a dimmer switch, that either you're strongly attracted to either men or women. But, in fact, it might turn out to be much more complicated." "What percentage are you?" he was asked.

"It depends on whether you mean behavior or fantasy life or identity, but in the end ... roughly 85 to 90 percent."

The next night at the Loeb Boathouse there was an American Foundation for AIDS Research benefit. Fashion designer Betsey Johnson said she was 49 lesbian, 20 percent "gay man" and 51 percent straight. O.K., so it didn't add up—that's ambiguity for you. Singer Foxy Brown was "100 percent heterosexual." Chris Eigeman, who played the Wildean wit in *Metropolitan* and a gay nightclub promoter in *The Last Days of Disco,* said he was 0 percent. Why? "Because I'm married, obviously," he said. Lisa Ling, the new, 25-year-old addition to ABC's *The View,* said she was 1 percent gay. And actress Liv Tyler, whom the paparazzi caught mid-smooch with Drew Barrymore at the Oscars? "That's my business!" Ms. Tyler said. "I love everybody—man, woman, I find women beautiful, I find men beautiful, I find animals and trees—I'd like to shag a tree sometimes!"

A bemused Jay Shaffer, the owner of Shaffer City Oyster Bar and Grill, was taking it all in. "We're all a little gay," said Mr. Shaffer, 46. "We all look at a man and say, 'Gee, that's very attractive—he's got great biceps, he's got great muscle structure.' We're not necessarily looking at his manhood." He put himself down for 20 percent gay. "That means you have enough control and understanding of your femininity, that you can cry, you can create, you can go like this"—he flipped his hand up and down—"like some sort of flaming faggot."

At a restaurant called Baby Jupiter on Orchard Street, a 23-year-old woman from London, who did not want her name used in this article, said she, too, thought we all have a little gayness in us. "I've never slept with a woman but I'd say 7 percent," she said. "I

> "They had a photo of Brad Pitt the other day," said Bob Grant, the very conservative talk-show host on WOR-AM. "I said, 'Gee, I wish I had that waistline, I wish I had that chest.' But that doesn't mean I want to go up to Brad Pitt and give him a big hug." He was asked if he might be 2 percent gay. "I couldn't even quantify it," he said.

can't say I've never thought about it, so it doesn't make me 0."

When she was 14, this woman was a tomboy, and her mother made her take ballroom dancing classes. Her best friend attended the class, too. "I'll never forget that girl," she said. "In the dance sessions you had to have a partner, so, of course, Lisa was my partner. We would dance together and spin each other around. I was still a virgin, I didn't even know what sex was. We danced together very closely, and it was like a form of communication without speaking. Dancing is a very intimate thing ... so we got very into the closeness of it all, and we'd practice dancing very close and no one else was in the room. It was just the two of us. I remember feeling something that I'd never ever felt before, like everything passed through my body, moving, like it never moved before, like feelings and areas, and we never said anything but we danced very well together, and every time she came up close, we'd nearly kiss each other, and she would just touch my breasts, touch my bum, or move around the front. She would just do that, and I would do the same to her. I've never told anyone this story. We would touch each other and then after the weeks went on, I remember volunteering to go back there, not just being forced to go back there. We tried to take all our clothes off. It was showing each other parts of our body we'd never shown each other before, and experiencing parts of our lower regions without really knowing. I just remember her touching me down below and feeling like this warm, and I'd do the same to her. We never said anything—that's the weirdest thing. I was overwhelmed. At 14, I knew what I was doing was wrong. I knew I wasn't supposed to be with a girl. I felt naughty, I felt dirty, I felt wrong. But I'm glad it happened."

Another believer in the continuum theory of sexual orientation is Brad Gooch, author of *Finding the Boyfriend Within.* "I think now with the whole gay liberation movement, people are getting to the point that the relief of coming out as gay isn't really the total answer or the end of the line or something. There's more to it than we think," said Mr. Gooch.

I reached Michael Thomas Ford, the 30-year-old author of *Alec Baldwin Doesn't Love Me* and *That's Mr. Faggot to You* by phone. He was at home, on his bed. "When you grow up, people give this either-or scenario, so when you pick one there's this intense pressure to stick with it, like taking piano lessons or something. I would say I'm 99 percent gay, but I would like to reserve that 1 percent if Gillian Anderson, the *X Files* girl, decides she wants to call. And Xena, who wouldn't want to sleep with Xena?"

What's with Alec Baldwin?

"Until I wrote the book, I thought I was the only guy who thought Alec Baldwin was really hot, and then I got hundreds of letters saying, 'Stay away from him, you bitch, he's mine.'"

AUGUST 2, 1999 BY GEORGE GURLEY

THE OBSERVATORY: Allan Block Is Worth More Than $100 Million and He's Seeking a Wife in New York

ALLAN BLOCK IS 44 YEARS OLD. He's worth over $100 million. Since 1985, he has come to Manhattan nearly every weekend from his hometown of Toledo, Ohio, to give small dinner parties ... and to find the right woman.

Mr. Block is a nice enough guy, a man who doesn't believe in the one-night stand, and he's beginning to be frustrated by the fact that he has not yet found the woman who will be Mrs. Block. Over the years, he has dated scores of women in Manhattan, taken them to Cipriani and '21', and he has spent many late nights searching solo, at places like Nell's and Le Club and Au Bar, but no wife yet.

"I would say I wish I had been married before now," said Mr. Block, driving down Route 27 in a rented Ford Taurus on his way to Southampton one recent Saturday. "I never thought I'd be this age and never been married. It was never my plan, you know. I think the conditions, the way it is today, is the reason. I think there's a war between the sexes going on. I think the female part of the population has been waging a war against the male part. Male and female have always been equal, you cannot compare gender to race, that was never

a valid analogy or comparison. There was never a deliberate effort to hold women down. Feminism is basically wrong."

Mr. Block has a girlfriend who lives in Milan, Italy, but he's still in the marriage market. He sees the woman from Milan every month, but she may not be too enamored with the idea of setting up house in Toledo. And that's part of the deal for any woman who marries him. Toledo will likely be her home base.

"I'm proud to be a native of Toledo, Ohio," he said. "It makes me angry when I hear people who have never been there making statements, 'That must be one of the worst places in the country!' One person, one girl, a dumb girl, said, 'That must be a really awful place!' And I said, 'It's a major metropolitan area! 800,000 people, two major universities, an independent medical college, top museums, outstanding zoo, a museum of science and industry, nice parks, a Great Lake and all the recreational opportunities that that represents. Toledo might be a great place to be married with kids."

It's not really so easy, being a wealthy, single man in 1999.

"I would have rather been single in 1950, 1955," said Mr. Block. "I would rather have been dealing with the woman who wanted to get married or had to get married. I think it would have been a lot easier. I can't run a house, I can't even have a nice apartment. I can sign the check. "

In a 1993 article, *Forbes* magazine put the worth of his family business—the Toledo, Ohio-based Blade Communications—at $600 million.

AUGUST 9, 1999 BY FRANK DIGIACOMO

THE TRANSOM: TINA BROWN, LATEST MIRAMAX STARLET

THE NARCOTIC BASSLINE OF ERIC B. & RAKIM'S "PAID IN FULL" HOOKED them as they stood staring at the stage that bore the rapper-turned-talk-show host Queen Latifah. At various places in the crowd, wild-haired Salman Rushdie, former mayoral candidate Andy Stein, and *Nation* editor Katrina vanden Heuvel, in a dress that showed off her tattoo and her ass, skanked to the rhythm with varying degrees of subtlety and dignity. Socialite writer Lally Weymouth and art dealer Arne Glimcher did not.

By sunset, when the ferries started leaving Battery Park for Liberty Island, the buzz had reached the kind of levels that Miramax reserves for its brightest Oscar hopefuls. And many of those who had not been invited to the *Talk* celebration had spent the afternoon desperately searching for someone with an extra ticket.

Later that night, Ms. Brown would describe the guest list as "totally insane eclecticism" and admit: "I know that I've left off mighty people who will cut me forever."

Yet, though the party's organizers had rounded up enough respectable celebrity tonnage (especially for August, when most of the meritocracy has left town) to generate ample publicity for the event, one key opportunity was lost. Both Ms. Brown and the Miramax boys have long known how to build a party crowd to make a statement. But any clues that could have been gleaned about the actual point of view of *Talk* magazine were lost in the darkness and wide open spaces of Liberty Island.

AUGUST 23, 1999   BY NICK PAUMGARTEN AND TINKER SPITZ

WELCOME TO 24-HOUR WALL STREET WORLD!

BACK WHEN MARIA S. WAS MAR-ried, before she gambled away $3.5 million, she was a stock market addict, a fool for the action. At Advest Inc., the securities firm where she worked, she traded all day, then went home and thought about stocks all night. She wore earphones to bed so she could tune in to the radio and listen to the stock market reports. She didn't even take them off for sex.

Maria was way ahead of her time. She was a stock market junkie before it was really possible to be one. She could not trade at night. She could not trade at home. So she took up gambling and ruined her life that way instead. Now, at 56, she's a homeless ex-con who attends regular

Gamblers Anonymous meetings in a midtown Manhattan hospital (hence the anonymity).

Accessible now to anyone with an Internet connection and a credit card, the stock market has become a universal distraction, a ubiquitous entertainment, a sanctioned narcotic. You are either plugged into it or made constantly aware of how foolish you are not to be. In hospitals and schools, in dens and kitchens, the amateurs are mainlining stocks. They have one eye on their day job and the other on their stock portfolio, posted in red and green on their computer screens. Once a barometer of the country's work, the market now is yet another way to play.

◇◇◇◇◇◇◇

SEPTEMBER 6, 1999   BY ALEXANDRA JACOBS

Women Warriors Invade the U.S. Open;
How Coach Brad Gilbert Remade Agassi's Game

TWENTY YEARS AGO, YOU WENT TO THE U.S. OPEN TO SEE BJORN Borg, John McEnroe and Jimmy Connors. Now you go to see Anna Kournikova, Venus Williams and Martina Hingis–a triumvirate Ms. Hingis cheerfully dubbed "the Spice Girls of tennis."

If to sit in Arthur Ashe Stadium at the height of the tournament as airplanes roar past is to feel that one is at the very heart of the urban jungle—forgetting for a moment the 45-minute subway ride to Flushing—then these young women are its new rulers, its lionesses. They're the ones strutting and preening and stalking the baseline while the rather simian Pete Sampras, the newly hairless, emasculated Andre Agassi and that wussy Aussie Patrick Rafter, with his pliés, his zinc oxide and his topknot, do their thing and quickly flee the court.

The new, big rackets—which have rendered the men's serves unreturnable and their rallies short and boring—are *feminine*. Their sweet spots are larger. Gone is the old racket press, a sort of corset.

Tennis, as a spectator sport in America, is mostly accessories, body parts and attitude. So: The sports bra has replaced the tennis sweater. The long, waxed thigh has replaced the hairy, clay-smudged calf. And the brattiness that Mr. McEnroe made acceptable has given way to the schoolgirl insouciance of Ms. Kournikova, Ms. Hingis and their juicy pop-culture counterparts.

JULY 26, 1999 BY FRANK DIGIACOMO

JOHN KENNEDY, NEW YORKER

NEW YORK DOESN'T HAVE ROOM TO BURY ITS VERY important dead. Ulysses Grant, of course, is up on Morningside Heights. A few old bishops rest in the crypts at St. John the Divine, and some cardinals lie under St. Patrick's. Some dusty patriots fill the yard way down beside Trinity Church. But when Gershwin or Jacqueline Kennedy Onassis or even Thurman Munson dies, they're honored here, then sent away for burial in greener, more sacred ground, and New York feels palpably lonely without them. This morning, New York feels older without him.

John Kennedy led an exterior, sometimes sunny life in this sometimes dark city. He was part of the brotherhood of his family, but he also lived a life apart, which was his own, and the city helped to set him apart. The New York of John Kennedy stretched from the duchies of Upper Fifth Avenue, where he grew up, to the warehouse district of Tribeca, where he lived his married life; from the green football fields of Central Park to the wrought-iron gates at Collegiate School on West End Avenue; and from the bright, flag-flying offices of *George* magazine, where he was founding editor, to the perky murals in the Bemelmans Bar at the Carlyle, where Ludwig Bemelmans figures of little, snow-dotted, sledding New Yorkers recall the elegance and fun and playful wit that was New York before ... everything. John F. Kennedy Jr. lived his life bathed in so much unwanted light that it is almost impossible to imagine him searching the opaque darkness over the Atlantic for some recognizable glimmer that would help him re-establish his bearings.

He lost his reference, the aviation experts speculated as the 24-hour cable news coverage desperately chased their tails. He could not find the horizon. These were odd phrases to hear in connection with a man whose inner compass rarely failed him when the eyes of the world were watching. And usually when the world was watching, the pictures and words were coming from New York, the city that Mr. Kennedy had called home since 1964. Here in this metropolis that has consumed so many wealthy, handsome scions with vainglorious notions of power and mortality, Mr. Kennedy had actually managed to define himself, not as some media-inflated myth, but as a man of his own design, right down to the ever-present chain that connected his wallet and keys to his belt.

His mother brought him and his sister to New York to achieve a kind of privacy, and they got that. But Jacqueline Kennedy Onassis insisted that her son become part of the city, and he did that as well. He made the city his Forest of Arden, his Emerald City. And, in a surprisingly optimistic period, John Kennedy made of New York a palace, not a prison—shooting to Yankee Stadium by subway, making Olmsted's park a playing ground, surfing the rivers of traffic. And when the city conspired to confront him—when the paparazzi assaulted not just him, but his wife, Carolyn Bessette—he went one-on-one; a fair fight between the best-known-guy-in-the-world-in-a-ski-hat up against the mob of the voracious, vulturing press corps. New York liked it. And as an embodiment of New York, he was exactly emblematic of the New York that had taken over from the old, ethnic melting pot. Manhattan in the 90's became the capitalist capital of the world—it was no longer a place your grandparents had come to; it was the place a generation was setting up camp to remake the urban experience. And John Kennedy lived here like nobody else—and like everybody else. He started a business; tried out suspenders; wore crutches, evening clothes, bandannas; moved on wheels, walked the dog, held the door for his wife, yelled at the paparazzi, fought with his partner in the hallways of Hachette, did quiet work for charities, and avoided phoniness on every front. So he became more than a New Yorker; he became a quintessential New Yorker. He did the whole thing: By day, he was the working stiff, Bruce Wayne going to the office. By night,

in a formal suit, he looked like a Rolls coming around the corner. Vital, vigorous, full of fun, generous, confrontational, an unsentimental existential lesson in the joy of daily living. At a Municipal Art Society gala at Grand Central Terminal, Mr. Kennedy pulled aside a waitress. Osso buco had been served that night and he wanted to know if she would put together a bag of leftover bones for his dog, Friday. Larry King and Dan Rather asked him about being the little boy who had saluted, but New Yorkers of his generation didn't think of him that way; New Yorkers saluted him, sometimes with a wave, sometimes with an envious middle finger, but saluted him nevertheless. When he flopped—like the New York bar—he passed the New York test by non-aversion, meeting reporters head-on. And when he succeeded—most of the time—he averted ever so slightly. By that definition, Mr. Kennedy was very much a New Yorker. Unlike the celebrities whose relationship with the city is an antiseptic one, buffered by town cars and bodyguards, Mr. Kennedy had become intimate with the asphalt in a way that most rank-and-file New Yorkers do not even achieve. He rode its subways and traveled its roads on bicycle and Rollerblade. Chanel president Arie Kopelman remembered that Mr. Kennedy once rode his bicycle to Rao's restaurant in East Harlem to meet him for dinner. "I said, 'John, come on, riding a bike in the city is crazy enough, but coming all the way up here? I don't think it's safe.'" Mr. Kopelman said that Mr. Kennedy laughed and said, "It's the only way I can get some great exercise." As he roamed our precincts, Mr. Kennedy became a poster boy for the new New York that had risen up during the reign of Rudy Giuliani. As he played shirtless in Central Park or braved the paparazzo gantlet at a black-tie gala, Mr. Kennedy sent the message that New York was a playground, not a prison. The world was watching, but those paying the closest attention were those who, like Mr. Kennedy, had been born at the tail end of the baby boom and had settled in the city.

Now, in their mid-30's and early 40's, they saw Mr. Kennedy as a point of reference—albeit an exceedingly handsome one—for what they hoped to achieve. Mr. Kennedy certainly had the looks and the surname to be head of the class. On these attributes, let alone the wealth that he had inherited, Mr. Kennedy could have coasted through life, ending up one of the many titled hollow men who haunt the city's nightspots with gin and bitterness on their breath. But those who knew Mr. Kennedy said he loved to confound expectations. "He was determined not to do what people expected him to do," said Joe Armstrong, senior vice president and group publisher of Capital Publishing, who knew Mr. Kennedy and his mother, Jacqueline Onassis. It's unclear how much of Mr. Kennedy's need to this was the result of the proto-*Truman Show* life he lived. Unlike the fictional Truman Burbank, however, Mr. Kennedy knew that he was constantly under surveillance by the media. It was a pressure that he dealt with indifferent ways, but rarely did Mr. Kennedy crack. He had his father's temper, and occasionally his arrogance, some have said

> *John Kennedy led an exterior, sometimes sunny life in this sometimes dark city. He was part of the brotherhood of his family, but he also lived a life apart, which was his own, and the city helped to set him apart.*

who worked with him, but the media did not see it. Mr. Holtzman, who got to know Mr. Kennedy later in life, said that he was "well aware of the contract" that existed between him and the press. He recalled leaving a Naked Angels benefit and getting into a cab with Mr. Kennedy a few years ago, then watching it become surrounded by paparazzi. "The cab's window was open and one of the photographers just shoved his lens inside and started shooting away. The flash was going off in the car and the guy wasn't even looking into his viewfinder," said the friend, who ended up getting hit in the head with the camera. "I took the camera and shoved it out the window. And as the cab pulled away, John looked at me and said: 'I can't do that.'" Photographer Victor Malafronte remembered a moment in the early 1990's when he was chasing Mr. Kennedy down a Soho street. Mr. Malafronte was on foot and loaded down with three cameras. Mr. Kennedy was on rollerblades and losing his pursuer. "I'm trying to get this gorgeous image of the man skating down West Broadway," remembered Mr. Malafronte, when suddenly Mr. Kennedy turned and started skating toward him. "I thought he was going to grab me," said the photographer, but instead his quarry stopped within a few inches of Mr. Malafronte and stuck out his right hand. "He says in the soft-spoken voice, 'Hi, I'm John.'" Mr. Malafronte said he managed to stammer back, "I know." But, really, he said, "I was blown away." Mr. Kennedy let Mr. Malafronte get the shots he wanted, which, he said, made the covers of the *New York Post* and *People*. And then he skated away. Mr. Malafronte saw another side of Mr. Kennedy a few days later when he and a documentary crew staked out Mr. Kennedy's apartment in a van. Mr. Kennedy snuck up on the crew and gave them a tongue lashing. "He had had enough," Mr. Malafronte said.

In late 1997, just months after Diana, the Princess of Wales, had been chased to her death by paparazzi on motorcycles, Mr. Kennedy confronted a group of photographers outside his apartment building by training his own video camera on the group. "You're looking for a harassment lawsuit," he told one of them. Mr. Kennedy could have hid behind lawyers and a publicist, but he did not. Just as he did not duck reporters in 1990 when he failed the New York bar exam for the second time. "I'm very disappointed. But you know, God willing, I'll go back there in July and I'll pass it then. Or I'll pass it the next time, or I'll pass it when I'm 95," Mr. Kennedy told the press phalanx that had gathered outside 1 Hogan Place. "I'm clearly not a major legal genius. I hope the next time you guys are here will be a happy day." In 1995, Chris Cuomo, who is related to the Kennedy family by marriage, said that he was studying for his bar exam when Mr. Kennedy contacted him. "He said, 'I know you're nervous about this test because of what happened to me. Don't sweat it.' He said, 'Listen, as long as you know who you are and you behave that way, everything will be fine.'" Added Mr. Cuomo: "I think that was the key to his dignity." When Mike Nichols spoke from the Book of Revelations at Jacqueline Onassis' funeral in May 1994, his voice a shipwreck, he said: "There will be no more death." But here we are again, and this time it's us, our generation, and so the loss, the sense of vulnerability, is ours to bear. We're all older now. And somehow, New York's 21st century seems a little colder and more distant knowing that John Kennedy—who was supposed to be in our future, who may be irreplaceable in our lives—is contained forever, back here with our youth, in his father's century, the 20th. If only he had been able to look out the window of his Piper Saratoga and seen the striated lights of the World Trade Center towers, the glow of the Chrysler Building's Art-Deco hubcaps, the white streams of the avenues, the Empire State's block of blue-lit limestone and the streaked spider webs of the Manhattan, Brooklyn and Triborough bridges. Then west to the river and home.

SEPTEMBER 27, 1999 BY PHILIP WEISS

THE OBSERVATORY: GET READY, MR. PRESIDENT, FOR CHAPPAQUA ALIENATION

I DON'T HAVE MUCH SYMPATHY for Bill Clinton, but after spending two days in Chappaqua my heart goes out to him. He's getting socked away down a cul-de-sac surrounded by McMansions. If his last house was done over, with provincial nuttiness, by Kaki Hockersmith, his new house has been done with bourgeois opulence that screams "rich doctor." Central air, custom moldings, giant addition and swimming pool. Not a lot of imagination.

Dentition, one real estate agent told me, describing the dental form of the moldings. Another agent said the kitchen is new and perfect, and the master bedroom suite is two stories. But if Bill gets bored in that bedroom he can't go out the back door, because that's the woods. It's a cul-de-sac with a perfect yellow gravel driveway and specimen plantings, as they say in Chappaqua, whatever specimen plantings are. And no blacks. This is probably the first place Bill Clinton will live without black people around.

If he did manage to escape, there's nothing for him to do. This is not old-line suburbia, not Cheever's Ossining or Key Party, Conn. Chappaqua is a family community in the woods. Everyone there tells you that. People move there for the

schools, and there's a stern family feeling about the place. Sheltered meritocracy gone nuts. I bumped into a 9-year-old in the little village, wearing a bicycle helmet and riding a bike with training wheels. Shades of my own bike-fearing Jewish childhood. The real estate agents hand out sheets listing where all the '99 high school graduates are going to college.

"Everything here is for the kids, there's nothing for adults," one longtime resident told me. There's no action. Chappaqua is not even a village, it's a hamlet. It shuts down at 9 o'clock at night. To make as much money as you have to, to live in Chappaqua, you have to be a mensch in the substantial sense of the word. The men are solid-citizen types, and the women drive SUV's, and many of them have put aside good careers to raise their children. It has that conservative feeling, even though it is Democratic. A man I ran into at the temple offered that he thinks Bill Clinton's "conduct" was "a great pity—despicable." The Baptist minister in town said the thing with the little girl last year took the wind out of his sails.

The Clintons don't have taste, don't have time for taste, something they insist on proving again and again, with Monica Lewinsky, Bill's neckties and Hillary's colorful capes. When they get something right, and they do, it is assigned taste, conventional taste.

That's what the Weisberg house looks like: conservative, perfect bourgeois taste, sitting uncomfortably on its tiny one acre, with tacky McMansions around it, and the cul-de-sac, and buses of Japanese tourists already arriving to swing around the bulb end of the cul-de-sac to gawk at the columned porch.

OCTOBER 25, 1999 BY JOHN HEILPERN

AT THE THEATER WITH JOHN HEILPERN:
Hello, Possums! Dame Edna Spreads Gladdies Everywhere

WELL, POSSUMS! LET US NOT delay the happy news for a second. The Broadway debut of Dame Edna Everage is a complete triumph.

Who—or what—is the dame? These are challenging questions, not easily answered. I'm resisting the coy when I say that Dame Edna can't be pinned down. She's such an outrageously unique self-invention, she resists classification. She was born in Australia. She is played by a man, Barry Humphries, and, as Dame Edna puts it, "If it wasn't for him, she wouldn't be where she is today."

A star in England, Dame Edna may have put Australia on the map. John Osborne of *Look Back in Anger*, an early fan, wrote ad-

miringly 30 years ago: "Her poetic instinct and genius created something that was not there before. That is to say, Australia." She says she is a housewife, investigative journalist, social anthropologist, swami, children's book illustrator, spin doctor and icon. She lists her hobbies as counseling royalty, redefining cultural strategies and posing for photographs with refugees.

Her motto is: "I'm sorry but I care." We might feel a little uneasy in her company, but she means well. I last saw her in London 20 years ago, God love us and save us. Then she was more Auntie Dame Edna; today she's a granny. And, as Dame Edna would put it: I mean that in the nicest possible way.

NOVEMBER 29, 1999   BY AMY LAROCCA

HEJ-HEJ, GAP! SEXY, SERIOUS SWEDES INVADE MANHATTAN WITH H&M STORES

ON THE FOURTH FLOOR OF an office building on Fifth Avenue, 50 New Yorkers were preparing to depart for a three-month boot camp in Stockholm, Sweden—land of Ikea, Nokia and Volvo. The traveling troops—the newest employees of Hennes and Mauritz, Sweden's version of the sprawling, low-priced, high-style chain stores—were watching a training video. On it, H&M's goateed chief executive, a 35-year-old named Fabien Mansson, was discussing fashion trends and ethics in manufacturing.

Fade to H&M's 65 young designers—all Swedish and wearing tight black pants and sneakers with very big soles—sketching away at their blond wood drafting tables. They were working together. With each other. With the fabric buyers. No egos. No competition. Not a break-out-on-my-own instinct among them. It was like some Scandinavian dream of enforced social compact brought to Manhattan.

"People will look and say, 'That is not the price,'" said Per Darj, the lanky, turtleneck-wearing Swede sent by H&M to spread the seed in New York. "But it is!"

◇◇◇◇◇◇◇

NOVEMBER 29, 1999   BY WILLIAM BERLIND

THE NEW YORK WORLD: NEW YORKERS LAUGHED AT Y2K HYPE, BUT NOW THEY'RE FINALLY SCARED.

OVER THE PAST YEAR NEW YORKers have heard dire predictions about the millennium—from computer meltdowns, to power outages, to economic collapse—and they were blasé. They figured it was all hype. Let the rubes spend New Year's Eve in a bomb shelter with their canned goods and transistor radios. We'll be just fine, thank you. If the computers want to make like it's 1900, we can play along. We'll just listen to Scott Joplin and wear boaters and spats and go for a stroll in the park.

And yet ... and yet ... well, there is the small matter of the American Red Cross—not known as a particularly alarmist organization—telling people to make preparations. "Stock disaster supplies to last several days to a week," goes the advice on the www.redcross.org Web site.

While some citizens remain less than impressed by the possibility of some Y2K-related disaster, the city is taking the matter seriously, fearing that something could go wrong when those estimated one million people celebrate in Times Square on New Year's Eve.

According to Brendan Sexton, the president of the Times Square Business Improvement District, there will be about 5,000 police officers on duty that night, when the crystal ball drops—2,000 more than last year.

Mr. Sexton said the blocks around Times Square could be emptied in 90 seconds or less. You know, just in case.

"But what could go wrong?" Mr. Sexton asked.

Rudy's Bunker: The mayor's command center at 7 World Trade Center

DECEMBER 13, 1999 BY FRANK DIGIACOMO

THE TRANSOM: It's the Last Party of the Century

THERE IN THE GREAT HALL OF THE METROPOLITAN MUseum of Art, Mick Jagger loomed above them all. Mr. Jagger was dressed in a white Kangol newsboy's hat, a white double-breasted jacket with dark piping, orange pants and a sheen of sweat, and his arms, legs and even his magnificent lips seemed to be flying off in different directions before a sea of rapt Rolling Stones fans. Back in the late 70's, some photographer had clicked his shutter and captured an explosion-a conflagration of sex and abandon, charisma and style that, even in two-dimensional photographic form, still thrills.

On Dec. 6, that image of Mr. Jagger, projected two stories high, served as a counterpoint and a challenge to the sleek crowd of 850 people who had gathered below for the Met's celebration of its new Rock Style exhibition.

Though the hall was packed with hundreds of tycoons (Peter Brant, Ted Forstmann) and actors (Charlize Theron, Milla Jovovich, Natasha Richardson, Liam Neeson) and designers (Gucci's Tom Ford, Calvin Klein, Dior's John Galliano) and models (two words: Kate Moss) but curiously few rock stars, the room was not emitting one-tenth of the electricity that that 20-year photo of Mr. Jagger had captured.

That's because the gentrification of celebrity that began in the 1990's—with the rise to power of the fashion stylist and the publicist—is essentially complete. Slowly, the sex, passion and spontaneity of celebrity have been supplanted with the more calculated qualities of taste, stylishness and ironic detachment. Sometimes one gets the sense that the whole celebrity sweepstakes is rigged. As when subscribers to *Vogue* got their January issue announcing the winners of the VH1-*Vogue* Fashion Awards days before the live event was cable-cast.

And the Met's Rock Style exhibition itself turns out to have been the perfect complement to New York's last big celebrity party of the millennium. All of the outrageousness—the Bob Mackie dresses and the Elvis jumpsuits—was kept behind a thick wall of glass.

And celebrities who embody the Age of Calculated Detachment were front and center at the gala. At the end of the red carpet, past the greeting line formed by the gala's co-chairs—*Vogue* editor Anna Wintour, Estée Lauder's creative marketing executive director Aerin Lauder and fashion designer Tommy Hilfiger—were Jerry Seinfeld, the master of ironic indifference, and his fiancée, Jessica Sklar, and Gwyneth Paltrow, the tidy sex symbol of the moment. There was also billionaire Ronald Perelman, his steady, actress Ellen Barkin, and Miramax Films co-chairman Harvey Weinstein and his wife. Elsewhere were actress Heather Graham and her boyfriend, director Ed Burns, who were certainly not behaving with detachment, according to those who saw the couple giving each other mutual tonsillectomies near one of the bars. Also in attendance were former Secretary of State Henry Kissinger; actress Elizabeth Hurley; husband-and-wife singers Whitney Houston and Bobby Brown; and socialites Patricia Buckley, Nan Kempner and Alexandra von Furstenberg, who wore a floor-length leather dress.

They were at the last party of the millennium, looking back at the year and trying to make sense of it.

For Gucci's Mr. Ford, the year was about exorcising the past. "Every decade matures at its end," said Mr. Ford, who noted that much of the culture of the 1990's was about revisiting trends of earlier decades. And here, just a few weeks from the end of the year, he added,

"Everything around is looking real tired." Yet here in this crowd, Mr. Ford said he did not see the past, but rather the future. "I look around and I don't see many people here who are going to be dropping dead anytime soon," Mr. Ford said. "We're it."

Mr. Ford was certainly it when it came to *Vogue* editor at large André Leon Talley, who was wearing a full-length couture leather tunic designed by Mr. Ford that had been embroidered with gold flowers in what Mr. Leon Talley called "Renaissance Baroque" style. "Feel the softness of the leather," said Mr. Talley, who was wearing matching leather slippers, also couture. Mr. Leon Talley's effusiveness attracted the attention of designer Arnold Scaasi, who said to him: "Are you trying to explain that drag?"

Meanwhile, Mr. Seinfeld was doing an expert job of not having to explain his and Ms. Sklar's plans for the future. When the Transom asked the couple, "Have you set your nuptials?" Mr. Seinfeld replied, "I'm wearing boxers tonight." Ms. Sklar doubled over at the punch line, as she seemed to do every time Mr. Seinfeld cracked a joke.

As Ms. Paltrow walked into the dinner with her father, Bruce Paltrow, the Transom asked her whether 1999 had been more about the past or the future for her. "It's been mostly about the present," she said. "That's my best achievement ever."

Taking up that Zen-like theme, a saucy-looking Elizabeth Hurley told the Transom, "I've been living day to day, thank you very much."

GEORGE GURLEY INTERVIEWS TERRY GOLWAY

I can tell you a little bit about the old days, pre–Graydon Carter. I started at the paper in April of '90, I was 35, the staff was Michael Tomasky, Charlie Bagli, Clare McHugh, Helen Thorpe, Robin Pogrebin. Most in their early 20s; Bagli was maybe 36. Ken Paul was managing editor and John Sicher, who was Arthur Carter's lawyer, was the editor and was also the editor of the Connecticut paper Arthur owned, *The Litchfield County Times*. Really, Ken Paul was the guy who made the paper run. He had run *Newsday*, he'd been in papers for years. *The Observer* back then was very low-key, very discursive, the headlines were very earnest. It didn't have the attitude.

The staff was crowded into half a floor of the 64th street townhouse. We were one on top of each other. This was of course before voice mail, and even though I was older and more experienced than the three women, I was still low man on the totem pole. I sat next to Bagli, who was always working the phones, and anytime another call came in on his other line, he would snap his fingers at me to pick up the line. And I did it! Until finally once I said to him, "Charlie, I can't do it!" And that was it. He never did it again. Charlie is this sort of rabid reporter digging out things, which I never was; I was a writer more than I was a reporter. September of that year Tomasky left, so now all of a sudden I got the Wise Guys column and I was expected to write a 1,500-2,000 news story a week in addition to Wise Guys, which was 1,800 words. It was a lot of stuff to write, and some of it was good and some of it wasn't. It always wound up being true at *The Observer*, you didn't have the luxury you thought you were going to have—"Oh, I work for a weekly, I'll take two or three weeks to work on a piece." That never really happened there. The workhorses of the paper were expected to produce. The paper was best known back then for Michael M. Thomas, who did the Midas Watch, and Hilton Kramer, the art critic. And Michael was a bomb thrower. Richard Brookhiser was there—he was sort of the young hotshot new William F. Buckley. And then we had John Hess on the left, an old lefty *New York Times* guy, and we had Howard Fast—who was a communist! Sid Zion was here, briefly. So Graydon comes on. Arthur does this purge in 1991, where Sicher gets his throat cut and Graydon gets put in,

> *There was that brief period where we thought, did we just send a 23-year-old down to his or her death?*

and talk about oil and water. Graydon Carter and Ken Paul—you could not have asked for a worse mix. I remember once Ken was trying to conduct an editorial meeting with Graydon there and Graydon made a few asides at Ken—a little sarcastic. Ken was very sensitive and politically correct and Ken was describing a story where he wanted to hear some African-American voices or Hispanic voices, that was the new New York, and Graydon said something like, "Yes, I guess we should get somebody handicapped in there, too." Something like that. Then at one point we had a story about Al D'Amato and in the headline Graydon wrote something like, "You say D'Amato, I say tomato." And Ken—this just did not compute! I remember Ken being very upset about that and I think that might have been his last issue.

Graydon was fantastic to me. Look, I was covering nitty-gritty Manhattan politics. At one point I presented a story idea and I was naming people like Hank Sheinkopf, who of course later becomes much better known. Graydon said to somebody afterward, "I had no idea who Terry Golway was talking about, but you know it sounded like a good idea." So Graydon left me alone, and after he left he actually asked Arthur Carter to give me a raise. And Arthur brought me in and said, "I want you to know, Graydon left a present for you." So I've always had a warm spot in my heart for Graydon. We had a nice ride there, it was only about a year. He left abruptly.

I started in newspapers when I was 17 years old, in 1973, doing sports. I started at the *Staten Island Advance* the day before I graduated high school. I was a 17-year-old nerd and most of the sports reporters at the *Advance* were ex-jocks. I played sports in my day but I'm not, you know, 6-foot-2. But there was one sport that was opening up, and that was high-school girls' sports. No one wanted to cover them. I mean, I was 17! These girls were only a year younger than me! I said, "I'll cover high-school girls' sports!" Are you kidding me! I'll get a byline, I might even get a date!

I've read newspapers since I was a kid. Some of my first memories are reading about John Kennedy's assassination. So we always had newspapers in the house. When I was in my senior year of high school, one of my teachers, I knew he was a part-time sportswriter at the *Staten Island Advance*. It was April of my senior year, I was working at the A & P making $1.05 an hour, and I was the worst stock clerk in history—in four weeks, I had to go on sick leave twice, because I had dropped a carton of Coke bottles—they didn't have plastic back then—and I scratched my eye. And then once when I was mopping the floors, I pulled my back. I remember thinking, I gotta do something else. So I cornered this teacher and said, "Mr. Berganzi, is there any chance I can get a job at the *Advance*?" I was

---

Terry Golway is director of the Kean Center for American History at Kean University and author of several books, most recently *Fellow Citizens: The Penguin Book of U.S. Presidential Addresses*, with Robert Remini.

of a sudden we've got Bagli and we've got [Michael] Powell and myself and we've got all these other good young reporters, and they're given this latitude. I think the other newspapers, but particularly *The New York Times*—I think [*New York Times* executive editor] Howell Raines stood up and said, "Yeah, that's what I want."

What do you remember about 54 East 64th Street?

For years, I would come in every morning with a bag of doughnuts that this Egyptian coffee guy used to give me, on Lexington Avenue. I would get off the 63rd Street stop and I was one of his last customers, I was getting in about 10 o'clock, and every day he gave me his leftovers. So my routine for years was I had the doughnuts, I laid them out. But on 9/11—I had no idea what happened, and I was on a train in the New Jersey Meadowlands when that first plane hit. And you remember it was primary day in New York, and I was reading *The Times*, thinking about Mark Green and Freddy Ferrer, because I know I'm going to do that story tonight. And I hear somebody say, "Oh my God, a plane just hit the World Trade Center." And I didn't even go to look. Because I thought it was a little Cessna. I'm thinking, I gotta find out everything I know about Mark Green. So then I go to Penn Station, I go to the Q train, and there's an announcement—because of "an incident"—I'll never forget it—"because of an incident at the World Trade Center, all subway trains downtown are delayed." So I said, O.K., well, that doesn't affect me, you know, I go uptown. I get out and here's this Egyptian guy and he looked at me—he only had one eye, the other was a glass eye, but they were wide open. I remember him saying, "They're going to blame us. They're going to blame me." I said, "Mohammed"—that's what his name was—"what are you talking about?" He said, "Don't you know what happened?" This is the guy who told me. So anyway, this was the guy who gave me the bag of doughnuts every day.

So you get into the office and ...?

Kaplan was stuck on a train outside the city—all the trains had shut down. The editors who were there—myself, Mary Ann Giordano, Peter Stevenson—made the decision to send all these young reporters downtown. And then the towers collapsed. We were wondering whether any of our reporters were killed. There was that brief period where we thought, did we just send a 23-year-old down to his or her death? Somehow, Kaplan made it into the city, gave me a big hug and we started to put together the Sept. 11 issue, which went to the printers that night.

The paper changed a lot over the years. Graydon was invaluable in what he did at the paper. He began to make the paper what it became; Susan Morrison also. When Peter Kaplan came, that's really when everything begins to change, because Peter was a political guy, unlike Graydon and Susan. He and I had grown up reading the same people—we read Teddy White, we read Richard Reeves, and that was the kind of political writing we wanted to do. But unfortunately, not long after Peter got here in '94—you know, I always feel that in some ways I let down the team a little bit, because by '96 or '97, I had pretty much lost interest in New York politics. I still feel badly about it because Peter was giving me everything I wanted or at least thought I wanted. I thought I wanted to be Richard Reeves, and if only an editor would give me, had the confidence in me, and say, "Yeah, go! Go ▶

at the *Advance* a month later. I wound up staying in the sports department for five years and then I went on to cover news. I became city editor and political columnist, jack of all trades. I left the *Advance* in '86 or '87, I was editor of a magazine called *Empire State Report* and then I came to *The Observer*. I was a kid from Staten Island. All I ever wanted to do was work for a newspaper in Manhattan and none would hire me, and I felt privileged every day I went to work at *The Observer*. I never forgot what it was like to get those goddamn rejection letters from editors at the New York City newspapers, dailies—I applied to all of them. Now, eventually, I got job offers from all of them, as a result of working at *The Observer*. Basically I've had a byline in all of them

At *The Observer* we played pretty straight under Ken, but once Graydon came, the rules changed and we were able to open up the paper to more opinion, more *Observer* attitude, and that was great. We didn't have to write these cold, objective news accounts—he said, she said, you figure out the truth—we were able to bring an attitude that, if you look at the way *The Observer* started to transform under Graydon Carter and then you look at the Metro section of *The New York Times*, *The Observer* attitude is there. And it's not a coincidence either. *The Times* wound up hiring so many *Observer* people. Once Kaplan gets here, the mid-'90s, and all to the conventions, go up to Albany, interview Mario Cuomo, get on the plane and fly with George Pataki." Around '96, we wanted to do a big profile of Pataki. And Kaplan said. "Get on his plane, he's flying out somewhere." Because we were making Pataki out to be, you know, the next president! And my son had just been born, November of '95. And I remember thinking, yeah, that's what I should do. I should get on that plane, I should follow George Pataki around, as he's trying to build a national base—and I don't want to fricking do it. And I don't ever want to do it again. I was 41 and it was right around that time that I got my first book contract, and I realized that that was what I wanted to do. Michael Powell came on board not long afterwards and started writing wonderful political stuff and I changed my role. But I always felt badly, because Peter was giving me the keys at a time when I had moved on. Five years earlier, oh my God, I would have been on that plane in a heartbeat. But I was beginning to get these book deals. That's what I really enjoy doing. I did kind of miss it this year. I would've liked to have been up in New Hampshire, I would've liked to have covered McCain and Obama and Hillary. But I moved on.

You got along well with Arthur Carter?
I've had a wonderful relationship with Arthur, but my favorite story is: Between Hillary Clinton's election in 2000 and her being sworn in 2001, the *Daily News* ran a series of stories about the fact that Bill Clinton had pardoned a couple of crooks who had given Hillary money. So Arthur was outraged. Arthur was just pissed off. Arthur has a real moral core to him. So he calls me up, "Let's do a big editorial saying that if Hillary Clinton had any shame, she would resign." And she hadn't even taken office yet! Or she had taken office maybe that week. "So let's do it big," he said. And my attitude always was, as an editorial writer—the editorial page is the publisher's. It isn't mine. I'm a hired gun. Now if I was offended by some position that Arthur or Jared Kushner took, they would not force me to write it. But it's never happened. Cultural issues are not something we do. We're offended by bad government, we're offended by corruption, and I'm offended by it, too, so I have no problem. Did I think Hillary Clinton should resign? No, I didn't! But you know, if that's what Arthur wants to say, I'm going to make the best goddamn case I can. So I did. We started off by saying, "Remember, New York, how you feel today and how you feel having elected this woman whose husband did this and that." And then it went on. Arthur just loved it. It was on page one of the paper. The next day Rush Limbaugh read that editorial over the air every hour on the hour. Our Web site crashed. We had something like a million hits. *New York Observer* calls on Hillary Clinton to resign!

Even though we hadn't technically said that; we'd said if she had shame, she would resign. And I have to admit, Arthur and I were astonished at the reaction. We just never expected—the thing I love about Arthur is one time

> *Did I think Hillary Clinton should resign? No, I didn't! But you know, if that's what Arthur wants to say, I'm going to make the best damn case I can. So I did. The next day Rush Limbaugh read that editorial over the air every hour on the hour. Our Web site crashed.*

[Mayor] David Dinkins called him to complain about a story I had written about him. And he says, "David, David, what are you so upset about? It's only in *The Observer*." So, you know, Arthur had that, like, "O.K., it's this little toy I have and whatever goes on, goes on." He loved that kind of stuff. So Arthur calls me after the Hillary editorial and asks me to lunch. Which he did from time to time. We went to some Italian place under the Queensboro Bridge. And he's got a glass of vodka, and he had this smile on his face: "Can you believe the reaction?" he said. "Terry, did we call on Hillary Clinton to—am I missing something?" I said, "No, Arthur. I mean, if we wanted Hillary Clinton to resign, we would've said, 'Hillary Clinton must resign.' But our words really were misconstrued." Well, yes, we were being mischievous. Absolutely. But Arthur loved it. So we had this great lunch and he had two vodkas, which is the most I've ever seen him have.

Corruption really did offend him. He was offended by shady dealmaking and bad government and wasteful government—it bothered him. Arthur liked bomb-throwing writing. Rarely, I think, would you say that Arthur would say, "That was a well-reported story." I mean, he knew what a well-reported story was, but he liked attitude. And although a succession of editors can certainly get the credit for installing that kind of attitude, let me tell you that it did come from the top. Arthur knew he wanted lively writing.

Another Arthur story. Once we went to the opera, and Arthur's got the best seats in the house. *La Boheme*. It's my wife and I and here we are, and it's probably our first time at the Metropolitan Opera. That box of his is for about 16 people. So we're with the New York crowd. And Arthur could not have been nicer. But in the middle of the opera, I guess we're getting to the third act and we're going to go to dinner at Arthur's place afterward. It's 11 o'clock—*La Boheme* is a long opera. So he said, "You know, listen, we're going to dinner now, it's 11 o'clock, and if you want to stay for the last act, that's O.K., but they all die in the end, so let's go eat."

My other favorite Arthur story is that he was trying to steal Ron Perelman's chef. I guess when you're trying to steal someone's chef, you have that person come in and cook you a meal. So this guy cooked pheasant for Arthur, and he brings it out and I guess—you know, I've never had pheasant—but I guess there's the bird and Arthur takes off the wing or the leg, as you would with a turkey, and starts eating it. And apparently the chef says, "You do not eat the leg of a pheasant! I am not going to work for this!" So the chef wouldn't work for Arthur, and Arthur told that story about himself, which I love. The fact that he would tell that story—he's basically saying, "Can you believe what a shmuck I am?"

You wrote angry columns about Brits in New York ...
It offended me that these Brits can come into New York and assume

that they can write about New York. As Pete Hamill once said—he is Irish-American, his parents were from Ireland—he would never presume that he could go to Dublin and edit the *Irish Times*. I, as an Irish-American historian—I know more about Irish history than many Irish people—the idea of going to Ireland and covering Irish politics? I can't imagine it. But what the Brits have done—and maybe this is genius—is that they figured that there is this global, international tabloid culture, where it doesn't matter whether you're at the *New York Post* or the *News of the World*—that it's all generic. That there is this culture out there, and it's driven by American popular culture, and New York is the capital of it—so, "Let's go to New York and you know, write about New York." That offends me on any number of levels. And Tina Brown posing as a mediator of American politics—again, I can't imagine going over to the U.K. and trying to mediate between the Labor Party and the conservative party, but there she is, she thinks nothing of being this, this pundit on American politics. Now I don't deny that you can learn, but they thought and acted as though they can walk right in with their posh accents, and they felt that every American they met would fall for their accents.

Basically, they're the Greeks during the Roman Empire, and to them we are the uncivilized Romans; they're going to come here and teach the colonials how to be civilized. I'm talking about everyone from the Tina Browns of the world to the latest Brit import at the *New York Post*. And it's not a coincidence that tabloid television and the tabloiding of America takes place in the early '90s, with this British invasion. All of a sudden you're reading about things in the *New York Post*, and then the *Daily News*, they've been Britified. Maybe I'm living in a romanticized world of 1950s New York, you know, the guy comes home with the tabloids stuck in his back pocket, and he picks it up and he's reading about bread-and-butter issues or crime, which is what tabloids are for, but to me I just felt that something changed in tabloid culture that was bad, that was brainless, that was not good for New York.

Who made you laugh in the office?

Windolf and Stevenson, I mean, they really did miss their calling. If we had any kind of vaudeville today ... They were hysterical and they added a lot of life to the place. The mid-'90s was a fun time at the paper. That was sort of where felt I was kind of handing off what I wanted to do to Greg Sargent and Josh Benson. They became the young political reporters in my place. I'm proud to call them my protégés; they were great. So now all of a sudden I was the city editor. I'm still the only person who ever had that title. I felt *The Observer* had maybe gone a little too far on the advocacy end of political coverage, that we were leaning kind of toward *The Village Voice* and I felt we had to bring it back toward the center. I didn't want every week to be "Giuliani is a bum, Giuliani is a bum." You know that there is plenty of bullshit to go around, and let's call it when

we see it. Nothing ideological or partisan about it. So I had Josh and Greg and Andrea Bernstein and myself. I think we succeeded around maybe '98 or so in making *The Observer* less ideological and more of a keen, witty observer of politics.

At that same time, Candace Bushnell shows up.

I remember hearing about this woman Candace Bushnell, who was literally sleeping on a floor in an apartment, and she just wanted to be a writer. And she was willing to sacrifice for that. And I remember admiring that, even though she was writing about a world I knew nothing about; I said, "Here's a woman who's making a sacrifice I would never make in a million years." There did come a point—I think Bagli and myself and some of the hard-news types—we were a little envious of the publicity Candace got. We felt that the Sex and the City column was overshadowing some other really good stuff that we were doing, but we didn't blame it on Candace. It bothered us that people were paying more attention to Candace than they were paying to local politics.

One day I was doing an interview with Pat Moynihan—and I used to talk to Senator Moynihan about once a year and we always had great conversations—I just thought he was the greatest—so I'm interviewing him, we're in the middle of this conversation, I've got the phone and I'm taking the notes—and in comes Candace to that front room. And Kaplan's there, he's talking to Bagli—and Candace just starts screaming at the top of her lungs. *Ahhhhhhhhhhhhh!!!!* Now that may have been the day she got her book deal. So she just starts screaming and Kaplan, God bless him, starts screaming back. *Ahhhhhhh!!!!* And I'm on the phone with Pat Moynihan talking about whether we should put another tunnel under the Hudson River, and I can't hear him. It's my one interview a year. So I say, "Excuse me, Senator, hold on one second." I cup the phone, and I stand up and Candace is right there, and I yell, "Shut the fuck up!" And I get back down and continue, "Senator, as we were saying ..."

All of the tensions and all of the resentments that I had about New York and the media just exploded. Here was this woman—and I really didn't resent her fame—but here was the symbol of what I felt was shallow in New York media. There was she was, live in front of me, and she was disrupting my interview with Pat Moynihan, and I wasn't going to take it anymore. I feel very badly about that, and I do respect the fact that Candace is leading a life that she actually did imagine and that she worked hard for and she got it, and it doesn't happen all the time.

What's *The Observer*'s legacy?

The Observer changed journalism. We showed how you can be substantive, fun and write with an attitude, and I think it's not a coincidence that so many *Observer* people wind up at *The Times* and other places. We've changed the standard. You can now write and have some fun. You couldn't do that in 1989.

> *I do respect the fact that Candace is leading a life that she actually did imagine and that she worked hard for and she got it, and it doesn't happen all the time.*

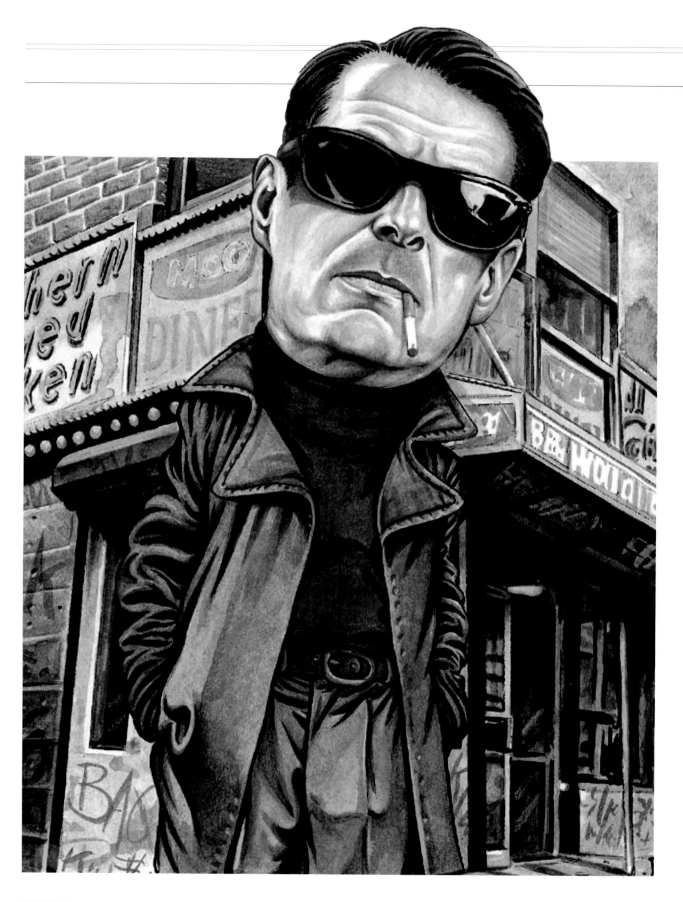

2000

▶ **Al Gore takes fashion advice for Naomi Wolf and hands the presidency to George W. Bush**

▶ Rudy Giuliani runs for Senate, drops his wife and gives the seat to Hillary Clinton!

 ▶ **George Bush rises above his Skull and Bones past to win the presidency**

▶ Georgette Mosbacher starts a trend of Stepfordizing New York Ladies

▶ **Christopher Walken gets his own cable chef show, *Cookin' With Walken***

▶ Designer Isaac Mizrahi  declares that history has ended and so has fashion

▶ **Super-investor J. Shelby Bryan loses $60 million but gets *Vogue* editor Anna Wintour**

▶ Billionaire Mort Zuckerman unloads  on billionaire David Bradley

2000

JANUARY 9, 2000 BY JOHN HEILPERN

FULL OF SOUND AND FURY, SIGNIFYING NOTHING

THERE WAS TIME ENOUGH during Andrei Serban's ludicrous 3-hour, 40-minute production of Hamlet at the Public Theater to wonder why nobody ever boos anymore.

It goes like this: "Boooooo! Boooooo! Get it off!" Or, as Shakespeare himself put it: "Pish! Pish for thee! O poverty in wit! Go mend, go mend! Froth and scum! By cock and pie! Peace your tattlings!"

My friends, never have I witnessed such pishy tattlings as Mr. Serban's lunatic display of directorial folly with *Hamlet*. As the Bard said elsewhere: "I have seen drunkards do more than this in sport."

Though it gives me no pleasure, I can boo in print, if I must. But I see you slumped in numbing disbelief at what you're witnessing, and do you utter a peep in protest? Do you dare? I've wondered before why audiences at the theater are so docile. Why should passionate disapproval from the paying customer be considered shocking?

The last lonely boo I heard at the theater was several seasons ago at the end of John Guare's unfortunate *Four Baboons Adoring the Sun*. Music to the ears! That boo, pish, raspberry, bird, heckle, protest vote and finger pointed at the Emperor's suit of clothes was brave in its way, discerning, and certainly of an independent mind. I am for uproar in the theater. I am for the boo. I am for all audiences who put drama critics out of business.

What acquiescent wimps we've all become at the theater! We wouldn't boo a goose, let alone *Hamlet*. If we can cheer, why can't we pish?

JANUARY 30, 2000 BY GEORGE GURLEY

Georgette Mosbacher Rides With McCain

GEORGETTE MOSBACHER—THE FORMER REPUBLICAN SUPER wife now serving as the main New York operative for insurgent presidential candidate John McCain—was talking about her 1998 divorce from oilman Robert Mosbacher, a Texan preppy who served as George Bush's secretary of commerce.

"When you've been married so long," she said, "you think you have a strong identity—but all of a sudden you have to find out who you are all over again. You have to build another life."

With the help of Mr. McCain and the role he has given her in his campaign—she's a big fund-raiser and his informal adviser—she is in the process of building that new life and remaking her reputation. "There are very few women who are big political fund-raisers," she said.

Ms. Mosbacher, 53, was wearing a brown tweed pant suit that showed off her figure very well. Her red hair was up in a French twist. Her bangs covered her red tattooed eyebrows.

From 1988 to '92, she was a supreme Washington wife, pilloried in the press for embodying the excesses of the age. She has fond memories of that time, the dinner parties with Margaret Thatcher and all that.

"Oh, Margaret Thatcher! Here was a woman who never ever apologized for being a woman, never made excuses for being a woman. ... She found my dinners interesting, because they were not the usual social babble, but that I do orchestrate my dinners to be a forum, if you will. That's why I always have everyone at one table, round table, and always throw a question on the table and allow everyone to participate, and that's my dinner party! She said, to go to a formal dinner party and be challenged intellectually, she said I did it very well. I think she used the term salon. ... And now the last time I sat with her she was very intrigued with McCain. She said, 'You know I think this McCain, you've got a winner there.'"

JANUARY 31, 2000   BY GEORGE GURLEY

SHE'S SEXY AND OVER 50

LAUREN HUTTON, WHAT A woman, my God, what a woman. She was in a studio on West 29th Street, on a break from a health-and-fitness-magazine shoot. The 50-something model was wearing jeans and white shirt, through which I could see a bright-colored bra.

She was moving around in her chair a lot, being all peppy and glamourous, winning me over, making me laugh and messing with my brain. My mouth was slightly open the whole time.

Besides modeling, she said she'd been writing her autobiography and spending time on her 300-acre Rattlesnake Ranch in the Southwest, where she drives a "hellacious" truck

and an "even meaner" Jeep, rides motorcycles and hot-tubs naked. As well, she spends a fourth of her time underwater, scuba diving with ex-Navy Seals and sharks.

"That's one of the reasons you go down," Ms. Hutton said. "A day without sharks is a very bad day—all day in kindergarten. Oh, no, they're great. You want to go down with schools of sharks."

Can you say anything you enjoy doing sexually?

"You are so cute! You are so cute. Well, one time I was wooed and won for about six years by a guy who just looked me in the eyes, and I was barefoot at the time, and he grabbed a foot and started sucking my toes. That was it! It was over. Now, he was extremely good at this, and he was good at an awful lot of other things, too! You better know what you're doing before you grab someone's big toe and pop it in your mouth!"

Best compliment you ever received?

"Yes, I was told that my butt was like a rare fruit. But if you put it in there, it will be stolen, it'll be all over, it will be just like calling someone 'swell.'"

She was being beckoned back out of the office. She popped out and came back.

"You're much cuter. I like you much better, I'm staying with you," she teased me, laughing.

Even with my extra 20 pounds?

She got up from her chair and made like she was going to attack my belly rolls: "Oooh, just get my fingers and toes in there! Nibble, nibble, nibble, nibble, ha-ha!"

Two fellas came in, and she kissed them goodbye. Now she was standing, jumping around like a hyperactive kid.

Ever been in an orgy?

"Well, let's see, I have a feeling that those are a lot better in theory than in practice. What do you think?"

It was time for her to get back.

That's a good way to end.

JANUARY 31, 2000   BY RON ROSENBAUM

The Edgy Enthusiast
Clinton Scandals, Stage III: The Buff Moment

WE ARE NOW ENtering Stage III in the Natural History of National Scandals: After the Huh? Moment comes the Buff Moment.

I love the Buff Moment. I am a student of buff moments, having written about assassination buffs, Watergate buffs, Philby-Angelton-mole war buffs, Mary Meyer buffs (the J.F.K. mistress whose murder in Georgetown in 1964 is still officially unsolved—although I know who did it), Danny Casolaro buffs (the reporter whose 1990 death under mysterious circumstances in a West Virginia motel is regarded as the work of a vast "Octopus conspiracy" by some buffs).

I suppose you could think of me as a buff buff (if I were in better shape I could call myself a buff buff buff). The difference between a buff and a buff buff, I would say, is that the buffs are almost all convinced they have the truth, an alternate truth, a suppressed truth, a conspiratorial truth, but the truth. They know the answers. The buff buff still has questions, the buff buff is willing to admit uncertainty, to evaluate both the evidence and the fantasies of the buffs for what they tell us about the thing itself—the crime around which the subculture of buffdom has bloomed. And for what they tell us not just about the buffs, but about ourselves, about the fantasies, the longings and the consolations that are embodied in buff theories.

Disney prez Bob Iger with host Regis Philbin

FEBRUARY 7, 2000   BY JIM WINDOLF

IT'S TOM WOLFE VS. THE 'THREE STOOGES'

I N NOVEMBER 1998, JOHN UPDIKE OH SO QUIETLY KILLED *A Man in Full*. It was a clean kill. Issued from Mr. Updike's *New Yorker* pulpit, the review of the big Tom Wolfe novel seemed mild, gentle and fair: "*A Man in Full* still amounts to entertainment, not literature, even literature in a modest aspirant form. Like a movie desperate to recoup its bankers' investment, the novel tries too hard to please us." Soon after, in *The New York Review of Books*, Norman Mailer aggravated Mr. Wolfe further by calling him "the most gifted best-seller writer to come along since Margaret Mitchell." Mr. Mailer hit upon that zinger only after a long review that seriously took into account Mr. Wolfe's strengths. "Extraordinarily good writing forces one to contemplate the uncomfortable possibility that Tom Wolfe might yet be seen as our best writer," Mr. Mailer wrote midway through. "How grateful one can feel then for his failures and his final inability to be great—his absence of truly large compass."

Mr. Updike, 67, and Mr. Mailer, 77, smelled blood. Both reviews moved in on Mr. Wolfe's greatest weakness: his quivering need to be perceived as a great author. For all his bluster and devil-may-care attacks on literary establishments from *The New Yorker* to the American Academy of Arts and Letters, Mr. Wolfe, at age 68, is desperate to be accepted into the literary pantheon. He longs for, lusts for, posterity.

Sensing his ambition, Mr. Updike, in his quietly devastating way, and Mr. Mailer, in his best barroom-brawler style, used their reviews to deliver the bad news, leaving Mr. Wolfe as wounded as the high school valedictorian who receives in the mail a thin envelope from Harvard.

Over a year later, Mr. Wolfe is still stung by their words. "There are these two old piles of bones, Norman Mailer and John Updike," he said in a November 1999 interview with *The Charlotte Observer*. "Updike took nine pages in *The New Yorker*, Mailer took 11 or 12 pages in *The New York Review of Books*, to try to say this is not literature."

He went on to argue that Mr. Updike and Mr. Mailer won't take any best-selling book seriously—a pretty shaky line of attack, given that both Mr. Updike and Mr. Mailer have had their No. 1 hits.

Enter John Irving, on behalf of the "two old piles of bones." Asked, on a Canadian TV talk show, *Hot Type*, to comment on the "war" Mr. Wolfe was having with Mr. Mailer and Mr. Updike, Mr. Irving said, "I don't think it's a war, because you can't have a war between a pawn and a king, can you?"

Then the 57-year-old author of *The World According to Garp* and *Trying to Save Piggy Sneed* called Mr. Wolfe's novels "yak" and "journalistic hyperbole described as fiction." Asked if he disliked Mr. Wolfe because of his popularity, Mr. Irving said, "I'm not using that argument against him. I'm using the argument against him that he can't write. ... It's like reading a bad newspaper or a bad piece in a magazine. It makes you wince." He added that on any page of any Tom Wolfe book, he could "read a sentence that would make me gag."

Mr. Wolfe soon visited the set of *Hot Type*, for a retaliatory interview. "Let's take Irving," he said. "He's our prime subject today. His last, *A Widow for One Year*, is about some neurotic people in the

Hamptons. They never get to town. They're in the house. They're neurotic. ... Irving is a great admirer of Dickens. But what writer does he see now the last year constantly compared to Dickens? Not John Irving, but Tom Wolfe. ... It must gnaw at him terribly." (Nice stuff. Never mind that, even in reviewing Mr. Irving's Long Island novel, critics continued, knee-jerk, to compare him to Dickens.) Mr. Wolfe also lumped Mr. Irving in with Mr. Updike and Mr. Mailer. "I think of the three of them now—because there are now three, as Larry, Curly and Moe—it must gall them a bit that everyone, even them, is talking about me."

Before giving that interview, Mr. Wolfe took on Mr. Irving in a statement from his publisher: "Why does he sputter and foam so?" The same rhetorical question could certainly be asked of Mr. Wolfe himself. And Mr. Wolfe has been foaming and sputtering, a full year after those reviews were published, because of his need to convince everyone—himself and the world—that he is no mere journalist or social satirist but a real artist, and one for the ages.

Alongside his main writings, Mr. Wolfe has made a kind of shadow career as a polemicist. The underlying purpose of this shadow career has been to teach people—critics and readers—how to appreciate Tom Wolfe. Through lectures and essays, the author provides his audience with an easy, step-by-step system for seeing Tom Wolfe's writing as art.

FEBRUARY 14, 2000   BY ANDREW GOLDMAN

Atoosa, Former High School Loser, Is Hearst's New Cosmogirl Queen

FROM BEHIND HER DESK, ATOOSA RUBENSTEIN TOOK A DEEP breath and knitted her brow, a signal that the 28-year-old editor in chief of *Cosmogirl* magazine was going to get serious and talk about that night a decade ago. Prom night. "You know, at the end of the day, it was fine ," she said of the prom, to which nobody at Valley Stream North High School in Long Island bothered to invite her. She was nodding her head in earnest. "It was fine ." Back then, Ms. Rubenstein was not the porcelain-skinned, 5-foot-11-inch woman with a wild mane of black hair falling over an Alessandro dell'Acqua sleeveless shell. Instead she was an unpopular, gawky immigrant from Iran in the days when Americans were convinced that Iranians were the only thing that sucked more than disco. "Ayatolla Atoosa," the kids called the girl from the strict Muslim home who was forbidden to shave her legs (much less pluck her eyebrows) and who had to be in the house every night by 6 p.m.

But now, Ms. Rubenstein is indeed a prom queen of sorts: In late 1998, Hearst Magazines president Cathie Black plucked her from her senior fashion editor job at *Cosmopolitan* and ordained her the youngest editor in chief in Hearst memory. (She was 26.)

Powered by some ugly adolescent memories, Ms. Rubenstein has positioned herself to be a Tony Robbins for the zitty, the unpopular and the flat-chested, someone they can look to as an exemplar of one who emerged from the same crap-ass situation, and got beautiful and rich. And married.

◇◇◇◇◇◇◇

MARCH 26, 2000   BY NYO STAFF

AT J.F.K. JR.'S LOFT, IT'S OFFICIAL: ED BURNS IS IN, HEATHER GRAHAM IS OUT

FOR THE RECORD, FILMMAKER Ed Burns got the keys to the former loft of John F. Kennedy Jr. at 20 N. Moore Street on May 9, just two weeks after he was approved by the building's co-op board and about the same time he and actress Heather Graham split.

While angling for the title of Hollywood's "it" couple in April, Mr. Burns and Ms. Graham took a tour together of the 2,400-square-foot penthouse apartment with a private elevator and a wall of windows to the east. To observers, they seemed almost beautiful enough to inherit the former home of Kennedy and his wife,

Carolyn Bessette Kennedy, the late Prince and Princess of Tribeca.But then it seemed like someone yelled, "Cut!" The board didn't want a part-time owner, and actors, directors and writers like Mr. Burns are known to be on location.

"We're not thrilled to have lots of attention," said one tenant who was tormented when people mourning Kennedy and his wife made pilgrimages to the address last year.

On June 8, a resident of 20 N. Moore told *The Observer* that Mr. Burns, a Queens native, had already moved in—alone. He

bought his new apartment, on top of the nine-story building near Varick Street, for just under the $2.4 million asking price, said brokers. Mr. Kennedy bought it for $700,000 in 1994.

MARCH 17, 2000
BY KATE KELLY

Lizzie Grubman and Peggy Siegal: P.R. Marriage of Year

A WEEK INTO THE NEWLY formed Lizzie Grubman Public Relations-Peggy Siegal Company, the two women were eagerly making the point that theirs was the best formula in the best of all possible worlds. The sunny view: Ms. Grubman, a dark-rooted 29-year-old with a successful three-year-old public relations company and a Rolodex full of music and nightclub clients, would join forces with Ms. Siegal, the 50-ish doyenne of the Manhattan movie premiere with a penchant for sit-down dinners at Le Cirque.

"What's great about me and Peggy is, we really complement the other one," said Ms. Grubman, who was dressed in a turtleneck sweater and tight, dark blue jeans. "O.K., we totally have—not totally, to a degree—we have different lists, and when we put them ..."

"No, no, excuse me. We don't know the same people," Ms. Siegal said. "Would you write that down? We ... do ... not ... know ... the ... same ... people. O.K."

"Yeah, we don't, O.K.," said Ms. Grubman. "I'm more young Hollywood, she's more established Hollywood."

"She was gonna say old," Ms. Siegal said, eyebrow raised. "But she held her tongue."

MARCH 27, 2000 BY RON ROSENBAUM

INSIDE GEORGE W.'S SECRET CRYPT

WHERE IS THE ALL-GIRL BREAK-IN TEAM NOW THAT we need them? Where are the intrepid young women who had the nerve and daring to pull off one of the great investigative coups of our era: to sneak into the triple-locked "tomb" of Skull and Bones, the secret citadel, the sanctum sanctorum, the heart of the heart of the Eastern Establishment, the place of weird, clandestine, occult bonding rituals that has shaped the character of American ruling-class figures from the 27th President, William Howard Taft, to the 41st, George Herbert Walker Bush and perhaps the next one, too: George W., Skull and Bones 1968. The place where generations of Bushes, Tafts and Buckleys and the like lay down in coffins and spewed the secrets of their sex lives. The place where many of America's top spies and spy masters were initiated into their clandestine destinies. The place where all conspiracy theories converge. The place where the people who shaped America's character had their character shaped.

But the superspooks of Skull and Bones had nothing on the all-girl break-in team, which managed to outwit their security, slip into the tomb and take pictures of each and every sacred ritual room. Including that dread enclosure I call the "Room With the License Plates of Many States."

I know because I once held in my hands the fruits of the all-girl break-in Skull and Bones raid. Yes, there came a time when I gazed at some glossy black-and-white prints that revealed the innermost sanctums of perhaps the most secrecy-shrouded interior in America, the interior of the Skull and Bones Tomb on the Yale campus in New Haven.

It is a space that is likely to have even more attention focused on it in the coming months because an initiate once again is poised to become President. And because of the imminent release of a film called *The Skulls* transparently based on Skull and Bones. But it was only recently that I began thinking about the all-girl break-in team, which was, I believe, inspired by something I'd written—the first and I think still the only outside investigation of Skull and Bones, its secrets, its legacy, its powerful subterranean influence on American history.

In fact, it is my belief that the all-girl break-in team might be doing W. a favor by demystifying this black hole in his biography: the occult rituals he engaged in twice a week in the bowels of the Skull and Bones tomb in the crucial 21st year of his life.

In fact, if I might engage in a speculative digression about W., who was my college classmate, though barely known to me—I have a feeling there is a part of him that might secretly have approved of the all-girl break-in team's act of clandestine mischief. An irreverent spirit, something I thought I glimpsed in a chance encounter with him and Hunter Thompson a quarter-century ago at a Super Bowl in Houston.

I can't recall who was hanging out with whom, but it was January 1974, it was in the atrium of the Hyatt Regency, the Super Bowl headquarters hotel (I was there to write about the spectacle that featured Dolphins versus Vikes that year) and I think it was a mutual friend, a fun-loving preppy guy I knew from college who also somehow knew

Hunter and W., who brought us all together in a room in the Hyatt. I don't remember exactly what went on, but I do remember coming away with a favorable impression of W.

I remember thinking he was one of the preppy types I'd always kind of liked, the hang-loose, good-ole-boy types, many of whom took the interregnum on careerism, which the war and the draft mandated as a cue to break out of the mold a bit, wander off the reservation, poke into the sides of life their trust funds otherwise might have sheltered them from. I sensed what W. liked about Hunter Thompson was that Hunter too was another button-down good old frat boy (once) who went weird but in a good-old-boy way.

This, in other words, was W. II, the kind of a guy who just might have seen through all the suits and trappings of moral seriousness Skull and Bones attempted to imbue its initiates with, one who might have seen it as a bit silly and pompous and who might have preferred, like some of his fellow preppy prince Hals, to spend time with Falstaffian misleaders of youth such as Mr. Thompson.

If you think of W. I as the guy who was tapped for Skull and Bones at Yale, W. II was a kind of counter-W. I. We know W. II was soon to be replaced, because he's told us he stopped doing any Bad Things in 1974. Except liquor: It was then he turned into the hard-drinking W. III. To be succeeded in 1986 when he gave up spirits as well by the solemn and preachy W. IV we have today.

My feeling is: Bring back W. II!

APRIL 17, 2000 BY ALEXANDRA JACOBS

The Observatory; Remember the Royalton?

THE CONDÉ NAST CAFETERIA has only been open a week, but it's already clear which part is Siberia.

The 10,000-square-foot, Frank Gehry-designed, track-lighted, fourth-floor space is dominated by a raised dining area enclosed by thick glass petals. The effect is slightly vaginal, accented by hanging chrome lamps that look like Fallopian tubes or sea anemones. Approximately two thirds of the restaurant's 200 diners will be eating inside this elevated region. Huddled therein on an ecru banquette with one's morning paper splayed out on a sunny yellow table, watching the late-morning rush of young mermaids picking up their fruit smoothies ($2.75) against a backdrop of sinuous titanium-blue walls, one might conclude that the architect had achieved a peaceful underwater effect.

But at the height of lunch hour, 1 p.m., noise collects inside the aquarium, and fast. Suddenly you're trapped amid the peasantry, with its lunch pails and clattering forks. Glancing down at the unfinished pale wood floors, you realize you're at the Royalton by way of Ikea. The occasional loudspeaker announcement of "fire drill on the 32nd floor" does not add to the atmosphere.

The cafeteria—called, of course, Cafeteria—is run by Restaurant Associates, a company that owns some dependable, two-star restaurants in New York such as Cafe Centro and Brasserie, and R.A. has stocked the room with lots of employees in matching gray shirts who lurk and linger, like a troop of super-efficient Oompa-Loompas, ready to wipe down your table the instant you make for the door. You bus your own table, by the way, depositing your tray on a three-tiered conveyer belt. Some Condé Nast employees seem to think this beneath them.

JULY 17, 2000 BY TISH DURKIN

The Hidden Hillary: First Lady Speaks, Very Carefully

THERE WAS SOMETHING about the sunglasses. "I think that one of my problems in communicating effectively is that I assume too much," mused Hillary Rodham Clinton, her eyes obscured behind a pair of electric-blue lenses. It was Sunday, July 9. The first lady was seated at a picnic table at a park in Van Buren, New York, after what felt like her 40th—but was in fact her fourth—Democratic picnic during a five-day upstate campaign swing.

"I have been around so long, I have been in so many battles ... I think I assume that people know more about what I believe and what my deepest convictions are and what motivates me to do this than perhaps it is fair to assume," she said.

It wasn't that the sunglasses appeared out of place. Though the weather had been in a mood of rain and wind for most of the day, the sun had just made a sufficiently bold appearance for Mrs. Clinton to ask an aide to bring her a straw hat to protect her complexion. In fact, the problem with the sunglasses may have been how very right they looked.

◇◇◇◇◇◇

SEPTEMBER 18, 2000 BY ANDREW GOLDMAN

WHO'S IN THE KITCHEN WITH WALKEN? ALL OF US, AND HE'S READY TO COOK

CHRISTOPHER WALKEN PULLED out a package of jumbo shrimp from the refrigerator and, grasping them in his hands, cut through them with the butcher knife, then ran them under water.

"This is a little dangerous," he said. "You know you're never supposed to cut like this. You can cut your hand off. You see, you butterfly it. And then there's this vein in there. You want to get rid of that. It's guts, I guess. You want to get those nice and clean."

Christopher Walken laid the shrimp into a sizzling frying pan, in which he had sautéed some garlic in olive oil. He squeezed an orange into a coffee mug that read "Notre Dame High School, 25th Class Reunion, Class of 1967."

"I'm going to throw a little more garlic in there," he said.

OCTOBER 2, 2000
BY LANDON THOMAS JR.

BRYAN HITS THE WALL: HANDSOME INVESTOR'S $60 MILLION GOES POOF! AS HE TAKES DOWN MALONE WITH HIM

J. SHELBY BRYAN IS TALL, smooth and charming—seductive, even. He is an incomparable salesman. A blend of old Texas money and East Coast establishment gloss, the 54-year-old Mr. Bryan offers something for everyone.

Vogue editor Anna Wintour left her husband for him. President Clinton shmoozed Manhattan Democrats in his Upper East Side salon. And on Feb. 29, cable titan and notoriously discerning communications investor John Malone took a $500 million stake in his high-flying Colorado-based telecommunications company, ICG Communications Inc.

Finally, though, Mr. Bryan had offered more than he could deliver.

When Malone's investment vehicle, Liberty Media, and two other blue-chip investors—Thomas Hicks of Texas-based Hicks, Muse, Tate & Furst Inc., and former Morgan Stanley mergers and acquisitions ace Eric Gleacher of buyout boutique Gleacher & Co.—invested $750 million in ICG ($230 million from Hicks, $20 million from Gleacher), the stock was trading at $28. Today it trades at around 62 cents.

Socks the cat evades scooterful of celebs

◇◇◇◇◇◇◇

OCTOBER 16, 2000   BY ALEXANDRA JACOBS

Das Boots: Women Beg for Torture, Wrapping Calves in Tight Leather

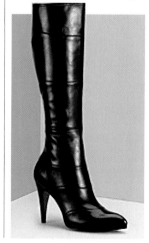

BOOTS ARE BACK. EVERYWHERE YOU LOOK, SOME WOMAN IS stalking around in a little not ing of a skirt and tall, snug boots. Sexy, right? Not so fast.

Andrea Brake was sitting in the shoe store Otto Tootsi Plohound on lower Fifth Avenue early in September, ready to plunk down $300 for the right pair.

"I got about midway up my calf," said the lithe graphic designer and yoga enthusiast. "I was smooshing the flesh, to no avail." As indifferent salespeople rushed around trying to serve a crush of boot-mad New Yorkers, recounted Ms. Brake, "I developed a blister on my index finger."

Vanessa Mobley, a 30-year-old editor at Basic Books, recalled looking on, aghast, as a friend tried on boots at the Calvin Klein store in Soho. "They had been built to some arbitrary circumference. The people at the store tried to convince her that there was this whole method of squeezing her flesh like a sausage. They barely fit. And she bought them anyway!'"

The last time knee-high boots were this popular, in the hippie-dippy 70's, women had soft, ethereal, pliant calves. A couple of aerobic decades, however, have carved a new, firm, decisive calf. Which has left scores of women chagrined about not being able to zip up this season's boots.

NOVEMBER 6, 2000
BY FRANK DIGIACOMO

CAN GENIUS CHEF ALAIN DUCASSE RECOUP AFTER HIS GRAND BOUFFE ?

ALAIN DUCASSE AT THE ES-sex House, which is closed on weekends, was undergoing a deep cleaning. The restaurant's tables and harlequin-hued silk banquettes had been moved or upended so that a team of men brandishing vacuum nozzles and polishing cloths could do their stuff.

As Mr. Ducasse bid adieu to the men, he could not instruct them to suck up and take away, along with the fallen brioche crumbs and stray wisps of tartufi di Alba, the demi-glace of negativity that has clung to his first months of doing business in New York. In a city that loves its restaurants and has conferred rock-star status to many of the chefs behind them, the arrival of Mr. Ducasse—the only man in history to have earned eight Michelin guide stars for his work in Europe—should have been interpreted as further evidence that New York is the culinary capital of the world.

But something went missing in the translation. Though Mr. Ducasse was no stranger to this city, he landed here without having mastered its language, its culture and, most of all, its press. Within weeks of opening his doors, Mr. Ducasse was not feeding New York. New York was feeding on him.

NOVEMBER 6, 2000 BY NYO STAFF

It's Al Gore for 21st Century

BILL CLINTON'S PRESIDENCY WILL NOT BE REMEMBERED, IT is safe to say, for its reverence for tradition and for the majesty of the presidency. It's a job, the president has said of his office.

No, it is not. Harry S Truman and Ronald Reagan, two men from the apogee of the American Century, may not have agreed on much, but both revered the institution of the presidency and respected its traditions. Like Mr. Clinton, neither Truman nor Mr. Reagan came from elite backgrounds; they were not and did not aspire to be aristocrats, but they surely prized the nobility and dignity of the republic's highest office.

The restoration of that nobility, the return to a seriousness of purpose, surely must be among the priorities of the next administration. We believe Al Gore is best suited for that assignment.

Mr. Gore is not an ideal candidate. His eagerness to please can be grating, and has led him to make statements that are more silly than deliberate. Still, he is the superior choice. His Republican opponent, George W. Bush, may be charming, but he is a lightweight of scandalous proportions. (This is a man, remember, who wondered aloud if those of the Jewish faith were allowed into heaven.) Mr. Bush is inarticulate not because he has trouble expressing himself, but because he has nothing to express.

We'd prefer a serious, professional politician to a breezy, unfocused and almost gleefully ignorant cipher.

NOVEMBER 13, 2000
BY DEBORAH SCHOENEMAN
AND DEBORAH NETBURN

Manhattan Transfers

Heiress Libbet Johnson Creates Triplex Condo Priced at $62 Million

LAST YEAR, WHILE RENOVAT-ing her co-op apartment at the River House, 435 East 52nd Street, Libbet Johnson, an heir of the Johnson & Johnson family, rented a condominium in Donald Trump's Trump International Hotel and Tower at 1 Central Park West. She liked the hotel services (delivery from Jean Georges) and location so much that, over the past year, she has plunked down more than $50 million for a total of six apartments in the building.

Now, she's putting all but one of those back on the market for $62 million, the highest anyone has ever asked for an apartment in Manhattan—and much more than she will get, brokers said.

Ms. Johnson was in the middle of combining the apartments, more than 20,000 square feet spread over the 49th, 50th and 51st floors, when she fell in love with celebrity hairdresser Frédéric Fekkai. A source said that Mr. Fekkai likes more modest—or cozy—living and persuaded Ms. Johnson to keep only one apartment, which they now share, and sell off the other five. (Or maybe he'd just rather live somewhere else altogether?)

NOVEMBER 20, 2000 BY PHILIP WEISS

Who's Looking More Presidential: Al the

WHO CAN LOOK less Presidential? George W. Bush's charm has drained away. He's gray and his neck turtles out of his suit collar. He erupted in boils, and the photograph he staged of his transition team looked like a dinner-theater version of *The West Wing*. But at least Mr. Bush is halfway transparent. When Al Gore came out of the White House on Monday to talk liltingly about school children and the democratic process, you had no idea what he was really thinking or feeling. He grinned too much. His family touch-football game for the cameras had the same air of bizarre artifice, like marzipan figures of the Kennedys. And what is he bingeing on to keep all that weight when he works so hard?

It is not as if they are fighting over a principle or an ideology; the only principle is self-interest—on one side the old guard's dream of restoration, on the other the meritocrat's dream of advancement. Everyone looks so graspy. When Lawrence Tribe showed up on the streets in Miami, then on *Larry King Live*, it wasn't to speak of a stirring principle of civil rights. No, he was just a walking, talking Harvard want ad for the Supreme Court.

So many of the old faces of Impeachment are assembled, with all of Impeachment's emotion but with none of the gripping issues of Impeachment. One side is for holding the ball and running the clock out, the other is for playing on, but on only one side of the field. In a sense, we are learning now what Impeachment was about: about pure interest, one side against another, a complex factional and cultural struggle of the urban versus the non-urban, the new and the old. And espe-

cially now that the lawyers seem to have dug in, it won't go away, either. This is only the third quarter. We have another whole bitter quarter to go, and overtime, 2004 and beyond. Did your heart sink when you saw the red and blue map of the United States with county-by-county results? Mine did: that sea of Republican red across the middle of the country, the lakes and rivulets of Democratic blue along the coasts and the upper Midwest. It showed how polarized the country is, along deep lines coming out from the new economy and new sociology. There were any number of ways to look at this map: the city and the country, the Information

Age and the pre-Information Age, globalization and isolation, meritocracy and birth, and—especially in the light of Palm Beach—Jews and blacks against Protestant whites. Jim Baker is back, and who can ever forget Mr. Baker's comment about the political clout of the Jews: Fuck 'em.

During Impeachment I heard people brag, "I voted for Nader in '96, and I'm already feeling good about my Nader vote now." Nader voters defy those red-blue fault lines, they are true independents who have sympathy for both sides, a hard-core 2 percent who refused to be browbeaten out of their vote by the Gore people. The Gore people tried to caricature us

as elitists, presumably because Ralph Nader himself owned so much stock in Cisco Systems Inc., but the biggest Nader vote was in Alaska, hardly an elitist roost. Mr. Nader's vision of America was romantic and nostalgic, reflecting his small-town origins. He complained about the long commutes people have just to keep up with the new economy, and seemed to believe that people would sacrifice their standard of living for simpler lives. They won't; Americans like buying things too much. But Mr. Nader's message resonated because he had a grand passion, and the opposition had so little. Who will lecture me about the environment while driving

Snipper or George the Human Boil?

> *It is not as if they are fighting over a principle or an ideology; the only principle is self-interest—on one side the old guard's dream of restoration, on the other the meritocrat's dream of advancement.*

an S.U.V.? Who will lecture about public schools when their kids are in private schools?

The Naderites tried to straddle the vast moral divide between the reds and the blues. The seminal event for the reds was Waco in '93, and you can pile up lawyers' reports till doomsday but it will not remove the unease people out in the red territory feel over the government's actions in the deaths of 20-odd children. Blaring rock 'n' roll music all night long at them during an impatient siege. The blues never cared about Waco, and from '93 on Democrats were supposed to tamp down all feelings of discomfort with the administration because the econ-

omy was so good, and Bill Clinton was a global maestro.

The degree of loyalty maintained by the Democratic side was astonishing, through Impeachment and the campaign-finance scandals, the Sudan bombing, the destruction of women's reputations. Early on there was a contrary example in Treasury aide Josh Steiner sharing his diaries with Congress, diaries that undercut the official line, but Mr. Steiner was soon packing, and the loyalty mode was established. Trash the diaries or don't write them. Don't even think them. And so never during Impeachment did anyone say, "I'm embarrassed that I served as a conduit of rumors to destroy the reputation of a young woman— therefore I will resign." That red-and-blue map had already taken hold in people's minds, a feeling of us against them, expressed at once poignantly and ridiculously by Barbra Streisand, who said lately of Mr. Bush, "Our whole way of life is at stake." She wasn't just talking about abortion, but a whole set of shared values about how the world works. As if they are really in danger. The fury that Democrats turned on Mr. Nader, and then his supporters, during the late campaign is the freshest example of those loyalty demands. Here again they were largely successful. Mr. Nader had polled close to 5 percent and wound up with 2 percent. Much of Mr. Nader's losses were obviously Gore people coming home to the Democratic Party; still, it is remarkable to compare the Nader third-party movement with Ross Perot's and John Anderson's before. Those men routinely got 7 and 8 percent, even 19. Maybe Ralph Nader's movement was truly smaller. But the fact

is that blue culture is not really tolerant of dissent, and it hammered away at the Nader campaign through the final weeks, effectively. A letter by prominent progressive intellectuals caricatured Mr. Nader as an unstable nut ("dangerous," "wrecking ball," "unbelievable," "incredible"). In *The Times*, Janet Malcolm compared Nader to Roger Clemens throwing the shattered bat-head. Kate Michelman went on and on about abortion. It had the emotion of a family feud. The Nader chastisers were always somewhat parental. But, like parents, they just didn't get it. They imagined that they knew what was most important to us, so they could say that Al Gore was better on those issues. But Mr. Bush and Mr. Gore are hard to tell apart, harder than ever. And what if your issue is corporate influence of the political process? What if you are concerned that all the big media are owned by big corporations, and ideas are marketed like Cheerios? The other day, the *Times* Arts & Ideas page had a deadly story (by Alexander Stille) about progressive American intellectuals being completely ignored in the United States while their ideas are taken up in Europe. Arguments against bio-engineering, redistributive schemes to give every 18-year-old $14,000 to invest in a house or education. These ideas are actively discussed in Europe and shunned here. Because in the culture of globalization, they are heretical. They could send the markets down. And that was always Ralph Nader's strongest argument: Our democratic discourse is shriveling, it has no room any more for unorthodox ideas.

As a Nader voter, I feel a certain

detachment now, watching the factions, seeing the fixer Bill Daley come out with a gallows expression vowing trench warfare and Bob Dole with his strange face-lift warning about Republicans boycotting the inauguration. What hacks they are!

And sadly, Mr. Gore and Mr. Bush seem controlled by their factions. If one of them were presidential, he could lift us out of this. The Frank Capra moment could still happen. George Bush could say, "You know what? I lost the popular vote, and it sure looks like Florida didn't want to vote for me either, so I'm going to step back now and stop this mess." He would be the big winner.

For a while on election night, George W. Bush had even played the old-time hero who stands above the fray. When a reporter at the governor's mansion said that his whole future was on the line, Mr. Bush bridled. No it isn't! he said. My life will go on fine without this prize, he was saying. But that act vanished in a hurry. Now we see who he is, a nervous Nelly with his father's lineup card, and determined to win on a technicality.

Al Gore may still have his lofty opportunity to win by losing. But it doesn't look like it. Outside the White House, his relentless smiling seemed to mask disappointment and rage. What kind of winner will he be—how condescending—and how bitter a loser? Two princes, and not a noble drop of blood between them. They almost make Nixon look good. When he let go of the presidency, his parting words to his staff were poetic, and his wave from the helicopter door was brave and cleansing. Of course, that was his last act. We're going to have both these guys to kick around for a long time.

NOVEMBER 13, 2000
BY TERRY GOLWAY

She Wins! BushGore Are DarnClose

Hillary R. Clinton Belongs to You, New Yorkers; First Lady's Win Is Bigger Than Anybody Thought

IN THE FIRST ELECTION OF THE new century, New Yorkers chose First Lady Hillary Rodham Clinton as their first woman U.S. senator, while the presidential election lived up to its billing as Wednesday, November 8, chugged into the East Coast without a winner.

But New York had one. With more then 92 percent of the vote counted in New York, Mrs. Clinton had 56 percent of the vote, to Republican Representative Rick Lazio's 43 percent. In the astonishing presidential race that seemed destined to drag long into the morning, Texas Governor George W. Bush had 246 votes in the Electoral College, while Vice President Al Gore had 242. Mr. Gore saw an early lead, fueled by crucial victories in Michigan and Pennsylvania, disappear as states in the South and Rocky Mountain regions came in for Mr. Bush. As 1 a.m. approached in New York, the election hinged on Florida, where the vote was amazingly close.

NOVEMBER 27, 2000
BY AMY BERKOWITZ

CRUSHED UNDER THEIR TONS OF BOOKS, L'IL WONKS PUT WHEELS ON BACKPACKS

THE LATEST OBSESSION OF NEW York City's school kids is the rolly backpack, a backpack with rubber wheels and a retractable plastic handle so it can be towed around.

Macy's has been selling well over 100 a day.

"My old bag weighed about 45 pounds," said Chris Dietz, a sixth-grade student at Hunter College Elementary School. "It strained my back a lot."

◇◇◇◇◇◇◇◇

DECEMBER 4, 2000
BY DEBORAH SCHOENEMAN AND DEBORAH NETBURN

Manhattan Transfers

Richard Meier Builds Perry Street Palace For Calvin and Martha

CHEF JEAN GEORGES VONGER-ichten has reserved the 10th floor of the south tower of two Mr. Meier has designed at 173 and 176 Perry Street. Calvin Klein is spending about $20 million on a triplex penthouse in the south tower—and he's paying Mr. Meier extra to fix it up. Martha Stewart has dibs on the north tower's penthouse, which came with a $3.75 million price tag. And Mr. Meier has bought one apartment in the south tower for himself.

"The light off the river is so beautiful," he said.

DECEMBER 18, 2000   BY ALEXANDRA JACOBS

WHERE HAVE YOU GONE, DIANA VREELAND?

IT IS TEMPTING TO DISMISS *LUCKY*, WHICH IS REALLY MORE OF A telephone book than a magazine, a 200-page telephone book filled with merchandise hand-picked and baldly showcased by editor Kim France and her staff (which includes an Internet editor named Jenny B. Fine; can this person exist?). But think what it means.

It heralds, for one thing, the end of the women's magazine editor as celebrity; as domineering, matriarchal presence; as "editrix."

Since editors can't possibly compete with the ready-made narratives celebrities provide, they have slowly begun to erase themselves. The new model of the women's magazine editor is not a dictator, not a queen, but a girlish and conspiratorial chum. (How can you dictate, after all, in a world of eBay and casual Friday? How elite can you be when most socialites have day jobs?)

The youthful Ms. France is the ultimate self-erasing editor, posing for her editor's letter quite literally in the closet. "I'd like you to think of *Lucky* as your personal shopping playground," she writes, "overseen by that one friend who knows exactly which jeans are the most butt flattering."

Her magazine goes on to present no stories, no advice on job hunts, no how-to, no horoscopes (finally!), no vision of your ideal life, just first-person squibs from her editors accompanying photographs of items, items, items—the reason why magazines were existing all along. It's crass, perhaps—note the $68 dish-drying rack on page 104—but there's something honest about it. Something even brave.

Lucky is a women's magazine as project. By its editor's fiat, its pages are meant quite explicitly to be annotated, doctored, torn up and out. One of its pages is covered with peel-off stickers—a rip-off from the popular Bliss spa catalog, one person who worked on the magazine remarked—to flag the items that the reader wants to buy. In the initial test issue, the stickers read "maybe" and "yes"; one read "yes!"—to indicate, one supposes, that one must-have item. In the current issue, all the yesses are adorned with exclamation points. Shopping as never-ending orgasm.

DECEMBER 25, 2000   BY FRANK DIGIACOMO

Ring-a-Ding-Ding! Bill and Hill's 'Crat Pack' Blows In

HIGH ON THE 34TH FLOOR OF THE GRAND HYATT, DEEP WITHIN the force field of Secret Service men and federal agents in riot gear, they stood in a loose group around the woman who hours before had been elected New York's junior senator. Hillary Clinton stood staring at an open copy of a hot-off-the-presses *New York Post* that bore front-and-back "Election Extra" news covers. "CAPITOL HILL" blared one of the headlines above what is probably the most tasteful picture of Mrs. Clinton that Rupert Murdoch's tabloid has ever run.

Around her stood VH1 chief John Sykes, *Talk* magazine editor in chief Tina Brown, her writer-editor husband Harold Evans, actress Uma Thurman, mook thespian Joe Pantoliano, writers Lucinda Franks and Stanley Crouch, Democratic operative Patricia Duff, monologist Anna Deavere Smith, opera singer Jessye Norman, and Ben Affleck, who was getting the googly eye from Chelsea Clinton as they stood on the perimeter of the crowd.

"Now Rupert's got to like you," said Mr. Sykes to Mrs. Clinton.

She had won, and there in the suite at the Grand Hyatt, you could already feel the world changing. Her enemies were equivocating and her sycophants were drawing closer.

◇◇◇◇◇◇◇◇

DECEMBER 25, 2000   BY GEORGE GURLEY

THE OBSERVATORY: WARNING! WASPS ON THE WEB!

DAVID PATRICK COLUMBIA WAS SITTING at Swifty's, a clubby restaurant on Manhattan's Upper East Side, inches away from a table of society figures eating lunch. There was the ageless philanthropist Carroll Petrie; jewelry designer and walker Kenneth Jay Lane; cabaret singer Yanna Avis, wife of the rent-a-car mogul; fashion designer Mary McFadden, wearing a fur hat; and the slim, silver-haired society lunch date, John Galliher. As Mr. Lane broke into snatches of Cole Porter, Mr. Columbia leaned in and told me, "I'm not a part of society. I'm an outsider. I don't aspire to be an insider. I could be at that table and not feel like an outsider. But I am not an insider like those people are with each other. I like to see these people. Very powerful creative forces. Not writers of the great American novel, but characters in the great American novel, which is even better than the writer. Every single person at this table. Really interesting stories. Tremendous lives, big lives. Somebody else might read that and say, 'Yeccch, he respects them? If he knew what I know!' What they really mean is all these people have amazing powers. Because they do!" In September, Mr. Columbia created a Web site, NewYorkSocialDiary.com. Through the magic of digital photography and Mr. Columbia's late-night typing, each morning people can see what happened the night before at the Waldorf Grand Ballroom, at a ballet benefit or at an exclusive dinner party. But the real secret of Mr. Columbia's success? He's actually nice to the people he covers.

At 59, David Patrick Columbia is a big fella, 6-foot-4, with a deep voice that erupts into that WASP-y sound somewhere between a bark and a honk. At lunch, he was wearing a blue blazer, brown tie and khakis. "I sort of made my reputation being nice-ish," he said. "The world that I cover is often about vanity, greed and venality. But most of us don't get up in the morning and think, 'I'm going to be the biggest son of a bitch that ever lived today.' Most of us get up in the morning and think, 'How am I going to get through my day? How am I going to make my lunch on time? How am I going to pay the rent? How am I going to keep that secret? How am I going to hide this from him or from her?' So I sometimes feel if you're nice, you actually get a much clearer picture of what people are. Because a lot of people tend to behave very badly in New York. It's like when you see little children behaving badly and parents say, 'Stop that!' Well, these are giant little children who don't have parents to say, 'Stop that.' So I try to be the family counselor in my mind."

GEORGE GURLEY INTERVIEWS SUSAN MORRISON

with occasional words from John Homans

Could you talk about how you got the job?
At *Spy* we ran a regular column about *The Observer*, which had just started, making fun of the paper's boring-ness. The first one read, "It's about time this city had a weekly—a baby-aspirin-colored weekly at that—as compelling, as daring, as NOW as the tweedy readership whose minor woes it chronicles." We would then list some typical headlines, for example: "Consumer Official Threatens Milk Suit," "3-Card Monte: The Game of the Streets." So when Graydon Carter ended up leaving *Spy* and going to edit *The Observer*, it seemed shocking to all of us. But Graydon saw the paper as a bundle of potential, and he completely re-made it. After he had been there for a little more than a year, he was hired by S. I. Newhouse to edit *Vanity Fair*, and he called me and said, "I don't know what Arthur has in mind here, but you should really come and take this place over." I was having a lot of fun with Kurt [Andersen] at *Spy*, and I wasn't that interested initially. But, at Graydon's suggestion, Arthur called and summoned me to the office on 64th Street. The *Spy* offices had always been improvised, ramshackle affairs, with lots of wall board and cheapo architectural flourishes held together with Elmer's glue, but I had never seen anything quite like the *Observer* office. It was a beautiful old townhouse, but overlayed entirely with a kind of acrid '70s feel—there was mustardy-beige paint on everything and old dust-colored carpeting that had been worn down into something like felt. People were literally piled on top of each other trying to work. But Arthur's office was a vast paneled space out of *Masterpiece Theatre*, very polished and woody and calm. When I went to meet him that first time, one of the first questions he asked me was what my SAT scores were. (I later learned that he asked everyone this. I also learned that he had a deep fascination with admissions processes of all kinds—to Ivy League schools, private schools, Manhattan clubs. He loved stories about *getting in*—and, at his urging, the paper did lots of memorable pieces on the subject.) I was 32 and I was planning to be married in a month, so it wasn't the greatest time for me to make a big move. But Arthur was very persuasive and I accepted. One week into the job I went on my honeymoon.

Once I got to *The Observer*, I remember how every single person I hired always came in on their first day with the same look on their face: "Oh my God, what have I *done*?"

John Homans: I did. I left the building until they promised to build me an office. I came in and there was no light. It was a very unsavory situation. The first thing I saw when I went into the *Observer* townhouse was Rob Speyer of

---

Susan Morrison is articles editor at *The New Yorker*.
John Homans is executive editor at *New York*.

> *It was like putting on a show in the barn. It felt like there were no grown-ups around in some ways, and we were free to do whatever we wanted.*

---

the Tishman Speyer family, a very loud-voiced, long-chinned fellow who was at that time about 22. And Arthur had this Italian guy who dealt with supplies, Leon, who would guard the supplies. On my first day, Leon had one end of a carton of milk and Rob Speyer had the other end, and they were physically fighting over this carton of milk. And Rob Speyer is a billionaire. And I thought, *This is fucked up.*

Susan Morrison: On my first day, I remember saying, "Leon, can I have a box of paper clips?" And he went downstairs and came back and held out his palm and he had three paper clips in his hand. Leon was the requisitions officer. Veteran staffers used to joke that he was Arthur's father. He was kept in the basement.

John Homans: Along with Warren St. John's beer. When Warren St. John introduced himself, he said, "I'm a *poet* and a *brewer*."

Susan Morrison: Things were so overcrowded. I remember the elaborate plans for a Quonset hut that was going to be erected in the backyard, because we needed more space—we were having four interns use a door propped on two sawhorses as a desk. And the receptionists! Their names were Angie and Rosalinda, and they had one of those Lily Tomlin–era switchboards with plugs.

Arthur threw a dinner party at his apartment to welcome John Homans. We were all pretty young and poor, so even just going into Arthur's house, with all the servants and impressionist paintings, was a little overwhelming. After dinner everyone retired to the living room, and Arthur, who was trained as a pianist, started playing classical pieces. Then Michael Thomas and John Heilpern got him to switch to show tunes and tried to get everyone into a singalong. I think Heilpern was sitting on a lid of the piano. It was an odd, very boozy evening. I'm quite sure that "Old Man River" was performed.

We young folk were sitting on the couch and I remember you [Homans] looking horrified. I was afraid you were going to quit right then.

How did it flow from Graydon's tenure to yours?
Graydon made a great success at the paper—he jump-started it—and I built on that. He had treated *The Observer* like a big high-school newspaper for the Upper East Side and for the media, and that's why everybody picked it up. It had really good media news, and it happened to be a period where there was a lot of interesting stuff going on in the media. Tina Brown had just taken over *The New Yorker*, for example. One thing I learned at *Spy* was that it's easier to be an editor if you have no sacred cows, if you allow no one to be off-limits. So no one was off-limits. We covered Graydon and *Vanity Fair* as well as former business associates of Arthur's.

Graydon succeeding in making people read and talk about the paper, and when I got there, I wanted to make it younger. There was a sense, in 1992, that the Upper East Side had a bit of an ossified, geriatric, *Town and Country* feel—it was the world of Jerry Zipkin, Saul and Gayfryd Steinberg. I wanted to rid the paper of that feel and make it younger, more relevant. Like Graydon, I wanted it to be entertaining and mischievous. Lots of stories about little local conflicts—I remember assigning one of those interns to read the *New York Law Journal* every day to find obscure lawsuits that would be good stories. We did some oddball trend stories—Phil Weiss wrote, all those years ago, about the phrase "At the end of the day," which was just becoming ubiquitous. We had no money and no resources. I remember what a huge deal it was to send Frank DiGiacomo, who wrote the Transom, to cover the Oscars (or rather, we did a bake-off story comparing Graydon Carter's *VF* Oscar party to Tina Brown's *New Yorker* Oscar party). I think Frank was sleeping on someone's floor out there and he called in his story in the middle of the night. It was the first time we used this newfangled device that none of us had ever heard of, called a modem.

How was it working for Arthur Carter?

Arthur took a lot of risks. He let me hire anyone I wanted, and he let me fire anyone I wanted. There were some older columnists when I got there who, while talented, just weren't contributing enough fresh material. And I think I had to let Taki go. It was the third time I was responsible for firing him! When I worked for Tina at *Vanity Fair*, Taki wrote a column that I was editing, and one, I think, had too much in common with a piece someone else had written in the *Telegraph*. So that was that. Taki is an old friend of Graydon's, and he became a columnist at *Spy*, and again I edited him, and again we had that, uh, problem. When I got to *The Observer*, there he was again—writing the same columns (it seemed as if many of them included a reference to the socialite Porfirio Rubirosa balancing a chair on his erect penis).

What were some memorable pieces?

When Donald Trump married Marla Maples, they had a huge society wedding at the Plaza. I assigned Phil Weiss to go and hang out in the kitchen, to be there when the vans from City Harvest arrived to pick up the leftover food for the homeless. At about 11 p.m., the City Harvest people came and loaded up all the foie gras and lobster and steak and brought it down to the Bowery Mission. Phil went down, too, and stayed with the scene for about 36 hours, reporting as the cooks made all of those luxury ingredients into stew and then talking to the homeless guys who ate it—Trump's leftovers. It was a really good piece.

Anyone ever call up screaming?

We once reviewed a somewhat cheesy novel by Julie Baumgold, who was married to Ed Kosner, the editor of *New York* magazine. There was a line in the review describing the author as being in the tradition of Shirley Lord and Nancy Friday—that is, wives of important editors who wrote dirty books. Baumgold was furious. I remember Arthur coming to the office extremely gleeful the next

week. He said he had been at a party the night before and had been accosted by Julie Baumgold. She had seen him across the room and had screamed obscenities at him. Arthur loved it. Because I had been at *Spy* for six years, I was used to that sort of thing. I was used to writing those awkward notes to people or relatives of people who were being mocked in the magazine. I remember writing one to my old friend David Kissinger: "Dear David, just wanted to give you a heads up that your father appears on the cover of the next issue wearing a coconut bra."

Memorable columnists?

Lots. We had Harold Brodkey writing the Runaway Column. He was great. I had a very intense relationship with him. Editing him involved being on the phone with him for hours. Eventually, I gave up the phone and ended up going to meet him at Café Edgar on the West Side. Then he was diagnosed with AIDS. He got sick at the same time I became pregnant, and he liked to talk on the phone about it. He was fascinated, and, in a strange way, consoled by drawing parallels between the baby growing inside of me and the disease growing inside of him. I loved hiring people to write the New Yorker's Diary—in particular, Jim Collins, Patty Marx and Phil Weiss. John Heilpern was always fun and smart. I remember editing Heilpern over the phone. I would sometimes say, "John, are you lying down?" You could just hear it in his voice.

John Homans: What was his famous line—it has to be apocryphal—he was married to an editor at British *Vogue*, Joan Juliet Buck, and supposedly the last thing that happened, she said, "John, the difference between you and me is, I came to America to be a success, and you came here to be a failure." And he said, "And neither one of us succeeded in our game."

What was the atmosphere like?

We were sitting in a tiny, grungy office, a bunch of underpaid people saying, "Let's do this, let's do that." It was like putting on a show in the barn. It felt like there were no grown-ups around in some ways, and we were free to do whatever we wanted. That was all really fun. It was a little like *Spy*, but it was different because it was real news. We were trying to break news, and we often succeeded. For those us who had done time at Condé Nast, it was liberating. There was a lovely sense of camaraderie in all of that. I remember on the day after Thanksgiving (we had to work) lining up all of those doors on sawhorses that passed for desks and serving a turkey dinner to the staff. It was fun. But there was a downside to making it up as we went along. The resources were scant. There were times when I had to pay freelance writers by writing checks from my personal checking account (these would be in the high two figures, of course!) and then I would put their fees on my expenses. That was sometimes the only way I could get writers paid. It was a high-wire act: Just getting the damn thing out every week was a miracle.

2001

▶ The real millenium begins with Bush Inauguration

▶ Chappaqua quakes as Bill, Hillary find Starbucks

▶ 200,000 crush grass to hear Dave Matthews

▶ Inspired jeans designers introduce the Butt Zipper

▶ Super Senators duel for TV time

▶ PR princess Lizzie Grubman backs into Hamptons Club

◀ September 11, 2001

▶ Wall Street finds distraction in BlackBerry

2001

JANUARY 22, 2001   BY TERRY GOLWAY

Conquering Clintons Squat in New York

JANUARY 8, 2001   EDITORIAL

THE SHAMELESS MRS. CLINTON

IN THE SHORT PERIOD BE-tween being elected and being sworn in as senator, Hillary Rodham Clinton has already orchestrated two separate multi-million-dollar deals that raise serious questions about her personal ethics and her political loyalty to New York.

First, for those who were under the assumption that Mrs. Clinton was the next senator from New York, she has proven instead that she should properly be introduced as "the senator

from Viacom." It is stunning how quickly she sold her impartiality to the highest bidder—in this case, Viacom, the media giant that coughed up an $8 million advance for Mrs. Clinton's memoirs. *The New York Times* reports that Mrs. Clinton was pushing to collect more of her advance immediately, before taking office, when the Senate Ethics Committee might have had something to say.

Why are other senators remaining silent? Five years ago, House Speaker Newt Gingrich was tarred and feathered for signing a $4.5 million book deal with Rupert Murdoch. He returned the advance. Mrs. Clinton's equally sleazy deal has raised barely a peep. Two nonpartisan groups, the Congressional Accountability Project and Common Cause, have implored Mrs. Clinton to take only royalties, but she clearly has no intention of doing so.

Of course, the joke is on Viacom. Mrs. Clinton received her stratospheric asking price because she claimed her memoirs will address the Clinton administration's scandals. Who does she think she's fooling (besides Viacom)? The book is to be published in 2003, when Mrs. Clinton will be two years into her first term as senator. It would be political suicide for her to remind readers of even one hair on Monica Lewinsky's head.

FOR YEARS NOW, WE'VE BEEN watching Bill Clinton's approach into New York—fund-raisers and friends, birthday cakes at Radio City and nights at the Waldorf. He was like a lumbering Airbus circling the air lanes above Kennedy Airport.

Well, he's finally touched down.

And, in a weird act of synchronicity, he's preparing to settle into the very space from which his buddy, Miramax head Harvey Weinstein, and editor Tina Brown spawned their almost-monthly magazine, *Talk*, and from where, on the 56th floor of Carnegie Hall Towers at 152 West 57th Street, Ms. Brown hatched an almost-memorable profile of Hillary Rodham Clinton in *Talk* No. 1.

In those offices—for which the taxpayers may pay as much as $750,000 a year—the southern windows provide views of passing blimps and heartbreaking sunsets glinting off the Em-pire State Building; the western windows provide the Hudson River to the Meadowlands; to the majestic north, the former president will see Central Park itself in perfect green miniature, down to the skaters at Wollman Rink. The eastern windows peer down 57th Street, where power brokers live and work and eat.

And he will be among them.

Julian Niccolini, managing co-partner of the Four Seasons Restaurant, already has a table waiting for Mr. Clinton. And like a good many New Yorkers, he's expecting to see him sometime soon.

Beginning at noon on Jan. 20, 54-year-old Bill Clinton will be a former president and a New Yorker, a combination not seen since Richard Nixon spent some time on the Upper East Side and Herbert Hoover lived out his chilly exile in an apartment in the Waldorf Astoria.

FEBRUARY 12, 2001 BY GEORGE GURLEY

THE OBSERVATORY: MANHATTAN MINX

ELISABETH KIESELSTEIN-Cord, a 21-year-old socialite, was on the phone and pissed off. A reporter had been calling her friends. "I haven't done anything mean—to anyone, in my entire life—so I'm not concerned that someone's going to be like, 'Oh, she kicked me,'" she said. "It makes me feel very awkward. You know, I feel like this is the most invasive procedure that I've ever done. I really am being eaten up over this one.

"My life is not about cocktail parties," she continued. "That's why I don't feel comfortable being photographed at them. You know what, I'm a young girl, O.K.? And

the last thing I want is to have a bunch of obstacles thrown my way because someone has written about me in such a way that is—I'm very upset, I need to go."

She called back. "I really wish I hadn't embarked on this labyrinthine journey with you to begin with, because it's out of control in my mind!"

Ms. Kieselstein-Cord is tremendously skinny, with caramel skin, dirty blond hair, big hazel eyes and lips that were described as "doll-thick" by a character in Woody Allen's 1996 film *Deconstructing Harry*, in which she appeared as an extra.

Ms. Kieselstein-Cord's photograph has appeared in *Harper's Bazaar* and *W*. Her father, Barry Kieselstein-Cord, is a well-known designer of high-priced accessories—belts, handbags, jewelry, sunglasses—which are popular in Manhattan, but considered more stylish in places such as Houston and Dallas. Her mother, Cece, is an artist and a socialite.

While Ms. Kieselstein-Cord has been lumped with all the other dewy "It Girls" of New York circa 2001, she professes to be perplexed at the attention she's getting.

"I find it very bizarre when I go home and listen to my answering

machine," she said, "and there are all these messages from people asking to work with me, about different projects. And I think, 'Why in the world do they want to do this?' And I figure, I'm part of the things that make New York New York."

◇◇◇◇◇◇◇

FEBRUARY 19, 2001 BY FRANK DIGIACOMO

Jennifer Lopez Has a Big ... Week

LAST WEEK, MS. LOPEZ WAS INARGUABLY THE BIGGEST HOMEGROWN crossover star to hit New York since Barbra Streisand. Her Reddi-Wip of a movie, *The Wedding Planner*, was the highest-grossing picture in the country until Hannibal showed up; her album *J. Lo* was roaring through record stores in the city; her magnificent butt was staring out from store windows and street-vendor carts from Yankee Stadium to the Battery; and she mixed it all with coy sightings and non-sightings with her charged beau, hip-hop artist Sean (Puffy) Combs, ingraining her purity with the intoxicating arsenic trace of scandal that has turned a very few gorgeous big stars—from Clara Bow to Lana Turner to Marilyn—into dangerously heated superstars.

On Feb. 10 in New York, anybody with the inclination to do so could have luxuriated in the aura of Jennifer Lopez. That might have meant anybody's turning on the radio to hear her sing, "Even if you were broke, my love don't cost a thing," from the single from her second album, which had crested at No. 1 on the Billboard charts, but which had the mind-numbing pleasure-giving quality that only the most insipid gloss can provide. Anybody could have picked up a copy of *Rolling Stone* magazine and admired the photos of Ms. Lopez's butter-and-brown-sugar skin busting out of a series of scanty Xena-style costumes. Anybody could—and did—float toward the street vendor on Madison Avenue, who was selling watches and CD's but using a poster of Ms. Lopez looking over her shoulder and aiming her butt like a Martian death ray: the most lethal black-and-white sex poster since Raquel Welch wore a torn bikini in *One Million Years B.C.* Or turned on *Saturday Night Live* and watched Will Ferrell declare to Ms. Lopez that he was "deeply and totally in love" with her "jungle rump," then ogled as Ms. Lopez dropped her robe onstage to reveal the green Versace dress with the steepest, deepest cleavage tumble this side of Victoria Falls.

FEBRUARY 26, 2001   BY TANYA CORRIN

THE OBSERVATORY: THE HARRIS EXPERIMENT

GO TO WWW.WELIVEINPUBLIC.COM. THERE YOU WILL SEE JOSH Harris, sleeping in the master bedroom of his magnificent Soho loft. You will see his cat, Neuffy, jump onto the bed and curl up at his feet. I see him, too, though I'm a few blocks away, watching him on my laptop at 56k. Josh looks so vulnerable that for a brief moment I want to reach out and hold him. The moment passes.

A few days ago, I was lying next to Josh. You could log on and watch in full-motion video as I woke up, tossed on my purple robe, brushed my teeth and fed Neuffy. We'd planned to live together in public—every minute of our lives in the loft, documented by 32 cameras and microphones—for 100 days. By day 60, I had to get out. By day 78, still unable to find an apartment, I chose couch surfing instead of remaining in a very public nightmare.

For four years, Josh and I were Silicon Alley's "It" couple. We met in 1996, when he was running the Internet entertainment site Pseudo.com and throwing Warhol-scale parties. I loved his galvanizing personality and wild ideas. He said he loved my ambition and spunk. Soon, Josh had convinced me to quit my corporate job and start an online animation company to make erotica tailored to women. Silicon Alley was flush with cash. Anything was possible. I'd never been happier.

Then, last March, he told me that he wanted to find out if I was the one. We'd already tried living together three times, but I packed for what I hoped would be the last time. By then, Josh's first company, Jupiter Communications, had gone public, and he had worked himself out of a job as founder of Pseudo to become a "full-time artist." I had become an Internet TV producer, making digital videos and hosting my own show on Pseudo.

Two months later, instead of asking me to marry him, Josh asked me to go public.

◇◇◇◇◇◇◇

Mayor Giuiliani threatens funding for Brooklyn Museum

MARCH 5, 2001   BY JASON GAY

Meet Four-Eyed New Sex Symbol, 'Weekend Update' Anchor Tina Fey

SHORTLY AFTER IT WAS ANnounced that *Saturday Night Live* head writer Tina Fey would take over as co-host of the "Weekend Update" news segment this season with Jimmy Fallon, fellow writer Paula Pell cornered Ms. Fey in the labyrinthine NBC Studios at 30 Rockefeller Center.

"Paula threatened to beat the crap out of me as soon as she saw any change in my behavior," Ms. Fey recalled." She hasn't beaten me yet."

Still, Tina Fey has changed since last August, when *Saturday Night Live* creator Lorne Michaels gambled and gave the 30-year-old one of the show's most prominent roles. In the ensuing months, Ms. Fey has undergone a caterpillar-like transformation from a schlumpy, sweatpants-wearing writer to a comedy princess.

"She's transformed herself into a total hottie!" said *SNL* featured player Rachel Dratch.

Ms. Dratch described her friend's comedic style as subtle yet purposeful: She will insist on writing a sketch that has an underlying point or payoff, as opposed to just riffing on a single joke or character.

Despite her growing popularity, Ms. Fey said she doesn't get noticed on the street. Her life remains low-key. "Am I clubbing with J. Lo?" Ms. Fey laughed and shook her head. So no J. Lo. But if some people think that Tina Fey, the writer, is also a Saturday Night Babe, well, that's just fine. "She must be psyched about it ... anyone would," said Ms. Dratch. "But she doesn't walk around thinking, 'I'm hot!' I think it's kind of new for her, being a sex symbol."

MARCH 5, 2001
BY ALEXANDRA JACOBS

Tail Hook ...

THERE THEY WERE, ASCENDing the stairs of the Bergen Street station: pants that zipped up the rear. Is this what the female sex has come to?

Sara Federlein, a 29-year-old grant writer for the aptly named Aperture Foundation, defended her size-eight, navy wool butt-zipper pants, which she received in a clothing swap. "They're really flattering, because they zip up the back and are kind of low-slung," she said.

If they were so great, why did her friend give them up? "In truth, the zipper thing never really worked for me," said Francine Stephens, also 29. "The zipper part, my mom didn't like that at all. And she's very hip!"

MARCH 12, 2001 BY IAN BLECHER

ACID REFLUX, CHIC GASTRIC AILMENT, REPLACES THE ULCER—ASK GANDOLFINI

THE THING ABOUT THE MEN in gray flannel suits, who came home from World War II and got married and bought a house in Great Neck with its very own fall-out shelter, who lunched on Dagwoods and napped all weekend, who feared only the boss and the communists: They all had ulcers. Ulcers were all the rage among the high-powered neurotic set not so long ago—the Marx Brothers made a cartoon promotional film for *The Saturday Evening Post* called *Showdown at Ulcer Gulch*; James Gleason played a stressed-out newspaper editor with a hole in his stomach in *Meet John Doe*.

Then, in 1983, Barry Marshall made an amazing discovery. Contrary to medical opinion of the time, ulcers are caused not by stress, not by hoagies, not even by the Russians; they're caused by bacteria called Helicobacter pylori. Suddenly, they were curable

with simple antibiotics. Just as suddenly, they became passé. Who gets ulcers anymore?

The ulcer went the way of afternoon highballs, newsreels, Sputnik and fin-tailed convertibles. But now, the children of the ulcer age are claiming a digestive grievance of their own. Acid reflux, an ailment caused by the backup of stomach acids in the throat, is becoming the ulcer of the New Age. And just as the mere mention of ulcers conjures images from the mid–20th century, someday acid reflux will do the same for the early 21st: The stressed-out dotcommer, the harassed defender of the Clinton family, the edgy day trader—all of them reaching for brand-name capsules to relieve the sour, verklempt feeling in the throat.

MARCH 26, 2001
BY FRANK DIGIACOMO

TO LIVE AND DINE IN N.Y.

MIDWAY THROUGH OUR MEAL at the restaurant Daniel I asked Jean-Louis Palladin what goes through his mind when he is in the kitchen.

Mr. Palladin—the 54-year-old French chef formerly of Palladin, Jean-Louis at the Watergate Hotel, and now Napa in Las Vegas—bolted upright in his chair. He looked at Tanya Bogdanovic, his Greek-Yugoslavian girlfriend, a flirtatious woman with dark eyes and a boyish haircut.

"It's like making love to a lady like that," he said as his hand reached out and grazed Ms. Bogdanovic's slender arm.

A dark cloud of a thought formed in my brain: How can a man wrestling with death be so alive? If you were to see Mr. Palladin on the street, you would not think, There goes a sick man. But in December he was diagnosed with lung cancer, and by the time you read this story, he will be waiting to learn if his second round of chemotherapy shrank his tumor sufficiently to allow his surgeons to remove it.

And yet I can assure you that Mr. Palladin is a man more alive than either you or me.

"He's amazingly strong," said chef Eric Ripert. "He can still eat like a pig, fuck like a rabbit, drink like a fish."

APRIL 2, 2000 BY GEORGE GURLEY

25-YEAR-OLD BROKER LEE MUNSON IS SWAGGERING RELIC OF THE BOOM

LEE MUNSON IS A TALL, LANKY, swaggering 25-year-old who moved from California to Manhattan three years ago and became a stockbroker. Now he works at a top brokerage house in midtown, drives a BMW and is married to an attractive 27-year-old woman who works in the art world.

One recent evening, Mr. Munson was in a cab on his way to Bellevue, a bar on 40th Street and Ninth Avenue.

"I realized at a very early time moving to New York City that my life was going to be shit out of luck unless I did something that made more fucking money—or as much money—as a drug dealer," he said. "There was only one thing that you could do, other than being a drug dealer, which I have no aptitude for anyway. Selling stock. So during good times, I make as much as a top drug dealer or mob guy—legally! Ethically.

"I consider myself a capitalist,"

he said. "Purebred. And you know what, I think the world is sick. And communism is so concerned about the world and helping your fellow brother. Fuck you, my fellow brother sucks. Why do I want to help him? He's a scumbag."

The next day I called Mr. Munson's wife, Alison Bamert.

"Lee really rocks and he's totally interesting, but you have to keep in mind that he shouldn't always be taken, like, completely literally," she said. "He's very interested in playing mind games with people and seeing what reaction he gets. And if you don't realize that, that can really turn people off."

APRIL 30, 2001 BY CHRISTINE MUHLKE

The Observatory: Do-It-Yourself Dinner

IT FIGURES THAT AFTER nearly a decade of affluence, excess and hot-toweled pampering, a New York restaurant could come along and make a big splash simply by offering people the opportunity to fend for themselves.

That's much of the appeal of Craft, an oddly conceived new restaurant in the Flatiron district launched by Gramercy Tavern chef Tom Colicchio.

Craft, we are told, is built upon tenets of simplicity and selection. Diners are provided with hypersized menus that resemble spreadsheets and list dozens of meat, poultry, fish and vegetable options; meals arrive with ingredients plated one by one, near-naked, on plain white plates or in shiny copper pots.

In essence, Craft puts the responsibility for a high-priced meal not on the fancy chef, but on you, the fancy customer. Naturally, this makes the restaurant something of a haven for control freaks. Are you one of those people constantly pulling the waiter aside and ordering off the menu? Then step to the plate: Craft is your kind of joint.

"It seems like a natural New Yorker fantasy," said Style.com gossip columnist Jill Kopelman. "[New Yorkers] tend to be controlling—what they want, when they want it. Everything [at Craft] is so specific."

"There's this period where you're thinking, 'You've got to be kidding,' especially by the time you get to the dessert menu," said Mitchell Davis, a cookbook author and director of publications at the James Beard Foundation.

In fact, instead of being a heavenly gift, Mr. Davis thinks Craft is something of a comeuppance for control-freak diners. After all, people who go into restaurants and fussily make changes to the menu don't do it because they want something else, he said. "It's because of power." Craft calls the picky eater's bluff. "When they get so many choices, they don't want to eat anything."

If you do want to eat, however, you first must tackle your fear of screwing up. New York diners forever worry about the ordering mistake, the culinary faux pas that triggers a humiliating roar of laughter from the waiter and the rest of the table. With all of its menu options, the potential for screwing up at Craft seems far higher.

Mr. Colicchio sounded somewhat surprised at the suggestion that Craft was stirring up trouble. "People say, 'Ah, I see what you're trying to do. You're trying to–' And I'm like, 'I'm not trying to do anything! Make good food, that's it!'"

Still, Craft does represent a severe challenge not just to the culture of the star chef, but also to culinary submission. At Craft, Mr. Colicchio's talents are only part of the show; the diner has an equal responsibility in the success of a meal.

"What's funny is the name: Craft," said Mr. Davis. "'Craft' presumes there's a craftsman there making beautiful things. If you want to work your own lathe and make your own ugly chair, then don't call it 'Craft.'"

Whether Craft perseveres or becomes another bump on the New York restaurant road remains to be seen. But there is something very now about this restaurant—this notion that, after too much carefree extravagance, improvidence and heavy cream sauces, we want to take care of our spoiled little selves again.

"We maybe need to have a shrink on staff full-time," joked Mr. Colicchio. "It's definitely bringing up some issues."

APRIL 30, 2001 BY MOIRA HODGSON

LABOR OF LUNCH

"MY EX-HUSBAND WAS ALways a pain about his food," said an English friend over lunch at Craft. "He once actually asked a waiter if he could have the roast beef on the menu without the roast beef."

He would not have been considered a pain at Craft, a new restaurant in the Flatiron district. Here the menu just provides the bare bones. You put your meal together yourself.

As a friend and I tried to create an imaginative dinner for ourselves one evening, I wondered what the chef would do with customers who ordered, say, gnocchi and red cabbage to go with sweetbreads.

"If I were him, I'd refuse to cook for them, of course," said my friend, who had been eyeing the sweetbreads himself. "I'd come out of the kitchen with my knife and stare at them. You have to be fearless in this restaurant. It places the responsibility for your dinner squarely on your shoulders."

CRAFT ★ ★ ★

43 East 19th Street
(between Park Avenue South and Broadway)
780-0880

Dress: Casual

Noise level: Fine

Wine list: Excellent, with unusual wines at fair prices

Credit cards: All major

Price range: Main courses, lunch, $20 to $26; dinner, $20 to $30, excluding vegetables, which range from $6 to $12

Lunch: Monday to Friday, noon to 2 p.m.

Dinner: Monday to Friday, 5:30 to 10 p.m.; Saturday and Sunday, 5:30 to 11 p.m.

★ Good
★ ★ Very Good
★ ★ ★ Excellent
★ ★ ★ ★ Outstanding
No Star: Poor

JUNE 6, 2001 BY JOSH BENSON

SUPER CHUCK FLIES AGAIN!

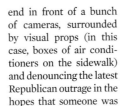

THE CAMERAMEN GATH-ered outside the P.C. Richard & Son appliance store on 14th Street were already griping. It was Memorial Day, and they were waiting for Senator Charles Schumer, who was disturbing their beach-and-barbecue day to talk about air conditioners.

Once Mr. Schumer arrived, he set about decrying President George W. Bush's efforts to roll back air-conditioning efficiency standards. This picture of the earnest, fist-pumping Chuck Schumer—clad in a stars-and-stripes tie and spending his holiday week-end in front of a bunch of cameras, surrounded by visual props (in this case, boxes of air conditioners on the sidewalk) and denouncing the latest Republican outrage in the hopes that someone was paying attention—seemed drearily familiar. But this time, things were different. "Today, I'm calling for the president to back off from his proposal," said Mr. Schumer, pausing as a bus roared by. "If he won't"—at this point the Senator broke into a broad smile—"as a member of the Energy Commit-tee, now in the majority, I'm going to call for hearings."

JUNE 11, 2001 BY ALEXANDRA JACOBS

Good Witch Glenda Comes to Bazaar as Classy, Chilly Kate Gets Gate

ON FRIDAY, JUNE 1, THE DREGS OF KATE BETTS' *HARPER'S BAZAAR* staff were summoned to their deposed editor's stripped-down office, where they confronted their new leader, Glenda Bailey, for the first time.

After a few jokes, the new editor in chief assured the assembled that she wasn't planning to turn the venerable fashion monthly, his-torically Pepsi to *Vogue*'s Coke, into another *Marie Claire*—the boppy, sexually frank Hearst title whose circulation she has increased more than 50 percent since she arrived from England five years ago.

The response: awkward silence. It was as if Glenda the Good Witch, with her cloud of frizzy, reddish hair and vivacious manner, had descended in a bubble to wave her wand over the ailing *Bazaar*.

As for the new editor in chief's personal image, which was causing some consternation among the lower ranks of the fashion commu-nity last week, it could be said that Ms. Bailey follows in the exuber-antly shabby tradition of the beloved Ms. Tilberis. Said one defender, "I think her hair looks best *wild* ."

◇◇◇◇◇◇◇

JULY 2, 2001 BY GEORGE GURLEY

Lights! Cameras! Hamptons Vérité !

ON A FRIDAY EVENING IN JUNE, TWO BLOND HEIRESSES WERE getting dressed for a party. Nicky Hilton, who is 18, and Amanda Hearst, who is 16, were in Ms. Hilton's parents' sprawling home in Southamp-ton. The only thing that made this scene any different from countless other summer evenings of countless young worthies getting dressed for a party near the beach was the presence of a Sony movie camera, a boom microphone and a film crew. The girls' pre-party ritual was being filmed for Barbara Kopple, the Academy Award-winning documentary film-maker. The cameras will roll until Labor Day, at which point Ms. Kopple will sit down in an editing room. Roughly eight months later, the result will be broadcast by ABC in four hours over two nights. The working title is *The Hamptons Project*.

Another of Ms. Kopple's characters is Joan Jedell, a photographer and the publisher of *The Hamptons Sheet*. Ms. Jedell had buttonholed Ms. Kopple's crew on the streets of Sag Harbor. "You should be talking to me; I'm the voice of the Hamptons," she told them. Ms. Jedell said she thinks Ms. Kopple should zoom in more on "the elitist kind of Hamptons."

"I don't get their point of view," she said. "Theirs is an all-around gen-eral non-glitzy focus, although the glitz will be part of it, but isn't all of it. Whereas in my life, it's all of it. I don't look at the fucking crap all over the place. I mean, I can look at that in Manhattan; I can go down to the Bowery if I want. The Latino dishwashers, the Mexicans, the fisher-men—I don't even focus on the locals. They hate us, anyway. If they're going to do something like this, and if they are going to include this well-rounded Hamptons, who's gonna care?"

JULY 16, 2001 BY FRANK DIGIACOMO AND DEBORAH SCHOENEMAN

Grubman Crackup: It Was a Bad Night at Conscience Point

LESS THAN 24 HOURS AFTER 30-year-old publicist Lizzie Grubman put her Mercedes in reverse and allegedly plowed into a bouncer and a group of 15 people who were waiting to get past the velvet ropes at Southampton's Conscience Point Inn, the damage to the well-worn Cape Cod–style nightclub had been patched up and painted over well enough that it was almost possible to forget the bloody faces and broken limbs of the previous night.

But four days into the media storm that was precipitated by the incident, it has become clear that repairing the human damage—to the injured, to Ms. Grubman's reputation and to the family, friends and business associates who have been affected by her actions—is going to require much more than shingles and nails. Already a small group of expensive men well acquainted with crisis—including public relations executive Howard Rubenstein, Southampton attorney Edward Burke Jr. and Manhattan attorney Edward Hayes—have begun plugging the ugly hole Ms. Grubman put into her well-manicured world, now that she has been charged with six counts of first-degree assault, one count of reckless endangerment, one count of second-degree assault and one count of leaving the scene of an accident involving physical injury. (Ms. Grubman posted $25,000 bail; a court date was set for Sept. 5.) And they are attempting to secure loose lips and quell angry voices in both the Hamptons and Manhattan, in the hope that eventually everything will seem as smooth and seamless as Conscience Point's shabby-chic façade.

But that is no easy task in this part of the world. For every acquiescent member of the New York establishment who's friendly with Ms. Grubman or her extremely successful father, entertainment attorney Allen Grubman, there is an ambitious, frustrated striver on the wrong side of the velvet rope looking to shake things up. For every couple that spends tens of thousands of dollars to summer in the Hamptons, there is a year-round resident who resents the conspicuousness of these weekenders. And for every publicist who shares Ms. Grubman's client list, there is one who covets her success.

AUGUST 6, 2001
BY ALEXANDRA JACOBS

THE OBSERVATORY: SAVING SILVERMAN

ON JULY 11, THE COMEDIAN Sarah Silverman made a typically kittenish appearance on the couch of NBC's *Late Night with Conan O'Brien*: She nibbled fruit, briefly clasped her breasts and performed a pre-scripted joke in which she uttered the word "Chinks," a slur for Chinese-Americans. It got a medium laugh.

A week later, Ms. Silverman woke up to a jangling phone in the airy lower-Broadway sublet she shares with her Chihuahua-pug mix, Duck. It was her mother calling. "She said, 'They were just talking about you on *The View!*'" said the sooty-lashed Ms. Silverman, at 30 still the gamine darling of the mostly male alternative-comedy world, but now the sworn enemy of Guy Aoki, president of the Media Action Network for Asian-Americans.

By the end of the next day, Mr. Aoki's demand that she apologize had spread to the national press. "When it was just *The View*, I was like, 'Oh, I better write this guy a letter,'" said Ms. Silverman. "And then by the end of the day I was like, 'This guy's a fucking idiot,' you know?" NBC quickly issued an official apology and vowed to expunge the joke from reruns. "The truth of the matter is, it's not a moral issue in terms of the network," said Ms. Silverman. "They may put this façade on that it is, but it's about advertisers and the F.C.C. and pleasing them. It has nothing to do with morals; they are void of morals. It's all about money. *It's all about money.*"

OUT OF OUR WAY, YOU @*?!& *!•⊕ WHITE TRASH!

VRRRROOM!!

SEPTEMBER 17, 2001 BY TERRY GOLWAY

September 11, 2001:
Infamy: Assault, Collapse at Twin Towers; City Girds

SPARED THE BOMBS AND SIEGES THAT scarred nearly every other world capital in the 20th century, New York on Sept. 11, 2001, suffered the most catastrophic attack on American territory since the Japanese attacked Pearl Harbor on Dec. 7, 1941.

Thousands of civilian men, women and children were killed and thousands more injured when two hijacked jetliners crashed into the World Trade Center at the beginning of what was to be just another day in pre-recessionary New York. The famed twin towers, dominant features of the downtown skyline since 1970, collapsed in a sickening heap about an hour after the crashes. Combined with a similar attack on the Pentagon, the casualties for Sept. 11, 2001, very likely will exceed the number of Allied casualties on D-Day, when 2,500 soldiers died and 10,000 were wounded. "The number of casualties will be more than any of us can bear," Mayor Rudolph Giuliani said during an afternoon news conference. "There was a large number of firefighters and police officers in harm's way. We don't know how many we've lost."

As night fell, thousands of families throughout the New York area prayed for loved ones they had not heard from, fearing the terrible news that might come with a phone call, or a visit from a clergyman. Downtown Manhattan, symbol of the resurgent New York, which gleefully laid claim to the title of "Capital of the World," had in an instant been rendered an appalling slaughterhouse.

President George W. Bush, who was told of the atrocities while he was reading to schoolchildren in Florida, promised to seek out the groups or people responsible. The president was flown to Nebraska, home of the Strategic Air Command, and then returned to Washington in late afternoon. By midday, F-16 fighter jets were patrolling Manhattan's skies, and all other air traffic throughout the nation was grounded. Sirens—suddenly reminiscent of air-raid warnings in London during the Blitz—replaced the honking horns and chaotic sounds of midtown as streets were shut down to allow access to emergency vehicles, some of them summoned from towns in Westchester County and New Jersey.

Doctors in St. Vincent's Hospital were, by late afternoon, awaiting casualties that were slow in coming. Dr. George Neuman, head of anesthesiology, said there was great concern about the number of injured people trapped under the massive rubble. The scene downtown was terrifying. People trapped in the towers could be seen leaping from windows, as witnesses on the ground screamed in horror. One eyewitness said one of the jumpers landed on a firefighter, killing both of them.

Crowds gathered in City Hall Plaza, several blocks to the northeast, to watch the tragedy unfold. At 10 a.m., they heard a terrible roar as the first tower, No. 1 World Trade Center, collapsed. Acrid white smoke quickly enveloped City Hall, and people began running north. Police officers shouted, "Move, move, move!" Some people sought refuge inside a subway entrance. Within minutes, the plaza was deserted. An ambulance was parked on a nearby street, seemingly abandoned. Soon, emerging from the thick smoke, refugees began streaming north towards City Hall. "I need a mask! I need a mask!" shouted an Emergency Medical Services worker. Somebody else shouted, "It's coming!"

Just after the first tower collapsed, grim-faced emergency workers and frantic family members tried to make their way south, while distraught survivors wandered uptown along the West Side Highway and other streets. Some of them were covered in dust and soot as they approached Warren and Greenwich Streets, when they heard a huge explosion behind them. The second tower had fallen.

Along Second Avenue on the East Side, people gathered around shop windows to watch televisions or listen to radios, an image associated with another era of strife. Scores of ambulances—many from the outer boroughs and beyond—raced down the avenue, which was almost devoid of normal traffic. With the subways shut down, people wandered the sidewalks, eager for news.

September 10, 2001 ... The Day Before

By Martin Scorsese Director, *Taxi Driver, Mean Streets, Gangs of New York*

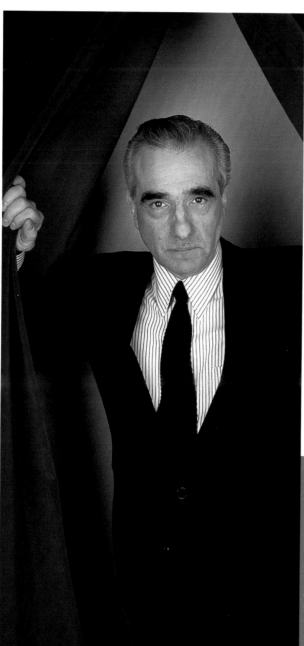

THAT MORNING, I REMEMBER BEING AWAKENED BY Silas the dog. Usually, my schedule is late morning to late night—I'm usually up until about 2 a.m—but Silas woke me at 8. The poor old dog. He's very sweet but, you know, he's had it. He's got eczema; he's scratching. I have eczema, too, so I understand. But he's on the bed scratching, and the bed's shaking.

I put him outside the bedroom. My wife, Helen, had already gone out. But then he started barking so I had to take him back in.

He woke me up twice.

So I was groggy, but I was also feeling an extraordinary amount of pressure. I usually exercise in the morning, but I didn't that day because I had to go to a photo shoot for *Talk* magazine. I had to get there by noon. But I was really consumed with *Gangs of New York*. We were preparing for a third rough-cut screening, which I think was going to be Sept. 20. The first cut of the film was three hours and 40 minutes. The next was three hours and 20 minutes. When you're cutting, you want to get as much as possible out. But first, the whole picture has to work before you can realize, "Oh, I don't need that scene."

I was eager to get back to the editing room, but between the photo shoot and the dog, I couldn't get there. The photo shoot, which I wanted to do, took place at the Peninsula Hotel, on the 23rd floor. When I got there, basically I was still sleeping. I met my editor, Thelma Schoonmaker, and publicist Larry Kaplan in the hall with my publicist, Lois Smith, and I didn't even utter hello to anyone. I hadn't even had my second cup of coffee.

Everyone else was already there: Griffin Dunne, Jay Cocks, Nick Pileggi, Nora Ephron, Paul Schrader and Jane Rosenthal.

I was still groggy but I was able to say hello to people. I said, "Actually, I'm not late. It was the elevator that was late." Which was true so I didn't feel guilty.

The photographer's camera and the giant silk had been set up on a terrace, near the edge. I looked at it and said, "I have vertigo." The

> "*I was really consumed with* Gangs of New York. *We were preparing for a third rough-cut screening, which I think was going to be Sept. 20.*"

safety barrier on the terrace was maybe up to your waist. It was like some nightmare: I wake up. I don't know where I am. I'm thinking of the cut of the film. I want to see the baby, Francesca. I've got a photo to do on the edge of a 23rd-floor terrace. I looked at the photographer. I said, "I don't think I can stand there."

They said, "O.K. we'll move the camera." I said hello to Griffin. I started to feel better. I hadn't seen most of these people for a while. While we were talking, Paul Schrader looked over the edge and said, "Look over there. There's the *Taxi Driver* suite." He was pointing at the St. Regis Hotel. When I was doing that film, the rooms I occupied were the rooms that had the oval windows. We were right across from them.

We started talking about *Taxi Driver* and about that summer in New York in 1975. It was a tough summer. Very hot. Lot's of rain. Lot's of edgy violence in the area. It made us all very nostalgic.

Shrader comes from the Midwest, but when he had written the film and had created Travis Bickle, we'd talked about doing *Taxi Driver* in a different city. We couldn't get the money to do it here. We thought San Francisco, but he said, "No, New York has the different neighborhoods." At that time, the stretch of Eight Avenue between 42nd and 57th streets was rough. Schrader said, "You cannot top that." And I said, "You're right, we've got to do it as a New York film." It was a defining time in my life, and Paul Schrader's life and De Niro's life. Even Cybill Shepherd's life.

And what happened right before the photo shoot was we all became very nostalgic about New York.

We just fell in love with New York all over again. We looked down past 55th Street, and we marveled at the buildings, at the extraordinary creation, which may be a little mad. People living 75 stories up. It's a little mad, maybe, but there's nothing like it ever in history.

It was quite an incredible moment. At certain points, you just remember why you're in love with New York.

I felt much better when I left the shoot. I could talk to people. I could breathe. I could see again. It was like a healing.

"We started talking about Taxi Driver and about that summer in New York in 1975. It was a tough summer. Very hot. Lot's of rain. Lot's of edgy violence in the area. It made us all very nostalgic."

SEPTEMBER 17, 2000
BY NYO STAFF

ON THE MIND OF LARRY KING JR.

I'M TIRED OF DINNER.

Is anybody else getting the feeling the Swedes are up to something?

Note to the movie stars: Take a small role now and then, like Bill Murray did in *Tootsie*. It makes 'em love you again.

I thought everybody had quit smoking. Then I watched an episode of *Big Brother 2*.

Cinnamon in my coffee? No, thanks.

My dad may have been cut loose by *USA Today*, but that doesn't change the fact that no one ever stopped reading one of his columns in the middle.

How much would it take for you to spend a night in an abandoned insane asylum? Me? No less than $5,000.

When the talk turns to David O. Russell, I always put in a strong word for *Flirting with Disaster* over *Three Kings*.

Rain is beautiful.

So when did bamboo stalks become the new flowers? And why wasn't I informed?

Would somebody please tell me how many bats live in Manhattan? It's something I'd like to know.

If you're in your 20's, do the rest of us a favor and quit yapping. We're not really interested.

Does anyone like George W. Bush?

I think my therapist has been "coasting" lately.

SEPTEMBER 24, 2001   BY GREG SARGENT AND JOSH BENSON

One City, Indivisible

HEADQUARTERS OF ENGINE Co. 22 and Ladder Co. 5 at Houston Street and Sixth Avenue, Sept. 11, mid-morning: An hour has passed since a pair of hijacked jetliners rammed into the World Trade Center, and Mayor Rudolph Giuliani and his top aides are taking refuge in this firehouse. Thousands of frightened people are fleeing north along Sixth Avenue, past the closed firehouse door. Mr. Giuliani is coated in ghostly white ash. Some stray arrivals to the firehouse are weeping. Fire Commissioner Thomas Von Essen is on the verge of tears, having learned that scores of firefighters are missing. Mr. Giuliani turns to Mr. Von Essen and hugs him.

"He had an instinctual emotional attachment to Commissioner Von Essen," Deputy Mayor Tony Coles, who was in the firehouse, later recalled. "He told him the whole city would work to get us all through this."

As Mr. Giuliani and his aides begin to figure out how to take command of a reeling city, they pause to consider that, moments ago, they almost lost their lives. They had arrived on the scene just after the second plane hit the south tower. They were in an adjacent office building when the first tower collapsed, shearing off a piece of their temporary shelter. The dust and smoke turned day into night. "It felt like midnight," one person present said.

Their room filling with smoke, they escaped through a warren of stairwells and walked uptown to the Houston Street firehouse.

Now, in the firehouse, Mr. Giuliani is scrambling to make telephone calls. Cell phones aren't working. There aren't nearly enough land lines in the firehouse. Throughout the morning, Mr. Giuliani will try repeatedly to contact President George W. Bush, but the president's aides are reluctant to reveal his whereabouts, because Mr. Giuliani's

phone lines are not secure.

Network news headquarters, Sept. 16, late afternoon: Nearly a week has passed since the disaster. Anchormen Tom Brokaw, Dan Rather and Charles Gibson are in their respective studios, each waiting for their own live-feed interview with Mr. Giuliani. The interviews were scheduled for 4:15, 4:30 and 4:50, after Mr. Giuliani fulfilled his promise to walk a bride—the sister of a Staten Island firefighter who died in the line of duty several weeks ago—up the aisle. But the wedding ran long, other matters arose and Mr. Giuliani was scheduled to attend to a mass in St. Patrick's Cathedral at 5:30. He skipped the interviews.

Two weeks ago, it would have been hard to imagine the networks clamoring for a piece of Mr. Giuliani's time. He was a lame-duck mayor who was preparing to hand City Hall to a successor. The only headlines he garnered, it seemed, were about his tumultuous private life and his quarrelsome demeanor. Despite the successes of his first term, he suddenly seemed irrelevant, a man whose second term was destined to be remembered as gossip, not as history.

Now, however, Rudolph Giuliani was a man transformed. In the midst of chaos, horror and unspeakable tragedy, he went far beyond the role of crisis manager, acting as the spiritual guide for an entire city. He rallied the city's spirit without inspiring any false hope or shallow optimism. He sought to assuage the city's fears while trying his best to indicate, ever so gently, that the 5,000 people missing very likely will never be found. He has handled the most grisly moments with grace.

Mr. Giuliani has, again and again, seemed more presidential than the president himself.

The Observatory: The Laughter, After

OCTOBER 22, 2001
BY CHRISTINE MUHLKE
WITH REPORTING
BY GEORGE GURLEY

THE OBSERVATORY: GET AWAY

JAN BARKER, A WRITER AND divorced mother of two who lives on the Upper East Side, has her bag ready to go. "I'm a very level-headed person, but I have children," she said. "Every parent I know is equally concerned. I have water, Power Bars—I figure we can live off those. I have a flashlight that's battery-operated that's also a radio, a siren and a clock. It's the coolest thing I've ever seen in my life. I have a first-aid kit, my antibiotics, Band-Aids and Neosporin. I have a little lightweight blanket and a camera. I have clean underwear and socks, Kleenex, toothpaste and toothbrush. The writer in me made me pack a journal and a book, *Five Little Peppers and How They Grew*, so I could read to my children. Extra batteries and a cell-phone charger. Then I put sweatshirts on top so we could tie sweatshirts around our waists."

Ms. Barker is one of a sizable number of New Yorkers who have taken things a bit further than pestering their doctors for Cipro, the antibiotic which can be effective against anthrax. Instead, they have packed survival bags—including a stash of Cipro, of course—and plotted escape routes in the wake of the Sept. 11 terrorist attack on the World Trade Center.

Does she carry the bag with her everywhere she goes? "No, I'm not that insane," she said.

IN THE AFTERMATH OF THE TERRORIST ATTACK ON NEW YORK, the Friars organization decided to go ahead with its annual roast, scheduled for September 29.

Gilbert Gottfried was the last man up to the podium. In his $11 gray shawl-collar tuxedo jacket with tails, black bow tie and Caesar haircut, Mr. Gottfried looked like he had just come from band practice.

"I have a flight to California. I can't get a direct flight," Mr. Gottfried said. "They said they have to stop at the Empire State Building first."

"Too soon," a man could be heard saying in the back of the ballroom.

When the booing started, Mr. Gottfried responded: "Awwwwwww, what the fuck do you care?" Silence fell once more.

"O.K.," he continued.

"A talent agent is sitting in his office. A family walks in. A man, woman, two kids, their little dog, and the talent agent goes, 'What kind of an act do you do?'" At the father's signal, Mr. Gottfried said, the family disrobes en masse. "The father starts fucking his wife," he said. "The wife starts jerking off the son. The son starts going down on the sister. The sister starts fingering the dog's asshole." Mr. Gottfried's voice was growing stronger. "Then the son starts blowing his father."

The Hilton's ballroom filled with the sounds of sudden exhalations. The comedians on the dais were bug-eyed with laughter and recognition. Mr. Gottfried was beaming.

Then he brought it home.

"The talent agent says, 'Well, that's an interesting act. What do you call yourselves?'"

Mr. Gottfried threw up his hands. "And they go, 'The Aristocrats!'"

There was a sound in the room that went beyond laughter.

Mr. Gottfried had gone to "The Aristocrats," the comedy equivalent of the B-flat below high C that Leontyne Price had sung at Carnegie Hall on Sunday.

Mr. Gottfried had used it to save himself, but also to lift the crowd to another place. A few minutes later, Alan King paid him a high compliment. "Forgive me," he said. "I'm just still a little touched by that asshole Gottfried."

NOVEMBER 19, 2001
BY SIMON DOONAN

THE OBSERVATORY: THE ELF-MADE MAN

FOR OBVIOUS REASONS, THIS year's holiday preparations were not the laugh riot they normally are. The destruction of the World Trade Center coincided with the start of holiday-window production at our display studio in the Daily News-Channel 13 building on West 33rd Street. Crafting papier-mâché reindeer and gluing pointy ears on elves while the worst domestic disaster in American history unfolded was a surreal and bleak experience.

For reasons best known to my subconscious, I had decided last February that the 2001 holiday windows needed a whiskers-on-kittens-ish traditional theme. In July, I sketched out the five Madison Avenue windows, each one focused on a different element of ultra-trad Xmas iconography—Santa Claus, elves, reindeer, etc. Then I Barneys-ized them into something called "The Groovy Grotto." The giant Santa would start things off. The elves would be celebs: e.g., Elf Saint Laurent, Elfis Presley, Marcelf Marceau, Dostoyelfsky, Donatelfa Versace, Missy Elfiot, Shields and Yarnelf, Steven Meiself. In the next window, "Mrs. Claus' Closet," 20 fashion designers from Vera Wang to Narciso Rodriguez riff on the same red-and-white theme. The reindeer in question would be Rudolph the Italian Reindeer (after our mayor). In the last window, Ruben and Isabel Toledo would create Trixie, the World's Largest Tree-Topper. (Guess her weight and win dinner for two at Fred's on the ninth floor.)

NOVEMBER 20, 2000

Tom Wolfe on the City of Change

HAS IT BEEN DULY recorded that everything in New York changed just before Sept. 11? Granted, it's hard to get the picture here in the Afghan glare of the TV set, but it looks like this:

Eighteen months before 9/11 and the death storm of ashes that rolled uptown from the World Trade Center, all of lower Manhattan's artists' quarters—SoHo, NoHo, WeVar, TriBeCa, the Village and Little Italy—were already history. The last stronghold, We-Var, a decrepit old warehouse area home to a hive of artists' lofts west of Varick Street and south of the Canal Street exit of the Holland Tunnel, was finally overrun by investment bankers, Silicon Alley then-fat cats and real-estate developers in the spring of 2000. Construction elevators started whining up and down the sides of the warehouses, and the victors' banners proclaimed FOR SALE NOW: HISTORIC OLD NEW YORK LOFT CONDOMINIUMS. The usual droves of young artists from the California Institute of the Arts to the Rhode Island School of Design and every M.F.A. program in between still arrive to storm the Manhattan art scene, but can no longer get even remotely within rent range and wind up in Williamsburg and Jersey City.

Twenty months before 9/11, Wall Street was already history, too. Wall Street hadn't been Wall Street since Dec. 31, 1999, when Nasdaq started the Street's great migration to Times Square. Reuters, Morgan Stanley, Lehman Smith Barney, Bear Stearns and Ernst and Young soon followed their lead. Today, out-of-town financial types must be perplexed to find the mighty Morgan Stanley shank-to-flank with a pink-neon

girlie bar called Runway 69.

A year before 9/11, that old standby of New York humor, folklore, fiction and drama—"the shrink," the Freudian psychiatrist with the couch—had already gone the way of the Irish cabby with the cap over one eye. When neuroscientists Paul Greengard of Rockefeller University and Eric Kandel of Columbia won the Nobel Prize in 2000 (along with Arvid Carlsson of Germany) for discoveries of how information actually circulates inside the brain, physiology and not Freud was king. The New York teaching hospitals were now training psy-

chiatrists who had actually been introduced to brain functions and the central nervous system. As the witticism went, going to a Freudian psychiatrist was like going to "a cardiologist who only knows about broken hearts and valentines." The psychiatrist who, in an ABC News conversation with Peter Jennings, referred to the World Trade Center as two towering "phallic symbols" subjected to "symbolic castration" came off as quaint. He would have done better on *The Sopranos*, the show that hasn't yet gotten the word about yakety-yak therapy.

Twenty months before 9/11, the

Democratic Party "organization," ruler of the city for half a century, had disintegrated thanks to, of all things, an oversupply of populous racial and ethnic minorities and wound up like the Republican Party and Liberal Party "organizations." The term limits that cleansed the City Council slates for the 2001 races were the mopping-up operation. Politicians still ran successfully under the Democratic Party banner, but only because they were neighborhood warlords who had to call themselves something.

Ten months before 9/11, New York City's architects, who only

A year before 9/11, that old standby of New York humor, folklore, fiction and drama—"the shrink," the Freudian psychiatrist with the couch—had already gone the way of the Irish cabby with the cap over one eye.

yesterday had battled so gloriously and avant-gardedly as the Whites (Richard Meier, Peter Eisenman, John Hedjuk et al.) versus the Grays (Michael Graves, Jaquelin Robertson, Robert Stern et al.), had already given up the cutting edge because they could no longer find one. When Cathy Lang Ho and Raul A. Barreneche set out to do a book on the edgiest residential designs in North America (*House: American Houses for the New Century*), they could find only three New York architects with houses actually built or under construction that deserved any such adjective: Toshiko Mori, Steven Holl and Michael McDonough, with his cyberspatial "e-House2000" (for Energy, the Environment and Exciting) in the upper Hudson Valley near New Paltz, built with SCADA software enabling the owner to (among other techie things) turn on the dishwasher from Tokyo. Two years before 9/11, contemporary American art, which in market terms had never recovered from the stock-market

and commercial real-estate nose dives of the early 1990's, went into sleep mode. Since the Brooklyn Museum's noisy Sensations show (all Brits) in 1999, the only thing causing anybody in the art world to open even one eye has been the wildfire rumor of a Guerrilla Art happening known as "Meat Shower" in a Brooklyn loft, at which brave and doggedly unclothes-conscious art worldlings ventured into a room wherein rained a drizzle of raw meat droplets created by high-speed electric deli knives shaving sides of beef. A full four years before 9/11, New York law enforcement had entered a new time zone: the epoch of the Latino cop. Irish cops still dominated the upper and older ranks of the NYPD, and they would show the world their legendary courage once again on 9/11, but the new legends were Latin. As a member of the brass at 1 Police Plaza, Irish himself, put it: "We still recruit Irish cops, but half of them are from the suburbs. These days, if you want a real old-fashioned Irish cop, you hire a Puerto Rican."

Eight years before 9/11, financial services and commercial real estate were superseded as driving forces in the New York economy by the restaurants appearing in boldface in Zagat's. The exodus of corporations from New York during the near-depression of 1992-95 was stanched by a single thing: lunch. The CEO's would do anything rather than give up the daily celebrations of their eminence at eateries in the town where the wining and dining were as good azagats. (I know, I know; just read it out loud.) The case could be made that any post-9/11 federal appropriations to prop up business in New York should go first to the places where you can get Chilean sea bass with a

Georgia plum marmalade glaze on a bed of mashed Hayman potatoes laced with leeks, broccoli rabe and emulsion of braised Vidalia onions infused with Marsala vinegar.

Four months before 9/11, figures came in to back up what every teacher and principal in the public-school system already knew: New York's great new wave of immigration is not black or Latino, much less Middle Eastern or European, but Asian, and especially Southeast Asian. Over the decade of the 1990's, the number of white students declined 10 percent (367,000 to 357,000), while the number of black students rose 4 percent (354,000 to 367,000), Hispanic students 22 percent (325,000 to 397,000)—and Asian students 67 percent (73,000 to 122,000). Brainy tyros they were, too. Each newly created trade school in the system had to enroll its share of students with subpar reading scores. Old hands knew that the trick was, in the words of one assistant principal, to "go down the lists and check off every Asian name you come to. If they have low scores, all that means is they just came through Immigration. Give them six months, and they'll lift your whole boat for you."

At least three years before 9/11, the mating game in New York got turned on its head. By this past summer, the ratio of girls to boys in Manhattan was so girl-heavy (as first reported in *The Observer* in July) that boys no longer even bothered expending the time and energy required to chat girls up in bars. They just handed every likely lovely their business card and waited for the calls, which they got with an almost lust-busting inevitability. The mantra for such young men about town had always been "You can't be too rich or too thin." Last summer,

they were all enrolling in fitness centers that looked like cocktail lounges with Cybex machines, and the mantra went: "Pecs, abs, delts, lats, obliques, traps and quads—you can't be too rich or too ripped."

Now that's changed.

The changes to look for next? It's hard not to see them coming. The girls will either read *The Rules*, which say that girls must never ring up boys, or else move to Boston and Cambridge, where, for some reason, when Cupid strikes, the targets stay struck and get married. New York's Asians will finally become a bloc no politician can write off, which will be obvious to all when the mayors start making ritual visits—and they will—to the other side of the international date line. Meanwhile, Latinos will take their turn dominating the ranks of public employees, from the marriage-bureau clerks to the school principals, just like the Irish, Italians, Jews and African-Americans before them. The Asians will get theirs later. The artists and architects will finally shake the overvalued urge known as "style" and head in a revolutionary direction known as "content." The cabby and the shrink will be succeeded as New York characters by the house-call computer swami and the diversity consultant. The bond market will become a heaving crap shoot, and the line bankers, as well as the I-bankers, will have themselves a boom with esoteric instruments such as Joshua Tree Federal 10-years. (I didn't say when.) The aging, flimsy glass-box office buildings of midtown and lower Manhattan will house artists' studios. (Nice light, but don't give up your lease in Jersey City yet.)

One thing won't change: lunch.

2002

Rudy Giuliani leaves the city to his designated mayor Michael Bloomberg ...

 ... who promises to bring a trimmer New York into the 21st century

Susan Lyne takes helm at ABC

George Pataki enters the elite group of three term N.Y. governors

New Yorkers stop cooking, go crazy for raw meats and vegetables

Jerry Seinfeld builds private garage on West Side for fleet of Porsches

Ann Coulter says that "you're never going to get rid of liberals altogether"

 We attend the wedding of Liza Minnelli and David Gest

2002

◇◇◇◇◇◇◇

JANUARY 7, 2002 BY GREG SARGENT

MIKE'S ICY INAUGURAL: BLOOMBERG SIGNS ON, ASKING FOR SACRIFICE

ON AN INAUGURATION Day charged with anxiety about the city's future and uncertainty about the abilities of its new chief executive, Mayor Michael Bloomberg offered the first hints of his leadership style, suggesting that he would subject the city government to the same sort of treatment that chainsaw-wielding CEO's bring to bloated corporations. He vowed to cut mayoral staff by 20 percent and challenged the public advocate, city comptroller and City Council to do the same—a pronouncement that didn't exactly inspire his bundled-up listeners to leap to their feet. Many of them, after all, work for the City of New York.

"We will not be able to afford everything we want; we will not even be able to afford everything we currently have," Mr. Bloomberg said.

Standing on a broad platform built atop the steps of City Hall, Mr. Bloomberg often seemed awkward and nervous, his head swiveling mechanically back and forth between two Plexiglas teleprompters that hovered at eye level on either side of the podium. The speech was larded with the sort of rhetoric one might expect from a second-tier candidate for student-council president, not the newly inaugurated mayor of New York:

"We will go forward; we will never go back."

"We can never abandon our future."

Meanwhile, there were signs everywhere that the third branch of municipal government—that is, the reporters who inhabit Room 9—was already trying to retake territory it lost during the Giuliani years.

Verbal scuffles broke out between reporters and harried Bloomberg aides. At one point, a reporter and a Bloomberg aide wrestled over a plastic cup brought in for the festivities; the goodies weren't for members of the press, the aide said.

At another point, a Bloomberg aide tried in vain to banish a group of reporters to a small space out of the way of visiting dignitaries.

"This is not the fucking Giuliani administration," one reporter snapped at the aide. "Things have changed now. It's morning in New York."

JANUARY 7, 2002 BY JASON GAY

NYTV: The Not-Quite-So-Idiotic Box: Television's Triumphant Return

HAS ANY INDUSTRY ENJOYED A BIGGER POST–SEPT. 11 REPRIEVE than television? Just four months ago, television as we had known it was presumed to be in its final lap, gray and limping for the home stretch, soon to be surpassed by delivery via the Internet, by broadband, by service on demand. So certain we were of the medium's imminent obsolescence that the very act of watching TV the old-fashioned way—sitting down on the couch for the early evening news or, heavens, a Thursday-night sitcom—had taken on an air of ritualized retro-quaintness, like drawing a bath or listening to a record by phonograph.

And then suddenly there we were, riveted, like we thought we'd never be again. News, of course, was the catalyst. Had anyone thought they'd see another moon walk, another television event that would match that 1963 bulletin from Dallas? Television felt as important as ever; the vaunted "shared experience" had returned. It also was in better shape than expected: Today's networks and correspondents, considered vapid underachievers compared to their forebears, managed to perform capably under trying circumstances.

A couple weeks back, Tim Russert had Jack Welch on his CNBC program, and television's reinvigoration came up. Mr. Welch, the former CEO of General Electric, the owner of NBC, had been a noted television hand-wringer: He was someone who could remember Edward R. Murrow's ashtray, and yet was utterly convinced of the medium's frailty. He had embraced the Internet, and rumors were persistent that he would have sold NBC to someone for the right price. And then there he was, three or so months after the attacks on New York and Washington, rhapsodizing the cathode.

"Television has a real place. It brings—it tells a story in a way nothing else does," Mr. Welch said. "Now, obviously, the Internet's going to have an enormous impact on regular communications and on other things, but it will become tied together. But you need the content, you need that to tell that story. You need to let people feel the emotion of what's happening when real stories break. And that's what television can do better than anything else."

JANUARY 31, 2002
BY GEORGE GURLEY

TALK STOPS, TO STUNNED SILENCE

THIS HAS BEEN A ROUGH SEA-son in the print media, but few were surprised by the deflation and slow settling to ground of the grand balloon known as *Talk*.

For like some turn-of-the-century hot-air balloon, there was something unwieldy about *Talk*: It didn't travel as fast as other, more modern forms of communication, or as fast as it should have to match its editor's aviatrix-like instincts. And as others of its style began losing air and drunkenly spiraling down, *Talk*'s short flight looked imperiled as well, despite the truly glittering smile of its captain, who continued to wave and express confidence all the while in its incessant descent until it dropped—*klump!*

◇◇◇◇◇◇◇◇

FEBRUARY 4, 2002
BY JASON GAY

NETWORK PRESIDENT PLANS TO RESTORE ABC'S HAPPIER DAYS

SUSAN LYNE, THE NEW PRESI-dent of ABC entertainment, was in a cheery mood. Ms. Lyne, 51, was sitting in her airy office on West 66th Street, mulling over ratings for the previous night's debut of *Rose Red*, a new Stephen King miniseries. The numbers looked solid.

But after riding Regis Philbin to ratings dominance in 2000 and early 2001, ABC's fortunes have fizzled. The network is currently mired behind CBS and NBC, and tangling with Fox for third place.

FEBRUARY 4, 2002 BY GEORGE GURLEY

How to Schwing Your Way Onto *Saturday Night Live*

AMY POEHLER, ONE OF the newest cast members of *Saturday Night Live*, was having lunch at Serafina on Lafayette Street. She wore a red sweater and jeans, said "Yes, sir" to the waiter and referred to me once as "the gentleman."

I told Ms. Poehler if I asked a question she didn't like, she could say "skip."

"'What's your bra size?'" Ms. Poehler said, erupting. "Skip! That's your first question: 'How do you like to do it?'"

After 11 episodes of *SNL*, Ms. Poehler, 30, is becoming more visible, appearing in as many as five sketches a show. But when she took a knitting class recently, the teacher was suspicious. The teacher asked Ms. Poehler: "They introduce you in the beginning?"

Recently, however, she had opened a bank account at Citibank, and the guy at the bank was impressed. "He goes, '*Saturday Night Live*! How'd you schwing that?'" Ms. Poehler said. "And I'm like, 'How did I schwing it? I just schwung it.'"

Ms. Poehler grew up in Massachusetts. Her parents were schoolteachers.

"My mother took too many Valiums and smashed the mirror," she said in a fake theatrical voice. "My father came downstairs, and he said, 'You stupid drunk,' and slapped her. And I ran to take the car and meet the teenage hoodlum by the Dairy Queen, and I got pregnant by my professor, robbed a liquor store. And I used to throw up in empty milk cartons and hide them under my bed."

She was kidding around, of course. Ms. Poehler attended Boston College, joined an improv troupe, got hooked and moved to Chicago in 1993 to study at Second City. She lived cheaply, rode her bike everywhere, did catering.

"I was never desperate," she said. "I sucked dick by choice, not by necessity."

In 1995, Ms. Poehler's group—the four-person Upright Citizens Brigade—moved to Manhattan, found an old burlesque theater, put on crazy fake heads and handed out fliers on Astor Place. U.C.B. turned into a major hit. Ms. Poehler still performs on Sunday nights at U.C.B.'s West 22nd Street theater, in an improv show called "A.S.S.S.S.A.T." She now lives in Tribeca, with two dogs and a boyfriend.

I had an "homage to Amy" I found on the Internet. Some guy had written a poem: "Methinks you truly are a goddess/ Thou are likened to a flower/ I hope I don't make you nauseous."

Ms. Poehler scanned the poem. "I like this," she said. "Oh, my! Wow, that's very nice. My father loves to, like, check out the news groups and tell me about it, and finally I'll just be like, 'I can't, I don't want to hear anymore about it,'" Ms. Poehler continued. "News groups are brutal: 'What's up with the ugly girl?!!! Her face looks like ...' or 'I'd fuck her, but only from behind!'"

Ms. Poehler said she's learned how to deal with fame, but she still gets annoyed. "There are certain professions where people feel like if they wanted to, they could do [it], which they could never do," she said. "Especially *SNL*–everyone's grown up with it, they've seen it, they have big opinions about it, and they think that you want to hear them. It's like, everybody I know that is successfully working has worked really hard and really paid their dues. I guess as you get older, it's like"—and here Ms. Poehler switched to a crazy-old-lady voice—"'I used to stand outside in Chicago 10 years ago and hand out fliers and nobody came.'"

Ms. Poehler paused. "It's like the banker guy asking me, 'How did you schwing that?'" she said. "Oh, I guess I worked 10 years to get on the show. I guess I gave up making money for 10 years. I guess I decided not to do what you did, which was to have a steady job and own a house. I gave up 10 years of that—so I guess that's how I schwung it."

MARCH 11, 2002 *BY FRANK DIGIACOMO*

THE OLD GIRLS' NETWORK

AT THE DRAMA LEAGUE'S ANNUAL GALA ON FEB. 25, singer Elaine Stritch stood on the stage of the Pierre Hotel's Grand Ballroom and talked about a good friend of hers. "She treats this town like Grover's Corners in *Our Town*," the 77-year-old Ms. Stritch said in her rat-a-tat-tat way. "She wafts her way in and out of Le Cirque like it was Starbucks, and she goes to Starbucks like it was '21.'"

Ms. Stritch was referring to gossip columnist Liz Smith, who was being saluted that night at the Drama League's annual benefit gala, but Ms. Stritch could have been toasting any of the Ladies Who Lunch in this town. And they deserve it. At this moment, when the alpha males who dominated the 80's and 90's are petering out, the grown-up women of Manhattan are surging once again.

New York is Biddy City—and before the Merriam-Websters start sailing this way, we mean that as a compliment. ABC News doyenne Barbara Walters, 70, and her colleague Diane Sawyer, 56, are knocking elbows over A-list interviews like it was the 90's; 79-year-old columnist Liz Smith is typing as fast as she can to bring the world scoops about Liza Minnelli's sideshow wedding. And Texas transplant (and former governor) Ann Richards moved to Manhattan with her own Biddy Creed: "Here's what I think about power. The more you give away, the more you get."

These women—and there are many more of them—are supplying this momentarily cold town with some welcome hot flashes. They set the agenda for what we discuss at cocktail parties, which media we consume and to which charities we give our disposable income.

So who's a Biddy? *New York Post* gossip columnist Cindy Adams is;

so is *WWD* Suzy columnist Aileen Mehle. So is Helen Gurley Brown. Real-estate mogul Elizabeth Stribling is a Biddy broker. Lynn Nesbit is a Biddy book agent. Former Texas governor Ann Richards is the new Biddy on the block. Socialite Brooke Astor is Biddy emeritus. Kitty Carlisle Hart is Biddy (ret.). Homemaking mogul Martha Stewart swings between Biddydom and alpha-girl tendencies, Wendy Wasserstein is the Biddy Boswell, and *The New York Times'* Alex Kuczynski is a Biddy in training. Rosie O'Donnell and Liza Minnelli aren't Biddies, but they are Biddy pets. Journalist Alex Witchel has the hottest novel on the Biddy circuit: *Me Times Three*, blurbed by Ms. Wasserstein and sexy Biddy Sarah Jessica Parker. Publicist Peggy Siegal is destined to become a Biddy. The recently departed Pauline Trigère was one of the original Biddies. Tina Brown was an alpha girl, but if she wants to—which she may not—she'll be reborn as a Biddy. Lincoln Center chair Beverly Sills was a Biddy who is looking more and more like a sputtering alpha girl. Male biddies? New York's got 'em. Phi Beta charmer and Sony chief executive Howard Stringer is among the most successful male Biddies. So is Barry Diller, as long as he's not screaming at someone in the office. *Vanity Fair* editor in chief Graydon Carter is a north-of-the-border Biddy. Mort Zuckerman is a Biddy, too, although he dreams about being an alpha boy. And the city's new mayor? Well, he does have Biddy tendencies. Biddies love to socialize, giving lie to the old Mark Twain adage that the wonderful part of old age is that you don't have to go out.

The patron saint of Biddyhood is Clare Boothe Luce, the author of *The Women*. Ms. Stritch—who's a Biddy—starred, along with Gloria Swanson, in a version of the play from which she was expelled in Warren, Ohio, and she's got a hilarious Biddy-laden story to tell about that experience in her show. For some time now, the Biddy Empress has been Ms. Walters, although she would never admit it. Through a spokesman, she declined to be interviewed for this article—which, to be fair to everyone who did talk to us, was characterized as a piece about grown-up women and power, not a feature on Biddy City.

Still, more than one person interviewed by *The Observer* recalled a 1996 *New York Times* piece by Judith Miller which intimated that Ms. Walters could eventually become the doyenne of New York society when Mrs. Astor relinquishes the role. The notion that Ms. Walters—who does precious little charity and board work because it might conflict with her reporting duties—could unite a modern social world that boasts as many niches as Time Warner's DTV has channels is a sign of how masterfully she wields her power.

And, well, Ms. Miller certainly turned out to be prescient when it came to anthrax.

MARCH 11, 2002 BY TOM MCGEVERAN

Seinfeld Builds a Parking Lot

TEN YEARS AGO THERE was a *Seinfeld* episode in which George Costanza was locked in an all-night parking siege over one crummy space, spurring a comparative consideration of the "pulling in versus backing in" approaches to parking. That same season there were episodes called "The Parking Garage" and "The Alternate Side."

Now Jerry Seinfeld seems to have resolved his parking obsession by building his own lot. He's planning 20 parking spaces, in his own garage, for his private collection of Porsches—in one of the best neighborhoods in Manhattan—for about $1.39 million.

Seismographs have already been set up on West 83rd Street between Columbus and Amsterdam avenues to guarantee the integrity of the neighbors' buildings.

Already two years in the making, the garage at 138 West 83rd Street—just three blocks from Mr. Seinfeld's $4.35 million duplex at the Beresford apartments—has faced delays, fines, denied permits and a neighborhood in need of placating ... all of which is nothing compared to the peace of mind that the semi-retired sitcom king will attain once he no longer has to get up at 7 a.m. to move the Boxster.

◇◇◇◇◇◇◇◇

MARCH 25, 2002 BY SIMON DOONAN

SIMON SAYS: COOKING IS SO TOTALLY OVER! NEW YORKERS LIKE IT RAW

THE NEO-HIPPIE MOVEMENT shows no signs of going away. Last year, it was the infernal Bikram sweaty-yoga craze; this year, New Yorkers are still cooking their bodies—but they've stopped cooking their food altogether.

With two restaurants and a catering service in Manhattan, the Quintessence mini-empire is the epicenter of the Manhattan raw lifestyle. I headed to the 10th Street branch, where I scrutinized the menu for clues and found the following screed: "We believe that by eating uncooked food long enough, we will regain the fifth element and the mystical

powers of our ancestors."

I tracked down one of the three owners, a Chinese lady who goes by the *Lord of the Rings*-ish name of Tolentin Chan, and found her less than keen to talk about that "fifth element" or her ancestral mystical powers. She was, however, a lot clearer about the overall benefits of raw food than some of her Seventh Avenue clients.

"I ate a standard American diet, and my health was terrible," said Tolentin, who in her pre-raw days suffered from asthma, thyroid problems and continuous colds. "Starch and dairy had coated my lungs with mucus."

MARCH 25, 2002 BY REX REED

Welcome to My Pew

LIZA FINALLY DID IT.

The fourth time, she got it right. The white and silver engraving on the invitation read: "Because you have shared in our lives by your friendship and love, we, LIZA MAY MINNELLI and DAVID ALAN GEST, invite you to share the beginning of our new life together when we exchange marriage vows on Saturday, the sixteenth of March, Two Thousand and Two, at five o'clock in the afternoon."

Since no cameras were allowed to provide photographic memories, I'm holding on to mine. I have to. I may never be invited to anything like this again. O.K., so Elizabeth Taylor demanded a Lear jet and couldn't get out of her chair; Chaka Khan requested a $300 per diem and got 86'd; and Whitney Houston got replaced by Natalie Cole as the wedding singer. O.K., so at a time when restraint has become mandatory, the words "gross" and "excess" emanated sotto voce from the church pews. O.K., so the guest list promised two presidents (Gerry and Bill), one senator (Hillary) and two mayors (Mike and Rudy), and none

of them showed up. O.K., so the groom ran the show and the bride didn't know half of the guests—not to mention most of her own bridesmaids. O.K., so "The Event of the Year" was maybe more like "The Event of the Year—So Far." (It's only March.) I'm here to tell you that when I arrived a block from ground zero on Saturday night, entered a rose-filled ballroom that used to be the first New York Stock Exchange and saw Martha Stewart dancing with Donny Osmond to the blasting "live" music of Little Anthony and the Imperials, with Margaret O'Brien on one side of the floor and Lauren Bacall on the other, I knew we weren't in Kansas anymore. On the curb, I overheard two jaded New York cops behind me: "How long do you give it?" "Six months or 5,000 miles—whatever comes first." I wouldn't bet on it. Knowing Liza, this story is just beginning.

In the cab home, Barbra Streisand (who declined her invitation) was singing into the New York dawn: So long, sad times. Go long, bad times. Happy days are here again. ...

MARCH 17, 2002 BY KATE KELLY

Danny Pearl, Reporter

DANIEL PEARL TOLD friends he was coming home. Pakistan was going to be his final fling with foreign journalism, he said; his wife, Mariane, was pregnant, and they were ready to rejoin the rhythm of American life.

"This was his victory lap," said Jeffrey Sonnenfeld, an associate dean at the Yale School of Management, who had befriended Mr. Pearl when the latter was a reporter in *The Wall Street Journal*'s Atlanta bureau and Mr. Sonnenfeld was teaching at Emory University. "He was almost done. This story ... he could have passed on it, and almost did. That's what makes it so tragic. I don't think he thought it was going to be risky."

And though a spokesperson for Dow Jones, *The Journal*'s parent company, said that there were no plans for Mr. Pearl to return to the U.S., sources said they understood he would be leaving Pakistan soon. On the day he was captured, Mr. Pearl spoke with a colleague who told him to drop the assignment he was working on—he was reporting on Islamic militants—and "get ready to come home."

He never got home, of course. And the kidnapping and execution of Daniel Pearl became a mournful event for the country, and a seismic event in journalism.

It had already been a grim month for *The Journal*, not to mention a grueling six-month stretch since the Sept. 11 attacks drove the paper from its downtown offices. When the news of Mr. Pearl's killing came, on Feb. 21, the Washington offices of the paper, where Mr. Pearl spent three years, was getting ready for a rare celebration: *WSJ* managing editor Paul Steiger was flying in to accept the Editor of the Year award from the National Press Foundation, and the staff

was supposed to have drinks in the newsroom at 5:30 p.m. before the black-tie event.

The day before, the world had learned that Washington bureau chief Alan Murray was leaving *The Journal*, his home for 18 years, to go to CNBC. In the early afternoon, Mr. Murray was taking down books from his shelves and packing. At 2 p.m., Dow Jones vice president Steve Goldstein came by to tell Mr. Murray what he'd learned: that the F.B.I. had contacted officials at Dow Jones with news of a videotape showing that Mr. Pearl had been killed.

To buy time for notifying the family and to prevent leaks to the press, Mr. Murray pretended that nothing was wrong. He kept packing. Later, he said this act

was "hard, but it gave me something to do."

At 4:15, Mr. Steiger arrived and spoke to Mr. Murray briefly in his office, then told the Washington staff what had happened. He spoke of the man Mr. Pearl was, of the "barbarism" of his death. Mr. Murray, in place of Mr. Steiger, put on his tuxedo and dragged members of his staff to the awards at the Washington Hilton, where they attended the ceremony and drank "way too much," then kept drinking in the hotel bar until Friday morning. A similar scene was being played out in New York, in a Soho bar, as those who knew Mr. Pearl gathered to drink and share stories of his life.

"He was the wrong guy in every respect for this," Mr. Murray said.

"He wasn't interested in danger. He wasn't a great patriot, and wasn't overly jingoistic in his writing. Folks in the bureau referred to him as 'Danny of Arabia.' We thought he'd gone native because he was so sympathetic and empathetic to that part of the world."

Since the initial report, the videotape of Mr. Pearl's killing, unseen here, has become the focus of scrutiny. The reports of its contents first appeared in the papers here on Saturday, Feb. 23, with a description of Mr. Pearl speaking and having his throat cut in mid-sentence. Later, a severed head appears. This was modified in the next day's newspapers, which reported that Mr. Pearl was forced to make a statement—"I am a Jew, my father is a Jew, my mother is a

> *But because Mr. Pearl didn't make it, didn't have a chance to win over his captors as people thought he might, the struggle to define his legacy has begun.*

Jew"—followed by a jump in the videotape and a shot showing Mr. Pearl unconscious, with what appeared to be a chest wound. The tape then seemed to have been stopped and started again as his captors videotaped his throat being cut. Then there was a last sequence in which his captors videotaped his severed head next to his body. According to one reporter working on the story, the initial accounts of the videotape came from Pakistani officials, including some who had seen copies of the tape. But it also came from others who were repeating second- or third-hand accounts, filling in the void of information while American officials refused to discuss its contents.

The reporter said the second, more accurate accounts originated in the United States, from law-enforcement officers seeking to correct the record, then were confirmed by Pakistani officials with more detailed knowledge.

No one knows what Mr. Pearl felt in those last hours and days. One former war correspondent, held by enemy forces in another war, described his captivity: "What

you feel is terror and guilt. After the initial fear goes, you feel guilty because of your family—especially your family. You start to think about your death and realize they may never know where your body is. Then the stupidity sets in. You think, 'Jesus Christ, how could I do something so dumb?'"

But because Mr. Pearl didn't make it, didn't have a chance to win over his captors as people thought he might, the struggle to define his legacy has begun. Because he was killed in a Muslim country, in a hot spot of unrest, Mr. Pearl has been transformed into a war correspondent, inextricably linked with the nine others killed in Afghanistan since the conflict started last fall.

Indeed, only the day after the revelation, *New York Times* columnist Nicholas Kristof wrote, "I didn't know Danny Pearl, but I feel as if I did." Mr. Kristof went on to detail his interactions over the years with war correspondents rushing off to cover the Congo civil war, and a journalist desperate to cover the Afghanistan conflict, ready to don a burqa and enter the country dressed as a woman. His death, Mr. Kristof wrote, was supposed to teach us "about the need to take a deep breath before allowing competitive instincts to direct us down a dirt track toward an uncertain story on the other side of a checkpoint manned by drunken soldiers."

It should be noted, though, that Mr. Pearl was nowhere near a front line or checkpoint manned by idiots drinking during their shift. As Mr. Murray put it: "He didn't want to be a war correspondent. The story he wrote about the town making the world's largest carpet in India, that was the kind of story he was in it for."

And as new information sur-

faces on how his captors lured him, Mr. Pearl seems less and less like a classic risk-taking front-line war correspondent. In e-mails from his abductors obtained by the *London Sunday Express* and printed in the Sunday, Feb. 24, edition of the *New York Post*, they make the interview he sought seem harmless, a formality. One dated Jan. 16 compliments him on his articles, saying: "I enjoyed reading them and I have passed them on the printout to Shah Saab [Gilani]. He has now gone to Karachi for a few days and I am sure that when he returns we can go and see him. I am sorry to have not replied to you earlier, I was preoccupied with looking after my wife who has been ill. Please pray for her health."

As Mr. Sonnenfeld put it: "He was going to a Western-sounding restaurant to meet somebody anchored in English. He had originally planned on taking Mariane. He wouldn't put her in jeopardy. He'd been set up for this."

And perhaps that's what hurts here. Take away Pakistan and the "war on terror" and what you have at its most rudimentary level is a writer betrayed by a source. In this light, Mr. Pearl becomes less like, say, Claude Cockburn, charging into the Spanish Civil War, and more like Bob Woodward, standing in a deserted parking lot, waiting for someone to deliver him the goods on Nixon.

"Here was a case," said Michael Massing, a board member on the Committee to Protect Journalists, "where a journalist was targeted because he was a journalist, because he was working on a specific type of story and because he was Jewish."

Of course, Mr. Pearl's death came at a time when this city's journalists, no longer earning

their bread and butter from stories chronicling Pets.com, had already begun to question what their livelihoods should mean. After all, we are only slightly removed from a time in which, as author David Halberstam said, "feather merchants were the most visible, and the rewards for doing sillier things and self-promoting were far greater than people covering Sierra Leone."

Those who spent the days after Sept. 11 running around with police ID badges and shaking the dust off of their clothes could claim the world had changed that day. But that's only because the events of the world—the real world—had come to New York. But Daniel Pearl had already left his country for it.

"He had an intense desire to find bridges between cultures," Mr. Sonnenfeld said. "He thought he needed to round himself out. He had gone to Washington"—from the *WSJ*'s Atlanta bureau in 1993—"to understand policy issues. He thought if he was going to understand globalization, he would have to live outside the U.S."

For his part, Mr. Murray had vehemently tried to dissuade Mr. Pearl from accepting a job on the paper's foreign desk in 1996. It had nothing to do with danger, he said. Instead, he told Mr. Pearl that he had a real future as a telecom reporter. The technology boom had already begun. There'd be plenty of stories in a very hot field. If he stayed, he told Mr. Pearl, there would be "be books in it and maybe more."

"He could have made a great career for himself doing that," Mr. Murray said. "He could have been our Ken Auletta. I really wanted him to stay. But he wanted to get out of Washington and report on the world."

APRIL 29, 2002   BY ALEXANDRA JACOBS

Clench Buttocks and Talk!

ON THE UNSEASON-ably hot April Thursday that *The Nanny Diaries* reached No. 3 on the *New York Times* best-seller list, media coach Joyce Newman was in an Upper East Side diner sipping iced tea, eating tuna salad and preening like a cockatoo.

"I want to show you what they wrote me," Ms. Newman said, pushing a copy of *The Nanny Diaries* across the table.

The inscription, in a girlish script, read: "To Joyce—our savior. You are the Easter Bunny, our Fairy Godmother, & Santa Claus rolled into one truly awesome teacher—we would be tongue-tied without you."

The long list of authors who have submitted to Ms. Newman's ministrations include Katie Roiphe, Simon & Schuster editor in chief Michael Korda and Helen Fielding, author of the blockbuster *Bridget Jones's Diary.*

A quick survey of the old school ran the gamut from unfamiliarity to dismay.

"What a terrible idea, oh dear," said John Updike.

"To tell the truth, I never heard the term before," said Tom Wolfe.

"I don't have, and never would think of having, a media coach," said Gay Talese. Told that Michael Korda had used one, he said: "But of course, he's a Hollywood guy!"

◇◇◇◇◇◇◇

APRIL 15, 2002   BY GEORGE GURLEY

THE BEST AND WORST MEN'S ROOMS IN NEW YORK CITY (AFTER MIDNIGHT)

THE BEST:

The Stanhope Park Hyatt
New York, Fifth Avenue at East 81st Street. Use the one by the bar. Nice and clean. Hotels are good in general, especially all those along Central Park South. Get in there no problem, sit down, kick back for 45 minutes.

Bungalow 8
West 27th Street between 10th and 11th avenues. Perhaps the best in Manhattan. Four private rooms, one of them big enough to take a nap on the floor. Dark in there. We like the black toilets with the dark toilet water. No one's gonna bang on the door because the cigarette girl outside will stop them. Take your time.

THE WORST:

The Village Idiot
14th Street between Eighth and Ninth avenues. No lock. Outhouse feel. Slidey floor. Vile.

Subway Inn
60th Street and Lexington Avenue. You come close to vomiting from the smell. Wear gloves, do not sit down. Real cheap drinks there, though.

Plug Uglies
Third Avenue between 20th and 21st streets. No lock. No stall. No privacy. Cop bar. Look out. Do whatever you gotta do fast.

The Liquor Store Bar
Corner of West Broadway and White Street. Only one bathroom. Big problem. Someone's always knocking on the door.

APRIL 29, 2002   BY TOM MCGEVERAN & DEBORAH NETBURN

MANHATTAN TRANSFERS: SOPRANOS SUBURB?

"THE DIFFERENCE BETWEEN you and me," shouts Carmela Soprano at her husband, Tony, on the HBO series, "is I'm going to heaven when I die."

The difference between the actors—Edie Falco, who plays Carmela, and James Gandolfini, who plays Tony—is now about five blocks, since both have recently purchased property in the far West Village.

On March 8, Mr. Gandolfini closed a deal to buy a 1,367-square-foot condo at 99 Jane Street. The purchase was made just three days before he filed for divorce from his wife, Marcy.

At just about the same time, Edie Falco bought a townhouse at 97 Barrow Street, between Hudson and Greenwich streets.

Though Ms. Falco made a bigger investment, the Jane Street condo is just the smallest piece of

Mr. Gandolfini's rapidly expanding real-estate empire spanning lower Manhattan and northern New Jersey—though all that might soon have to be divided with his wife.

In January of last year, Mr. Gandolfini bought a historic farmhouse in Chester Township, N.J. Three months later, the Gandolfinis reportedly moved from an apartment in the Village to a three-bedroom loft on Greenwich Street in Tribeca.

But Mr. Gandolfini seems to have missed the Village. Last July, he made a $300,000 deposit on an 1842 Greek revival brownstone at 138 West 13th Street, with a separate, small 1920's cottage at the back of the lot. The house belonged to Ethan Hawke and Uma Thurman, and when the deal unraveled, Mr. Gandolfini sued the couple for the deposit money.

Elvis Costello, master of pop and pain

JUNE 20, 2002 BY GREG SARGENT

The Rudy Team Has '04 Dream: Bush-Giuliani

BRUCE TEITELBAUM, RUDY Giuliani's most trusted political adviser, sidled up to a veteran New York operative recently and made a bold pronouncement.

"Bruce said, very openly, that if Rudy Giuliani wants it, he'll be the Republican Party's vice presidential nominee in 2004," the operative told *The Observer*. "And he said that he thinks Giuliani is going to be running in 2008 for president."

A mere six months after Mr. Giuliani left City Hall, there are increasing signs that he is seeking to ride his post–Sept. 11 popularity all the way to the White

House. Even as his allies boost his prospects among insiders, Mr. Giuliani has launched an open-ended national campaign, build-

ing a base in the Republican Party by stumping for candidates across the country and becoming one of the most effusive advocates for Mr. Bush.

Since leaving office, Mr. Giuliani has discussed his performance under fire before scores, if not hundreds, of audiences. It's a subject he never tires of addressing. It figures prominently in speeches and in commercials for Republican candidates across the country.

"Not forgetting it means not forgetting what actually happened," he said, "as opposed to some highly euphemistic version of it."

◇◇◇◇◇◇

JUNE 17, 2002 BY BLAIR GOLSON

MANHATTAN TRANSFERS: VILLAGE SWANK

MAY 20, 2002 BY JASON GAY

THE EVOLUTION OF JIMMY KIMMEL

"THIS MAY MAKE ME SOUND like a dickhead," said Jimmy Kimmel, "but I am not surprised at all. In fact, I was disappointed that it took this long."

It was Monday, May 13, and Mr. Kimmel, 34, was talking from his office in Los Angeles, where in a few hours he would hop a plane bound for New York City. The next day, the scruffy-cheeked ex–radio D.J. turned tele-chauvinist would step triumphantly onto the stage at the New Amsterdam Theater in Times Square to be crowned late-night television's Latest Shiny New Object. ABC had signed Mr. Kimmel to do a comedy show after *Nightline*, one to replace the never-really-worked Bill Maher and *Politically Incorrect*.

Mr. Kimmel had spent the past three years blowing up as host of Comedy Central's *The Man Show*, the weekly, wild testosterone release in which he and toothy co-host Adam Carolla, cheered on by an eager, beer-swilling audience, riffed upon subjects like urination, masturbation and farting while surrounded by half-naked side-kickettes called the "Juggies." Seen as a he-man rebuke of 90's political correctness, *The Man Show* was not high art. On one *Man Show* skit, a shirtless Mr. Kimmel—all 191 pounds of him—had dry-humped a live chimpanzee.

Now he will follow Ted Koppel.

WHEN THE CASTING CALL WENT OUT FOR WHAT WOULD eventually become the Oscar-winning film *Boys Don't Cry*, Hilary Swank was a Hollywood hopeful with little but her starring role in the fourth installment of the *Karate Kid* franchise under her belt—and barely enough money to make the round-trip flight to New York for the audition. She and husband Chad Lowe (Rob *frère*) have had no shortage of access to remunerative roles: She got her start as a ditzy minor player in the 1992 movie *Buffy the Vampire Slayer*; he's been on *Melrose Place*. But it was her performance as the transgender Nebraska teenager Brandon Teena and subsequent (though less notable) efforts—the fizzled bodice-ripper *The Affair of the Necklace*, the supernatural thriller *The Gift*—that seem to have made the 27-year-old actress' financial circumstances more comfortable: She's now preparing, with Mr. Lowe, to feather a cozy townhouse nest in Greenwich Village that came with a $4 million price tag.

"We always dreamed of having a place in New York," Ms. Swank told *The Observer*. "And as soon as I walked in, I knew this was it."

Ms. Swank and her husband recently signed a contract on this four-story residence on a tree-lined street. The house is full of original detail—from pocket doors and hardwood floors to etched moldings and multiple glass chandeliers. It has a large, landscaped garden, eat-in kitchen, wood-burning fireplace, and a large master bedroom with his-and-hers bathrooms. The house's parlor floor has a living room and library, and the children's floor has a large central skylight and kitchenette.

Both now seem to be hoping that the artistic mojo of the Village rubs off on them.

"It's all about balancing art and commerce," Mr. Lowe recently told a group of film students.

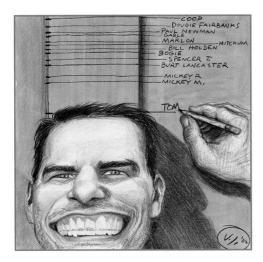

JUNE 24, 2002 BY JASON GAY

TOM'S CRUISE BLUES

AT THE ZIEGFELD THEATER ON MONDAY, JUNE 17—WHERE TOM Cruise's new movie, *Minority Report*, was getting the full premiere treatment—the red-carpet territory was calm until—*whoooosh!*—Jerry Maguire swooped in, shortish, friendly, black-suited, black-booted, scruffy, stubbly and looking like a World Cup goalkeeper. The place went nuts. Mr. Cruise poured himself into the willing crowd, clutching hands, swirling his name on glossy photos, flashing his midlife braces and sucking up so much Manhattan air that pretty much everyone else—including his boss, gray-bearded Steven Spielberg—had to feel a little oxygen-deprived.

He'll be 40 on July 3, and the media has generally agreed to state that he is the biggest star on the planet. Every one of his pictures is met with the deferential P.R. sound of non-rocking-the-boat commercial respect; the press is preconditioned to respect Mr. Cruise's professionalism and commercialism.

He looks great, he sounds great; sometimes you swear he even smells great. The 5-foot-7 Mr. Cruise is a little guy who doesn't play the little guy; he is popularity personified, and reminds no one of a person they ignored in high school.

Still, money and power and celebrity can be nasty buggers, and together they have conspired to trap Mr. Cruise in a neat box of fame that is good for the June 2002 market but possibly problematic for the actor himself over the long term. We are told repeatedly of how affable Mr. Cruise is by people who meet with him and know him, but to the public Mr. Cruise is now less a person than a fantastic performance car, fast and clean, with a controlled edge of recklessness. Mr. Cruise has become, essentially, a commodity, a living product placement.

He remains, on the cusp of his fifth decade, a youthful ideal, even as faint facial lines begin to appear and crow's feet form around his green eyes. He is, quite clearly, an adult, but still a tough sell as an adult. Perhaps this is why—rather than the knee-jerk belief that it would turn off audiences—Mr. Cruise has still yet to take that transformative role that allows boys to become men, as Paul Newman did with *The Hustler* and *Hud*.

JULY 15, 2002 BY JOE HAGAN

Martha Still Living

MARTHA STEWART may or may not wind up in deep trouble as a result of the current ImClone stock investigation, but the mess has already begun to impact a significant part of her media empire: print advertising.

Advertising drives *Martha Stewart Living*, so if the Krafts and Doves and Pepperidge Farms of the world decide to yank their ads, Omnimedia would be in for some serious pain.

Not surprisingly, Ms. Stewart's sales team is trying to stem the potential flow. According to several people who have met with ad reps from Ms. Stewart's magazines recently, the team is insisting that *Martha Stewart Living* is about the content of the magazine and not about the person—an argument that would have sounded ludicrous a month ago.

So far there are no measurable results upon *Martha Stewart Living* from June's onslaught of bad press.

Still, given their long lead time, ad buyers must now deliberate purchasing space in a magazine named after a woman who could be in serious straits by the time their advertisements appear. "If, in three months, she's really in deep shit, there could be a problem," said Joe Mandese, the editor of *Media Buyer's Daily*.

◇◇◇◇◇◇◇

JULY 22, 2002 BY STANLEY CROUCH

WHY I BUY HIS STORY

NO MATTER HOW ECCENTRIC Michael Jackson is, no matter how self-serving his charges might seem, he is bringing to the surface an old story, full of exploited figures, that is still very much alive—and among the lessons of his rise and fall from grace is a cold hard fact that black artists and entertainers have to grow up and realize: In show business nothing is guaranteed, regardless of the color of the person making the promise.

It was a little over a week ago that Mr. Jackson made the charge that the recording business is racist and that his case is about the essential nature of color prejudice. "If you're fighting for me, you're fighting for all black people, dead and alive," Mr. Jackson said.

What is most significant about Michael Jackson and his battle with Sony is what it says about the world we're still living in: When it comes to the music industry, even those who have brought in billions—even Michael Jackson—can find himself in a position to play the race card and deserve a hearing; the denigration of black people is far from over.

FEBRUARY 4, 2002 BY CLAY FELKER

CITY OF AMBITION WILL RISE FROM ASHES OF 9/11

AS THE HEAD OF CHASE MANHATTAN BANK, A GREAT International power, David Rockefeller's appointment book filled up as much as a year in advance. So I was surprised to receive an invitation to lunch with him at his headquarters near the southern tip of Manhattan.

It was the late 1960's, and his passion then was building the World Trade Center along with the governor at the time, his brother Nelson. I, on the other hand, was the editor at *New York* magazine, where we'd been questioning why the Port Authority wanted to engage in a real-estate project instead of improving mass transportation—its very reason for being. We were not alone. Local real-estate developers argued that the city had plenty of office space already and complained that the last thing they needed was a government agency to enter the game.

When I joined Mr. Rockefeller in his office at 1 Chase Manhattan Plaza, he took me to the window overlooking the construction site. Oddly enough, it looked much like ground zero today.

He understood that some people didn't share his vision, but he argued that it would be a great thing for the city, for the whole region. At lunch, he went into more persuasive detail. I was impressed with his commitment as a New Yorker to the future of the city as the great international financial capital it was.

But as we sat together, something else crossed my mind. Maybe he wanted to make his own mark, revitalizing lower Manhattan just as his brother Nelson had done to midtown with the construction of Rockefeller Center a few decades earlier.

Now the twin towers are no more, leaving us to wonder again about the direction of New York itself, the larger question whose answer will almost certainly tell us what to do with those 16 acres that, once more, stand nearly vacant.

It is becoming apparent that Lower Manhattan will not be the financial center that it was before. There is an inexorable movement away from it, not only to midtown or New Jersey, but also to the far-flung corners of an electronic world that no longer needs a grand metropolis from which to provide financial services.

As cruel as it has been, a disaster on the scale of Sept. 11 can be looked upon as an opportunity to recast the future. San Francisco, for one, has had its share of devastating earthquakes and fires, but emerged each time with new vitality and a new identity.

The economic promise of New York lies in its historic ability to adapt and re-create itself. After all, the great port that first gave the city its dynamism was superseded by manufacturing, then by financial services. Now, another future beckons—if it isn't already here.

Where are we headed? A good guess would be that the divinations of men who understood the historical currents of their times point the way.

Some years ago, I went downtown to have lunch with Felix Rohatyn at the investment bank Lazard Freres. We were joined by the head of the company, the legendary and massively powerful Andre Meyer. The process of consolidation among financial firms was picking up speed,

It is becoming apparent that Lower Manhattan will not be the financial center that it was before. There is an inexorable movement away from it, not only to midtown or New Jersey, but also to the far-flung corners of an electronic world that no longer needs a grand metropolis from which to provide financial services.

and Mr. Meyer wanted to talk about it.

"No matter what happens," he said, "people will always need expert advice. And Lazard will still be here to give it, when most of these others have gone."

Another glimpse of the future came in a conversation Tom Wolfe and I had with the visionary of the electronic age, Marshall McLuhan. He told us that in the future New York (meaning Manhattan) would become Disneyland.

When one would ask for clarification of his startling oracular bulletins, Mr. McLuhan, in his typically mystical manner, would simply say, "They are only probes." But what he was driving at was that the business of Manhattan would overwhelmingly become tourism. With its great hotels, restaurants, entertainment, cultural institutions and shopping emporiums, the island would become an enclave where only the privileged—and the temporary—could afford to live.

I saw something like this happening to Paris when the great designer Milton Glaser and I were asked by the publisher of *Paris Match* and the daily newspaper *Le Figaro* about the possibility of starting a *New York*–style publication there. The cost of living in the French capital was driving most ordinary people to the suburbs or the outskirts—so much so that even the French Disneyland was located well outside the city.

When fate takes a hand and speeds up the future, as it did on Sept. 11, the dimly sketched outlines of what was already occurring stand out more clearly.

New York is not going to become Disneyworld, of course, and for the most critical financial transactions—especially the kind of deal-making that requires face-to-face negotiations—Manhattan will remain irreplaceable. But visitors coming here to spend money, either as tourists or business people, will ultimately edge out financial services as the city's economic engine.

Right now, New York is currently the recipient of wide admiration and sympathy. But those sentiments will undoubtedly revert to more normal geocentric attitudes, and people will focus on their own self-interest. The rest of the country is fond of saying, "We're all New Yorkers now."

But they're not.

New York's historic role has been that of an idea factory, where ingenious and capable people, packed together, take raw materials from around the globe and transform them into products and services they sell back to the rest of the world—at higher prices. Whether it's managing money, designing fashions, solving knotty legal or marketing problems, or translating ephemeral ideas into art and entertainment, New Yorkers thrive by charging high fees for their advice and services.

This commercial alchemy—the advice and ideas—depends on a critical mass of ambitious and highly creative people, and New York is home to more of them than probably any other metropolis in the world. It may cause outsiders to feel jealous or inferior. But they'll seek it out anyway, with all its irritating confidence and street smarts.

That's what New York does.

AUGUST 12, 2002 BY GEORGE GURLEY

BARE TOES CLOSING IN ... FEEL FAINT

GIRLS, LADIES, WOMen of the city: I know you love your open-toe shoes, and so do I. They're very sexy! I love everything about you: the hair, the eyes, the lips, the shoulders, the arms—and you know I'm fond of the breasts, not to mention the belly, the curves, the hips, the rump, the Brazilian bikini wax, the buttery thighs, all the way down to the ankles, and oh—it is all good.

Except for one thing. There's just one little problem, something you haven't quite picked up on: Your feet, your toes, displayed so proudly, stuffed into $500 strappies or $10 flip-flops as if on a pedestal for all to behold and admire ...

Well, they ain't so cute.

You may not know it, but in the male mind they can ruin the rest of your physical charms. Yes, your huge, bony, milky-white feet, with enormous, mangled, red-toenail-painted toes—those frightening, E.T. -shaped, elongated toes, those *Alien*-like talons spreading out and creeping over the edge of your black slides, slithering out like sea monsters to snatch innocents up off the sidewalk, or like the claws of prehistoric birds, ready to grab us by the neck and carry us aloft and dash us against the rocks. ... Ladies whom I love, we're talking dread-primal fear—much more harrowing than Mr. Freud's vagina dentata.

But women in New York City seem to be blissfully unaware of this fact. Why else would 98 percent of them be wearing open-toe shoes, not knowing (or caring) that only 10 percent of those exposed feet and toes are appetizing, while 25 percent are merely tolerable? Which leaves an awful lot that are ... *scary*!

Spend an afternoon walking around Manhattan's verdant park land, and you will see legions of women who have kicked off their flip-flops in order to show off grubby, filthy feet slimed with bacteria—and worse—after a day traipsing around midtown, in the grimy subway, in fetid cabs, in anonymous bathrooms. ... And now check out these same dogs laid out on the soft green grass or a chair, being offered up for all to see, gnarly toes wriggling around, cooking in the sun, like crabs crawling toward me. ...

Don't they know what men are thinking as they check a woman out from head to toe?

It was only about two years ago that I became like this. Before then, I could actually attend a summer cocktail party in the Hamptons without vomit making it to the back of my throat several times.

Take, for instance, a party thrown in East Hampton on July 26 for Marian Wright Edelman, the president of the Children's Defense Fund. The party had actually been promoted as a "barefoot" cocktail party. I went with the grim, masochistic fascination that drives men to test themselves against the absolute worst.

I wisely kept on my loafers and argyle socks. My date's feet were exposed.

She volunteered that the shiny white stuff on them was wart medicine.

"It's becoming," I said.

Back in Manhattan, I thought I'd be safe. I was wrong. More terrifying than the movie *Signs* was the party after the premiere, held at the Metropolitan Club. It was over 90 degrees outside, and inside was an open-toe-shoe horror show.

There was socialite actor Matthew Modine, wearing sideburns, a pinstripe suit and Birkenstock-like evening sandals. How were his wife's feet?

"Well, she has dancer's feet, which I think are beautiful," he said.

Joni Wilkins, a 37-year-old woman wearing Gucci open-toe shoes, approached and said what a great actor Mr. Modine was. How did she feel about his feet?

"They're nice feet—needs a little bit of a pedicure, but nice feet," she said.

Had she ever seen gross feet?

"Absolutely," she said. "Wiggy toes. Wiggy toes don't line up straight. Nasty. You can cram them into a Manolo, but they're still wiggy toes. Wiggy toes are not cool."

Mr. Modine looked at me. "You are really hung up on this gross-feet thing," he said. "When you were a little boy, did you have a grandma kick you around the house that had nasty feet?"

I didn't care for his jokes, so I went to talk to his wife, Cari Modine. Ms. Modine said her own feet were "destroyed."

"I would definitely describe my feet as those with character," she said. "I think when you have ugly feet and you show them anyway, it's indicative of something in you, I think it's pretty brave."

She started to bring her feet out from under the table. I braced myself: flip-flops. But her feet were ... fine! And I told her so.

"It's the lighting, honey," she said.

On the way out, I passed Mr. Modine again. I told him his wife had beautiful feet.

"You're a sick man," he said.

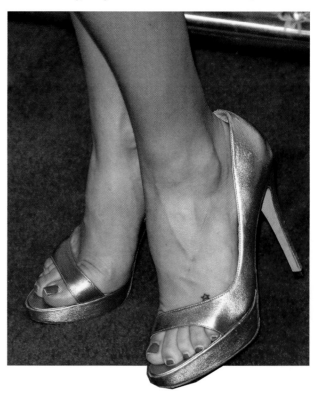

SEPTEMBER 2, 2002   BY GEORGE GURLEY

Coultergeist

SEPTEMBER 9, 2002
BY PHILIP WEISS

INTERVIEW WITH THE VAMP

ANN COULTER, AU-thor of the No. 1 best-selling nonfiction book in America—*Slander: Liberal Lies About the American Right*, a small book coruscating with giddy bile—was 20 minutes late to lunch at Michael's, the sunlit media-centric restaurant on West 55th Street. I'd been so excited to meet the glowing scimitar of the American right that I hadn't fallen asleep until 5 a.m. the night before.

Now I was worried that Ann had backed out. Had she figured she'd be un-welcomed, hissed at, throttled at the hub center of the media elite?

Her book has been No. 1 on the *New York Times* best-seller list for nonfiction since the first week it came out, in early July, which means that the people who dismiss her also have to deal with a secondary emotion: envy.

No one at Michael's really noticed Ms. Coulter when she showed up, a sluice of sweat dripping off her long, perfect New Canaan nose, apologizing profusely—radio interview, subway, late for everything. She was wearing a simple black dress and black closed-toe heels. She looked nice, not evil.

"I'm never an insider," Ms. Coulter said, looking around the room, not recognizing anyone. "No, I don't know who they are, I don't care who they are. I don't want to go to their cocktail parties, and I no longer want to bother writing articles they ask me to write, only to have them killed when they discover, 'Oh, maybe we don't want to publish a conservative after all.'"

So just write books? I chirped.

"That's right," she said. "That's right. The American people like me; editors don't. I've arranged my life so that I am unfireable. I don't have any bosses. The only

people who can fire me are the American people. That's part of the reason I'm not anxious to have a TV show. Who's gonna give me a TV show? I didn't work for an impeached, disbarred president who was held in contempt by a federal judge. That's what they look for in objective reporters."

In the cab, I told Ms. Coulter that although back in college I'd been comforted by writers like Tom Wolfe, Camille Paglia and Dinesh D'Souza ("I've dated him, I've dated every right-winger," Ms. Coulter said), I remembered feeling that that nauseating political correctness was the way the world was going to be and I had to accept it.

"And then you moved to New York and it was true," she said. "The rest of America hates New York," she said, laughing. "I love that, I find it very comforting."

There was nothing wrong with me?

"No, we're living in an insane asylum," Ms. Coulter said. She said she "takes joy in liberal attacks. It's like coffee. I mean, usually when I write up a column, I know what's going to drive them crazy. I know when I'm baiting them, it's so easy to bait them and they always bite. That is my signature style, to start with the wild, bald, McCarthyite overstatements—seemingly—and then back it up with methodical and laborious research. Taunting liberals is like having a pet that does tricks. Sit! Beg! Shake! Then they do it."

The cab stopped outside the Empire State Building. Her long, skinny legs stretched to the sidewalk.

"You're never going to get rid of liberals altogether," she said, laughing. Ann Coulter practically glowed at this thought.

I looked up at her from in the taxi. She seemed very tall against the sky.

A FEW WEEKS BACK, A FRIEND handed me model Janice Dickinson's autobiography and said it was a juicy tell-all, but under that was a cold understanding of the currency of fashion: the drooling agents and clients, the callous celebrities, the routine personal abuse, the blurred line between prostitution and modeling, etc.

I read *No Lifeguard on Duty* at once and wasn't disappointed.

Young Janice would break down doors to make it, dress like a French whore, do almost anything to get what she wanted. And so would the men she ran into. "You really can sing," Muddy Waters told her, and she believed him, and believed Bill Cosby when he told her the same lie—that is, until she didn't want to go to bed with him and he blew her off.

I called Regan Books and learned that Janice Dickinson was coming to New York. I could meet her at the Omni Berkshire Place on East 52nd Street.

I'd been in the Guggenheim room on the second floor all of 10 seconds when I understood Janice Dickinson's true nature: She's a viper.

The Gangs of New York gang:
Daniel Day-Lewis, Martin Scorsese and Leonardo DiCaprio

◇◇◇◇◇◇◇

SEPTEMBER 9, 2002 BY NYO STAFF

More Notions From Larry King Jr.

I HAVEN'T BEEN merry in years.

Do I want to overhear the conversation you're having in public? No.

How did cows survive in the wild all those years?

Those of you wearing CBGB's T-shirts purchased at Urban Outfitters are not fooling anybody. Not that you can win with the whole T-shirt thing anyway.

Swearing a lot is old hat.

Why doesn't Jerry Seinfeld buy the Mets?

I thank God for the overweight punk girls who slept with me in college.

I'm getting too thin-skinned to suffer through the ordeal of Starbucks.

Tom Golisano. Your punch line here.

Charlie Rose wasn't taking any chances with those replacement hosts, was he?

Women are beautiful. Men are ugly.

War and Peace is slightly better than *Anna Karenina.*

Why hasn't there been a new dance step in the last 10 years?.

I feel exhausted after reading movie reviews by Elvis Mitchell or A.O. Scott.

Everybody knows that TV is sapping our energy.

Note to 3:30 p.m.: You're an unpopular time of day.

Can't grocers make berry prices more stable?

Shakespeare could do it all.

Let's not commemorate Sept. 11.

I'm going to get up at 7 tomorrow and get things done. This time I really mean it.

If you don't love water, you and I have a problem.

OCTOBER 21, 2002 BY GREG SARGENT & JOSH BENSON

EL-IOT! CAN SPITZER GO TO 1600?

WHEN ELIOT SPITZER WAS growing up in the Riverdale section of the Bronx, he and his two siblings played a somewhat unusual game at the dinner table.

"We had an assignment process," said Bernard Spitzer, Eliot's father, a real-estate developer. "We would go around the table, and one of the three children would be asked to raise a topic for discussion."

Three decades later, the pressure is still on Eliot Spitzer, the state attorney general who is an overwhelming favorite to win reelection to a second term next month.

"Would I like him to become president? Of course," said the elder Mr. Spitzer. "I'd love to spend the night in the Lincoln Bedroom."

And would the attorney general himself like to be president?

"I think he would," the elder Mr. Spitzer said. "It's his very nature."

It's in Mr. Spitzer's nature to be ambitious—both for his office and for himself. He has transformed the attorney general's office from a sleepy patronage mill with little institutional power into the scourge of corrupt business leaders, producing headlines across the country. By using the attorney general's office to wage a one-man assault on Wall Street, Mr. Spitzer is turning himself into the Tom Dewey of the 21st century.

He won't talk about it, but he is almost certainly running for governor in 2006—provided, of course, that the current Democratic candidate, Carl McCall, loses to the incumbent, George Pataki—and his main selling point is likely to be his aggressive prosecution of Wall Street executives.

"He wants to be governor, for sure," said City Councilman Eric Gioia, who helped run Al Gore's New York operation in 2000. "Any governor of New York is automatically on the short list for President. It wouldn't surprise me if, in the back of his mind, he thinks that in 10 or 20 years the White House is a legitimate and obtainable goal."

DECEMBER 1, 2002   BY JOSH BENSON

GORE'S TV WAR: HE LOBS SALVO AT FOX NEWS

AMONG THE MANY PROBLEMS facing the Democratic Party, according to former Vice President Al Gore, is the state of the American media.

"The media is kind of weird these days on politics, and there are some major institutional voices that are, truthfully speaking, part and parcel of the Republican Party," said Mr. Gore in an interview with *The Observer.* "Fox News Network, *The Washington Times*, Rush Limbaugh—there's a bunch of them, and some of them are financed by wealthy ultra-conservative billionaires who make political deals with Republican

administrations and the rest of the media. ... Most of the media [has] been slow to recognize the pervasive impact of this fifth column in their ranks— that is, day after day, injecting the daily Republican talking points into the definition of what's objective as stated by the news media as a whole." Mr. Gore has been airing his views during a nationwide promotional book tour that marks his re-emergence in public life after a self-imposed exile following his loss in the 2000 presidential election. Now, as Mr. Gore considers

another presidential campaign, he's determined to confound his ponderous image by unveiling a new Al Gore—one who doesn't hesitate, as he puts it, to "let 'er rip." Hence his controversial criticisms of President Bush's foreign policy, and his surprise announcement in favor of a government-run universal health care system. And hence, in a phone interview with *The Observer*, his extensive criticism of the media, which is hardly a conventional way of launching a national political campaign. Ac-

tually, Mr. Gore may have little reason to hide his views about the media, for his re-emergence, while generating a massive amount of attention, has also inspired ridicule from commentators of all ideological persuasions. Conservatives seemed delighted by his return, remembering his awkward candidacy in 2000, and many liberals have been quite frank in wishing that he would simply disappear. But Mr. Gore has a bone to pick with his critics: namely, he says, that a systematically orchestrated bias in the media makes it impossible for him and his fellow Democrats to get a fair shake.

NOVEMBER 18, 2002   BY FRANK DIGIACOMO

Who's Master Now?

THE STORY OF COMEDIAN LARRY David's introduction to his friend and fellow comedian Richard Lewis' psychotherapy group is the stuff of show-business legend, but it's worth repeating, if only for the glimpse it affords into the mind of the guy who created HBO's *Curb Your Enthusiasm*.

"I introduced him to psychotherapy," said Mr. Lewis, who is a regular guest star on *Curb* and, by his own estimation, has been in therapy for some three decades. This particular episode took place many years ago in New York, from which both men hail.

"He only went once," Mr. Lewis said. After the traditional group session, many of the same patients would gather at an appointed destination "and sit around with coffee and donuts and have another two hours."

"I'll never forget: We were on the East Side, at someone's apartment after the therapy session. It was like 10 people moaning and groaning," Mr. Lewis said. "And Larry stood up and said: 'I can't stand this. I don't need this. I don't want to hear this.' And he ran out of this person's apartment.

"He had 10 neurotic people chasing him down First Avenue for al-

most like 30 blocks, thinking he was in denial—and he might have been— but he hated this form of therapy," Mr. Lewis said. "And he went into this phone booth—like Superman.

"I'll never forget it," he said. "We're all knocking on the phone booth, saying, 'Larry, we love you, come back, it's O.K.' And he said, 'No! Get away from me, you whack jobs.' And he never came back. He might have gone to therapy privately—I think he did," Mr. Lewis said.

"He just could not stand to hear people moan and groan."

Both men are now in their mid-50's and Mr. Lewis called it "heightened reality" when they have a scene together in *Curb*. "When I know what the scene is, the homework is so done. I'm me, he's him, 'Action,'" he said. He even likened it to appearing in the comedy equivalent of John Cassavetes' *Husbands*. "You know, there was that camaraderie between Peter Falk and Ben Gazzara in that movie in particular, and Cassavetes, that was just so astonishing," he said. "And that's because they were close and they did have those feelings."

GEORGE GURLEY INTERVIEWS PETER STEVENSON

Go on. Give me the goods.

George, don't eat a banana while you're interviewing me; it'll make me anxious. Is this on? Is it Radio Shack? O.K. I moved to New York, to Brooklyn, in 1985 and I worked at *Manhattan, inc.*, a magazine that covered New York business the way *Vanity Fair* covers Hollywood. Peter Kaplan was my boss. During the interview, he kept telling me not to take the job. I started as Peter's editorial assistant, Clay Felker was the editor, Kaplan was his No. 2. Clay brought the whiff of New Journalism with him, he was the real deal—he'd invented *New York* magazine, he had fans and real enemies, he'd dated famous actresses, he knew everybody—Gloria Steinem, Jimmy Breslin, Tom Wolfe, Rupert Murdoch, David Frost—his bark could knock you a foot off your chair, but he was also tremendously encouraging to young reporters. My first task was to type up cards for Peter Kaplan's Rolodex—he had hundreds of those pink message pads that his previous assistant had taken his phone messages on; he'd saved a stack of them, so I typed up the cards on an IBM Selectric II typewriter—the ones with the golf-ball-shaped gizmo that smacked the paper to leave the imprint of the letters. So I'd type in these names—Binky Urban, Nora Ephron, Wendy Wasserstein. The joke is, Peter has a photographic memory for phone numbers—if you tell him your number, he'll remember it for years. So he never actually looked at the Rolodex.

Kaplan had a distinct style at the time, sort of Camelot meets Warhol. Peter was, and is, very close with the Kennedy family—I think the family sees Peter as their resident Talmudic sage—and he'd also spent time with the Warhol crowd. So by the mid-1980s, his personal style reflected this tension inside of him. He was already wearing what he wears today—Paul Stuart blue blazer and khakis with scuffed leather belt and blue button-down shirts, club ties—but he also had vestiges of his 1970s self. The sandals—he wore these sandals he'd bought in Mexico, he wore them year round, rain, snow or shine. He didn't wear them with socks, at least he spared us that. And he wore this hat—it was very Carnaby Street circa 1969, this floppy hat, the kind of hat Marianne Faithful wore when she traveled with the Stones, maybe velvet, anyway very floppy. Peter called it a sombrero; of course, it was nothing like a sombrero, but try telling him that. Each day Peter would pin a carnation to the hat. It had to be a fresh carnation, and he was obsessive that it be a different color each day. Guess whose job it was to bring a fresh carnation to the office each morning? Luckily for me, I was living on West 19th Street by then, and the flower market is West 28th street, and it opens before dawn. I don't think Peter ever thought I'd be able to bring a different colored carnation in every day, for this hat, and so when I did—which also involved, by the way, lots of arguments because he'd fuss that the peach carnations were just day-old white carnations I was trying to sneak past him—when I succeeded at this absurd task, I think he started to see me as someone he might work with a long time.

Manhattan, inc. collapsed in the wake of the Black Monday stock market crash of '87, but at the same time Kaplan had been working on starting up an

Esquire-type magazine, *Smart for Men*, so I went to work as a writer there; we were told a Japanese group was funding us.

One day, a young woman named Candace Bushnell came bursting in, she had long blond hair and little round sunglasses, looking exactly like Meg Ryan in *The Doors* movie, and she calls out in this booming, reach-to-the-cheap-seats voice, "Which one of you is *Peter*?!" And Kaplan and I look at each other, we're both thinking, "*Here we go.*" And that was the beginning of a beautiful friendship. Candace and I went out to lunch to talk about story ideas; she drank vodka and ate a steak.

A few days before we were about to go to press with the first issue of *Smart for Men*, Peter and I went to see Scorsese's *Goodfellas* during lunch, and when we came back to the office we were told the magazine was folding—immediately. The Japanese money had vanished. The staff was told to leave the building, guards were watching to make sure no one took anything. So we hid the computer server, which had the text and photo and layout files for that first issue, in a gym bag and carried it out past the guards. Various articles in that issue were then published elsewhere.

After a few years of freelancing, I came here; Susan Morrison hired me as a writer in 1993. It was a pretty rough crew, a combination of real newspaperman like Terry Golway and Charlie Bagli, along with a row of pomaded interns who were sons and daughters of Arthur Carter's rich friends. And you're working on East 64th between Park and Madison, so every time you want to go out for a sandwich you're bombarded by the wealthiest ZIP code in the country. People in mink coats and bedroom slippers, that kind of situation. Susan was an unbelievable editor; she'd come from *Spy*, she had this lightning sense of humor. And even though we were a madcap publication, she always kept the drumbeat of a newspaper; no matter what you were reporting, you should have every detail *The New York Times* would have had.

This is also before the Internet was anything except a rudimentary e-mail service. There wasn't a Google, there weren't bloggers, there weren't news Web sites because newspapers didn't *have* Web sites, so if you were on a story, you knew—if you got there first, of course—that your story on someone really could become *the* clip on that person, or that event, for months or even years at a time.

Meanwhile you were always conscious of the fact that the paper was owned by this eccentric guy, Arthur Carter; he'd made a bundle on Wall Street in the 1970s, and he loved owning this newspaper that poked holes in the self-importance of Wall Street guys, society people, political players. We'd have lunch at Gino's, the place with the zerbras on the walls; he'd tell me how I was going about my love life all wrong. He'd order for you if you weren't quick enough to order for yourself—you had to know before you even walked in the door what you were going to order, and be ready to call it out the moment any waiter or busboy came within earshot; otherwise, you'd eat what Arthur decided you should eat. He's a very unpredictable, hilarious guy. One of his favorite things to do was to show up in the office on the Monday holidays, because we never got them off—Memorial Day, Labor Day—because of our deadline schedule. So you'd be sitting at your desk and all of a sudden, there'd be this guy who looked like a young Kirk Douglas in a cashmere

Peter Stevenson is executive editor of *The New York Observer*.

sweater standing next to your desk.

Then one day Kaplan shows up, after Susan left, so now you have a madcap eccentric owner *and* a madcap eccentric editor. Imagine Dennis Hopper and Crispin Glover in a two-man bass boat.

You and Jim Windolf played a lot of pranks.
It was like a smoking break, but good for your lungs. Windolf was the one who talked me into it. We invented a Singaporean gossip columnist, John Wu, who used to call people up; he'd say he had his own gossip magazine, *Night Beat*, and was doing an item on them, something completely fabricated, of course—like we'd call Glenn Birnbaum, the owner of Mortimer's, and say we heard there were a bunch of socialites playing in a baby pool there last night, and he'd be outraged, and we would still say, "O.K., so we can print that you deny it?" And of course that would push him over the edge. Later, we made John Wu a Singaporean billionaire who wanted to invest money in various projects. Other times

he was John Wu, guerilla publicist—we'd call people up and say, "I'm doing some guerilla publicity for you guys, when can I expect my payment?"

Tell me about an average day there. Where'd you go out to lunch?
Kaplan loved this coffee shop called the Gardenia, where it cost $20 for a sandwich; it had green walls, like it was designed by Laura Ashley on a bender. It was on Madison around 69th Street. Famous neighborhood people would be there, like Wayne Gretzky, Jackie Mason, Richard Lewis. Joe DiMaggio was there. The thing is, when Kaplan sees someone famous, he doesn't quietly stare, he'll see DiMaggio and boom out, "The Yankee Clipper!" He sees Kitty Carlisle Hart and shouts, "Mrs. Hart!" It's what everyone else is thinking, but Peter's like a kid, he blurts it out, gleefully, which is really funny.

You wrote the Monica Diaries column.
When the Clinton thing was breaking, one afternoon for some reason I started writing a parody of a 21-year-old Beverly Hills girl's diary of her affair with this cute guy who happened to be president of the United States. It probably said a lot more about my neuroses than Bill Clinton's. Monica's mother didn't like them, because she thought we were making her daughter sound like an idiot, so she wrote a letter. We stopped it—no need to upset the girl's mother.

Can you talk about some of the people you've edited? Alex Kuczynski?
Alex was a giddy blast. She always would have 10 ideas at story meetings and eight of them would be terrible and two would be brilliant. Once she found out that all these models were getting colonics to slim down; a bunch of the world's most beautiful women lining up in Soho for enemas is a funny piece.

Warren St. John?
One piece of his I edited was about Kathryn Harrison, who wrote a memoir called *The Kiss* about having an affair with her estranged father when she was in college. And Warren, being a good reporter, said, "Well, I'm going to find the father and get his side of the story." So he tracks the guy down, sweet-talking these file clerks with his Alabama twang; he finds the father, and it turns out the guy has no idea his daughter had written this book. And he gives Warren an interview. So we're about to go to press, and the day before we're getting calls from Kathryn Harrison's agent saying you can't publish this piece, because this man's new family doesn't know about this event in his past and it will shatter them. Now Kathryn Harrison was doing lots of publicity, she's going on *Good Morning America*. So we're thinking, if you don't want your dad's new family to find out about the book, it might not be such a good idea to talk to Diane Sawyer about it while America is eating Cornflakes. And indeed, it turned out the guy's kids *had* seen the ABC segment, knew all about it, before we ran our piece. So in that respect, we weren't villains, and yes, finding the dad was a cheeky thing to do, but it was also the right story to do.

Tish Durkin?
Tish, she went to Baghdad for us, right after the war "ended." We had to outfit her with $10,000 in cash that she wore in a body belt—credit cards weren't going to be much use over there—and she got herself to Baghdad and started filing terrific narratives. Baghdad was a pretty big bowl of fruit for *The Observer* to try and pick from, and Tish did beautifully. She also fell in love with an Irish-American guy over there and ended up marrying him. A few weeks before their wedding, their best man, who was Iraqi, was assassinated.

Sex and the City?
Candace Bushnell and I were friends, she'd been doing articles for the paper, and together with Candace, Kaplan and I came up with this column, and handed it to her, and it was like a race horse bolting out of the gate. On a weekly basis, she was coining terms like toxic bachelors and modelizers. She was always a tremendous pro, always filed on time. You know that Flaubert line, be bourgeois in your life so you can be violent in your work. Aside from her society nights, Candace has always had a real domestic side, cooking pork chops, cozy socks, Jane Austen novel by the fireplace. And I think that's what allows her to go so far out in her writing. My job as her editor was just to help Candace be Candace, help her trust her instincts. And I remember—in what seemed like a tremendously short span of time after the column started—one day coming back to the townhouse from some dumpy lunch place and there were the big lights and huge trailers and army of PAs blocking the sidewalks. It was HBO filming a scene from *Sex and the City*, right across the street from the stinky little office where we'd conceived the thing, and that image, the juxtaposition, stayed with me for days.

2003

◀ Casual use of F-word gains currency in polite society

▶ Architect Daniel Libeskind wins competition to reconstruct World Trade Center

▶ James Frey aspires to be greatest writer of his generation

▶ $1.8 billion AOL Time Warner Center is priciest single-building project in U.S. history

 ▶ Former Clintonite George Stephanopoulos joins Sunday-morning TV biz

▶ New Yorkers demonstrate against invasion of Iraq

▶ Anna Wintour hosts Goddess-themed ball; former assistant publishes roman à clef

▶ Veteran writer and editor Michael Kelly dies in Humvee crash

▶ Raines falls: Howell out, Bill Keller in at *Times* after reporter Jayson Blair's disgrace

2003

◇◇◇◇◇◇◇

JANUARY 19, 2003 BY TOM MCGEVERAN

THE MAN WHO IS ALMOST THERE

WHEN BERLIN-BASED AMERI-can architect Daniel Libeskind unveiled his plan for the World Trade Center site last month to members of families still grieving the loss of loved ones in the Sept. 11 terror attack, several of them wept.

Unlike any of the competing proposals, Mr. Libeskind's plan did something that had profound meaning for the bereaved: his design called for a new tower that would be set in the old foundation, which remained behind when the towers collapsed. The actual pit—the enormous bedrock-lined hole in the ground where the World Trade Center once stood—would be left virtually untouched, a testament to the memory of the dead.

For many of the families, Mr. Libeskind had deftly captured the emotional contradictions inherent in building a new commercial center on what is effectively a mass grave. His design embodied a series of wrenching questions: How can we merge mourning and morning commuters, retail and remembrance? If the site is made beautiful, is tragedy faithlessly forgotten? If it is raw, and bares the scars of loss too vividly, will it maintain the requisite respect for the

dignity of the dead?

Mr. Libeskind, the son of Holocaust survivors, a man who arrived in New York harbor by boat in 1960, is undoubtedly the man who has the best chance of uniting the cacophony of interests squabbling over the site's future.

Consider his design: It calls for a crystal spire whose foundation is firmly set in the pit—it has come to be known as "the bathtub"—a hole that is lined with ancient bedrock that, for millennia, has kept the waters of the Hudson River at bay. The spire rises up out of the pit, and as it does, it appears to repeat the lines of the Statue of Liberty, spiraling upwards and thinning out like the line from the strong shoulders of the statue to the hand held aloft, its torch topped by a copper flame. The upper stories are set off by gardens that seem to hang in the sky.

The beauty of the design is that by rising up out of the pit, it proceeds upward from memorial to cultural to retail to office uses. And so the business end of the new structure appears conceptually at the other end of a vertical spectrum that is grounded in the memorial. "I don't think there's a disjunct there," he said.

JANUARY 22, 2003
BY JOE HAGAN

MEET THE NEW STAGGERING GENIUS

AT 33, JAMES FREY HAS A HUM-ble ambition: He wants to be the greatest literary writer of his generation. Film director Gus Van Sant has compared him to "a young-guard Eggers"—which means Dave Eggers had better be prepared to, you know, throw down.

"The Eggers book pissed me off," said Mr. Frey, referring to the best-selling and critically beloved *A Heartbreaking Work of Staggering Genius.* "Because a book that I thought was mediocre was being hailed as the best book written by the best writer of my generation," he said. "Fuck that. And fuck him and fuck anybody that says that. I don't give a fuck what they think of me. I'm going to try to write the best book of my generation and I'm going to try to be the best writer."

Mr. Frey has thinning, curly hair, a slightly doughy build and a Southern California drawl. "And maybe I'll fall flat on my fucking face," he conceded, "but I'll fall flat on my fucking face trying to do it."

MARCH 16, 2003 BY JOE CONASON

IRAQ'S NUKE THREAT LITTLE MORE THAN MYTH

OF ALL THE CONSTANTLY CHANGING REASONS FOR WAR ON IRAQ that have emanated from the White House since last summer, there has been only one that ever sounded compelling: the prospect of an atomic bomb wielded by Saddam Hussein.

Biological and chemical weapons are frightening as well as illegal. Missiles and warheads sound scary. Shadowy links to terrorism raise the specter of Sept. 11. Yet as knowledgeable experts would explain, if they could get anyone to listen, Iraq lacks the capacity and the motive to attack us with chemical or biological weapons.

But if Saddam possesses a nuclear weapon—or could someday build a nuclear weapon—then he would be almost as dangerous as Kim Jong Il. If he got a nuclear weapon, Saddam could threaten Israel, or smuggle it into the United States. That's why hawkish pundits and politicians, including President George W. Bush, emphasize the potential Iraqi bomb as their favorite casus belli.

Uttered last September by National Security Advisor Condoleezza Rice, the best line has been repeated ominously many times since: "We don't want the smoking gun to be a mushroom cloud." Mr. Bush warned last fall that, according to our intelligence sources, "Iraq is reconstituting its nuclear-weapons program ... And he is moving ever closer to developing a nuclear weapon."

After three months of inspections by the United Nations—underwritten by the threat of military force—we now know that those warnings were grossly exaggerated. Iraq has not reconstituted the extensive nuclear-weapons program dismantled during the previous round of U.N. inspections. The facilities in the U.S. satellite photographs are still in shambles, and aren't being used for any illegal purpose. The aluminum tubes were unusable for uranium enrichment. And the documents that show Saddam tried to buy uranium from Africa, which were cited by the president in his State of the Union address? Oh, they were forged.

Those classified papers, provided by Britain's MI6 and then intensively reviewed by the C.I.A., were brandished as proof that Iraq had attempted to purchase uranium from Niger in 1999. Officials from both countries denied any such deal, and the U.N.'s independent experts confirmed their denials, finding that the documents had been crudely faked. (Another published description was "transparently obvious.")

So far, spokesmen for the U.S. and British governments have not tried to deny that the uranium documents were bogus. Asked about the fake papers by Tim Russert on NBC's *Meet the Press*, Mr. Powell replied blandly: "If that information is inaccurate, fine."

With all due respect to the secretary, the appropriate word isn't "inaccurate"—and it isn't "fine," either. It is horrific to contemplate that someone would fabricate a document to foment a war likely to kill thousands. It is humiliating to think that American intelligence services cannot distinguish a fake of that kind—or, worse still, would consciously pass along such a fake to an international authority. It is troubling to realize that the quality of information used by the president as he prepares for war may be no better than that.

And it is impossible not to wonder what other lies and myths are being spread to justify this war.

◇◇◇◇◇◇◇

FEBRUARY 2, 2003 BY TOM MCGEVERAN

Glass Menagerie

THE LARGE GLASS PANELS ARE WORKING THEIR WAY UP THE SKELeton of the AOL Time Warner Center, the mixed-use pair of obelisks stretching 80 stories into the sky over Columbus Circle. The progress is measurable daily. In fact, the massive mountain of commerce—now at its full height—stands confidently astride the street grid, as if it predated all the structures that have risen on the West Side since the grid was established in 1811. At $1.8 billion, it's the most expensive single-building construction project in U.S. history.

It remains to be seen whether New Yorkers will be impressed with the building's debut. Indeed, the marketing campaign for the AOL Time Warner Center does not intend to leave that to chance. Its promotional materials appear aimed as much at selling the building to New Yorkers at large as at reassuring its many tenants that theirs was a risk worth taking.

New Yorkers, after futzing for a year and a half with ground zero, are looking for something that will inspire. Will it matter to New Yorkers what the building means, or how AOL Time Warner is structured, when they enter the five-story glass atrium off Columbus Circle this fall?

MARCH 30, 2003   BY CALEB CARR

The Ferocious Spectacle In Baghdad

THE FEROCIOUS SPECTACLE BEING PLAYED OUT IN THE desert, marshes and cities of Iraq is a complicated psychological and spiritual gamble, one that may culminate, during the next few days, in a battle across a ring of chemical fire thrown by Saddam Hussein around Baghdad—his "red line." This last redoubt may or may not exist, but coalition forces and their civilian commanders have promised to move on the capital regardless, breeding fear throughout the world that civilization's cradle may soon become its coffin: The historical forces of modernism and medievalism may well have begun the first formal battle in a decisive war.

In planning for this battle, both the American-led coalition and Saddam Hussein have drawn inspiration and methods from the Middle Ages as much as from the Information Age. Yet neither modernism nor medievalism has consented to wear the uniform of just one side.

Consider, for instance, the ambitious opening effort by coalition forces to kill Saddam Hussein, his sons and their top advisers with cruise missiles and bunker-busting bombs. The move was referred to by the American military as a "decapitation attempt," a suitably anachronistic title for a tactic that looked for its inspiration and validation not to the modern age—during which such behavior has generally been viewed with distaste—but to medieval and even ancient times.

Subsequent attempts have been made to cut off all the many heads of the monstrous Iraqi Republican Guard, as well as those of Saddam's supposedly suicidal fedayeen and the various armed Baath political militias. The coalition relied again on its seemingly unlimited supply of technologically complex bombs whose "smartness" has done nothing to temper their essential and spectacular violence. Images of the resulting destruction were soon being shown by newspapers and television networks throughout the Muslim world. Exploiting the tools of information technology, these media organs worked hard and with considerable success to demonstrate that the allied coalition had returned to the old Western (for which read "crusading") habit of grinding enemy populations into the dust.

In the opening round, the coalition chose the weapons of modernism and the psychology of medievalism; the Iraqis reversed the equation and gained a momentary advantage.

Demonstrating that their embrace of progressive military methods in Afghanistan hasn't been a passing fancy, the coalition launched its ground attack into Iraq at the same time that its bombs were falling on the country's urban areas, in line with the fundamental principles of modern mobile, mechanized warfare established by the great armor campaigns of the Second World War. From the first, coalition forces emphasized speed and maneuver over attrition, the need to bypass enemy strongholds rather than subdue them, and a rampaging drive to get at the enemy's vitals before an effective defense of any one part of Iraq could be managed. But with dreadful suddenness, the age of the coalition campaign's operational ethos was revealed by Saddam's defensive plan, which is based on a more contemporary belligerent tactic: terrorism. El-

ements of the dictator's most vicious fighters had been detailed among the forlorn Iraqi regulars in the south, who were bypassed by the allies. As the armored columns sped towards Baghdad, the fanatics kept their weapons trained on their countrymen even more than on the invading enemy, and when the coalition lines of supply and communication had been stretched tight, they ordered the regulars to strike. If those hapless men would not obey, the Republican Guardsmen and fedayeen simply tore off their own uniforms and blended into the civilian population. They waited until the coalition had sent all but slender garrison forces ahead and then struck murderously themselves.

While the effect on coalition military might and progress was minimal, the psychological effect was maximized by a weapon that the coalition itself had unwittingly brought along, as if to allow Saddam some sort of handicap: the "embedded" television press corps.

With the decision to integrate both print and television journalists into military units, President George W. Bush and certain of his advisers demonstrated once again their belief that history has begun anew with them. In fact, the history behind this journalistic innovation is long, torturous and important.

From the beginning of organized violence, soldiers have viewed civilians as prey and spoils, while civilians have viewed soldiers as little more than rapacious criminals. So great did this mutual contempt grow that by the Middle Ages, philosophers, legalists and military men had begun to search for ways to limit the impact of the first group on the second.

In the West, this movement led to the professionalization of armies and accompanying codes of discipline for soldiers. Though these codes were often violated, outrages no longer occurred with anything approaching the regularity that they had in earlier cen-

Demonstrating that their embrace of progressive military methods in Afghanistan hasn't been a passing fancy, the coalition launched its ground attack into Iraq at the same time that its bombs were falling on the country's urban areas, in line with the fundamental principles of modern mobile, mechanized warfare established by the great armor campaigns of the Second World War.

turies. More and more, civilians learned of war from the work of writers who witnessed it rather than by hard experience.

Writers thus accrued a predictably large measure of influence over military affairs, based on how much they did or did not reveal about a given army's plans and actions. Indeed, so significant did this influence become that, by the time of the American Civil War, William Tecumseh Sherman declared that if he could, he would shoot all war correspondents as spies.

Generals of a different nervous temperament, however, learned not to despise but to manipulate the press: T.E. Lawrence, for example, could never have become the great legend of Arabia without the studious efforts of correspondent Lowell Thomas. Myths were not difficult to manufacture or fine-tune: The public's appetite for tales of martial valor only grew with its greater remove from the dangers of the battlefield.

Television altered this equation. On the one hand, stories of battlefield excitement could be illustrated as never before; on the other, televised images more often than not revealed that war was a terrifying, dangerous and often psychologically shattering experience. But for their new war in Iraq, Mr. Bush and his advisers jettisoned all the old qualms about allowing cameras to show too much. Convinced of the absolute moral rectitude of his struggle against Saddam, Mr. Bush apparently believed that embedded correspondents would only add to the campaign's glory by allowing the public to see the two undertakings—military and journalistic—as one great and just national mission. Instead, before the first week was out, the administration's new media policy became the factor most likely to complicate, frustrate and perhaps endanger the success of a military campaign whose brilliance cannot disguise the fact that it is, after all, a military campaign, and as such loaded with death, bloodshed, blunders and acts of betrayal as well as bravery.

The embedded journalist equipped with a video feed is a feature of war more suited to degenerate ancient Rome and its circuses of blood than to a modern, progressive army. Watching actual violence in real time may teach valuable lessons about war, but it spreads fear and eventually inures us to killing. "Embedding," as the name ironically suggests, is more than mere voyeurism: It is the pornography of the battlefield, and in the hands of amoral criminals such as America's current enemies, it will prove enormously and enduringly useful. The images born today will take a long time dying.

By allowing the embedding of journalists, then, our modern army is again embracing medievalism. Our enemy, meanwhile, has used the methods of the Information Age to turn the power of televised images against us. This will not be the last reversal of psychological roles that we experience in this war. When we discover weapons of mass destruction, and when we learn just how willing Saddam's legions are to kill their own merely to gain a temporary advantage, the moral momentum will shift back our way. But embedding has been an unnecessary and foolish experiment; and the sooner we pull the plug on it, the quicker we can go about the final, grueling business of subduing Saddam's minions.

MARCH 30, 2003

BY ALEXANDRA JACOBS

THE UNDERLING'S REVENGE, BY CONDÉ NAST'S WHISTLEBLOWER

The Devil Wears Prada,
by Lauren Weisberger.
Doubleday, 327 pages, $21.95.

THE COVER OF THIS BOOK BY A former assistant to Anna Wintour, the British editor in chief of the American *Vogue*, proclaims that it is "A Novel," no doubt in part as a legal precaution. It's been dangled before us for months as a roman à clef that will unlock the chilly glass doors of Condé Nast Publications to give us an inside look at one of the magazine industry's most famous and fearsome figures. You're not being sold the writing talent of the author, Lauren Weisberger, a young, beaming, blond Cornell graduate. No, the selling point of *The Devil Wears Prada* is Ms. Weisberger's presumably intimate knowledge of her mysterious ex-boss.

APRIL 13, 2003

BY CHRISTOPHER HITCHENS, MARGARET TALBOT, MICHAEL CRAWLEY

MICHAEL KELLY

FOR THOSE OF US hanging about the Kuwait Hilton and the military briefings in the past weeks, and paying the occasional easy-does-it visit to the frontier zone or to the safer bits of southern Iraq, the name of Michael Kelly was a frequent and somewhat guilt-inducing reference. In the first place, we had all read or were engaged in re-reading *Martyrs' Day*, his enviable account of the last Gulf War. In the second place, we knew that he was miles up the road ahead of us, at the sharp end with the Third Infantry Division. I don't approve of "embedded" journalism myself, but nor was I pretending that I'd have had the discipline or fortitude to go that way. So, as we fiddled with gas masks during mostly false-alarm air-raid warnings in Kuwait City, one would say facetiously to another: "Mike must be within commuting distance of Baghdad by now."

The longest time I ever spent with him was very different. He heard that I was going to a Farrakhan rally at the Howard University campus a few years back, and asked if he could keep me company. We ended up as the only white guys present during an especially lurid harangue from the late Khalid Muhammad. The atmosphere wasn't all that menacing despite some efforts in that direction, and afterward we spent a good deal of time talking to the organizers and the members of the audience. The rest of the night, we sat up forever while he told me of growing up in D.C., of being by family origin a member of the opposite Irish-Catholic faction to Pat Buchanan, and of going with his mother to early civil-rights rallies. His curiosity and his humor, and his quick impatience with bullshit, were all of a piece. I often thought he was wrong, but I never knew him to be wrong for an ignoble or cowardly reason.

–Christopher Hitchens

I MET MIKE WHEN I WAS on maternity leave with my first baby, and he had just been chosen as the editor of *The New Republic*, where I then worked. The prospect of squeezing myself into acceptable business attire, heading downtown for the first time since the baby, and making intelligent conversation with the famous journalist who was my new boss seemed hopelessly intimidating. Maybe Mike noticed my moment of hesitation; maybe he just intuited how I felt because he and his wife, Max, had a new baby, too. But the next thing I knew, he was proposing bringing lunch to my house in Bethesda, and the next day he was there, bearing pâté and a baguette and the ingredients for a lovely simple pasta, which he cooked for me while keeping up a riveting patter about all the things he wanted to do at the magazine. He never made a big deal about instituting a "family-friendly" policy at *The New Republic*, where the staff was young and childless; he just said

that, if I preferred, I could work at home a couple of days a week when I came back.

There are so many ways in which the public Mike will be remembered and deeply missed-as an extraordinary war correspondent, a charismatic editor, a passionate columnist and a beautiful writer. I will remember him as my beau ideal of a working father.

–Margaret Talbot

I MET MICHAEL KELLY when I was an intern at *The New Republic* in 1996 and he was the magazine's incoming editor. I wrote to him asking for a staff job. He responded by taking me to a nice lunch in downtown Washington. Our lunch confirmed everything you'll hear about his kindness toward aspiring young writers whom other editors might impatiently brush off. I was still just a punk, but he treated me like a serious person.

But that lunch was less interesting than the second conversation we had. Michael had offered me a job as a *TNR* fact-checker, with a chance to write on the side. I had another offer, to write about politics for an alternative weekly in Boston, and decided I couldn't turn down a full-time writing job. Not only did Michael understand my decision, he seemed to turn a bit wistful.

He was most passionate in urging me to devote myself completely to my work. Go to every last campaign event and city council meeting you can, he told me. If you have a girlfriend, drag her along. Work hard, he said. "You don't have as much time as you think you do."

–Michael Crowley

APRIL 20, 2003   BY FRANK DIGIACOMO

Back to the Couture

SOCIAL NAVIGATION REQUIRES a geisha's wiles, so it was startling to hear Nan Kempner speak her mind about the $3,500 dinner ticket that the Metropolitan Museum of Art is charging for its April 28 CostumeInstitute Benefit—the opening night of its Goddess exhibit, which will examine the way that "classical dress has profoundly inspired and influenced art and fashion through the millennia."

"What the hell, I might as well be honest," Ms. Kempner said by phone. "I just think it's terribly expensive, and I've been doing this party for God knows how many years." Ms. Kempner said that she'd been at it since the 70's and her name appears on the current list of benefit committee members. "It's always been fun and attractive, but it seems to me it's gotten a little out of hand," she said.

When asked if she meant that the ticket price seemed ostentatious against the backdrop of the war in Iraq and our foundering economy, she brushed that aside. "I think it was all planned before the war and the economy, and I don't think it has anything to do with taste or judgment. I just think it has to do with interest, and it has to do with desire to go," she said. "Who knows? Maybe it's Seventh Avenue blackmail. It's the old story: People love to see and be seen, and I guess if you have to pay that much to do so ... "

I told Ms. Kempner there didn't seem to be too many on the committee list who couldn't afford the price tag.

"Well, exactly," she said, "but maybe it's the same group of people that get asked to everything and feel they want to support everything, and sometimes maybe it gets a little out of hand."

MAY 25, 2003   BY SRIDHAR PAPPU

SO JAYSON BLAIR COULD LIVE, THE JOURNALIST HAD TO DIE

"THAT WAS MY FAVORITE," JAYSON Blair said. It was the morning of Monday, May 19, and the disgraced former *New York Times* reporter was curled in a butterfly chair in his sparsely furnished Brooklyn apartment. He was eating a bagel and talking about one of his many fabricated stories—his March 27 account, datelined Palestine, W.Va., of Pvt. Jessica Lynch's family's reaction to their daughter's liberation in Iraq.

Mr. Blair hadn't gone to Palestine, W.Va. He'd filed from Brooklyn, N.Y. As he'd done before, he cobbled facts and details from other places and made some parts up. He wrote how Private Lynch's father had "choked up as he stood on the porch here overlooking the tobacco fields and cattle pastures."

That was a lie. In *The Times'* lengthy May 11 account of Mr. Blair's long trail of deception, it reported that "the porch overlooks no such thing."

Mr. Blair found this funny.

It was now two weeks since Mr. Blair had been exposed and resigned from *The Times*. In that period, he'd become a journalistic pariah, entered and

exited a rehabilitation clinic, and wound up on the cover of *Newsweek*, smoking a cigarette. His actions stained *The New York Times*, turned his former newsroom upside down and called into question the future of his ex-boss, executive editor Howell Raines. *The Times'* publisher, Arthur Sulzberger Jr., had called his deception "a low point" in the paper's 152-year history.

But other than a couple of brief statements here and there, Mr. Blair hadn't talked publicly about what happened. Everyone still wanted to know: Why had he done it? Why had a promising 27-year-old reporter with a career in high gear at the most respected news organization in the world thrown it all away in a pathological binge of dishonesty?

Theories, of course, abounded. He was too young. He'd been pushed too far. He was a drunk; he was a drug addict; he was depressed.

These theories were all partially true, he said.

"I was young at *The New York Times*," said Mr. Blair. "I was under a lot of pressure. I was black at *The New York Times*, which is something that hurts you as much as it helps you. I certainly have health problems, which probably led to me having to kill Jayson Blair the journalist. I was either going to kill myself or I was going to kill the journalist persona."

He stayed with that concept. "So Jayson Blair the human being could live," he said, "Jayson Blair the journalist had to die."

AUGUST 17, 2003   BY TOM MCGEVERAN

SHMOMO ERECTUS

"IT'S A GAY WORLD AFTER ALL!" SCREAMS VH1 IN A press release pumping up their Aug. 18 documentary, *Totally Gay*. The show, VH1 says, will capture a phenomenon that has built to a fabulous crescendo this summer. "In the early 90's, the entertainment landscape was a virtual gay wasteland," the promoters scold. "Fast forward to 2003, where 'gay is the new black.'"

Gay is the new black.

In one sentence, they're telling us that the gay-rights movement has met its moment, and now stands to rank with the greatest culture war of our time, the civil-rights movement; and they're also telling us the movement is well-dressed. Is this liberation, or is it stereotype? Is the current increase in gay visibility progress, or is it a retrograde throwback to the homosexual caricatures of the 1950's, of a Nelly Nation of queens, hairdressers and interior decorators? Should we all just sit back and enjoy the show, as the caricature of the aesthetically obsessed, sweet-smelling gay man joins the American ranks of the non-threatening interloper: the funny little Jew, the tap-dancing Negro, and last year's model, the fumblingly illiterate Italian mobster—the lovable social misfits for a new age?

Not if we have anything to say about it. Call us the shmomosexuals: gay men who use the same moisturizer for their hands and face, if they use it to "moisturize" at all. Gay men who thrill to the prospect that Oscar, not Felix, might have been the latently gay character in *The Odd Couple*. Gay men whose daydreams of a wardrobe splurge are set against the efficient, Muzaked quietude of the Men's Wearhouse on Sixth Avenue in Chelsea. Joe Shmo, that is, but gay.

Much of the excitement over alpha gays and their "metrosexual" acolytes has been generated by America's most recent gay fetish object, the Bravo reality show *Queer Eye for the Straight Guy*, where five gay style experts make over a hapless straight guy in their own image.

The Fab Five and their helpful, helpful attentions to the grooming and manners of straight men: a safe and fun way to accept gays without having to admit they might be something like you—or that they might be people for whom civil rights are not an abstract matter of national policy or history, but a very real and personal question of self-determination or economic freedom.

And what is at stake for the wider culture? An opportunity, really, to do this one right, to admit gays into the full panoply of legal protections without forcing them to go through the minstrelsy phase: a little soft-shoe with your blowout, sir?

Shmomosexuals—untelegenic, too smart by half for the pop-mania version of homosexuality—have to steal a part of this limelight

> *Gay men whose daydreams of a wardrobe splurge are set against the efficient, Muzaked quietude of the Men's Wearhouse on Sixth Avenue in Chelsea. (It's all in one place!) Joe Shmo, that is, but gay.*

if the culture wars are not to devolve into wan affirmations from marketeers and product-pushers at the cost of rights granted by the government and supported by voters.

Massachusetts Representative Barney Frank is a shmomosexual of the first order. He said he was looking at his 1976 campaign poster as he was speaking to *The Observer* from his Capitol Hill offices.

"It's like the equivalent would be *Two Guys for the Poor Goys*, with Jewish people showing people how to cut corners and save money," he said of *Queer Eye*. "It doesn't have to do with effeminacy, it has to do with superficiality. The notion that gay men have a superior fashion sense is not true, and it's damaging. It's a way to marginalize people—you can treat them as pets."

In other words, it encourages the sentiment: What could they want with gay marriage or adoption or immigration rights for their partners, or the right to teach in our schools or serve in our military, when they're getting such fabulous publicity for their looks?

With all of this new visibility for gay men, this nationwide consensus on their cuteness and sartorial smarts, it has been difficult to find a prominent gay man—a gay man with any cultural or political power—speaking on television about the serious issues facing gays right now.

So recently, it seemed, it had been time to break out the Skyy Vodka and cranberry juice to cheer the Supreme Court's June 26 ruling in *Lawrence v. Texas,* which struck down the 17-year-old ruling in *Bowers v. Hardwick*, which upheld states' rights to outlaw sodomy. Fearmongers on the right, and their perennially hopeful counterparts on the left, were already talking about the inevitability of gay-marriage rights as a result of the majority's decision, which went beyond simply striking down the Texas law to offer gays a measure of the same "privacy" afforded women under *Roe v. Wade*. The decision placed gays' rights to determine the course of their own lives over the government's interest in preserving "morality."

But before long, a Gallup poll found an unexpected reversal in the country's feelings about gay marriage: In the space of less than two months, popular support for extending legal rights to gay unions had dropped eight percentage points, from 57 percent to 49 percent. Buzz-kill!

President George W. Bush was happy to end the party early. Answering a question from a reporter about homosexuality in a White House press conference on July 30, Mr. Bush told reporters: "I believe in the sanctity of marriage. I believe a marriage is between a man and a woman. And I think we ought to codify that one way or the other, and we've got lawyers looking at the best way to do that."

That such dark moments in the progress of gay causes can co-exist with a happy makeover show in which mincing style experts remake

straight men for the benefit of their wives and girlfriends shouldn't come as a surprise. If the straight world has long been willing to stomach the prospect of a gay man in the local hair salon or department store, it's another story when it comes to one's family, school or church. And to the extent that one allows gays into one's household—Vice President Dick Cheney, after all, has a gay daughter; George and Laura Bush are said to have included gay couples among their guests in the governor's mansion in Austin, Texas—it must not be publicly understood as an endorsement of their "lifestyle choice."

So it follows that what American families watch gays do onscreen, or in the privacy of their own living rooms, apparently is their business. But don't ask them to support gays' right to marry or to adopt children.

It's somewhere in the haze of the inevitable *Queer Eye* hangover that the politically significant work has to begin. It's probably useless to issue a call to arms to my fellow shmomosexuals of the world, to unite and take over; when the paint cans and the tinting solutions are cleared away and America has finished its country paté on little slices of baguette, sometime around the clever nightcap of this media homo-party, Congress will return to work and the right-wing stink tanks will start churning out the propaganda. And there is no hairstyle or stick of Ikea furniture that can protect us then; it'll mostly be us nursing America's belligerent hangover, because it's mostly, in the end, just us who are out there.

A Literary Lion in Winter: Norman Mailer

JULY 6, 2003 BY ALEXANDRA JACOBS & MARIA RUSSO

@#%*! IT'S A FOUR-LETTER SUMMER

ONCE THE ENGLISH LANGUAGE'S most shocking, egregious, off-limits word, it's become just another cultural noise, thrown around with the casualness of a summer softball, appearing on your TV, on your answering machine, at a newsstand near you, from the mouth of your son, your mom, your congressman, your philosophy professor, your dentist, your waiter, your basic innocent virgin on the street.

Note to the reader: Are we off page 1 yet? If we are, we might as well get on with saying what we mean:

It's the Summer of Fuck!

The door slams too loud, the waiter comes too late, the drinks are mixed too strong, the traffic's too bad on the L.I.E., the mother-in-law is coming, the Yanks are behind, the Mets are ahead, *T-3* is good, *The Hulk* isn't. You stub your toe—*fuck!* You hear good news—*fu-uhck!* You hear amusing news: *You're fucking kidding!* You hear amazing news: *No fucking way!*

The sex act it used to so scandalously denote is barely conjured by the word any more; it's a linguistic tailbone, the vestige of a previous incarnation. It's the word that Superman would use for emphasis if he could have: *What the fuck!* It's a stand-in for the black cloud that would rise above Charlie Brown's head in *Peanuts*: *Fuck me*. But it's lost its bite, its Anglo-Saxon threat. And what it's gained in currency—and a new range of multi-expressiveness—it's lost in its former beautiful, lupine lethality.

What the four letters express best, according to Aaron Karo, 23, a stand-up comic who lives in the Gramercy area, is "exasperation." Mr. Karo has found fortune in the word. He attended the Wharton School of Business, where he wrote a monthly e-mail newsletter called "Ruminations on College Life," famously signing off each column with the phrase "Fuck me." After Simon & Schuster made it into a book (excising the F-word), he quit an investment-banking job and is in talks to do a sitcom.

"I don't think fuck is the new damn," said Mr. Karo. "I think it's the new *the*."

Gosh.

◇◇◇◇◇◇◇

JULY 20, 2003 BY SRIDHAR PAPPU

King Calm Keller Takes Over Times, Quiets Kvetchers

AT 1 P.M. ON JULY 14, BILL KELLER stood before the top editors and managers of *The New York Times* in an 11th-floor dining room at the paper's West 43rd Street headquarters.

Like a latter-day Mikhail Gorbachev, charged with bringing reform and openness to the dark corridors of the Kremlin, Mr. Keller told them there would be no personal recriminations as a result of the previous scandal-rocked months at the paper under former executive editor Howell Raines, who was asked to resign when mounting trouble at the paper in the wake of the Jayson Blair affair threatened to swallow the paper's leadership whole. He would not, he told his new subjects as they ate their lunches, "divide the paper into Friends of Howell and Friends of Bill."

SEPTEMBER 14, 2003
BY GAIL SHEEHY

9/11/03: The Past as Pre-History

TWO WEEKS AFTER THE AT-tacks of 9/11 created a Ground Zero in New York, I went looking for the emotional Ground Zero in the suburbs. I found it in Middletown, N.J., only 20 miles across the bay in physical distance but as remote as one of the Trobriand Islands in its complacent consciousness. That was, before nearly 50 people were robbed from Middletown and environs.

I started my explorations of Middletown as a student of anthropologist Margaret Mead; I had learned that when a highly significant event opens a fissure in the normal patterns of life, a writer must drop everything and go to the edge, where she will see the culture turned inside out.

There is no middle in Middletown. It was a large, sprawling, fragmented township divided into 12 separate enclaves. The bigger the house and the broader the lawn, the less likely the occupants would know their neighbors or imagine they would ever need to rely on community. It was a microcosm of suburban America.

People ask me, *What can we do on 9/11?* The simplest act of recognition that we are now living in a New Normal would be to walk across the lawn to someone you don't know and say, "You've lived here a long time, and I've lived here a long time, and we don't know each other. I'd like to get to know you, so that if a day comes when we need each other, we will have already made the connection."

New Yorkers protest the Iraq war

◇◇◇◇◇◇◇

OCTOBER 5, 2003   BY ALEXANDRA JACOBS

KELLER'S PIPING HOT LAUNDRY!

YOUNTVILLE, CALIF.—"I'M TERRIFIED OF GOING BACK TO NEW York, New York," said Thomas Keller, the chef at arguably the best restaurant in America—and by the time his pastry guy's little bombardment of desserts has arrived, like a hail of bullets covered in sugar and gold leaf, who can argue?

"It's almost like this sport," is how Mr. Keller described cooking for strangers. "It just gets tough sometimes when you get into a situation where you don't know."

The next day he'd be leaving for New York, where he and several corporate partners plan to unveil an entity he describes as "the French Laundry, but not the French Laundry" on the fourth floor of the forbidding new Time Warner building in Columbus Circle. There is a tentative name picked out, a Latin word that he refused to divulge, fearing premature analysis from the city's notoriously oversalivating food press.

"It's a scary thing," he said

OCTOBER 5, 2003
BY SRIDHAR PAPPU

ANNA'S MINI-SHE: *TEEN VOGUE* EDITOR PREPS FOR WINTOUR

"I THINK THEIR LIFE IS SO hard," said Amy Astley as she sat talking about the young people who fill the pages of her magazine, *Teen Vogue.*

The hazel-eyed, blond-haired ballerina turned editor in chief has such confidence in the girls who read and appear in *Teen Vogue* that she speaks of being young as though it were synonymous with being talented.

"They're so young," she said. "Having grown up in the hothouse of ballet, I understand."

In June 2002, Condé Nast chairman Si Newhouse and *Vogue* editor in chief Anna Wintour pulled Ms. Astley, then nine months pregnant with her second child, to lead the company's charge into the *Gilmore Girls* set.

"People are always saying to me, 'Don't you miss *Vogue*?'" Ms. Astley said. "And I'm like, 'No, now I work with all the fresh talent.'

"I want another baby, but I can't. Because *Teen Vogue*'s my third baby. And I don't think I can take care of four babies."

OCTOBER 26, 2003   BY GEORGE GURLEY

My Vagina Monologue

THE OTHER NIGHT I SAW A TV COMMERCIAL WHERE TWO guys wearing overcoats go to a "streaking party." Five beautiful women wearing bathrobes open the door. The guys flash them; the women look down at the men's equipment and don't react. The guys get nervous and close their coats.

You can't get through one day these days without a reference to penis size. It's always been talked about, of course, but previously there was at least a sense of madcap fun: think of playboy Porfirio Rubirosa, whose infamous "giant pepper mill" Truman Capote likened to "an 11-inch cafe au lait sinker as thick as a man's wrist." Now penis size has become something of a giddy cultural obsession. In addition to constant reminders—on television, in movies, on giant billboard underwear ads—men learn of their probable shortcomings every morning in the form of spam.

"Are you hung like a gnat?"

Delete.

"Want to add three inches and fatten up your pipe?"

Delete, delete.

"Hey you! Want a huge trouser snake, an enormous Johnson, a purple oak?"

Delete, delete, delete.

Not true five, 10 years ago.

But what about the flip side, I've started to wonder: How come no one ever talks about a woman's "size"? Every straight man knows—even if he doesn't dare mention this to his wife or girlfriend—that ladies' packages come in different sizes. And we're not talking about external aesthetic differences: We're talking about ... the Grip.

I decided to ask men and women about this serious issue. So I put fresh batteries in my tape recorder and went out into the night. First stop: a fancy Fifth Avenue party.

Helen Gurley Brown—the original Cosmo girl!—was at the party, wearing a pink Chanel suit. "I don't think, for women, the size of her vagina is an issue, *ever*," she said. "Because she can fit anything into her, no problem. But all the propaganda about penis size not making a difference—I think that's just propaganda, because it does make a difference."

I called Dian Hanson, the former editor of *Leg Show* and *Juggs*, another woman who's has seen a lot of women up close.

"Of course there's vaginal variation, and probably as much as penile variation," she said from Los Angeles, where she's an editor at Taschen books.

"I think women can pretty smugly go about their lives not worrying about it," she said. "Because, historically, guys are so happy to be allowed in there that if the walls are a little loose, they're just going to adjust their thrust and think they have a small penis."

She did say that heavy women tend to be tighter.

"You're going to see the most cavernous ones on little, tiny, slender women," she said. "This is where, to the pornographer, these things become apparent: You say to the girl, 'O.K., bend over, put your chest on the bed and let your butt stick up in the air.' These little skinny girls? That thing will blow up like a balloon."

I met actress Jackie Clarke, 28, for a drink in Chelsea. Last year she wrote and performed *Mail Order Family*, a one-woman show at the Upright Citizens Brigade Theatre. The original title had been Big Vagina Monologues, but, Ms. Clarke said, Eve Ensler's lawyers made her change it. In the show, she had a riff about her "crazy" father, who had married a Filipino woman whom he'd ordered from a catalog.

"I guess I was 8 or 9 at the time," she said. "And my stepmother had visited the gynecologist, and she was crying in the kitchen. Apparently, the doctor had made her feel really bad because he was complaining how she was too small and his medical tools wouldn't fit inside of her.

"So my dad just started going off trying to make my stepmom feel better. He kept saying, 'What do you want to be, an American wom-

an? You know, American women, by the time they're 30, they have mustaches and enormous vaginas. Enormous, floppy vaginas!'

"So she's feeling a little better, and I'm starting to get a little antsy, because I know I'm a full-fledged American and all I can see myself as is a 30-year-old woman with a handlebar mustache and just a gaping oasis canyon of a vagina."

Now that she's all grown up, she said, "I've never had any complaints. I think if a guy's complaining, he's probably too tiny."

Later, at the restaurant 66, I found myself sitting across from hair-salon owner Joel Warren and his Asian model girlfriend.

"I've always thought it was not fair to pick on men and not talk about women," he said. "It's a big thing."

Dean Winters, an actor who played Ryan O'Reily on the HBO series *Oz*, joined me for a cigarette outside; he said he agreed with me "a hundred percent."

"Every guy at some point in his career has been with a woman and it was like making love to a glass of water," he said. "I remember one time, I really felt like I was just seriously yodeling into the abyss."

OCTOBER 5, 2003   BY DAVID MICHAELIS

THE LAST GENTLEMAN

IN THOSE DAYS, *THE PARIS REVIEW* OCCUPIED A ONE-ROOM ground floor office on the East River with a lion-tamer's chair hanging from the ceiling. George lived upstairs in a duplex. His first wife, Freddy, and oldest daughter, Medora, lived up there, too, but the first floor of the Plimpton apartment, with its pool table and club-green walls and hunting trophies and general flavor of Harvard and Hemingway, was such a pure expression of George that the whole of the first floor had simply remained a bachelor pad—a clubhouse.

In those summer mornings, the managing editor, Molly McKaughan, all bustle and energy, opened the office. Next came the three editorial assistants; one with a desk (Jannika Hurwitt), one with a rolling chair (Lucas Matthiessen) and one perched uncertainly between the tiny bathroom, the front door, and the sliver of a storage room (me). I came in one morning to find a rat swimming in the office toilet, which caused hardly any commotion, it turned out, so unflappable was the staff of George Plimpton's literary magazine.

By mid-morning, George showed up, looking surprised and amused to find us there: still at work, or at work already. He himself was half-dressed; pale blue Brooks Brothers boxers and a hastily buttoned dress shirt, his hair a mop of semi-tarnished silver, his nose, like the beak of a wading bird, rising as he peered into the office with furrowed forehead. The idea was that he, too, should already be hard at work, but, alas, here he was, just another boyish Upper East Side WASP male in stocking feet, guiltily retrieving the morning paper from the vestibule instead of getting down to work at the bank.

Half-dressed George would fold himself into his armchair, gloomily pulling on his glasses to look at the topmost query on the pile. Almost immediately a phone would ring, but no one would answer it—it was the Plimptons' private line. After an interval the intercom would buzz from upstairs, and George would be needed on that line. George's voice heard up close for the first time in a quiet room made you complicit in a strange phenomenon. Was he serious? "No one who talked the way George did could ever be serious," the poet Donald Hall recalled thinking when he first met Plimpton in the '50s. Where was that Brahmin drawl from? Kurt Vonnegut called it a "honk"; it was thought to be "British." George himself described it as "Eastern Seaboard cosmopolitan." What people didn't understand was that although it was not a put-on, Plimpton's accent had a playful aspect that took some getting used to.

In any case, he made deliberate use of his voice, and what he most often did with it—at least when he was feeling generous—was to make you an intimate by letting you in on the joke. The joke was that stuffy as he sounded, George Plimpton had in fact made a career by taking stands against the professionalism and adultism that was the bane of his generation.

He triumphed uniquely in this because his career was founded on the expectation that he was not in the end going to win. He did hard work and made it look easy. He had the ability to impart lightness in the form of a touch of self-amusement. He had both the courage to enter worlds where well-trained professionals risked blood and guts and the wit to look at their struggles with the kind of bemusement

that puts life itself into perspective. He stepped into the boxing ring with the light heavyweight champion Archie Moore, took the mound as a major league pitcher, and sauntered onto the field as the third-string quarterback for the Detroit Lions—all at a time when sports were becoming increasingly professional and obsessive. Plimpton single-handedly returned sports to pure pleasure, but with a twist, and with hard work.

The twist was in his generous fascination with the way people did things. In a culture that cares more for who people are than for what

they do and how they do it, George peered curiously, and with great respect, into the way the game was played. He conveyed the work that went into the game. He revealed both to the players he played with and the readers reading him a new idea in American sports writing: Winners rarely feel like winners. Victory is what the onlooker feels, not the participant. From his vantage point inside the game, Plimpton could see that triumph was expressed not by the exhausted warriors but by their spear-carriers, the fans. Victory had become something to go out to the stadium to see, no longer earned only on the field. His work conveyed, above all, an almost melancholy sense of the price paid by the man in the dust of the arena.

Journalism set Plimpton apart, and therefore placed him in his natural element, which was to be isolated and alone even among a crowd of people. Of all the things George Plimpton did, and the *Paris Review* office was nothing if not a living museum of the artifacts of a singular career, the magazine itself was always closest to his heart. "I would feel that a limb had been amputated," he once confided, "if *The Paris Review* stopped."

Once, in 1960, it almost had. After 25 issues, the editors, now in their 30s, with careers and families, met in New York to decide the magazine's future. Matthiessen and Guinzburg had both moved on to newer projects and voted for closing down *The Paris Review*. Plimpton, still the editor, was held to account for the lateness of issues and general inefficiency. For his part, George was frustrated and angry at having been abandoned by the other founding editors; he wanted everyone to stay on and work harder. Factions formed, tempers flared, everyone had too much to drink. Finally the poetry editor, Donald Hall, soothed the room with a speech about the magazine's first principles. George, left with the choice to shut the shop or carry on alone with new talent, credited Hall as "the man who saved *The Paris Review*." But it was Hall who got closer to the truth that defined Plimpton's whole life: "George never gives up on anyone."

George invented himself. In Paris at the age of 26, he had no idea what he would do with his life. He thought maybe he would come home and get involved in television, the coming thing. Then he stumbled on his first real invention, "the *Paris Review* interview."

George and the other editors created an alternative to criticism. They let the authors talk about their work themselves. *The Paris Review*'s first issue featured an interview with E. M. Forster, in which the old King's College don demystified the Malabar Caves scene in *A Passage to India* by revealing that he had consciously created it as a substitute for violence. The *Paris Review* interviews, Writers at Work, are the indispensable companion to postwar world literature. Plimpton, who interviewed Ernest Hemingway for issue No. 18, thus made an art form of going to writers better than he and talking about what it was really like to write. There, in other words, was the template for his

Journalism set Plimpton apart, and therefore placed him in his natural element, which was to be isolated and alone even among a crowd of people.

whole career as interested participant on Centre Court at Wimbledon or at the 18th hole at the U. S. Open or in the backfield of the Detroit Lions football team.

As with so many things in his life, the New York of the 1960s and of his prime was the sunlit city of pretty girls in their summer dresses. He seemed merely amused by pretty girls: He concealed how hard he had taken it when the love of his youth jilted him. The story was allowed to show its nose, but that was all: At Harvard, a faunlike Radcliffe girl named Bea was smart, with a purpose in life besides getting a man. The romance was serious on both sides, but Bea was cautious—perhaps she could see that being married to this young man was a career in itself—and turned George down.

He was a celebrity in a minor key. He was famous in a gentlemanly way. He was criticized for being a publicity hound, but in fact, though George loved being famous and worked very hard at it, he never opened the windows on his private life. He never alluded to his childhood, or to episodes of personal pain. He was always George Plimpton, Amateur, and he lived in a world in which painful passions do not exist on the page.

George talked incessantly about money. Money was a routine topic of conversation in *The Paris Review*'s editorial office—a surprise to me, at eighteen. In my own middle-class family, the subject of money was an embarrassment. George had an aristocratic unembarrassment about money.

His concern about money centered always around the baby he'd fathered in Paris and been stuck with by his fellow founders. He worried, perhaps, again, out of guilt: George always knew that of all the choices in his life, the "most sensible one," he once told me, "would be to drop *The Paris Review*." But he didn't, and from the moment he tapped Prince Sadruddin Aga Khan, his Harvard roommate, to be *The Paris Review*'s first publisher while they were running with the bulls in Pamplona, to the somewhat less glamorous but no less loyal publishers of the 1970s (Ron Dante, the music producer and creator of the Archies; Bernard F. Connors, the Canadian soft-drink king), to the creation in the 1990s of a sensibly endowed Paris Review Foundation, fund-raising was foremost on his mind.

Money is the key theme—dignity the dominant gift conferred—in his final note to subscribers. It arrived the week before his death as a small printed insert accompanying the dazzlingly chic invitation to the magazine's gala 50th anniversary revels. Under *The Paris Review*'s insignia—talon-gripped dip pen and liberty cap with tricolore cockade—George took note of the fact that the party on October 14 was going to be, in fact, a fund-raiser and that, for some, the ticket prices would be "relatively high." Was George taking pity on the poor subscriber in Kansas City, Kansas, because the cheapest seat would be $500 and it's a long way to New York? Well, no, probably not—but he wanted us all to know that we were welcome, and he turned what might be seen as condescension into a high compliment: "We tend to think of our subscribers as those we would like to have with us at such an occasion and thus the invitation." And having done the cosmopolitan thing, he then wastes no more time before pointing out that if you happen to be unable to come, you still have several options: You might like to make a contribution to the Paris Review Foundation; or simply buy an extra subscription for a friend through *The Review*'s new Web site; or—the purest of Plimptonian salutes—"simply raise a glass on the 14th of October." He signs off in even purer faith, a classically wistful-sounding Plimpton promise: "In any case, the 50th anniversary issue will be reaching you next month."

DECEMBER 21, 2003   BY TISH DURKIN

Saddam Bagged, Bizarre Baghdad Doesn't Bug Out

BAGHDAD—IF YOU DIDN'T KNOW THE DEVIL himself had been put behind bars, you never would have guessed.

The jig was up, the news was out, the DNA was in, the dictatorial hair had been probed for lice on international television. ... Yet, to all outward appearances, the streets of Baghdad did not know and did not care.

I had gotten into a car for a vivid, perhaps even dicey, ride through Saddam Hussein's capital after its last piece of sky had fallen. It turned out to be a scavenger hunt for signs of anything at all.

I went to Al Sadr City, the massively Shia, largely impoverished area where the resilience of sewage has long since tempered the euphoria of liberation—but where the waning of affection for America has, nonetheless, done little to dilute the venomous hatred of Saddam. There, the streets were quiet—but not, it bears noting, one murmur more quiet than usual. The shops that were always open late were open late tonight, and through their windows could clearly be seen one vignette after another of business as usual: a storekeeper putting cans on the shelves; a shoe salesman accepting dinar notes for plastic sandals.

On the way home, on a flashier, busier thoroughfare, I came across a merry convoy of about a dozen cars with their horns blaring, full of singing, waving passengers. Sure enough, one of the passengers had a foot-high hairdo and a sugar-spun veil; it was a wedding procession.

In context, the insistence of normality seemed all the more bizarre. Iraqis, as the wedding indicated, are great markers of milestones. Weeks before, when their national soccer team had won a big game, these same people had erupted in celebratory gunfire that was so loud and lasted so long that I truly, if briefly, believed that the civil war had come at last. Moreover, since the occupation began, many Iraqis had given many indications that the capture of Saddam would be the biggest milestone of them all.

Perhaps the Iraqis' ambivalence now has less to do with what they are facing than with who they are—or who they think they are. And, in many of their own minds, who they are seems surprisingly hard to sever from who Saddam is.

Which is not to suggest that they don't hate him and want him dead.

It's complicated.

"What is complicated?" asked Ahmed Chalabi, the Pentagon's favorite member of the American-appointed, pre-emptively marginalized Iraqi Governing Council. This was on Sunday afternoon, right after the announcement, and Mr. Chalabi was standing outside the marble headquarters of the 25-member council.

Mr. Chalabi, along with several colleagues, had been wandering now and again out of the building to meet the gathering press. The complications he was dismissing were not emotional but judicial, and they were already bubbling up on the burner of What Next For Saddam.

"There is a process," he said, referring to the war-crimes tribunal that had been set up. "There is an investigation."

"There is going to be a trial," an aide pointed out.

Given the young fellow's excellent grooming and the perfect English in which he swirled such phrases as "phoner with Stephanopoulos" into his mobile telephone, it was hard to imagine that he and his boss had never heard of O.J. Simpson, and therefore of the potential for the trials of celebrities—let alone allegedly genocidal celebrities—to spin off in ways that were unpredictable, even dangerous, for society as a whole.

In any event, they would be learning about this phenomenon soon.

The complications arising from the spectacle of Saddam, captured alive and kept that way for months at least, range from the wildly colorful to the dry but defining. On one side of this spectrum, there is the wild, wild card of how Saddam plays as a defendant. If catching Saddam can have its public-relations perils for the Americans, it is foolhardy to assume that trying Saddam will not. Until Sunday, I must admit, I would have laughed at the notion of negative fallout from either one, except among those Iraqis who have supported Saddam all along.

Then the Americans pulled him out of a rat hole looking like hell, and televised him getting his tongue depressed and his tonsils lit up.

Fascinatingly, no matter what the regime had done to them or their relatives, almost no one I spoke to seemed to be reveling in his humiliation, and many seemed to feel that they somehow shared in it.

This does not mean that people don't want him punished, but it does suggest the possibility for public sentiment toward captive and captors alike to change in the coming months, depending on what is done with Saddam.

Not even the people who helped formulate the war-crimes tribunal are clear on how it will work or what its limits will be. On Monday morning, Dara Nooraldin, a judge and a member of the Governing Council, gave an interview to three Western reporters.

"This is not a revenging court," he declared.

Then one of the reporters asked whether the Iraqis might consider doing something along the lines of the Truth and Reconciliation Commission in South Africa, in which members and enemies of the apartheid regime fully confessed to their former crimes, in exchange for which many were pardoned.

"In South Africa, were the same crimes committed as were committed here?" he asked.

Well, some pretty serious stuff went on there, the reporter replied.

"Did they used to bury them alive?" Nooraldin challenged. "Or kill children with poisonous gas?"

The reporter then allowed as how they used to stick tires around people's necks, douse them in gasoline and set them on fire.

"And they were forgiven for these crimes?" asked the judge.

"Yes," said the reporter—correctly or incorrectly, I don't know.

"Oh," said the judge, and then paused for a moment, as if this revelation were a freshly formed cushion and he needed to sit back on it for a second. This he did.

"Maybe the same thing will happen here."

And maybe, all present thought but did not say, it won't.

Power Punks! Chelsea Clinton, Gifford Miller, Adrien Brody, Jay-Z, Chloë Sevigny, Drew and Karenna Gore Schiff

GEORGE GURLEY INTERVIEWS CANDACE BUSHNELL

**What was life like before you came to
The New York Observer?**
I moved to New York at 19. I was doing a lot
of fiction writing, and I went to acting school
for a couple of months—I had an agent and this idea that I would do TV
commercials to support myself as a novelist. The first writing I ever got
paid for was a children's book for Simon and Schuster. It was *Dress the
Bear* instead of *Pat the Bunny*. I got paid a thousand dollars; I don't think
they ended up publishing it, but I got paid. Then in the early '80s, I was an
assistant at *Ladies Home Journal* and *Good Housekeeping*, then a staff
writer at *Self*, writing about everything from micro-
waves to relationships to fashion designers. And I
freelanced for places like *Mademoiselle* and *Esquire*.
I was friends with Morgan Entrekin and Jay McInerney and Bret Easton Ellis, so I knew people in publishing. You know, for me, that time was glam but no
money. I had this little studio apartment, a girlfriend
and I lived in the same building and our apartments
were never quite finished; she never had a kitchen
sink, I didn't have a bed—I had a piece of foam. We'd
go to Kentucky Fried Chicken on the corner of 74th
and First Avenue. We never got our hair done, we
didn't get manicures. It was a struggle and there
were times when it was frightening. My apartment
was robbed and they took my mink coat, some old
ratty mink coat.

> *If there was
> something about
> Mr. Big in the
> column, I would
> show it to him
> and he would
> always say, "Cute,
> baby, cute."*

**But you still found yourself at fancy black-tie parties, like at the
Met's Temple of Dendur?**
Occasionally. I would go to Saks and buy a frock that was 80 percent off
and pretty much got around New York the way young, determined people
get around New York. And I had lots and lots of girlfriends. And it was fun!
New York's celebrities then were restaurateurs and writers, journalists like
Tina Brown and Graydon Carter. And there were all these restaurants—the
McNally brothers opened a restaurant every six months. Like Indochine.
Everyone went to restaurants every night. They were like little clubs, you
saw people you knew, lots of table-hopping, they were theater! And you
could *smoke* in restaurants. One time Morgan Entrekin and I went to one
of those restaurants in Tribeca, and it started pouring rain, and they just
cranked up the music and everybody started dancing, because it was
raining too hard to leave and it was two in the morning. People would
stay at restaurants drinking until *one!* There were cell phones but only a

Candace Bushnell wrote the Sex and the City column for *The New York
Observer*; her most recent novel is *One Fifth Avenue*.

few investment bankers had them, and they were as big as a brick. And
so in order to communicate, to know what was going on, you had to be
there. You couldn't read about it on the Internet. It was about being there.
So with *The Observer*, what happened was Peter Stevenson and I had a
mutual friend, Laura Yorke, a young editor at Simon and Schuster, and I
sent her 100 pages of a novel I'd been working on. And she said, "Well, I
don't think I can publish this, but I have a friend, Peter Stevenson, he's an
editor and you should meet him." And Peter Kaplan and Stevenson were
restarting a magazine called *Smart*, and I had a meeting with them. But
their Japanese backers disappeared, vanished. Then Stevenson went to
The Observer and he called me up. They were in that
townhouse, they didn't even have cubicles, it was a
mess. John Homans was there in his dirty Converse
sneakers, there were old pizza boxes and bags of
food, and that *bathroom*! God forbid you should ever
go to that bathroom. My first piece was called "Manhattan Transfers"; it was about these kids, like Nicky
Beavers—who unfortunately, as you know, ended
up killing himself, which was really, really sad—and
they had gone to rehab in Minnesota at Hazelden.
And Hazelden had told them that they should live in
Minneapolis, away from New York and temptation.
So there was a group of about 20 young New Yorkers
who were expats in Minneapolis, being sober. But the
problem was that *The Observer* didn't have money
for expenses. They were going to pay me $500. I had
$300, so I took the $300 and I got a cheap flight to Minneapolis and my
sister was living there, so I slept on her couch. I wrote the story and Susan
Morrison, who was the editor of the paper, liked it. *The Observer* was the
place for quirky characters and quirky pieces, and there was a lot of freedom in how the pieces were written.

How did Sex and the City get started?
By that time Peter Kaplan had become the editor, and I guess he felt that
the stories I was doing were popular, people were talking about them, so
he and Stevenson asked if I wanted to do a column. We came up with the
title Sex and the City and for the first column, they made me go to that
sex club Le Trapeze. So I went, I reported it, I did the story. I actually felt
we were going to run out of material in about two columns. But after that,
I really knew what I wanted to do with the column. First of all, it's *The New
York Observer*—it was never going to be sexually explicit, ever. It was about
what happened, in a sense, before and after sex. Social anthropology, people jockeying for position. We set out to write about things that could only
happen in New York—for instance, the second column was about a serial
dater, this guy had dated *20* women that I knew. And of course all the girls
were friends, and in fact a lot of the women had become friends because

George Gurley Interviews Candace Bushnell

What was it like being with Mr. Big, writing about him? And Mr. Big was based on?

[*Vogue* publisher] Ron Galotti. I was crazy about him and I was in love with him. We were together for a year and a half. If there was something about Mr. Big in the column, I would show it to him and he would always say, "Cute, baby, cute."

You think sex and relationships are less messed up than they were 15 years ago?

Oh, no, I think that they're probably just as messed up. It may even be worse because young women say that they don't even go on dates.

What about Peter Kaplan?

Ahh, the mysterious Kaplan! We always wondered if he ever read anything that went into the paper. Kaplan would always have his door closed, pulling his hair out. And then if you had a meeting with him, he would always say something really unfathomable. The big-picture thing! You'd come out and be laughing and wondering, "What the hell was he talking about?"

If you wanted to have a meeting with Kaplan, you had to schedule a meeting—and then he'd never be there! Stevenson and I would have lunch and Kaplan would come, at this lousy little cheap French bistro on Madison Avenue. But the bottom line about working for *The Observer* is that it was really *fun*. And it was hilarious! There were always funny things going on. We used to try to find out what pieces *New York* magazine was doing and we would try to scoop them. And Maer Roshan was working for *New York* and once he had a big story due on a Thursday. And we came up with this plan: I went out with Maer and I made him stay out all night. And then he was so hung over, he couldn't make it to work, and he couldn't get his story done. Very fiendish stuff.

Why do you think the column became a hit so fast?

It was the '90s, and there were all of these single women in their 30s who hadn't found Mr. Right. And that was, at the time, somewhat of a phenomenon. Nobody really knew what to *think* about these women—because there weren't supposed to *be* single women in their 30s. When I first started writing the column, that really got around: The frightening *truth* of being a single woman in your 30s! And when I wrote about the toxic bachelors, I interviewed different men, and they said, "If a woman's over 35, I don't know that I want to date her." So there were things in that column that were frighteningly real. And I think the column touched on a lot of things that we're still talking about. From the beginning, there were women who read that column and felt it addressed their secret fears, and made them feel as if they weren't alone, like they weren't the only ones having these thoughts. Every column was in a sense a little morality tale. The story about the modelizers, for instance, ends pretty grimly, with the modelizer saying that he got this girl pregnant, she wants all this money and she's having a baby, and he's 32 years old and he feels like an old man. So I would always try to have a little twist at the end, as if to say, you know, *everybody's* a little fucked up.

they'd all dated this guy. I got the women together and interviewed them about this guy. So at the start, the column was very journalistic. In a piece about threesomes, I sat in a room with guys and interviewed them. Later some of the columns were completely fiction, like the one where Carrie and her friends go to the baby shower in Connecticut. For me the column really evolved from journalism to fiction—writing the column was my way around all the obstacles I faced in becoming a novelist. And the biggest obstacle was nobody was interested in publishing a novel by a young woman about people in New York City; those weren't the kinds of books they were publishing. Anyway, I got the Sex and the City book deal after six or seven columns. I told Bret Easton Ellis that I thought Morgan Entrekin was interested in buying it, and he said, "You've got to get an agent!" Bret called up ICM, spoke to three agents, and one of them, Heather Schroeder, called me back in 30 minutes. And she's still my agent. One thing that was interesting about the column was that it was really written for a very small audience, the audience that read *The Observer*, which was a small, sophisticated—I would say fairly well-heeled—audience. It was insidery. And for the audience it was written for, I think that it felt like the truth about their lives, that knife's edge where ambition meets frustration and where you have people who want things but getting them is complicated. One thing that was a little perplexing, when the book first came out, bookstores would put it in the sociology section.

2004

The Brits are back—again: Charles and Camilla tour our shores

Ugg! Fuzzy shearling boots blight city

Absolut rip-off: Nightclubs spin patrons in $200 jeans with $300 "bottle service"

The most lusted name in news? Anderson Cooper is CNN's new superstar

 Comedian Chris Rock knocks 'em dead with Black Ambition tour

Caitlin Flanagan chronicles domestic life as pallid emo boys frustrate New York women

Retired GE chair Jack Welch charges up his babe Boswell, Suzy Wetlaufer

 Right-wing commentator Bill O'Reilly sued for sexual harassment

Loafer-clad Republicans pad over alien planet New York City for political convention

2004

◇◇◇◇◇◇◇

JANUARY 5, 2004   BY ALEXANDRA JACOBS

Ugg!
Fuzzy Boots Blight City

IS THERE ANYTHING MORE TO say about Ugg boots, the heinous shearling footwear that women are wearing all over Manhattan, even in the formerly delicate-ankled quarter of Nolita?

How about: Stop wearing them? How about: Be glad that the boots are back-ordered from the manufacturer until the spring; be glad that they're going for three times their $150 price on eBay. That's good. It will give you time to stop and think before you buy, you big ol' fashion sheep.

Ugg boots originate in Australia, but like many other "but they're sooo comfortable" trends of the past year—velour track suits, etc.—the blame for their popularity may be pinned squarely on Southern California. Embraced 25 years ago by shaggy, tolerant surfers, Uggs caught on more recently with celebrities like Jessica Simpson and Pamela Anderson. Their sleek Barbie beauty is supposedly thrown into stark relief by the dowdy boots—which simply make the rest of us look like militant lesbian activists.

Uggs are, in a word, awful.

I Love Ali

JANUARY 19, 2004   BY GEORGE GURLEY

'SPLAIN IT, ALI!

THE MORNING SHOW *LIVING It Up!* with Ali and Jack, which debuted last Sept. 15, hadn't been on CBS for two weeks before the critics were bitching away.

Some were kind, but numerous others pointed out the lack of chemistry between Ms. Wentworth, 39, and co-host Jack Ford, 53, and noted the "nonexistent" ratings. In early December, the *Daily News* reported "rumblings" that if Martha Stewart beats her insider-trading case, CBS will return her show to the Ali and Jack time slot.

I began trading e-mails with the show's publicist in hopes of meeting Ms. Wentworth, an actress, author of *The WASP Cookbook* and wife of the former Clinton adviser George Stephanopoulos, who hosts the Sunday-morning political talk show *This Week on ABC*.

Last summer, there had been rumors in the *New York Post* about the couple. Their marriage was in trouble. George resented Ali's success. Ms. Wentworth decided to take action and told *The Washington Post*, "Come on, do you know of many strained marriages that make love twice a day?"

Mr. Stephanopoulos is a constant on *Living It Up!* He gets mentioned several times an episode. Ms. Wentworth thinks they complement each other well.

"He's much more serious, and news is much more devastating to him, and I kind of lighten that up," she said. "But vice versa: He has gotten me much more immersed in 'Wow, this happens in Palestine?' But it's a good balance. I think if we were both, you know, 'Whoa-ho-ho-ho!' about everything, we would be the most annoying couple."

FEBRUARY 2, 2004
BY PHOEBE EATON

THE HOLLYWOOD BEAST ROARS

IN MARCH 2001, JOE ESZTERHAS was diagnosed with throat cancer. It was now or perhaps never to release *Hollywood Animal* (Alfred A. Knopf), a 736-page monster truck of a memoir that lumbers into bookstores this week.

In the 80's and much of the 90's, Mr. Eszterhas was Hollywood's best-paid screenwriter, sometimes receiving more cash for a script than the film's director. Some of these movies were hits. Some weren't. One could count on seeing cartons of militantly smoked cigarettes and, in his late-period panty movies, ruttish lesbians and multiple grand-mal orgasms.

How insufferable was I? he asks several times in the course of the book's introduction. The answer is all too apparent, but he clearly prides himself on the particulars: the Concorde tickets, the "A-list pussy" that rubbed up against his leg. Mr. Eszterhas' movies grossed more than $1 billion, so he comes by his bragging rights honestly. Still, one can't help but wonder if it was merely an accident of geography that neighbor Bob Dylan's mastiffs often chose to relieve themselves in front of his Point Dume house.

FEBRUARY 9, 2004 BY FRANK DIGIACOMO

The Bling of Comedy

IN ONE OF THE BACKSTAGE hospitality rooms of the Theater at Madison Square Garden, Chris Rock sat on an ass-battered couch, arms folded tightly, and talked about the ambition in his "Black Ambition" tour.

"I want to have it so tight that it works in front of every audience: rich, poor, a strip club and the Senate. Literally like that," he said. "If only smart people like your shit, it ain't that smart." He let out a laugh, a heh-heh-heh that was a cross between Eddie Murphy and Phyllis Diller. *Heh-heh-heh.*

"The greatest artists of our time were pop. Beethoven was pop!" Mr. Rock said, putting an emphasis on that last word as if he were participating in a poetry slam. "Beethoven was the fucking Justin Timberlake of his time. You know what I mean? Louis Armstrong, that shit was pop! It wasn't like just some cool-shit jazz people that listened to it. That shit was pop. Picasso was pop. Motherfuckers are eating burgers and going, 'That Picasso shit is good.'

"So, that's what you strive for," he said.

When I said he had talked a lot about President Bush, Mr. Rock stopped me. "I'm talking about the president. In my last special, I talked about Clinton. I haven't picked a side. I'm still where I've always been. It's my job to talk about the president, no matter who he is," he said. And a little later, worried that he'd be perceived as being co-opted, he said what generations of comics have said, "You want me to take a political stance. That's career suicide."

Well, did Mr. Rock think that Republicans or Democrats were better at creating the kind of distractions to which he was referring earlier? "People like distraction," he said with a smile that suggested he was not going to be fooled into committing career suicide. "Nobody likes to sit down and write a novel. You can't wait for something to distract you." He laughed. "Nobody wants to do work. Hard work ahead of you? Look, a bunny rabbit!"

But Mr. Rock has clearly not given up on good old American democracy. During his show, he says something that seems shocking at first—then he explains himself. "I love to see the flag burn, because it lets me know I'm in the right spot," he says. "People only hate the winners. People hate the Yankees. People hate the Cowboys. People hate the Lakers."

In other words, Mr. Rock, like the other big comedians in the Pantheon—Redd Foxx, Bill Cosby, Lenny Bruce and Will Rogers—likes being in the free speech vortex of the world. "Come to my show, laugh," he said. "I kind of write a show the way I write it because I don't really take any laughs for granted. My whole philosophy is even if you don't think it's funny, hopefully you think it's interesting."

"It's jokes, man," he said after the show. "It's jokes.

"Look at Bill Cosby. Look at Dick Gregory. As far as who's the bigger activist, who's got more stuff done." Mr. Rock cupped his hands around his mouth and whispered, *"Bill Cosby."* Then he said, "That's how you do it. Do I want to march down 125th Street or do I want to put myself in a position to give Tuskegee [University] $40 million? That's where it's at. That's the real gangster shit. That's the real activism."

MARCH 1, 2004
BY RACHEL DONADIO

Naomi Wolf Makes Much Ado About Nuzzling At Yale

NAOMI WOLF WAS ON THE phone on Feb. 24 speaking about her cover story in this week's *New York,* in which she accuses literary scholar Harold Bloom of having placed his "heavy, boneless hand" on her inner thigh when she was an undergraduate student in 1983. In it, she also depicted Yale University as an environment where sexual "encroachment" is tolerated, and where, to this day, students are afraid to come forward about their troubling experiences.

But in opening up a 20-year-old case of sexual harassment at Yale, Ms. Wolf had also opened up any number of questions: about the university, about Professor Bloom, about her own journalistic techniques, and about the reliability of using older anecdotal memories brought to bear on long-buried circumstances.

Apparently banking on the fact that Ms. Wolf's celebrity—as well as that of her accused sexual "encroacher"—would blind readers to the fact that neither Ms. Wolf nor *New York* magazine made any attempt to find any other accounts of Mr. Bloom behaving in a sexually inappropriate manner toward a student, the piece converted Mr. Bloom instantly from best-selling Shakespeare authority to sexual predator. *New York* didn't offer Mr. Bloom a conventional journalistic forum in which to respond, such as by having a disinterested reporter report and write the piece; instead, Ms. Wolf acted as a combination memoirist and reporter.

MARCH 15, 2004   BY CHOIRE SICHA

MR. ANDERSON COOPER, SUPERSTAR

THE DAY BEFORE HIS FIRST vacation in a good while, in a jewel box of a West Chelsea teahouse, Anderson Cooper sat reading *The New York Times* beside a small reflective pool. Sleek in his near-black pinstriped suit, he looked like a commercial. The teahouse was otherwise empty. The titanium-haired CNN anchor was drinking from an obnoxiously tall glass of juice with humongous chunks of fruit in it—and he was pulling it off with élan.

Two origin myths of Anderson Cooper are propagated; both are true. In the newsworld version, he's a scrappy youngster who paid his dues with a borrowed camera on his shoulder. He slept on hotel roofs and worked the Third World crisis tour until someone would put him on TV. He's a hard-core news man with the blood on his Betacam to prove it.

Then there's the Page Six version of Anderson Cooper: flashy Manhattanite in sharp tailored suits. Dalton fed him to Yale. Not only is his mom the designer-jean queen, his great-aunt Gertrude founded the Whitney Museum. He writes for *Details,* for chrissakes. All this means that Mr. Cooper is, in fact, the epitome of the East Coast media elite that Fox News and their gang harp on. "I'm sort of guilty on all those counts—I'm from New York and

went to an Ivy League school. I do think how one is born and how one chooses to live one's life are often two different things—or should be two different things," said Mr. Cooper. He seems in his chronically polite and understated way to be saying by this: Fuck off.

Last September, CNN plunked down the contradictions of Mr. Cooper in the middle of their evening lineup and threw a buttload of money into advertising, promoting his elite face in a 7 p.m. show that consciously traffics in the meanings of his double life. The show is self-conscious and self-referential, very nearly MTV-styled. It begins in breaking news and ends with just-shy-of-cruel digs at pop culture. Mr. Cooper is far from traditional anchor material, which makes the show inherently interesting.

But as far as numbers go, the experiment hasn't worked yet. In the cable ratings war, CNN has been thrashed. Mr. Cooper pulls a bit under half a million viewers. In the same slot over on Fox News, Shepard Smith gets around three times that. Still, focus-group research released in house at CNN last week shows Mr. Cooper testing strongest of all their anchors, a CNN source said, and the hope at CNN is that ratings will follow.

Never mind: At a time when cable news is a cesspool of partisan shit-stirring, rehashed war feed and cheery, white-toothed weatherman smiles, Mr. Cooper distinctly stands out. He's turning out to be something even more unexpected than the Gen-X sex symbol/anchor of his do-me CNN marketing: the return of the TV journalist as humanist.

APRIL 12, 2004   BY RACHEL DONADIO

Breslin Bites Back

IT WAS ONLY A SMALL HEADLINE, BURIED DEEP IN THE METRO section of *The New York Times* on April 8—"Minister Says Breslin Falsified Interview About Homosexuals"—but as a sign of the newest chapter in the history of American journalism, it might as well have been a front-page splash.

Whatever its outcome, the flap represented a peculiar clash of journalistic cultures: between the once bold and brash, now old-school narrative New Journalism of Jimmy Breslin's generation, and today's newspaper journalism, which in its sobriety and extreme attentiveness to accuracy is more akin to the old old school.

Mr. Breslin comes from another tradition—the one of Damon Runyon (whose biography Mr. Breslin wrote), Joseph Mitchell, A. J. Liebling, Meyer Berger, Murray Kempton and Pete Hamill—terse, atmospheric writers who celebrated ordinary people in the bars, offices and waterfronts of a New York where the Irish, Italians and Jews were still considered ethnic. That New York is irretrievably lost, and gone with it are the columnists who helped create the myth.

Mr. Breslin did not think the kind of operatic stories he specialized in are rarer these days. "If you keep fucking looking, you'll get them! You gotta look!" Does he have a formula for bringing life to his columns? "Yeah," he said with a growl more ebullient than menacing. "Writing!"

APRIL 19, 2004   BY ALEXANDRA WOLFE

SEXY SCIONS SELL SELVES

SITTING IN HIS WHITE MINImalist corner office in his company's 30th floor headquarters on East 57th Street, Eric Villency, the president of Maurice Villency, a home-furnishings business started by his grandfather, looked like a man who had recently had a manicure. Since he joined the company in 1999, Mr. Villency has been working at rebranding it, and the plan has meant spiffing up not just the furniture, but himself as well. Leaning back in his chair next to the wafer-thin conference table he designed, Mr. Villency smiled behind his nerd-chic dark-rimmed glasses and said, "I think every single person has a personal brand,

and it represents who they are in their professional life."

Mr. Villency's girlfriend, Olivia Chantecaille, knows all too well the pressures he faces. Though it might seem that Ms. Chantecaille's forte is her regular appearances in *Gotham* and *New York*, a fact that she wishes were better known is that she is also the creative director of her family's high-end makeup line, Chantecaille.

She knows that she hasn't made it to the level of the Lauder cosmetics dynasty yet, but she likes to think that she and Estée Lauder's granddaughter, Aerin Lauder Zinterhofer, the company's vice president for advertising and a kingpin of the New

York social circuit, could be in the same league: "I think people kind of think of us together, kind of like the makeup sisters."

Ms. Zinterhofer may be the closest thing to the Brooke Astor of her generation. Like Mrs. Astor, Ms. Zinterhofer's name is synonymous with upperclass elegance; she attracts the right kind of guests, those who would go to the New York Public Library spring benefit but could skip Paris Hilton's birthday party. But the difference between Ms. Zinterhofer and Mrs. Astor is that the latter didn't have a product to hawk—and that divide says everything about how New York society has changed.

APRIL 26, 2003   BY GABRIEL SHERMAN

THE NETFLIX NEUROSIS

WHEN KURT ANDERSEN WANDERED INTO THE LIVING ROOM AT A recent Manhattan dinner party and noticed a stack of firehouse-red Netflix DVD envelopes sitting on the coffee table, he felt an instant sense of belonging.

In the mental iconography of the New York culture junkie, the Netflix queue has joined the line of must-have life accoutrements. The kind of person who fixates on arranging just the right titles on his built-in bookcases now spends countless hours searching the Netflix Web site.

The queue, according to many Netflix addicts, has its own existential pleasure. Sure, you can only have up to eight Netflix DVD's out at once—but with more than 18,000 movies beckoning you to click your mouse and virtually no limit to the number you can keep in your online queue, it's not hard to see why Netflix has inspired a citywide frenzy of cinematic aspiration. Never mind the mundane reality of actually finding the time to watch them.

"It's just so easy to keep a constant Netflix queue running in your head," said Jodi Kantor, the *New York Times* Arts and Leisure editor.

◇◇◇◇◇◇◇

APRIL 19, 2004   BY SHEELAH KOLHATKAR

Suzy Wetlaufer Preparing To Be 'Neutron Jackie'

ON A RECENT AFTERNOON, SUZY Wetlaufer walked into her kitchen and started screaming.

"Oh my God!" she shrieked, staring at a large cardboard box that had arrived via FedEx from Saks Fifth Avenue. "It's my wedding dress! It's my wedding dress!"

It was two weeks before her wedding to retired General Electric chairman Jack Welch, and Ms. Wetlaufer, the 44-year-old former editor of the *Harvard Business Review*, had plenty to do.

"It's going to be a beautiful wedding," she said. "But it's not about the wedding, it's about the *marriage*."

And what a courtship it has been. Ms. Wetlaufer met Mr. Welch in October 2001, a month after he retired as the head of G.E. She was then editor in chief of the Harvard Business Review; her intention was to interview Mr. Welch for a cover story. But they became romantically, infamously involved while working on the article. Mr. Welch's second wife, Jane Beasley Welch, found out about it by reading their e-mails and telephoned the *Review* to complain. Ms. Wetlaufer lost her job in the ensuing scandal and was portrayed in the press as a promiscuous gold-digger; meanwhile, the details of Mr. Welch's lavish retirement package were scrutinized as he and his wife haggled over his fortune, estimated to be between $450 million and $900 million. Their divorce was settled on undisclosed terms in July 2003.

When I asked later whether she and Mr. Welch had paid a high price to be together, Ms. Wetlaufer smiled and said, "What do you think, having seen our life?"

MAY 3, 2004   BY SHEELAH KOLHATKAR

Bottle Boobs Buy $300 Vodka

IN THE EARLY HOURS OF A RECENT Sunday morning, the plebeian masses outside Marquee were growing restless. Women teetering in heels pleaded with the gatekeepers while their menfolk placed frantic cell-phone calls. Most aspirants were turned away; the place was already throbbing and packed to the rafters, threatening to explode and spray sweaty prepsters all over West Chelsea. The only hope for many outside was to wave a credit card and utter the only password that comes close to guaranteeing passage into Manhattan's inner nightlife sanctum these days: "*Bottle service!*"

The time-honored New York City tradition of velvet-rope profiling based on looks, coolness and connections has given way to a cruder calculus: In the ultimate triumph of money over beauty, the willingness to drop hundreds on a bottle of Absolut has become the major criterion for admittance to the city's desirable nightspots, especially for those who would otherwise be rejected for the old reasons. Like Vegas high rollers, cretinous bores with a little space left on their MasterCards rule the night—until that bottle of Grey Goose goes empty.

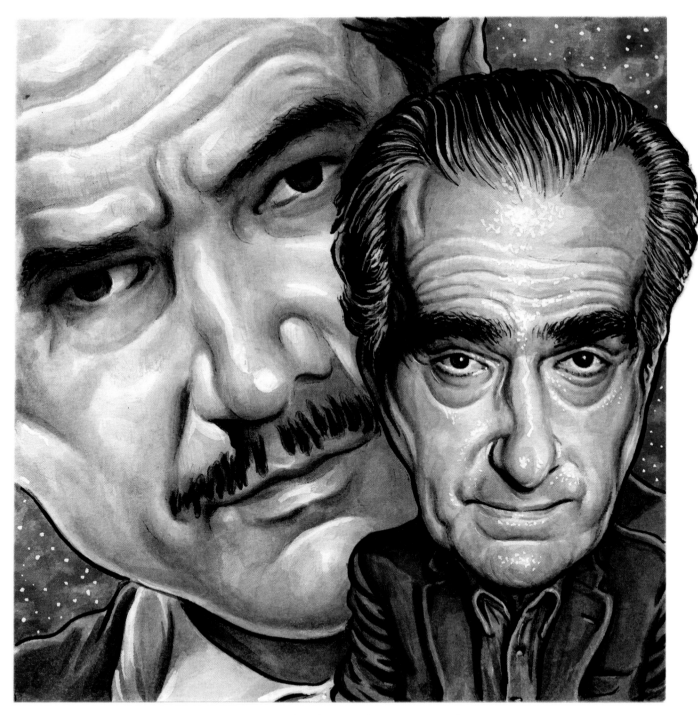

Director Howard Hughes inspired Martin Scorsese's The Aviator

MAY 10, 2004 BY CYNTHIA OZICK

THE MODERN 'HEP! HEP! HEP!'

WE THOUGHT IT WAS FINISHED. THE OVENS ARE long cooled, the anti-vermin gas dissipated into purifying clouds, cleansed air, nightmarish fable. The cries of the naked, decades gone, are mute; the bullets splitting throats and breasts and skulls, the human waterfall of bodies tipping over into the wooded ravine at Babi Yar, are no more than tedious footnotes on aging paper.

It has awakened.

In "The Modern Hep! Hep! Hep!"—an 1878 essay reflecting on the condition of the Jews—George Eliot noted that it would be "difficult to find a form of bad reasoning about [Jews] which had not been heard in conversation or been admitted to the dignity of print." She was writing in a period politically not unlike our own, Disraeli ascendant in England, Jews prominent in liberal parties both in Germany and France. Yet her title points to something far deadlier than mere "bad reasoning." Hep! was the cry of the Crusaders as they swept through Europe, annihilating one Jewish community after another; it stood for *Hierosolyma est perdita* (Jerusalem is destroyed), and was taken up again by anti-Jewish rioters in Germany in 1819. In this single raging syllable, past and future met, and in her blunt, bold enunciation of it, George Eliot was joining bad reasoning—i.e., canard and vilification—to its consequences: violence and murder.

As an anti-Semitic yelp, Hep! is long out of fashion. In the 11th century it was already a substitution and a metaphor: Jerusalem meant Jews, and "Jerusalem is destroyed" was, when knighthood was in flower, an incitement to pogrom. Today, the modern Hep! appears in the form of Zionism, Israel, Sharon. And the connection between vilification and the will to undermine and endanger Jewish lives is as vigorous as when the howl of Hep! was new. The French ambassador to Britain, his tongue unbuttoned in a London salon, hardly thinks to cry Hep!; instead, he speaks of "that shitty little country." European and British scholars and academicians, their Latin gone dry, will never cry Hep!; instead they call for the boycott of Israeli scholars and academicians.

In the time of Goebbels, the Big Lie about the Jews was mainly confined to Germany alone; much of the rest of the world saw through it with honest clarity. In our time, the Big Lie (or Big Lies, there are so many) is disseminated everywhere, and not merely by the ignorant, but with malice aforethought by the intellectual classes, the governing elites, the most prestigious elements of the press in all the capitals of Europe, and by the university professors and the diplomats.

The contemporary Big Lie, of course, concerns the Jews of Israel: they are oppressors in the style of the Nazis; they ruthlessly pursue, and perpetuate, "occupation" solely for the sake of domination and humiliation; they purposefully kill Palestinian children; their military have committed massacres; their government "violates international law"; their nationhood and their sovereignty have no legitimacy; they are intruders and usurpers inhabiting an illicit "entity," and not a people entitled as other peoples are entitled; and so on and so on. Reviving both blood libel and deicide, respectable European journals publish political cartoons showing Prime Minister Sharon devouring Palestinian babies, and Israeli soldiers bayoneting the infant Jesus.

Yet the modern history of Jews in the Holy Land overwhelmingly

refutes these scurrilities. It is the Arabs, not the Jews, who have been determined to dispose of a people's right to live in peace. Is there any point now—after so many politically willed erasures of fact by Palestinian Arabs, Muslim populations in general, and a mean-spirited European intelligentsia—to recapitulate the long record of Arab hostility that has prevailed since the demise of the Ottoman Empire?

What use is there, in the face of brute political and cultural intransigence, to rehearse the events of 1948? In that year Arab rejection of an independent Palestinian state under the UN partition plan led to the invasion by five Arab armies intent on crushing nascent Jewish sovereignty; whole sections of Jerusalem were destroyed or overrun. Nineteen-forty-eight marked the second, though not the first or the last, Arab refusal of Palestinian statehood. The first came in 1937, when under the British Mandate the Peel Commission proposed partition and statehood for the Arabs of Palestine; the last, and most recent, occurred in 2000, when Arafat dismissed statehood in favor of a well-prepared and programmatic violence.

And though the Oslo accords of 1993 strove yet again for negotiations, most energetically under Ehud Barak, both the Palestinian leadership

> In "The Modern Hep! Hep! Hep!"
> —an 1878 essay reflecting on the
> condition of the Jews—George Eliot
> noted that it would be "difficult
> to find a form of bad reasoning
> about [Jews] which had not been
> heard in conversation or been
> admitted to the dignity of print."

and the Palestinian public chose killing over compromise—this time with newly conceived atrocities through suicide bombings, always directed against civilians, in buses, cafés, restaurants, supermarkets, or wherever Israelis peacefully congregate.

This is the history that is ignored or denigrated or distorted or spitefully misrepresented. And because it is a history that has been assaulted and undermined by worldwide falsehoods in the mouths of pundits and journalists, in Europe and all over the Muslim world, the distinction between anti-Semitism and anti-Zionism has finally and utterly collapsed. It is only sophistry, disingenuousness and corrupted conscience that continue to insist on such a distinction. To fail to trace the pernicious consistencies of Arab political aims from 1920 until today, despite temporary pretensions otherwise, is to elevate intellectual negligence to a principle. To transmogrify self-defense into aggression is to invite an Orwellian horse-laugh. To identify occupation as Israel's primal sin—the most up-to-date Hep! of all—is to be blind to Arab actions and intentions before 1967, and to be equally blind to Israel's repeated commitments to negotiated compromise. On the Palestinian side, the desire to eradicate Jewish nationhood increases daily: It is as if 1948 has returned, replicated in the guise of fanatical young "martyrs" systematically indoctrinated in kindergartens and schools and camps—concerning whom it is cant to say, as many do, that they strap detonators to their loins because they are without hope. It is hope that inflames them.

Among the sophists and intellectuals, the tone is subtler. Here it is not Jewish lives that are put in jeopardy so much as it is Jewish sensibility and memory that are humbled and mocked. Pressing political analogies, however apt, are dismissed as "confused" or "odious." When history is invoked, it is said to be for purposes of coarse extortion: Israel is charged, for instance, with "using" the Holocaust as sympathetic coinage to be spent on victimizing others.

I would not wish to equate, in any manner or degree, the disparagement of Jewish memory and sensibility with anti-Semitism, a term that must be reserved for deadlier intentions. Disparagement is that much lighter species of dismissal that is sometimes designated as "social anti-Semitism," and is essentially a type of snobbery. Snobbery falls well short of lethal hatred—but it conveys more than a touch of insolence, and insolence in a political context can begin to be worrisome. It vibrates at the outer margins of "that shitty little country"; it is, one might say, not helpful.

It is long past time when the duplicitous "rift" between anti-Zionism and anti-Semitism can be logically sustained. Whether in its secular or religious expression, Zionism is, in essence, the modern flowering of a vast series of diverse intellectual and pietistic movements, all of them steeped in the yearning for human dignity—symbolized by the Exodus from slavery—that has characterized Jewish civilization for millennia. Contempt and defamation from without have sometimes infiltrated the abject psyches of defeatist Jews, who then begin to judge themselves according to the prevailing canards. Such Jews certainly are not what is commonly called self-haters, since they are motivated by the preening self-love that congratulates itself on always "seeing the other side." Not self-haters, no; low moral cowards, rather, often trailing uplifting slogans.

Still, one must ask: Why the Jews? A sad old joke pluckily confronts the enigma:

The Jews and the bicyclists are at the bottom of all the world's ills.-Why the bicyclists?-Why the Jews?—implying that blaming one set of irrelevancies is just as irrational as blaming the other. Ah, but it is never the bicyclists and it is always the Jews. There are innumerable social, economic, and political speculations as to cause: scapegoatism; envy; exclusionary practices; the temptation of a demographic majority to subjugate a demographic minority; the attempt by corrupt rulers to deflect attention from the failings of their tyrannical regimes; and more. But any of these can burst out in any society against any people—so why always the Jews? A metaphysical explanation is proffered: the forceful popular resistance to what Jewish civilization represents—the standard of ethical monotheism and its demands on personal and social conscience. Or else it is proposed, in Freudian terms, that Christianity and Islam, each in its turn, sought to undo the parent religion, which was seen as an authoritative rival it was needful to surpass and displace.

The riddle of anti-Semitism—why always the Jews?—survives as an apparently eternal irritant. The German-Jewish philosopher Franz Rosenzweig, writing in 1916 of "hatred of the Jews," remarked to a friend, "You know as well as I do that all its realistic arguments are only fashionable cloaks." The state of Israel is our era's fashionable cloak—mainly on the left in the West, and centrally and endemically among the populations of the Muslim despotisms. But if one cannot account for the tenacity of anti-Semitism, one can readily identify it. It wears its chic disguises. It breeds on the tongues of liars. The lies may be noisy and primitive and preposterous, like the widespread Islamist charge (doggerelized by New Jersey's poet laureate) that a Jewish conspiracy leveled the Twin Towers. Or the lies may take the form of skilled patter in a respectable timbre, while retailing sleight-of-hand trickeries—such as the hallucinatory notion that the defensive measures of a perennially beleaguered people constitute colonization and victimization; or that the Jewish state is to blame for the aggressions committed against it. Lies shoot up from the rioters in Gaza and Ramallah. Insinuations ripple out of the high tables of Oxbridge. And steadily, whether from the street or the salon, one hears the enduring old cry: Hep! Hep! Hep!

MAY 24, 2004   BY CHOIRE SICHA,
WITH SHEELAH KOLHATKAR AND GABRIEL SHERMAN

YIKES! YOU'RE IN ÜBERCLASS CITY, POST-CAB HIKE

THREE NEW FURIES HAVE SUD-ddenly appeared over Manhattan, inducing faux-shock in the media and nervous laughter at parties. Please welcome the million-dollar apartment, the $200 pair of jeans and the $10 crosstown cab fare—you'll be seeing a lot of them.

The taxi-fare hike was eight years in the making, but it arrived exactly as the dam was breaking—the one that, for a couple of years there, held prices in the city fairly steady. The result has been a new flood of price hikes in everything from a bagel and cream cheese at Murray's on Sixth Avenue (now $1.75, up 35 cents from a year ago), to a martini at Whiskey Park ($12, up from $10), to a pedicure at Avon Salon & Spa ($58 for the basic; last year it was $56).

As a city, New York is no longer upper-middle-class—it's über-middle-class, and the shifting of the ground under our feet is just beginning to register.

"Average income in Manhattan is the highest in the country, at $92,000," said W.

Michael Cox, the senior vice president and chief economist at the Federal Reserve Bank of Dallas. "A person earning $100,000 in Dallas needs to make $266,000 in New York just to maintain the same lifestyle."

Mr. Cox actually seems to think Manhattanites have a sickness. He cites an issue of *The American Economic Review* of June 1991: "The authors compared consumers in New York and Moscow. In Russia, if you told two people they could both become richer, but one would become wealthier than the other, they would take the proposition, no problem. In New York, people surveyed rejected this scenario. Only in New York would people rather be poorer, if they knew that at the same time, someone else wasn't getting ahead either."

Well, exactly! How are the bankers going to plant their seed in the perfect blond receptacle if another man, who's got more hair and better cufflinks, has just bought a larger apartment?

MAY 24, 2004 BY KATHERINE ROSMAN

Long Before the Hiltons ...

LONG BEFORE THE SYKES, THE MILLERS OR THE HILTONS, THERE were the Harveys: Evelyn, 87, and Jacqueline, who turns 90 on June 1. One worked for Condé Nast till she could take it no longer; the other climbed the ranks as a publicist. One went through man after man until she settled on one 15 years her junior; the other had a brief, exotic stint as an executive's wife in the 'burbs. They were Manhattan's original fabulous sisters. Still are. While the Sykes prance before Patrick Mc-Mullan's camera and the Hiltons dance on sticky tables, the Harveys exert their "It"-ness the old-fashioned way: They apply red lipstick and saunter to one of their two preferred "watering places"—the bar at the Gramercy Park Hotel, or Gramercy Tavern—and get properly soused on stiff gin martinis: stirred, not shaken.

On this particular evening, the Harveys had opted to dash out to the hotel bar, just across the southernmost block of Lexington Avenue from the 950-square-foot Gramercy Park apartment they've shared for 40years. Jacqueline, who when standing is shaped like a comma, was escorted by the sisters' 30-year-old afternoon aide, Fernela Frederick. The spryer Evelyn zipped ahead to secure their preferred perch: two red velvet brocade chairs situated in a corner that allows for easy storage of their walkers. "It's impossible for the Harvey sisters to walk into the room without people taking note," said Danny Meyer, the co-owner of Gramercy Tavern (which the sisters simply refer to as "the Tavern"). "Our staff loves serving them, our guests love sitting next to them, and our bartenders love stirring martinis for them," Mr. Meyer said.

"His great thing is he knows exactly how to train his people," Evelyn remarked a bit patricianly.

◇◇◇◇◇◇◇◇

Big Met Meet-Up: Renee, Anna, ALT and Hugh

JUNE 7, 2004
BY PHILIP WEISS

Roger W. Straus Adored A Rascal—And So Did I

ROGER STRAUS' FUNERAL WAS a dirgelike gathering at Temple Emanu El with solemn talk from the rabbi about Guggenheims and the Torah and Roger's Calling. The newspapers have kept up a Gregorian chant as well. Next fall, there will be some packed memorial where the Gods of Literature descend on golden wires to extol Roger's contribution to the culture.

That is all well and good. Roger was a great publisher. But to know Roger, and love him, wasn't really about Literature and Culture. I'm trying to remember if I ever saw him wield a pen. Roger loved pleasure and fun and mischief, Roger fled bores like the plague. Roger never had a pious, sober or correct thought in the three years that I hung around him. Why is it that the people who do anything interesting seem to take themselves so unseriously? Roger W. Straus Jr. was an elegant rascal; Roger was bad.

He squirmed when writers wanted real money, but he loved to tip them grandly, like waiters. My wife shook Roger down for $2,000 for a book party, although Roger then instructed her carefully on how to throw it.

"Invite everybody and don't get too big a room. I like a party where everyone had to breathe at the same time. Don't spend anything on the wine. Have you ever been to a cocktail party where someone said, 'Oh boy, this wine is good!'" Laughing his velvet laugh. "Now that is a bad party."

MAY 31, 2004   BY DALE PECK

DROWNTOWN LOCAL

ROLAND EMMERICH HAS A PARticular jones for seeing New York City burn. *The Day After Tomorrow* is his third film to feature scenes of the wanton demolition of New York. Unlike the wave in *Deep Impact*, the wave in *The Day After Tomorrow* is just high enough to wet the face of the Statue of Liberty, but leaving her head and upraised arm sticking out of the water. I was reminded of a beachgoing mom who's decided to smoke and swim at the same time, determinedly holding that cigarette above the waves.

Alas, Lady Liberty's torch seems to have gone out long ago. The statue's dousing failed to achieve cinematic impact, eliciting little more than slightly embarrassed titters from the Ziegfeld audience. The laughter was a reminder that New Yorkers, living under the continually implied threat of actual destruction, no longer seem to invest much in mocked-up cinematographic fantasies of that end.

The point is not that New Yorkers are living in fear, but that we're not. We are neither offended nor horrified by these particular images because we have disinvested in the idea of our own destruction, opting instead for the safety of statistics. Another way of saying that 2,801 people died in the World Trade Center is to say that seven million New Yorkers didn't. This is one of those rationalizations that is either very brave or very foolish, but it is, to all appearances, and for all intents and purposes, the way things are now.

John'ed at the Hip: Kerry and Edwards

◇◇◇◇◇◇◇

JUNE 7, 2004   BY ANNA SCHNEIDER-MAYERSON

The Public Life of Joyce Wadler

ON THE AFTERNOON OF MAY 26, *THE NEW YORK TIMES*' BOLDFACE Names columnist, Joyce Wadler, arrived at Cipriani 42nd Street to cover furrier Dennis Basso's fall fashion show, toting a leopard-printed umbrella and pen-marked leather bag. In a crowd that included Ivanka Trump, Chloë Sevigny and P. Diddy's mother, Janice Combs, Ms. Wadler, 56, had an incongruously auntie vibe with her carrot-colored shag hairdo, shoulder-padded black pantsuit and men's Cole Haan loafers, which she bought after too many years of jamming C-width feet into narrow shoes.

Later, Ms. Wadler got confused, pointing to a dark-skinned Indian woman and thinking she was Padma Lakshmi. Told that it wasn't, the *Times* woman was unperturbed. She has mulled wearing a button to such events that reads "Who the fuck are you and why should I care?" "This is my life at these things. I stumble through," she said. "Who? What?"

"This is *The Times*' excuse for a gossip column. They don't want to do gossip—they're afraid of it," said the *New York Post*'s gossip eminence, Liz Smith, over Memorial Day weekend, speaking by phone from ABC reporter Cynthia McFadden's house in Connecticut. "They don't let what's happening be the story," she continued. "They thrust themselves into the story. And then they complain in the column that nobody will talk to them and treat them right, and then if anybody does talk to them, they make them sound like idiots."

JUNE 7, 2004 BY RACHEL DONADIO

THE ANTI-FEMINIST MYSTIQUE

"THE CARDINAL RULE TO LEADing a happy life is that you must never, under any circumstances, Google yourself." Newly minted *New Yorker* staff writer Caitlin Flanagan—provocatrice, chronicler of contemporary domestic life, self-described anti-feminist—was speaking on the phone from her home in Los Angeles.

She was discussing what she has learned in the aftermath of her controversial March cover story in *The Atlantic Monthly*, "How Serfdom Saved the Women's Movement," a sprawling, 12,000-word polemic in the guise of an observational essay. Ms. Flanagan argued that upper-middle-class women have achieved their goal of having both a career and a family more often than not by employing—or, she maintained, exploiting—other women lower on the class ladder: nannies, on whom they don't always bestow the same benefits they demand for themselves, like Social Security and maternity leave.

Tapping into the turgid well of upper-middle-class women's guilt, the piece drew "an extraordinary number of letters," according to Julia Rothwax, a spokeswoman for *The*

Atlantic Monthly Two years in the works, the nanny story is her longest essay and by far her most problematic. In it, Ms. Flanagan confessed that not only did she stay home after her twin boys were born, but she also employed a nanny to help care for them, and someone else to do domestic chores—in fact, she confessed that she has never even changed a sheet since she got married. Then she wrapped it all up with a zinger: "When a mother works, something is lost." And added, "If you want to make an upper-middle-class woman squeal in indignation, tell her she can't have something. If she works, she can't have as deep and connected a relationship with her child as she would if she stayed home and raised him."

This did not go over well in many quarters. A common reaction was: Who is this privileged woman to suggest that because I go to work, which I have to do out of necessity, I am not connected to my children? And since when is hiring a nanny necessarily exploitation? Or, as one blogger wrote, "How to Make a Caitlin Flanagan / Take: / One jigger of [anti-gay activist] Anita Bryant / One jigger of [actress and children's advocate] Jane Russell / One jigger of [right-wing firebrand] Ann Coulter / A dash of pretentious language (for faux sophistication and New Yorker credentials) / One quart of self-entitlement, an expendable income / Mix. Serves establishment."

Ms. Flanagan appears to be reeling still. "The nasty things they write!" she said in her breathy, high-pitched voice. "They really hate me!"

JULY 5, 2004   BY ROBERT SAM ANSON

Bill Tells All ... Stop Him!

OUR 42ND PRESIDENT IS FAMOUS.

Famous for putting duties off to the last possible moment (and sometimes beyond). Famous, too, for the fact that when he finally gets around to whatever he's supposed to be doing, be it going after bin Laden or telling the truth, any shortcomings will be excused, rationalized, blamed on others. Most famous, perhaps, for inflicting on one and all the intimacies of a life untidy in the extreme. That's part of why he's so hypnotizing. Who can turn away from a 10-car pile-up?

All these traits (and a number of shining ones besides) are neon-lit in *My Life*, the most exhaustive explication yet of the tangled psyche of William Jefferson Clinton—though assuredly not in ways intended.

Since the Monica dish is the principal reason Knopf's already booked a record two million–plus orders, let's get that out of the way first:

Bill had to sleep on the couch for a stretch after fessing up that there was more to his acquaintance with "that woman, Miss Lewinsky" than he'd been letting on—news, he writes, that left Hillary looking "as if I had punched her in the gut." A year plus of once-a-week, all-day counseling sessions (far more attention than terrorism seemed to be getting at the time) banished the first lady's divorce musings.

As for what got him into this fix in the first place, Mr. Clinton unfurls a Couch Canyon laundry list. There's the "old demons" that have always haunted him; the "parallel lives" he alternates between (sunny on the outside, tormented on the in); the "Don't ask, Don't tell" credo he learned as a child; the determination to "drain the most out of every moment of life" that was the legacy of his father's early death; perhaps even a bit of the fright that Mr. Clinton remembers accompanying his sexual awakenings.

Once the Dr. Phil recitation is over, though, Mr. Clinton piles opprobrium on himself. As he phrased it during his *60 Minutes* sit-down with Dan Rather on Sunday evening, "I think I did something for the worst possible reason—just because I could."

About Monica herself, we learn next to nothing. Her entire life is summed up in part of one sentence on page 773 giving her employment history at the White House and Pentagon.

Much of what we do learn about the events that gained her book royalties and a handbag company that's reportedly on the rocks is not new. Nor are Mr. Clinton's self-diagnoses. *The Washington Post*'s former White House correspondent, John F. Harris, notes that in his 1992 campaign biopic, *The Man From Hope* Mr. Clinton speculates that growing up in an alcoholic household made him eager to please. He also points out that in 1998, shortly after he'd admitted to lying about Monica, Mr. Clinton told his cabinet that beneath the genial surface lurked deep anger that resulted in liaisons with Ms. Lewinsky.

He's succeeded, at least, in polarizing literary opinion. Dan Rather awarded *My Life* "five stars on a scale of five," hailing Mr. Clinton's craftsmanship as the equal of the acknowledged genre master, Ulysses S. Grant. But in her front-page *Times* review, Michiko Kakutani pronounced the same book "sloppy, self-indulgent and often eye-crossingly dull—the sound of one man prattling away, not for the reader, but for himself and some distant recording angel of history." And that was just throat-clearing.

Much has also been made of the Exxon Valdez of bile Mr. Clinton dumps on Ken Starr, the point man of the vast right-wing conspiracy. This one, you gotta feel Bill's pain. If somebody turned your sex life in all its kinkiness into a libel-proof best-seller; nearly got you fired; locked up one of your close friends for a year and a half because she wouldn't blab; dragged your wife before a grand jury through a howling mob of reporters; drained your life savings in legal fees; made you a national laughingstock; and put an asterisk after your name that will remain until the end of time—you might avail yourself of payback opportunities, too.

One comes away from this book with the same feelings one has for its author: so many gifts, so appallingly squandered.

If ever there were a chance for Mr. Clinton's redemption, *My Life* was it. Months ago, James Carville called this book "just the biggest thing in his post-presidency." Mr. Carville was on the money. So, too, were the friends who urged him to reflect, take greater care, stop wasting critical time introducing a Rolling Stones concert and palling with hangers-on not fit to shine his shoes. Mr. Clinton ignored them, as he did in the White House, and does still.

All that's left is the "Why?"

That question Bill Clinton's answered: "Just because I could."

NOVEMBER 7, 2004   BY PETER W. KAPLAN

SEE YA, EAST 64TH ST.! 17 GIDDY YEARS IN DOTTY SQUALOR

FOR 17 YEARS, SINCE *THE NEW YORK OBSERVER* entered city life in 1987, it has existed within a red brick and white-marble-stepped townhouse on East 64th Street. When I entered for the first time, I had an enzymatic sensation I think was shared by many people who worked here—some to their pleasure, some to their horror: I'm home. I'd worked at plenty of publications in New York, but never in a house. As Polly Adler, the great Manhattan bordello madame of the 1920's, said of her own business, a house is not a home. Except in our case.

We worked in a home. Four floors, a giant alimentary center-hall staircase, caked moldings, brass chandeliers, glass-fronted oak cupboards, *The New York Observer* sometimes felt like a Henry James society home or a 70's swinger pad, with reporters stacked and stuffed in its confines like Hong Kong tailors. Our legal reporter set up his computer in the fourth-floor closet, near the tuxedo that was used by whomever had to go out to a formal evening.

When I walked in, Mr. Charles Bagli and Mr. Terry Golway were stuffed back-to-back in the front living room, reporters were so close that one yammering diva could stop work for the entire room, turning the whole floor into an instant Eugene O'Neill parlor trauma. Later, a strange and occasionally brilliant agglomeration of writers and editors built up; pretty often, some were seduced to go off to slicker, better-paid indenturements. We lived together like vaudevillians at an actors' boarding house.

At this very moment, there are around 20 former Observer employees at work at *The New York Times*, inmates at *The Wall Street Journal*, countless refugees in the Condé Nast Building, but does one of them relieve him or herself in a singing office toilet that gurgles 23 hours a day? For ambition's sake, they cashed in their chance to shower midday in a claw-footed bathtub, or to spy with a vengeance at courtyard transgressions like *Rear Window*'s L. B. Jeffries: One night, one editor called the cops when he saw a new mother leave her baby on the fire escape. Another editor was almost tempted to sin with a writer when an ancient brass door fixture snapped, trapping them inside.

Visitors invariably had the same reaction on entering the house: It's so cute! And it was. But the response of editors and writers, who trundled through, tromping on worn carpet, cursing the vents, wondering if the auditory carrying capabilities of the air-conditioning vents would carry conversations to other departments, was baleful. Phone books and files were occasionally hurled from the fourth-floor window onto the 64th Street sidewalk like a faithless lover's pajamas.

Visitors stopped by. The writer Veronica Geng lived down the street and used to offer advice, bartering it for a day with one editor who drove upstate to empty her country house. Down the block, the great luxury mastodon 32 East 64th, home to Mrs. Kitty Carlisle Hart, whose trim gams took her on their evening constitutional past the office every night; she would nod and ask, "How's the paper?" Across the street, the vaguely decadent Plaza

Athénée, with its leopard-skin benches and $12 martinis.

Movie shoots were common: Al Pacino shouting spittle into the afternoon air, Keanu Reeves grinning at our young reporters. The pavement on 64th Street was wide and clean, a province of billionaires strutting down the street—Ron Perelman and David Geffen. Chanel suits, Giorgio Armani and La Perla, the ritzy underwear store. Next door to the newspaper itself, and down some steps, a ritzy veterinarian, where endless pet crates were carried, and slinky septuagenarian Lauren Bacall looking left, looking right, heading down.

While up into our building trooped writers: the cheeky, the depressed, the jolly, the mission-driven, the perky. On the first floor, in what had been a grand dining room, the production department: hot waxers reminiscent of—not reminiscent of, identical to!—your high-school paper's.

One flight up, the mandarin office of the publisher, a huge Oriental frieze staring down at the participants below, black-and-white photographs of Thomas Mann and Einstein smiling down at the whole enterprise. Across the hall, ad salespeople: glamorous, dark and shiny ladies with a sheen, first single, then married, then single, with dangerous ebony hairdos like movie noir heroines.

Cranking up and down, a cage elevator, witness to God knows how many muttered or screaming conversations, creaking up and down among the four floors and the cool basement, where checks were cut that soothed tempers on the other floors.

Highest of all in this crazy little enterprise, the dotty fireworks of the fourth floor, where politics were dissected, plots hatched, sociology sprinkled, coffee guzzled and names thrown around: Mario, Harvey, Rudy, Jerry, Puff, Woody, Punch, Si, Liz, Rupert. Hidden calls from psychiatrists, occasional nervous breakdowns not-so-manqué, pranks of Homeric intricacy, involving a floating cast of characters that appeared to the in-house residents of the house like the offstage stock company in a sitcom during the Seinfeldian 90's. Story subjects called and screamed; others showed up for some mischief: Bill Murray, Mike Wallace, the occasional mayor. Norman Mailer, clanking in on a cane to bring draft after draft of his cartoon

"Puffs." Bill O'Reilly and Carol Channing were on the phone. Martinis were served in summer, and "Sex and the City" came and went. And then the giddiness came to a freeze-frame on Sept. 11, 2001. The smoke from the south of Manhattan hung acrid above 64th Street as editors slumped on their desks.

There was Leon the office-supplies guy, who gave out pencils one at a time, and Angie the switchboard operator, who shrieked the editors' names up the stairwell like Stanley Kowalski, and the young intern who everyone was afraid might have explosives strapped under his shirt. But nobody brought out the curious empathy of the building like the librarian who sat in her cubby making small cooing noises like a pigeon and one day just fluttered away without notice, leaving behind the French-fairy-tale possibility that she had been a bird all along.

Now we're moving downtown, to a classy old skyscraper two blocks south of the Flatiron Building, in the neighborhood of the Gramercy Tavern and Eisenberg's, but not the magnificent coffee shops Gardenia and the Viand, where big Pete and smooth George respectively presided. The girls will be younger downtown and not as well dressed, but not as dressed. The billionaires will still be there, but their drivers will be waiting to take them back uptown.

Around the corner and up the street from us was a tall, distinctive luxury building with a Citibank, its first floor faced in blue bricks, an anomaly of bad taste in our chichi neighborhood. Its brazen cluelessness made it stand out like a structure in Munchkin Land, the sector of L. Frank Baum's Oz that was all blue among the high-rises of the Emerald City. They could never fill the joint up, and the Europeans eating lunch at La Goulue used to stare up at its strange refusal to be tasteful as though it was the public-school girl in polyester at the Cotillion. Now the owners, finally wised-up, have caved, and they're refacing it in mud-brown brick, another Madison Avenue makeover.

Goodbye, blue-brick poseur, goodbye, red-brick townhouse; we're heading south, toward Broadway. There are fresh, grotesque and homely anomalies downtown.

While up into our building trooped writers: the cheeky, the depressed, the jolly, the mission-driven, the perky. On the first floor, in what had been a grand dining room, the production department: hot waxers reminiscent of—not reminiscent of, identical to!—your high-school paper's.

JULY 26, 2004
BY RACHEL DONADIO,
SHEELAH KOLHATKAR
AND ANNA
SCHNEIDER-MAYERSON

STUFF IT, EMO BOY!

RECENTLY REBECCA HACK-emann, a 32-year-old artist, had a distressing third date with a banker type she'd met on Nerve.com. He flipped out when Ms. Hackemann showed up 20 minutes late after some trouble on the subway. "You know, you just can't be late like this," whined the athletic, 42-year-old fellow after she had sat down and apologized profusely. "You don't know what it does to me emotionally," he continued. "Next time, we're just going to have to make sure you're on time."

"It's partly to do with my past," he added after they had placed their orders.

The banker is emblematic of an alarming moment in gender relations here in New York: the rampant spread of the emo man (or perhaps more appropriately, emo boy). Originally referring to a floppy-limbed, "sincere" indie-rock movement, emo gathered speed during the Clinton feel-your-pain era. Now it has landed squarely in the laps of disgusted Manhattan women like Ms. Hackemann.

OCTOBER 25, 2004 BY JOE HAGAN & SHEELAH KOLHATKAR

REVOLT OF FOX'S HENS

THIS HAS BEEN A BLOODY AND unpleasant couple of weeks at the Fox News Channel. A producer named Andrea Mackris brought a sexual harassment suit against Bill O'Reilly, the Fox News Channel brand-name host of *The O'Reilly Factor* and inventor of the TV territory called the "No-Spin Zone."

The details of Ms. Mackris' complaints are grisly and involve late-night dinners, dirty conversations and an electronic apparatus that no boss should ever recommend to an employee as office equipment. For his part, Mr. O'Reilly was prepared with a preemptive suit; the Fox News Channel almost immediately attempted to surgically remove Ms. Mackris from the company, implausibly asserting that her dismissal had nothing to do with her court complaint against Mr. O'Reilly.

But when Fox News' highest-profile female journalist, Greta Van Susteren, host of *On the Record*, was asked about Andrea Mackris' sexual-harassment suit against Mr. O'Reilly, she threw the ball elsewhere.

"I have an open door all the way to the top in this company," she said, "and I've got nothing about walking right through that door. If I heard about it, believe me, I would not look the other way. I would speak up. I don't want that in my environment, and I would raise hell. I wouldn't raise hell in the newspaper, but I would

raise hell in the organization.

"Which is what I did at CNN."

Ms. Van Susteren, who became a legal analyst at CNN in 1991, said she "left CNN because of the way they were mistreating people. I'd do the same here. I'd walk out of here. If I heard about a situation that was not being addressed—I don't sit back. I'm a lawyer." Ms. Van Susteren's complaints about CNN didn't include the dinners, telephone calls and electric vibrators that show up in Ms. Mackris' suit against Mr. O'Reilly.

But they suggested the same principle that many women interviewed by *The Observer* have asserted since Ms. Mackris' vivid charges against Mr. O'Reilly

have been reported: TV news is a generally inhospitable place for women to work. It often involves unequal pay for comparable work. It nurtures and inspires sexual harassment in a pressured, heightened environment filled with risks and rewards, highs and lows, and often staffed by malleable younger women producers and assistants assigned to the care and feeding of outsized male egos.

Few women under the age of 40 were willing to speak on the record for this piece about their harassment experiences, or even the sexist culture of TV news in general. But this was a shockingly easy story to gather anecdotal material for, on background.

"The television industry in general is rampant with sexual harassment, and it's very difficult for women at a low level to complain or do anything about it," said Lisa Bloom, a Court TV anchor and sexual-harassment attorney. "As you can see with what's happened to Andrea Mackris, it's brutal. That's why they don't come forward. They put up with it, they change jobs, engage in avoidance. It's a small industry in New York, especially in cable news, and we all know each other. You move around a lot, and your reputation follows you. And if you offend the top brass at one TV network, they're very tight with top brass at other networks. Word will spread, and you'll have a hard time getting a job."

The Baby Botoxers: Prep school gals seek radical cheeks

SEPTEMBER 6, 2004   BY PHILIP WEISS

Invasion of Bushy Snatchers

AN EMPIRE REQUIRES an imperial city, and the Republicans turned New York into the backlot for *Julius Caesar*. They used the grand scale and took over the grand elegant spaces as backdrop. Their bridle-bit loafers passed softly over the worn marble and mosaic floors of high culture. Once everyone who lives here fled town, they took over. The city they occupied and remade wasn't quite New York, it was more like Neo York. Grand but toneless, a little off.

There was to be nothing ideological or even conservative at the New York convention. They wanted the tone of New York's liberalism to rub off on them, too, the way cultural conservatives want their hair cut by a gay hairdresser or to hear a little Philip Glass in the middle of an all-Sousa concert. They needed it. New York's sophistication. They wanted that to help their image. The Republicans do not want to seem narrow to America, beady-eyed and dangerous. They don't want to feel that way about themselves, either. They want the pleasure of thinking of themselves as New Yorkers are able to think of themselves: clued-in, toney, broad-minded, triumphant. They wanted to put on New York airs. And they have.

On Monday night they took over both the Metropolitan Museum of Art and the Central Building of the New York Public Library. Corporate lobbyists threw big parties for the Congressional leadership under lemony light against old stone. The Met was the fancier event. Tom DeLay at the Temple

of Dendur. Tom DeLay under glass, facing Fifth Avenue and the entrance to Central Park, acquiring international culture and the history of the ages at the Met, just south and west of the building from which Jacqueline K. Onassis used to stare down at the park.

The word went out among the Republican wives to wear black to the Met. This is New York, you wear black. Black is the sophisticated color in New York.

So a procession of Republican women went up the great steps of the Metropolitan, almost all of them in black. Black pantsuits. A short black dress. Another black pantsuit. Yes, now

and then a howler: pinstriped pants, as if she had gotten on half the Yankees' home uniform. But most of the ladies had gotten the signal right and worn black. A cropped black jacket, gathered at the back, with the long dangling ends of the string, capped in silver, dancing naughtily against the lady's pert black rump. Very empire.

Some ladies, under the black suits, had put on tangerine or sky-blue blouses. Tangerine. See, there was something off.

And sad, too—not chipper and conventiony, but sad. You walked through the city and it was no longer yours. Anybody with New York in the spirit had

decamped, and now the Republicans were doing their best to imitate the departed, and not quite making it. The country singer Lee Greenwood had come into Cipriani 42d Street to sing his hit "God Bless the U.S.A.," with the Harlem Boys Choir behind him. The crowd sang along with him, and the boys and girls of the choir watched him with smiling befuddlement.

Lee Greenwood was a star out of his element. He wore a new New York jacket and fiddled nervously with the buttons. He's from California. Usually he wears jeans and cowboy boots and a five-day growth. He had put on this stiff new jacket over a fine

cotton shirt and a blue jacquard tie, and seemed a mannequin in the Italian-made clothes, the country star lost in New York. See, there was something off.

Bo Derek held forth at a press conference in a side room. Well, actually, she doesn't hold forth. She's a demure sort, in pastel paisley. She carried a bone-colored purse and said with a bashful sweetness that she was voting for George Bush because of his courage.

A reporter baited her. "Are you the right wing's answer to Susan Sarandon?"

Bo wasn't built for New York sarcasm, and her self-esteem cratered.

> *Yes, and they have the worst judgment of any leaders since Vietnam, and all the world hates us, and our young men and women are dying by the handful for no good or clear reason. But an empire requires an imperial city, and there is only one.*

"Absolutely not! She's so smart, she's so brilliant. Look at me, I'm blond!" She sent her shoulder-length hair flying with a hapless fling of her hand. "No one should vote the way I vote!"

A blond joke, on herself. See, there was something off. It wasn't savvy, even as it tried to be. Bo Derek wasn't a stand-in for Susan Sarandon, and Lee Greenwood wasn't comfortable in a landmarked bank building across from Grand Central. It occurred to you that in Vichy Paris they still had croissants and coffee, baguettes and nightlife, but it wasn't the same there, either.

"I've never seen the city so deserted," said one of the Republican organizers, dejectedly. "We decided to come here as a way of saying thank you. That was the whole point.

"And it all backfired because of the people who are protesting. The anarchists. So New York is being hurt instead."

She enjoyed saying that word, "anarchist." All the Republicans did. But that was disingenuous. Whatever fears had sent New Yorkers out of town, the New Yorkers were gone, and that was the way the Republicans liked it. It fit in with their worldview. It was like having Disney World open to just your family on a Sunday. They were free to use all the locations. If waiters at Butter, the boîte next to the Public Theater on Lafayette, snickered at the guys in khakis who were ordering mojitos, so what? That was an inside joke among the passive resistance.

Meantime, the Republicans would use New York to make themselves seem worldly, broad-minded. It was funny

and it was painful. And so a place that is the embodiment of intellectual life, the Central Building of the New York Public Library, had gone goofy.

Probably they were cowed by New York. Isn't everyone when they get off the boat? Of course they were, as scared as a New Yorker in Texas seeing a gunrack in the pickup. They didn't feel right, even stepping up the Metropolitan steps in new Manolo Blahnik shoes, having heard about Manolos on *Sex in the City*. They did not feel hip even as they tried. But that's not the point. Something was working for them in these locations, and they did what everyone does in New York, they imagined themselves in a new way. They imagined themselves open-minded and sophisticated.

A pretty Senate operative from California had ordered Chinese at 2 in the morning from her hotel room—"because I could," she announced triumphantly—and got an irritated look when you said the word "abortion." "We come here as an exercise in patriotism and duty, not because of any ideology."

So the Republican had pro-choicers give speeches on the opening night and their pro-choice group co-hosted a rock concert at the Beacon. And at a big gathering for women in the Waldorf-Astoria—"W Stands for Women"—Vice President Cheney's straight daughter talked about her four kids and used the word "gender" 100 times, signaling to right and left, while Mr. Cheney's wife said that women in Afghanistan no longer had their fingers amputated for wearing fingernail polish.

Fingernail polish in Islam. See, there was something a little off

about that. A little tone-deaf, as a human rights message.

A lady from Orange County, Mary Young, wore a giant button saying Red Hot Republican.

"Mary, you know what that means in New York," a reporter said. "You're saying you're sexy, you're hot."

Mary dissolved. "Oh no. That's not why I bought it. I'm a dyed-in-the-wool Republican, a red-blooded Republican, hot-blooded Republican."

The convention's position on the Iraq war was also shrewd. It was a position meant to play outside the New York Public Library. We all can disagree. Yes, George Bush has made some tactical mistakes. Rudy Giuliani said, None of us is always right. Lindsey Graham said, George Bush has had to make decisions every day, day in and day out. Not everyone is going to like you.

But why question the president's decisions? They came out of resolution, courage, firmness. Male virtues. When the fires of hell rose from New York. This great city that belongs to all of us.

"We live in times of peril," Lynne Cheney said at the Waldorf-Astoria, "and it is such a comfort to all of us to have these good men who are so solid, so stable, leading our country. And both these men are surrounded by strong women."

Yes, and they have the worst judgment of any leaders since Vietnam, and all the world hates us, and our young men and women are dying by the handful for no good or clear reason. But an empire requires an imperial city, and there is only one. Ladies, when you go to the Temple of Dendur, wear black.

2005

Dan Rather retires as anchorman of *CBS Evening News* after forged-memo controversy

Mayor Michael Bloomberg ratified in landslide reelection victory

 Guarded by dashing doorman Armin Amiri, Amy Sacco's Bungalow 8 rules the night

Generation Zzzzz: New Yorkers curl up with gentle sleeping aid Ambien

Pitt splits! Brad and Jennifer Aniston split as maneater Angelina Jolie muscles in

Web wars: HuffPo is left's answer to Drudge; Nick Denton builds online empire

The Plame game: *Times* reporter Judy Miller plugs White House leak with 85 days in jail

Hurricane Katrina leaves New Orleans flooded, bereft

 JetBlue flight broadcasts own emergency landing on DirecTV; *Observer* editor lives

2005

JANUARY 16, 2005   BY ANNA SCHNEIDER-MAYERSON

PUSSES IN BOOTS, '05

NICOLE LEACH, A PETITE PER-oxide blonde of 25, was standing inside the slick 10th Avenue bar Glass on a recent sodden evening, looking a bit like a risqué elf in a black camisole and bright red pants ... tucked into knee-high, rubber-soled, maroon suede boots from Macy's. "It's about style, not something you're wearing because it's cold," said Ms. Leach, who said she makes her living as a "performer." "I like the way it looks. It evens your whole leg out."

In Manhattan these days, it's hard to find a girl who isn't doing the Tuck. Across West Chelsea bars, sleek boutiques in Madison Avenue and grungy boîtes of the Lower East Side, the women of the city can be found peg-legging their jeans and parading around with them scrunched into the legs of their boots like crumpled bed sheets. They're pulling sculpted stiletto boots up over trousers and walking around with them in plain view, like a pair of knee socks. Or they're rolling their jeans up so that they rest just where the boot ends, thus shortening the appearance of their legs by about 40 percent. And somehow they seem to think this is a good idea.

MARCH 6, 2005   BY PHOEBE EATON

Anthony Weiner, In Mayoral Run, Models On Koch

WOODY JOHNSON WAS at the annual winter cocktail party for the Queens County Democrats, making the rounds, cranking up support for a stadium on the site of the M.T.A.'s West Side railyards. Only suddenly, he had a gate-crasher: Days earlier, Cablevision offered $600 million to the M.T.A. to plunk some apartments and offices on the site—six times more than what Mr. Johnson was bidding. Trans-Gas would soon be flashing $700 million at the M.T.A., too, and the State of New Jersey was jumping up and down to sell the Jets on a less magnificent setup entirely. It was turning into a messy food fight, and everyone knew it.

Congressman Anthony Weiner was cheering all of this mayhem from the sidelines. Though he hadn't yet declared his candidacy, Mr. Weiner was very publicly running for mayor, largely on the issue of where Mr. Johnson could stick his stadium.

Somebody finally dragged Mr. Weiner over to shake hands with Mr. Johnson. There was some strained chitchat about Chad Pennington's injured throwing arm before the elephant in the room laid a great big fart: "It's gonna be terrific to just get on the No. 7 and go right to the stadium," another guest said to Mr. Johnson.

"Yeah," Mr. Weiner chimed in, "even if you're going in the other direction!" Mr. Weiner plucked two cubes of cheddar off a tray and headed for the door.

Diane Sawyer makes nice in the morning

MARCH 13, 2005 BY MARK LOTTO

HACKS OF PASSION

ON A SLOW NIGHT, ANNE, A 23-YEAR-OLD ASSISTANT AT an art consultancy, will get drunk at home with her friends and, instead of watching a movie or gossiping about men, they'll break into one of their old boyfriends' e-mail accounts. "My friends and I have a few glasses of wine, and it's like, 'Let's go read [his] e-mail!'" Anne said, making an inbox sound like a pirated cable box—free of charge, only slightly criminal and endlessly engaging. The girls guffaw at his misspellings and giggle about his dating mishaps. They are as careful as cat burglars and never get caught. According to Anne, "It's fun! It's so entertaining."

And also rather common. Manhattan marriage counselor Sharyn Wolf, author of *Guerrilla Dating Tactics: Strategies, Tips and Secrets for Finding Romance*, said that a lot of her clients have either committed this crime or had it done to them. "Men's passwords are the easiest to figure out," Ms. Wolf said. "Go home and change yours tonight!"

But who says passwords need to be guessed, anyway? Who says e-mail accounts need to be hacked into? These days, girlfriends and boyfriends, husbands and wives, girlfriends and girlfriends, casually swap the passwords to their Gmail, AOL and Yahoo! accounts out of convenience—or they lovingly swap to prove their intimacy and their absolute confidence in the relationship and in one another.

"There's a level of trust in relationships where, if I'm with someone for a while, yeah, I give them my fucking password, because I want them to know I'm not hiding anything," said Anne's roommate Jennifer, 26, who works at a corporate law firm and is blond, frightfully smart (though not about this) and *Maxim* beautiful.

E-mail intimacy hasn't brought couples closer together; instead, it has broken hearts, wrecked long marriages and crippled new relationships. In truth, swapping passwords or sharing computers is actually less a signal of faith than it is a test, too tempting and too easy to fail.

"When you snoop, you're not looking for the concert seats he's going to surprise you with, you're looking for something that's going to break your heart," Ms. Wolf warned in her best Cassandra mode. "When you snoop, you will always find something. You snoop to confirm something. It will always be there."

And then there's that rare situation where deception brings two people closer together. Molly, a 24-year-old writer, found her new boyfriend's e-mail open on her computer. They'd only been dating a few weeks, and he checked his mail just before getting into bed. Even though her boyfriend was lying a few feet away from her, she just couldn't help herself.

"It was the sent e-mail, the e-mail from him, that really interested me," she said. "I wanted to go back to the dates around the beginning of when we met and see what his impressions of me were, and what he said to people about me."

What she found was an e-mail he had written to one of his friends around the time of his and Molly's second date, something to the effect of: "She came over last night. Well, you know, physically, she's not everything I would want, but I find her so amazing in so many other ways that I just want this."

Molly sat there for a while, frozen, not knowing what the hell to do next: "I mean, also because it was exactly what I was looking for. There it was, a very concise statement of what his impression of me was—to a friend, being very candid."

To snoop or not to snoop, to confess or not to confess: Molly's dilemma is typical. In the end, what's worse? Breaking into someone's e-mail, violating their trust, looking like a psychopath? Or is the ugly truth discovered in the purloined e-mail the real infraction?

Or maybe not. When Molly got into bed, she lay there for a while, stiff as board, completely confused. Her boyfriend noticed immediately that something was wrong, and when he probed her, she confessed what she'd done.

"To my shock, he didn't back off at all, he didn't shy off at all," Molly said. He told her: "I did write something about you not being my physical type, and it's true. You're not the type of girl that I've gone out with before, and you've completely shattered my type."

Before Molly, he'd mostly dated "gym rats, all-American blond waifs." Molly is more voluptuous than waifish, her hair a very dark shade of honey blond—she's plenty cute enough to inspire conversions. Finally, after hours in bed fighting and talking, he convinced her that he was one of the sincerely converted. He wasn't angry; more than anything, he seemed "scared" that what he'd written would cause him to lose her.

"After that, I felt invincible, I really did," said Molly. "I felt like I'd opened the closet and looked at my worst fear, and there was nothing else to fear after that. I guess that's not totally true—there's infidelity."

Molly then vowed never to snoop again, but she speaks of it with the eloquent nostalgia of a drug addict just barely clean.

"It's a thrill," she said. "Especially having him in the room while I was doing it. It was a weird high. I felt thrilled."

APRIL 3, 2005
BY GEORGE GURLEY

Bungalow Gate

"RESERVATIONS ONLY, RESERVA-tions only. I can't, sorry, man, we're packed inside. Guys, we are packed. We have no more tables. We're done."

It was late Friday night outside Bungalow 8, the super-exclusive nightclub where New York's most glamorous and beautiful young people enjoy conversation, flirting and something stronger than soda pop. Located on a bleak stretch of West 27th Street between 10th and 11th avenues, the club can hold at most about 150 people and turns away the great majority of the people who wish to enter.

Armin, the dashing 33-year-old Iranian doorman, was wearing a fur hat and a blue cashmere coat over a $1,800 suit. He was standing behind the velvet rope he's manned since the club opened in 2001.

"This place has given me a pow-er more than I could ever imagine in my life," he admitted. "I've had congressmen's offices giving me a call trying to get people in. Then you have President Bush's daugh-ters coming in: sweethearts. I don't care what people say about Bush, here comes his daughters and I'm this refugee boy. I wasn't letting them in the first couple of times, until I got a call from Fa-bian Basabe. ... That's the beauty of America, do you know?"

APRIL 3, 2005
BY BEN SMITH

REALLY RICH RUDY

IN 2001, RUDY GIULIANI WAS *Time* magazine's Person of the Year. By 2002, he was *Consult-ing Magazine*'s Consultant of the Year. And in another year or two, it was widely assumed, he'd be on another step in his rise, whether as vice president or in a cabinet post. Then it would be on to the White House.

Instead, Mr. Giuliani has dug into his position in the private sector, where he has found un-precedented success in a new kind of consultancy that sells to-day's highest-valued commod-ity: pure, crystalline security.

Mr. Giuliani has become a tycoon.

◇◇◇◇◇◇◇

APRIL 17, 2005   BY JAMES KAPLAN

MR. BELLOW'S PLANET: AMIS, McEWAN SNATCH SAUL'S HERRING SOUL

ONE OPENED *THE New York Times* expectantly, two days after Saul Bel-low's death, ready for the Op-Ed trib-utes that seemed as certain to ap-pear as *The Times* itself: Surely one or more of American literature's surviv-ing phallocrats, a Mailer or a Roth or an Updike, would contribute a brief but feeling essay, hastily composed yet sharply observed, glittering with wit and fond (or double-edged) remembrance of the tart-tongued, pint-sized titan, that pluperfectly penetrat-ing colossus of our native literary landscape. Surely there would be four or five hundred words by Bellow's biographer, James Atlas, or conceivably a feeling homage by a younger American novelist whose life had been changed by reading Henderson the Rain King. One could imagine it all, down to the small, boxlike dimensions of the essays, placed (of course) respectfully high on the page.

Instead, we got Ian McEwan.

When Ian McEwan started rhapsodizing about that barking dog in *The Dean's December*, all I could think of, for some reason, was a piece of herring: the herring snack that Charlie Citrine, in the incomparable *Humboldt's Gift*, eats at his kitchen counter as he reads the obituary of a Princeton professor who once interviewed him for a teaching job.

In the novel, that herring, to-gether with Charlie's afternoon whiskey, becomes a Proustian de-vice for stirring up memories of the late poet Von Humboldt Fleisher, the fictional stand-in for Saul Bel-low's real-life friend, the doomed, dazzling Delmore Schwartz.

Yet that herring is more than a Proustian device. It's also an actual piece of herring—a quint-essentially Jewish food, a nosh which I suspect is, in its homely Yiddishkeit, quite beneath the notice of the likes of Messrs. Amis and McEwan, who prefer meta-phorical dogs and the full pitch of "cerebral endeavour."

There was something even nearer and dearer to Saul Bellow than herring, metaphorical or actual, something I surmise high-toned British writers also have trouble with: the human soul.

We have nothing over the British any longer: We've found our own ways of being soulless. Unfortunately, we're now also Saul-less.

APRIL 24, 2005
BY SHAZIA AHMAD

Generation Zzzzzz

JUST OVER A MONTH AGO, A young man found himself in an uncomfortable sleeping arrangement. After a night out with a group of friends, he found himself alone in the home of a senior editor at a well-known fashion magazine. The woman was in her early 30's, attractive and, according to the young man, angling for some action. But then she said something.

"She was laying there," he said, "and had taken her clothes off. Then, in completely slurred speech, she said: 'I just took two Ambien, so anything you're going to do, you better do it before I pass out.' She said she hadn't slept a night in seven years without her Ambien."

The young man had come face to face with a member of the Ambien Generation, where being turned on takes a back seat to being able to turn off. In this edgy, post-9/11 city, sleep is more and more seen as an inalienable right: Tossing and turning is for suckers. Though Ambien has been on the market since 1993, it's increasingly begun to occupy the same place in many New Yorkers' lives as coffee and cigarettes. The city that never sleeps is becoming the city that can't wait to go to sleep.

MAY 9, 2005   BY GEORGE GURLEY

BOB SAGET'S FULL MOUTH

BOB SAGET WALKED into the lobby of the Hudson Hotel and thrust out his hand. The tall, fit 48-year-old was wearing a zip-up sweatshirt, faded jeans and Converse loafers. I was eager to ask him to tell a famous dirty joke, a joke so well known among comedians it's the subject of its own documentary, *The Aristocrats*, which comes out in July.

In the film, Mr. Saget is one of 100 comedians who each tell their own version of the bawdy yarn. His version, I'd been told, was the filthiest—not something you might expect from a guy who beamed into prime time as the sitcom dad on ABC's *Full House* and the corny host of *America's Funniest Home Videos*. Who was the real Bob Saget?

"Saget was famously dirty in college, 30 years ago," said the comic magician Penn Jillette, who produced the documentary. "The joke is not that in an R movie, Bob Saget gets dirty; the joke is that in the world, Saget got clean."

"It's not appropriate for any mass consumption," Mr. Saget said. "This joke is like 70 years old, and the point of it is that it's the most offensive thing that you can make up. The purpose is to offend, and that nothing is too offensive—nothing.

"My justification is that I find stuff that is horrific funny. I find things that are terrible—terrible, terrible, terrible—hilarious, because how could people be so horrible? It's my defense. I could sit around crying all day. I'm a very sensitive person."

He said that he'd never let his kids or his parents see *The Aristocrats*.

"I can't really tell you the joke," he said. "I'll explain it. It won't translate on paper. So, O.K., a family goes into an agent's of-fice. ..." He paused. "This is not a good joke, by the way. ... O.K., a family goes into an agent's office, and they say, 'We'd like you to represent us.' It's a mother, a father and a few kids. And the agent's got a cigar, he's a big guy behind a desk. He says, 'Whatya do?' The father says, 'What do we do? Watch this.' And they all strip naked and start having sex with each other. The mother and her kids, you know, everybody's going at it: They're all having sex. I'm not going to go into the horrible dirty details. ... The bottom line is the family is having horrible sex with each other. It goes on and on. And eventually they freeze in place and go, 'Ta-dahhhh!' And the agent says, 'This is very interesting. Uh, what do you call yourselves?' And the father goes, 'The Aris-tocrats!' That's the joke.

"The purpose of the joke, what I thought was funny about it, is that people will do anything to make it in show business," Mr. Saget said. "Because everybody wants to be famous. Not everybody—smart people don't. And this is how low someone will go to be famous. They will have sex with their own family. What I find funny about it is the desperation."

"Saget is the dirtiest mother-fucking cocksucker that ever walked the face of the earth!" said Mr. Jillette. "Doing those little bullshit family shows, playing the retarded fucking squeaky dickless dad—that's not Saget! That's a joke. You go to a restaurant with Saget and before he orders food, he'll be talking to the waitress about fucking his daughters in the ass."

MAY 22, 2005 BY TOM SCOCCA

Metaphysics of a Magazine

THE INVITATION—MY INVITATION—to the relaunch party for *Radar* magazine arrived in the form of Martha Stewart's head, in stiff paper, with a stick to glue it onto. Other invitees apparently received other celebrities, but mine is Martha: luridly colored, like a tinted Daguerreotype, and with the eyes cut out to serve as a mask.

The head of Martha on a stick, with its empty eyes, is an unpleasant icon. Ms. Stewart herself is more ordinary at first sight. When she presented herself on stage last month at the National Magazine Awards to claim the trophy for *Martha Stewart Weddings* it took a second to figure out what was going on. Is that ... ? Did she ... ? The gathering buzz in the hall certified her identity. Magazine editors and executives applauded.

Martha Stewart is a celebrity who publishes magazines. The magazines exist because the brand identity of Martha

Stewart is behind them. At the awards ceremony, a series of video montages had played, interlacing news footage with images of significant magazine covers from various eras. Before Ms. Stewart got up on stage, the clips had reached the mid-80's. The old covers, previously an assortment of striking single images, had begun to converge on a new look. Stark blank space was filled in with an ever-thickening collection of cover lines, the burgeoning text framing not an illustration but a photograph, and a specific kind of photograph: a portrait of a celebrity.

Radar magazine, editor Maer Roshan said in a phone interview, is "alternately amused and appalled" by celebrity. The cover of the upcoming issue features a not-too-smooth photo composite of President George W. Bush hanging a medal around the neck of Paris Hilton. "No talent? No problem!" the cover line says. "How to be FAMOUS for doing nothing at all."

This, *Radar* knows. After producing a pair of sample issues in 2003, Mr. Roshan kept *Radar* hovering in the public consciousness for nearly two full years without actually printing any more magazines. Now, with the backing of Mortimer Zuckerman and Jeffrey Epstein, the operation is up and running. The summer 2005 issue is due on newsstands next week.

But in the meantime, *Radar* has quasi-accidentally evolved into a new kind of thing: the celebrity magazine has become a celebrity/magazine. *Radar* is a celebrity.

"You need a lot of buzz to sell advertising," Tina Brown said. "You can't sell advertising without buzz."

JUNE 19, 2005 BY BEN SMITH

THE ODD COUPLE '08

HILLARY CLINTON HASN'T HAD HER HAYMAN ISLAND MOMENT. YET.

Hayman is a resort off Queensland, Australia, to which Rupert Murdoch flew Tony Blair in 1995 for the annual conference of his right-of-center media megalith, News Corp.

It was a crucial step in the complex and surprising negotiation between the two men that would boost Labour's Mr. Blair up the little stoop and through the door at 10 Downing Street two years later.

Now, the specter of an alliance between Mrs. Clinton and Mr. Murdoch is beginning to whet the appetites of the chattering classes.

At the moment, the two speak of each other (through surrogates) in notably similar terms:

"Senator Clinton respects him and thinks he is smart and effective," said a spokesman for Mrs. Clinton, Philippe Reines.

"Rupert has respect for her political skills and for the hard work that she's done as a senator," said an executive vice president at News Corp., Gary Ginsberg.

What a couple they'd make! For the 74-year-old native of Australia, an embrace of Mrs. Clinton would be only the latest in a long string of daring and (mostly) winning political plays. For New York's junior Senator, it would be the perfection of an art that she and her husband have practiced for more than a decade: keeping your enemies close.

"They are very similar—both hard-nosed characters," said Nicholas Wapshott, who was at *The Times* of London when Mr. Murdoch arrived in 1980. "They would understand each other perfectly. Absolutely perfectly."

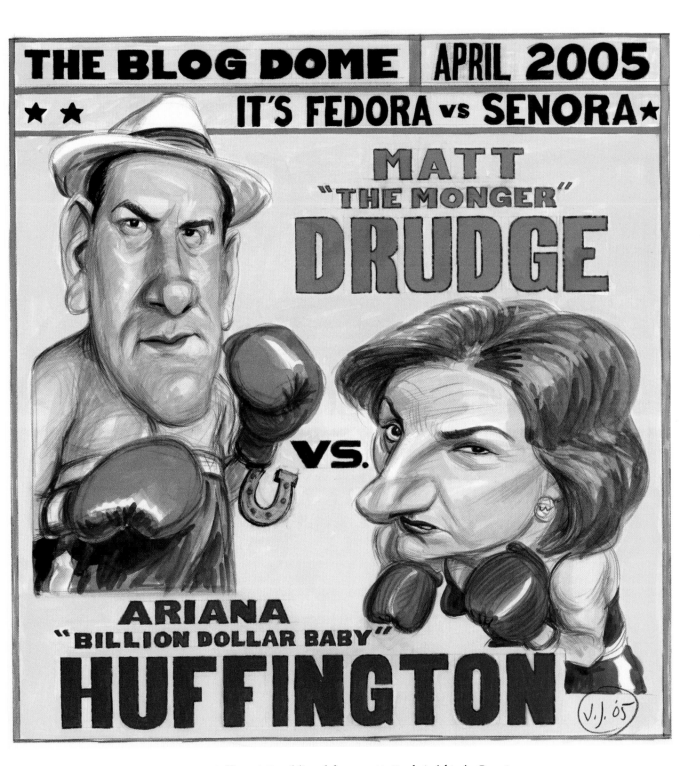

Huffington's Post delivers left uppercut to Drudge's right-wing Report

SEPTEMBER 12, 2005   BY CHRIS LEHMANN

The Story of the Hurricane in Washington, Lies, Third Worldliness—George W. as Imelda M.

THE TRAGEDY OF NEW ORLEANS IS NOT THAT DESPER-ate need turned the city's overwhelmingly poor and black flood survivors into "the Third World," as so many put it. Rather, it was that the federal government feels free to behave like a tin-pot Third World regime in responding to crises involving its neediest citizens.

First there were the lies: President Bush's false claim to Diane Sawyer on *Good Morning America* that "I don't think anybody anticipated" the breaches in New Orleans's levees, and Homeland Security chief Michael Chertoff's repeating of that big lie on *Meet the Press*. And somehow, Federal Emergency Management Agency head Mike Brown said on CNN last Thursday that he had not until that day seen any intel indicating that the New Orleans Convention Center had been designated an emergency evacuation site.

Mr. Brown also spoke glibly of the flood victims left in New Orleans in Katrina's wake as "those who chose not to evacuate, who chose not to leave the city," as though the flood victims in one of America's poorest cities stayed home on some sort of madcap lark and now had to own up to the consequences of their poor individual judgment.

Yet Mr. Brown is at least as outrageous for what he represents as for what he says. The college roommate of former FEMA head Joseph All-baugh, Mr. Brown perfectly embodies the thoughtlessly privileged yet reflexively punitive outlook of the Bush administration's entire policy elite. Indeed, Mr. Brown has presided over the misguided patriation of his agency into Homeland Security and the corresponding shift of its chief mandate from disaster preparedness to terror response.

FEMA has worked toward an overarching approach of "disaster mitigation," says Walter Gillis Peacock, who directs Texas A&M University's Hazard Reduction and Recovery Center. The idea of mitigation is to develop a comprehensive "all-hazards" strategy for minimizing death and property loss.

"We ought to be building back better; we ought to be restoring re-sources as we rebuild," Mr. Peacock said, speaking of the pre-Bush ethos of the agency. "But now the agency has been folded into D.H.S., and it's forgotten its real mission. Actually, that mission has even been pulled away from it. That whole component has been ripped out."

In its place is a single agency mandate to structure all agency efforts to address the terror threat.

As FEMA has been systematically hollowed out, the bulk of disaster-mitigation work falls to state and local jurisdictions. And this is the state of affairs that now permits administration apologists to cynically claim that Louisiana Governor Kathleen Blanco and New Orleans' patchwork of underfunded parish and city authori-ties bear primary responsibility for the calamity after the flood. (Then again, maybe city residents just "chose," in that feckless way of theirs, not to earn enough money to support a surrogate

Corps of Engineers or FEMA directorate in their midst.)

Foreign critics of the Bush administration are quick to point out that such devolutions of power are commonplace in other parts of the globe. It's hard not to see the fortunes of FEMA as a "parable" of sorts, according to longtime international-aid critic George Monbiot, author of the recently published *The Age of Consent: A Manifesto for a New World Order* and a columnist for *The Guardian*. "You could begin it, 'Once upon a time, there was a government which tried to serve its people's needs ... ,'" Mr. Monbiot said.

And the moral: "One thing that keeps occurring to me over and over again as I watch the coverage: This is what happens when you have minimal government. I mean, you have maximum government in the U.S. when it comes to things like foreign investment, but minimal government when it comes to providing essential services." Mr. Monbiot referred to early Katrina reports that described FEMA workers arriving on the scene in New Orleans with anti-anthrax and chemical-weapons kits. "When people were asked what they were doing with all this, they responded, 'Well, this is what we've been told to bring.'"

Mr. Monbiot sees such grotesque mismatches as of a piece with the thwarted priorities of traditional "Third World" powers, preoccupied with distant threats and indifferent to economic inequities within their own borders. "The prime example would be Ferdinand Marcos in the Philippines," Mr. Monbiot said. "Here was a regime which invested in military power on a massive scale. You had huge weapons-buying programs for complete white elephants; you had nuclear-power stations that were built on earthquake fault zones. So profoundly callous and neglectful was he that his wife, Imelda—she oversaw construction of a new sports stadium for the Asia Games. Workers fell into concrete—into the wet cement—and died, and she instructed the project contractors not to take them out, simply to press on and stay on deadline. It was a government which couldn't give a damn about its own people, yet invested massively in prestige projects. And that's what you're seeing here."

Anthony Borden, who directs the London-based Institute for War and Peace Reporting, which coordinates coverage of humanitarian-aid efforts across the globe, saw much of the Katrina coverage while on a trip to the institute's Johannesburg office. "My African friends—their jaws are dropping. People have never seen poor folk in stadiums starving in the U.S. They just think it's completely amazing. You never see it, this version of America, on TV in other parts of the world. You might know, intellectually, that it exists. But you never see it."

"With Katrina, right now," Mr. Borden said, "I think you're seeing that same confidence and competency gap. I mean, it's true in any disaster situation: A reasonable amount of shit happens. But in our reactions,

> *First there were the lies: President Bush's false claim to Diane Sawyer on* Good Morning America *that "I don't think anybody anticipated" the breaches in New Orleans's levees, and Homeland Security chief Michael Chertoff's repeating of that big lie on* Meet the Press.

I think there's a certain level at which we can learn from this. I asked my friends, 'Would you jump to the conclusion that you're seeing a case for multilateral collective security'—of the 'soft power' versus the 'go-it-alone' superpower model? Does this enter into the discourse? I think it does at some point. I mean, look at the tsunami. There you had a more complicated disaster covering a greater stretch of territory, but aid got through pretty efficiently. It's definitely confusing to see a response like this in New Orleans. It may be feeding a big dilemma for the U.S.: As a global emperor, you have a clothing problem. Are you clothed?"

There does seem to be a careful coordination of effort in one sphere, however. When the president finally managed to land on the ground at hurricane-devastated sites in the Gulf, presidential flacks and handlers made certain he was surrounded by impressive amounts of supplies and equipment, symbolizing federal commitment to the relief effort. It appears, however, that this equipment was chiefly mobilized for the purposes of photo-op display.

A German TV crew in Biloxi reported that a relief station was erected behind the president, even though Biloxi is a site where relief had managed to reach citizens in a somewhat timely fashion last week and therefore had few victims on hand to gratefully accept the feds' symbolic largess. When the president moved on, ZDF correspondent Christine Adelhardt reported that the Potemkin relief stations were promptly dismantled.

Likewise, when the President toured the breached 17th Street levee, construction equipment bulked significantly around him as he burbled that "there's a flow in progress." Yet in a blistering press release issued over the weekend, Louisiana Senator Mary Landrieu, who had accompanied Mr. Bush to the levee, said that the critical breach-repair equipment had flowed away.

"Touring this critical site yesterday with the president, I saw what I believed to be a real and significant effort to get a handle on a major cause of this catastrophe. Flying over this critical spot again this morning, less than 24 hours later, it became apparent that yesterday we witnessed a hastily prepared stage set for a presidential photo opportunity; and the desperately needed resources we saw were this morning reduced to a single, lonely piece of equipment."

A week ago Tuesday, after Hurricane Katrina's landfall, Mr. Bush delivered his most hubristic speech yet on the Iraq war, using the 60th anniversary of the end of World War II to liken that epic struggle with the Iraqi occupation, and to liken himself to a latter-day F.D.R.

But a fortnight later, the nation's worst natural catastrophe has blown away such fond reveries once and for all. Peel away the stage sets, the rote platitudes, the crony appointments, the stage-managed intelligence and precooked casus belli—and there stands Imelda Marcos.

JUNE 4, 2005 BY MARK LOTTO

Nude York, Nude York!

AFTER THE BIG JANUARY BLIZZARD, MANY BUCKETS OF purgatorial rain, a chilly, leafless spring-summer, suddenly. Greenhouse gas has cooked Manhattan into a tropical isle; all the hot, half-dressed girls have returned like robins. It's getting so there's no place you can rest your eyes without being assaulted by a salvo of flesh. The subway poles are like strippers' poles, encircled with the most marvelous and terrifying variety of breasts; but don't look down, because there's always that flurry of filthy, flip-flopped feet. And in every other direction: man ass. "Ass cleavage is really in right now," said Antonio Jeffery, a national denim specialist at Diesel Jeans in Union Square. Ass cleavage, like regular cleavage, used to be strictly for women. Even the least careful observers of fashion will recall that a few years back, the rises on women's jeans plummeted with the stock market; at one point, pants got so low that Christine Aguilera was literally prancing in assless chaps. This summer, it's the men who are artfully displaying the tops of their bottoms, as dudes, gay and straight, squeeze themselves into ever-lower-riding jeans from Paper, Prada and Levi's. Even the Gap's in on the action, selling its "1969 extra low boot fit (burnished sky)" denim.

Man ass is suddenly everywhere, from the chichi shopathons of Soho to the hipster suburbia of Williamsburg. Just last Friday night, on the Brooklyn-bound L train, an Asian dude posed, scruffy and tan: Between his too-short olive tee and his too-too-low gray Diesel jeans, the buttresses of his pelvic muscles flared architecturally. Try to ignore his pubes. And then, when he exited at the second stop into Williamsburg, his leather shoulder bag shifted just so, revealing the Metallica keychain dangling conspicuously out his back pocket, above which: a full inch of ass crack—at least.

This is becoming the norm—and, according to denim expert Mr. Jeffery, the waists of men's jeans have actually been sinking like Venice for some time now.

"The rises have progressively dropped lower over the past five or 10 years. We've seen the rise go from the belly button to the hips, to right below the hips," he said. "It has definitely picked up a lot of steam over the past few years."

The disappearing pants seem to be a part of a much larger wave of disconcerting male fads. Lately, it's as if men will accept whatever fashion trends are imposed upon them as happily and willingly as Vichy collaborationists. American men have come to vanity late and practice it with the zeal of the newly converted. And, frankly, it seems to be driving them a little bit nuts.

JULY 10, 2005 BY LIZZY RATNER

WELCOME TO MURRAY HELL!

THE STRIP OF THIRD AVENUE that runs between 29th and 38th streets in Manhattan is more than 1,500 miles from Club Med Cancun, but on sticky summer nights it could easily be mistaken for that spring-break frat-trap where youth is ascendant and every hour is happy hour. On almost any evening, the bars lining the strip pump and grind to the beat of screechy-boozy flirtation, while "Mambo Number Five" blasts over the sound system like a bad bar mitzvah memory. Girls in Seven jeans nuzzle up to banker-boys in baseball caps. The boys ply girls with Raspberry Stoli. Everywhere the night gyrates with the sound of suburban kids at play in the big city.

And yet, despite the riot of youthful hormones, there is something about this neighborhood, known as Murray Hill, that

eerily resembles a Florida retirement resort. Perhaps it's the dedication to challenge-free living, or perhaps it's the abundance of ready-made leisure activities. But swap happy hour with the early-bird special, and it's little Boca in the big city.

Never mind that Murray Hill has as much metro-cred as a cul-de-sac in Great Neck. Or that its new residents wouldn't have survived a night in New York 15 years ago. The young Murray Hillites seem perfectly content with the mini-Manhattan theme park they've created, which allows them to feel like they're living the Big Apple experience while safely ensconced in a bubble of familiarity. Indeed, what's so jarring about Murray Hill is that its young people, who've been treated to everything from the best colleges to trips to Europe,

have as much interaction with their adopted city as tourists on urban safari.

"Murray Hill has more young people that just graduated from college than any other neighborhood in the city," said Kevin

Kurland, the president of the eponymously named Kurland Realty Inc. "This is where they land, their first stop. ... I would say 90 percent of the clients I've placed are between 21 and 25 years old."

SHOULD I GET MARRIED? MY HILLY JOINING ME IN COUPLES SESSION

DR. SELMAN WEL-comed us into his office, and Hilly and I sat down on a couch. He leaned back in an easy chair, popped the top off a Diet Sunkist, and asked what had brought us to see him.

GEORGE: I think we probably had some disagreements. Nothing that specific. Not one incident. Just general patterns of behavior. Maybe me being irritable, that kind of thing.

DR. SELMAN: Whose idea was it to go to couple's therapy?

HILLY: A couple months ago, George was talking about maybe seeing someone yourself, and I said I thought it might be a good idea, because you get sad a lot. I said if you want, I'll go with you.

GEORGE: It was a mutual thing.

DR. SELMAN: You think he gets sad a lot?

HILLY: Sad and anxious and irritable and angry. I mean, not all at once.

GEORGE: Most of the time, I have a great time with Hilly, think of her as my best friend, and we have our own little special language. But part of me is ... troubled. Just about ... all kinds of things. General feeling of malaise and uncertainty. Not knowing how to have a stable emotional tie here. I don't know if I've ever had that. I wonder if I can establish that with anyone.

DR. SELMAN: So why don't you just go for individual therapy?

GEORGE: Maybe I can do that, too.

DR. SELMAN: Going for therapy like this can open up a Pandora's box.

GEORGE: The other day, Hilly came over to my apartment, my little "sanctuary," and started ironing and—do you want to tell that story?

HILLY: You can. Well, I just started ironing and I blew a fuse and—it's actually one of my goals: "I'd like to minimize the number of George's grumpy outbursts"—so anyway I blew the fuse, the air conditioner turned off, and he got really mad. He sat on the couch and he couldn't even look me in the eye.

GEORGE: I knew as soon as I went into the bathroom, you'd start doing something, snooping around.

HILLY: His face kind of turned red and he got really upset. And I said, "Well, George, haven't you ever blown a fuse before?" And he said, "No! Not in my entire life!" And I said, "Well, George, don't worry—it's really easy to fix it. All you have to do is find a panel and switch the fuse thingy." So we just sat there and then I thought, "Well, it's probably in the basement." So I went down there and found the fuse box. Then I switched it off and switched it on and then I went back

upstairs and I said, "Is it back on?" And you said, "No, no—now you turned my computer off, too!" So I went back down and tried it again, went back up and it still wasn't working. And I said, "Well, maybe you should call your super." So he called his super—still couldn't look at me—then he threw the phone down and said, "On vacation for a month!" And I said, "Maybe I should go and talk to the neighbor—"

GEORGE: No, you didn't say that—you just went and did it.

HILLY: I did—you just didn't hear me. So I walked outside down the hall and I knocked on the neighbor's door, and as soon as I did, I heard George back in his apartment screaming, "Get back in here RIGHT NOW!" And as soon as he said that, the door opened and this guy—this bodybuilder bald man—was staring at me thinking I was a battered victim or something. And I was just laughing. He told me there was another fuse box in the kitchen, so everything was fine after that.

GEORGE: She fixed it. I know the retelling of it sounds gruesome, but soon after we were laughing about it. We went on to have a nice dinner, right?

HILLY: Mmm-hmmm. Yeah, but that kind of stuff happens frequently. These short bursts of anger and frustration.

DR. SELMAN: How often do you think it is like that?

GEORGE [to DR. SELMAN]: Can I go get one of those Diet Sunkists?

DR. SELMAN: Sure.

[GEORGE rises, walks to a small kitchen next to the waiting room, gets a Diet Sunkist, returns.]

[To be continued]

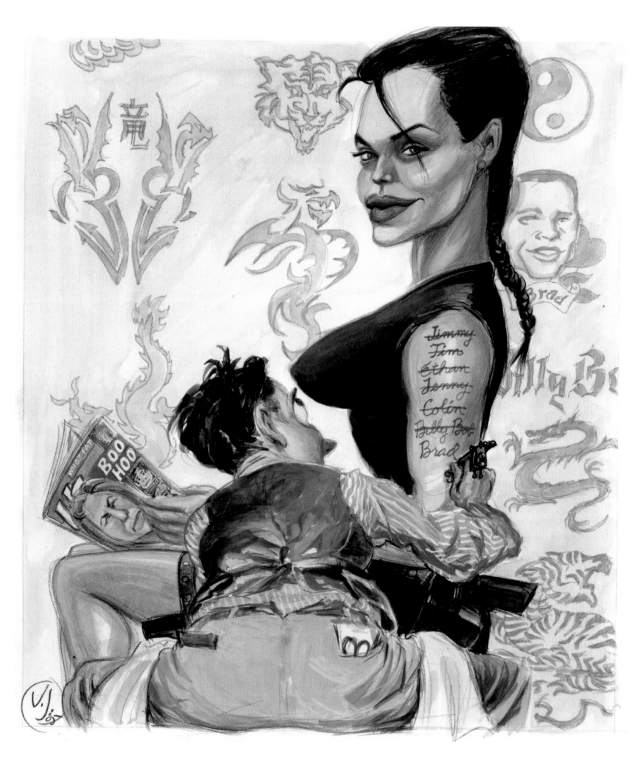

Tattoo Boo-Hoo! Brad bows down to Angelina as Jen weeps

OCTOBER 2, 2005 BY TOM SCOCCA

THE GAWKER KING

Nick Denton Is Either the Luce or Hefner of New Age, But He's Building Web Empire on Gossip, Sex, Smarts; Inspiring Tale of Skinny Bloke With Oxford Honor

ON SEPT. 21, ARIANNA HUFFINGTON, THE LOS ANGELES SOCIAL catalyst, former California gubernatorial candidate and self-appointed anti-Drudge of Web hostesses, tore off her shoes, jumped up on Nick Denton's coffee table and anointed him: Mr. Denton, said the Amazonian queen of L.A. society—a world that one of Mr. Denton's 14 Web sites assesses and reports on—is "the Rupert Murdoch of the blogosphere."

Mr. Denton, her 39-year-old host and the publisher of Gawker Media—the combination steroid and tonic that both inflates and slaps down societies in New York, Los Angeles and Washington, as well as the borderless society of Web-porn fans—was ostensibly welcoming Ms. Huffington to New York. Really, he was throwing his own coming-out party, and had opened the doors of his Soho apartment to some of the mob that clicks on the Gawker site five, six, seven times a day.

He pulled out a much-folded piece of paper and began to read excerpts from a hostile notice that the celebrity-heavy Huffington Post had gotten on its debut. His hands shook just a little. Nikki Finke had declared the site "horrific," adding that Ms. Huffington—"the Madonna of the mediapolitic world"—had "undergone one reinvention too many." The disaster that was the Huffington Post was "unsurvivable."

"I think contrition is in order from the doubters, including Nikki Finke," Mr. Denton said. The partygoers applauded.

But the contrition could have been self-administered. Like so many rising press lords, electronic or not, Mr. Denton had gotten in the business of celebrating what his own publication had recently stomped. Gawker.com had sneezed at the Huffington Post's debut: "When important celebrities have a platform from which to dispense their well-informed opinions, everyone wins!"

Within two days, many of the party guests would receive e-mailed invitations to join an exclusive-but-not-too-exclusive group of readers who would be allowed to post comments on Gawker.

One of them was Nikki Finke.

JULY 10, 2005 BY ANNA SCHNEIDER-MAYERSON

Cool Hand Judy

Talk About a Failure to Communicate! Miller's Tale Climaxes: Love Letter From Scooter, Reporter Sprung, 43rd Street Meeting; Zenger Time It's Not—Why Did Sulzberger Allow Collapse?

ON OCT. 3, *NEW YORK Times* executive editor Bill Keller announced to the staff that at 3:30 that afternoon, reporter-cum-story-cum-victim-cum-witness Judith Miller would be making her return appearance in the newsroom, after spending 85 days in jail. "[S]he would like to thank you," Mr. Keller wrote in an e-mail, "for standing by her during an ordeal that—as you know from the vultures still circling—is not entirely over."

But who was circling? Special prosecutor Patrick Fitzgerald was done with Ms. Miller; his grand jury had collected her notes and her long-delayed testimony three days before. Whatever Mr. Fitzgerald had wished to know about Ms. Miller's role in the White House's leaking of C.I.A. agent Valerie Plame Wilson's identity, Mr. Fitzgerald presumably now knew.

That appeared to leave the public and the press in the role of scavengers—and Ms. Miller, Mr. Keller and publisher Arthur O. Sulzberger Jr. in the role of rotting meat.

The trio held forth near the national-desk area, in the spot where the editors stand to announce the Pulitzers. Ms. Miller described prison as a "soulless" place and described her love of the newsroom. A witness described the applause as "above polite but below wildly enthusiastic."

It was a Judith Miller moment: part crisis, part special occasion. The event captured the singularity of Ms. Miller's standing inside *The Times*—an insider with the publisher, she had become an outsider to her colleagues. For the past 12 months, she had been cast as a journalistic everywoman, standing in for all her fellow *Times*ians. But what had she stood for?

One of those colleagues, Adam Liptak, could be seen at the afternoon fête, hovering at the front, taking notes—presumably attempting to find out. Mr. Liptak is part of a multi-reporter team working on *The Times*' own wrap-up of the Miller case—"a thoroughly reported piece in the pages of *The New York Times*," as Mr. Keller was quoted promising in *The Times*' own Oct. 4 story about Ms. Miller's return to West 43rd Street.

If *The Times* does come up with a thorough and satisfying account of Ms. Miller's journey from the St. Regis Hotel, where she had her first conversation with Vice Presidential Chief of Staff I. Lewis (Scooter) Libby; to the Alexandria Detention Center, where she served her sentence; and finally to the witness stand, it would be the first one.

Until she tells her story in full, herself, her colleagues and readers of *The Times* will have to rely on the tidbits that have so far been revealed about Ms. Miller, Mr. Libby, Vice President Dick Cheney, former ambassador Joseph Wilson, First Amendment law, imaginary uranium and the rest of Mr. Fitzgerald's portfolio. And the more of them that emerge, the less sense the entire story seems to make.

OCTOBER 9, 2005
BY GEORGE GURLEY

GEORGE AND HILLY

IT WAS OUR FIFTH COUPLES-THERAPY SESSION ...

DR. SELMAN: It would be interesting—how do you think it would be different if, let's say, George didn't have these moods? Didn't have mood swings? How would that affect the relationship?

HILLY: I think it would be great!

GEORGE: Right.

DR. SELMAN: Well, in my experience, geographical cures don't work. But there are medications that people can take to—

GEORGE: This one? [*picking up a brochure*] Effexor?

DR. SELMAN: The problem with antidepressants is that they usually take a few weeks before they can work. So if you take it for a week or two—

GEORGE: So a month.

HILLY: Can't you try Prozac?

GEORGE: Ahh! I don't want to take these things. Hmmm.

HILLY: What about homeopathics, natural remedies?

GEORGE: St. John's wort?

DR. SELMAN: St. John's wort does not work. Effexor is a good antidepressant. It might be a reasonable thing to do. Drugs like that tend to work better than Prozac.

GEORGE: But if I start getting in a good mood all the time, does that still count? I mean, you're taking a drug for it.

DR. SELMAN: So? If you had high blood pressure, would you take medication to lower your blood pressure?

[To be continued]

OCTOBER 16, 2005 BY CHOIRE SICHA

The Great Gay Outdoors

AT 5:30 A.M. ON OCT. 6, TWO MEN were shot and robbed in Prospect Park.

"The men were engaged in a sex act," the *Daily News* reported. They were shot, in fact, as the 78th Precinct confirmed, prior to being robbed.

On the gloomy Saturday afternoon that followed, just a muddy little twirl of yellow police tape was tangled in the bushes. Nearby, a cop sat idly in a car; two generators rigged to floodlights, now dark, marked a spooky triangle of forest.

And not far away from the crime scene, under a brutal steady rain, a few men loitered and paced, dressed in their Brooklyn casuals, looking for "sex acts."

That these woods immediately returned to regular use as a cruising ground isn't unusual. Areas like this are the decrepit, unchanging standbys of man-on-man match-ups. Online message boards regularly update men on conditions in similar places: Have they been raided recently? Are the men hot? Anybody, you know, been shot?

But outdoor Manhattan proper is changing, and rapidly. Rezoning—and zoning variances—in many neighborhoods are turning manufacturing districts that were desolate and therefore randy in the dark of night into Dullsville, U.S.A.

◇◇◇◇◇◇◇

NOVEMBER 13, 2005 BY BEN SMITH

WELCOME TO BLOOM-BURG
Mayor Wins Historic Victory in Both Parties; It Only Cost About $100 a Vote, a Bargain! What Will Mike Do With Massive Mandate?

MICHAEL BLOOMBERG IS not a man who confuses the trappings of power for power. But on the eve of his re-election, as he stood on the observation deck on the Empire State Building, at the top of the city, the symbolism of his mastery was irresistible. The new Bloomberg L.P. tower stood out behind him; his city was sprawled around him. But after a single glance, the mayor turned away from the view.

Early returns showed Mr. Bloomberg well on his way to the sizable victory foreseen in the pre-election polls. At press time, the incumbent had more than 60 percent of the vote.

The landslide ratifies what may be the most powerful mayoralty in New York City history and anoints Mr. Bloomberg as the city's first true Imperial Mayor. Not since Ed Koch's victory on both Democratic and Republican lines in 1981 has a mayor emerged from an election with no coherent opposition.

But unlike Mr. Koch, Mr. Bloomberg steps into a Mayoralty re-engineered for power by a 1989 reform of the City Charter that removed the "upper house" of New York's legislature and with it most of the checks on the mayor's power to set budgets and make policy.

"The mayor is unrivaled. It's total primacy. There are no competing centers of power," said Fred Siegel, a historian at the Cooper Union. "If you have someone who seizes the power inherent in the office, they can be a hegemon."

NOVEMBER 13, 2005
BY DAISY CARRINGTON

Red Diapers, Platinum Umbilical

THIS WEEK, FAIRCHILD PUBLI-cations is introducing a horrify-ing new magazine called *Cookie*, featuring $900 strollers and hair gel for 3-year-old boys.

But could this be the very magazine that New York City parents deserve? Have you no-ticed how parents are increas-ingly using the bellies of inno-cent babes as their own personal billboards?

Take David Moore, 37, a cre-ative director at Publicis Ad-vertising, who likes to dress his 2-year-old son, Conrad, in a T-shirt stenciled with the clas-sic image of Marxist revolution-ary Che Guevara. "It seems like pretty much all parents in Brook-lyn have something similar," Mr. Moore said.

"I don't think many of our cus-tomers are communists," said Harald Husum, founder of Ap-paman.com, which distributes the T-shirts. According to Mr. Husum, he's sold nearly 6,000 Che products since his company was launched in 2002, despite a smattering of protests from Cu-ban-Americans.

Mr. Moore's wife, Francesca Castagnoli, a writer, wearily es-timates that one in 10 kids in her hood own the Che shirt. "Some people probably think it's an icon of what's cool," she said, adding (without apparent irony): "Also, you sort of want that independent spirit for your child."

DECEMBER 4, 2005   BY MARK LOTTO

WELCOME TO SCHNOOKLYN

ON A RECENT SUNDAY AFTER-noon in Cobble Hill, Brook-lyn, every street corner along Smith Street was set and lit like a Norman Rockwell. But. The signs in the windows all read: "Wanted for Sexual As-sault. Reward of $12,000. Name: Peter Braunstein."

It's not Whitechapel during Jack the Ripper, but ever since the former *Women's Wear Daily* reporter allegedly assaulted a woman in her Chelsea home on Halloween night, Peter Braun-stein has been spotted sipping lattes and annoying dry cleaners all over Cobble Hill. Every day

the police dragnet continues, and every day drags nothing up.

But Alberto Braunstein, the suspect's dad, knows that Pe-ter wasn't the suspicious coffee drinker or the irate dry-cleaner customer. His son wouldn't be caught dead outside Manhat-tan. "I have never known my son to even go to Brooklyn," said Mr. Braunstein. "So I was stunned."

Forget the massive manhunt. Is Peter Braunstein the last free-lancer in New York who thinks he's too good for Brooklyn?

It would have seemed that, by now, few New Yorkers still

cling to the old anti-Brooklyn bigotries. Who persists in see-ing the borough as little more than Manhattan's waiting room, its discard pile, its backwater wilderness? Even prejudiced Manhattanites are migrating en masse to Brooklyn.

This hegira has been going on for years, but can no lon-ger be understood simply as the search for cheap, mythi-cally large apartments; rents in Brooklyn are nearly as high as those in Manhattan. It's dif-ferent now. People aspire to Brooklyn. The vector of the city has reversed itself.

OCTOBER 2, 2005 BY ALEXANDRA JACOBS

Yes, I Flew JetBlue Flight 292: *Gleeful Survivor Tale; 'Tis*

A S WE PASSENGERS JOYOUSLY DISEMBARKED FROM JetBlue Flight 292 on the evening of Sept. 21, 2005, one of Los Angeles' gorgeous toxic sunsets was illuminating the kindly, ruddy, handsome faces of the suddenly superfluous but very welcome emergency personnel gathered on the tarmac. They all looked like 1940s movie heroes reduced to skycap duty.

We were shepherded into shuttle buses with big glass doors, where we sat making call after happy call on our cell phones or just staring stupidly into space as we were driven to the terminal. There, as if at a particularly festive wedding, we were greeted by a receiving line consisting of JetBlue executives wearing shiny blue ties, L.A. Chief of Police Bill Bratton (remember him?) with chest puffed out in a natty suit, and a curly-haired, diminutive gentleman in rolled-up shirtsleeves who kindly offered to help me find my husband. As he walked away, a couple of remote synapses clicked in my addled brain. "I think that was the mayor," I told a bearded fellow who had been sitting across the aisle from me on the plane. "No," he said. "Really?" Yes, in spacy, decentralized Los Angeles, Mayor Antonio Villaraigosa, elected last May, commands approximately the same amount of recognition as the actress Taryn Manning—also on the flight, with her publicist, who must've been thrown into severe shock by what happened; how else to explain the over-24-hour delay in shoving Ms. Manning before the television cameras?

Alas, I was not quite so restrained. Indeed, after eschewing another adrenaline-fueled flight to J.F.K. in favor of a tearful reunion with my spouse, I made a quick decision: I was not going to allow myself to be spirited away back to normalcy, dinner and the indifferent mews of our two cats, but would rather plunge shamelessly headlong into the mosh pit of waiting news media, starting with John Broder, L.A. bureau chief of *The New York Times*, and quickly following up with an Aaron Brown–Anderson Cooper sandwich on CNN. Surrounded by these and other enthralled suitors, I felt like Scarlett O'Hara flouncing her petticoats at the Twelve Oaks barbecue. Fiddle-dee-dee—I was alive! The hot flash of the cameras felt like a mother's kiss. That landing was scary, sure—but even scarier was how quickly I transmogrified into a total media whore. Yet it seemed a fitting coda to an ordeal that was amplified to the nth power because so many of us had, now famously, watched it on television. For those who have never flown JetBlue: One of the company's major selling points is the small televisions on the back of each passenger's seat, which offer a selection of free channels via DirecTV satellite. I have complained about these TV's before, mostly because of the ambient noise that emanates from the cheap plastic headphones they distribute; there is nothing like trying to sleep to the tinny sounds of your seatmate enjoying VH1's Metal Mania. But this time, believe it or not, I was grateful to have them. Because guess what? After the initial alarm of seeing the very plane we were occupying filmed circling around LAX on MSNBC and Fox and ABC—a garish spotlight trained on the faulty nose-gear, the news of our possible plight crawling along, incredibly, in the same text zipper as Hurricane Rita—the testimony of the aviation experts summoned by the news programs proved largely reassuring.

To answer some frequently asked questions: What was the mood in the cabin? Um, it was tense. Very tense. Though not as bad as you might

Pity I'm a Media Whore; Some F.A.Q.'s on My Landing

think: I tallied no screams nor frenzied clicking of rosary beads. As we glided along at 5,000 feet, there were scattered tears, subdued prayers and even jokes from a few wizened, seen-it-all-before road warriors—you know the type. I was far from being able to joke, but I did remark to one of my row mates, a handsome, clean-cut man with a wife and two young daughters waiting for him at home, that at least if I perished in a fiery inferno, there would be the satisfaction of knowing that I had conclusively won an ongoing argument with my husband about whether a fear of flying is justified. "Small consolation," he said. But he knew exactly what I meant.

What did the flight crew tell you? The announcements from the cockpit were warm, yet crisp and businesslike. At first, slowly rising over the dusty hills of Palmdale, we thought the problem was merely landing gear that wouldn't retract (much less of an issue, surely, than landing gear that wouldn't extrude), or possibly even a mere signal glitch. Then a low fly-by at Long Beach Airport, during which our plane's underbelly was inspected from the ground with binoculars, revealed the cockeyed nose gear. Is this the moment to admit that I had never really realized before that planes have nose gear? Somehow I had always thought that they alighted on their back feet—like birds. We were informed about the plans for an emergency landing at LAX, which is not a JetBlue hub, but whose facilities could better accommodate our wayward aircraft. "We're going to do our best to make this a positive situation," said pilot Scott Burke, inciting hollow laughter in the cabin, along with a few groans.

In the closing minutes, we were instructed on how to use the rubber slides, if necessary, what to do if we smelled smoke (calmly find another method of egress), and to remove sharp objects and high heels from our person—in essence, a refresher course on those indecipherable little cards they stuff in the seatback pockets, where the paper vomit bags used to be. I quietly congratulated myself on having selected 13D, an aisle seat directly behind the emergency-exit row, and on wearing the sneakers and sweatpants that I had hitherto dismissed as inappropriate, "ugly American" flying wear, but adopted with the excuse of my six-month-old pregnancy.

Who informed the media? I have no idea, and have been unable to find out. What was the landing like? As we glided toward earth, pilot Burke

> Um, it was tense. Very tense. Though not as bad as you might think: I tallied no screams nor frenzied clicking of rosary beads. As we glided along at 5,000 feet, there were scattered tears, subdued prayers and even jokes from a few wizened, seen-it-all-before road warriors—you know the type.

said, "Flight attendants, prepare for arrival," which set off a fresh round of hollow laughter in the cabin. Then there was mostly silence, except for the attendants' powerful and surprising incantation of "Brace, brace, brace!" I am not a religious person, but I will admit to mumbling "Please, God," several times through clenched teeth as the smell of scorched rubber—but, blessedly, no actual smoke—filled the aircraft. Time had an amazingly rubato quality during this whole experience; the hours of circling had gone incredibly quickly, while the final minutes seemed extremely slow. It was a much gentler, if hotter, landing than most. At the time I attributed the heat to anxiety, and the discontinuation of the pressurized air-conditioning. Later, I saw the footage of fire shooting under the plane. When we came to a solid stop and realized that we weren't going to die, nor was the plane even going to break apart, the silence ended in a loud, collective, spontaneous *Whooo! Yeaah!*

What is JetBlue providing as compensation? A refund, plus two free round-trip tickets to the destination of one's choice, and service representatives bearing goodie bags filled with snacks, a free car service and little clucks of sympathy. The airline is classless, so forget about lifetime upgrades, but at a certain point I felt that I could demand just about anything—massages, male escorts, a lifetime supply of Terra Blues potato chips—and it would be mine. I didn't want to take advantage.

I did, however, take advantage of the numerous opportunities for on-air time that continued to cascade my way. But who, exactly, was taking advantage? *Good Morning America* booked me, along with two other talkative passengers, at 3 a.m. Pacific Standard Time. I consented to this unholy hour partly because the studio where ABC tapes remotes is on Prospect Avenue, about half a mile down the hill from our house in Los Feliz. I figured I wouldn't be getting any sleep anyway. At 2:45 a.m., the over-solicitous bookers sent a stretch limo—the kind they use at proms, with shaded windows and fake "stars" dotted on the ceiling. At 5:45 a.m., a smaller car came to take me to CNN's *American Morning*, where I reiterated the same things I'd said to Anderson and Aaron (I think we're on a first-name basis now), much less articulately, I'm afraid, to Miles O'Brien. The passing hours had transformed them into bullet points. Catharsis via mass talk therapy had become simple exhaustion. As the day progressed, the phone kept ringing: the Fox News Channel, the A.P., NPR, *USA Today*, The *Daily News*, *Ellen: The Ellen DeGeneres Show*, *The Tyra Banks Show*(!), *Le Parisienne* and too many podunk radio stations and small local gazettes to count. I marveled at how deep the media's penetration was, yet how pointillist. Via e-mail, I was hearing from friends I hadn't spoken to since seventh grade, from locations as far-flung as Africa and South America, but it would take me well over a day to locate my own parents, who were visiting London with a new, tricky cell phone. Has communication ever been simultaneously so efficient and so inefficient?

I was taking a call from a jocular New Zealand disc jockey as my husband drove us back to where it all started, the Bob Hope Airport in Burbank, where there was a big billboard advertising the airplane thriller *Flightplan*, starring Jodie Foster. It would turn out to be the weekend's top-grossing movie. Sitting on a brand-new JetBlue Flight 292, we held hands and admired a cute picture of ourselves in the *L.A. Times*, then dozed as my image flickered across the tiny screens.

GEORGE GURLEY INTERVIEWS FRANK DIGIACOMO

Who are some of the celebrities and socialites you covered?

I loved the social women, those really wonderful characters who sort of deserved their stature. Pat Buckley—I was very fond of her, even though I can't say that I was close to her. Ninety-nine percent of the women who call themselves socialites today—it's more of a branding term than a cultural one—couldn't hold a candle to her. Mrs. Buckley had a great sense of humor and a fierce intellect. On the record, she was self-deprecating, but off the record, after a glass or two of white wine, she could be wonderfully wicked. I remember once writing that she was like a Mafia captain. If you tried to talk to her about "society," she would essentially, say, "I have no idea what you're talking about, dear boy." And then she would laugh. She had this amazing laugh that was somewhere between Lauren Bacall and Charles Nelson Reilly. She would laugh and completely disarm me. With her it was a chess game. She gave up very little, and yet she still gave me these great quotes. She enjoyed the game as much as I did, talking to me while she was in her rose bed in Connecticut pruning her roses. And that was the thing that I loved—love—about my job: The access it's given me to worlds that I would never, ever have seen otherwise. Ever.

Julian's Schnabel's a guy who I had a very stormy relationship with. But I was always fascinated by his supreme self-confidence. Most people, when you challenge them a bit—especially if you're a reporter—they either run or they cut you out. They marginalize you. You stopped getting invited to their parties. And Schnabel always—well, he did stop inviting me to his parties—but whenever I ran into him, he would sit me down and try to explain his point of view, usually with a great deal of contempt and condescension. I think that probably has a lot to do with why he's such a good filmmaker.

One of the most memorable stories I did was the week I followed Martin Scorsese for our Millennium issue. That was when the *Observer* staff tracked all these different New Yorkers over the course of seven days during the last weeks of 1999. The thing about Scorsese is, if you're Italian-American, it's hard not to have him as one of your heroes. I mean, here's this guy who has done these amazing, visceral films that really convey the anger and blood lust and distrust that I have in the Sicilian subdivision of my genes, and yet, at the same time, he has transcended all of that primal, cologne-and-cuff-links goombah stuff. He's a scholar who just happens to be fluent in the language of mook, you know? His knowledge of film and literature and history is pretty breathtaking, and, on top of that, he knows his rock 'n' roll. And I don't know if this makes sense, but interviewing him was both incredibly exciting and yet also depressing. I probably sat with him for a total of two hours over the course

> *Off the record, after a glass or two of white wine, Pat Buckley could be wonderfully wicked, like a Mafia captain.*

of the week and spoke to him on the phone for maybe another 45 minutes and the guy just blew me away with what he'd read and what he knew. After I left my first interview with him, I remember actually feeling guilty about all the time I'd wasted over the course of my life. I was thinking, Jesus Christ, he was very gracious about it, but this guy seemed to have completely maximized every potential educational opportunity that came his way. No slacking for Scorsese. And even though during that first interview, he told me more than once that he was feeling tired, when he got onto a subject that excited him, it was evident that he's a man of great energy. I know why he was tired, too. He'd just become a father again. His wife was there and she brought out their baby daughter, Frances is her name, and in retrospect, maybe Scorsese was directing the scene, but his wife handed him the baby while he was standing in front of this huge, amazing poster for Jean Cocteau's *Beauty and the Beast*. You know, there's Scorsese, fumbling a bit with his daughter—the beast and his baby beauty—and I was standing there thinking, "Well, I've got my last graf."

Can you talk about some of the great parties?

In 2000, when Hillary Clinton ran for the Senate and Al Gore ran for president, Harvey Weinstein and Tina Brown threw an election-night party at Elaine's that was sponsored by *Talk* magazine. I think Georgette Mosbacher and Michael Bloomberg's media company were involved as well. This was before Bloomberg was mayor, and I remember him walking around the room and, at one point, refusing to talk to me for my story. Anyway, Hillary's victory was apparent pretty early on, but Gore and Bush were back and forth, and I remember Harvey [Weinstein] saying something into his cell phone—he was asking about electoral votes. I don't know who he was talking to, but he said something like, "See what you can do," as if he was instructing some secret operative to goose Gore's numbers. That was when Harvey was totally embroiled in Hillary's campaign and campaigning for Gore in Florida with Robert De Niro and Ben Affleck. So they have this great party, and at the end of it, Hillary was supposed to come to Elaine's with Bill Clinton, but she never did. This couldn't have made Harvey and Tina happy because, if memory serves correctly, it had been implied in the days leading up to the party that they were going to deliver Hillary and Bill—the meta-message being, I guess, that *Talk* magazine delivers. So, God knows what kind of negotiations went on, but at some point, a decision was made that Harvey and Tina Brown were going to hand-pick a group of people to go down to Hillary's suite at the Grand Hyatt hotel. I remember Harvey pointing to people in the crowd and then pointing to me. And thinking, "All right, I've got it!" And then, once we got to the hotel and the Secret Service let us into the suite, the thing that stayed in my mind was Bill Clinton chatting up Uma Thurman while Harvey debriefed Hillary. Uma looked radiant that night, but I think what she really wanted to do was impress the president with her intelligence, not mesmerize him with her beauty. One of my biggest regrets is that I couldn't hear what she

---

Frank DiGiacomo is a contributing editor at *Vanity Fair*.

was asking him—if I moved in any closer, I would have ruined the moment—but she was behaving in that way that actors do when they're trying to sound like they're well informed. Clinton reminded me of Snoopy when he used to imitate the vulture. Only this time, the vulture was smiling.

Speaking of Uma Thurman, there was a period around the breakup of her marriage to Ethan Hawke when Hawke seemed to be at an event in the city every night. I'm exaggerating, but, for a time, I could literally run a picture of him at some shit-ass event every week in the Transom. And I did. Kaplan once told me that he never wanted the party pictures to just be party pictures. He wanted them to be about something. You know, once Robert Benton did this great photo spread in *Esquire* called "Happy Marriages Are All Alike" in which he photographed couples such as Mickey Hargitay and Jayne Mansfield and Xavier Cugat and Abbe Lane and the whole point of the spread—and you could kind of see it in the body language—was that these couples weren't happy. Well, I was trying to do a much dumber version of that. You know, I think Ethan Hawke is a really fine actor. I thought he was great in *Before the Devil Knows Your Dead* and *Training Day* and *Gattaca*. And I guess my perspective was, people who are that talented don't need to go to parties celebrating the unveiling of fountain pens or the opening of Brazilian bikini wax salons or wherever he was going. So, when he started making countless public appearances, I decided to have fun with it. I invented some kind of title or nickname for him—I can't remember what it was—but I mocked him for a while. I don't seem to recall that he curtailed his public appearances any, but the weird thing is that one night, I was at a party, and a woman came up to me and grabbed me by the hand and said, "Are you Frank DiGiacomo of *The Observer*?"

And I said, "Yes." And she said, "O.K., could you wait right here? Someone wants to meet you."

And after a few moments, Uma Thurman walked up to me and just stared at me. She didn't say a word to me; she just stared for, like, 5 or 10 seconds and then she walked away. I assumed it had something to do with the pictures I was running of Ethan Hawke, but I couldn't tell if she was secretly happy that I was twitting her ex-husband or if she was being protective of him. But it was weird. It was almost as if she was going to keep an eye out for me now.

Did you ever have any tense moments covering the Oscar parties?
One year, I'd co-authored a piece on Harvey and Bob Weinstein. The gist of the story was that there was a correction going on at Miramax and, I think, that Bob was asserting himself. I went out to the Oscars, and the day before the awards ceremony, Miramax would do this cocktail party where nominated actors such as Dame Judi Dench would do skits from Miramax films. It became a huge thing that we covered every year, and so I walked into that party, at the Mondrian's Sky Bar in L.A., and Harvey made a beeline towards me with his protectors; I think at one point he had me by the lapels, or maybe he was poking his finger into my chest, but I distinctly remember him saying, "You don't know me. You don't know me." He wasn't roughing me up, just getting in my face, and I remember giggling awkwardly, because I didn't really know what to do. I wish I could say that Dame Judi was standing next to him wearing a pair of brass knuckles, but she wasn't.

Harvey was very serious. He was very angry. And then when I laughed, I think he just realized this was not a good way of dealing. And he just backed away and let it go. And you know what? Maybe I didn't "know" Harvey, but I think I got him. I think that's why he kept letting me cover him. Lucky me. Seriously, I have some pretty great memories from the Miramax Oscar-night after-parties. There was always the party and then the much smaller after-party that went until almost dawn. I remember Winona Ryder sitting on the floor of a suite at the Beverly Hills Hotel—or maybe it was the Mondrian—by the CD player rocking out to the Replacements' "Bastards of Young," which is one of my favorite songs. The year that *Shakespeare in Love* won, Tom Stoppard was at the breakfast buffet and asked me to hold the Oscar he'd won for the screenplay while he filled up his plate. There's something about the heft of those awards that makes you feel like a million bucks. Peter Kaplan was there with me that year and I remember him telling me that he saw Stoppard in the men's room standing at a urinal holding his Oscar in one hand and his Johnson in the other. Kaplan asked him how he felt and he said, "Fantastic." And another year, I'll never forget Sir Ian McKellen and his boyfriend slow-dancing with each other as if there was no one else in the room.

Can you tell me about the *Pulp Fiction* party, that Oscar party?
All I remember was that Kaplan kept calling me on my massive cell phone and telling me to steal an ashtray from Chasen's. And I couldn't. You know what was interesting about that assignment, for me as a writer? I feel like Peter Kaplan pushed me to another level. That was the second Oscar party that I did. The previous Oscars, the story was Tina [Brown, then editor of *The New Yorker*] vs. Graydon [Carter, editor of *Vanity Fair*]. And I did a very skeletal job. The *New Yorker* party, which was Tina's gig, was a week before Graydon's party. The night of Graydon's party—the Oscars were on a Monday then and I had to file the following day—the Sunset Marquis, where I was staying, had this Oscar disco party going on outside my window, and it kept me up all night. By the time I got up to write, my nerves were all jangled. So the next year, Kaplan kind of sat me down and re-framed the story. Tina had decided not to do a party, but Miramax was doing one at Chasen's, which was about to close. Kaplan knew somehow that there ▶

was a caricature of *The New Yorker*'s Harold Ross, who was an investor in Chasen's, on the second floor of the restaurant, and using that as an entry point, he spun out this whole thesis about New Yorkers in Los Angeles—you know, outsiders storming Hollywood on its most sacred night. The light bulb went on in my head. I knew where to take it from there—except Kaplan kept calling me about that ashtray.

What kind of pep talk would Kaplan give you before you'd go cover the Oscars?
Well, the thing was always, he would get in front of you and say: "Listen to me. Listen to me. Listen to me." It was at least three times. And then he would look me in the eye really sternly and say, "Do you understand I'm being perfectly straight with you here, Frank?" And that's when I knew that I'd better listen carefully to whatever he said next. It was like a Vulcan mind meld. Then he would say, "This is what I want you to get—an ashtray from Chasen's." Part of the genius of this guy is that he made you feel like you were doing something important: You were contributing to literature. *The Observer* remains the favorite time of my career. I had the most fun, the most freedom and I grew the most as a writer and a reporter.

What percentage of the stories you did just came to you, as gifts on your voice mail? Or did it always require getting on the phone, seeing what was going on?
There weren't that many gifts. I guess there was a point when some came in. Once we got into that 1996-1998 sweet spot, there was stuff coming in. After Graydon and Susan [Morrison] got it rolling and then with Kaplan, the paper achieved this critical mass. One thing I remember—you know that Mr. Jenkins ad? It was a gin ad. He was this white-haired cartoon figure portrayed as cutout marionette. It was a really annoying ad and, for a while in the '90s, it was everywhere. And Stevenson went off and did this great thing called "Killing Mr. Jenkins": There were three or four scenarios on how to kill the guy, and they were really very funny, witty. And I remember coming in the day after it was published and the ad agency called up and they were trying to be cool about it, but they were furious and it was just great. It was one of those moments—like when Windolf and Stevenson correctly named all the winners of the National Magazine Awards before they were announced. That was huge.

There was another piece you did on *The New Yorker*'s 70th anniversary party—people like Harrison Ford, Rudolph Giuliani, Barry Diller, Larry Tisch, Joseph Mitchell. You wrote about the feeling of disconnectedness and you had a quote from a veteran journalist: "[Tina Brown] invited all the right people but then left no room to invite some of the wrong people."
That's a great line about New York because as Kaplan used to say, New York is about "shit and perfume." And it's true, with New York you've gotta have both. And that's why right now, New York is a very sterile place, because there's no fringe area. Even Brooklyn. It's about money—it's all about money now.

Tina Brown was a recurring subject in *The Observer*.
She was. Which is one reason she called me a scumball. "You're just a scumball," she said. I think she meant to call me a scumbag, but I got the point. It was at a party and there were one or two members of her public relations team around, and they were put in that weird position of supporting her even as they were wincing at what she'd said. So that was interesting. I will say this about Tina. Most people in our business can throw a punch, but they can't

take one. Tina can. She really got battered near the end of *Talk*'s run—and if I'm going to be completely honest, I was part of the mob that thrashed her. But she picked herself up off the canvas and she's still out there swinging.

Can you say something about getting that sort of frosty reception and *The Observer*'s reputation?
Look at Letterman, look at *Esquire* in the '60s, look at *The Observer*. They were all places that were accused of being mean-spirited, and in the end it's undeserved, because when people drink the Kool-Aid at a point in the culture, you need someone to say, "Hey, wait a minute here, this is all bullshit." And everyone else is so invested in the bullshit, they try to kill the messenger.

Anything else about the energy back in the mid-'90s compared to now?
You know what started to creep in—and I wrote about this when I first noticed it in the Hamptons. Suddenly, it wasn't enough to throw a party. Your potato chips—you know those multicolored potato chips, Terra Chips? They began to sort of advertise those at parties. Everything was marketing and product placement. It wasn't a party anymore. It was a Skyy Vodka party. And I remember that same weekend going to a Donna Karan boutique opening where this singing messenger showed up with the DKNY logo shaved into his head, and that was the moment for me when parties weren't fun anymore. I mean, on some level, parties are usually about selling something—even if it's just the host's ego—but in the '90s they became particularly brazen. They were pure business. And you were only invited if you could in some way contribute to whatever the endgame was. I remember a number of phone calls during which publicists fairly pleaded with me to mention the name of some brand or another that had provided the alcohol for an event. And that's where I think things started to go off the rails for New York. The other thing that happened is that, at some point, people started paying publicists to curate their parties, and the crowds became homogenized and dull.

Tell me about [*Observer* founder and owner] Arthur Carter ...
Arthur was very good to me. Most newspaper owners look at their gossip columnists as necessary pains in the ass. They're good for business because they bring in readers, but they also generate countless angry phone calls from the owner's rich and powerful friends who are inevitably the targets of the columnists. Arthur was remarkably fearless in that regard. I'm sure he got plenty of those calls, but they didn't bother him. In fact, I think he kind of liked them because they told him that people were reading his paper. Another thing I'll always remember about Arthur was that when I first started at the paper, I would sometimes run into him outside the *Observer* townhouse in, say, August, and I would be sweating through my T-shirt. And he would be wearing a sweater and there would not be even a bead of sweat on him.

You want to say something about what the 64th Street office was like then?
At first I was a little intimidated because everybody was real literate, dressed real nice, but fairly quickly, I felt at home. It was after the first few columns that I did. They had gone over pretty well, and Susan Morrison, who had hired me away from the *New York Post*, was really supportive and she immediately kept her promise to get me writing features. And yet, though *The Observer* was as serious as a heart attack when it came to journalistic standards, there was a slight whiff of Animal House about the place. Warren St. John, who was

a reporter then, had brewed homemade beer with a Barry Blitt caricature of Arthur Carter on the label. You could regularly hear the political editor Terry Golway yelling "Buuulllshit!" at the top of his lungs whenever something didn't pass his smell test. And there were some world-class pranks being pulled by [writers and editors] Peter Stevenson and Jim Windolf. Also, remember what we used to do? Drinks in the backyard after closing. On like the second or third Tuesday that we were out there, the deputy editor, John Homans, came up to me. Stevenson and Windolf always used to describe Homans as standing with "arms akimbo" because he stood a certain way, but he was one of the people who initially scared the crap out of me because he didn't mince words and had the physique of a Parris Island boot camp sergeant. Anyway, he complimented me on some item I'd written that week and I remember standing there with my bottle of beer, thinking: "This is so cool."

You called Elaine Kaufman the patron saint of journalists. Was Elaine's your favorite?

Elaine's and the Four Seasons were probably the two places where—even if I hadn't gotten a single story out of them—I felt part of the city. Elaine's was the only place I ever felt I belonged—that and *The Observer*. I once said to Elaine, "Why have you always been so kind to me?" and she said, "You seem like a nice kid." I'm glad she didn't think I was a "yutz," which was a word I once heard her use to describe someone she didn't like. One night, I was at a party downtown and I was talking to [Page Six editor] Richard Johnson and he was with [his then-wife] Nadine, and Nadine had these models that she was repping. And I was with my wife. And we said, "Let's go to Elaine's!" There were so many of us that we got split up. So I walk into Elaine's with Richard and two beautiful models—both three feet taller than I was—and Elaine gave me the hairy eyeball and wouldn't come over to our table. She was really cold to me. Fifteen minutes later, my wife showed up and Elaine was fine. That's when I realized that Elaine has a moral code that's very interesting. She also has one of the best shows in town: I've seen Al Pacino there; Woody Allen. I met Phil Spector there; Peter Wolf and Robert Altman; Anna Strasberg; Esther Williams. I've dined with Bobby Zarem; Gay Talese. And I swear I once saw Tony Danza sit down with Arthur Miller. The sad thing is, I'm at a stage now where I have an 11-year-old son. I can't afford to eat at Elaine's as much as I once did. And I miss it.

I can't afford the Four Seasons anymore, either, although one of my favorite things in life is to sit at the bar, order a martini straight up with lots of olives and just take in the sights. I could stare at those undulating chain-mail curtains for hours, but what I really love is to watch the two general managers, Alex von Bidder and Julian Niccolini, deal with all the egos who swan into their little kingdom. Alex is courtly, precise and has impeccable manners. My sense is that he caters to that portion of the power crowd that wants their dining experience to be soothing and self-affirming. But Julian is all about drama. Like many Italians, he's a bit of a sadist. He isn't cowed by power, and he has a pretty wicked grasp of politics—the backroom kind. The Four Seasons is his domain and when you go there, you must submit to his rule, no matter how powerful you are. If you understand this about him, he will make you feel like royalty. If you don't, well, you'll probably never go there again. I also think

Julian knows that, despite their charmed lives, a lot of his customers are bored out their skulls.

What was the strangest story you ever did?

One of the most bizarre stories I ever covered was the Jackson family reunion at Madison Square Garden. The concert must have fallen right at the beginning of September 2001. Drew Nieporent, the restaurateur behind Nobu and Corton, invited me. The show was built around the fact that Michael Jackson and his brothers hadn't performed together in many years, but there were also some special guests. And one of the first persons onstage was Marlon Brando. He was big and wearing a massive pair of sunglasses. And when he came out, he didn't say anything. He just took off his watch and stared at it for at least a full minute. Not surprisingly, the crowd started to get restless. There had been this Michael Jackson look-alike—or maybe it was really Michael—popping up in different sections of the Garden driving the crowd into a frenzy, but now they've got Marlon Brando staring silently at his watch. Eventually, he did speak and that's when things got really freaky.

Brando started talking about how in the amount of time he had been silent, dozens or maybe hundreds of children had been hacked to death with machetes—I definitely remember him using the word "hacked." Drew and I were both looking at each other like, "Did he just say what we think he said?" Maybe Brando was making some appeal to charity, but all he did was succeed in confusing and angering the crowd. I mean, they had come to see Michael Jackson perform "Beat It" and "ABC" with Marlon and Randy and Tito, but instead Marlon Brando, whom most of the crowd probably remembered from his insane performance in that remake of *The Island of Dr. Moreau*, is lecturing them on murdered children. The whole thing was incredibly jarring. Well, the rest of the concert didn't exactly reach that what-the-fuck level, but then there was an after-party at Tavern on the Green that was like a Fellini film. I wasn't invited but I got in. I can't tell you who let me in because to this day he will get in trouble, but the

> *Uma looked radiant that night, but I think what she really wanted to do was impress the president with her intelligence, not mesmerize him with her beauty.*

crowd was just the most perplexing collection of celebrities I've ever seen. On one hand you had this amazing cross-section of ham-and-cheese actors and singers from the last 20 years of show business: William Shatner, David Hasselhoff and Kenny Rogers. The age of irony was represented by Paul Shaffer and then you had this gaggle of old-school actresses that included *Psycho*'s Janet Leigh and Ann Miller. Liz Taylor may have been there, too—I know she was at the concert. The scene was weird enough, but then the night climaxed in this really unsettling scene where a crowd of fans swarmed Michael Jackson and his security intervened. Jackson was just being pulled and torn like a rag doll and he looked genuinely terrified beneath his kabuki makeup. People were screaming. It was supposed to be the cover story for the issue that came out on Wednesday, September 12, 2001. I hadn't finished the story that Tuesday morning when the planes hit the towers, and I didn't want to finish it, because, you know, the subject matter suddenly seemed irrelevant. I remember, after we closed the paper on September 11, Peter Stevenson and I walked together to the Upper West Side because that was the only way you could get home if you didn't have a car. I've never heard the city as quiet as it was that night.

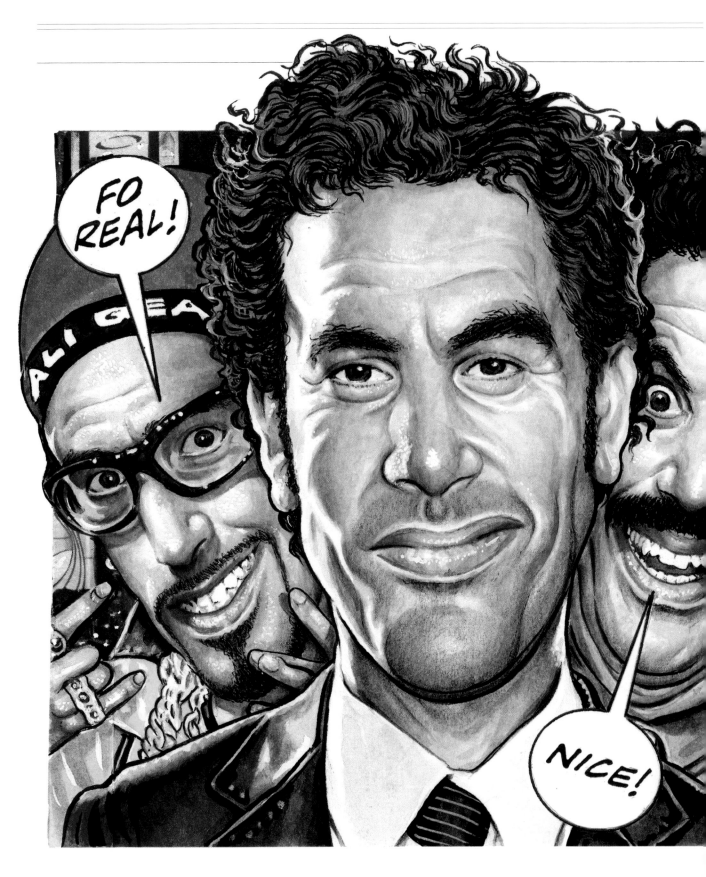

2006

◀ Brit comic Sacha Baron Cohen does boffo box office as Borat

▶ Best-selling memoirist James Frey outed as liar

▶ Another inconvenient truth? As eco-documentarian, Al Gore is bigger than ever

▶ Billionaire Ron Burkle accuses *New York Post* columnist Jared Paul Stern of extortion

▶ Katie Couric leaves *Today* show for *CBS Evening News*

▶ Sweet embraceable YouTube: Disposable culture achieves permanence online

▶ In time of war, *Us* editor Janice Min dictates Jessica, Jen, Jolie

▶ Stork spin: Docs sell baby sex selection on East Side

▶ FAIRWAY Brooklyn beloveds fondle fruits at new Red Hook Fairway

2006

⬦⬦⬦⬦⬦⬦

JANUARY 26, 2006 BY TOM SCOCCA

The Awful Untruth

You've Probably Had It on Phony Memoir—But Frey Fraud Was Worse Than You Know; Was Explosion Just Delayed W.M.D. Reaction?

"THAT THIS MAN IS STANDING in front of me and everyone else in this room is lying to us is heresy. The truth is all that matters. This is fucking heresy."—James Frey, *A Million Little Pieces*, page 178

First things first: James Frey is a liar. To say someone has lied, flat-out lied, is to make a claim about that person's internal moral workings: The person knew something was false and said it anyway, de-liberately, with intent to deceive. That's a tough standard. Better to say that what the person said "appears to contradict" the facts—

Enough. James Frey is a liar. (By the way, so is "James Frey.") His best-selling memoir, *A Million Little Pieces*, is a fraud. It is a seamless mass of falsehoods, told deliberately, for the purpose of making money.

"I still stand by the essential truths of the book," Mr. Frey told Larry King on Jan. 11. Mr. Frey invoked "essential truth" seven times in an hour. It was his main talking point, his defense against an ever-growing port-folio of specific untruths. Essentially, Mr. Frey seems to be, as his book claims, an alcoholic and probably a drug abuser, who went through rehab in Minnesota in the late fall and winter of 1992. Essentially.

That plain essence, however, would not have rung cash-register bells for the publishing industry. It would not have gotten Mr. Frey to the top of the best-seller lists and into Oprah's Book Club. So the book includes: a double root canal for Mr. Frey, done without anesthetic under treatment-program rules. An illicit romance between Mr. Frey and a beautiful, doomed crackhead-prostitute fellow patient. A series of scuffles between Mr. Frey and various ward mates, some leading to injury. A back story of a child-hood as an outcast, of the tragic death of his first love—above all, of wanton, precedent-breaking drug abuse and crime that left Mr. Frey a wanted man in three states and would eventually send him to jail for three months. None of that happened.

JANUARY 29, 2006
BY BEN SMITH

GORE IS BIGGER THAN EVER!

A CROWD OF NEARLY 500 IN the Library Theater in Park City, Utah, stayed on through a standing ovation and into the question-and-answer session as Al Gore restated his warnings about the "planetary emergency," global warming.

Mr. Gore is the star of a docu-mentary entered in the Sun-dance Film Festival, *An Inconve-nient Truth*, and all the questions were for him.

Mr. Gore had been haunting Sundance since it kicked off, popping in at the *Entertainment Weekly* party to chat with A- and B-list celebs, but this was the former vice president's big day. That morning, his new publish-er, Rodale, had announced an Andrew Wylie–brokered book of the same title as the film, to be released in April.

At the question-and-answer session, the reporters wanted to know about Mr. Gore's pros-pects. Was the film itself cov-ered under campaign-finance laws? Would he be endorsing another candidate for Presi-dent in 2008—like, say, Robert F. Kennedy Jr.? (It was, after all, the Hollywood press.)

"I won't be endorsing a candi-date," he said. "I am a recovering politician."

JANUARY 29, 2006   BY LIZZY RATNER

BARON FRANCHETTI GETS READY
29-Year-Old Beauty Boy Brings Own Bread to Bernardin, Wants to Teach Manners

AT AN APPROPRIATELY SOPHISticated hour on a recent Tuesday evening, 29-year-old Cody Franchetti relaxed at his table at the four-star restaurant Le Bernardin, explaining what it means to be an Italian aristocrat in 21st-century New York.

"I am an elitist," he said in his basso Italiano, as a small fiefdom of waiters in neat black suits whisked silently about the restaurant. "I believe in an elite, I believe that people want an elite ... because there's always been one, whether it be an oligarchy or a dictatorship. Those who don't have want to have more"— he paused as a French-accented black waiter deposited a pre-appetizer in front of him—"and those who have, have different pursuits."

As an unrepentant member of the latter category, Mr. Franchetti has spent much of the last decade carefully honing such "pursuits"—none, of course, resembling anything so functional as a profession. He has read the books in his "extensive library," collected rotary phones, studied the different kinds of marble, experimented with modeling and made weekly trips to his tailor—all in happy, anachronistic anonymity. But of late he has begun cultivating a new interest: He has resolved to make himself a reality-TV star.

"This is a place of display, therefore you display yourself," he said.

By his own estimation, Mr. Franchetti took his most successful stab at provoking such discussion in *Born Rich*, the 2003 documentary-cum-therapy-session made by Johnson & Johnson heir Jamie Johnson. In the film, the former model's stratospheric wealth was exceeded only by his ability to offend. "I find guilt [over wealth] absolutely senseless. It's basically for old women and nuns," he said in one scene as he sat in his book-lined West Village apartment, a black Hamburg Steinway off to his right.

But his most notorious line was his attempt to invoke the modern aristocrat's great struggle between his dueling low and high impulses. "I'm reading a book and I'm thinking about a pussy, but I find when I get the pussy, I'm thinking about the book," he said.

◇◇◇◇◇◇◇◇

JANUARY 29, 2006   BY MICHAEL CALDERONE

Woody ♥ New York
His $26 M. Townhouse Buy Sets an Expensive Trend

IN *HUSBANDS AND WIVES*, MIA FARROW'S CHARACTER memorably tells her husband, played by Woody Allen, that he isn't serious about moving to Europe, because he "couldn't survive off the island of Manhattan for more than 48 hours."

Nevertheless, it has been rumored from time to time that the acclaimed director might someday go through with the move across the pond.

Most recently, such speculation was fueled by the fact that the 70-year-old auteur used London as the location for two feature films, the critically acclaimed *Match Point*, released last December, and the forthcoming *Scoop*.

Although Mr. Allen temporarily took up residence during shooting in a ritzy neighborhood near Hyde Park, he won't be giving up on New York just yet: The ink just dried on his $25.9 million townhouse contract, as *The Observer* reported on Jan. 19.

Whether or not the real estate market is slowing down "dramatically" (says Mayor Bloomberg) or simply has cooled a bit, there are very few trophy homes to go around for the most discriminating buyers. So, despite the fears of a bursting bubble, such properties have still been moving. Since last fall, five townhouses have sold for above $20 million, with three on East 64th Street alone.

Although Mr. Allen's deal certainly won't break the overall record price paid for a townhouse—the $40 million dropped on the Duke Semans mansion—there is little doubt that it will smash the current townhouse record for price per square foot.

In early November, Louise Beit, of Sotheby's International Realty, listed the 20-foot-wide townhouse for $25.9 million. At that considerable price, the luxurious residence—measuring 6,400 square feet, according to city records—is asking $4,047 a foot.

While several ritzy developments have yielded sales at that lofty price point, the previous townhouse record for price per square foot was $2,471.

Hillary in Wonderland, met by confounding Cheshire Democrat Obama

FEBRUARY 12, 2006 BY MICHAEL CALDERONE

MANHATTAN SWEPT UP IN ZILLOW'S MIDNIGHT RIDE

AT MIDNIGHT ON FEB. 8, THE MYSTERIOUS NEW WEB SITE CREATED by the swashbuckling Web entrepreneur Richard Barton was scheduled to go live. If all goes as planned, it's going to be a weird moment.

The story of Zillow.com has been, from start to finish, an anachronism: a stealth start-up formed in a whorl of rumor by an old god of the Internet boom; funded in a venture-capital frenzy; and launched far ahead of schedule as competitors got wind of the plan and raced him to the market.

The icing on the cake is that, this time, the whole thing is founded on speculation about one of the most hotly contested sectors of the economy: the real estate market.

"Zillow.com today announced the launch of its beta real estate site, offering free, unbiased valuations on more than 40 million homes across the United States, with data on an additional 20 million homes. All consumers need to do is enter an address."

Creepy! The number it crunches out for the address you type in even has its own name: It's the property's "Zestimate."

It will include historical value changes for each home. It will find data on all comparable home sales in an area. It will offer satellite and aerial views of each home. And it will include individual data on each home.

Is this what everyone was so nervous about?

◇◇◇◇◇◇◇◇

Swiss hunk Roger Federer ruled the U.S. Open

MARCH 26, 2006
BY JASON HOROWITZ

City Girl Squawk: It's Like So Bad—It. Really. Sucks?

"I LAAAAAHV A DIIIIIVEY BAAA-aaahr," said a girl with a voice that could crack the ice in her vodka tonic. It was her third drink. She was in her late 20's, had thick, dark eyebrows and straight, shiny brown hair worn in a long ponytail. She looked like a million other girls in New York: attractive but not pretty, stringy but not skinny, smart but not all that intelligent.

"People're li-yike, 'Oh my Gaaaaahd. You luh-iiiiive abu-huuuuv Fawer-teeeeenth Sh-treeeeet?'"

More than the pearls or the diamond-stud earrings, what really identified this New Yorker was her voice: those long, whiney vowels; that touch of an early-morning grumble; that lazy, whistling "s" and glottal stop that hushes the "t," even in such cherished words as "bachelorette."

Is it a new dialect? A new accent? Or is it The Affect? Whatever it is, a distinct group of young women in the American Northeast are speaking with warped syllables that are a linguistic love song to their own exclusive milieu.

MARCH 26, 2006
BY LIZZY RATNER

CITY HEALTH CHIEF: IF BIRD FLU COMES, COVER YOUR MOUTH

AS APOCALYPTIC HORROR FANtasies go, the threat of an avian-flu pandemic remains blessedly hypothetical. Before it can wreak havoc on a city like New York, it must jump through a tangle of if/then hoops, including (but hardly limited to) morphing into a virus that can hop from human to human and making landfall in the United States. But should if become then, then New Yorkers had better hope it doesn't happen within the next year or two. At least.

"If it comes, then it's going to be incredibly difficult to deal with," said Thomas Frieden, the city's commissioner of health and mental hygiene and flu-fighter in chief. "If it were to happen in the next year or two, it's not likely that we would have either effective vaccines or effective vaccinations that would be in use to be taken by the general public. So the most important messages may be very simple messages, such as cover your cough, wash your hands, and don't go out if you've got a cough and fever."

As the bird flu continues its pathogenic march around the globe, this is not exactly the kind of message that jumpy New Yorkers want to hear.

"GOOD EVENING I'M... I'M... BOB...UM"

APRIL 9, 2006   BY REBECCA DANA

Katie Cronkite

Good Night, and Good Pluck! Couric Is Moving to CBS News; It's Being Announced This Morning—Even as You Read This! Worst-Kept Secret in New York Blows, and Schieffer Loves It

KATIE COURIC WILL ANNOUNCE HER INTENTION TO LEAVE NBC on the *Today* show the morning of April 5, according to a source with knowledge of the network's plans.

The announcement will come at 7:30 a.m., amid on-air festivities marking Ms. Couric's 15th anniversary with *Today*. Staffers said that a highlight reel of her work has been prepared for the occasion. Chances are there will be cake.

And then Ms. Couric will be on her way to anchor the *CBS Evening News*. A corresponding announcement from CBS will come later in the morning, according to a source familiar with CBS's plans.

The announcement would cap a veiled but intense image-management campaign on Ms. Couric's behalf.

Beyond the debates about whether a chipper morning anchorwoman can make suitably serious faces at the evening cameras, there's the question of what Ms. Couric's full role at the *CBS Evening News* will be. Will she be a true managing editor, running meetings and setting news agendas like the men who came before her? Or will she be a pretty headline-reader—"perky," to use her least-favorite word—the network equivalent of a shiny hood ornament on a rusty Cadillac?

APRIL 16, 2006   BY CHOIRE SICHA

IN JARED'S COTTAGE

WHEN THIS THING DROPPED down on me," said Jared Paul Stern, "it made it sound like the cops were on the way to lock me up."

It was cocktail hour inside Mr. Stern's home in the Catskills on Monday, April 10, a little after 5 p.m. There are no fewer than three bars on the house's first floor; his Macallan is 12-year. Now it was gin and tonic for him, and a Bombay gin martini with "the bad olives" for his wife, Ruth Gutman, a farm girl from Maine who is known to the gossip community by her husband's pet name for her, Snoodles.

"But it's funny," Mr. Stern said. "You know, I am optimistic that by the time all this is done, really, I won't be damaged goods. I'll be better known—and, if anything, at least back where I started, if not better."

The phone had been ringing and would keep on ringing through the evening with calls from dozens of reporters.

As Mr. Stern absorbed the initial shock of being a front-page scandal, he had decided he was at war with Ron Burkle, the California billionaire who recorded conversations between the two and accused Mr. Stern of extorting cash for favorable coverage in the *New York Post*. On Saturday night, over the phone, Mr. Stern had said that soon "the story will have shifted off of me and on to more juicy targets."

And so on Monday he was advancing his version and also suggesting to reporters who called some things he thought they might be interested in printing.

Mr. Stern said that his real friends had stuck with him since the story broke last week. He said one friend, the director Whit Stillman, had told him, "This is going to be the best thing that ever happened; this is great for the clothing line. And I want the movie rights."

10¢ WEIRD EXTORTION APRIL — "BUGS BURKLE" "SHAKES" STERN — THE POST-MAN ALWAYS RINGS TWICE

APRIL 25, 2006 BY JASON HOROWITZ

HONOR THY TALESE

The Serendipiter Explains His Journey: 'If You Figure Destination, What's the Point?'

"JOURNALISM IS VERY SERIOUS, AND WHEN DONE WELL," said the 74-year-old writer Gay Talese, "it is beautiful."

On Monday, April 17, Mr. Talese was in his bright East 61st Street living room, perched on a cracked brown leather couch and under an oil painting depicting a snowy Central Park. He had a strong Calabrian nose, a small, thin mouth, fine white hair and brown eyes that he shielded with his hand when he sought out a memory.

He struck such a pose when he recalled being a young reporter in the 1950's, fresh out of the University of Alabama, and surrounded by the clacking keys and ringing bells of typewriters on the third-floor newsroom of *The New York Times*.

"Though I was doing daily journalism, I thought it would be a reference point for the future," said Mr. Talese, remembering a day in which he was taking a characteristically long, long time to tinker with a story. That's when a "third-string labor reporter" began badgering him.

"He was saying, 'Come on, young man—you are not writing for posterity, you know,'" recalled Mr. Talese, dressed now in a sand-colored three-piece worsted suit that's kept the crease well for its 25 years. "It was a revelation, and not a welcome one."

A half-century later, and Mr. Talese is still missing deadlines because he labors over sentences for so very long. His ponderous nature and tendency to procrastinate are offered in ample portions in his sprawling new book, called *A Writer's Life*. And what a life it is, brimming with failures, missteps, false starts and other assorted frustrations.

Yet Mr. Talese, speaking with unwavering earnestness, apologizes for none of that.

"You are going along for the trip," he said. "You can't have a destination. If you have figured that out, then what's the point?"

Among other things, the book reveals that even Mr. Talese, who is canonized in journalism textbooks for his *Esquire* profiles, needs to compose the dreaded pitch letter. Granted, these pitches are addressed to acquaintances and editors such as Norman Pearlstine and Tina Brown. But his ideas are shot down. The words don't come easy. ("Writing is not fun. It is not supposed to be fun.")

Thanks to *A Writer's Life*, more than a decade of Mr. Talese's pursuits have now seen the light of day. Here is a disgraced Chinese soccer star, a haunted building and the restaurants that inexorably fail in it, a sociological study of *The New York Times*, civil rights in Selma, and Lorena and John Wayne Bobbitt.

On the afternoon of April 17, he was happy that the book was done. Mr. Talese sipped sparkling water from a wine glass and talked about heading to the theater that night with the writer David Halberstam, an old *Times* colleague. He sat by the phone, anxious not to miss a call from his wife, Nan, an editor and publisher at Doubleday.

As he sat, elbows on knees, on the living-room couch, he spoke about the last time he succumbed to the pressures of a deadline. He had already left *The Times* by then and was writing for famed

Esquire editor Harold Hayes.

In the 1960's, Hayes had given Mr. Talese a last-minute assignment to fill in for James Baldwin, who wrote a story different than the one Hayes had envisioned, and for which the editor had already set the plates for photographs. Mr. Talese wasn't particularly proud of the piece, "Harlem at Night," but he got it in under deadline.

During a chance meeting some weeks later, Hayes approached Mr. Talese and criticized the piece. He said that he'd seen better.

"And I said, 'Fuck you, Hayes,'" Mr. Talese recalled. "I never met another deadline again. I said I'm never going to make another deadline, and I never did."

That might be one of the reasons Mr. Talese has had such a tough time publishing of late. While his commitment to research is the stuff of legend—spending years at a time getting to know the characters of a story—it raises the question of when process stops and procrastination begins.

"Time is always a factor," said Mr. Talese, specifying that he meant not only the time devoted to writing, "but before writing—to thinking."

JULY 31, 2006   BY TOM SCOCCA

OFF THE RECORD: The YouTube Devolution

Want to See Zidane Head Bump, Exploding Mentos, Cringeful Dennis Miller? Come to YouTube, Video Web Site Where Bad Culture Is Reborn Forever

ONCE UPON A TIME, it would have meant something to have watched the Zidane head-butt in the World Cup final live on TV. I did see it. I missed the first 85 minutes or so of the match, then tuned in for the critical juncture. *Pow!* Right there.

But who cared? The blow was right there—and there—and there: Almost instantly, it was all over YouTube. Anyone in the world could click and replay it. It didn't matter when or where.

I already knew this when I'd watched the moment live. I realized what YouTube was doing to television when I found myself watching Dennis Miller as he conducted a post-performance interview with the now-canonized turn-of-the-90's band the Pixies on his talk show. He strolled up to the mike and introduced himself to the lead singer, Black Francis.

"Black, I'm Embarrassingly White Dennis," Mr. Miller said, and I cringed. Fourteen years after the fact.

The thing about television used to be that once you saw it, it was gone. It was disposable, and it was mostly dispensed

Pixies - Planet of Sound

with—the old signals, from what we used to watch, streaming out past the Oort Cloud, carrying Lancelot Link, Secret Chimp away into infinity.

Print could aim to be stolid and enduring, piling up in libraries or, at worst, on microfiche. TV made its getaway. If you weren't right there and watching with everyone else when something happened, you didn't see it. Reruns or syndication could give you another chance, but you still had to catch the moment.

The VCR only stalled it a little. Your friend's mother could watch her stories on Saturday, after working the day shift all week. If somebody had had a tape running, you might get to rewatch a Tyson fight or when that dude broke Geraldo's nose with the chair, until somebody forgot which tape it was or recorded over it.

After that, people would do what they did with everything on TV: talk about it for a while, then mostly forget about it. TV moved on, in its infinitely renewable present. The main points—Kojak: bald guy—went into the collective consciousness; the rest faded into the dimness of individual semiconsciousness.

Suddenly, via YouTube links, those lost moments click back into view, as if a telegram from your great-grandfather were showing up in your e-mail. When the Pixies popped up on my laptop, playing on Dennis Miller, I was transported: I was standing in front of my dorm-room television, 14 years in the past, in the peach-tinged glare of an early-generation halogen torchiere. The Pixies more or less invented what would

Diet Coke + Mentos

be called alternative rock, but broke up before it finished becoming a viable commercial category; they were not a band you heard much on the radio, let alone saw on a talk show.

I felt a gleeful kick as Black Francis scurried up to the mike and announced they were covering a "Reid Brothers song"—a secret handshake to us viewers who not only knew the Jesus and Mary Chain, but knew the Jesus and Mary Chain's names. The band tore through "Head On," just like they'd torn through it in 1992.

But then Mr. Miller—the sly rebel comedian, the *Saturday Night Live* legend, who knew enough to book the Pixies on his own show—came over to greet them. And he was ... a tool. He was smarmy; he was stilted; his floppy West Coast suit was ridiculous. He wasn't funny.

He wasn't funny? I was sure Dennis Miller was funny in 1992. I remembered it. He came on funny in the 80's, with force. We all watched "Weekend Update" and recited back the best parts between bells on 10th-grade Mondays. Then when we were in college, the talk show was funny too, even if it did bomb. He only

descended into unfunniness over the next decade, taking the wrong projects, hardening into a cranky, right-wing bore. But I knew he was funny before that, just like people knew Brando wasn't a fat blob in *A Streetcar Named Desire.*

Nope. He was lousy. YouTube had him dead to rights. There was another clip of him, from earlier, sitting down with David Letterman at the height of his *SNL* fame. Mr. Letterman? Funny. Mr. Miller? Lousy, lousy, lousy. Everything that would make him a washout on *Monday Night Football* was already on display: the obviously canned pop-culture references; the clumsy timing; the attempt to mask his stiffness and incompetence with smugness. What had the 20-year-old me been thinking? How could I have been so wrong?

In *The Life of Samuel Johnson,* Boswell describes the hero having fled the room while someone was reading one of his old works aloud—"and somebody having asked him the reason of this, he replied, 'Sir, I thought it had been better.'"

Memory has always been a shaky witness. But writing was

Frank Zappa on Crossfire

> *Suddenly, via YouTube links, those lost moments click back into view, as if a telegram from your great-grand-father were showing up in your e-mail.*

checkable, to one degree or another. There could be differences of taste or opinion, but there was the text lurking, waiting to settle the question. If you told someone else a piece of writing was good (or gorgeous, or moving, or persuasive), that claim would have to survive the other person's reading of it.

The Internet left writers more exposed than ever. If you were published from the mid-90's onward, you ended up in a text-based panopticon: At any time, someone, somewhere, could conceivably be reading something you had written. No longer would people have to go to the library to find old arguments and past errors. Every few months, I get an e-mail from a reader responding to something or other I wrote eight years and three jobs ago. Thanks to a retroactive Web-archiving initiative, a college intern from last summer could crack wise

about something I'd written as an undergraduate myself.

Video had always been more elusive. It defeated secondhand reports; a critic might describe a scene, but the moving image was unquotable. The original moment was transformed by the telling into something else—probably something funnier or more original or more shocking.

But now the moments—all the moments, even the ones thought lost—have begun looping back around for public inspection. You can relive the bubble-gum commercial wars of the 80's (they even call them the bubble-gum wars on the Web). You can test which sketch-comedy shows hold up (*SCTV*, yes; *The Kids in the Hall*, not so much).

These opportunities represent, in part, a surprise victory for library science. As we plunged into the digital age, one of the great fears was of format obsolescence: People would throw out old-fashioned paper in favor of electronic archives, only to suddenly find that they had all the works of human knowledge stored on five-and-a-quarter-inch floppies

zinedine zidane headbutt world cup final

and nobody was making floppy drives anymore. But with Web video, people are raiding their personal, inaccessible stashes of VHS tapes, winding through them till they find the important bits, and transferring them from a near-obsolete medium to a current one.

So TV's past is being clipped and replayed and distributed by anyone with a computer, to anyone with a computer—the professional TV product mixed in with home videos and Web-cam feeds and amateur animation. There are too many video sites to keep track of: Google Video, Veoh, iFilm, Evtv1, Go-tuit, blip.tv.

YouTube, though, is the one that everyone talks about, even if they're talking about the other sites. It has the grab-bag quality the good sites had back when the Internet was exciting. It keeps getting busted for copyright problems and throwing out the problem content, as people paste up more and more new stuff.

The other sites may have their advantages: better-synchronized sound and video, cleaner pictures, more violence and nudity than the scrupulously PG-13 YouTube offerings. YouTube, though, is the phenomenon; YouTube is the one the *New York Post* reported was being bandied about as a billion-dollar property, even though (or because?) it has no discernable revenue model.

It has even already begun acting out the Web-downfall script by being undermined and co-opted. This summer, marketing and publicity took off around video of Mentos dissolving in Diet Coke to make violent foun-

welcome back kotter joke

tains—an established Web-vid genre, like parking-lot car-drifting videos. A YouTube competitor, Revver, staked its claim on public attention with the most elaborate Coke-spout clip, and Mentos bought ad space.

YouTube stands as the opposite of old television because, above all, it's easy. It doesn't demand that you install a player; it doesn't crash your browser. It embeds in blogs and plays there, freely.

What it does, then, is break the synchrony of television. It makes television work like text. Last month, on the 20th anniversary of Len Bias' death, newspaper let me down. *The Baltimore Sun* had no stories that described the Bias I remembered, the basketball player before he became a cocaine casualty. So I went to YouTube. And there he was, alive if a little blurry, on the court at No. 1 North Carolina, making the greatest sequence of plays I'd ever known: burying a shot, then flashing to steal the inbounds pass, rising up and—with the assurance of a man who did not know what limits were on a basketball court—dunking it, two-handed, in reverse.

APRIL 30, 2006   BY ANNA SCHNEIDER-MAYERSON

Mrs. Spitzer Suits Up

*Attorney Silda Wall Never Counted On Becoming—
Eccch!—a Candidate's Wife*

LAST WEEK AT THE CONTEM-porary photography gallery at Christie's, an Elizabeth Montgomery look-alike named Silda Wall took the podium before a polished mix of lawyers, Wall Streeters and politicos. She wore a crisp cream-colored shift and slingbacks, and her honey-brown hair was set in a perfect Samantha flip.

Meanwhile, her husband—ruddy-cheeked, handsome and working his way through a glass

of white wine—stood joking near the bar with an old friend, playing the cheerfully obedient spouse. But his presence was hardly incidental, to this or any other public or private evening in Manhattan these days at which the couple turns up. Ms. Wall's husband of almost 19 years is Eliot Spitzer, outgoing state attorney general and the favorite to become the next governor of New York. And many of the deep-pocketed minglers gathered that night at Christie's had helped fuel his surge to the top of New York politics.

The couple had been married for six and a half years when Ms. Wall gave birth to their third daughter, Jenna, in May of 1994. A week later (or before—neither can remember), Mr. Spitzer announced that he was running for attorney general.

"This was not something that I had anticipated," said Ms. Wall. "Certainly not at this stage of life, with the children at the ages that they are. It was not my expectation that Eliot would be running for office. So I had to process that."

"I don't think Silda had ever expected that I would be in politics or government in an elected capacity," Mr. Spitzer, 46, said, calling from his cell phone two days later. "And frankly, that's because I had never anticipated that that was the direction my career would take. At the end of the day, the most important point was that her conclusion was: If I wanted to do it, it was necessarily the right thing to do. Because she didn't want the dream to be unfulfilled. Win or lose, her attitude was: If the passion is there to try it, you've got to try it."

MAY 21, 2006   BY SUZY HANSEN

BROOKLYN CIVIL WAR: IT'S NORTH VS. SOUTH, RATNER AGAINST LEDGER

JOHN FLANSBURGH, OF THE band They Might Be Giants, was on the phone. "I have mixed emotions about 'fabulous' Williamsburg," said Mr. Flansburgh, 47, who has lived in that neighborhood for over 20 years, watching as bars and boutiques began to choke Bedford Avenue. "It's quickly becoming a life-size replica of St. Marks Place, and honestly, I've never wanted to live on St. Marks Place."

None of the elite streaming out of Manhattan and over the pretty bridge to the mirror world on the other side want to live on St. Marks Place. But what do they want exactly? Brooklyn isn't a united front. The North Brooklyn of do-it-yourself fashion and vinyl siding (Williamsburg, Greenpoint, Bushwick) just feels separate from brownstone South Brooklyn (from Fort Greene to Park Slope). South Brooklyn is rich and pretty; North is rougher-edged and moody.

"I'm firmly committed to the notion that there's an unbridgeable divide," said a 27-year-old Bushwick resident, who explained that he even feels this way about "literary-minded, quasi-hipsters" like himself who live in the nether regions of the Hills and Slopes and Heights. "I've always felt deeply uncomfortable in Park Slope. And for everything that's hateable about Williamsburg, I have this feeling that they're my people."

Of course, all of gentrified Brooklyn is somewhat similar. It's mostly white. It's mostly partial to some form of indie rock. Refugees from small colleges like Vassar and Wesleyan may trudge North; shiny Ivy Leaguers could prefer the South—but the bottom line is that they all attended fancy colleges.

Southerners reluctantly fork over deceptively low salaries for DVF dresses and Paper, Denim, Whatever jeans; Northern chicks would rather jump off the Williamsburg Bridge than wear something they didn't iron on themselves.

But they all care a lot about what they wear. So why can't they get along? It might be that development, from Ratnerville to waterfront condos, threatens the borough's beloved low-rise lifestyle.

The gentrifiers are being gentrified.

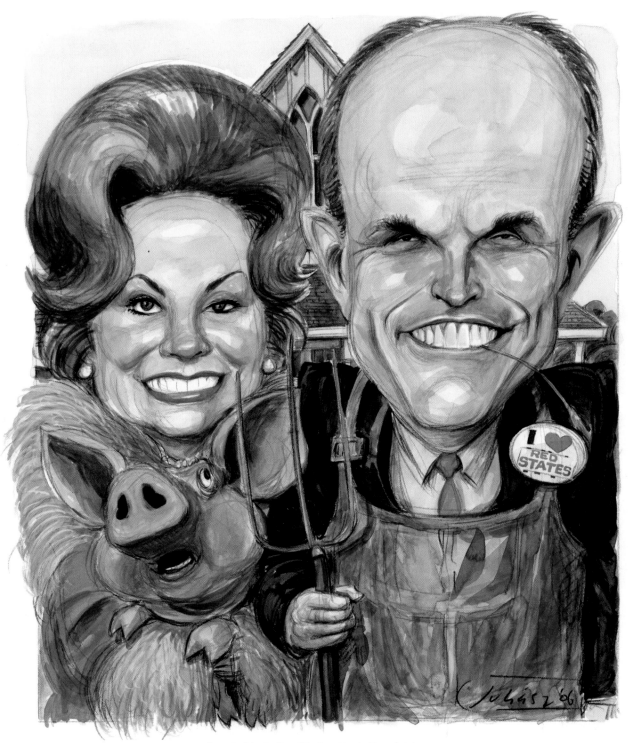

Gotham Gothic: Judi and Rudy cotton to the red states

Clockwise from left: Marla Maples, Ivana, Ivanka, Donald, Jr., Donald, Melania and baby Barron

JULY 10, 2006   BY GABRIEL SHERMAN

Us Editor Janice Min Dictates: In Raw Times, Jessica, Jen, Jolie

"THE WHOLE AGE OF THE SOFT interview is gone," Janice Min said.

Ms. Min, 36, is approaching her third anniversary as editor of *Us Weekly*. She ascended to the job in July 2003, the same month that George W. Bush, savoring a quick and tidy army-on-army victory, dared Iraqi insurgents to "Bring 'em on."

Ms. Min has had a better three years than Mr. Bush. Circulation has doubled, to 1.75 million. Since January, *Us*—"the *Newsweek* of celebrity," in Ms. Min's words—has pulled in some $107 million in revenue. *Rolling Stone*, Wenner Media's flagship, which makes room for war and politics, has

made $70 million.

"It's not a pick-me-up to read about American soldiers get-

ting beheaded," Ms. Min said.

Ms. Min, a onetime reporter for the *Reporter-Dispatch* in Westchester County, was cheery and matter-of-fact. On June 5, the magazine had put out its best-selling issue ever, with Janet Jackson on the cover: "How I Got Thin: 60 Pounds in 4 Months!"

Magazines are magazines; either people read them or they don't. And people want—at this moment in history, when *American Idol* outdraws the evening news 7 to 1—to read *Us*, with its flurries of exclamation points, its snappy captions, its photos of the famous on the hoof with the franchise slogan: "Stars —They're

Just Like Us!"

And who cares to read a soft piece about one of us? *Us* deals in escapism, but an escape into drama and conflict—human-shaped conflict, if not exactly human-sized. The plot lines are coupling and uncoupling, childbirth and divorce, recounted with cynical affability and enthusiasm for minute detail. "Entertainers are themselves the entertainment," Ms. Min said.

"I guess in an era when probably politicians and many people [are] wishing people would be involved in the Iraq debate, you know, people are more interested in debating did Jen Aniston get the shaft?"

◇◇◇◇◇◇◇

JULY 24, 2006   BY LIZZY RATNER

Brave New Boutique: Baby Sex Selection Sold On East Side

LAST WEEK, BRITAIN'S HEALTH Minister Caroline Flint announced plans to ban the brave new reproductive practice known as elective gender selection. Raising the specter of a slippery ethical slope, she warned that it could usher in a new era of gender inequality and, newspapers reported, "designer babies."

But while the Brits were digesting this sad news, the story made barely a ripple across the Atlantic. In America's high-tech baby capitals, the thorny but potentially lucrative business of choosing a child's sex was chugging away as merrily as ever.

A controversial West Coast

fertility pioneer named Dr. Jeffrey Steinberg was finishing a license application to open up his first satellite office in the heart of Manhattan's Baby Belt.

"Everybody's saying, 'Open in New York, open in New York!'" said Dr. Steinberg, who already runs clinics in Los Angeles, Las Vegas and Guadalajara, and who estimates that from 5 to 10 percent of his sex-selection patients come from New York. "We've had a huge demand from Europe, and there's a lot from New York ... a lot from the Upper East Side and quite a few from Queens.

"It's about convenience for the patients," he said.

OCTOBER 2, 2006 BY HOOMAN MAJD

Mahmoud and Me
Ahmadinejad's Wild Week, by His Translator: 'I Heard You Sounded Great!'; Meet the Wife; Asks for Michael Moore; Big Dinner at Hilton

ON TUESDAY, SEPT. 19, THE DAY OF HIS NOW-FAMOUS speech, Iranian President Mahmoud Ahmadinejad entered the General Assembly at the United Nations and sat down with his foreign minister and the Iranian U.N. ambassador. He waved in my direction, and I waved back. Me and Mahmoud, I thought to myself.

I had seen the text of Mr. Ahmadinejad's speech before he'd even arrived in Manhattan on Monday, Sept. 18: I was his interpreter, or at least his English voice, at the U.N.

My father was an ambassador under the Shah, and I've spent most of my life in the U.S. After a career in the entertainment industry, I had written about President Khatami for U.S. publications and made contacts within his government. That experience, along with my credentials as an apparently trustworthy Iranian, led to my invitation to be Mr. Ahmadinejad's translator, and to attend some of his public pit stops, as well as an Iranian-only (and media-free) celebration at the Hilton. There, I thought, I'd glimpse the real Ahmadinejad.

His speech used the simple "man of the people," anti-intellectual language that Mr. Ahmadinejad is known for, and was translated expertly. Any nuance would be in Mr. Ahmadinejad's tone or body language, neither of which I would be able to reproduce from my booth overlooking the General Assembly.

Nuance in Persian is difficult to translate, but it can be most misleading—sometimes comically so—during interviews with the American press. When Brian Williams of NBC asked about Mr. Ahmadinejad's attire— a suit rather than his trademark windbreaker—the Iranian president replied, "Sheneedem shoma kot-shalvaree hasteen, manam kot-shalvar poosheedam"—which was translated as " ... you wear a suit, so I wore a suit." The phrase is actually much closer to " ... you are a suit, so I wore a suit."

And when Mr. Williams asked if he wanted to see anything else in America other than Manhattan, the president's response was yes. Pressed for details, Mr. Ahmadine-

jad stuck firmly to generalities, but also said, "Albateh, esrary nadareem," which was correctly translated as "Of course, we're not insistent." But the meaning was closer to "Of course, we don't really care." While Mr. Ahmadinejad thought America might be interesting, it's apparently not that interesting, at least to him.

Perhaps Mr. Ahmadinejad just didn't want to tarnish his revolutionary credentials by showing overt eagerness, but the president neither ventured to any Manhattan landmarks nor expressed a desire to do so. Instead, limited

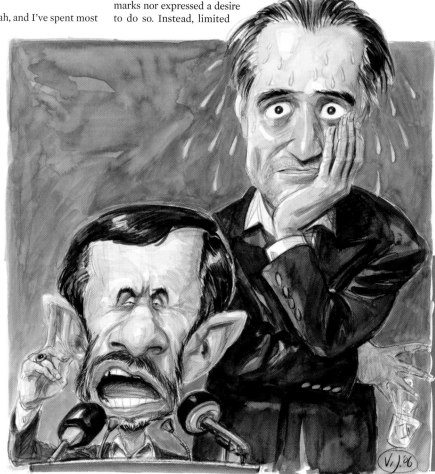

by his special visa to a 25-mile radius from U.N. headquarters, Mr. Ahmadinejad spent most of his first day less than a mile away, ensconced in his suite or in meeting rooms at the Intercontinental Hotel on Lexington and 48th, which had been turned into a fortress. Midtown Manhattan through the tinted, bullet-proof windows of a government-supplied limousine is just about all that Mr. Ahmadinejad has ever seen of America—other than his rides to and from J.F.K., which have been under cover of darkness.

COCA LEAVES AND CHADORS

The Tuesday afternoon before his speech, President Ahmadinejad didn't seem particularly concerned that he was missing both a luncheon given by Kofi Annan (the fact that wine was being served may have had something to do with his absence) or President Bush's own highly anticipated speech at the U.N. Mr. Ahmadinejad and I spoke briefly about his own speech, before he was whisked away by his minders.

An hour later, I made my way to the floor of the General Assembly and sat on one side, flanked by two Iranian diplomats and facing Evo Morales of Bolivia. I was more than a little nervous. I fought the temptation to ask if I could have my picture taken with the Bolivian head of state (which would have been a certain hit with some friends) and, since I was in the midst of a nicotine fit, to also ask him if I could bum a coca leaf or two. (He later brandished a leaf during his speech.)

Anxious, I decided to take a walk around the hall and came across Mr. Ahmadinejad's wife, milling about in full black chador, protected by a lone female Secret Service agent. I knew that she, unlike the wives of previous Iranian dignitaries, had accompanied him on his trip. It would have been both un-Islamic and rude of me to approach her, so I watched as Mrs. Ahmadinejad made her way to a row of seats off in one corner behind the podium to wait for her husband's speech.

Attendance was curiously sparse, perhaps because of the evening hour and the fact that the speech was being carried live on CNN.

> I began to sweat. The realization hit me that whatever I said would be heard the world over, and all I could think of was Ronald Reagan's infamous "We begin bombing in five minutes" quip into what he thought were unplugged microphones.

The Iraqi delegation, however, was in full attendance. Presumably they were not willing to offend their true patrons.

I began to sweat. The realization hit me that whatever I said would be heard the world over, and all I could think of was Ronald Reagan's infamous "We begin bombing in five minutes" quip into what he thought were unplugged microphones. I had no intention of veering from the text, but it was both tantalizing and terrifying to know that a few extra words here and there would create headlines and headaches across the globe, if not land me either in Gitmo or Evin prison in Tehran.

In fact, I remember little of Mr. Ahmadinejad's speech or my reading of it; I was far too busy concentrating on listening to him in one ear, checking where we were in the text, and watching him out of the corner of one eye. After the address was over, I was stopped by an African U.N. security guard; he begged me for a copy of the speech, saying it was the best he'd ever heard. I had left my copy behind in the booth. The Iranian diplomat with me promised him a personal copy on Islamic Republic of Iran letterhead.

Mr. Ahmadinejad, although mobbed by a throng of well-wishers, thanked me rather graciously. "I heard from everyone you sounded great," he said. "Thank you so much." When he speaks to you (and maybe this is more relevant if you're a fellow Iranian), Mr. Ahmadinejad is not only charming, but his tone is one of genuine friendliness—a remarkable ability to make you think he relates to you. Even his dress—the simply cut pale gray suit, one of three that he apparently owns, as well as the windbreaker and the inexpensive loafers (the better for slipping on and off for prayers)—seem less like political affectations and more a reflection of who he really is: a regular Muslim guy who happens to be the president of a now-powerful nation.

The following morning, Mr. Ahmadinejad held a 7:30 a.m. breakfast meeting, again at his hotel, with American academics and journalists. Earlier, he had expressed some interest in having Michael Moore attend, and although attempts were made to reach him (even by myself, since I was asked), they were unsuccessful. I was seated between Gary Sick (of Columbia University) and Jon Lee Anderson (of *The New Yorker*), and three hot issues were covered: nuclear power, Israel and the Holocaust.

Mr. Ahmadinejad didn't seem to tire of repeating the responses he had given over and over. The participants were polite and respectful, and if they held any misgivings about breaking bread with someone seemingly reviled by a large number of their fellow New Yorkers as not only perfidious but extremely dangerous, they didn't show it. Anderson Cooper of CNN posed the softest if not most pro-Iran question of the morning when he asked about the country's rather under-publicized but valiant efforts at fighting the Afghan opium trade. I realized later that the question must have been intended to help land the unscheduled short interview that Mr. Cooper conducted for CNN that night.

As he left the breakfast, Mr. Ahmadinejad once again thanked me for my U.N. performance and said that he had heard from all over the world—specifying Senegal, which he had visited on his way to New York—that the speech was really beautiful.

BIRKE 06

AUGUST 21, 2006   BY RON ROSENBAUM

THE EDGY ENTHUSIAST: Drama King

Entourage's Explosive Johnny Drama Is the Man for This Season: Icon of Irritability, Newest Masculine Ideal in Brutal Age– Kevin Dillon's Caffeine-Addled Loser Hero a New American Winner

JOHNNY DRAMA: WHAT A GREAT character! I'm surprised that more attention hasn't been paid to Kevin Dillon's brilliant embodiment of comic/pathetic irritability on HBO's *Entourage*. It's not only the best thing on that otherwise uneven show, but Johnny Drama, pissed-off wannabe star, may be the most resonant new icon of the American character on TV.

But maybe Johnny Drama's time has come. I guess it depends on how you regard the recently announced deal for a series of special four-minute cell-phone download "Johnny Drama" episodes for Cingular.

I don't know if competing with the ring-tone market on a four-inch square screen is a portent of cutting-edge spin-off success—

or more of a Johnny Drama–like "success" comparable to his (fictional) Valtrex commercial.

But either way, it's an exemplar of the growing recognition of Johnny Drama, Icon of Irritability. And the growing recognition of the Johnny Drama type offers an occasion to reexamine irritability itself as a characterological trait. Irritability has long been treated as a character flaw. But irritability isn't mere anger, the same way that rock music isn't mere noise.

And who among us, except those irritating people smugly carrying yoga mats in their oh-so-special bags, isn't at least a little irritable? You virtually have to have had a lobotomy not to be irritable in this world and this city.

AUGUST 21, 2006 BY SUZY HANSEN

THE OBSERVATORY: Fairway Day!

On weekend days, the comfortably cloistered couples of Brooklyn stroll the aisles of the new Fairway Supermarket in Red Hook, practicing a level of House Connoisseurship that would make Martha Stewart blush

ON A RECENT SUNDAY AT THE NEW FAIRWAY SUPERMARKET IN Brooklyn, a pale, reed-thin man, pointy-nosed and wearing glasses, was contemplating a Portugal Serpa. This is a spicy, strong-smelling cheese made in southeast Portugal from ewe's milk. Here in this Epcot Center of a cheese display, the Serpa bordered on a Torta del Casar, which I took to mean "wedding cake," but which subsequent research showed to be another ewe's-milk cheese from the nearby Extramadura region of West Central Spain, and—lo!—a cruelly named Aged Balarina.

Moments later, the thin man's girlfriend was beside him, just checking in, just saying hi, just seeing what he was up to. He pointed to his purchase, tentatively, which was being carefully sliced and packaged behind the counter.

"A quarter of a pound of Portugal Serpa," he told her, in a whisper, as if not to disturb this bit of cross-cultural commerce. She nodded, or said "good"—whatever, she was satisfied—and left him to his further responsibilities, perhaps somewhere in "Ham, I Am" Land, or toward the giant round fish station, mobbed all around by a heaving, panting mass of Brooklynites.

Even a couple months after it opened in May, the pious whispers can still be heard on the F train, recounting visits to the Fairway like pilgrims bearing witness: "Have you been to the new Fairway yet?" As though the Cathedral of Notre Dame had just been erected in their backyards.

A visit to Fairway on a weekend day in Brooklyn these days is a redundant proposition. A weekend day is Fairway day. And in the religious calendar that has formed among the Brooklyn faithful, for whom a certain connoisseurship of groceries serves as a stand-in for the contemplative life, Fairway Day is a holy day of obligation.

APRIL 25, 2006 BY REBECCA DANA

NYTV: Life of Brian

NBC Anchor Williams, Bronzed, Burnished, Brokaw-Bred, Contemplates Big Battle: 'Go Ahead, Touch My Peabody'

"TOUCH MY PEABODY," BRIAN Williams said.

The award sits on a small glass table by the door of the *NBC Nightly News* anchor's third-floor office at 30 Rockefeller Plaza.

Mr. Williams won the prize this year for NBC's coverage of Hurricane Katrina, the national calamity during which the boy-journalist personally groomed by Tom Brokaw demonstrated that he was finally an Anchorman: the mature face of a major network, a manly monument around which the chaos of the day's news swirls.

Mr. Williams was discussing his work on the afternoon of Aug. 21, before the 2:30 story meeting. The one-year anniversary of Katrina was on its way, and so was Katie Couric. On Sept. 5, Ms. Couric is due to make her debut on CBS, facing off against Mr. Williams and ABC's Charlie Gibson in the evening, backed by a multimillion-dollar promotion budget and the belief that the nation is ready for something new to replace the figure of the old, stiff anchorman (emphasis on man).

Mr. Williams' oft-repeated reaction to the hubbub about the evening news is: "A rising tide lifts all boats." He wore an eggplant-colored tie that offset a deep tan—a tan acquired on a recent trip to the Middle East. He has a well-calibrated seriousness, leavened by periodic visits with talk-show funnymen. He is not so self-important that he couldn't joke about his Peabody,

the highest honor in broadcast journalism. He wasn't bragging about it. He was merely mentioning it—offhand, a little lewdly—as it sat there, inconspicuous but unmissable. Katie Couric, if you're counting, has one, too, for her 2000 series on colon cancer.

NBC's official position on Ms. Couric's debut, and the year-long multimedia rollout that has preceded it, is unqualified joy.

"Our philosophy has been that, look, we're thrilled to have such strong competition," said Steve Capus, Mr. Williams' old friend, former producer and the president of NBC News.

"I feel terrific," Mr. Williams said. "I'm a very competitive animal." (Growl!)

"Walter Cronkite called us a headline service," Mr. Williams said. "He called us the supplement to a good daily newspaper. Well, add to that a good selection of Web sites and other sources of information and he's still right."

◇◇◇◇◇◇

OCTOBER 25, 2006 BY GEORGE GURLEY

I AM CHARLOTTE BOCLY: LIKE, DRAMA DRAMA DRAMA!—MEET '06 GIRL OF YEAR

ON A RECENT SUNDAY NIGHT, CHARLOTTE BOCLY, WHO IS A 19-YEAR-old sophomore at Marymount Manhattan College and lives on Park Avenue, swept into the bar at the Carlyle Hotel. She laughed, ordered a chamomile tea, and said that Matt Dillon had just tried to pick her up.

This past July, her partying had gotten out of hand and Charlotte checked herself into the Silver Hill rehab clinic in New Canaan, Conn.

"I've never really liked alcohol in general until I started drinking, you know, and then, you know, smoking a joint," she said. "You find a level and you like it and, like a lot of kids growing up in New York City, you find it appealing, because it's so easy to do it."

The summer of 2006 had started out quietly enough. At her family's house in Bridgehampton, Charlotte floated around in the pool, played tennis in a bikini, had lunch with her friends at the Maid-stone Club. Then, one evening, she had some friends over ... then more friends. Then it was off to a nightclub.

"It was just a crazy, crazy time," she said. "Somehow, everyone ended up at my house, and everyone's in my pool, everyone's naked, Paul is naked—this is at 5 in the morning, by the way—then Alexandra drove up. Out of nowhere, there are like 20 cars. Alexandra disappeared with a house guest, and I disappeared with this boy I thought was cute—a good-looking boy who I found out was in high school the next morning, but looked much older. And then Emily goes off with Paul—Paul!—and I'm in my underwear and a bra and I'm chasing after this guy, and I'm on the lawn—this is a little scandalous. My father comes out in his underwear, and he was yelling in French and everyone was out of there. The world was shaking. Then I passed out in bed. That was a great night, for the Hamptons."

NOVEMBER 6, 2006   BY CHOIRE SICHA AND JOHN KOBLIN

Obama in Orbit

BARACK OBAMA—DELIVERED FEET-FIRST ON OPRAH'S COUCH AND tickled on *Meet the Press* and then highly buffed by *New Yorker* editor David Remnick before the magazine editors of America—has enjoyed the best-orchestrated product reveal since the iPod.

Now Mr. Obama is the only author with two books among the top 50 sellers on Amazon.com. Two weeks after the release of *The Audacity of Hope*, it is in its sixth printing, with 725,000 books in print.

America can't tell the difference between the book and the candidate. That may be because the book itself is the perfect campaign speech, and is one of the reasons why everyone keeps talking about Mr. Obama and '08.

"Primaries are 13 1/2 and 14 months away, and there are full teams in New Hampshire and Iowa already," said pollster John Zogby. "And Hillary, who is a household word, and Kerry and Edwards and Gore, who have run before—this is the time to get the word out, and this is the trial balloon."

The Obamamania trial balloon has gotten oohs and ahs from wonks and dreamers alike. But, with so many donors locked down by Hillary Clinton, and with a few hopelessly devoted to various non-celebrity candidates, is there affection—and wallet—enough for Mr. Obama to raise real money for a campaign? Why, yes! Yes, there is. Sort of.

"I think the execution of phase one of this rollout is obviously a huge success," said Tom Ochs, of McMahon, Squier and Associates. (Mr. Ochs did Howard Dean's D.N.C. chair campaign in 2005.) "He has people talking about it, and in a way that diminishes all the other candidates—except Hillary."

So far, the book, and the accompanying publicity campaign, has worked very well. "I would say it has fulfilled our most optimistic best-case scenario," said Steve Ross, senior VP and publisher of Crown.

The escalating talk of a presidential run "was more like icing on the cake," Mr. Ross said.

NOVEMBER 6, 2006   BY SARA VILKOMERSON

Beneath Their Stations

While Connecticut snobs bask in Grand Central's marble glow, New Jersey and Long Island commuters have to brave dingy Penn Station. But, as SARA VILKOMERSON reports, this delicate caste system may be facing a rail revolution

DURING A RECENT AND RAINY RUSH HOUR AT PENN STATION, dripping umbrellas and dirt tracked in from squeaky sneakers and soggy loafers added to the standard feeling of despair among New Jersey Transit and Long Island Rail Road commuters trying to get home. The air was thick and humid with anxiety, and it smelled like a combination of wet hair, hot dogs and defeat.

Meanwhile, across town at Grand Central Terminal, Metro-North crowds moved easily beneath the aquamarine astronomical ceiling, so high and domed that all sounds below took on a civilized hush.

The chasm between rail-rider identities is already a natural caste system deriving from where one commutes from: scrappy/trashy New Jersey and Long Island versus WASP-y old-money Connecticut. John Updike as opposed to Bon Jovi, *Peyton Place* compared to *The Sopranos*, and so on.

◇◇◇◇◇◇◇◇

NOVEMBER 27, 2006   BY REBECCA DANA

NYTV: If They Did It

But They Didn't: Rupert Pulled the Plug on O.J., Regan Long After Barbara Walters Considered It, Passed; Fox News Team Trounces News Corp. Boss Chernin

IN APRIL 2006, CELEBRITY PUBlisher Judith Regan began working on what she called "Project Miami." It would be a book by O. J. Simpson in which he would not not confess to the 1994 murders of Nicole Brown Simpson and Ronald Goldman.

Four months later, Ms. Regan began to shop an interview with Mr. Simpson around the broadcast networks.

She approached Barbara Walters at ABC.

Ms. Walters was intrigued, but needed to know exactly what revelations the book, called *If I Did It*, would contain.

Ms. Walters was sent an excerpt, which she read, sources said.

She spent no more than 10 days, by one informed account, in consideration, weighing these factors as well as a personal distaste for the enterprise. Ms. Walters declined the interview. So Ms. Regan set out to find a less ideal host.

Spy Guys, in Ties: Graydon Carter and Kurt Andersen fete book

2007

Life in the fast Lohan: star Lindsay's daddy Michael vows to make good

Hillary Rodham Clinton and Barack Hussein Obama begin epic presidential campaign

Vanity Fair editor Graydon Carter opens Waverly Inn, the Village's answer to Elaine's

Condé Nast percolates *Portfolio*: hyped-but-secretive biz mag; Tom Wolfe steps up

The boho-cialite! Hippie heiress Arden Wohl is Manhattan's answer to Paris Hilton

High-end designers,  celebs produce "masstige" lines for Target, Kohl's, H&M

Mayor Bloomberg's congestion-pricing plan gridlocked by Shelly Silver

The New York Times leaves 229 West 43rd Street for swank new Renzo Piano digs

New York loses longtime fixtures Brooke Astor,  Norman Mailer and Linda Stein

2007

◇◇◇◇◇◇◇

JANUARY 1, 2007 BY REBECCA DANA

NYTV: Balmy Weatherpeople Fête Toasty Winter as the World Burns

DEC. 18 WAS ANOTHER TERRI-fyingly mild day in New York City. At noon, the temperature in Central Park was a toasty 58 degrees. Somewhere near the North Pole, another giant hunk of ice may have been melting off into a swelling Arctic Ocean, but over on 10th Avenue, the Channel 2 afternoon news team was busy wrapping up a package on holiday hassles.

After a few seconds of cheerful nattering about long lines at the post office, they kicked it over to meteorologist Audrey Puente for her forecast.

"If the line extends out the door, no problem!" said a glowing Ms. Puente. "Because the temperatures will be nice and comfortable for everyone waiting on those lines, whether it's at a store or the post office today!"

Global warming may be turning the earth into a shriveled, flooded, lifeless swamp faster than Al Gore can jet around the country trying to stop it. But then also, the sun is shining; the skies are clear. There are no blizzards, no rain and no snow for the TV weather folk to report. Manhattan has all the balmy imperviousness of Venice before the plague.

On Dec. 11, the National Center for Atmospheric Research released findings showing that because of greenhouse emissions, the retreat of Arctic sea ice is increasing so rapidly that there won't be any ice left in the Arctic Ocean in the summertime in 2040. On Dec. 19, government and private researchers projected the heat spell will last well into January. Someone named Mike Palmerino of the private firm DTN Meteorologix pronounced the chances of anyone in the Northeast enjoying a white Christmas "very unlikely."

So put away those parkas and go for a stroll, New York! The only thing better than last-minute Christmas shopping is doing so on the eve of the apocalypse.

"In terms of people being out and about, shopping for the holidays, looking at the tree in Rockefeller Center, this is great weather, especially for tourists," said Janice Huff, a meteorologist for WNBC. "I know some people are wondering, 'Oh, is the world coming to an end?' I say, 'Enjoy it while you got it.'"

JANUARY 8, 2007
BY SPENCER MORGAN

THE TRANSOM: MS. HEDBERG PRESENTS

"HELLO, I'M ASHLEY BUSH," said a fresh-faced brunette, extending an arm sheathed in white kid. A native of Houston, the granddaughter of former President George H. W. Bush, 17, was among those chosen to represent the United States at the 52nd Annual International Debutantes Ball at the Waldorf-Astoria Hotel on the evening of Dec. 29.

At 7 p.m., the queue to meet these eligible society bachelorettes and their supporters stretched into the hallway outside the hotel's main ballroom and down the stairs. The proceeds of the ball, which is expected to net $300,000 after expenses, principally benefit the Soldiers', Sailors', Marines' and Airmen's Club on Lexington Avenue.

FEBRUARY 4, 2007   BY JASON HOROWITZ

BIDEN UNBOUND: LAYS INTO CLINTON, OBAMA, EDWARDS

SENATOR JOSEPH BIDEN DOESN'T THINK HIGHLY OF THE IRAQ policies of some of the other Democrats who are running for president. To hear him tell it, Hillary Clinton's position is calibrated, confusing and "a very bad idea." John Edwards doesn't know what he's talking about and is pushing a recipe for Armageddon in the Middle East. Barack Obama is offering charming but insubstantial fluff. And all of them are playing politics.

"Let me put it this way," Mr. Biden said. "You didn't hear any one of them get in this debate at all until they announced for president." Mr. Biden, who ran an ill-fated campaign for president in 1988, is a man who believes his time has finally come, announcing this week that he was filing papers to make his 2008 presidential bid official.

Although he admits to a tendency to "bloviate," he thinks that an aggressive advocate with rough edges might be just what the party needs right now. "Democrats nominated the perfect blow-dried candidates in 2000 and 2004," he said, "and they couldn't connect."

Though Mr. Biden, 64, has never achieved his national ambitions, he has in recent years emerged as one of the party's go-to experts on foreign policy. In the past week, he has spearheaded the Democratic pushback against the president's plan to increase troop levels in Iraq, opposing the move with a nonbinding resolution that his party has rallied around. On a recent weekday afternoon, he was discussing his rivals over a bowl of tomato soup in the corner of a diner in Delaware, about a 15-minute drive from his Senate office. Mr. Biden, the chairman of the Senate Foreign Relations Committee, is firmly in the thick of a pack of third-tier candidates. Still, he thinks that at such a precarious point in the nation's history, voters are seeking someone with his level of experience to take the helm. "Are they going to turn to Hillary Clinton?" Biden asked, lowering his voice to a hush to explain why Mrs. Clinton won't win the election.

"Do you want to be in a place where 100 percent of the Democrats know you? They've looked at you for the last three years. And four out of 10 is the max you can get?" Mr. Biden is equally skeptical—albeit in a slightly more backhanded way—about Mr. Obama. "I mean, you got the first mainstream African-American who is articulate and bright and clean and a nice-looking guy," he said. "I mean, that's a storybook, man." But he doubts whether American voters are going to elect "a one-term, a guy who has served for four years in the Senate."

◇◇◇◇◇◇◇

FEBRUARY 9, 2007   BY REBECCA DANA

NYTV: Katie Go-Nightly

KATIE COURIC, THE ANCHOR OF THE *CBS EVENING NEWS*, WAS IN Georgia on Friday, Jan. 5, in a car parked outside a Nathan's hot-dog stand.

She had started this job four months ago, at a salary of $15 million a year, with a contract of four years. The network spent around $10 million advertising Ms. Couric and refused millions more from advertisers in the form of in-house spots.

Ms. Couric was en route from Fort Stewart—where she had interviewed a raft of servicemen and their families—to Savannah, where she would catch a plane home.

"Sorry," she said. "I've thought about it a lot, and I do think, for security reasons, it's sometimes hard for journalists to get a broad perspective of what's going on in Iraq."

Ms. Couric is responsible for obtaining and quickly disseminating some such broad perspective to approximately 7.5 million American television viewers every night. She is the first solo female anchor of a national network newscast, and that suits her in that she must be what she mostly already was: starlet, cultural icon, feminist pioneer, media doyenne and, now, theorist of the war.

Her loaded-up dog arrived at last. "Isn't television glamorous?" Ms. Couric asked.

Her lunch called to mind an old joke about what the Dalai Lama said to the hot-dog vendor: "Make me one with everything!" Only in this case, Ms. Couric isn't looking for spiritual unity. She actually wants everything.

♪THERE'S SUCH A LOT OF WORLD TO SEE...♪

Speech bubble: I'LL MAKE YOU AN OFFER YOU CAN'T REFUSE

FEBRUARY 18, 2007   BY JASON HOROWITZ

It Takes a Chill

Senator Clinton Comes Up With Press-Control Method: Freeze 'em! Cipriani to Nashua, She Beats the Press; Ann Lewis: 'Most People Prefer Information Firsthand'

HILLARY CLINTON DROPPED HER SHOULDERS AND WHIMPERED.

She was reacting, with comic theatricality, after a guest at a fundraiser on Friday night asked her about the perception in the media that she was cold and calculating.

"I am aware of the story line, and I very much am conscious of how I have to work to make it clear to people who I really am," said Mrs. Clinton as she walked around a "Hillary for President" stage in the midtown Cipriani ballroom. "That doesn't mean everybody is going to like me or vote for me, but at least it gives me a better chance to stand on my own bearings."

She was speaking at an event packed with ticket-holding supporters and almost entirely free of reporters.

Mrs. Clinton, the front-runner in the race to win the Democratic presidential nomination, controls her statements and image more than perhaps any candidate that has come before her.

Her disciplined and highly touted communications operation keeps the media at arm's length, reflecting the wariness of a woman who has been the subject of more press scrutiny than just about any other elected official in the world. At the same time, her press people have arguably emerged as the most aggressive of any on the Democratic side, criticizing opponents John Edwards and, this week, Barack Obama for their perceived mischaracterizations of her complicated position on Iraq.

Now, as reporters observe and deconstruct Mrs. Clinton's every gesture and syllable from the wings, she simply isn't playing along.

FEBRUARY 18, 2007   BY GEORGE GURLEY

BUNGALOWING IRAQ

IT WAS AFTER MIDNIGHT LAST Saturday, and Bungalow 8 was filling up. I wanted to ask the famously exclusive nightclub's regular patrons their thoughts about Iraq.

John Flanagan, a 40-year-old nightlife impresario, was sitting with a large group drinking $350 bottles of vodka.

"I'm upset for the American lives that are lost, and the Iraqi lives," he said. "It makes me feel confused about the direction we've taken and whether it was for the right cause."

He referred to the war as an "unpleasantry of life."

"I'd rather not be talking about this," he added. "I'd rather talk about helping out Darfur, helping victims of Katrina."

By the bar stood Laura Choi, a 25-year-old wearing a black-and-white-striped Marni dress. She said she did not support the war. "Living in Europe, I feel like I always have to defend myself, and people are always attacking me," she said. "I mean, I'm in Paris, I'll sit down for dinner with a bunch of French people, and they'll just attack Bush. I'm not a Bush supporter, and yet I feel, as an American, I have to defend my country."

Interior designer Brinton Brewster, 38, was also very upset.

"We were brought into the war under false pretenses, the public was lied to, and we're creating another generation of terrorists," he said.

"Unfortunately, the 'fabulous people' get a bad rap," he continued. "Just because we live life in a certain way, they think we don't have compassion for other people. It's just not the truth. But you know, what really upsets me, honestly, is the propensity of the media to focus on Lindsay Lohan going in and out of rehab. I don't care about celebrities and what they're doing. I've met them all."

Emily, a history major at Princeton University, took a seat. "I am upset by the Iraq war, but I don't focus on it, because it's a negative energy," she said. "I think we are overanalyzing the situation. I mean, here we are at Bungalow 8!"

FEBRUARY 25, 2007   BY MARK LOTTO

I Am George Jetson

MEET GEORGE JETSON; JANE, HIS WIFE.

Their deluxe apartment in the sky, you must admit, boasts quite the view. Rockets whiz past condos the shape of flying saucers. Stars flutter and flicker, and below the clouds are frozen like rivers.

Tonight's another of George and Jane's keycard parties. Pretty swingin'. Plenty of futurific fun to be had, here in the 21st century.

Or not. The actual 21st century, our 21st century, has been—not to put too fine a point on it—a real clusterfuck. Like kids outgrowing Santa Claus, we've spent the past seven miserable years learning to stop dreaming about the World of Tomorrow.

Why would we? In the continued absence of solar-paneled jetpacks, plutonium-powered time machines or even fully electric (forget flying) cars, most of us still arrive at our still-earthbound offices via that great marvel of 1904, the subway. Which rarely gets faster, cleaner, cheaper or more frequent, but instead everyday further erodes, like the ruins at Troy. The news isn't any better above ground: just look at the hole still sitting at ground zero—and the monolithic monstrosity we'd like to fill it with—for definitive proof that the cultural capital of the world hasn't managed to keep its imagination running, that we've sputtered to a stop.

Americans have always assumed that one day we'd awaken in our utopian future, like tourists at Disney World wandering happily from Frontierland into Tomorrowland. But we took the future for granted, as if it were a wife. And maybe it escaped this neglectful marriage, changed its name and skipped town.

◇◇◇◇◇◇

MARCH 11, 2004   BY ANNA SCHNEIDER-MAYERSON

IT'S OBAMALOT! HARVARD LAW MAFIA LED BY LARRY TRIBE RESURRECTS OBAMA TIES

LAURENCE TRIBE, THE CELEBRATed liberal constitutional scholar, was looking at a black plastic "Countdown Clock" that sits on a desk at his home in Cambridge, Mass. "Time until Bush goes," reads the legend accompanying the digital read-out.

Mr. Tribe's former research assistant, Barack Obama, is now the leading contender against Senator Clinton for the Democratic presidential nomination in 2008, and Mr. Tribe is working furiously on behalf of his favorite alumnus.

On March 20, Mr. Tribe will finally get to co-host a party for more than 150 guests, at the Cambridge home of his law-school colleague David Wilkins, that was originally scheduled for this past weekend.

Several of Mr. Obama's former professors are expected to welcome their prodigal son back to Cambridge for the event, an intimate, $2,300-a-head affair.

Several Harvard Law School faculty members who got to know Mr. Obama before he graduated in 1991 have spent the last 20 years eagerly watching his star rise. The presidential campaign has become a culmination of the old New England bastion's affection for a favorite son.

And at this early date in the campaign, their favors are about more than Mr. Obama's image, as they and their cohort scramble to meet the maximum donations to his war chest before a March 31 deadline, when all agree that the viability of his candidacy will really be determined.

EVERYBODY COMES TO GRAYDONS!

MARCH 18, 2007 BY SPENCER MORGAN

This Is Cafe Society?

AT AROUND 11:30 LAST SATURDAY NIGHT, TWO MEN OF EQUALLY modest stature—one in a gray suit, the other in jeans and a worn jacket—were enjoying a cigarette on the corner of Bank Street and Waverly Place.

The better-dressed man was the actor Sean Penn. His companion, Pearl Jam lead singer Eddie Vedder.

Then a third, taller man approached.

"Hey, fellas, can we get a group shot?" asked one of the paparazzi. He spoke in a foreign accent.

"O.K., just one and then you'll leave, right?" said the actor Tim Robbins. "I feel like I'm at a premiere," Mr. Robbins added. "We're out on the streets."

Mr. Robbins and his famous friends were on the street in front of the Waverly Inn, a West Village pub recently reborn as the city's latest clubhouse to the rich and famous under the direction of its host-with-the-mostest, *Vanity Fair* editor Graydon Carter.

In many respects, dining at the Waverly is very much like being at a premiere. Adjacent to Messrs. Penn, Robbins and Vedder's table was Mr. Penn's *21 Grams* co-star, Naomi Watts, dining with a gaggle of girlfriends.

Toward the back of the restaurant, in the big booths adjacent to the bathrooms sat the likes of rock star Lenny Kravitz, rap mogul Russell Simmons and celebrity photographer Sante D'Orazio.

And shadowing them all was the Edward Sorel mural, commissioned by Mr. Carter and featuring caricatures of Anaïs Nin, e.e. cummings, Jackson Pollock, Bob Dylan, William S. Burroughs, Eugene O'Neill and others. Mr. Sorel said he charged Mr. Carter the "very cheap" price of $50,000 for the mural. "The only change Graydon made was that he had me take him out of it," he said. "I had drawn him as a bird with a martini."

Mr. Sorel added, "Sometimes, when I go there, I am the only person I don't know."

MARCH 18, 2007 BY NICOLE BRYDSON

THE SMUG TUG

MEN OF NEW YORK! WHY ARE you no longer throwing your scarves carelessly, rakishly over your shoulders, ends trailing in the wind?

Why are you now pausing to double those scarves, holding the looped end at one side of your necks, then drawing the ends primly through so that they form a little bundled knot in front?

From the warmth of our cubicle we did a little research and found out that the loopy new trend has a name: the Hoxton knot, after the hipster district in London. It's also known by the even poofier, vaguely scrotal-sounding moniker, the Snug Tug.

Whatever it's called, we don't like it. The old way of tying a scarf suggested that a fellow had somewhere to go, and more important things to think about than meticulously showcasing his knitted goods. Whereas the Snug Tug, well ... it's more like the Smug Tug: self-satisfied, static. Luckily, spring is nigh.

◇◇◇◇◇◇

MARCH 25, 2007 BY MICHAEL CALDERONE

PORTFOLIO STAFF GETS A GAG ORDER ON QUIET LAUNCH
As Magazine Prepares a 'Quasi-Beta' Issue, Tom Wolfe Steps Up

WHAT GOES INTO *PORTFOLIO*'S new business journalism? Mr. New Journalism himself, for starters: "I'd been poking around on the subject of hedge funds," Tom Wolfe said, "so I agreed to do 2,500 words."

The hyped-yet-secretive new Condé Nast business magazine is sending its first batch of pages to the printer this week, in order to get the 300-plus-page debut issue onto newsstands by April 24. Editor Joanne Lipman, who came to the startup from *The Wall Street Journal* in a roar of publicity, has put a gag order into effect—ordering the people assembling *Portfolio* on the 17th floor of 4 Times Square not to breathe a word about it in the hallways.

Mr. Wolfe reported from Greenwich and New York for his piece, which will run outside that crowded feature well—even though he filed long.

Mr. Wolfe said he was re-cruited by *Portfolio* staff writer Alexandra Wolfe. Ms. Wolfe has a front-of-the-book piece in the launch. "It's kind of like a father-daughter field entry," Mr. Wolfe said. "It's like when you have two horses in the same stable."

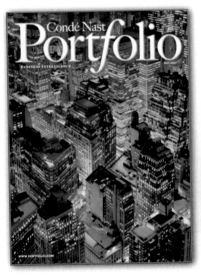

Tricky Dick and ... Hic! Was George W. tippling again?

APRIL 8, 2007 BY MICHAEL CALDERONE

The *Times* Machine

"SOME DAY WE'LL ALL BE READ-ing our papers electronically," said Arthur Gelb, who started his career at *The New York Times* in 1944 and served as the paper's managing editor from 1986 to 1990. "That's just the way. Am I happy about it? No, because I lived my life with the wonderful past of the printed newspaper."

Mr. Gelb, who chronicled his life at *The Times* in the book *City Room*, offered his reflection on the future of newsprint in the context of what might otherwise appear to be an unrelated topic: *The Times*' move this year from its century-old headquarters at 229 West 43rd Street to the gleaming new 52-story tower on Seventh and Eighth avenues, between 40th and 41st streets.

But nobody at *The Times* seems to be able to talk about the new building without talking about the future of the newspaper—or rather, the future of the news organization. Amid harangues from rogue shareholders that

the newspaper isn't mak-ing enough money, and amid dire predictions for the future of the "dead-tree" media indus-try, publisher Arthur O. Sulz-berger Jr. is moving his com-pany into a building that will demand the kinds of changes he has been trumpeting for more than a decade.

The old building at 229 West 43rd Street—the noisy, hulking bricks-and-mortar newspaper factory chronicled by Mr. Gelb —is still essentially an indus-trial building; the new one is an airy, transparent embodiment of Mr. Sulzberger's post-news-paper newspapering plans for *The Times*.

Cascading style sheets replace plates; pixels stand in for ink, the virtual for the physical.

The move to the new building will force a change in the news-paper's basic DNA. The product of *The New York Times* is no lon-ger a newspaper but the news itself, in whatever form it takes.

APRIL 15, 2007 BY SPENCER MORGAN

ARDEN OF EDEN

HERE'S A NEAT TRICK TO TRY next time you're at a swanky downtown fund-raiser gala: Ask Arden Wohl—the 24-year-old as-piring filmmaker, philanthropist and accomplished (whether she likes it or not) socialite—what she thinks about, say, New York's current obsession with "It" girls.

Then see how quickly your head starts to spin.

"I just feel like, with anything, things go in and out of inter-est, and in and out of fashion. The age of technology, people are drawn now to the Internet, so they gain access to things. People are obsessed with things that are not important—money, and imaginary lives that people don't really live. And I think that 10 years ago it was magazines, it was these imaginary lives, what people would look at, and it was

models. It would be supermod-els, and it was a great, trendy thing, and now there's like five supermodels that die a year, and they're all faceless, skinny girls who are like 15 who were prob-ably sex-trafficked and abused, and they probably come here and are stuffed with drugs and put on the runway and, like, are an-orexic and they're all underage, and they're faceless. And now people are like, 'The new trend now is socialites,' and people like to blog, and people like the Inter-net, to talk about who they know, people that they've met."

On March 31, *The Observer* met Ms. Wohl outside her favorite bead store, Beads of Paradise on 17th Street, and persuaded the waifish heiress to partake in an interview and a whiskey at the Old Town Bar.

Before agreeing to answer questions, Ms. Wohl had one of her own: "Why me?"

It's a fair question.

"I think that people should pay more attention to the people that are actually making a difference and the people that are actu-ally working their asses off," Ms. Wohl said. "And the people that are actually working really hard to save the environment. People don't pay attention because they're not fashion designers or because they're not pretty—or because they're not something. Those people are there; it's just that our society chooses to es-cape into the fantasy world of something that isn't real.

"I'm not saying that I wish girls wearing gowns would care more about a cause," Ms. Wohl went on. "But Paris Hilton, or some-one like that, if she believed in something, she could make a difference. She's fabulous, she's great—she's great? You know, I don't know. Whatever."

MAY 7, 2007 BY NICOLE BRYDSON

KATE MOSS GOES MASS!

IN 1996, THE ACTRESS SHARON Stone made the minimalist statement of the decade when she eschewed her favorite designer, Vera Wang, and wore a Gap turtleneck with a ball skirt to the Oscars; now, the Gap sells a cut of jeans called "Williamsburg," and Ms. Wang, the empress of bridal wear for the Park Avenue set, has produced her own cheap line, Very Vera, for Kohl's, as if she were Jaclyn Smith or something.

As for Ms. Stone, no one would be surprised if she dipped a toe into the clothing biz. After all, every other celebrity on earth has.

On May 8, Barneys—Barneys!—will begin selling cheapo clothes that the only temporarily disgraced model Kate Moss designed for the British chain Topshop, a favorite of Gwyneth Paltrow. And M by Madonna is but the latest offering from Ms. Moss' erstwhile employer H&M, one of whose stores is on the site of the old (sniff!) Daffy's on Fifth Avenue.

Gone is the late-1990's frisson of sifting through bins of last season's discount designer rejects; with the sudden ubiquity of fast-food fashion, one can have a reasonable facsimile of the latest thing, right now, with minimal effort.

And the ladies are lovin' it. "I want this!" said Jenya Walters, 17, a high-school student who was shopping at Target.

◇◇◇◇◇◇◇

MAY 28, 2007 BY GEORGE GURLEY

RED EYE FOR THE STRAIGHT GUY

"I'VE GOT TITS. I'VE GOT *FUCKING TITS.*"

Greg Gutfeld, host of Fox News' bawdy, blogger-friendly 2 a.m. chatfest *Red Eye with Greg Gutfeld*, was smoking outside the Landmark Tavern in Hell's Kitchen on a recent Sunday night and talking about the changes wrought on his physique since his TV show debuted in February.

"I've completely stopped exercising," he continued. "I have not thought about going to a gym. My diet has gone to hell; I smoke more. I don't think my drinking has gotten worse; it's just more intense. I need it—and I've never needed it. The one thing I hate about it is, the people around you, who you love, you end up being kind of mean to them. Because you feel they don't understand. And it's a very wrong kind of thing."

If *Red Eye* isn't quite Fox's answer to *The Daily Show,* the show's giddy roster of New York–area media stars and camera-craving bloggers, who are probably unknown and unattractive to the vast majority of Fox viewers, is evidence that Fox wishes to make itself a respectable place to do business for the next-generation New York media elite.

So far, about 300,000 viewers are tuning in to the show, which is taped at 8:40 p.m. and airs at 2 a.m.

JUNE 12, 2007 BY PETER W. KAPLAN

TONY'S BLACKOUT

'Sopranos' Auteur David Chase Left a Majestic Wrap-Up, But His Onion-Ring Existentialism Causes a Panic—Where's Dr. Melfi? It's a Media Anxiety Attack!

WHAT ROUGH BEAST IS DAVID CHASE RIDING? He seems to have understood the mood of his nation better than anyone since Mario Puzo and Francis Coppola forecast the fate of the American empire in *The Godfather*.

And he has world leaders mouthing his dialogue, day and night. Here is Nuri Kamal al-Maliki, the prime minister of Iraq, in *The New York Times* yesterday: "There are two mentalities in this region," he said. "Conspiracy and mistrust."

Baghdada-bing.

The rest of the world was muttering about Tony Soprano's final blackout, but Mr. Maliki proved once more that David Chase has been battling for something worth fighting for. What do I mean, battled?

Try David Chase himself, as interviewed cathartically and perceptively by the hardest-working man in Sopranos land, Alan Sepinwall, the TV critic for Tony Soprano's end-of-the-driveway hometown paper, *The Star-Ledger*: "No one was trying to be audacious, honest to God," Mr. Chase said. "We did what we thought we had to do."

He had completed his story, but he was giving us a gift in the last scene: He was telling us more. What happened in the four last minutes was plenty of information, and not of the conspiracy-theory type: We got to see the world as Tony does, suffused with anxiety and some amusement and apprehension. It took David Chase eight years to get Tony in and out of therapy, and he was improved about as much as a patient can be improved, maybe 2 to 5 percent.

"It felt like ginger ale in my skull," he told Dr. Melfi in the first episode. *The Sopranos* ended up as it began—not with a bang, but an anxiety attack.

Only this time it was ours. This time we blacked out.

"I was shocked by the ending," said Peter Bogdanovich, the movie director and film historian who played Dr. Elliot Kupferberg, Tony's therapist's therapist. Mr. Bogdanovich said he had shot another scene that didn't make the final episode, in which he was comforting an exhausted, bereaved Dr. Melfi.

"It ends at that moment because that's his life," said

Mr. Bogdanovich. "He's anxious about getting blown away, the F.B.I. is going to indict him, Syl is going to die, everything is insecure and tense. It kept going, and the insert shots kept making you feel it was the last thing he was going to do. Endings, endings, endings. The little things in life are the last thing you are going to do. In fact, that's his life."

"He didn't give you what you expected—instead of a Hollywood ending," Mr. Bogdanovich said, and so the viewer was left with "any number of imaginings, so you ask, 'What the fuck happened?'"

"David has been consistent by doing everything with a vengeance he was not allowed to do on network television, so he gave you a very ambiguous ending," he continued. "Which is not what the American audience is used to."

The entire business history of American television has been a conspiracy toward two ends:

(a) the resolved ending, generally happy;

(b) destroying ambiguity.

Life and art weren't supposed to jibe when it came to commercial entertainment. It's not that David Chase was the first guy to come up with ambiguity and moral relativism on TV, but he may have done it with the most vengeance of any television writer since Rod Serling.

You may have noticed that the guys in the safe house where Tony was hiding were watching an episode of *The Twilight Zone*. It's a 1963 episode called "The Bard," and it was written by Rod Serling, the patron saint of television auteurs. In it, a failed playwright summons William Shakespeare from the dead to write his TV pilot for him. Shakespeare, needless to say, sells it, then is compromised and crushed. On Mr. Chase's soundtrack, you could hear the agent lecture the writer: "The television industry today ... is preoccupied with talent, looking for quality ... the television writer is a major commodity." Television writer ... commodity. It is the voice of the network slaughterer.

Now the tabloid writers are mad at him. They wanted the show to splatter. As John Candy and Joe Flaherty used to say on *SCTV*, they wanted it to blow up real good. Mr. Chase inspired the ire of Yahoo nation by bagging and dumping what he wanted to avoid: The dark bedtime-story end of *The Sopranos* was in great demand, and he provided it—splattt!—under the wheels of Phil Leotardo's Ford Expedition.

But he also provided the first really grown-up summation in the history of American television: The subjective shot of Tony experiencing the American influx of diners at Holsten's restaurant was news, as was his inglorious humanity. The final shot of Tony before the black, if freeze-framed, is a human image more photojournalistic than dramatic. If you have that particular device, take a look at Tony, the woolly mammoth in freeze-frame before the Ice Age, another human in anxious abatement in the Age of Ambiguity.

"It is the most subversive television series ever because it makes you like the monster," said Mr. Bogdanovich, who was still mulling the last scene. "You don't know what you're waiting for. It's the perfect use of suspense. You are trapped, not wanting anything to happen, but wanting something to happen. It's very vicious. You're left with any number of imaginings. What the fuck happened? Which shows you're bloodthirsty also."

We saw the two things that were preoccupying Tony: the one unambivalent relationship of his life, the adoring Meadow, his only true believer—she decided to become a lawyer when she saw her daddy taken away in cuffs!—and the assassins around him.

The Chase Gang gave us all the information we needed in the hour: indictments, threats, business, A.J., Carmela, Janice, it was all wrapped up. I was always certain that someone was going to clue Carmela in on the murder of Ade, but it didn't happen. When Carmela entered Holsten's, she entered in long shot, and her friendly, reassuring smile to Tony was casual and loving, but quick. A.J. entered with what looked like a potential assassin, his effective twin. But it was Meadow who re-

Tony and the Boss: Sopranos auteur David Chase's subversive finale made panicked millions shriek, lunge for remote control.

ceived the Hitchcockian treatment of threat: Would she be able to park? Was she about to be locked in by assassins? Would she make it across Broad Street, on which she seemed to be in as much jeopardy as was Janet Leigh in *Psycho*?

"Anybody who wants to watch it," Mr. Chase told Mr. Sepinwall in *The Star-Ledger*, "it's all there."

The Sopranos could have made it in the Clinton years, but it could only have become the deeply troubling comedy it was in the Bush era. Not because of the White House so much, but because of the viewer's complicity in the dirty brew of power that flowed from this White House. Not because of the war, but because of the public sense of responsibility for this war.

"Oh," says Carmela when she's trying to talk A.J. out of joining the army, "you want to get your legs blown off?"

"Always with the dramatics," he says.

But not really.

Earlier, at Bobby Bacala's funeral, A.J., who truly did seem to relax and inhabit his own body once more after his yellow S.U.V. exploded, had a peroration for the commercial landscape the show inhabited: "America," he said, "is still where people come to make it. It's a beautiful idea. And then what do they get? Bling and come-ons for shit they don't need and can't afford?" Paulie mocked him and descended into a Norm Crosby routine.

But David Chase fought for and won a strange moment of pure insight into the American process. It was romantic, bleary, filthy, piercing. It was as much a comedy of American sobering up after 9/11 as *Dallas* was a comedy of America getting drunk on the Reagan years. But Mr. Chase fought a battle and won: He created a last shot on television that was one of the best close-ups in movie history, the snapshot of Tony taking in American ambiguity: the Boy Scouts, the killers, the gangstas and the one person toward whom he had little ambiguity. Like the final image of Antoine Doinel in *The 400 Blows*, he captured all the intimate uncertainty of his age, in a room that could have been heaven or hell, but with good onion rings.

It was, so far, the best last episode in TV history—better than *The Mary Tyler Moore Show* or *All in the Family* or *Seinfeld*, despite all the screaming about it from plotmongers who wouldn't have been happy with anything short of the conflagration from the end of *Scarface* or Tony whacking Dr. Elliot Kupferberg before he entered witness protection. Paradox, moral relativism, internality. All the stuff that network television has battled and ejected in the past 60 years—except in a very few instances—is the essence that David Chase brought to his 86 hours. David Chase's enduring triumph in American television is that he embraced ambiguity and looked for poetry in the Bush administration.

Paulie Walnuts thought he had seen the Virgin Mary, and Tony mocked him; but in fact, Tony had seen the other side of mortality as well, and almost was cajoled by Cousin Tony—a spectral Steve Buscemi—into entering that big, well-lit house in his coma dream, after Junior shot him. But he didn't, he re-entered the living and went on. That was, he knew somewhere, his task, and it's why the cozy, dark ordinariness of Holsten's restaurant in Bloomfield, N.J., was a terrifying but immensely moving way station.

Orson Welles once said that "Every story essentially has an unhappy ending. If you want a happy ending it all depends on where you stop telling it." David Chase's triumph was that he had the balls to stop telling it right h

JUNE 25, 2007 BY AZI PAYBARAH AND ANDREW MANGINO

Shelly's Gridlock

ALBANY—EARLIER THIS MONTH, Michael Bloomberg and Eliot Spitzer emerged from the governor's midtown office with great fanfare and announced that they were ready, in principle, to support City Hall's sweeping plan to reduce traffic and air pollution in New York, which includes a proposal to charge cars for entering midtown Manhattan.

Not that it mattered.

The real show took place in Albany this week, where a stoop-shouldered, graying cipher of a man shuffled down the hallway in the State Capitol behind the Assembly Chamber, and slowly mumbled to a handful of reporters in a gravely voice, "We're going to conference it," and "We're going to talk about it."

Thus spoke Sheldon Silver, the 63-year-old Democratic State Assembly speaker who led his party during the dark years under Republican Governor George Pataki and who has stubbornly refused to fade away now that, technically, there's another Democrat in Albany that outranks him.

◇◇◇◇◇◇

JULY 16, 2007 BY HILLARY FREY

GRILLING GORDON

RECENTLY ON FOX'S REALITY COOKING CONTEST *HELL'S KITCHEN*, Gordon Ramsay, the multiple Michelin Star–winning Scottish chef, screamed at Melissa, a struggling contestant: "Listen, listen ... If you just shut the fuck up for 30 seconds you might learn something!"

A few days later, on a broadcast of his BBC America show, *Ramsay's Kitchen Nightmares*, in which the chef helps faltering U.K. restaurants get back on their feet, he counseled a distressed chef, a "big friendly giant" named Stuart White: "You deserve to make [the restaurant] yours. Stick to what you know, you can do properly, and stand firm."

Who exactly is Gordon Ramsay? Is he the obnoxious, permanently exasperated Simon Cowell caricature on yet another American reality series—a series which happens to be winning its Monday night time slot among the 18-to-49 demographic? Or is he a nurturing, wickedly talented food expert who wants to save wayward restaurants? Is he an ambitious 40-year-old chef de cuisine who wants more than anything to woo and conquer New York City—or just a greedy blond bastard?

JULY 16, 2007 BY LIZZY RATNER

THE NEW VICTORIANS

ON A BALMY MORNING IN JUNE, Rebecca Miller, a petite 26-year-old actress and Brown University graduate, was perched on a wooden bench in the East Village, just a block from the apartment she shares with her fiancé and two cats. By the looks of her outfit, she was firmly grounded in the 21st century, just another hip lass with loose curls, a scoop-necked top and denim skirt with naughty front slits.

Then she opened her mouth, and it was as if one had been transported back—oh, 150 years or so. "We had been talking about getting married since we got together," Ms.—or perhaps we should write Miss—Miller said.

There was a time, not too long ago, when the young and the aimless hightailed it to New York City in pursuit of an altogether different urban experience than the domestic bliss enjoyed by Miss Miller and many of her bosom companions. High on a cocktail of recklessness and aban-

don, they came here to find their id, lose their superego, shake up the world, or simply shake their thang. Then they promptly chronicled these exploits in confessional sex columns.

But recent years have seen a breed of ambitious, twenty-something nesters settling in the city, embracing the comforts of hearth and home with all the fervor of characters in Middlemarch. This prudish pack—call them the New Victorians—appears to have little interest in the prolonged puberty of earlier generations. While their forbears flitted away their 20's in a haze of booze, Bolivian marching powder, and bed-hopping, New Vics throw dinner parties, tend to pedigreed pets, practice earnest monogamy, and affect an air of complacent careerism.

As one soon-to-be-married, female 26-year-old online editor who lives in Williamsburg put it: "It's no longer cool to be a slacker and be living in your basement."

JULY 23, 2007 BY ANONYMOUS

MUSINGS OF OSAMA JR.

DON'T YOU SIMPLY HATE IT when you find yourself no longer in the mood for the Netflix movie you requested on the very day of its arrival?

Certain New York cab drivers seem to be under the impression that their backseat air-conditioners are powerfully blowing jets of cool air when, in fact, they emit only the weakest lukewarm puffs. And they grow offended when you roll down the window!

There are those who (rightly, I suppose) deplore the treatment of women in certain Islamic nations, but it seems to me that the widespread and rather gleeful mockery of Paris Hilton is borne of much the same impulse—that is, to keep female sexuality in check, wherever its power is on display.

I found *Ratatouille* to be

charming indeed! Not only that, but the film was quite original and not so very formulaic. It strikes me that the built-in audience for animated children's pictures allowed Walt Disney/Pixar to take more risks than the other big studios did with their summer-blockbuster fare.

I agree that the heliport on West 30th Street is quite annoying for those of us making use of the riverside bike paths and such. A device that will make the problem disappear very quickly is the over-

the-shoulder antiaircraft gun. Simply fire the missile and —after the initial blast—no more noise!

Many New Yorkers love Daniel, where the waiters serve the tables in choreographed teams. While I certainly do enjoy Chef Boulud's cooking, I must say I find the presentation more befitting a restaurant in a provincial town such as Las Vegas than one in the nation's most sparkling jewel of urbanity.

How I hate all the scaffolding on the sidewalks when the day is sunny and bright! I feel as if I am walking through some tunneled city. But how I love it when the rain pours down and those planks help to keep my clothing and head dry. There is, perhaps, a lesson in that somewhere.

Allah be praised.

◇◇◇◇◇◇

SEPTEMBER 17, 2007
BY SARA VILKOMERSON

Members Only

IN ONE OF THE MANY STARTling scenes in the new HBO drama *Tell Me You Love Me*, which debuted Sunday night, a young, attractive married couple sit side by side on a sofa, watching a boxing match on TV. The wife unbuckles her husband's pants, and after some noisy kissing, she pulls away and says, "I want to see it." She sees it and—*holy cow*—so do we.

Over the past few months, the buzz on the show has centered on its frank sexual content. Throughout the hour, as bodies moved and eyefuls of flesh flashed, it was the sight of that erect penis being clinically manipulated into a graphic orgasm that prompted did-I-just-see-what-I-think-I-saw gapes from less action-packed couches nationwide.

AUGUST 27, 2007 BY SARA VILKOMERSON

The O.C. Goes N.Y.C.

AT AROUND 3 P.M. ON FRIDAY, Aug. 17, things were looking a little dicey for the cast and crew of the new CW show *Gossip Girl*. The day's schedule was running a little late. Curious tourists flashed pictures; bored-looking kids milled about; a banker-y fella pretended to read the *Financial Times* while gawking at the bright lights.

It's unlikely that any of these observers realized that they were watching a scene from what is sure to be a monstrous megahit this fall. From the frighteningly fertile young mind of *The O.C.* creator Josh Schwartz, 31, and fel-

low *O.C* writer-producer Stephanie Savage, *Gossip Girl*, which will premiere on Sept. 19, has all the same elements that made *The O.C* must-see TV: a young, attractive cast of as-yet mostly unknowns, a unique universe of privilege, wealth, social-striving and exclusivity (trading the sandy shores of Orange County for the limestone-and-Town-Cars enclave of the Upper East Side), a pounding musical score of of-the-moment music, and campy over-the-top drama involving sex, scandal and betrayal, all set in the inherent tragedy of private high schools.

JUNE 26, 2007 BY GAY TALESE

THE KINGDOM AND THE TOWER

On Thursday, June 21, *The New York Times* spent its last day at 229 West 43rd Street. Gay Talese, *The Times'* greatest chronicler and a former reporter there, returned to the gothic newspaper castle that housed Sulzbergers, Adolph S. Ochs' 10-foot grandfather clock, thousands of journalists, massive underground presses that still ooze ink and defined an era in journalism

WHEN ARTHUR GELB JOINED *THE NEW YORK TIMES* as a copyboy in 1944, the uniformed elevator men wore white gloves, the desk editors donned green eye shades and reporters making phone calls from the third-floor newsroom had to be connected by one of the dozen female operators seated at the 11th-floor switchboard (perhaps the most vibrant center of gossip in all of New York); and up on the 14th floor, adjoining the publisher's office, was a private apartment visited on occasion by the publisher's mistress—and there was also nearby a bedroom for the publisher's valet, a gentleman of high moral character and undaunted discretion.

The Times' citadel of communication, whose neo-Gothic finials, scallops and fleurs-de-lis at 229 West 43rd Street were in accord with young Arthur Gelb's vision of himself as an aspiring vassal in the House of Ochs, is now operational within *The Times'* recently occupied skyscraper on Eighth Avenue between 40th and 41st streets, thus terminating Mr. Gelb's ties to where he had invested 63 years of his working life and left him at his current age of 83 as the most enduring employee in the history of the paper.

Having risen from copyboy to reporter in 1947, and from metro editor in 1967 to managing editor (1986-1990), and thereafter a fixture in the corporate hierarchy overseeing the paper's scholarship programs and other forms of munificence, Mr. Gelb now continues his relationship with *The Times* as a consultant and, for whatever it is worth in an age when the journalism he knew and practiced may be on the cutting edge of oblivion, he exists as the institution's éminence grise and one of its ceremonial hosts for such events as last Thursday evening's farewell party to the chateau of the Good Gray Lady on West 43rd Street.

Hundreds of the paper's employees and their guests were invited to dance in the aisles and drink beer in the vacated third-floor area where Mr. Gelb had once overseen the Metro staff and where his present-day successor, Joe Sexton, a physically fit and bespectacled man of 47 who had a salt-and-pepper goatee and was wearing a light blue cotton shirt darkened with his perspiration, danced with such tireless vigor around the room that he got the attention of someone with a digital camera and, promptly, his picture was available around the globe via Gawker.

Watching from the sidelines, with his facial expression suggesting benign noninvolvement, was Mr. Gelb in a suit and tie chatting with some of *The Times'* veterans, myself included, with whom he had dined an hour earlier at Sardi's on West 44th Street, next to the rear entrance of the Times Building. At the dinner, Mr. Gelb had begun by expressing condolences over the deaths of such Timesmen as David Halberstam, R.W. Apple Jr.,

Sammy Solovitz (a pint-sized lifetime copyboy) and Abe Rosenthal, who had preceded Mr. Gelb as the Metro editor and whose leadership in the newsroom was often defined by the staff as a reign of terror.

After leading the way out of Sardi's, he paused on the sidewalk to remove from his pocket a key that he said held special meaning. "This key was given to me many years ago by [then publisher] Punch Sulzberger and it provides a shortcut from Sardi's into *The Times*, meaning you don't have to walk all the way around the block to get in. Oh, I've used this key thousands of times, and now, on this night, I'll be using it for the last time."

He then inserted the key into the lock of a metal door that was a few steps above what had once been a loading dock for *Times* delivery trucks, and soon we were following Mr. Gelb through the mail room, which was directly over where the huge printing presses used to function until this operation was transferred in 1997 to plants out of town. Still, as we passed one row of tanks, there was evidence of ink oozing out.

Following our ride on one of the back elevators up to the third floor, we immediately heard the loud music blaring from two self-powered Mackie speakers affixed to 10-foot-high tripods that overlooked the Metro desk, and the L.P. records spinning around on two turntables sequentially introduced us to the voices of James Brown, Aretha Franklin, Michael Jackson, Diana Ross, Justin Timberlake and the Temptations. In rhythm with all of this music was the redoubtable Joe Sexton, and within the crowds of other dancers and onlookers—it was not easy to distinguish between them—were such newsroom notables as the executive editor, Bill Keller; a managing editor, John Geddes; and an assistant managing editor, William E. Schmidt.

The evening was very successful, in the opinion of Charles Kaiser, a writer who had worked as a Metro reporter for *The Times* until 1980, having first gained Mr. Gelb's attention in the early 1970's, when Mr. Kaiser was a Columbia student serving as a stringer. "What we saw in this place tonight was what you'd never have seen when I started as a reporter here in 1974," he said, adding, "You saw all these young people of color, and people of all kinds dancing with one another—men dancing with men, men dancing with women, women dancing with women—and it really reflects the fundamental change in *The Times* since Arthur Ochs Sulzberger Jr. became the publisher [in 1992]. When he started out here in the early 1980's as an assistant Metro editor, he figured out who all the gay reporters were, and then he took each of them to lunch, and one by one he said: 'I know you're gay—don't worry about it. When Abe Rosenthal leaves I'll make sure that the fact that you're gay will make no difference in your career.'"

After the music stopped, most people left the building; but others were free to roam around, and even wander up to the executive suite on the 14th floor, as I did, to get a final look at the exalted domestic quarters occupied many years ago by the publisher, the publisher's mistress and the publisher's valet. Although the beds are gone, I assumed that what I saw was pretty much as things looked a half-century ago, notwithstanding the fact that there are draperies sprawled along the floor, and the ornate chandeliers were dislodged from the ceiling, and a few plush chairs, tables and other furniture were scattered here and there and sometimes turned upside down.

The Times' new headquarters building on Eighth Avenue, a 52-story "shimmering tower of transparent glass" (words by Paul Goldberger), has already received much welcoming attention from architectural critics and has elicited few negative comments from members of the staff, even though the top editors were more prestigiously endowed when they were at 229 West 43rd—which is to say that in the old place anyone holding the rank of managing editor or above had offices with private bathrooms. But not in the new place. Not even Mr. Sulzberger will have one, as he apparently wishes to convey his egalitarian sensibilities, whether they truly exist within him or not, and at the same time he emphasizes his paper's devotion to transparency by making it virtually impossible for any reporter or editor in this glass-walled emporium to enjoy a single moment of privacy—be it a furtive gesture of flirtatiousness expressed across the aisle toward a co-worker, or an upraised index finger in the face of an irascible colleague. But it behooves me not to enlarge upon my meanderings, for I have only briefly visited the new premises, having done so during the past weekend while accompanied by Mr. Gelb and two amiable *Times* escorts who deal harmoniously with Mr. Sulzberger.

In the lobby of the new building, as Mr. Gelb and I headed home and thanked our escorts for showing us around, I noticed a bronze statue of Adolph S. Ochs that had held the preeminent position in the lobby of 43rd Street, but now in the new building it was positioned at an oblique angle behind the reception desk, with the statue's foundation wrapped in packing cloth, and the imperial gaze seemingly adrift.

"Where's that going to go?" I asked one of the escorts.

"We don't know yet," he replied.

The Times' *citadel of communication, whose neo-Gothic finials, scallops and fleurs-de-lis at 229 West 43rd Street* were in accord with young Arthur Gelb's vision of himself as an aspiring vassal in the House of Ochs ...

NOVEMBER 5, 2007
BY DOREE SHAFRIR

The Bicycle Thief: Philip Gourevitch's *Paris Review*

PHILIP GOUREVITCH, THE EDItor of *The Paris Review*, can be blunt about the magazine bequeathed to him in March 2005, two years after the death of longtime editor and co-founder George Plimpton.

"I thought the magazine was physically unattractive," he told *The Observer* on a recent rainy afternoon. The 45-year-old Mr. Gourevitch is, like the young Plimpton, personally attractive and preternaturally successful. He also writes for *The New Yorker*, and his book about the Rwandan genocide, *We Wish to Inform You That Tomorrow We Will Be Killed With Our Families*, was well received. His hair is a curly black mop, his dark eyes piercing; he moves his hands when he talks. When Mr. Gourevitch took over the highbrow literary magazine, he was charged with the formidable—some might say unenviable—task of revitalizing a magazine that had for decades been the expression in print of George Plimpton, arguably New York's most fashionable and well-loved arbiter of literary taste.

NOVEMBER 12, 2007   BY SPENCER MORGAN

LYDIA UNLEASHED

LYDIA HEARST LEADS A RIDICUlous life.

She is a successful model—despite being 5 feet 7 inches short. She often has her pick of runway shows and photo shoots around the world. In the past two months, modeling has taken her to Paris, London, Florence and Los Angeles. She designs handbags for Puma, and is putting finishing touches on a line of Puma fitness wear. She sometimes stays up all night looking at color swatches. And she writes a column for the *New York Post*'s *Page Six Magazine*, called "The Hearst Chronicles." She writes it sitting at her desk, which belonged to her great-grandfather, William Randolph Hearst.

"I try to sleep at least five hours," she chirped in her crisp New England accent.

At the tender age of 23, she tries not to let her family's great wealth and illustrious history cloud her judgment.

"I tell her, 'Listen, you're a socialite, it's a fair enough description, you come by it honestly,'" said her mom, Patricia Hearst-Shaw. "For 'heiress' we usually substitute 'airhead' around here. Just on general principle, lest anyone get too full of themselves."

"I am definitely not a socialite," Ms. Hearst explained over dinner recently in Soho.

⬦⬦⬦⬦⬦⬦⬦

Wild Cards: Yankees Derek Jeter and Alex Rodriguez

NOVEMBER 12, 2007
BY STEVEN GAINES

MY LINDA STEIN: POWDER KEG FULL OF SOUND, FURY

ONE OF THE MANY THINGS I'LL miss about Linda Stein was dropping by her comfy Fifth Avenue penthouse on late weekday afternoons where an impromptu salon of sorts would form. There was always an unexpected collection of people—real estate brokers exchanging co-op board and sales gossip, a pop star down on his luck, a billionaire from Australia to whom Linda was trying to sell a $20 million apartment, or a pot dealer from Harlem whose pager number she had called.

It's inconceivable to me now to imagine Linda Stein dead in that elegant apartment lying facedown in a pool of blood, bludgeoned to death with a jagged weapon, perhaps a hammer, the hood of her sweatshirt presumably pulled by her murderer to cover the horrible wounds.

Who could have killed Linda Stein this violently? Why? Did she have enemies? Plenty—the line forms on the right. There were dozens of people who were furious with her. But was there anyone who could have been angry enough to kill her?

A lot of her intimates think the answer is yes.

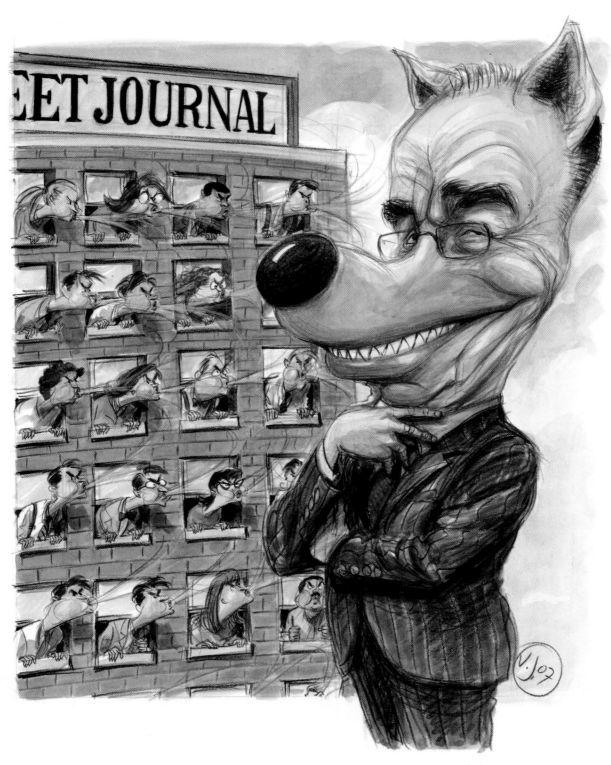

He'll Huff and He'll Puff and He'll ... : Dow Jones' new owner, Rupert Murdoch

NOVEMBER 26, 2007   BY LEON NEYFAKH AND DOREE SHAFRIR

If She Did It

Judith Regan has theories of who drove her from HarperCollins; here are some: Kerik, Ailes, Giuliani, Murdoch, Jane Friedman; retribution is her plan

ROBERT GROSSMAN

"I ALWAYS GOT ALONG WITH creative people," said Judith Regan, the 54-year old former book publisher who has brought a $100 million lawsuit against News Corporation, its book publishing division HarperCollins, and HarperCollins president and CEO Jane Friedman.

That is Judith Regan 2007 speaking. About a year ago, Ms. Regan was head of her own imprint, ReganBooks, at Harper-Collins, granted by News Corp. chairman Rupert Murdoch himself in 1994. Earlier that year, she completed her staff's move to Los Angeles, and dark-sheened, glossy-lipped, hard-nosed Judith Regan was doing what Judith Regan would do in L.A., signing authors and making deals. She

also had a radio show, on Sirius Satellite Radio, that she recorded in her new offices.

It seemed as though the whole impetus behind the L.A. move—the synergy that would package the entire Judith Regan style, a raw, unflinching, sexy, direct, aggressive curiosity, a dismissal of prissy publishing convention, a roaring office manner, a personal voraciousness, a good old-fashioned vulgarity—might actually work in Hollywood.

She had booted the New York stiffs and taken her business to L.A., where they didn't know from publishing convention, and where a tough boss could yell like a studio executive as long as she was a success. And if there was one thing Judith Regan knew it

was how to make best sellers—four *Times* best sellers in 2006, though that was a drop-off from the previous year, when she'd had 14.

And then, last year, it crumbled around her.

In November 2006, Harper-Collins provoked a public outcry when it announced plans for ReganBooks to publish a bizarre "hypothetical" tell-all by O. J. Simpson, in which he described the steps he might have taken had he killed his ex-wife Nicole Brown and her friend Ron Goldman. The royalties of *If I Did It* would go to a trust for his children. To accompany the book, Fox would broadcast a two-hour interview that Ms. Regan had conducted with Mr. Simpson, after Barbara Walters and ABC had backed out, in which she asked him about the murder and just about got him to confess.

Cue public outrage, stoked by, among others, Fox's own Bill O'Reilly, who declared on air: "I'm not going to watch the Simpson show or even look at the book. I'm not even going to look at it. If any company sponsors the TV program, I will not buy anything that company sells ever."

When the dust settled, Ms. Regan was out of a job, amid accusations from HarperCollins, which she has denied vehemently, that she had referred to a group of HarperCollins executives and a prominent New York literary agent as "a Jewish cabal."

That was that: There was an order sent by Rupert Murdoch to Ms. Friedman, the Harper-Collins chief, and Century City was no longer Judith Regan's second home.

DECEMBER 24, 2007
BY NINA ROBERTS

PAD GIRLS! ATTACK OF THE 21ST-CENTURY FALSIES

TO THE LONG LIST OF THINGS making New York City more homogenous—funky brownstones razed in preparation for high-rise condos, chain-store franchises displacing neighborhood favorites—add women's breasts.

Have you noticed? Increasingly, the ladies of this town have been sporting remarkably similar pairs of perfect, pert globes: rounder, higher and larger than ever before. There has been an absence of breast individuality such as lace, seams, overflow, jiggle and, most notably, nipple.

The flawless orbs that have been parading around the city are achieved by strapping on a "lined," "T-shirt," or "contour" bra. These are marketing terms for what is essentially a modern padded bra. This is not the quilted number of years past, but rather a smooth, immaculate device with foam-infused breast cups. Each cup is preformed, creepily having the same shape on or off the body. These lined bras have eased out simple cotton, silk or lace bras, and comprise about 90 to 95 percent of the bras for sale in Victoria's Secret, the Gap, or any of the mainstream department stores.

DECEMBER 18, 2007 BY JASON HOROWITZ

Raucous Caucus

IOWA HAS EIGHT DEER HUNTING seasons: Shotgun, muzzleloader, early muzzleloader, bow, youth, disabled and special November and January antlerless seasons. I learned this from Mark, the taxi driver who picked me up from the Des Moines airport and drove me to see John Edwards, who was campaigning in Indianola on Thursday afternoon. Mark had just finished pointing out a few deer grazing on the icy fields along the road when I learned something else about Iowa: Kamikaze wild turkeys will spring out of ditches, smash your windshield with the force of a cannonball and almost kill you.

On the side of the road after the accident, Mark and I dusted off the blue shards of glass that had sprayed onto our clothes and examined the few feathers and innards stuck in the cratered windshield. I asked if the last black wing-beats I saw before the impact didn't belong to a pheasant. But Mark said it was a turkey, and Mark is from Iowa, so it was a turkey. With that settled, he called me another cab, and we stood outside the car, where everything around us—the farm's wooden fence, the spindly tree branches and corn stalks shooting though the snow—wore a coating of glistening ice. Then we did what you do in Iowa in late December, three weeks before one of the most anticipated caucuses in decades. We talked politics.

Mark liked all the Democratic candidates, and he knew without my prompting that Mr. Edwards had an event out in Indianola. He said that, personally, he leaned toward Hillary Clinton because he liked her experience. The cab driver who came to retrieve me, and drive me the rest of the way out to the Edwards event, said, "Mark is a moderate liberal; I'm so far to the right that you can't see me. I'm almost a fascist."

He was serious. He believed that Islamofascist terrorists, as he called them, would destroy America and bring about the end of days if not stopped by the full force of the American military. He wanted Iowa to secede from the union if the next president proved incapable of beating the terrorists back. I asked him which Republican candidate he liked. "None of them," he said. I said that he sounded like a Rudy Giuliani voter, but he said Mr. Giuliani was too soft on terrorism for his taste, which is something you rarely hear about Rudy Giuliani. Bob also had a problem with the default Republican position on immigration, but not the problem I expected. He called the idea of building a wall to stem illegal immigration between Mexico and the United States ridiculous. "It would divide two Christian countries that needed to unite to fight the Islamofascists," he explained.

Bob dropped me off at the museum in Indianola, which had Edwards lawn signs stuck in the snow around the parking lot and icicles hanging from the rafters. "I better get out of here—enemy territory," he said, laughing.

Mr. Edwards spoke at the Warren County Historical Museum, the central exhibit of which was an installation of opposing cubicles

showcasing different collectibles—old medicine bottles, retro dresses and "maternal corsets," a barbershop chair—to evoke an old-fashioned main street.

Later that weekend, Mrs. Clinton appeared at the Antique Car Museum of Iowa in Coralville, where families piled into a red 1909 Reo, a green 1913 Rambler, a black 1924 Hupmobile and dozens of other old automobiles, and honked their horns when she was introduced.

Johnston, Dec. 17

Hillary Clinton is a human being.

That may sound like an oddly obvious message for a presidential campaign, but for Mrs. Clinton, who has faced six weeks of bad press coverage and 15 years of cartoonish characterizations from all across the political spectrum, it is an essential point that she is now emphasizing in an attempt to right the direction of her presidential bid with three weeks before the Iowa caucuses.

"Here in Iowa I want you to have some flavor of who I am, you know, outside of the television cameras when all the lights and cameras disappear," she said softly, in an unprecedentedly personal speech this morning to announce a new Web site called TheHillaryIKnow.com. "What I do when nobody is listening, taking notes or recording. Because it's hard in public life to have that kind of sharing experience."

Standing in a barn in front of about 150 people and dozens of reporters, Mrs. Clinton was introduced by four of her friends, each of whom swore to her, well, humanity.

One old friend and former Clinton Justice Department appointee, Bonnie Campbell, called her a "human being who is so empathetic, so compassionate and so supportive of others."

The final speaker to introduce the candidate, Betsy Ebeling, became teary as she discussed her lifelong friendship with Mrs. Clinton. "Friendships are the things that maintain you through good and through bad," she said. "She is loyal to her friends, she remembers them, she remembers their kids.

"Do all of you understand that she is a mom, she is a daughter?" she said.

When Mrs. Clinton took the microphone, she spoke gently and thanked her friends. She picked up on an element from her old stump speech, that many people in America are "invisible," and said that her life's work has been "to try and help people who are doing the best they can, but life sometimes has a way of hitting you upside the head."

She then ventured into what is for her mostly uncharted territory, talking about her own experiences growing up: how, for example, she wore thick glasses in junior high and high school and how that made it tough for her to meet boys.

"We're not all the same in every setting we find ourselves, are we?" she said, arguing that people are composites of the many different faces "that all add up to the people we are."

AUGUST 20, 2007 BY FRANCES KIERNAN

GOODBYE MRS. ASTOR: On Aug. 13, the city lost its most gracious dowager: unfailingly generous, tirelessly sociable, enduringly chic

"MONEY IS LIKE MANURE, IT SHOULD BE spread around," Brooke Astor took to saying in later years. In 1986, when she accepted an award from the American Academy of Arts and Letters for "Distinguished Service to the Arts," she attributed the remark to Thornton Wilder; in fact she was paraphrasing the words of the turn-of-the-century Yonkers widow Dolly Levi, eponymous heroine of *Hello, Dolly*.

For more than four decades Mrs. Astor captured the attention of New Yorkers with words more in keeping with her public demeanor. "Good manners come from a good heart," she liked to say. She was also the published author of two novels, numerous essays and articles, and two book-length memoirs, as well as a devoted friend and daughter, a self-professed romantic, an accomplished hostess, an intrepid dancer, and a valued guest who thought nothing of attending as many as four parties in one night. But, above all, she was a world-famous philanthropist. For 37 years, as president and guiding spirit of the Vincent Astor Foundation, she devoted the better part of her life to this city—securing funding and also ensuring attention for causes she deemed important. "I never give to anything that I don't see," Mrs. Astor liked to say. For her philanthropy was always personal.

REMEMBERING MRS. ASTOR

BARBARA WALTERS **TELEVISION HOST**
One sometimes hears, "Who will be the next Brooke Astor?" But there will never be another Brooke Astor. She was unique —charming, wise, funny, elegant and, most important, generous. Even her very long life was unique. To have her for a friend was a privilege.

ROBERT SILVERS **EDITOR, *THE NEW YORK REVIEW OF BOOKS***
She was in no way remote from the world. She knew very much what was happening. And this was, after all, indicated by this fact that she had taken an interest in this paper which had been put on the newsstands once. ... She took the initiative, she wanted to see it, she wanted to be part of it, she wanted to invest. ... At a later point, one of her businesspeople said, you know, you've been going on for years and the paper is doing well, and she wants to make her shares available to you at low cost ... and she just gave it back to us, really.

KENNETH JAY LANE **JEWELRY DESIGNER TO THE SOCIALITES AND FRIEND OF MRS. ASTOR'S FOR 40 YEARS**
One thing she always used to say all the time, even in her old age, was, "Kenneth, do I flirt too much?" And I'd say, "No, Brooke you flirt just enough. You better not stop."

NOVEMBER 19, 2007 BY PHILIP WEISS

OH NORMAN, MY NORMAN: His New York Jewish Public Self Was American Triumph

NORMAN MAILER'S JEWISHNESS WAS A DOORWAY TO the world. He gave his talents to mankind and felt no special obligation to the people from whom he came. He wasn't a self-denier, he knew the marvels of being Jewish—"My Jewishness was a great asset in my work, because it gave me a certain sensitivity to the world. It is not easy to be a Jew without thinking about the world a great deal of the time, given the classic situation of Jews in history," he said in an interview I did for *The Observer.*

But Jewish history is filled with assimilation, especially by literary stars from Spinoza to Heine to Nathanael West. Assimilation is older than any other Jewish social dream, older than Zionism, communism, or, today, neoconservatism. Mailer said once that being a bookish Brooklyn kid felt like a limitation to him, and certainly he rebelled against it. Mailer wanted—like the Zionists—to be a man of action, and for a while, the writing was dwarfed by the extravagant life: the marriages, offspring and fights (on the Town Hall stage with feminists, and on the Hamptons turf with Rip Torn).

There was a lot that was Jewishy about the book that made him a celebrity: *The Naked and the Dead,* published in 1948. Mailer did not experience much combat in the South Pacific; but in one World War II reminiscence, I read that Mailer the young reporter used to pop into other guys' tents and ask questions, listen to the stories. In the novel, Mailer's ego is parceled out, like cabalist shards of the godhead. Goldstein the Jew from Brooklyn is a smaller character than the book's hero, Lieutenant Hearn, a gentile who went to Harvard.

Charles McGrath wrote in *The Times* that Mailer never wrote the great American novel, and this must be conceded, though he died trying. He told Charlie Rose earlier this year that he waited three years to write the sequel to *The Castle in the Forest.* But "I know enough about being 84 to know that if you're a ping-pong ball you can roll off the table at any second."

From the time he was in South Pacific tents, the journalism and novels bled into and out of one another, but my generation was more turned on by the journalism. When Mailer was tied down by fact and his own experience, it made the work more alive. We were electrified by the journalist insisting on his own experience in *The Armies of the Night* and *Miami and the Siege of Chicago*—trying to breathe the hot air in Miami and saying it was like making love to a 300-pound woman who decided to get on top.

"There are two kinds of ways for novelists who have some talent to go," he said in my interview with him for *The Observer.* "One is to use their experience as their private gold mine, and they search more and more deeply into that gold mine. That is one way to be a serious novelist. Another way was to use your personal experience as a springboard to go quite a distance into the outside world. That was my preference. ... But I have never wanted to write about the near things. My personal experiences are crystals to beam my imagination into far off places."

I wish he had tried to integrate those experiences more, the personal life of being a rabbi's grandson, then an American celebrity with all the women and children. He emulated Tolstoy, but Tolstoy seems to have injected more of himself and his life into his novels. He said he never went to Israel because he knew he'd have to write a book about it. So he turned away from vital material. Mailer wanted to wrestle more with history than with himself.

Mailer was more American than Jewish. He was granted a passport out of his Harvard/Brooklyn petri dish by two great democratic experiences, Army service in World War II and the celebrity that followed from that. He made his own choices in Jewish and American history, and he didn't look back.

GEORGE GURLEY INTERVIEWS JARED KUSHNER

Can you tell the story of how you bought the paper?

Well, I heard the paper was for sale and I'd obviously heard of the paper, mostly when I picked it up when I was going up to college on the LaGuardia-Boston shuttle. They always had great caricatures in front, and I remember seeing an article about the "power seders" in New York; the paper was different, exciting and interesting. So I heard it was for sale, and it seemed like a very cheap price for a New York paper, based on what I had read in the press. I called up Arthur Carter, whom I'd met a few times through my father, and said, "I'm reading in the papers that you're selling *The Observer*." And he said, "It's not really for sale; I'm not sure what I want to do." So I kept calling, saying, "Arthur I want to meet with you, I want to make you an offer." He'd say, "I'll call you if I'm interested." I think at the time he had a deal to sell it to Robert De Niro and his people.

Then out of the blue, I got a call one day and Arthur said, "I can sell you the paper, but you have to do all of your diligence over the weekend." I said, "No problem." That Saturday night my girlfriend and I were at the movies and I got an email on my BlackBerry with the contract attached. I left in the middle of the movie, went into the city, read the contract, did all the diligence the next morning. We worked through Sunday and by Monday morning, we had a contract that was close to executable form.

I met with Arthur that Tuesday, sat with him and [his daughter] Mary Dixie, and I'd brought Clive Cummis, one of my father's lawyers, who is well respected and wears a bow tie and has gray hair, a real gentleman—I figured he'd give me some sense of credibility with Arthur. We sat down, and I put down on the table a check with the full purchase price and a signed contract, and I said, "Listen, I'm ready to go." And we spoke for an hour and I said, "I really do want to buy this paper, I've got all these plans." I had put together a full PowerPoint presentation about how I can improve circulation, I can improve ad sales, I can make this thing great, I can make it hip, I can do this—I didn't know what I was talking about, I'd never done any of these things before.

I left and thought, you know, it was a good meeting, and I went back to my summer internship at a start-up private-equity fund, and I got a call in the afternoon and it's Arthur, and he says, "Jared, I'm going to sell you the paper." And I said, "Well, O.K.!" I'd been pursuing him for six months and I thought I had a one-in-a-million chance of doing it, so I was shocked. I thought, "Well, now I actually have to do all these things that I said I knew how to do!" It was like I was airdropped behind enemy lines without knowing that many people in New York. I was excited, enthused, scared.

That night I went to the lawyer's office and we finished up the documents, down on Wall Street, and I walked out at 5:30 in the morning and was walking through the streets of New York, which were very dormant and quiet and it was just starting to get light outside, because it was the summertime, and I remember looking up at all these buildings and saying, "Wow, I just did something that really is significant in this city." That day I called my boss at the private-equity firm and said, "I've got to quit; I just bought a newspaper." He was very supportive and told me no one had ever quit on him before for that reason. He remains a friend.

Jared Kushner is the owner and publisher of *The New York Observer*.

I was totally unprepared for what happened next, and was overwhelmed by the media interest. I didn't know how much the media cared about media. I didn't know what Gawker was, and all of a sudden they start writing about you.

The most important thing that happened in that regard was that the reporter who called first was [*The New York Times*'] David Carr, who's a phenomenal journalist. And I was very lucky to be working with [public relations executive] Howard Rubenstein, and Howard said, "I think you should do the first interview with him since he called first." So I sat down with David on a Sunday, and for me it was weird because there's a photographer taking pictures of me and I'm thinking, "What the hell is going on?" The article came out well, and I think it made a difference because David took me seriously. He could very easily have said this is a *kid*, he's 25 years old, what the hell does he know? But instead, he really listened to what I was saying and, by David Carr taking you seriously, I think it set the tone for a lot of the press that was to come. So I always appreciate that he took me seriously, and I was serious about it, so I think he got it right.

Why do you think you've been able to manage a business at a young age?

My father instilled in my siblings and myself a good work ethic. He taught us not to take anything for granted. A day off from school wasn't an excuse to bum around—it was a mandate to get up early and go to work with Dad and listen in on his meetings. Sundays, my friends would be at football games with their fathers; I'd be in the back of my dad's car with my pair of mini construction boots, walking job sites. Later, when I was in college and I bought some buildings, I figured, "Well, I know everything there is to know about real estate; I've been exposed to it all my life." Truth is, I didn't know anything. The best thing that I learned from my father through these experiences is not solutions to individual problems; instead, he gave me a set of tools with which to deal with problems, and with which to analyze situations. And that tool kit is applicable to a lot of different situations.

And my father gave me a real sense of personal accountability, in the sense that it's so easy in life to pick a million reasons why a person's doing well and you're not, or why this or that happened—you've just got to say there are things that I can control and things that I can't control. You can only worry about the things that you can control. However, you actually control more than you think you do. So if the newspaper doesn't get out on time—yes, it's because a series of people missed responsibilities. I can get mad at them, or I can say to myself, "This is actually *my* fault that this didn't happen." Then I could sit with them, create together a system and say, "This is how it's going to be from here on. I'm going to monitor you and I'm going to reward and punish you accordingly, and we're going to make it happen." So instead of saying, "That's your problem," and yelling at individuals, I can say "This is my problem; let's work to find a way to solve it."

What were your first days at *The Observer* like?

Everything was chaotic. I didn't have an assistant, I was just learning the office, I was learning the people, and before you figure out the business side—the best thing to do is: listen. So I was trying to meet with everybody, understand what they were doing, what they thought of others, who's bullshitting, who's not bullshitting. I was working crazy hours, probably 15-, 20-hour days trying to get my arms around everything. I knew that the paper needed big changes and it had to start with the product, which had become dull from the uncertainty and

George Gurley Interviews Jared Kushner

lack of direction surrounding the business.

Something came together one night. My father had extra tickets to the Yankees playoff game against the Tigers, and the banker who was going to use them canceled. So I called Peter Kaplan and said, "What are you doing tonight?" He told me he had to be home with his family, and when I told him I had two front-row seats for the Yankees, he said he would call me back in five minutes, as Lisa would understand. So we went to the game and we were sitting there, eating hot dogs and drinking beers, and it was drizzling and we start talking and it was just *pouring*. We didn't realize it; we were just talking about the paper. At one point, I looked around and Yankee Stadium was empty because everyone was underneath the bleachers. We were the only two people in heavy rain, without coats, just sitting in the front row of Yankee Stadium, having beers and getting waterlogged. And we talked about what the paper could be and what it meant. We got on the same page that night and were able to spend the focused time together that really made a difference.

Peter's a phenomenal guy, and a guy who's out of *The New York Times'* mold, where journalism is incredibly important. I've had to shake him up a little bit and say, "Journalism's important, but it's also a business and we've got to run this in certain ways, and there's this thing called the World Wide Web and it has actually some pretty interesting ramifications for newspapers." Then we got to the redesign of the paper. I challenged Peter to show me what the next generation of the paper was to become. The paper had become stuck, in the sense that the articles were way too long, it wasn't visually stimulating, and I thought that people today are more responsive to shorter, easier pieces like they get on the Internet. When you want to do something long, deliberately do that, but for the most part, stay within the mold and give the reader what they are looking for with minimum effort. Reading shouldn't be hard. You should be able to lay things out, present things to people in a way that it's easy. I said, "I want a paper that readers will be able to read and enjoy. I want a paper that advertisers will be proud to put their advertisements into."

The Observer had so much smartness to it, but it was putting forth the material in a way that was hard to decipher, and we didn't have a design director. It was a rough diamond that needed to be cut properly. So we brought in Nancy Butkus, who's absolutely brilliant, has a great eye and an aesthetic, and we worked with Nancy and Tom McGeveran to come up with the tabloid idea. I thought it was absolutely phenomenal. We were a bit nervous that people wouldn't understand a classy tab, but we kept saying, "Think *New York Post* goes to college." Visually it read much better, it gave us the ability to have a full back section, which we turned into our version of a sports page: real estate. Peter and Nancy were the brains behind the operation. I was more the critical pain in the ass. I would suggest things—"Let's do it like this," and they'd explain why you can't do that in newspapers. And I'd say, "Well, let's try that anyway." We quickened the pace of the paper, more short pieces, more images, easier entrances to the pieces.

To use a Peter phrase, we really changed the DNA of the product. We really crashed the staff and we went from producing 30 items a week to almost 50 items a week in the paper. The metabolism of the newsroom changed dramatically. From there on out it was a mandate to close the paper on time, on budget—which is something that they never were very good at before I got there. The first week we went out with the tabloid, Peter and I went hawking papers in the snow outside Grand Central Station. I realized where the pecking order of a newspaper fell when I was trying to hand out papers and the guy next to me was handing out NYC Condoms and he was getting a lot more takers than I was at first. We later had a big party at the Four Seasons for the staff to thank everybody.

When we were designing the tabloid version, out of respect, I kept calling Arthur and saying, "Arthur, I really want to come and show you the new paper." And he kept saying, "I'll call you; we'll make a date." And he just wouldn't make a date. So I said to Peter, "Why does Arthur not want to see me?" And Peter said, "Well, Jared, it's kind of like meeting your ex-wife's new husband. For Arthur, he loves the paper, he built it." But Arthur called me the morning the tabloid version came out. He said, "Jared, I got it and I love it. I think it's great."

Can you think of editorials you've been excited about?

We were the first New York paper to endorse Obama. It was hard for me to do, because I really like Hillary [Clinton] a lot and respect her, and she's as stand-up as they come as a person and I really respect her. But I felt that Obama would be a great president for the country at the time. One Sunday I was in the office and I went across the street to get a sandwich, and there were about 200 kids in the freezing cold running around with "Obama '08" T-shirts. And I said to myself, my generation is so apathetic about politics in America, it's amazing that a politician could inspire this reaction.

With the editorial page, we get calls both positive and negative about the stuff we write, and one of the great things about the paper is that it really does matter to people who are important throughout the city. When you get a call from the mayor or the police commissioner or the school chancellor or any other number of people, and it happens with frequency, it's good to feel like you've got a voice. When I first bought the paper, I didn't get any of these calls, and now they come weekly. For me, it's a great barometer of the impact and influence that the paper has. Furthermore, editorially I'm always proud when we do clever articles, like the one about how *Saturday Night Live* was freaking out because they didn't have an African-American to play Obama in skits. It's stuff like that that epitomizes how clever the paper is.

The best thing about all the reporters we have is that they're a lot smarter than I am. We have a great stable of young aggressive reporters. One time there was a reporter working somewhere else, whose stuff I liked, and I said, "Peter, we should look at hiring him." And Peter said, "I would, but he violates the one principle I have: Against the hiring of assholes." The culture of the paper is really unique, and I hope that we can keep that for many years to come.

So in two years, you've remade, redesigned, refocused *The Observer*. Any last thoughts for today?

The thing about the redesign that is special is that it really came from Peter's brain, but I think that my youth and inexperience and desire to be open-minded is what beat it out of him. It was a great combination of my inexperience and Peter's vast experience coming together to form something very special. For me, these past two years at the paper have been like going to publishing school. These are interesting times in the newspaper business, but with hard work, and continued devotion, I think we have the chance to come away from this turbulence stronger than ever.

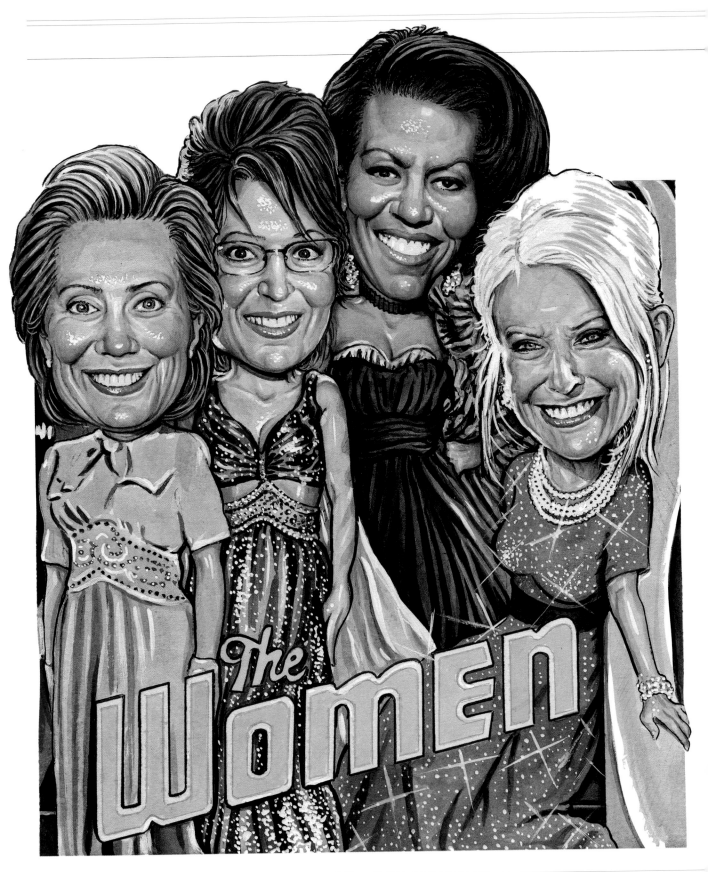

2008

McCain running mate Sarah Palin fries feminist circuits

 Governor Eliot Spitzer ousted in prostitution scandal; David Paterson sworn in

Kiss my Facebook! Proud media hermits resist online social networking site

Movie star and erstwhile Brooklyn dad Heath Ledger found dead in Soho apartment

Climate-change couture? Fashionistas don sleeveless coats, toeless boots, wool shorts

Bear naked tradies: Wall Street crisis starts with sale of Stearns to JPMorgan

 Park Slope power moms pine for *Mad Men*'s Don Draper

Weeknight update: Jimmy Fallon chosen as Conan O'Brien's late-night successor

City cheers as Barack Obama elected 44th president

2008

◇◇◇◇◇◇◇◇

JANUARY 21, 2008 BY CHRIS SHOTT

Travis Bickle Suite

*Moroccan Tiles, Tibetan Rugs, $725 Rooms, You Talkin'
to Me, Sir? Once Stars Closed Bars, But Robert De Niro,
Jay-Z, Giorgio Armani Are in Warm Towel Rack,
Cold Champagne, Full-Minibar Business*

ACTOR ROBERT DE NIRO USED to be just another famous guest in the world of swanky hotels.

Now, he's opening his own posh lodge in downtown Manhattan.

Standing seven stories high at the corner of Greenwich and North Moore streets, Mr. De Niro's roughly 75,000-square-foot Greenwich Hotel, scheduled to open this spring, will include all the world-class amenities that one might expect from a wealthy, two-time Oscar winner: Moroccan tiles, Tibetan rugs, French doors, Siberian oak floors—even a fancy Tuscan-style restaurant and chichi Shibui Spa.

Room rates will be just as extravagant, starting at $725 per night.

And people will probably pay it—if not for the stylish surroundings, then perhaps because every other decent place in town is either entirely booked or equally expensive.

The annual average room rate in Manhattan has escalated more than 50 percent since 2003, to nearly $300 a night, according to the city's latest figures.

Mr. De Niro isn't the only A-list luminary looking to get in on the lucrative action.

Hip-hop mogul Shawn Carter, a.k.a. Jay-Z, perhaps foreshadowed his own foray into the business when he first unleashed the

celebratory rap lyric "after the show it's the after-party and after the party is the hotel lobby."

The Grammy-winning former president of Def Jam records and part-time party promoter announced this past December that he, too, is planning to build a new high-end hotel in Manhattan with the help of CB Developers.

The reported $66.4 million, 150,000-square-foot project, located on the site of an old warehouse and parking garage on West 22nd Street, will serve as the flagship for a whole new chain of luxury lodgings called J Hotels. "Everything is in a very developmental stage," noted Mr. Carter's publicist, who declined further comment.

Fashion designer Giorgio Armani, meanwhile, is searching for a chic spot to create a New York counterpart to his opulent Armani Hotel & Residences in Dubai.

JANUARY 7, 2008 BY ELIOT BROWN

ELIOT SPITZER, BUILDER
THE GOVERNOR'S SIT-DOWN:
HE SEES PENN STATION AS A KIND OF HELL

The son of a real estate developer, Eliot Spitzer became governor one year ago this week. Since then, he's yanked the plug on a large-scale Javits Center expansion; accepted five bids for the West Side rail yards; and negotiated insurance settlements at ground zero What's next?

THE CITY HAS ASKED the state to be a 50/50 partner with Governors Island, but last year the state gave less money than the city. Will the state be matching the city's commitments this year?

The deal is a 50/50 partnership, and we will do that in due course. I think the time lag until now has been the failure to define with any specificity what we're doing. We're fully funded for the next two years in terms of our ability to do the design work, the environmental reviews that we need. We're going to be there doing our part. We have a $4.3 billion deficit right now, but in the long haul, we'll be doing our part.

About the Javits Center expansion—is a renovation of the facility the most likely option at this point? [*Editor's note: On Dec. 20, the day after this interview was conducted, Governor Spitzer's development chief Patrick Foye said at a State Assembly hearing that the state would scrap any large-scale expansion plans for Javits.*]

This has been a difficult analytical process, primarily because the cost structure turned out to be very different from what we were told and what we expected. ... The numbers were not what we were led to believe they were, and I don't say that to impute anything improper; but the numbers—when people went back and we said, 'Check the numbers, make sure we're dealing with data that's good'—the cost structure came in in a very different place than we anticipated, so that required some reexamination of some of the premises and some of the financing decisions that had been made.

Though isn't an expansion a pretty strong driver of economic development?

That's actually something that's been a topic of significant debate. I think for different cites, the role of [a] convention center plays a different role. ... With hotel occupancy rates what they are, with the draw to New York what it is for people, tourists—44 million tourists a year, I think, is the number—it may be less critical that we actually have a convention center that is the largest in order to keep our hotels filled and to keep the tourists coming here.

The city has tens of millions of square feet of commercial development planned, but we still have, overall, fewer jobs than in 2000. Do you think the city could be overdeveloping?

I don't want to quite say that if we build it, they will come; but, certainly, if we build the additional commercial space that we project we need, I have no doubt that it will be filled.

HEATH LEDGER, 1979-2008

ON THE AFTERNOON OF TUESDAY, JAN. 22, THE ACTOR **HEATH LEDGER** was found dead, reportedly in a fourth-floor apartment at 421 Broome Street between Crosby and Lafayette, with pills near his body, by a masseuse and the housekeeper who'd admitted her.

By around 6:30 p.m., barricades that had been erected around the building to keep gawkers and fans clear were being removed, and the body had been taken out of the building by the county medical examiner.

Mr. Ledger leaves behind a 2-year-old daughter, Matilda, with former fiancée **Michelle Williams**. An actor from a young age, he got his Hollywood break in the teen flick *10 Things I Hate About You*, and an Oscar nomination for his performance in the 2005 film *Brokeback Mountain*. He settled temporarily with Ms. Williams in Boerum Hill and joined in local protests against the development of the Atlantic Yards by real estate developer **Bruce Ratner**.

Mr. Ledger's last big role: the Joker in *The Dark Knight*, director *Christopher Nolan's* second installment of the Batman series, slated for release on July 18 by Warner Bros. "Our hearts go out to his family and friends," said studio brass in another statement.

◇◇◇◇◇◇◇◇

Feeling Queasy ... : The Good Ship HRC

JANUARY 21, 2008
BY GILLIAN REAGAN

Facebook Holdouts: Proud Media Hermits, Clutching At Privacy

There are still a few proud New Yorkers who resist conducting their social lives online, putting up their pictures and preferences for all the world to peruse. Herein, they explain their rationale

IT SEEMS THAT MOST URBAN SOphisticates these days, from politicians and celebrities to coworkers, have a profile on Facebook, the social networking Web site. The C.I.A., I.R.S., Time Inc., even MySpace, Facebook's ostensible competition, have job networks there. To the site's enthusiasts—and there are many; the site has 60 million users so far, with 200 million projected by the end of the year—there is no reason not to partake.

But not all of us are signing up: clicking on that grassy-green button that allows one to join a so-called "exclusive club" in which one may receive pertinent updates of some "friend's" baby pictures, a new veggie burger someone tried last night, and who is slinging electronic "poo" at whose profile.

JANUARY 28, 2008   EDITORIAL

ON FEBRUARY 5, OBAMA

LOST AMID THE SOUND AND fury of this year's primary season is the certainty, not the promise, of change. For the first time since 1952, there is no heir apparent to the administration in power.

The stakes have rarely been higher in a presidential election. The question is not if there will be change in American leadership, but what kind.

And the change that is being offered has a focus and intelligence that is kindred to the best American traditions. It is embodied by one candidate in the Democratic Party who is offering a reinvigorated America: Senator Barack Obama.

The New York Observer urges New York Democrats to support Mr. Obama in the state's presidential primary on Feb. 5.

New Yorkers might ask why they should not pull a lever for our junior senator, Hillary Rodham Clinton. While Mrs. Clinton is an extraordinary United States senator for New York, we believe that Mr. Obama can be a great president for the United States of America.

Most of the other candidates have absorbed, assimilated or ap-

propriated Mr. Obama's issue of change. It is a powerful concept. But a great deal of the argument for Mr. Obama's candidacy is about one great issue in American life: restoring and reinvigorating American democracy.

Democracy is the greatest strength of this still-young nation. Its living enactment is our gift to the world. It is the product of our best instincts and most powerful ideals. But it has been polluted, sullied and compromised by an obstructive administration that seems to have no particular regard for its attributes.

It is difficult to remember the last national candidate who has charged and jazzed the democratic system as Mr. Obama has. Partly as a result of his candidacy, college campuses have remembered why they are proud of the United States, kids are going door to door, runners are handing out leaflets on weekends, racial lines have been culturally melted and the electoral approach to presidential campaigning has been reborn.

And, as more than one commentator has said, America is being reintroduced to the world.

FEBRUARY 4, 2008   BY NICOLE BRYDSON

Globally Warmed:
The Couture of Climate Change
With increasingly erratic winter temperatures, short-sleeved and even sleeveless coats are starting to make a crazy kind of sense to many New York women

TO THE LONG LIST OF OXYMO-ronic garments produced by our novelty-desperate fashion complex—corduroy culottes! Uggs in Malibu!—now add sleeveless coats. "They look great!" enthused Kasia Steczyk, 27, a special-events intern at the Brooklyn Academy of Music who owns a whopping 10 of 'em.

What's the latest thing in fashion these days? Buying stuff that requires you to buy ... more stuff. Think iPod accessories, those little clip-on gew-gaws now available for Hermès Birkins, and these baffling arm-exposing coats that appeared on the Marc Jacobs fall '06 runway and have been spotted everywhere from high-end stores like Opening Ceremony and Miss Sixty to Forever 21, H&M and Club Monaco.

One can't help but think the trend has something to do with increasingly erratic winter temperatures.

For all the eco-conscious magazine theme issues and organic parties (waitresses in hemp dresses! Greentinis!), the fashion industry's basic response to Al Gore and his sufferin' polar bears has been: Hey, New Options! Witness the spread in the August *Vogue* that blithely declared: "As the planet heats up, the jacket is stealing the coat's thunder. ... It's got every age and sensibility stylishly covered." We may not be able to unmelt the polar ice caps—but we'll be damned if we can't find a style solution in the interim.

Helena Fredriksson, designer of the eponymous label H Fredriksson, who has designed coats with shorter sleeves, called the category "the new in-between piece."

"The short or no sleeve has felt a bit unpractical previous seasons with cold fall and winters," she said. "Now in our current times of global warming, they do make more sense."

And there are aesthetic advantages as well. "The three-quarter sleeve can give a more interesting shape in terms of design, and it's easier to make sense with a volume three-quarter sleeve than a full length," Ms. Fredriksson said. "It also gives an opportunity to show longer gloves, which I like, and it gives a less bulky feel when wearing. The short sleeve and no sleeve is not as interesting in terms of sleeve design to me, but I do like the simplicity of it."

Of course, the style has its detractors.

"Those coats drive me crazy!" said Julie Gerstein, 29, a writer for *OK!* magazine. "I saw a woman today in a floor-length sleeveless fur coat. So tacky and wrong on so many levels."

FEBRUARY 11, 2008 BY FELIX GILLETTE

NYTV PRIMARY SCREAM

Chris Matthews, MSNBC's Manic Oracle of American Politics, Has Been Through a Lot of Elections, But 'I've Never Seen Anything Like This! This Is–' What? 'Bigger Than Kennedy!'

CHRIS MATTHEWS WOKE UP ON SUPER TUESDAY AT THE RITZ Carlton on Central Park South. For breakfast, he tore into a bowl of Raisin Bran with skim milk, slurped down a cup of coffee (no cream, no sugar) and attacked a stack of newspapers. Moving from story to story, he scribbled notes directly onto the newsprint, circling important facts and figures and jotting down the occasional exclamation points. He particularly liked an article in the *Daily News* by Rich Cohen suggesting that Barack Obama should be president, and Hillary Clinton his chief of staff.

Afterward, MSNBC's prizefighter—the political pundit who knows more and filters less than anyone else in the business and who with his manic emotional odes to a certain senator from Illinois has become a fascinating sideshow attraction in this crazy primary circus—had hoped to go for a morning constitutional.

But this morning, in lieu of going for a walk, Mr. Matthews, who is 62, called the South African embassy. Recently, MSNBC announced that Super Tuesday would be broadcast live in South Africa, and Mr. Matthews, who spent two years in the Peace Corps, "spreading capitalism in the bush," wanted to greet properly his faraway viewers. The nice woman at the embassy signed off on Mr. Matthews' phrase of greeting: *Sanibonani*! Mr. Matthews planned to use the phrase later that night.

In the meantime, he continued to ponder the big factors in the campaign. History. Courage. Change. Hope.

"I've been following politics since I was about 5," said Mr. Matthews. "I've never seen anything like this. This is bigger than Kennedy. [Obama] comes along, and he seems to have the answers. This is the New Testament. This is surprising."

It was the morning of Super Tuesday. Everything was still in play.

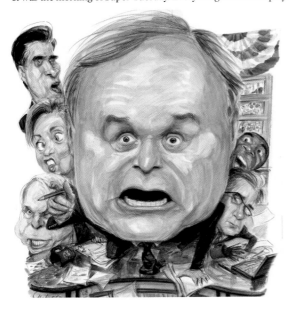

MARCH 17, 2008 BY AZI PAYBARAH

The Touchable

Eliot Spitzer, Tortured Straight-Arrow Governor, Becomes Client 9 Forever

IN RETROSPECT, ELIOT SPITZER'S first year in office—during which time he lost high-profile fights with the Democratic Assembly and the Republican Senate, and introduced an initiative so toxic it nearly derailed Hillary Clinton's presidential campaign—only seemed like a disaster.

The revelation, broken this week on the Web site of *The New York Times*, that he paid thousands of dollars for a prostitute to meet him in Washington is the real thing.

It's not simply that Mr. Spitzer has systematically alienated virtually everyone in Albany—Republican or Democrat—meaning that he has no political allies in his time of need. Or that he has managed to turn his considerable popular mandate to dust.

The worst thing about Mr. Spitzer's transgression is that it finally, definitively and, barring a miracle, irreversibly destroys the premise of his political existence.

A clean-as-a-whistle crusader, he's not.

"I have acted in a way that violates my obligations to my family, and violates my—or any—sense of right and wrong," Mr. Spitzer said during a brief appearance in his midtown office on March 10, as his red-eyed wife stood behind him. "I apologize first and most importantly to my family. I apologize to the public, whom I promised better."

It was the most coherent part of a vague and largely defensive-sounding statement that satisfied exactly no one.

Afterward, some officials offered rote statements of sympathy for Mr. Spitzer's family while politely avoiding the issue of whether he should resign.

MAY 20, 2008   BY DOREE SHAFRIR

What, Me Host?

Why Was Guileless Jimmy Fallon Hired for Conan's Late-Night Desk? 'I Got the Sense He Was Built for It,' Says Producer Lorne Michaels; 'You Get to Tell Jokes, Meet Cool People,' Says Scruffy Ex-SNL Guy

LAST WEEK, AT A PRESS CONFERENCE AT NBC HEADQUARTERS AT 30 Rockefeller Center announcing that he would take over for Conan O'Brien on NBC's *Late Night* next year, when Mr. O'Brien moves into Jay Leno's big chair, Jimmy Fallon looked just a little sheepish.

"I'm very excited about this," he told the crowd of reporters. "I hope to make this the best show, and the show to make everyone choose me to fall asleep during." The crowd laughed politely. On the podium with him was his mentor, NBC comedy guru Lorne Michaels, who produces *Late Night*, which airs nightly at 12:30 a.m., and who had selected Mr. Fallon as its new host, just as he had anointed an unknown 30-year-old Conan O'Brien 15 years earlier.

A week later, on the phone from the Los Angeles home he shares with his wife of five months, the movie producer Nancy Juvonen, and their dog, Lucy, Mr. Fallon reflected on his decision to take the job.

"It's a comedian's dream where you can get a job where you can tell jokes on national television," said Jimmy Fallon. "It's amazing. That's why comedians work comedy clubs. They work any room they can get a laugh! I missed that. I missed the applause, and I missed working with writers and getting out there and telling jokes and doing bits. Late-night television is responsible for some of the best moments on TV! And you get to meet a bunch of people. I find people interesting. I really do. I think I'm looking forward to that as well, so much. It's almost like, what don't you like about the job?"

MARCH 24, 2008   BY AZI PAYBARAH

HIS EXCELLENCY

Governor David A. Paterson: Whap! The full-frontal download of his past has charmed Albany and stunned New York

ADMITTEDLY, IT'S HARD TO KNOW EXACTLY WHAT TO MAKE OF David Paterson's unorthodox debut as governor.

An attempt to preempt a wave of press speculation about his personal life by granting an interview to the *Daily News* on March 17—the day he was sworn in—put the issue of his extramarital activities in play without putting it to rest, leaving out the name and professional position of the woman he had been sleeping with.

From here, the scenario goes like this: The press, free now to address in print what they've been talking about in private for a while already, plumbs the depths of Mr. Paterson's relationships in search of overlap with his role as a public official and his access to campaign funds and public money.

And here's the likely ending: Mr. Paterson survives. The thing he has going for him, above all, is that no matter what the press turns up, none of the big players in Albany has an interest in seeing Mr. Paterson fail.

For the Democrats, an early exit for David Paterson would mean Governor Joe Bruno. For Mr. Bruno it would mean a level of scrutiny that he, even more than Mr. Paterson, is ill-prepared to endure. And for the public, it would mean yet another scandal after an exhausting (and deeply unappealing) week of stories about Eliot Spitzer and prostitutes.

And besides, just about every elected official, interest group and lobbyist in Albany seemed far too occupied adjusting to Day One, Part Two, to do anything but pursue their business as usual.

APRIL 7, 2008

BY JOHN KOBLIN

OFF THE RECORD: MAG AS HELL! WHERE WILL MAGAZINES BE 10 YEARS FROM NOW?

IN THE NEXT FIVE YEARS IN Graydon Carter's world, you'll walk onto a plane, or a subway, or a soon-to-be-invented mode of transport, and you'll tuck a little electronic book under your arm. Inside that little book, which will be very expensive at first but soon will cost $150, there'll be a series of mylar "pages," and there will be small buttons off to the side, and once you hit one of them, whoooosh, words and photos from *Vanity Fair* will suddenly appear.

"In a decade time frame?" asked Chris Anderson, editor of *Wired*. "No. Technology adoption happens slowly. This is the editor of *Wired* telling you no. Obviously, newspapers are going to be changing dramatically over the next few years, but magazines are not newspapers. And I think magazines 10 years from now are going to look something like they do now."

Interviews with editors of magazines like *Wired, Rolling Stone, The New Yorker, Us Weekly* and several others elicited more of the same: Magazines are not, for the most part, worried about the Internet.

Most magazine editors seem to have emerged from 10 years of mostly noncommittal fiddling around with the Web confident that the magazine of the future will be largely the magazine of the present. That is, when they are willing to look past the next print deadline to contemplate the magazine of the future at all.

Isn't It ... ? HBO hired Tina Brown and Frank Rich

◇◇◇◇◇◇◇

JUNE 2, 2008 BY JOHN KOBLIN

OFF THE RECORD:
The Times Magazine Dapples Sunlight on Its Memoirist

THIS PAST WINTER, PAUL TOUGH, A STORY EDITOR AT *THE NEW York Times Magazine*, brought Emily Gould, a recently retired editor of Gawker.com, to the sixth floor of the paper's skyscraper on Eighth Avenue. Sometimes, writers meet with the magazine's editor in chief, Gerry Marzorati, and this was one of those times.

Mr. Marzorati had never before heard of Ms. Gould, he told Off the Record. They talked for around an hour about her "wanting to write some memoirish piece about having lived a fair amount of her life on the Internet in her first years in New York; I was interested."

The task of illustrating fell to Elinor Carucci, a freelance photographer who said she does mostly fine arts work and spent several hours over two days in a one-on-one photo shoot at Ms. Gould's apartment in Brooklyn.

Mr. Marzorati said his instructions were "to try to convey this sort of intimacy and dreaminess and sort of intimate detachment—if that's a meaningful oxymoron—that is in the piece. They worked that out together."

And this is how an image of Ms. Gould, poured upside-down onto a rumpled bed wearing a camisole, no bra and a come-hither look, landed on New Yorkers' laptops and brunch tables over Memorial Day weekend. The writer was involved in winnowing the photos to a dozen, Ms. Carucci said. Still, "when I saw the cover, I was shocked," Ms. Gould said on the phone from Bryant Park on May 27. Did she feel a tad exploited? Ms. Gould paused. "Yeah, I really don't want to talk about it."

JUNE 2, 2008 BY GILLIAN REAGAN

THE OBSERVATORY: GET PLENTY OF IRONY! THE GOLDEN ARCHES, ARCHLY

Three-star pigs in a blanket, $55 mac 'n' cheese with truffles, peanut butter and foie gras: When did eating in Manhattan become so demandingly witty? GILLIAN REAGAN longs for the days when a Twinkie was just a Twinkie

FROM MAY 28 UNTIL JUNE 2, visitors to the first-floor atrium at Henri Bendel on Fifth Avenue, weaving through perfumed salesladies at a trunk show for Gold Skin Care, will find Sarah Magid, an organic baker from Greenpoint, Brooklyn, selling her most popular item, a "Goldie"—a cylindrical chocolate sponge cake filled with buttercream that retails for $8.

"People see it and say, 'Oh my God, is that a Twinkie and it's ... organic?'" said Ms. Magid. When she started making the confection two years ago, she dubbed it a "Tweenkee," but she eventually changed the name in less direct tribute to the Hostess pastry, and perhaps a nod to the phrase "golden oldie." Enthusiasts include staffers at *Women's Wear Daily* and Ed Bucciarelli, the CEO of Bendel. "They just laugh and then they eat it," Ms. Magid said. "It brings a sense of humor to the food."

Not everyone is amused, however. Such gourmet gimmicks are increasingly common in New York's rarefied circles, where dining outside the home has become a prolonged and occasionally wearying exercise in wit and detachment. We have entered an era of Ironic Food, with chefs taking working-class staples, citifying them into nearly unrecognizable form and serving them with a wink and a smile to the upper crust.

At BLT Market, Laurent Tourondel serves "pigs in a blanket": prime cuts of beef and pork cuddling in a delicate puff pastry, served as a complimentary start to a meal. Daniel Boulud, Olde Homestead and the Wall Street Burger Shoppe have all done burgers of varying degrees of unaffordability. And at Graydon Carter's Waverly Inn, the once-mocked $55 plate of truffled mac 'n' cheese has become one of the restaurant's defining dishes.

Combined with the brigade of Park Slope mommies pouring "evaporated cane juice" (a.k.a. sugar) down their children's throats, it's enough to send anyone scurrying over to the nearest Dollar Menu.

JUNE 9, 2008 BY MEREDITH BRYAN

Ben-Her Friends, Romans, Ladies!

*Friends, Romans, Ladies! Why Are Gladiator Sandals Hot Shoes for Women Warriors This Summer?
They're Sexy, Powerful, Flat! Says Cynthia Rowley: 'Orthopedic Spartan Shoes'*

ON A RECENT SUNDAY EVENING, AT THE PRIVATE CLUB NORWOOD on 14th Street, designer Michael Kors was explaining the appeal of the gladiator sandal, the shoe New Yorkers are not going to be able to escape this summer. "It's comfortable and powerful," he said. "What could be better? Sexy, comfortable and powerful all at once. It works with any length; you can wear it with a short dress, wear it with a long dress, wear it with shorts. ..."

This was a party honoring the Council of Fashion Designers of America Awards nominees, and the aggressive accessory du jour was out in full force, encasing the feet of everyone from the actress Ashley Olsen (high-heeled, black and strappy, paired with short shorts and a blazer) to the female servers wearing spare, proletarian versions as they proffered pork skewers.

Designer Cynthia Rowley sported a pair of her own design: nude platforms with a faux armor-plate stretching over the front of her foot and extending to the ankle. They looked like a softer version of the now-impossible-to-find black $770 Dior Extreme Gladiators worn by Sarah Jessica Parker in the new *Sex and the City* movie. "These are sort of orthopedic Spartan shoes," said Ms. Rowley, who said she'd been inspired by the 2006 film *300*, about the 480 B.C. Battle of Thermopylae.

Of course, the Spartans were Greek, which gladiators were not, but no matter: Footwear is having an ancient moment.

◇◇◇◇◇◇◇

JUNE 9, 2008 BY DANA RUBINSTEIN

CLIENT 9 TO 5
Eliot Spitzer's got a new day job at dad Bernie's real estate empire. But will Big Business welcome former Sheriff of Wall Street?

BY ALL ACCOUNTS, ELIOT SPITZER NEVER IMAGINED that Spitzer Enterprises would be his life's work. His father Bernie's real estate empire, the one he built from scratch, would finance Eliot's ambitions. Not circumscribe them.

But that was then. This is now. And apparently, the deposed governor is adjusting.

Mr. Spitzer, who just a few months ago was said to contemplate White House ambitions, now ascends every weekday to the top of the Crown Building, according to sources familiar with the Spitzers. More precisely, the ex-governor reports to the 22nd floor of 730 Fifth Avenue, the French Renaissance-style masterpiece his father co-owns with the Winter Organization.

It's apparently the closest thing to a nine-to-five job Mr. Spitzer has had since his hypocrisy and lust transformed him from a left-wing hero into the left's own version of the Rev. Ted Haggard—a man guilty of doing that which he so publicly condemned.

But what, precisely, is Mr. Spitzer doing in his father's office?

Mr. Spitzer wouldn't tell us. A call to Spitzer Enterprises at 2:30 on Monday afternoon revealed he was there and in a meeting. He never called back.

But a real estate insider close to Bernie Spitzer said the family was trying to suss things out.

"He's going into a fully established real estate empire. It's all there for him," said a real estate consultant. "No one in the real estate world will, pardon my French, give a shit about the prostitutes."

In fact, given the back-slapping, meat-and-potatoes culture of New York real estate, Mr. Spitzer might even find himself a star.

"Guys in our industry, if he started attending real estate board functions, they'd get a kick out of it," said the consultant. "We live in this sort of perverted, celebrity-driven world."

Centerfolds just a few floors down from his desk. Central Park just two blocks away. A view of the city from his window. Forget the past, Mr. Spitzer. You've got it made.

A selection of favorites by RJ Matson

JUNE 30, 2008 BY SPENCER MORGAN

Bear Naked Tradies
The professional death of a brilliant Bear Stearns salesman

"ANYTIME BEAR WAS INVOLVED with another bank—we always had to go a level deeper, even though at the end of the day it does not matter, but the idea was to prove that we were better than the other bank," said a junior investment analyst, who jumped ship just as the ship was sinking.

Being the best on the trading side was a little trickier. Bear didn't have a lot of liquid, so to make the big bets that would feed the Bear, everything had to be leveraged to the gills.

Enter Ralph Cioffi (pronounced Cho-fi). A Bear man through and through. Born in South Burlington, Vt. Running back at Rice Memorial High, St. Michael's College in Colchester, studied business and bodybuilding, too.

Like everyone else, he was looking to take advantage of the housing boom, but do it better, riskier, more profitable—the new Bear man. So he creates a new type of collateralized debt obligation, CDOs, which are mortgage bonds that are sliced and diced into bundles with differing default risks. They're called Klio Funding, and they were catnip to the $2 trillion mother lode of money-market accounts. And mortgage bonds have the highest ratings, so they could be leveraged up the wazoo. In some cases, banks like Citigroup and Barclays were giving out loans of 20 bucks to 1. And why not, the housing market is booming, prices are going up. If a guy defaults on his loan, well, he or the bank can sell the house at a profit. The more mortgage bonds Bear buys, the more fees banks make, and the more likely they are to want to make more loans to make more fees.

A guy who worked with him said the thing about Mr. Cioffi, which is symptomatic of the Bear culture, is that he was promoted from a salesman position to a money manager position.

"So what does he do in this new position? He sells, sells, sells his fund on investors, and then leverages the investments, basically raising money very successfully."

Other investment banks began to buy these bonds. Bear the scrappy pit bull had the white shoes tap-dancing to its tune. Man, that must have felt good.

Then the ass fell out of the housing market. People couldn't afford their mortgage payments, the ratings of the bonds went down. Investors tried to get out while they could, but the raging pit bull had a problem. The trick about mortgage bonds is that you have to be able to sell them, and when they're leveraged 20 times over, the price can only fall so much before you lose money. So they lost everyone's money. Everyone's.

In March 2007, Mr. Cioffi told a colleague, "I'm sick to my stomach over our performance in March." And he wasn't kidding. And because he was a Bear man, he felt more than a little sick. How sick? Bear sick.

JUNE 23, 2008   BY FELIX GILLETTE

NYTV: TIM RUSSERT, MAN OF AMBITION

AT 1:30 P.M., THE LINE OF mourners on Mount Saint Alban in Washington, D.C., for Tim Russert, NBC Washington bureau chief and host of *Meet the Press*, who died so suddenly last week at the age of 58, stretched all the way from the front doors of the St. Albans School Refectory out to Wisconsin Avenue.

'IF IT'S SUNDAY, IT'S *MEET THE PRESS*'

When he first took over as moderator of *Meet the Press* in 1991, the chance that he would give new life to the long-running program was considered a long shot at best.

At the time, *This Week With David Brinkley* was the dominant force in Sunday morning public affairs programming. The previous year, *This Week* on ABC averaged roughly 3.6 million viewers, compared to *Face the Nation* on CBS, which had averaged around three million viewers. *Meet the Press* was limping along with a meager 2.6 million viewers.

By May of 1992, Robert Novak and William Safire were lining up with a bunch of Beltway tastemakers to declare Russert the next big thing. Within a year of Russert's on-air debut, *Meet the Press* was regularly beating *This Week* in the ratings in the D.C. market. By 1995, Russert and Co. had racked up a number of weekly wins against *This Week* in the national ratings. By 1996, Russert had essentially chased Mr. Brinkley into retirement.

Before he ever set foot in the *Meet the Press* studio, Russert spent years devising press strategies for Senator Daniel Patrick Moynihan, Governor Mario Cuomo and eventually for NBC News. "When Tim was wearing his old hat of press strategist and campaign strategist, we had many conversations about the press and how it works," said *The New Yorker*'s Ken Auletta. "He was a great tactician. He was a very shrewd political press guy."

JULY 14, 2008 BY PETER W. KAPLAN

NEVER HOLD YOUR BEST STUFF: CLAY FELKER'S NEW YORK WAS POPULATED BY HEROES AND SCOUNDRELS, DUCHESSES AND BEAUTIES

WHEN I THINK OF CLAY FELKER, WHICH is often, it's at the Peacock Alley in the Waldorf Astoria. I had just come to *The Observer* in 1994 and I was scared and sweating. Clay offered to meet with me once a week and kick around story ideas. I used to bring a stack of napkins. They were, by the end of breakfast, black with scrawl: call David Garth, Milton Glaser, Mrs. Astor; water, Moynihan, women and money, Brooklyn as the new Paris, Columbia vs. N.Y.U., water mains, Murdoch, CBS News, power.

There were Felkerian adages:

1. Never hold your best stuff.
2. Put something shocking at the top of the page.
3. Women are the best reporters.
4. Point of view is everything.
5. Personal is better.
6. Never hold your best stuff.

There were instructions about calling writers, some of them too young, some too old, some cronies, some princes, some just right. There were design edicts about tearing the front page into pieces, using more illustration, less photography, bigger type. There were declarations about making the paper more "female," with more ideas.

"It's a newspaper of interpretation," he used to say. Then: "Point of view is everything."

The last statement is as true as anything I know about the kind of journalism Clay Felker taught a generation of reporters and editors. For him, point of view was everything. It was not only an edict, it was a revolution. Clay came from a generation that was killing the newspaper writer, in which the dominance of *The New York Times* and the mystical insularity of William Shawn's *New Yorker* were so powerful that the blaring, clattering bumptiousness of New York newspapers that had come to dominate the press in the 19th century through the Menckenian 1920s was being squashed into a white-collar, gray-suited blur.

Clay Felker, of Webster Groves, Mo., son of the managing editor of *The Sporting News* and the women's editor of the *St. Louis Post-Dispatch*, of Duke University, of *Life*, *Esquire* and the *New York Herald Tribune*, had a different point of view. Somewhere on this earth and even within this city there are still men and women who remember when Clay Felker was a giant with a delicate smile whose melodic, brassy belt could stop New York cold; there are fewer who remember before that, when he still was a jostling, ambitious, impossible tyro, whose ambition—which he would turn into a journalistic petrochemical—was still burbling: He was the young *Life* magazine reporter who ended Joe DiMaggio's reign in center field at Yankee Stadium by proving that his arm was ailing. Clay liked to tell the story of Gary Cooper showing up at a photo shoot near the end of his life and creating the illusion of vitality with an almost indiscernible move of the tip of his cowboy boot.

But nothing Clay did was a tiny tip of a boot. Clay reinvented the American magazine in *New York* magazine with huge type and big noises, journalistic ambition, the salvaged egg he pulled from the ashes of the collapsed *Herald Tribune*. Vitality was his game, ambition was his fuel, manliness was his strength. As a younger man, he was a blasting force of nature; as an older man, he became the sweetheart of the Western world, beloved to students, girl reporters and acolytes.

He reinvented the American magazine, not just in New York with *New York*, but with his noise and chest-bumping assault on the power structures in the city. Clay Felker, who you may not have heard of, but who was the last great magazine editor of the 20th century, was a strange amalgam of exuberance, innocence and pragmatism.

Clay wrote two pieces for this newspaper. He never seemed quite as certain about himself as a writer as he might have, and I'm sorry, for one, that he didn't complete the autobiography he started. But his Felkerian ideas were as vivid on the page as they were when he belted them. He wrote this soon after Sept. 11, 2001:

"The people who come to New York will continue to be ambitious, looking for more than just work, looking for advancement and the possibility of realizing their dreams. The city thrives on the young, the marginalized and the outcasts—people who live on the edge, driven by necessity to creativity.

"Once more, New York now faces the dangerous opportunity of creative destruction. For people accustomed to living on the edge, out of the terrible tragedy can come the spark of creativity that will give rise to something new: a new belle époque, such as those in the late 40's and 50's, and again in the 90's. It will take a while. But a new city will grow out of the shell of the old. ... The ambitious, striving, swarming culture of this wounded place is what will re-create New York City, once again, as the world's greatest."

And he wrote this three months later:

"New York's historic role has been that of an idea factory, where ingenious and capable people, packed together, take raw materials from around the globe and transform them into products and services they sell back to the rest of the world—at higher prices. Whether it's managing money, designing fashions, solving knotty legal or marketing problems, or translating ephemeral ideas into art and entertainment, New Yorkers thrive by charging high fees for their advice and services.

"This commercial alchemy—the advice and ideas—depends on a critical mass of ambitious and highly creative people, and New York is home to more of them than probably any other metropolis in the world. It may cause outsiders to feel jealous or inferior. But they'll seek it out anyway, with all its irritating confidence and street smarts.

"That's what New York does."

That's what Clay Felker did.

Hosanna! Obama rides triumphantly to the Democratic convention in Denver

SEPTEMBER 1, 2008
BY FELIX GILLETTE

NYTV:
It's a Maddow, Maddow World; MSNBC's fresh-faced host glows under the hot lights in Denver

A FEW MINUTES BEFORE 11 P.M. on Aug. 25, Rachel Maddow was sitting behind a desk in a double-decker, alfresco television studio her television network, MSNBC, had erected near the old train tracks that cut through downtown Denver, from which Ms. Maddow was to punditize to the public from the near environs of the Democratic National Convention.

Just a few years ago, the 35-year-old Stanford University graduate, Bay Area native and Rhodes Scholar hadn't even been in journalism. But then she gave up academics and activism, and somewhat improbably landed a talk show on the liberal radio network Air America. From there, she parlayed her success into regular appearances as a progressive political pundit on the cable news shows.

And now she was charged with doing what former MSNBC general manager Dan Abrams had failed to do—that is, hang on to Mr. Olbermann's younger viewers in the crucial hour following MSNBC's hit show *Countdown*.

SEPTEMBER 9, 2008   BY JONATHAN BINES

THE NEW YORK WORLD: BLACK COMIC INTRODUCES MCCAIN

What up, RNC!
(cheers)
You white motherfuckers!
(laughter)
This conference so white, Helen Mirren tried to snort it!
(laughter)
Y'all the whitest white people in the history of white people. Even Barbara Bush sitting here right now going: 'These are some *white* motherfuckers.'
(laughter)
Look at this place. I can't *believe* this shit! Y'all couldn't find one single brother?
(shouting)
There is? Where?
(shouting)
Yo, what up, brother! Looks like you the only chocolate chip in the cookie.
(laughter)
You look like a fly in a glass of milk, yo. Swim! Swim for your life!
(laughter)
Alaska in the house!
(Cheers)
Where the baby daddy at?

Where he at?
(crowd noise)
You knocked her up, man? That's cool. That's cool.
(silence)
You know that word 'abstinence'—you know that mean 'no fucking,' right?
(laughter)
I guess they didn't make that clear at the *seminar*.
(laughter)
'So I just use this *abstinence*, that mean we can fuck all we want, right?' *No!*
(laughter)
But you know I *feel* you, man. I do. Because the fact is, you live in motherfucking *Alas*ka! What else is there to do but fuck?
(laughter)
Just fuck! That's all there is to do! Just fuck!
(laughter)
That's all Alaska is. Just a bunch of crazy white people fucking!
(sustained laughter and applause)
And you know he got to marry

that girl, too. Because ... her momma done shot a *moose*.
(laughter)
'Cause when a girl's momma shoot a moose, that's, like, a red flag for me. I take that shit into consideration. I do! It's like, 'Yeah, you fine. No doubt. You *real* fine. And you got a great personality. *And* you drunk. But ... ain't your momma the one done shot a *moose*? I'll be seeing you later on.' I practice *abstinence* with moose-shooting-momma-having bitches.
(laughter)
But it's time to bring out the white man you've all been waiting for. This man is so white, he makes y'all look Mexican.
(laughter)
He spent five long years locked up in a POW camp, and returned a national hero.
(applause)
And fucked every white woman in America.
(sustained applause)
'Cause five years—that makes you horny. And women, they *looove* to fuck war heroes. Basically, if you were white and female in 1973, you were fucked by John McCain.
("USA! USA! USA!")
And then he married a fine rich white girl whose daddy owned a beer company.
(laughter, applause)
And he wants to be president? *Sheeet*, you already got money, beer *and* pussy! What the fuck you want with the *presidency*? Quit while you're ahead! You're 72 years old—just drink, fuck, and play golf, you dumb white motherfucker!
(raucous laughter, applause)
Ladies and gentlemen, the next president of the United States of America, John McCain!

SEPTEMBER 15, 2008   BY DOREE SHAFRIR

FEMOCRACY '08

Sisterhood Is Powerful, But McCain Running-Mate Sarah Palin Has Fried the Circuits of Post-Clinton New York Feminists

SINCE AUG. 29, WHEN JOHN MCCAIN ANNOUNCED HIS SELECTION of Alaska's governor, Sarah Palin, as his running mate, the news cycle has been consumed by Ms. Palin's politics, her family, even her eyeglasses. The speech she gave at the Republican National Convention was perfectly calibrated to appeal to two core constituencies: the evangelical base that Mr. McCain has had so much trouble attracting, and women—hopefully former Hillary Clinton voters among them—who might look at balancing her day job (governor!) with her five children, including a baby with Down syndrome and a 17-year-old daughter with a baby on the way, and think that in Ms. Palin they had finally found someone in national politics whom they could look up to and admire.

In the days after Ms. Palin's saucy Minneapolis salvo, underneath the giddy left-wing blogosphere blowback and smug IM banter—she looks just like Tina Fey! Imagine what *Saturday Night Live* is gonna do with *this!*—there were distinct rumblings of self-doubt. Had the feminist narrative suddenly been seized from the Democrats, who in their anxiety to "inspire," have been not thrilling but simply inspiring—i.e., exhausting (and clunky-shoed in the bargain)?

SEPTEMBER 22, 2008   BY ADAM BEGLEY

D.F.W., R.I.P.

A DOZEN YEARS AGO, I SPENT three weeks with David Foster Wallace. Not the guy—not the man who hanged himself, age 46, on Sept. 12—but the writer, the novelist who invaded my house with a huge, wonderful, impossible book, *Infinite Jest.* For 20 days or so I did virtually nothing but read and re-read the 1,079 pages of a novel that thrilled and infuriated me. There were long hours, pinned on the couch under his 3-pound, 5-ounce tome, when I hated him with a pure and righteous rage—my wrist hurt from holding the thing, my brain was weary from the footnotes and the cleverness and the strangeness of the world he'd plunged me into. I think I was dazed by the tenacity of his obsessions (drugs, tennis). But even when I hated him, I never doubted, after the first day, that I was reading an amazing book and that the 33-year-old author was some kind of wild genius.

Death is gruesome. I don't have the talent (or the heart) to make Wallace's suicide seem funny. Wallace could have done the job himself—and who knows? His auto-obituary, a piece of writing that will heal the hurt of his sudden absence, may be among the works published posthumously.

Until then, I'd urge anyone who wants to mourn David Foster Wallace to go back to "Forever Overhead," a gorgeous story from *Brief Interviews with Hideous Men* (1999), about a boy on his 13th birthday at a public pool just west of Tucson, Ariz., who screws up his courage, gets in line, and climbs to the top of the tower for the high dive.

Wallace leaves him up there, on the board, clenched by fear.

But first he gives us the climb to the top of the tower's ladder: "The rungs are very thin. It's unexpected. Thin round iron rungs laced in slick wet Safe-T felt."

The boy is disturbed (and so are you) by the two "dirty spots" at the end of the board: "They are from all the people who've gone before you. ... They are skin, abraded from the feet by the violence of the disappearance of people with real weight. ... " And below? "The square tank is a cold blue sheet. Cold is just a kind of hard."

Goodbye, David Foster Wallace.

SEPTEMBER 29, 2008 BY JASON HOROWITZ

Mayor Bloomberg: Suddenly Seer of Financial Crisis

MAYOR MICHAEL BLOOMBERG shrugged his shoulders, turned up his palms and rolled his eyes in what is now his well-practiced impression of an exasperated person.

It was another question about whether he would consider helping the next administration by swooping into Washington to rescue the economy as secretary of the Treasury or as the appointed overseer of a proposed $700 billion fund to buy and resell troubled mortgages. This time, a reporter wanted to know if he felt qualified for the job.

"It's sort of pressing it to say that I was interested in running a mortgage business, which I don't have the expertise in, incidentally," Mr. Bloomberg said over a dozen tape recorders resting on his podium.

Standing alone on a stage in a gleaming new terminal at Kennedy Airport, the mayor turned to take the next question. "Yes, sir," he said.

But then he couldn't leave it there.

He had one little qualifier to add to that lack of expertise he had just mentioned: "I could get it, I assume."

That Mr. Bloomberg is now wording his answers with all the care of a cabinet nominee at a confirmation hearing says something about the perfect storm that has swept him up since Wall Street melted down.

Without actually doing much to stoke it—just by being there, really—Mr. Bloomberg has somehow become a catch-all messiah, coveted by both major-party nominees, cited by federal officials on either side of the aisle and wielded by pundits as a syn-onym for fiscal expertise and market wisdom.

"It's one of the oldest games in the political book," said Ralph Schlosstein, a former White House aide in the Carter administration and co-founder of the private-equity group BlackRock, explaining the ongoing political stampede in Mr. Bloomberg's direction. "You like to have your name associated with talented, popular leaders."

As with all commodity bubbles, there is something more than slightly irrational in the current mania for all things Bloomberg.

It is likely, even, that Mr. Bloomberg, who made his fortune by inventing and marketing the Bloomberg Terminal, knows this—as evidenced by his half-retracted admission that he's not actually a mortgage expert at all.

But for now, as a practical matter, it's not really important whether expectations about Mr. Bloomberg's ability to heal the financial world are realistic. Given the mayor's current circumstances—term-limited mayor seeks options for prolonging time in current office or obtaining national one—it's all upside. And the mayor, quite naturally, has taken to his role enthusiastically.

SEPTEMBER 29, 2008   BY MAX ABELSON

MRS. ASTOR'S PRODIGAL SON COMES HOME—TO SELL IT

Anthony Marshall never spent a night in his mother Brooke Astor's Park Avenue apartment. Now, Max Abelson tours it and talks to the son: 'You can't change the past'

ON SEPT. 17, JUST AS HIS LATE MOTHER BROOKE ASTOR'S $46 MILLION duplex co-op was coming back on the market after a summer hiatus, and one day before a court appearance, Anthony D. Marshall slouched in his white living room armchair, one hand resting on his neck. The senatorial 84-year-old, unsmiling and handsome in his gold-buttoned navy blazer, blue-checked white shirt, pressed gray-striped pants and black loafers, said he had regrets. "Oh, yes. But that's awfully ..." He paused. "To be retrospective about anything is being retrospective."

"You can't change the past."

Nearly a year after pleading not guilty to a 16-count criminal indictment that accuses him of stealing millions from his mother while she was suffering from Alzheimer's, American-born but Victorian-voiced Mr. Marshall still makes the Metropolitan Museum's outgoing director, Philippe de Montebello, sound like a barfly: His "yes" can arrive in two distinct syllables; his "past" rhymes with "lost." Does he wish things were different at the end of his mother's life? "Yes," he said. "But I can't comment any more than that."

Mr. Marshall wouldn't speak about the charges, but he was very gracious about sharing his memories of his mother's apartment at 778 Park Avenue and its six terraces, five wood-burning fireplaces and one very famous red-lacquered library.

"Do you want to begin or shall I?" he said. Ms. Astor bought the place in 1959, although her only son never slept over. "Sleep there? Never did, no. Well—I was an old man by then."

There's just one real bedroom in the whole duplex. Four rooms went to maids; a bedroom upstairs was turned into a second sitting room; two bedrooms downstairs are office and storage space.

OCTOBER 6, 2008   BY JOHN KOBLIN

OFF THE RECORD: THERE GOES *THE SUN*

INSIDE *THE NEW YORK SUN'S* spacious Chambers Street offices on Tuesday, Sept. 30, the old-fashioned journalistic decorum that had defined the paper's culture was nowhere in sight. The 20-somethings that made up the reporting ranks were in for one last time wearing blue jeans and T-shirts—a far cry from the conservative broadsheet's long-standing dress code, which required reporters to come in with polished shoes and nice suits. "It's the casual Friday that *The Sun* never had," said Grace Rauh, the 29-year-old city hall reporter.

Staffers seemed in buoyant spirits, some even laughing.

It was a far cry from the month-long anxiety that had followed editor and founder Seth Lipsky's announcement that the paper was in danger of closing at the end of the month if it didn't find new financiers.

As early as Sunday night, informal e-mails began circulating to that effect. "I look forward to working with you at my next post," wrote Rebecca Fox, associate features editor, in a missive to business contacts.

But all day on Monday, Sept. 29, there was not a word from Mr. Lipsky. Would there be a lifeline?

Then, at about 4 p.m., Mr. Lipsky told reporters and editors to drop their phones and gather round in that office, the size of a big, bright lunchroom.

Whatever funding Mr. Lipsky was hoping for had not arrived, and it probably didn't help that at the moment he was waiting for a last-ditch investor to save the paper, the Dow Jones plunged 777 points. Mr. Lipsky, who had described losses as "substantial," told Columbia journalism students back in 2006 that the paper lost up to $1 million a month, according to *The Columbia Journalism Review*.

Money wasn't the only thing expended.

"There's always been a ton of amazing energy—in an era when newsrooms are being gutted and shrunken down, and *The Sun* had this amazing can-do spirit," Ms. Rauh said.

◇◇◇◇◇◇◇

OCTOBER 6, 2008   BY PETER W. KAPLAN

THE OBSERVATORY: PETER W. KAPLAN
DESCRIBES A FEW LIFE MOMENTS HE SHARED WITH PAUL NEWMAN IN 1983

DON'T GET ME WRONG, I DIDN'T KNOW PAUL NEWMAN. But I spent a few weeks with him in 1983, when I went down to Florida to watch him direct a father-and-son picture he had also co-written and produced, *Harry and Son*, with himself, Robby Benson, Wilford Brimley, a young lop-smiled actress named Ellen Barkin and Joanne Woodward. Movie sets, as you might know, are excruciatingly boring places where time moves slowly, really underwater, and the director asks for the same thing over and over until whatever he or she wants revealed shows up.

Paul Newman's set was a happy set. The weather was good, the actors were kind to each other and every day at 3, three or four giant Hefty bags of popcorn made by the director showed up. My memory of the director and his wife—with his taut, focused affection and her internal discipline, goodwill and generous warmth—was watching an undemonstrative, unbroken marital choreography of intimacy and regard. Newman implausibly died at the end of the movie, but you've never seen an expiree so tanned and vital. It seemed impossible that his corpse wouldn't come back in the last reel and whip all the other actors in a speed-round of tennis.

After the shooting weeks, I went to see him race his cars in Georgia: a movie actor doing his best to escape the fetid weight of fame, enduring a hovering reporter from *Life*, which even in its diminished state was still a name he had to put up with. He was completely consumed with his racing team. One afternoon I met him at his motel, in Athens, to drive him into Atlanta to meet his wife. He came out of his motor court door looking like the usual trillion bucks and had big racing sunglasses on. It must have been around 5; he said he was late for dinner with Joanne. I told him we'd get there faster if he drove; I have to admit, I wanted to see what my budget-priced rental car would feel like being handled by Paul Newman.

The last time I saw him was up in Westport, Conn., at the musty old narrow summer stock theater where he played the Stage Manager in *Our Town*, much more a member of the Westport community than Hollywood legend. It was a deeply democratic performance, the Stage Manager less as omniscient codger than as another slightly addled human.

Almost at the end of the play, standing in the dark in his collar and vest, he got to answer Emily's big question as she surveys her former life from beyond: "Do any human beings ever realize life while they live it—every, every minute?"

"No—" the Stage Manager says, "Saints and poets, maybe—they do some."

Paul Newman came close on both.

APRIL 28, 2008   BY DOREE SHAFRIR

The Brooklyn Literary 100

The idea of a Brooklyn literary "scene" is one that has become so ingrained in the city's consciousness that, in true Brooklyn style, it has now become fashionable to consider writerly Brooklyn in an ironic manner, to comment on the ridiculousness of the idea that a place can, in fact, be said to help define a literary community. Take, for example, Colson Whitehead's cheeky *New York Times Book Review* essay—"I Write in Brooklyn. Get Over It"—from last month, in which he questioned the very idea that the borough could be said to inspire any kind of literary imagination. He wrote: "There was the famous case of the language poet from Red Hook who grew despondent when the Shift key on her MacBook broke. She couldn't write for weeks. Overcome by melancholy humors, she jumped into the enchanted, glowing waters of the Gowanus Canal, her pockets full of stones. And ... she was cured! The metaphors came rushing back. With eccentric spacing between the letters, but still."

Of course, as Mr. Whitehead himself tacitly acknowledges, writers have long found refuge across the East River (if often for financial reasons). Norman Mailer held his famous late-night parties in a Brooklyn Heights brownstone (his neighbor, for a time, was the playwright Arthur Miller); Truman Capote lived in the neighborhood in the '50s and '60s; poet Hart Crane lived in Brooklyn Heights for part of his short life. Poet Marianne Moore lived in a Fort Greene brownstone for decades. In Brooklyn Heights, at 7 Middagh Street, was a writers' and artists' commune of sorts that at various points in the 1940s counted Carson McCullers, Richard Wright, W. H. Auden, and Jane and Paul Bowles among its residents. ("I think Auden was kind of the father to the house," said Evan Hughes, a 32-year-old writer in Fort Greene who is writing a history of literary Brooklyn. "He made sure the bills got paid and whatnot.") And of course, no mention of literary Brooklyn is complete without reference to its patron saint, Walt Whitman, who first moved to Brooklyn at the age of 4 and made his living as a journalist at a number of local papers while writing poetry.

Still, it's true that Manhattan—especially the Upper West Side and Greenwich Village, and Elaine's—for years occupied a special place in the city's literary landscape, and still, today, it's not surprising

to find those neighborhoods clinging to the tops of mastheads, with older authors and senior agents and editors living in the Classic 6 on West End Avenue, where they've been since the 1970s. But making the jump across the East River, and onto Carroll Street and Clinton Avenue—along with the assistants and junior staffers and newly minted MFAs—are now the likes of (No. 1 *New York Times* best-selling author!) Jhumpa Lahiri; Jonathan Safran Foer and Nicole Krauss, who famously bought a Park Slope townhouse for $3.5 million in 2005; and the veritable Renaissance man Kurt Andersen, who makes his home in Carroll Gardens. And so they clack away on their MacBooks at Ozzie's or the Tea Lounge in Park Slope or the Central branch of the Brooklyn Public Library at Grand Army Plaza, and do readings at Pete's Candy Store in Williamsburg or the Brooklyn Lyceum, and contribute to A Public Space or One Story or n+1, and meet their editor for drinks at Union Hall, and play football in Prospect Park on the weekends and tutor kids at 826NYC and buy their friends' books at the

Community Bookstore or Book Court and raise money to fight the Atlantic Yards project by contributing essays to a book called *Brooklyn Was Mine*, published by Riverhead in January

Thus a Brooklyn literary community has, stubbornly, taken root, despite Mr. Whitehead's disavowals, and yet, we wondered just who the members of this community were—everyone from its longtime to its newest denizens. Preemptively, we must warn the reader that the Brooklyn Literary 100, like any list of the Best or Worst, or Most Important or Most Popular or Most Expensive, is necessarily arbitrary to some degree. That being said, there were some criteria that we attempted to hew to. We restricted the list to people we (again, somewhat arbitrarily) deemed "literary." If a writer, preferably he or she has published a book and/or regularly contributes to a well-known publication, be it magazine, newspaper or blog; if an editor, someone who is either prominent in his or her field or recognized in the book or magazine publishing world as a comer; if an agent, someone who has a client roster that would be at least somewhat recognizable to the average literary follower. But prospective listees also got points (on an undetermined scale in this reporter's head) for other literary endeavors beyond writing and publishing, such as hosting parties known for their writerly attendees. We surveyed our own bookish acquaintances and trolled the Internet in search of hints that list-worthy people might live in Brooklyn. (Though sometimes our suppositions were wrong: *Believer* editor Ed Park, for example, lives on the Upper West Side; *Harper's* literary editor Ben Metcalf, Chelsea!) But we must also, once again preemptively, say that we of course missed some people who deserve to be on the list. Next time! And, yes, Mr. Whitehead is on there. Much to his chagrin, we suppose.

Brighton Beach Lara Vapnyar, author

Brooklyn Heights Elizabeth Gaffney, editor, A Public Space; author • Philip Levine, poet • Norris Church Mailer, author • Dinaw Mengestu, author • Simon Rich, author • Valerie Steiker, editor, *Vogue*

Boerum Hill John Cassidy, staff writer, *The New Yorker*; author • Sarah Crichton, editor, Farrar, Straus & Giroux • Emily Gould, blogger, Galleycat; author • Courtney Hodell, editor, Farrar, Straus & Giroux • Samantha Hunt, author • Scott Malcomson, editor, *The New York Times Magazine* • Lawrence Osborne, author • Jonathan Lethem, author • Katie Roiphe, author • Jonathan Burnham Schwartz, author • Craig Seligman, critic, Bloomberg News; author • Elizabeth Spiers, contributing writer, *Fortune*; author • Michael Thomas, author

Carroll Gardens Kurt Andersen, author; radio host; editor at large, Random House • Joshua Ferris, author • David Grann, staff writer, *The New Yorker*; author • Phillip Lopate, author and essayist • Richard Nash, editorial director, Soft Skull Press • Vijay Seshadri, author

Clinton Hill Molly Barton, editor, Penguin • Susan Choi, author • Laura Ford, editor, Random House • Fiona Maazel, author • Benjamin Nugent, author • Meghan O'Rourke, literary editor, Slate;

poetry editor, *The Paris Review*; poet • Anna Stein, agent, Irene Skolnick and Associates • James Surowiecki, staff writer, *The New Yorker*; author • Matt Weiland, editor, *The Paris Review*

Cobble Hill Geoff Kloske, publisher, Riverhead • Stephen Metcalf, critic-at-large, Slate • Nathaniel Rich, editor, *The Paris Review*; author • Eric Simonoff, agent, Janklow & Nesbitt • Alex Star, editor, *The New York Times Magazine* • Paula Fox, author

Ditmas Park Roger Hodge, editor-in-chief, Harper's

Dumbo Michael M. Thomas, author and essayist

Fort Greene Jennifer Carlson, agent, Dunow, Carlson & Lerner • Bryan Curtis, contributing writer, *The New York Times Magazine* • Jennifer Egan, author • Sarah Fan, editor, New Press • Ryan Fischer-Harbage, agent, • Fischer-Harbage Agency • Melissa Flashman, agent, Trident Media Group • Amitav Ghosh, author • Emily Haynes, editor, Plume • Brigid Hughes, editor in chief, A Public Space • Trena Keating, editor in chief, Dutton • Chris Knutsen, editor, *Vogue* • Jhumpa Lahiri, author • Simon Lipskar, agent, Writers House • Sarah Rainone, editor, Doubleday • Rakesh Satyal, editor, HarperCollins • Emily Takoudes, editor, Ecco • Toure, contributing editor, *Rolling Stone*; author • Colson Whitehead, author

Gowanus Paul Ford, editor, *Harper's*; author; blogger

Kensington Daniel Radosh, author; blogger

Park Slope Paul Auster, author • Jonathan Safran Foer, author • Mary Gannon, editor, Poets & Writers • Ben Greenman, editor, *The New Yorker*; author • Colin Harrison, editor, *Harper's*; author • Kathryn Harrison, author • Steven Berlin Johnson, author; blogger • Edward Kastenmeier, editor, Knopf • Porochista Khakpour, author • Nicole Krauss, author • Megan Lynch, editor, Riverhead • Sarah McGrath, editor, Riverhead • Suketu Mehta, author • Elissa Schappell, contributing editor, *Vanity Fair* • John Sellers, author • Darin Strauss, author • Alexandra Styron, author • Bill Wasik, editor, *Harper's*; author • Larry Weissman, agent, Larry Weissman Literary

Prospect Heights Mike Albo, author • Julia Cheiffetz, editor, Random House • Becky Cole, editor, Broadway Books • Keith Gessen, editor, n+1; author • Philip Gourevitch, editor in chief, *The Paris Review*; staff writer, *The New Yorker*; author • Mark Kirby, editor, *GQ* • Larissa MacFarquhar, staff writer, *The New Yorker* • Rick Moody, author • George Packer, staff writer, *The New Yorker*; author • Matt Power, author • Laura Secor, author • Paul Slovak, editor, Viking

Red Hook Philip Nobel, architecture critic; author • Jody Rosen, music critic, Slate; author

Williamsburg Jami Attenberg, author • Philip Dray, author

Windsor Terrace Aaron Gell, editor, *Radar* • Myla Goldberg, author

OCTOBER 20, 2008   BY IRINA ALEKSANDER

Mad About the Man: What Do Women Really Want?
Mad Men's *Don Draper! He's the Man in the Gray Flannel Suit With a Package! Whining About Stepford Dads: 'It's Not Terribly Erotic'*

"DON DRAPER IS EVERY PARK Slope mom's fantasy," said Paula Bernstein, a 40-year-old author who lives in Brooklyn with her husband, a video editor, and their two children. "The fact that he is so emotionally withholding and mysterious is frustrating, but women are intrigued by men like that, and as much as they say they want a sensitive guy who's going to let it all hang out, there is an appeal to a man with *secrets*."

Ms. Bernstein was speaking about the darkly compelling protagonist of Matthew Weiner's 1960s advertising drama *Mad Men*, which airs every Sunday on AMC, transporting scores of New York women into a haze of longing for an era they never knew and a type of man to whom they definitely aren't married. Who, in fact, may no longer exist.

Don Draper is a bastard, most of these women will concede. He cheats on his pre-Friedan-ized wife, Betty, going through mistresses like packs of Lucky Strike cigarettes. He is stoic, handsome, emotionally stunted.

But he also reminds us of a time before suits were replaced by messenger bags and Converse sneakers. Before hairless chests and Cialis; before men knew pop-psychology phrases like "displaced anger" and "defense mechanisms" and talked about how their parents fucked them up; before Dr. Phil; before dads posted photos of themselves with their babies on their Facebook pages; before paternity leaves—there were men like Don Draper.

"If you just compare him to, say, Patrick Dempsey on *Grey's Anatomy*, Dr. McDreamy comes off as a whiny little sensitive *bitch*," said Lindsay Robertson, 31, resident of Carroll Gardens and a self-described member of the "Draper estrogen brigade."

OCTOBER 27, 2008
BY MEREDITH BRYAN AND
JOE POMPEO

NINTH INNING
No Yankees, No Mets, Just a City Compulsively Clicking: RCP, Drudge, HuffPo, Politico and FiveThirtyEight.com; 'Telling People Not to Give Into Anxiety Makes It Worse'

IT WAS AN UNSEASONABLY WARM evening in a courtyard behind a midtown dive bar called Rudy's, and a casual after-work crowd of Obamaphiles was bathed in the light of a Florida State football game projected on the wall, talking politics over $9 pitchers of beer. The mood was festive, anticipatory, measured. With just a dash of paranoia.

For the overwhelming number of New Yorkers who support Barack Obama, the news has been *allll good* lately. Numbers up. Lookin' sharp. McCain flailing. So why can't everyone just sit back and relax?

We'd be the last to argue that New Yorkers' overproduction and overconsumption of media is news. But there's a strange, unsettling feeling behind the great campaign obsession of 2008: *sincerity*.

Let's admit it: Many cynical, hardened New Yorkers are experiencing a refreshing surge of *actual emotion* toward their Ivy-educated, book-writing, multiracial, bar-admitted candidate!

Perhaps all this frantic clicking and neurotic number-crunching and magical thinking, then, is simply a way of shielding these rarely exposed soft spots. "It's like when I fly in a plane," said a lawyer, 35. "I know rationally that chances it will crash are next to nil, but looking outside again and again, checking the wing flaps, is reassuring emotionally."

NOVEMBER 10, 2008   BY FELIX GILLETTE

NYTV: A Star is Reborn
So 2008 restored Couric's star status; 'Give me an hour,' she says

ON THE AFTERNOON OF FRIDAY, OCT. 31, KATIE COURIC SAT DOWN IN the Olympic Flame diner at the corner of 60th Street and Amsterdam, and ordered a cup of coffee.

O.K., Ms. Couric, it's trick or treat time: What would you want from CBS, the network that paid you a reported $15 million a year to lure you from your perch at NBC's *Today*?

"I'd like an hour," said Ms. Couric.

She's already getting that, albeit on an ad hoc basis. On Monday, Nov. 3, the night before the election, the network was giving the *CBS Evening News* (which is typically a half-hour long) twice its usual length, said Ms. Couric. She was looking forward to the extra real estate. In an ideal world, if she had her druthers, the expansion would be permanent.

"I really would like more time," said Ms. Couric. "Because I think time is not our friend at the *Evening News*."

Not long ago, the suggestion was put about that time was not on Ms. Couric's side at CBS. According to various news reports back in April, CBS, disappointed with her performance but unwilling to pay the ghastly sum the premature termination of her contract would entail, was letting her run out the clock and then planning to cut her loose. Or it was she, frustrated with the network's handling of her and her show, who was planning to cut the cord at the earliest possible moment.

But against the odds—she wasn't allowed the opportunity, for instance, to anchor a single presidential or vice presidential debate for CBS—Ms. Couric has used the 2008 presidential elections to make herself a commodity again. Not the too expensive piece of furniture the Tiffany network had bought and regretted, but the game-changing political journalist she aspired to be when she first took the *Evening News*. Hers was the most memorable interview of the 2008 election. Über political blogger Mark Halperin named her one of the five most important people in politics not running for president.

NOVEMBER 17, 2008   BY GILLIAN REAGAN

THE OBSERVATORY: RAHM POKED ME!
Barack Obama's White House Is the First Facebook Administration—From Jon Favreau to Austan Goolsbee!

LAST WEEK, JUST MINUTES after winning the presidential election, Barack Obama sent an e-mail—to me.

"I'm about to head to Grant Park to talk to everyone gathered there, but I wanted to write to you first. We just made history." We did, didn't we? "We have a lot of work to do to get our country back on track, and I'll be in touch soon about what comes next." Signed: "Barack."

I've been on a first-name basis with Barack, our president-elect, since he announced his candidacy nearly two years ago. And in recent months, I've received a "personalized" e-mail, Twitter tweet, YouTube video or Facebook update from Mr. Obama or his campaign staff almost daily, assuring me that we were in it together, that we could bring about the change that was so often referenced in 2008. Like my friends and big brother, Barack Obama is part of the Facebook generation.

And so it holds that a good chunk of the folks Mr. Obama will take to Washington with him in January are children of the Internet as well. Let's call it the Facebook Administration. Sure, politicians have had Web pages and e-mail addresses for years. But so many of those fall easily out of date; their owners treat them with neglect and even contempt. This is different. For the first time, a White House administration is happily online, their profiles—personal and political—there for our perusal; we can express support, irritation or anger for our leaders, and the public, to see. Want to link to Obama Chief of Staff Rahm Emanuel's Facebook page? Or tell him you hate his guts? He's there on Facebook. Go for it!

And there are many other Facebookers whose names are being bandied about for top administration posts: Jason Furman, a senior economic adviser during the campaign (his profile picture is a snapshot of his baby girl); Jon Favreau, Mr. Obama's head speechwriter, who has almost 600 Facebook friends; and Reggie Love, the president-elect's personal aide, who is friends with *Harold and Kumar*'s Kal Penn!

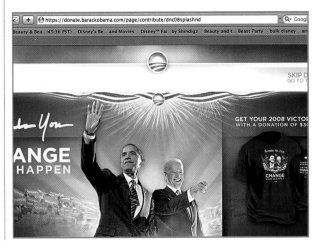

DECEMBER 1, 2008   BY JOHN KOBLIN

OFF THE RECORD: The Web Guru

As Media Shatters, Jeff Jarvis Is Ideologue Seer of New Age; 'Journalists? They're Community Organizers!' Says Professor; 'He and I Edged Closer,' Says Bill Keller; 'Bullshit,' Says Jarvis

IF YOU WANTED TO WIPE OUT the American media establishment in one blow, you might have targeted the Grand Ballroom on the third floor of the Plaza hotel at around 9 a.m. on Nov. 12.

The Foursquare Conference was organized by media mogul Steve Rattner's Quadrangle Partners, and had the kind of exclusive list Mr. Rattner is known for. Barry Diller attended the conference, as did Lachlan Murdoch, Arthur Sulzberger Jr., and Tribune chief Sam Zell.

It was just the place for Jeff Jarvis, the tall 54-year-old professorial-looking guy who was looking intently through unfashionable glasses at the par-

ticipants of a panel discussion on the state of American media, from his perch up front.

The blogger, professor and media consultant has, through his Web sites, seminars, journalism classes, panel-discussion appearances and the occasional flamewar, preached for some time now the gospel of New Media. These days, it's taking hold—and not just among the patchwork constituency of media studies majors, technophile utopians and media malcontents left and right. To oversimplify it: The old business of journalism has failed. It was full of monopolies, a lot of egos, a lot of overhead; presided over by a medieval guild of pro-

tectionist editors, copy editors, managers; staffed by reporters who were doomed to stand alongside "competitors" to cycle

out the same press-conference reports for only marginally different audiences.

A new model of journalism, one that starts in his West 40th Street classroom, begins with new ideas, a smaller staff and a direct cooperation with the public to contribute stories, ideas, videos and more.

If newsrooms are getting smaller, anyway, it's time to rethink them. Critics, opinion writers, lifestyle writers are all a waste of space. In an industry with few resources, throw them overboard first. Editors just get in the way. They should teach the public how to report for itself, instead of coming between them and the news.

◇◇◇◇◇◇◇

DECEMBER 8, 2008   BY DANA RUBINSTEIN

BROKERS AS SHRINKS

Hardened commercial brokers find themselves empathetic 'hand-holders' to jittery Masters of the Property Universe

DO YOU FEEL BURDENED WITH AN EMPTY STOREFRONT? ARE YOU convinced you're the only landlord saddled with too much debt? Do you feel terrified that the bottom of this infernal market will never come? Are you anxious? Depressed? Lonely?

Call your broker.

The plunging market has turned commercial real estate brokers—those hard-nosed, pinstriped wheeler-dealers who play by few rules but their own—into purveyors of comfort and wisdom. It's an activity that brokers, being brokers, have archly dubbed "hand-holding."

"The landlords, the owners, the developers, they are in need of constant hand-holding and assurances," said Faith Hope Consolo, chairwoman of the retail leasing and sales division at Prudential Douglas Elliman. "Now, to hear from a landlord five times a day is not unusual. The same landlord. And asking the same questions over and over. If they ask you the same question at 9, they ask it again at 11:30."

Of course, absent a triplicate prescription pad, there's only so much a broker can do to calm a client's nerves. And, thankfully, not all clients are equally panicked.

"All that's happening now is that people want information," said Simon Wasserberger, senior vice president at CB Richard Ellis. "Nobody's jumping out a window, at least that I know of."

DECEMBER 1, 2008   BY GEORGE GURLEY

THE NEW YORK WORLD: HOW TO BE BROKE AND NOT BE A SUCKER

S O I'M BROKE. I HAVE A NEGATIVE balance. Minus $9.44.

Nothing to do, nowhere to go, imprisoned here on Roosevelt Island. Back in '99 I bought a $400 bottle of wine at Raoul's to impress what I thought was my girlfriend. Turned out I was merely one of three dudes she was nailing. And now I can't even afford giant litter box liners. The cat's been wobbling around making it real clear she's not happy about the litter box situation. Tried to do a makeshift job with

pieces of garbage bag and Scotch tape but it's just not working. Cat's giving me funny looks. Translation: Mama, I'm gonna drop some dookies in your bathtub again.

So this morning on the way out I stopped at the A.T.M. in the lobby. No real need to—I knew I had at least $140, I'm on top of things, got my life under control, but why not withdraw $60? That's when things get fuzzy. First, shock, then a real sinking feeling of hopelessness. Is this rock bottom or the beginning of the end? What will happen? Will I starve or go mad? Coal mines, tenements, Third World countries. So much for cat box liners—that's out. All a sudden, a woman screamed into my ear, "Max! Max!" Her little boy was just down the hall. Too deflated to scream back at her: "Hate to break it to you, lady, but odds are Max will turn out to be a complete dope. Maybe next time go with a goofy lower-expectations name like Buford or Dippy."

Had an endoscopy. Was worried I had Barrett's esophagus and gout. Gastroenterologist Dr. Bamji gave me a clean bill of health. So decided to celebrate last night, stayed out until 10 a.m. Pretty sure at 6:30 a.m. I was talking to Lydia Hearst on the phone in Madrid and that I'm invited to her Xmas costume party. All day been burping, gurgling and tooting even after popping Beanos, Gas-X and Tums. An endoscopy is when they cram a black tube down your throat. Was paranoid about anesthesia so asked for smallest dose, which meant I was conscious the whole procedure and gagging. Sexy Asian nurse kept telling me to "Just relax" during the deep throatage. Dr. Bamji promised to put a finger in my ass next time. May cancel. Well, for six weeks I was waking up at like 6 every morning from the gurgling sounds in my throat. I'd sit up, burp 20 times, then drift off before another episode. Dr. Bamji has outlawed spicy, fried, fatty, tomato-based foods; citrus, caffeine, carbonated drinks; onions, garlic, chocolate, smoking and binge drinking. Have to switch from Metamucil to FiberCon.

So Malcolm Gladwell has another best seller and everyone's slobbering all over him, except the lady from *The Times*, who called it clumsy, glib and thoroughly unconvincing. Makes me feel better about the $4 million advance. Maybe I should write *Broke: How to Unlock the Unlimited Power of Being Fucked.* Never read anything by Gladwell, though I think I'm one of his "connector" types who start trends and have a special gift for bringing the world together like Paul Revere. For example I invented that late-night party game "Band Names A-Z."

Later soaked in the tub and read an old review of a Poussin exhibit by Robert Hughes and thought how we both banged the same woman, me circa 1995. He got in there a good 15 years before me, but my significant

other didn't catch me in the act and wave a machete around like his did. Also on the same layline as Quentin Tarantino, Chuck Scarborough and I'm pretty sure Matt Dillon. Wonder where that frisky cougar from the class of '71 I hooked up with at our reunion in '91 is. Could not close the deal. So many things I can't do now. Eleven months ago I was yacht-hopping in St. Barts and having conversations with Leelee Sobieski, Nick Rhodes, Terrence Howard, Amy Poehler, George Soros; I had thousands of euros to blow. Now look at me.

Ever worry you're gonna towel your balls off too hard and one of 'em is gonna fall off?

So the lady at the deli spreads a paper-thin layer of cream cheese on bagels. People have started to complain. So she charges another 50 cents for "extra cream cheese!" By extra she means the amount of cream cheese a normal decent American would spread on a bagel. Has nothing to do with the economy.

Never been much for S&M. Never been tied up, worn diapers. Went home with a girl circa '97 who in retrospect suspected was a dominatrix. She cranked up Brian Eno's "Here He Comes," danced around naked in her living room, ordered me to sit on the couch and whack it. Next morning her phone started ringing. A lot. Oh, and earlier she kept going into her closet and coming out in different outfits.

I know about shame now. Know what it's like to be poor. I was outside a Sbarro in midtown, jiggling quarters in my pocket, pacing like I'm outside a porn emporium 'cause I know someone might see me. Screw up the courage, take a deep breath and go in and order a slice and stack up quarters. Guy behind the counter gives me a pitying look and THEN the place starts filling up! Five, six people see my pathetic stack of change and the slice takes a long time. Then I start feeling inexplicably better. I sit down and what song comes on? "I Can See Clearly Now." Positive vibes wash over me.

For the past few weeks I've been setting my alarm at 10:55 a.m. to watch you, Elisabeth Hasselbeck, on *The View*, thinking about you nonstop throughout the day, and YouTubing clips of you late into the night. Damn, you are one adorable pint-size dynamo. And stacked. I like how you've never changed your look. You still dress cute and feminine, and I really like your bottle-blond hairdo. But we still know the curtains don't match the drapes! Oh boy. Be cool to have a tiny version of you sitting on my keyboard right now, blabbing away, and if it got on my nerves I could flip a switch—but I don't want a doll like my Ann Coulter doll. It's got to be you. Carry you around in my pocket. I can relate—I used to interview Republican pundits, then receive up to a thousand nasty e-mails from readers. "You are a fucking idiot," one of them read in its entirety. You got the toughest job on TV. Case closed. Almost forgot. Here's a nice vid of you in a blue satiny waist-high number and for a split second you can see the white panties. Just thought I'd pass that along. Lotsa weirdos out there.

NOVEMBER 10, 2008 EDITORIAL

PRESIDENT O. **It's Barackfest in New York!**
Voting mobs, parties, ad-hoc exit polls; Chris Matthews, Matthew Modine, Susan Sarandon, Michael Bloomberg, Harvey Weinstein, Bob Caro, Jill Abramson, Austin Scarlett Go Gaga for New Era

AS ELECTION NIGHT NEARED, NEW YORK'S POWER elite—but also its creative class, its political class, its partying class, lurched to find the center of gravity for election night.

The premonition that New York's obvious choice, Barack Obama, was likely to win was not the smallest consideration here.

And then there were those who attempted to provide the city with its own massive town square, to hold election night, for the first time in eight years, as a massive, citywide, public event.

ABC did Times Square, NBC of course did Rockefeller. Harvey Weinstein and Georgette Mosbacher cultivated a list, checked it twice, added a bunch of plus ones and basically accounted for every boldface name in town.

Then there were the churches, the political power centers of Black New York, which suddenly realized they might have the first black president on their hands. Charlie Rangel would spend some time in midtown with the Democrats, but then planned to go uptown, and try to move the center of gravity there.

Every neighborhood bar put up a sign: free hot dogs, CNN all night. And New York put on its suits and frocks and went out for a risky, big, historic night.

But the day began early in the morning, with floods of New Yorkers eschewing habit to pull themselves out of bed well before the break of dawn to get themselves to their polling places, often, like Joseph and Mary, in some obscure neighborhood they have long since outgrown, and sometimes, in the very same place their family has voted for generations. The lines were long and the passions were high—ask Tim Robbins!—but the historic day had begun.

O Beautiful!

Harlem, before 6 a.m.

Sixty-four voters waited on a line outside an elementary school polling place on West 134th Street before 6 a.m. on Election Day.

Carole Branch, a 41-year-old project architect who lives around the corner in the Lenox Terrace apartments (where the Rangels also live), got there first.

"My mother-in-law told me to wake up early and beat the rush," Ms. Branch said. She said she didn't want to wait in line "but would have" to cast a vote for Barack Obama.

Election officials wouldn't open the site till after 6 a.m. But soon after they did, Mr. Rangel appeared. The line had by now grown to about 200.

"This is beautiful. This is exciting," he said. "Who would have thought it?"

Mr. Rangel, wearing a black overcoat, yellow tie and carrying a *New York Times* tucked under his arm, said, "I've never seen anything like this."

He had little doubt about the prospects of his candidate, Barack Obama, on Election Day.

"No, no. He's ahead in almost every poll."

"Those Europeans never thought the slaves would be in charge," Mr. Rangel was heard telling the young woman in front of him.

—Azi Paybarah

Union Square, Noon

The Rub DJs, along with DJ Rekha and Chez Music's Neil Aline, were starting an afternoon DJ party at the Raise the Volume Election Day Party at the Virgin Megastore in Times Square around 1 p.m. On the decks: "Elected," by Alice Cooper; "I Believe" by Simian Mobile Disco; "Funky President" by James Brown; "Please Please Please Let Me Get What I Want," by the Smiths; George Clinton's "Paint the White House Black" and more. Start your own playlist!

—Gillian Reagan

Harlem, Midday

Governor David Paterson walked into the voting booth with his wife, Michelle, today, but said afterward, "I pulled the lever myself."

Mr. Paterson did not use a Braille ballot when voting for Barack Obama. (He doesn't read Braille.) Mr. Paterson conducted a walking press conference with reporters while on line to vote at the same Harlem elementary school where Representative Charlie Rangel voted hours earlier.

"I've never seen so many people stand on line for so long and be so excited," Mr. Paterson said. "I've never seen so many people look so happy, even though they have to wait over an hour to vote." He said the "struggles" of African-Americans, women, Hispanics, the disabled, elderly and others "may all be congealed in this sort of symbolic moment. But symbolic moments have often been the catalyst for great change in this country."

—Azi Paybarah

Harlem, afternoon

In some Harlem precincts, as the day progressed, it became not so much a question of whether Barack Obama will win, but how his victory will be thwarted.

"I think it's going to come down to a mess-up in the voting," said 70-year-old Ervin McLean, a golf caddy who lives in the neighborhood.

Thomas Mullins, a 52-year-old fellow caddy, was less pessimistic.

"I definitely think they're going to throw a monkey wrench into the machine," he said, but, "I don't think there will be no disarray. There will not be unrest, but there will be a lot of disappointed people."

He added that if Mr. Obama loses, and it's blamed on voting irregularity, it will "stay in the consciousness of America's mind."

—Azi Paybarah

The Lower East Side, 4:30 p.m.

By late afternoon on Essex Street, the line to vote at Public School 20 was nonexistent, and voters trickled out at five-minute intervals.

Which is not to say voting here was entirely seamless.

"The machines were weird," said neighborhood resident Nikki, 30, emerging from the gymnasium in a black puffy jacket after voting for Mr. Obama. (She asked that her last name not be used.)

Lower East Sider Danny Rivera, 23, had also voted for Mr. Obama, but not with a lever. "My name wasn't on the list, so I had to do an affidavit," he said. He thought perhaps it was because he hadn't voted in the last election, because he knew he was registered. He was with Maritza Alimonte, also 23, who had voted for Mr. Obama earlier in the day in the Bronx. They couple was confident Mr. Obama would win, but they were not Obamaphiles.

"I don't trust him," said Ms. Alimonte. "I don't trust any of them."

—Meredith Bryan

Chelsea, 7 p.m.

A little before 7 p.m., Matthew Modine was watching the TV screen at the Half King bar on 23rd Street in Manhattan, a few blocks from where he lives.

"I tell you if Obama loses and there's a sense that there's been some funny business, there's going to be fucking riots," said the 49-year-old actor.

Earlier that afternoon he had accompanied his 18-year-old daughter to a voting booth in the East Village. He said she doesn't really get what the big deal is.

"It's amazing how things have changed," he said. "The other day she was doing her homework and the TV was on and she looked up and said, 'Did you hear what he just said?'" The newscaster had just noted that Mr. Obama would be the first black president. That fact had apparently not struck her up to that point.

—Spencer Morgan

Soho, 8 p.m.

A cheer went up at 8:15 p.m. at the party for Huffington Post humor site 23/6, as MSNBC called Pennsylvania for Senator Obama. Looking over at Wolf Blitzer and Anderson Cooper projected on another wall, a guest was overheard asking, "Where are the holograms?"

"I feel absolutely confident that Obama will win," said Penelope Bunn, a 51-year-old journalist. "I travel abroad and the whole world wants this." Asked if she felt at all fatigued by the long campaign, Ms. Bunn fairly beamed, "It seems like he just got started yesterday!" She added, "McCain's not a bad guy. It's just not his time."

—Matt Haber

Harlem, 8:31 p.m.

As the jumbotron on 125th Street showed CNN announcing that Barack Obama is leading in Florida, the crowd here cheered.

But 27-year-old arts administrator Daisy Rosario of Harlem pressed a blue Obama poster over her mouth and tried not to cry.

"The last eight years have been awful," she said. "On September 11, I was in the first tower that got hit. Since then," she went on, referring to the Bush years, "it's been a long, sad journey."

She added, "I just want it to be over."

—Azi Paybarah

Index

Index

The future of newspapers? Father of the press Benjamin Franklin